W9-CNI-007

"Bill O'Shaughnessy's editorials make his New York TV counterparts look like so much mish-mash."

—*The New York Times*

"He has great style. And so does his writing."

—Sirio Maccioni, Le Cirque 2000

"Bill O'Shaughnessy's three books are a monumental trilogy and the stuff of history. Oscar Wilde in his aphorisms held that 'Anybody can make history; only a great man can write it . . . and that puts O'Shaughnessy on sacred ground."

—Monsignor William B. O'Brien, founder, Daytop International

"Bill O'Shaughnessy maneuvers words like Nelson Riddle arranged notes. And sometimes he even uses them like Errol Flynn wielded a saber. In his very best moments he resembles Ed Murrow broadcasting from the rooftops of London. He's that good."

—Tony Malara, former president, CBS

"His editorials and interviews, like fine wine, become better with time."

—Joseph Reilly, President, New York State Broadcasters Association

"These interviews, tributes, essays, and thoughts off the top of Bill's handsome head are the stuff of New York history, direct from his radio bully pulpit."

—Liz Smith, nationally syndicated columnist

"His writings, manner of expression and social conscience are incisive and important."

—Rabbi Amiel Wohl, Rabbi emeritus, Temple Israel

"An interesting, accurate inside look at riveting characters and colorful times."

—Walter J. P. Curley, former Ambassador to France and Ireland

"I enjoy Bill O'Shaughnessy's books of 'character' portraits. I even relish his sketches of people I've never met. They are rather like potato chips in that you can't stop with only one! And his portrait of Nelson [Rockefeller] is still second to none."

—Henry A. Kissinger, former Secretary of State

"Bill O'Shaughnessy should be required reading in every English lit and writing class at journalism schools. Superb craftsmanship."

—Arnaud de Borchgrave, President/CEO, United Press International

"He presides over the front-running suburban radio station in this whole country!"

—Larry King

"He is the conscience of broadcasting."

—Patrick Maines, president, The Media Institute

"A handsome book chock full of wonderful memories, vignettes, and wise insights."

—The Nelson A. Rockefeller Public Policy Institute of Government

"Our profession is privileged to have a man of Bill O'Shaughnessy's stature. He is one of the giants. At a time when the trivial and nonsensical seem to make headlines and profits, his always wise words on the air and in print give the rest of us hope that the pendulum will swing back in the right direction."

—Deborah Norville, "Inside Edition"

"This may be blasphemous . . . but I haven't enjoyed a book this much since Fulton Sheen or Norman Vincent Peale! O'Shaughnessy is a dapper guy who looks like a movie star. But the book is very . . . *spiritual.*"

—Joe Franklin, Bloomberg radio legend

"I know I will enjoy this book. I have already savored the warm references to a former president in his previous works."

—President George H. W. Bush

Vox Populi

ALSO BY WILLIAM O'SHAUGHNESSY

AirWAVES!:
A Collection of Radio Editorials from the Golden Apple

It All Comes Back To Me Now:
Character Portraits from the Golden Apple

More Riffs, Rants, and Raves

Serving Their Communities:
A 50-year History of the New York State Broadcasters Association
(Edited) with Stephen Warley and Joseph Reilly

VOX
VIP

Vox Populi

THE O'SHAUGHNESSY FILES

WILLIAM O'SHAUGHNESSY

FORDHAM UNIVERSITY PRESS

New York 2011

Photographs by Don Pollard, Courtney Grant Winston, and Wendy Moger-Bross, Rockefeller Family archives, Steve Barkaszi, and the Whitney Media archives.

Library of Congress Cataloging-in-Publication Data

O'Shaughnessy, William.
Vox populi : the O'Shaughnessy files / William O'Shaughnessy.—1st ed.
p. cm.
Collection of interview transcripts, editorials, essays, and observations made after 2004.
Includes index.
ISBN 978-0-8232-3247-5 (cloth : alk. paper)—ISBN 978-0-8232-3249-9 (ebook)
1. United States—Politics and government—1989——Anecdotes. 2. United States—Biography—Anecdotes. 3. New York (State)—Politics and government—1951——Anecdotes. 4. New York (State)—Biography—Anecdotes. 5. Interviews—United States. 6. Politicians—New York—Interviews. 7. Freedom of speech—United States. 8. Freedom of the press—United States. 9. O'Shaughnessy, William. I. Title.
E839.4.O843 2011
973.928—dc22

2010038219

Printed in the United States of America
13 12 11 5 4 3 2 1
First edition

For my children, in whom I'm so well pleased:

MATTHEW THAYER O'SHAUGHNESSY

DAVID TUCKER O'SHAUGHNESSY

KATE WHARTON O'SHAUGHNESSY NULTY

And for my spectacular grandchildren:

TUCKER THOMAS NULTY

ISABEL GRACE O'SHAUGHNESSY

FLYNN THAYER NULTY

LILY ANNA O'SHAUGHNESSY

AMELIA JANE NULTY

I've been blessed . . .

And one more:

For NANCY *with the laughing face*

CONTENTS

FOREWORD
BY GOVERNOR MARIO M. CUOMO

Bill O'Shaughnessy's previous books were so good, I couldn't put them down. This one, when you put it down . . . you literally can't pick it up again! If they get any thicker, we'll have to put them on wheels!

Bill's personal commentaries, written with casually elegant language, make you wish the whole country was hearing and reading his work. Actually, the whole world can now savor his genius thanks to the Internet and wvox.com. He is a journalist, commentator, connoisseur, a strong political presence, and a forceful advocate of great causes.

During his remarkable fifty-year run as the permittee of WVOX and WVIP, O'Shaughnessy has used his great Gaelic gift of words, a sharp mind, deep conviction, and the capacity for powerful advocacy to inspire the fainthearted, guide the eager, and charm almost everyone he meets. As a broadcaster and author, he has written and spoken simple truths and powerful political arguments with a good heart.

As an interviewer, Bill O'Shaughnessy is a magic miner of fascinating nuggets coaxed from a host of extraordinarily interesting people, some of them celebrities and others previously undiscovered neighborhood gems. O'Shaughnessy is among a select few who create magic with their words. He always brings us a rich flow of genuine American opinions and sentiment.

Few people have or had as rich a talent for "writing for the ear"—Charles Kuralt and Charles Osgood, certainly. Also the late, legendary Paul Harvey. And Bill O'Shaughnessy.

He can't describe a scene as well as Jimmy Breslin. He's not as "easy" a writer as Pete Hamill. But when he's on his game, Brother Bill is better than anyone on the air or in print.

We don't always agree politically. But O'Shaughnessy has never lost his instinct for the underdog. He is a constant reminder of a Republican Party that was much better for this country.

He's also an elegant, entertaining, and spellbinding speaker. He might have taken all these gifts and made himself a great political leader or a very rich captain of industry. Instead, fifty years ago he devoted himself to what then was a small and struggling radio station, and ever since then, thanks to his brilliance and dedication, he's created what has become his much-praised WVOX/Worldwide and the highly successful and innovative WVIP, where many different and emerging new voices are heard in the land.

Somebody said to me about his previous three books, "That's quite a body of good work O'Shaughnessy has put together. All the while we were dazzled by only his high style and glittering persona." I guess that's right. But it is not the body of work; it's the *soul* of the work that I have always been more attracted to.

And that's what O'Shaughnessy does. He doesn't deliver homilies about it. Maybe he doesn't even know it fully. But he is a lover. He loves people. He loves understanding them. He loves not just the big shots, but he loves all the little people, too. And that is all in this new book. And you can see it, you can read it, you can *feel* it, and you can hear it on the radio.

The man is a lover. He uses one word few people in our society use regularly (unless they are in the apparel business): "sweet." The highest compliment he can give you is not to tell you this guy is bright, successful, dazzling in his language or ability, but that he's sweet, or that she's sweet, or that it's sweet. Well, that, in the end, is what I like about him. He understands life, he understands love, and he knows how to portray it.

And always—if you push the discussion with him—you find, not far from the surface, a profound yearning to use his own great gift of life to find more sweetness in the world or perhaps even to create some himself. I know him. And he will find a way or he will spend the rest of his life trying.

So it's all here: O'Shaughnessy the businessman, reporter, gadfly, commentator, friend of politicians of all stripes, religious leaders of all stripes—and even an occasional politician "in stripes"!

So, I've given you no new knowledge of Bill in this foreword to his new book. But custom requires that I repeat the obvious, if only to remind ourselves why we are so pleased he was persuaded to assemble another dazzling anthology of life in Westchester and New York state (and beyond).

One of his great passions is the First Amendment, that nearly sacred guarantee of our unique American freedom of speech and expression, which is being challenged at the moment by government agents seeking to make themselves the dictators of public tastes and attitudes. And Bill O'Shaughnessy is one of the few respected authorities on the subject who have spoken out against these powerful and dangerous political forces, even at the risk of reprisal.

His speech "Obsequious Acquiescence" has been widely read and admired by some of the best legal minds in America, including the estimable Floyd Abrams, the distinguished national First Amendment expert. Indeed, for his lifetime of work on free speech issues, Bill was called "The Conscience of the Broadcasting Industry" by the prestigious Media Institute think tank in Washington.

He's also a philanthropist and humanitarian. And the down and out in the broadcasting profession have been the beneficiaries of his dynamic and creative fundraising efforts for the Broadcasters Foundation of America, which he presently serves as chairman of its Guardian Fund to assist the less fortunate in what Brother Bill calls his "tribe."

In *The Screwtape Letters,* the great C. S. Lewis wrote that what the devil wants is for a man to finish his life having to say I spent my life not doing either what is *right* . . . or what I *enjoy*. For the many years I've known him, Bill O'Shaughnessy has spent most of his time doing things he ought to have been doing and enjoying them immensely.

I have myself been blessed with a glittering array of loyal friends from every phase of my already long life. People willing to weigh my many inadequacies less diligently than they assess what they find commendable. None of these friends have tried harder than Bill O'Shaughnessy to give me a chance to be useful. He is a man of his words. But I'll never have the words I need to express my gratitude adequately to him.

Everyone in our family calls him "Brother Bill." By any name, he is very special, as you will discover in this, his fourth book, so aptly named: *Vox Populi.*

Mario Cuomo, the fifty-second governor of New York from 1983 to 1994, has been called "the great philosopher-statesman of the American nation" by the *Boston Globe*. A national journal recently said, "Every pronouncement from his bright, fine mind glistens with the sweat of moral conviction." He is seventy-seven years old and practices law at Willkie, Farr & Gallagher in New York City when he is not out making speeches to uplift and enlighten his admirers and the whole country.

PREFACE

I owe a great deal to the wonderful people of Westchester, who have been willing to weigh my many inadequacies less diligently than they assess what they find commendable in my stewardship of their radio stations WVOX and WVIP.

I began my career in radio during the summer of 1957. And our listeners here in the Golden Apple and throughout the tri-state New York metropolitan area have somehow tolerated my enthusiasms and endured my pronouncements for a long, long time. I have been at this profession for more than fifty years.

Obviously, I never took John Gardner's advice that one should change careers every four years or so. So I'm glad I stuck to my last, which has enabled me to amplify the sweet voices of some remarkable men and women whose goodness you'll discover in these pages. Radio has also provided me with an enormously influential soapbox from which to confront and challenge some of the great societal and civic issues of my time.

Although I have been fortunate beyond anything I deserve in my career and professional endeavors, my life has also been attended by some sadness over the years. I've walked down center church aisles behind the coffins of my mother, Catherine Tucker O'Shaughnessy (1906–91); my father, William Mac O'Shaughnessy (1904–74); and my only brother, John Thomas O'Shaughnessy (1940–98); I've stood in rural cemeteries in Friendship, Waverly, and Peekskill, New York, and watched as gravediggers threw dirt on them as they went back into the earth. And there was the untimely passing of my son Michael Pasquale (1982–2005). I also remember—and I've written of it in a previous book—the day some son of a bitch blew John Fitzgerald Kennedy's brains out in Dallas. And the call from Joe Canzeri at 1:30 in the morning: "Billy, Nelson [Rockefeller] died last night." And I saw Bobby Kennedy dying on a greasy kitchen floor in Los Angeles.

There was also a time, with Nancy, in the White Plains hospital, trying to save a baby I hoped would look like her. And the night Mario Cuomo lost his bid for a fourth term as governor of New York.

So there have been some moments of sadness with it all. But as I finish this fourth volume and my mind drifts back over my years as a community broadcaster in the New York area, I am well aware of my great good luck that I've been privileged to be the permittee of WVOX, WRTN, and WVIP.

In all my broadcasts, editorials, essays, and writings and in my talks on college campuses, I always refer to what I do as a "profession." Many/most of my colleagues call it an "industry" (the Southerners prefer "in-*dus*-try.") By *any* name, radio has been very good to me and mine.

Charles Osgood, of CBS's "Sunday Morning," once said, "Television is OK, but radio is magic." To this day he signs off every broadcast with his famous "See you on the radio." Proof that even in this high-tech, speeded-up, cyber day and age, radio is still the medium closest to the people. It is the friend and companion of the poor, the hurting, the misunderstood, the forgotten, the lonely, and the disenfranchised in our society. Therein lies its potential. Broadcasters have a real opportunity, perhaps an obligation, to be more than entertainers or peddlers of distraction; more than transmitters of slogans, headlines, and catch phrases; more than messengers of commerce. Radio, as the great Mario Cuomo often reminds us, can amplify "the goodness of the people and make a community better, stronger, *sweeter* than it is." It can be more than a jukebox. Or as E. B. White suggested, it is not just a kitchen appliance. I have always believed a radio station achieves its highest calling when it resembles a platform or forum for the expression of many different viewpoints. One of our recurring themes over the years has been "Where Many Voices Are Heard in the Land."

Radio, as I try to mention in every lecture or classroom talk, is like Lazarus in the Bible. You can't kill it. Television and cable couldn't do it in. Nor could the Internet. So we can agree that radio is resilient, widely available, and durable, with a remarkable ability to uplift and inspire as well as entertain.

But for all of radio's attributes—its vaunted immediacy and potential for doing good and motivating people—the product of our daily enterprise is instantly carried off via the airwaves and driven up into the ether, where it floats casually like the wind through the ionosphere, never to return.

But now, because there have occurred so many wonderful moments that were captured by our microphones over the years, I've tried to gather some of the highlights and preserve them. My first three volumes for Fordham University Press—*AirWAVES!, It All Comes Back to Me Now,* and *More Riffs, Rants, and Raves*—were generously received, quite beyond their due, as you will notice in the blurbs and encomiums in the front and at the back of this fourth volume.

Every book is a reflection of a writer's life and experience. And a lot has happened in the world since my last collection was published, in mid-2004. Most of the broadcasts, speeches, interviews, and occurrences in this book took place in the past several years, at the beginning of the new millennium. That realization and the ticking of the clock made me dig a little deeper into our archives and tape library. Thus, this fourth volume includes some extraordinary broadcasts, which I thought I'd run by you one more time.

In the end, I make my living with words, and so do all the others I've included in this volume. Quite apart from my own meager and inartful contributions, it has been a privilege to amplify the voices of so many wonderful and intelligent souls who have sat before our microphones.

Sooner or later everyone peddling a proposition, an idea, a book (or a candidacy) finds his or her way to Westchester County because that's where the money and the influence reside: between the Hudson River and Long Island Sound, in the Heart of the Eastern Establishment, the privileged area they call the Golden Apple.

So make no mistake: Radio is my first love, for all the reasons I've given here. But I love *books*, too. And I owe them a great debt. I never attended a day of college (something I hope my listeners will not hold against me). The books I've read and collected, as well as the five or six newspapers I read each morning, gave me a valuable education.

So I have a real thing for books. And libraries where they reside. And bookstores where they first see the light of day after they are bound and published. Books have staying power. And when I'm not writing or reading them, I sometimes "rescue" them—like for instance a few weeks ago, when I visited a country fair in the Litchfield Hills of Connecticut and was immediately drawn to a tent filled with "decommissioned" library books from the Goshen Rural Free Library. There, for $1 each, I lugged home the writings of Camus, a biography of Tip O'Neill, Jack Newfield's magnificent memoir of Bobby Kennedy, Ben Bradlee's autobiography of his life at the *Washington Post,* a novel by Pete Hamill, a collection of Jimmy Breslin's columns, and *Jinx,* a fifty-year-old book about Jinx Falkenburg, who left us a few years ago and for whom Nancy and I had great affection.

Most of these and the others I loaded into the trunk of my 'Vette were published some thirty or forty years ago. And after languishing in that country library, they now have a new life in my own personal library and here at the radio station, where they'll never be "decommissioned."

I thought about that day at the country fair as I was putting the finishing touches to *Vox Populi: The O'Shaughnessy Files.* I believe there is some fine stuff in this book that is worth preserving. But the judgment as to its merit and ultimate staying power won't be made by me or even by the readers of this first edition, which will see the light of day in the fall of 2010, but rather by someone who wanders into a tent at a country fair many years from today. I pray this book commends itself to their favorable judgment. And to yours.

Westchester, the Golden Apple
A summer day in 2010

P.S. I have to confess that I also see this book as an opportunity to do something for an organization I have long admired. The Broadcasters Foundation of America, based in New York City, will again receive all royalties from this book. A few years ago it occurred to Ward Quaal, the legendary gray eminence of our tribe, that not everyone makes the big bucks that flow to the brilliant likes of Don Imus, Howard Stern, Oprah, or Scott Shannon. So Mr. Quaal, together with well-known broadcast executive Gordon Hastings, and helped by the generous purse of Patricia McLaughlin and her husband, Ed, discoverer of Rush Limbaugh, took a tired, fading organization called the Broadcast Pioneers and turned it into the Broadcasters Foundation of America, a first-class and highly effective national charity that operates as a safety net for our colleagues all across the country who have fallen on hard times, many of them obscure "sidemen" in orchestras long dispersed.

The present board of the foundation includes Joe Amaturo, David Barrett, George Beasley, Philip Beuth, Richard Bodorff, Del Bryant, Rick Buckley, Carl Butrum, Gary Chapman, Edward Christian, Larry Dunn, Erica Farber, Dick Ferguson, Joe Field, Skip Finley, Andy Fisher, Dick Foreman, Alan Frank, Ralph Guild, Wade Hargrove, Esq., Paul Karpowicz, Scott Knight, Jerry Lee, Jerry Levy, Edward McLaughlin, Deborah Norville, Stu Olds, Joe Reilly, former Senator Gordon Smith, Jeff Smulyan, Peter Smyth, George Stephanopoulos, Dennis Swanson, Nick Verbitsky, Diana Wilkin, and Ed Wilson. These generous souls have again wisely elected Phil Lombardo, the dynamic former head of the National Association of Broadcasters and Citadel Television, as a member of its executive committee and chairman of our foundation, which I have been privileged to serve as chairman of its Guardian Fund.

It's a very worthy, focused, and well-run charity. And thus I hope you won't mind my suggesting that if you're sitting on a few bucks and want to do something to help some radio and TV folks who have entertained and informed you over the years, only to have been dealt a poor hand as a result of sickness or loss of a spouse, please consider calling Jim Thompson, our president, at (212) 373–8250. He and Chairman Phil Lombardo, a relentlessly generous guy in his own right, will be glad to tell you about the wonderful work of a great charitable organization. For those who are more "technologically savvy" than I, the email address is citnyltd@aol.com.

ACKNOWLEDGMENTS

For openers, I'm grateful, beyond my capacity to express it, to Fordham University Press, the great Jesuit publishing house in New York City. Operating from their ancient three-story building just off the Fordham campus in the Bronx, the Press has earned an international reputation for scholarship—which I hope I have not damaged or diminished with my clumsy efforts.

The Press's former director Saverio Procario, an old Rockefeller Republican, has been my friend and mentor for many years. During his tenure as director, the Press grew in stature and influence; it now publishes more than forty books of scholarship and regional history each year.

Mr. Procario's unique genius has been continued by his successors and their talented associates. And by five other great souls at the Press to whom I'm indebted for their extraordinary interest in all four of my books. Margaret Noonan is the great definer and protector of Fordham University Press (when she's not rooting for that other magnificent Bronx institution, her beloved Yankees). Kate O'Brien uses her considerable influence with booksellers and the media to find shelf space for my books all over the country. But first we had to produce the four books that bear my poor name and Fordham's prestigious imprimatur, and for their production and design I was privileged to rely on the creativity and judgment of Loomis Mayer, who knows all the levers and secrets of publishing. I'm especially grateful to Loomis, and to the Press's brilliant new director, Fredric Nachbaur. I liked Fred instantly when I came bearing my latest manuscript, and this book would not have had a chance without his blessing and encouragement. And for his relentless genius, good humor, and dazzling skills as a copy editor, I'm immensely grateful to the Press's managing editor, Eric Newman, for cleaning up my act and making it worthy of a great publishing house with an international reputation.

All their worthy and scholarly publishing activities and literary efforts are, of course, informed by the example and vision of two extraordinary educators: Father Joseph O'Hare, S.J., who is universally admired for his public service in New York City as well as for his academic leadership, and Father Joseph M. McShane, S.J., a brilliant and, if he will permit me, a saintly man, as well as a great educator and administrator, who is Father O'Hare's successor as president of Fordham University.

The jacket and the interior of this fourth volume were designed by the legendary Rich Hendel of Chapel Hill, North Carolina. One of the most prolific and heralded in his field, Rich Hendel actually "wrote the book" (no pun intended) on the subject with his classic text *On Book Design* for Yale University Press. His genius at layout and design is everywhere apparent in this new anthology, and I am grateful to the elders at Fordham University Press for persuading this great artist to put his imprimatur on our efforts.

The great barroom philosopher Mr. Bernard "Toots" Shor once famously observed, "Me and my pals won't read a book that doesn't have an *index* so we can look up our names without having to waste time on the rest of the stuff!" I took the hint. And I'm grateful to the great researcher Jennifer Rushing-Schurr for identifying not only the marvelous *characters* found on almost every page of this, my fourth, anthology, but also for identifying and organizing the *themes* contained herein. She's the best in the business.

Cindy Hall Gallagher has been my friend, confidante, and Executive Everything for thirty-three years. As an amanuensis and personal assistant, she has no equal. Dwight Eisenhower and, later, Nelson Rockefeller enjoyed the brilliant service of the legendary Ann Whitman to run their offices and lives. And Mario Cuomo, during the various seasons of his life, relied on Mary Tragale, Pam Broughton, and now the estimable Mary Porcelli. As great as all these women are, they can't compare to Mrs. Gallagher. Cindy's intuitive powers and wise judgment inform everything I do. And my family shares my admiration and affection for this marvelous woman who has devoted herself to me and mine for almost four decades.

Anthony Chiffolo is an author of many inspiring prayer books and works on the lives of the saints, not to mention two cookbooks! He is also a gifted editor whose brilliance is reflected in my second anthology, *It All Comes Back to Me Now.* Anthony has also done books on two pontiffs—John XXIII and John Paul II. How can you argue with a guy who has edited two popes? I don't even try.

I should also acknowledge the many contributions of Don Stevens, our Whitney Radio chief of staff, whom I literally found among the smoke and ruins when the former WVIP in northern Westchester burned to the ground. Don was the last man standing at that fabled community station. He is a great and dedicated advocate for radio, and when he is not presiding over WVOX and our new WVIP, Don counsels and instructs young broadcasters at Dick Robinson's highly regarded Connecticut Schools of Broadcasting. We are all his students.

For the purpose of running Whitney Radio, the people of Westchester and I are fortunate to enjoy the enterprise and selfless service of my son David Tucker O'Shaughnessy, Judy Fremont, John Harper, Bob Marrone, Richard Littlejohn, Nick Sarames, Stephanie Lombardo, Kevin Elliott, Debbie Schechter, Chris Conway, Chris Clarke, Sara Caldwell, Chuck Donegan, Nick Golden, Russ Mafes, Chris Sylvester, Bud Williamson, Dennis Jackson, and Clif Mills Jr., most of whom, like Judy, John, and Richard, have been with us for many, many years.

We are also blessed by the enterprise and creativity of the incomparable Gregg Pavelle, Irma Valencia, William Kennedy, Dave Piwowarski, Mark Cheetham, Jesus Valencia, Vee Peterson, Betty Ann Mummert, and Thomas Johnson, all of whom excel in those many areas where I come up short. I'm grateful for their presence in our lives.

As the permittee of WVOX and WVIP, which, as of the fall of 2010, are just about the last remaining independent stations in the New York area, I'm immensely grateful to several other talented folks—experts in the law, real estate, finance, and architecture who help us keep these two stations relevant and away from the speculators, predators, and absentee owners who have descended on our tribe since consolidation began in the 1980s. Those generous souls, who over the years have "adopted" our radio stations, include Judge Charlie Gill, Anita Oken, Judge Ann Dranginis, William Plunkett, Jeff Bernbach, Joe Reilly, General Joe Spinelli, Alan Rosenberg, Ken

Raske, Michele Silva, Michael Fasano Sr., Elliot Wiener, Judge Samuel George Fredman, Henry Berman, Frank Connelly Jr., Kathleen Plunkett O'Connor, Chuck Strome, Patrick Carroll, John Vasile, Bill McKenna, Bep McSweeney, William O'Neill, Emilie O'Sullivan, Jean Ensign, John Van Buren Sullivan, Erwin Krasnow, Jules Cohen, Bernie Koteen, and the late Rainer Kraus.

Pierre Teilhard de Chardin, the great Jesuit philosopher and paleontologist, wrote of the "diminishments" we all suffer as we get older. I've been very fortunate during my already long life to have encountered some terrific medical practitioners who help me confront those diminishments. I've written previously of my great admiration for Dr. Richard Rocco Pisano, who, with his wife, Cathy, runs a modest but thriving "mom-and-pop" medical office. He still makes house calls and does a lot of *pro bono* work in the wilds of Westchester. That alone should recommend the guy, in an age when a lot of doctors are in it strictly for the bucks. The elders at John Spicer's Sound Shore Medical Center, the best community hospital in the New York suburbs, have previously elected Dr. Pisano chairman of the medical board. Forget all those long-overdue honors and encomiums. When you're scrambling and in trouble, you couldn't have a brighter, more caring fellow on the case. Thank God, I've had to "scramble" only a few times in my seventy-two years. And as I sit here at my desk early on a September morning in 2010, I am also aware of my debt to Dr. Marc Eisenberg, Dr. Fritz Ehlert, Dr. Paul Pellicci, Dr. Bernard Kruger, Dr. Steven Butensky, Dr. Kevin Falvey, Dr. David Breindel, Dr. Kenneth Porter, and Dr. Sandy Mirabile. They are all legends in their fields. They deserve their international reputations. And my thanks.

I would also beg an author's privilege to tell you of my tremendous pride in my children: Matthew Thayer O'Shaughnessy; David Tucker O'Shaughnessy and his wife, Cara Ferrin O'Shaughnessy; Kate O'Shaughnessy Nulty and her husband, Jerry Nulty; and my late son Michael Curry Pasquale. They are good, strong souls, and each one is more attractive and loving than the next.

And like all grandfathers everywhere, I'm crazy about Tucker Thomas Nulty, Isabel Grace O'Shaughnessy, Flynn Thayer Nulty, Lily Anna O'Shaughnessy, and Amelia Jane Wharton Nulty. A New

York power broker I know—Jim Gill—recently wrote an entire four-hundred-page paean to his grandchildren. I'll just do this meager paragraph and go back to thinking up ways to see them often. And I just want to stick around long enough to walk each one of them into "21" for the first time.

For the sweetness of his friendship and constant inspiration, I owe an incalculable debt to a failed baseball player with too many vowels in his name. Governor Mario M. Cuomo is the most impressive public figure I've encountered during my time at the people's business. I was raised by a father who idolized Franklin Roosevelt, Al Smith, James A. Farley, and Jimmy Walker. And as a young man, I was greatly enamored of the Kennedy brothers and so I eagerly embraced the appellation "Kennedy Democrat." After they were taken, I slowly drifted toward the dazzling persona and dynamism of my incomparable Westchester neighbor Nelson Rockefeller, who was so wonderfully supportive of our local radio stations. And so over the years, I became a self-styled "Rockefeller Republican," which progressive label I proudly wear to this day.

However, as much as I admired Jack and Bobby Kennedy and the great Rockefeller, they did not have the profound, lasting impact on my psyche and soul as has Mario Cuomo. When he served as governor of New York for twelve years, from 1983 to 1994, I was not at all popular with his counselors, retainers, and senior staff, because I was all the while insisting that the mundane minutiae of his job was not worthy of his stunning talents.

In the years since he left Albany, Mario Cuomo has become not only America's greatest orator but also, I'm persuaded, the greatest thinker of the late twentieth and early twenty-first century. Week after week, month after month, this great and good man is out on the road—in lecture halls and on college campuses—peddling the Eternal Truths and fundamental values to all who will listen. Despite the importunings of his party and admirers, he never made it to the White House or the Supreme Court. But his goodness, his teachings, and his example will, I'm sure, endure long after the public record and pronouncements of any of our presidents or Supreme Court justices. Cuomo is the best politician—public servant—during my time. His wisdom will endure through the ages. I'm absolutely certain of it.

Essentially, I think, Mario Cuomo is a *teacher* of rare gifts who is possessed of great eloquence and a wonderful soul. And I recall a conversation some years ago with a high-ranking member of our Roman Catholic Church in which we agreed that Cuomo seemed to be irresistibly drawn to the great moral issues of the day in his pronouncements. And when I suggested that perhaps the "unease" some in the Church hierarchy harbored about the governor was attributable to his great mind and brilliance, this high-ranking churchman said, "Oh, no, O'Shaughnessy, they're afraid of his *goodness*."

Mario Cuomo has inspired so many during what he calls his "already long life," and I am obviously among them. I would not have found the resolve and focus to do this book—or the first three volumes, for that matter—without the governor's gentle urging and consistent encouragement. In case you haven't noticed: I love the man.

F.O.B. (FRIENDS OF BILL)

I'm also grateful to those generous individuals who have indulged my passions and enthusiasms during my professional life of some 50 years. All my writings, broadcasts, editorials, pronouncements, and speeches—indeed, my whole *life*—have been instructed and enhanced by their kindness and, in many cases, by their love.

Each has weighed my faults and shortcomings less diligently than they have assessed what they find commendable in my stewardship. And so I'm immensely grateful to them . . . collectively *and* individually. It's not so hard making your way in life with these dear souls cheering for you.

Bob Abplanalp; Michael Ackerman; Cindy Adams; Jazzy Adams Jr.; Juicy Adams; Roger Ailes; J. Lester Albertson; Harry Albright Jr.; Col Allan; Snoopy Allgood; JR Allen; Mel Allen; David Allyn; Warren Alpert; Gregorio Alvarez; Miosotis Nuñez Alvarez; Lynne Ames; Phil Amicone; Louise and Captain Joseph Anastasi; Kelly and Ernie Anastos; Robin Andersen; Kristine Anderson; Walter Anderson; Senator Warren Anderson; Dean Andrews; Judge Dan Angiolillo; Joe Angiolillo; David Annakie; Joe Apicella; Peter Applebome; Bob Armao; Louis Armstrong; Judy and Mickey Arons; Brooke Astor; Monsignor Terry Attridge; Ken Auletta; Al Ayers; Nadar Aziz; Paul Aziz; Peter Aziz; Jon Ballin; Whitney Balliett; Petey "Bananas"; Frank Bandy; Steve Barkaszi; Ed Barlow; Tim Barrett; James Barron; Mary and Bruce Barron; Jean and Ralph Baruch; Maureen Bateman; Frank Becerra; P. J. Bednarski; Charles "Bill" Bell; Rocco Bellantoni Jr.; Gerald Benjamin; Danny Bennett; Richard Rodney Bennett; Tony Bennett; Kara Benorth; Max Berking; Hilda and Bill Berkowitz; Randy Berlage; Fran Berman; Richard Berman; Ronnie and Henry Berman; Andrea Bernacchia; Robin and George Bernacchia; Karen and Jeffrey Bernbach; Jerry Berns; Steve Bernstein; James Berry; Dominique Bertolone; John Bertsch; Terry Betteridge; Phil Beuth; Mario Biaggi; Ken Bialo; Ron Bianchi; Stanley Bing; Richard Biondi; Ira Birnbaum; Paolo Biscioni; Joseph Biscoglio;

Junior Jawara Blake; Bob Blank; Robert Blau; Valerie Block; Michael Blitzer; Joan and Lou Boccardi; John Bodnar; Bill Boggs; Mary Ann Bonito; Tyrus Bonner; Tradeep Bose; Pierre Bouvard; Frank Bowling; Barbara Boxer; Michael Boyle; Frank Boyle; Jack Boyle; James Brady; Noam Bramson; John Branca; Lydia and Sergio Braszesco; Paul Braun; Dr. David Breindel; Jimmy Breslin; Jimmy Breslin Jr.; Judge Evans Brewster; Colonel Paul Breyer; William Brick; Judge Charles Brieant; Stefano Briganti; Lois Bronz; Jill Brooke; Alexander Brooks; David Brown; Ed Brown; Gary Brown; James Brown; Les Brown; Marilyn and Warren Brown; Michael Brown; Roberta and Rick Brudner; Bob Bruno; Rick Buckley; Adam Buckman; Judge Valerie Bullard; Tom Buono; Peg and George Burchell; Johnny Burke; Patricia and Barrett Burns; Colin and Janet Burns Sr.; President George H.W. Bush; Jodi and Jonathan Bush; William "Billy" Bush; William Butcher; Di and Steven and Maxwell Butensky; John Cahill; Frank Calamari; Kimberly Callet; Bob Cammann; Angela Campbell; Inez Candrea; Jimmy Cannon; Trish and Joseph Wood Canzeri; Tony Capasso; Kylie and Louis Cappelli; Paul Capelli; Danny Capello; Nat Carbo; Anthony Carbone; Governor Hugh Leo Carey; Leslie and Peter Carlton-Jones; Jim Carnegie; Father Michael Carnevale, OFM; Oreste Carnevale; Michael Carney; Peter Carpenter; Kathleen and Patrick Carroll; Maurice "Mickey" Carroll; Arthur Carter; Dr. Frank Cartica; Bill Cary; Matthew Cashman; Dan Castleman; Sabrina and Charles Barton Castleberry; Ray Catena; Father Joseph Cavoto; Bill Cella; Louis Ceruzzi; Jeff Champion; Ken Chandler; Richard Chapin; John J.J. Chapman; Dr. Alan Chartok; Jessica and Mark Cheetham; Jody Chesnov; Anthony Chiffolo; Paul Chou; Sir Harold Christie; Kristen Cilento; John Cilibergo; Jim Cimino; Casper Citron; Joe Claffey; Andy Clark; Bill Clark; Bobby Clark; James Mott Clark Jr. ; Richard McC. Clark; Pastor Valentine Clark; Lynn Claudy; Gayle and Linden Clay; Tony Cobb; Mike Cockrell; Jules Cohen; Stanley Cohen; Judge Nick Colabella; Anthony J. Colavita; Anthony Colavita Jr.; Kenneth Cole; Maria Cuomo Cole; Nat "King" Cole; Andre Coleman; Dr. Robert Coles; Brian Collins; Michael Collins; Pat Collins; Alan Colmes; Cooper Colwell; David Patrick Columbia; Rick Condon; Tom Condon; Cheryl Connelly; Frank Connelly Jr.; Monsignor Edward Connors;

Katherine Wilson Conroy; Jimmy Cosgriff; Tom Constantine; Elaine and E. Virgil Conway; Dorothy and Burton Cooper; Tino Cornaccio; Frank Corvino; Richard Cotter; Jack Coughlin; Tom Coughlin; Andrea Stewart-Cousins; Rev. Lester Cousins; Jay Couture; General Richard Crabtree; Judy Craig; Ted Crane; Jeff Crawford; Fran and D. Bruce Crew III; Guido Cribari; Dan Cronin; Betsy and Walter Cronkite; Jerry Crotty; Lynn Crystal; Matthew J. "Joe" Culligan; Jerry Cummins; Bill Cunningham; Jim Cunningham; Pat Cunningham; Andrew Mark Cuomo; Christopher Cuomo; Governor Mario M. Cuomo; Matilda Raffa Cuomo; Steve Cuozzo; Ambassador Walter J.P. Curley; Dave Curran; Father Charles L. Currie, S.J.; Bernard F. Curry Jr.; Bo, Jack, Cynthia, and Bernie Curry; Joe Curtis; Connie Cutts; Dominick D'Agostino; Alfonse D'Amato; Ken D'Ambrosio; Joan and Richard D'Aronco; Armando D'Onofrio; Florence D'Urso; Rocco Dalvito; Stacey and Marvin Dames; Tony Damiani; Jerry Danko; Fred Danzig; Esther Davidowitz; Electra Davis; Emery Davis; Ernie Davis; Evan Davis; Ossie Davis; Arnaud de Borchgrave; John Dean; Morton Dean; John Dearie; Ruby Dee; Margaret DeFrancisco; Vincent de Jager; C. Glover Delaney; George Delaney; Dee DelBello; Jerry DelColliano; Franco Delle Piane; Cartha "Deke" DeLoach; Ed Dennis; Matt Dennis; Matt Denti; Becky Deo; Joe DePaolo; Andrea and Richard Derwin; Abramo DeSpirito; Allison and Matthew Deutsch; Judge Charlie Devlin; James Diamond; Fred Dicker; Mary Dickson; Tara and Arthur Hill Diedrick; Max DiFabio; Bernie Dilson; Fiorita and Michael DiLullo; Joseph Paul DiMaggio; Lynn DiMenna; Giovanni DiNardo; Mayor David Dinkins; Dave DiRubba; Charles Dolan; Father Charles F.X. Dolan, S.J.; Father James Dolan, S.J.; James Dolan; Judge Denny Donovan; Robert Royal Douglass; John E. Dowling; Michael Dowling; Hugh A. Doyle; Judge Anne Dranginis; Brother John Driscoll; Sean Driscoll; Dr. Ronald Drusin; Owen Duckett; John Dudley; Bobby Duffy; Steve Dunleavy; Larry Dunn; John R. Dunne; Joan Dupay; Bruno Dussin; David Dziedzic; Dick Ebersol and Susan St. James; Cashie and Tom Egan; Edward Cardinal Egan; John Eggerton; Fritz Ehlert; Gregory Ehrlich; Lee Einsidler; Marc Eisenberg; Peter Elliot; Kevin Elliott; Lee Elman; Arnold Elser; Chris Elser; Edward E. Elson; Arthur Emil; Bill Ennis; Jean T. Ensign; Jaime and Alfonso Escobar; Lee Evans; Linda

Evans; Ed Evers; Junior Ewart; Terry Ezekiel; Kate and John Fahey; Lucille Falcone; Jinx Falkenburg; Kevin Falvey; Bill Fanning; Erica Farber; Joe Farda; Steve Farrell; Michael Fasano Sr.; Mario Faustini; Norm Fein; Matt Feinberg; Paul Feiner; Shirin and Frédéric Fekkai; Steven Fendrich; Massimo Ferragamo; Rich Ferrara; Linda and David Ferrin; Giancarlo Ferro; Bram Fierstein; Suzi Finesilver; Mike Finnegan; Brad Firkins; Jim Fitzgerald; William FitzGibbon; John Fix III; Mary and John Fix Jr.; Adrian Flannelly; Doug Fleming; Guillermo "Memmo" Flores; Barbara Fluker; Charles L. Flynn; Ed Flynn; Dr. Thomas Fogarty; Marty Fogelman; Trevor Forde; Richard Foreman; Bob Forstbauer; George Forstbauer; Arnold Forster; Joe Fosina; John Fosina; Al Fox; Ray Fox; Roy Fox; Paul Francis; George Frank; Jon R. Frank; Sidney Frank; Joe Franklin; Frank Franz; Ann and Dr. Richard A.R. Fraser; Joe Fredericks; Justice Samuel Fredman; Roy Fredriks; Maurice Freedman; Louis Freeh; Judy Fremont; Richard French; Emily Freund; Ralph Freydberg; Adam Friedlander; Sharon Friedlander; Michael Friedman; Richard Friedman; Martha Dale and Eddie Fritts; Alan Fuerstman; William Denis Fugazy; Bob Funking; Chris Furey; Frances Fusco; Judge Louis Fusco; Mario Gabelli; Judge Joseph Gagliardi; Anthony Galetta; Bernard Gallagher; Cindy, Kevin, Kevin Jr., Joseph, and Alicia Gallagher; Jay Gallagher; Jim Gallagher; "Scoop" Gallello; John Gambling; Dave Gardner; Jack Gardner; Rev. Richard Garner; Marina Garnier; Karen Gavell; Ira Gelb; Leon Geller; Dr. Irwin Gelman; Harold Geneen; James Generoso; Jean and Sal Generoso; Arthur Geoghegan; Dr. Viji George; Paul Gerbi; Edward "Ned" Gerrity; David Ghatan; Mark Giannini; Commodore William Gibbons; Marjorie and Dick Gidron; Kathie Lee and Frank Gifford; Lou Gigante; Joan and Phil Gilbert Jr.; Jim Gill; Joan and Judge Charles Gill; Ben Gilman; Martin Ginsburg; Fred Gioffre; Louise and Anthony B. Gioffre; Dr. Bernard Gitler; Robert Giuffra Jr.; Billy Gleason; Chris Godfrey; Marla Golden; Judge Howard Goldfluss; Marvin Goldfluss; Bruce Golding; Kevin Goldman; Martin Goldsmith; Larry Goldstein; Terry Golway; Peter Goodman; Senator Roy Goodman; Bryon Gordon; Marsha Gordon; Rob Gordon; Andy Gorran; Jim Graham; Murray Grand; Bob Grant; Emily and Eugene Grant; Louie Grant; Ralph Graves; E. T. "Bud" Gravette Jr.; Bill

Greenawalt; Bernadette Greene; Robert Greene; Teddy Greene; Jeff Greenfield; Jon Greenhut; Fred Greenstein; Lee and Jim Greenwald; Cristina Greeven and Chris Cuomo; Regina and Rainer Greeven; Jamee and Peter Gregory; Bill and Peter Griffin; Dr. Ray Griffin; Steve Grossman; Rich Guberti; Tony Guest; Thomas Guida; Tonny Guido; Claude Guigon; Ralph Guild; Charlotte and Denny Haight; Pete Hamill; Adam Handler; Lynn and Jerry Handler; Joseph Hankin; Anne Harmon; John Harper; Patricia Harper; Fred Harris; Ron Harris; Michael Harrison; Kitty Carlisle Hart; Professor Willem Hart; Constance and Jack Hartnett; Graham Hastedt; Lynn and Gordon Hastings; David Hauk; Cindy and Carl Hayden; Chris Hazelhurst; Vernon Headley; David Hebert; Mark Hedberg; Paul Hedberg; George Helm; Darryl Henline; John Hennessy Jr.; Jim Henry; Joyce Hergenhan; Scott Herman; Patrick Hermanto; Ralph Hersom; Fr. Rusty Hesse; Nat Hentoff; Jamie Hewitt; Neil Hickey; Ernest Hickman; David Hicks; Bob Himmelberg; David Hinckley; Father Michael F.X. Hinkley; Milton Hoffman; Tom Hogan; Earl Holding; Alisa Holland; Philip Hollis; Phil Hollis Jr.; Jim Holm; Napoleon Holmes; David Honig; Al Hood; Valerie Hovasapian; Cheryl and Bill Howard; Debby and Jim Howard; Karen and Stanley Hubbard; Ed Hughes; Wally Huffman; Bobby Hutton; Paul Hutton; George Hyde; Bob Hyland; Tim Idoni; Don Imus; Michael Israel; Dennis Jackson; Mary Ann Jacon; Barbara Curry James; O. Aldon James Jr.; Peter Jarjura; Dr. Joel Jarolimek; Senator Jacob K. Javits; Marian Javits; Joan Jedell; Ralph M. Jennings; Evan Jerome; Marc Jerome; Steve Jerome; Harry Jessell; Coula and Steve Johnides; Sessa and Richard Johnson; Tom Johnson; Margo Jones; David Josey; Jim Joyce; Judy Juhring; Jack Kadden; Milton Kael; Charles Kafferman; Larry Kaiser; Peter Kalikow; Jason Kam; Noel Kane; Peter Kanze; Peter Kaplan; Rick Kaplar; Mel Karmazin; Paul Karpowicz; Farooq Kathwari; Dr. Neil Katz; Elaine Kaufman; Msgr. Charles Kavanagh; Walter Kaye; Gerald Keane; Ralph Kebrdle; Nancy Q. Keefe; Pat Keegan; William W. Keifer; Paula Kelleher; Bob Keller; Dan Kelly; Ed Kelly; Jane and John "Shipwreck" Kelly; Keith Kelly; Linda Kelly; Sue Kelly; Irving Kendall; Walter Kennedy; William Kennedy; Andy Kenney; Doug Kennison; Aaron Kershaw; Ray "Doc" Kiernan; Corey Kilgannon; Jim Killoran; Guy King; Larry King; Mike Kinosian; Les

Kinsolving; Claude Kirchner; Henry Kissinger; Seiji Kitavato; Ruth Kitchen; Marv Kitman; Dr. Larry Klecatsky; Jeff Klein; Karen Klein; Sam Klein; Ira Kleinman; Carolyn Klemm; Fred Klestine; Winnie Klotz; Jack Knebel; Virginia and George Kneeland; Norman Knight; Scott Knight; Steve Knoll; Mayor Ed Koch; Peter Kohler; Oliver Koppel; Burt Korall; Peter Korn; Jay Kos; Robin Kotz; David Kowalski; Kate Kowalski; Laura O'Shaughnessy Kowalski; Carmela Kozinski; Larry Krantz; Erwin Krasnow; Emily Kratzer; Rainer Kraus; Pete Kreindler; Arthur Jerry Kremer; Dr. Bernard Kruger; Dave Kufeld; Marina Kuliakov; Cathy Kumbios; Bill Kunstler; Lisa Kushner; Cappy LaBarbara; Rita La Duc; Albert LaFarge; Ray Lahey; Denise Lally; Barry Landau; Andrew Langston; Jim Lanza; Joseph Lanza; Bob Lape; Marguerite Lascola; Tony Lash; George Latimer; Ron Leal; Susan and Jerry Lauren; Rena and Leonard Lauren; Connie Laverty; Patricia and Rick Lazio; Joseph Lazzaro; Thomas F. Leahy; Peter Leavey; Barbara Leavy; Michael LeBron; Jerry Lee; Louis Lefkowitz; Francine LeFrak and Rick Friedberg; Sam LeFrak; Richard Leibner; Laura Accurso and Scott Lennon; Paul Lenok; Jacques LeSourd; Mike Letis; Father Peter Levierge; Ellen Levin; Jan Levin; Mel Levin; Arthur Levitt; Jerry Levy; Marcel Levy; Mel Levy; Don Lia; Lava Libretti; Mike Licalzi; Mary Ann and Lewis Liebert; Scott Liebovitz; Alice and Allen Lin; John V. Lindsay; Mary Lindsay; Lionel; Robert Linzey; Jim Lisa; George Lisojo; Richard Littlejohn; Father James Lloyd; John Lehman Loeb; Stephanie Lombardo; Jimmy LoPilato; Jim Lowe; Nita and Steven Lowey; Luca; Charles Luce; William Luddy; Craig Lundquist; Dan Lynch; Peter Maas; Rita Mabli; General of the Armies Douglas MacArthur; Gavin K. MacBain; Joe Maccarillo; Egidiana and Sirio Maccioni; Lauren and Mario Maccioni; Bernard Luckner; Marco Maccioni; Mauro Maccioni; Nicola and Olivia Maccioni; Paul MacLane; Margaret and Howard Maier; John Mainelli; Patrick Maines; Jim Maisano; Tony Malara; Tim Malsbury; Ed Mancuso; Nick Manero; Squeegie Mangialardo; Jim Mann; Archbishop Henry Mansell; Ann and Wellington Mara; Steven March; Carl Marcucci; Tom Mariam; Don Mariani; Bob Marrone; Kevin Marquis; Charles Massimi; Charles Masson; Martin and Rose at Kennedy's; Douglas Martin; Joe Martin; Julie Martin; Angelo Martinelli;

Ralph A. Martinelli; Ralph R. Martinelli; Archbishop Renato Martino; Mike Martinez; Eve and R. J. Marx; Charlie Massimi; Val and Nick Mastronardi; Colonel Jim May; Walter May; Loomis Mayer; Judy Mayhew; Lowry Mays; Tom Mazenis; Bill McAndrew; Charlie McCabe; Kevin McCabe; Senator John McCain; Joyce and Carl McCall; Bishop James McCarthy; Brother James McCarthy; Michael McCarthy; Mary and Bob McCooey; Brian McCormick; Tim McCormick; Bernard McCoy; Bob McCurdy; Mary and Chief Justice Francis McDonald; Claudia McDonnell; Susan Mara and John McDonnell; Tim Mara McDonnell; Edwin McDowell; Bill McElveen; Kieran McElvenie; Steve McFadden; Jim McGinty; J. Raymond McGovern; Father Felix McGrath; Kevin B. McGrath; Bill McGrory; Mary McGrory; John McGovern; Bryan McGuire; Bill McKenna; Dave McKenna; Don McKenna; Gerald McKinstry; Renate and Thomas McKnight; Sandy McKown; Paul McLane; Pat and Ed McLaughlin; Randolph Scott McLaughlin; Rosemary and Charles McLaughlin; Stu McMillan; Patrick McMullan; Bruce McNichols; Father Joseph McShane, S.J.; Bep McSweeney; Karren and Dennis Mehiel; George Melkemus; Myron Melnikoff; Bruce Merbaum; Mabel Mercer; Ian Merlino; Marian and Robert Merrill; Jack Messmer; Bill Meth; Judith Meyer; Marcia Meyers; Frank Micelli; Mary Middlemiss; Paulo Midei; Edwin Gilbert Michaelian; Luigi Miele; Mike Miele; Barbara, Joseph, Mama Rose, and Mario Migliucci; Ray Miles; Cay Miller; Elmer Miller; Henry Miller; Luther Miller; Marcia Egan Miller; Mark Miller; Sandy Miller; Stella Miller; Clif Mills Jr.; Philip Milner; Dr. Richard Milone; Jackie and Judge Roger Miner; Peter Mintun; Bob Minzesheimer; Vincent Mirabile; Howard Mirchin; Lee Miringoff; Jay Mitchell; Marian and Bob Mitchell; Adriana and Robert Mnuchin; Shelby, Bill, Leslie, and Mitchell Modell; Heather Moe; Stan Moger; Chris Mohney; Mel and Stephen Moliterno; Joe Mondello; Joe Montalto; Louise Montclare; Nino Monte; Joseph Montebello; Bill Mooney; Garry Moore; Heather Moore; Robert Moore; Walter Moore; Mark Moran; Thomas Moran; Archbishop Eugene Moreno; Tom Moretti; Robert M. Morgenthau; Mike Moritz; Billy Morley; Geoffrey James Morris; Martha Evans Morris; Heather Morrison; Michael Mortara; Beverly and John Woodrow Mosch; Heather Moss; Arthur H. "Red" Motley; Carl Moxie; Senator

Daniel Patrick Moynihan; Liz Moynihan; Bill Mullen; Thomas Mullen; Brian Mulligan; Judge William Hughes Mulligan; Bill Mulrow; Betty Ann Mummert; Rupert Murdoch; Paul Murnane; Dan Murphy; JoAnn and Joe Murphy; Kent Murphy; Mark Murphy; Ray Murray; Patrick Muscillo; Peter Mustich; Fredric W. Nachbaur; Trish Nachstein; Helaine Naiman; Catfish Nardone; John Nashid; Vincent Natrella; Jimmy Neary; Gustav Neibuhr; Roxanne Neilson; Sheila Nevins; Jack Newfield; Dean Newman; Ambassador Edward Noonan Ney; Vu Nguyen; Julian Niccolini; Judge Frank Nicolai; David Nolan; Margaret Noonan; Alex Norton; Deborah Norville; Richard D. Novik; Jim Nugent; Amelia Jane Nulty; Flynn Thayer Nulty; Kate O'Shaughnessy Nulty; Jerry Nulty; Liz Nulty; Tucker Thomas Nulty; Briana Alvarez Nuñez; Jack O'Brian; Monsignor Bill O'Brien; Archbishop Edwin O'Brien; Des O'Brien; Father John O'Brien; Kate O'Brien; Bob O'Connell; Brother John Justin O'Connor; John Cardinal O'Connor; Kathleen and Kevin O'Connor; Madeline and Brian O'Donohue; Father Joseph O'Hare, S.J.; Michael "Buzzy" O'Keeffe; Monsignor Jack O'Keefe; Valerie Moore O'Keefe; Rita O'Mara; Paddy O'Neil; William O'Neill; Bill O'Reilly; Admiral Andrew O'Rourke; Ashley Elizabeth O'Shaughnessy; Cara Ferrin O'Shaughnessy; Catherine Tucker O'Shaughnessy; David Tucker O'Shaughnessy; Isabel Grace O'Shaughnessy; John Thomas O'Shaughnessy; Julie O'Shaughnessy; Kelly and John O'Shaughnessy Jr.; Laura O'Shaughnessy; Lily Anna O'Shaughnessy; Matthew Thayer O'Shaughnessy; Nancy Curry O'Shaughnessy; Taylor Meghan O'Shaughnessy; William Mac O'Shaughnessy; James O'Shea; Emilie O'Sullivan; Jim O'Toole; Tom O'Toole; Christiana Oakes; Sidney Offit; Anita Oken; Stu Olds; William Olson; Catherine and Gregory Oneglia; Ellen and Ray Oneglia; Rod Oneglia; Suzi Oppenheimer; Frank Orlando; Jorge Ortega; Nick Orzio; Congressman Richard Ottinger; Senator Bob Packwood; Len Paduano; Carl Pagano; Bob Paley; William S. Paley; Father Bernie Palka; Steven Palm; Cheryl Palmer; Fabian Palomino; Louis, Joe, and Robert Panico; Joe Parisi; Richard Parisi; Rev. Everett Parker; A. J. Parkinson; Richard Parsons; Michael Lawrence Pasquale; Vincent Pastore; Ron Patafio; Governor George E. Pataki; Libby Rowland Pataki; Ken Paul; Leo Paul; Amy Paulin; Gregg Pavelle; Jean and Jim Pawlik;

Carole Peck; Walter Peek; Steve Pellittieri; Eileen Perrotti; Vee Peterson; Rich Petriccione; Augie Petrillo; Alex Philippidis; Jacqueline Philpotts; Didier Picquot; Pat Pignatore; Joe Pilla; Cheryl Pinder; Marco Pipolo; Albert Pirro; Jeanine F. Pirro; Senator Joseph Pisani; Kathy and Richard Pisano; Donna and Dave Piwowarski; Caryl and William Plunkett; Erin Plunkett; Jake Plunkett; Patrick Plunkett; Rosemary and Kevin Plunkett; Ryan Plunkett; Tim Plunkett; Don Pollard; J. William Poole; Jean Poole; Mary Porcelli; Cole Porter; Kenneth Porter; Tom Poster; Irene and Fred Powers Sr.; Chris, Jeff, Fred III, and Stephen Powers; Ginny and Frederic Powers Jr.; Frances Preston; Lorenz Pretterhofer; Elaine Price; Hugh Price; Norman Pride; Al Primo; John Pritchard; Saverio Procario; Dominic Procopio; Ward Quall; Judge Kevin Quarante; Jim Quello; Milan Radolovic; Ian Rae; Joe Rao; Ken Raske; Jean and Dan Rather; M. Paul Redd; Mary Jane and Jack Reddington; Dr. George Reed; Rex Reed; Dana and Christopher Reeve; Mary Louise and Ambassador Ogden Rogers Reid; Carol Fernicola Reilly; Joseph Reilly; Daniel Reingold; Phil Reisman; Steven Reitano; Ron Rettner; Antonio Reyes; Eric Rhoads; Anthony Riccardi; Mike Richards; Rev. W. Franklyn Richardson; Murray Richman; Louise and Leonard Riggio; Joe Rinaldi; Monica and Judge Vincent Rippa; Eddie Robbins; Chris Roberts; Dick Robinson; Joseph Rocco; Col. Marty Rochelle; Happy Rockefeller; Laurance Rockefeller; Mark Rockefeller; Governor Nelson Aldrich Rockefeller; Nelson Rockefeller Jr.; Dotty Roer; Tom Rogers; William Pierce Rogers; Tim Rooney; Janine Rose; Rita and Phil Rosen; Pam Rosenberg; Wendy and Alan Rosenberg; Robert Rosencrans; A. M. Rosenthal; Phil Rosenthal; Steve Rosenthal; John Rotando; Kyle Rote; William "Billy" Rowe; CynDee Royle; Bruce Rubino; Kevin Ruddy; Anthony Rudel; Michel Rudigoz; Susan and Jack Rudin; Nancy Rutigliano; Dotore Natale Rusconi; Sylvia and Justice Alvin Richard Ruskin; Tim Russert; Liz Russo; Rich Russo; Tim Russo; Jack Rutledge; Ed Ryan; Tony Ryan; Dirk Sabin; Walter Sabo; Steve Sachler; Marcy Sackett; Steven M. Safyer, M.D.; Al and George Salerno; Arlene Salman; Joanna and General David Samson; Howard Samuels; Irv Samuels; Louis Sandroni; Ralph Sanzeri; Nick Sarames; Steve Savino; Frank Saxe; Steve Sayles;

Rosario Scandarito; Angela Scarano; Jack Scarangella; Chuck Scarborough; Judge Anthony Scarpino; Jon B. Schandler; Dr. Stanley Schneller; Edwin K. Schober; Cheryl and Barry Schwartz; Gil Schwartz; Jonathan Schwartz; Larry Schwartz; Louis O. Schwartz; William "Kirby" Scollon; Jim Scott; Justin Scott; William Scott; Paul Screvane; John Scroope; Mike Scully; Sue and John Scully; Dominick Sedita; Harold Segall; Phyllis and Ivan Seidenberg; Ginger and Honda Bob Seiperman; Rob Seitz Bruno Selimaj; Nino Selimaj; Grace Sensbach; Tony Serrao; Benito Sevarin; Gail Sevarin; Charlie Sgobbo; Hugh Shannon; Trish and Michael Scott Shannon; Charlie Shapiro; Alan Shayne; Wilfrid Sheed; Bob Sheppard; Val and Judge Preston "Sandy" Sher; Dr. Dan Sherber; Allie Sherman; Daryl Sherman; Dr. Shirley and James Sherwood; Bernard "Toots" Shor; Bobby Short; John Shuster; Michele Silva; Dr. Norman Silver; Fred Simon; Mark Simone; Francis Albert Sinatra; I. Philip Sipser; Marie and Brad Skinner; Curtis Sliwa; Ray Slobodzian; Brad Smith; Emily Smith; Francis and John Smith; Jan Johnson Smith; Liz Smith; Michael Smith; Professor Richard Norton Smith; Sally Bedell Smith; Shepard Smith; Terrence K. Smith; Walter "Red" Smith; Meredith Smulian; Tommy Smyth; Bruce Snyder; Jane Wharton Sockwell; Ellen Sokol; Scott Solomon; Tony Spadacini; Sam Spady; Andy Spano; Brenda Resnick Spano; Domenico Spano; Len Spano; Michael Spano; Nick Spano; Mayor John Spencer; Jerry Speyer; Rob Speyer; Cathy and John Spicer; Michael Spicer; Sue Spina; General Joseph Spinelli; Eliot Spitzer; Jeffrey Sprung; Neal Sroka; Tara Stacom; Gary Stanley; Dr. Frank Stanton; Sheila Stapleton; Jeannie Stapleton-Smith; Michael Starr; Charlie Steers; Ariana Steig; George M. Steinbrenner; Garry Steinhart; Andrew Stengel; Rene and Stuart Stengel; John Sterling; Howard Stern; Claire Stevens; Don Stevens; Gary Stevens; Steve Stickler; Martin Stone; Roger Stone; Allison Struck; Howard Sturman; Ellen Sulzberger Straus; Ambassador R. Peter Straus; Chuck Strome; Father John Sturm, S.J.; Bill Stutler; Barbara and Edward O. "Ned" Sullivan; Joan and John Van Buren Sullivan; Bishop Joe Sullivan; Arthur O. Sulzberger; Frederic Sunderman; Norman Sunshine; Teddy Suric; Seymour Surnow; Marianne Sussman; Ernie Sutkowski; Brad Sweeney; Stephen Sweeny; Marcy Syms; Sy Syms; Tony Taddeo;

Laurence Taishoff; Laurie and Rob Taishoff; Martha and Randy Taishoff; Sol Taishoff; Gay Talese; David A. Tanner; Albert Tarantino; Peter Tartaglia; Joan and Val Taubner; Eloise and James Taussig; Chris Taylor; Eddie Taylor; Sherill Taylor; Tom Taylor; Oren Teicher; Steve Tenore; Ann Wharton Thayer; Harry M. Thayer; Jeanne C. Thayer; Thomas Courtney Thayer; Walter Nelson Thayer; Deborah Thomas; Lowell Thomas; Maria Thomas; Jim Thompson; Kevin Thomson; Donald Thurston; Marnie and Adam Tihany; John Tolomer; Setrak Tokatzian; George Torello; Tony Torres; Neal and Tolly Travis; Alexander "Sandy" Treadwell; John Trevenan; Diane, John, Alex, and Kate Trimper; Frank Trotta Jr.; Billie Tucker; Carll Tucker Jr.; Father Robert Tucker; Hy B. Turner; Randy Tuttle; Mayor Joe Vacarella; Joe Valeant; Irma Valencia; Jesus Valencia; Lynn and Jerome A. Valenti; Ken Valenti; Lionel VanDeerlin; John Vasile; Linda and Roger Vaughn; Patrick R. Vecchio; Lloyd Veitch; Elian and Jose "Pepe" Vega; Bonnie and Nick Verbitsky; Carl Vergari; John Verni; Lillian Vernon and Paolo Martino; Davey Vichram; Lorenzo Viani; Wendy and Mike Victor; Lisa Vierling; Lloyd Vietch; Floyd Vivino; Margaret and Michael Vivolo; Sean Vokhshoorzadeh; Alex Von Bidder; Vic Vuksanaj; Joyce Wadler; Mario Wainer; Dr. Mary Beth Walsh; Paula Walsh; Claire and Howard Walsh; Judge William Walsh; Billy Walters; Calvin Walton; Emmanuel Wansi; Frank Ward; John Ward; Claudia and George Wardman; Father Robert Warren; Jim Watkinson; Craig Watson; Rosemary and William Weaver; Christa Weaving; Chris Webb; Karl Wellner; Charles Wendelken; Marty Weisberg; Richard Weinstein; Walter Weiss; Wes Weiss; Don West; Dr. Tom West; Merold Westphal; Jerry Whelan; Jack Whitaker; Bruce J. White; Ed Whitman; Ambassador John Hay Whitney; Margarita and Tom Whitney; L. H. "Hank" Whittemore; Ronny Whyte; Duffy Widmer; Chuck Wielgus; Elliot Wiener; Dr. Peter Wiernik; Frank Williams; Ken Williams; Bud Williamson; Ogan Williams; William B. Williams; Governor Malcolm Wilson; Matthew Withers; Rabbi Amiel Wohl; Fran Wood; Jonathan L. Wood; Minister C. V. "Jim" Woolridge, CBE; Bill Wright; Greg, Mark, and Dave Wright; Frank Young; Leigh Curry Young; Ryan Christopher Young; Tony Yurgaitis; Nina and Tim Zagat; Steven Zelicoff; Robert Zimmerman; Sid Zion; John Zogby; Susan and Art Zuckerman; Giuliano Zuliani.

Vox Populi

I BROADCASTING, CENSORSHIP, AND THE FIRST AMENDMENT

THE SILENCING OF IMUS

Censorship from corporate timidity in the face of economic boycotts is just as dangerous as the stifling of creative and artistic expression by government fiat, decree, sanction, or regulation. Here is our commentary from April 16, 2007.

Howard Stern, Opie and Anthony, Bob Grant, Bill Maher, Chris Rock, George Lopez, and even—God forbid!—Rosie. We've always had terrible examples to defend. And Don Imus has given us another stellar example. But defend it we must.

Not the hateful and discomfiting words. But the right of the social commentator to be heard, and the right of the people to decide.

Don Imus is a performer, a disc jockey, a humorist, and a provocateur with a rapier-sharp wit. Unlike many of our colleagues, he avoids raucous vulgarity or incendiary right-wing rhetoric directed at immigrants, illegal aliens, and other familiar targets of our tribe.

Throughout his brilliant career, Mr. Imus has been an equal-opportunity offender, poking fun at the high and mighty as well as at the rest of us for our foibles and pomposity. He may have occasionally gone too far. Were his comments about the Rutgers basketball team racist or mean-spirited? Only Imus knows for sure, but we doubt it. Were they funny? No.

His *mea culpa* and apologies seemed sincere. We had thus hoped his sponsors and the executives at CBS, WFAN, MSNBC, and all those local affiliates across the country would stand up to the pressure and continue to carry the I-Man.

So many successful performers take and put nothing back. Imus has been extravagantly generous to a number of worthy causes, often without fanfare.

Imus claims he's been active in our profession for 30 years—actually, it's closer to 40 since he came roaring out of Cleveland. By our calculation, that's about 8,000 broadcasts, with some 2,400,000 ad libs. Admittedly, none as insensitive as his reference to the Rutgers team.

This was a misfire. And it was to be hoped the executives at CBS and NBC would act accordingly.

Here's a baseball analogy. Suppose you had a pitcher, with remarkable stamina, who threw 8,000 innings. Many of his pitches will miss the strike zone. A few may even hit the poor batter. And during those 8,000 innings, spanning 30 or 40 seasons, he may even bean the umpire! But he's still a great pitcher.

With the possible exception of overnight broadcasting, from dusk until dawn, morning drive is the toughest shift in radio. And when Imus plops those well-traveled bones into a chair, straps on his earphones, and throws his voice out into another morning, armed only with his humor, wit, and irreverence, he may even be compared to a Franciscan priest dragging himself up into a pulpit after 30 or 40 years to pronounce the Good News before a sparse, sleepy congregation at an early Mass.

But Imus strives only to make us laugh or think. That's a pretty good way to make a living. And he should thus be protected from those unforgiving critics who heaped scorn and derision upon him as a result of this controversy.

The guy misfired. But he should not have been fired.

Censorship from corporate timidity in the face of economic boycotts is just as dangerous as the stifling of creative and artistic expression by government fiat, decree, sanction, or regulation.

That's just as treacherous as any racism, sexism, or bigotry.

THE UNDOING OF DON IMUS

Jonathan Bush, author of this commentary, is a brother of President George H.W. Bush, an uncle of President George W. Bush, and the father of rising TV–radio star William "Billy" Bush. His own father was the U.S. senator from Connecticut Prescott Bush. Jon is a successful investor based in New Haven. He and his wife, Jodi, never fail to remind us that their son and heir, Billy, got his start at WVOX. Young Mr. Bush is destined for even greater stardom. Jim Griffin, the uber-agent at the Paradigm Agency, told me that Billy Bush could be the next Johnny Carson. Meanwhile, his classy father retains a keen interest in the great issues of the day. This was his take on the silencing of the I-Man.

Much has been written and much said about the firing of Don Imus. After the recent appearance of Hillary Clinton at Rutgers, opportunistically pandering away, if a little late, about rising up against those who might disparage minorities or women, I felt compelled to speak up. So here goes.

About ten years ago, my company moved from New York to New Haven, and I undertook the daily grind of a forty-minute morning drive to work. In that first year I tuned my radio to Don Imus and have listened to him at least two or three days a week ever since. At times I found his show funny; at other times I would turn off the radio violently as he talked to politicians who did not exactly share my point of view. The show offered a welcome escape to the caged listener.

From laugh-out-loud-funny skits to serious political discussions to interviews with politicians to authors of books to country and western singers, no show presented an attention-getting format remotely close to that of "Imus in the Morning." Through it all, the mercurial Imus rode with effortless charisma, guiding the program with a sure hand and a deft instinct for humor. His long-suffering support staff stood ever at the ready to bail the chief out if he had gone too far.

Part of the schtick centered around Imus's fecklessness, such as a recent episode that focused on an invitation to Imus from Brian Williams to join him on a trip to Iraq. Naturally, the cast of characters discussed the idea that Imus was afraid to go. Imus, in a sense, was playing the role of everyman but with one exception: Imus's equivocating was delightfully funny.

Occasionally, Imus, speaking probably ten million words a year or more, would stray close to the line of decency. But listeners didn't particularly care. They tuned in to hear Imus's wit, Imus's charm, Imus's intransigence, Imus's melodic baritone voice—in short, Imus, warts and all.

Now on Thursday April 5, 2007, Imus, in a brief snippet of humor, let slip a demeaning phrase. He referred, jokingly, to the Rutgers women's basketball team as "nappy-headed hos." Could any sensible person think he meant this disparagingly? Of course not. However, he immediately apologized, subsequently almost falling over backward apologizing, even going on the radio show of one of the nation's leading mountebanks, the Reverend Al Sharpton. (As an aside, has anyone yet heard Sharpton apologize for his hand in the deplorable Tawana Brawley affair?)

So what happened? NBC turned off the cameras on MSNBC. Then CBS suspended Imus for two weeks. Then, knuckling under to pressure from a few big advertisers, themselves afraid of losing African American customers through a threatened boycott by Sharpton and the Reverend Jesse Jackson, Les Moonves of CBS canceled the entire show. Poof! Gone.

One thing amazes me: that in a country that prides itself on free speech, a gifted performer who brightens the lives of millions of listeners every morning could be snuffed out in an instant.

Of course cowardice gained the victory—the cowardice of Mr. Moonves, who knuckled under, and the cowardice of the advertisers who feared a boycott if they continued to sponsor Imus. However, far worse seems the cowardice of all those who fed at Imus's table only to abandon him when the tables turned against him. Where were those men and women whose voices should have spoken out against the firing?

On his program, Imus frequently used the term "weasel" to refer to those of whom, for one reason or another, he was being critical. Little did he know that the term would apply to all those people who toadied up to him, who leapt at the opportunity to appear on his program, only to run from him when their support was called for.

There exists one vast constituency who would gladly speak up for Imus had they but a voice so to do so—namely, the millions of listeners who have been denied the joy of hearing "Imus in the Morning" and who are wondering what happened to the idea "Let he who is without guilt among you cast the first stone."

BOB GRANT ON THE IMUS CONTROVERSY

It takes one to know one. Bob Grant has been pilloried, castigated, censured, and denounced by our colleagues in the public press. So it was to be expected he'd get his ire up when Imus was on the ropes. This is the interview he did with us on April 20, 2007.

WILLIAM O'SHAUGHNESSY (W.O.): In our profession, the Imus controversy lingers. The I-Man is silenced. For how long? Nobody knows. And we're going to switch now to New Jersey for the dean of talk show hosts, the great Bob Grant. We are all your students, sir. How do you see this controversy with Imus?

BOB GRANT (B.G.): Well, actually, after reflecting on it, I'm not really surprised. That doesn't mean I approve of what happened. But Don has lived on the edge for a long time. And, of course, when I heard about all this, I immediately thought about what happened to me eleven years ago.

Naturally, I understood when he said he was shocked because I was, too. Neither of us ever intended to get people so angry they would want us fired.

W.O.: Bob Grant, you, too, have been the victim of intimidation and coercion.

B.G.: Well, yes indeed. (*laughter*) So many things were broadcast with humor and then perceived to be very serious. I remember asking a program director, a very nice, sympathetic guy, "What are they taking this all so seriously for?" He replied, "Hey, wait a minute! That means you've achieved your goal!" And as far as Don is concerned, I believe certain people have taken him way too seriously.

W.O.: Should they have fired Don Imus, Bob Grant? MSNBC and CBS? Should they have thrown him off the air?

B.G.: Well, I thought they would suspend him. Matter of fact, I predicted, "Well, one week, maybe two." But, apparently, the pressure was so intense, sponsors were dropping like flies, and that's what did it. Purely economic. I'm sure the honchos at NBC and CBS weren't that offended in the beginning.

W.O.: What do you think about the heat he took from Jesse Jackson and Al Sharpton?

B.G.: Well, I've talked to people who say these guys didn't really care about the sensitivity of the Rutgers basketball team. But it's a great opportunity to insert themselves into a controversial issue and ride to the rescue of the damsels in distress.

W.O.: Bob Grant, it's so wonderful to hear your strong voice. Do you miss being on the radio?

B.G.: Yes. (*laughter*)

W.O.: Well, what does the lion do in the winter? Is there really a famous diner where you're the king?

B.G.: No. (*laughter*) As a matter of fact, it's not that close to where I live now.

W.O.: We're speaking to you from the Jersey shore?

B.G.: That's right. And I spend a lot of time at my new home in Florida. I love to travel, and I'm having fun just doing things I postponed for all those years.

W.O.: But, Bob Grant, if WABC or WOR called, would you saddle up again, strap on the earphones, and go back to a regular gig?

B.G.: I don't know about that. But maybe a part-time thing, once or twice a week.

W.O.: Are you going to tell us how old you are? Or how young you are?

B.G.: I'll say it indirectly. I made my entrance into the world on March 14, 1929, the birthday of Albert Einstein.

W.O.: Bob Grant, you graced our airways for a long, long time. You got some people mad at you. You made us all think. Has it changed over the years? I remember the great WNEW, and you were at WMCA, the Ellen and Peter Straus station. Do you still listen to the radio?

B.G.: I'm a little embarrassed to tell you, hardly at all. If I jump in the car, maybe I'll put something on.

W.O.: What do you watch on television in your Florida home or on the Jersey shore?

B.G.: Well, naturally, I watch CNN, MSNBC, and Fox News Channel. I'm addicted to the news channels. (*laughter*)

W.O.: Mario Cuomo, your old nemesis, I guess he's about seventy-four now. Did you ever make up?

B.G.: Well, no, we never did, and it's kind of sad in a way because at one time, I felt a great fondness for him, and he was a good friend. And when I say "good friend"—you know they throw that word around loosely—but one time, he really was.

The man has a great sense of humor. We had lunch together a couple of times. Then, I started kidding around, and over time, some people thought it was a shootout at the OK Corral. But I really bear him no malice whatsoever, and he would probably be surprised if he heard that. No, in many respects, he's a remarkable man.

W.O.: Bob Grant, I won't keep you long from your sojourn on the Jersey shore. I get a flash of déjà vu when you used to take callers, and I'm a little nervous interviewing the legendary Bob Grant. But it drove you nuts when they'd say, "Hi, Mr. Grant. How are you?" You couldn't stand small talk. Remember that?

B.G.: Well, that was only on the air. In real life, I'd give them a traditional response. But many times on the air, in the beginning of my career on the West Coast, they would start off by saying, "How are you?" and the next thing you know, they're attacking me! So my attitude was, "Let's dispense with the formalities," and my stock reply was, "What's on your mind, pal?"

W.O.: Bob Grant, I just want to hear you say it one more time for the record, "Get off my phone!"

B.G.: I'd be happy to! I might be out of practice, but I'll give it a shot. "Get off my phone, you creep!"

W.O.: Bravo! You still got your fastball! The great Bob Grant. Thank you, sir.

OBSEQUIOUS ACQUIESCENCE

This commentary, which was prepared for an NAB (National Association of Broadcasters) Summit, "Responsible Programming," held in Washington on April 7, 2004, was widely circulated in our broadcasting fraternity and quoted in all the major communications journals. We called it "A Runaway Freight Train Heading Straight for the First Amendment." I am indebted to Patrick Maines, Erwin Krasnow, Don West, Harry Jessell, John Eggerton, Floyd Abrams, Nat Hentoff, and several other First Amendment voluptuaries for their counsel and suggestions on this essay.

A runaway train is headed straight for our profession, with a head of steam from the FCC (Federal Communications Commission) and Congress. The passenger list includes misguided regulators, legislators, concerned citizens, and even some broadcasters. We have to stop this train to preserve our politics, governance, economy, and culture.

The people, our ultimate authority, must have freedom of expression. This extraordinary gift, the right to speak, to advocate, to describe, to entertain, to perform, to dissent?to sing?is more than a wonderful privilege; it makes this democracy a miracle.

The Founding Fathers gave us freedom of expression without nuance or conditions, but plainly and purely.

Some broadcasters, through excessive bad taste, reckless reporting, pervasively biased opinions and analysis—yes, palpable *un*fairness—have invited laws and rulings the Founding Fathers would have abhorred.

Still, we must stop this train.

We must continue to protect the broadest possible freedom of expression for the press. All of it, written and electronic. It is the coin of our democratic realm. But the flip side of that coin is responsibility.

As editors, as broadcasters, as permittees of the instruments of communication that are in our care and keeping, we should monitor ourselves to avoid retaliation. We have the power to transform our audience of millions and make them fuller, surer, sweeter.

As long as we treat our power and our privilege with the respect it deserves, we'll preserve for ourselves, and our posterity, the freedom to develop the richest and wisest culture ever.

In an election-year frenzy, Congress may crack down on broadcast "indecency" with scant regard for the robust tradition of free speech at the core of American values. If vulgar, outrageous, and tasteless speech isn't protected by the First Amendment, then the amendment has lost its meaning.

The prohibition against "indecent" speech does not apply to newspapers, magazines, books, or pamphlets. It does not apply to the Internet. It does not apply to satellite television, or cable or satellite radio. At least not yet.

Traditional, terrestrial broadcasting is currently exempted from equal protection. A lot of people think that is right and proper. They are wrong. In an age when all media is "electronic," it's increasingly difficult to justify this approach.

Does that mean radio and television will become as free as newspapers? Not likely. In today's climate, it could be the other way around. Will those who cheer as Congress clamps down on broadcasting have second thoughts when their favorite newspaper columnist is muzzled? It could happen.

As the revered Supreme Court Justice William O. Douglas once observed, "The fear that Madison and Jefferson had of government intrusion . . . was founded not only on the spectre of a lawless government but [on the spectre] of government under the control of a faction foisting its views of the common good on the people."

The First Amendment was enacted to prevent that. Yet an FCC policy against "indecent" speech, already dangerously vague, is expanding to include "profane" speech, with strict enforcement.

It has happened before. The Nixon FCC in 1971 declared that a broadcaster should carefully listen to, and understand, all the lyrics in a song before playing it, or else it would "raise . . . serious questions as to whether continued operation of the station is in the public interest."

In response, as Professor Lucas A. Powell Jr. noted in his book *American Broadcasting and the First Amendment*, station WNTN in Newton, Massachusetts, simply eliminated *all* Bob Dylan songs "because management could not interpret the lyrics!"

The FCC should not be the national arbiter of indecency and obscenity. With its inherent power to browbeat industry executives by bestowing, renewing, and revoking licenses, and to grant waivers of ownership rules, the FCC used to regulate by "raised eyebrow," but today, a more apt characterization might be by "sledgehammer."

These issues should be decided by the courts, applying the wisdom of the First Amendment, instead of the FCC, a politically appointed body. Indeed, the courts are the forum for obscenity and indecency regulation on cable, satellite, film, and the print media.

You can tell a lot about a nation, and the world, from what you hear on the radio. The current "indecency" campaign is led by some of the brightest and most capable leaders on the commission and in Congress. I admire their passion to heal an ailing world. But I disagree with their remedy.

"Indecency" should not be the subject of government regulation. If the central concept of our Constitution is liberty, its most important working principle is freedom of expression.

The Founding Fathers knew that, certainly. With a blunt and fundamental clarity, they wrote, "Congress shall make no law respecting an establishment of religion, or prohibiting the free exercise thereof; or abridging the freedom of speech, or of the press. . . ."

They understood that an oppressive government could not stifle the truth, or distort it, with a boldly free press. People could say what they wanted, when they wanted. Accurate or not. In good taste or bad. To give two sides of an issue, or only one. All in the name of freedom.

Over the years, the government dared to impose on broadcasters a standard of "right conduct" unthinkable for the print media and other forms of expression.

The reason the Founding Fathers left the balancing and filtering to the people, instead of to the politicians, applies perfectly to electronic broadcasting as well.

Censoring electronic speech seizes an important sector of our freedom and delivers it to a government we already distrust. It substitutes the opinions of faceless and unaccountable bureaucrats for our own.

As Mario Cuomo constantly reminds us when we seek more civility in our lives, we embody an extraordinary contradiction: a desire for what disgusts us, a disgust for what we desire.

Every age struggles with its own disorder, crises, and calamities, but the world we live in now is so disorienting, it frightens even the historians. This urgent desire to wrestle our society back to the "good old days" is occurring among inherently liberal officials. Thus, our fear has transcended our political opinions.

The American people are so traumatized by the terrible syndrome of drugs, guns, and violence, they are desperate for bold action. In their anxiety, they confuse displaying this chaos with encouraging and disseminating it.

As radio broadcasters, we must acknowledge our failures. We've done some really stupid things. The Opie and Anthony copulation stunt in St. Patrick's Cathedral is just one episode we'd like to forget. But our radio tribe has also been tarnished by the medium of television.

For at least a generation, ever since the advent of deregulation and the birth of cable, television has become a vessel of escalating narcissism, exhibitionism, prurience, degradation, humiliation, and sexual dysfunction.

With greed and lust in the lead, the seven deadly sins are on parade morning, noon, and night. Viewers all across the land encounter a dreary cavalcade of unwed jilted mothers on "Maury," geriatric strippers on "Jerry," and a long chorus line of promiscuous midgets, cross-dressing male prostitutes, and toothless, white-trash, trailer-park hags at all hours of the day and night.

And it's not just the tawdry Jerry Springer freak shows. It's the mean-spirited sitcoms, the suggestive commercials, and the ever-expanding, mind-blowing realm of "Reality TV," the boiled-down essence of experiments in sadomasochism by half-crazed psych majors.

In this sad age of rapidly diminishing cultural standards, television reflects who we are and where we stand in our history. It shows a nation of tortured souls filled with anger and self-loathing.

But if radio broadcasters seek the protection of the First Amendment for our shock jocks, then our television colleagues are entitled to its embrace for their "Reality TV."

Of only this we can be sure: We've always had terrible examples to defend. The great Sol Taishoff's son and heir, Lawrence, told me so when, as founders of *Broadcasting* magazine, they were our sentinels on the Potomac against government intrusion. But even now, the government must acknowledge freedom of speech and expression.

Even now . . .

A lot of us would like to limit the sex and profanity, as well as disrespect, cynicism, and emptiness. But in any society, the fine line of taste constantly changes. The populace redraws it every season, and we can't stop it.

Imagine if the FCC of the Fifties had tried to codify indecency according to the mores of that era. Television might be restricted to endless reruns of "Ozzie and Harriet" and "Leave It to Beaver."

For many years, Puritan America banned the word "hell" on radio. Indeed, and somewhat ironically, the word "virgin" was also considered taboo.

Listen again to Noel Coward's "Don't Put Your Daughter on the Stage, Mrs. Worthington." Listen again to the great Cole Porter song "I Get a Kick Out of You" with the line "Some get a kick from cocaine," and listen to the orgasmic suggestion and pulsating rhythm as the airplane goes higher and higher. Or the girl in *Kiss Me, Kate* who is "always true to you, darling, in my fashion." Or "Love for Sale." Or "Let's Do It." And that lovely song, "Bewitched, Bothered, and Bewildered": "He's a joke, but I love him . . . because the joke's on me."

Didn't William Shakespeare, the revered Bard of Stratford-on-Avon, call someone "a hoarsome bitch"? Benjamin Franklin wrote songs that would shock FCC bureaucrats and senators.

And so did Ogden Nash.

And "The Ballad of the Joking Jesus" was not written by Michael Jackson or Prince, but James Joyce.

Restricting language works only in a totalitarian atmosphere where one mode of communication predominates. So, no, you can't sing an off-color song in Bulgaria, and yet, even without such songs, they have drunkenness, adultery, and suicide, but not on the radio.

Commissioner [Michael] Copps, Senator [Sam] Brownback, Congressman [Fred] Upton, and their colleagues, with my considerable admiration, want the atmosphere and the milieu of their homes to prevail in society at large. They are of good heart and motive.

We all want our ideas to predominate, to be the ideas of the marketplace. But that wonderful, warm, stable, secure atmosphere in the Copps home, or the Brownback and Upton residences, is different from the atmosphere confronting a ghetto kid in Harlem, or a farm boy in Bismarck, or a beach boy in Berkeley, or even an oil-rig worker in Houston or Alaska.

The commissioner and Congress want an uncomplicated world for their children, without pain, obscenity, or profanity. But their children, *our* children, are finding those very influences in the real world we are trying to shield them from. Indeed, if you've ever listened to children returning from summer camp, you will realize they make up their own songs, a lot worse than those on the radio!

We are concerned about our children, our most precious possession. We can only hope what we teach them at home will prevail and carry them through life.

If parents give their children the right kind of vehicle, their kids will float on any kind of debris. The censors and the bluenoses can't, however, get rid of the debris. It's part of the landscape. It's called *Life*.

I respect and admire Michael Copps and his formidable intellect. But really, Commissioner, should the FCC judge and punish "utterances"?

Richard Nixon once established a "Presidential Commission on Pornography." And when its report stated that pornography provided an outlet for passions and prevented violence, the president, the story is told, used some unprintable words himself.

Well, we survived Richard Nixon's colorful language, and we will survive Janet Jackson's breast and Bono's curse word.

However you may feel about Howard Stern, you must acknowledge he is more than a vulgarian. He entertains, performs, and provides cutting-edge comedy and social commentary. If you succeed in silencing him, you silence all of that.

To many, Stern's "trash mouth" is not worth defending. But freedom of speech is. This election year's crusade against "shock jocks" and talk show hosts can have far-reaching consequences.

Some people enjoy confronting the broadcast establishment as it seeks to renew its licenses via "obsequious acquiescence." But it may prove to be incredibly expensive entertainment. Once freedom is eroded, it will be difficult, if not impossible, to restore it. And America will never be the same.

America is wandering a little. Now we, the people, on our own, without a censor's sharp prod, must choose the right course. That's our hope toward a perfect world, or even a world free to be just a little imperfect.

With all the talent our industry possesses, surely we can help stop this train and set it on the right track.

FREE SPEECH

I jotted down these thoughts early one morning after a sleepless night. I thought they would make a great poster. I still do.

Some of it ain't so pretty . . . but all of it needs to be protected.

Words that are alliterative, amoral, anarchistic, anti-religious, appropriate, awkward, barely audible, bawdy, beyond the pale, biased, blunt, brave, charming, chaste, clumsy, coarse, crude, cutting, cutting edge, dangerous, desperate, disappointing, discursive, disgusting, disjointed, dismissive, dissonant, dolorous, doughty, dreary, droll, dull, enteric, excessive, exhilarating, ferocious, florid, halting, harmful to the community, horrific, humorous, ignoble, immoral, improper, in error, inane, inappropriate, inartful, inarticulate, incendiary, incorrect, indecent, insane, inspiring, insulting, jumbled, just plain silly, long-winded, loud, lusty, lyrical, meaningless, moral, nasty, noble, not serious, nutty, obscene, offensive, out of bounds, over the top, overblown, passionate, pedantic, pointed, pointless, political, popular, provocative, prurient, pungent, rambling, raucous, religious, resolute, revolting, ribald, risqué, rough, sacrilegious, scary, scintillating, serene, serious, sexual, sexy, slanted, sloppy, soaring, soothing, stupid, sublime, subtle, suggestive, sweet, thoughtful, tormented, truthful, un-American, unclear, uncomfortable, unfair, uninhibited, unpleasant, unpopular, vague, vulgar, witty, and X-rated are all part of the essential language of America.

The language of America must be protected.

All of it. By all of us.

CENSORSHIP IN PARADISE

It is our privilege on WVIP (93.5 FM) in the New York area to amplify the sweet, vibrant voices of many emerging "new Americans" who, while providing our country with their labor, genius, and brilliant music, continue to retain a keen interest in the beautifully endowed island nation whence they came. Government censorship has no place in the Caribbean either. It threatened to put a chill on the warm Jamaican culture. Here is how we responded, on February 23, 2009.

The new "rules" announced on Saturday by the Jamaican Broadcast Commission to *ban* songs and music videos in that magnificent island nation are ill advised. And dangerous.

Prime Minister Bruce Golding is a man of intelligence and character who does not need to be reminded about the wisdom of our First Amendment, which has served America so well for so many years. It is thus to be urgently hoped the prime minister will "crack down" on his own government regulators who are trying to stifle free expression.

The broadcasters of Jamaica are "permittees" and "trustees," with a fiduciary relationship to the airwaves that rightly and properly belong to the people of their country. Most of them believe that a radio station achieves its highest calling when it resembles a platform, a soapbox.

Someone has to tell the Jamaican Broadcast Commission in no uncertain terms that the popular songs of the day deserve protection—no matter how gross, raucous, raunchy, vulgar, outrageous, or "explicit."

Some of it ain't so pretty . . . but *all* of it needs to be protected.

A song is like an eyewitness report. The writers of those songs write of life in Jamaica, the daily passions of their compatriots, the milieu in which they live. They write in the vernacular and with the currency of the day.

In any society there's a fine line of taste that constantly changes. The populace redraws it every season, and government can't stop it.

People have been making songs to reflect their environment since the beginning of time.

Jamaica has given wonderful gifts to the world, from the collective genius of Bob Marley, Byron Lee, Jimmy Cliff, Peter Tosh, Desmond Dekker, and Bunny Wailer. *They* wrote and sang in the vernacular and with the currency of their day.

Nothing "encourages" people to sin or commit crimes. Songs are signs, banners: They do not make history.

Restricting language is possible only in a totalitarian atmosphere. It was possible in Germany, in Bulgaria, in Cuba. It is possible where only one mode of communication dominates. So, no, you can't sing an off-color song in Bulgaria. But even without such songs, they have drunkenness, adultery, and suicide—just not on the radio.

Apparently, the Jamaican Broadcast Commission wants a world that is uncomplicated, without pain for their children, not obscene, not profane. But it is a great mistake to blame songwriters, musical performers, and broadcasters for the coarsening of the culture that is occurring worldwide.

John Updike writes that "popular" composers, from generation to generation, "if they do not teach us how to love, do lend our romances a certain accent and give our courting rites and their milieu . . . a background of communal experience."

It should never be left to government to decide what is "worthy" or meritorious, even one as wise and prescient as that presided over by Prime Minister Golding, who, after only one year, seems so well begun in the hearts of his compatriots and in the eyes of the world. Nor should it be the province of a regulatory authority to decide what is *not*.

Let the people of Jamaica exercise the only permissible form of censorship—that of tuning out offensive material.

Jamaica should get out of the business of censorship and stick to the vital business of hospitality and tourism for which it is so justly renowned.

NANCY PELOSI V. JAMES MADISON

Re: The Unfairness Doctrine—these remarks of July 25, 2008, are based on my response to the blogs of Jerry DelColliano, who came out of Philadelphia. He was a disc jockey in the City of Brotherly Love before he became a nationally known radio programmer. The guy has had many lives. For many years he published Inside Radio, *a widely read trade newsletter that railed against the evils of consolidation. A few years ago, Professor DelColliano moved to the Arizona desert and commuted to the University of Southern California to teach the next generation of communicators and journalists. Jerry has been a contrarian in every season of his life and has many admirers and scores of detractors. I have been among the former.*

An influential communications blog recently called for the reimposition of the so-called Fairness Doctrine, suggesting that House Speaker Nancy Pelosi might favor the effort: "It will not surprise us if the Fairness Doctrine returns and we wouldn't get all that upset about it. Speaker Nancy Pelosi wants it back on the books. It could be good for broadcasting."

I'm absolutely opposed to this, and just to make myself clear, we'll refer to it henceforth as the *Un*fairness Doctrine.

The misnamed doctrine was struck down on August 4, 1987, by an enlightened FCC of its day. And although the damn thing sometimes resembles the biblical Lazarus in that it keeps jumping up again and again, I hope we won't associate ourselves with any recurring assault on the First Amendment rights of broadcasters, no matter how agreeable and deceptively named.

It's very simple and very fundamental: The FCC and Congress should not be allowed to dictate our agenda or shape our priorities. Our opposition to any unfairness doctrine is based, in every season, on the bedrock, fundamental wisdom of the Founders: "Congress shall make no law. . . ." You know the rest.

The bloggers may have Nancy Pelosi on their side. I'm afraid I have only James Madison.

In our best moments we are electronic journalists at the people's business. And clearly, it (any doctrine by government fiat or decree) would be an impermissible intrusion into the editorial process and an inhibitor rather than promoter of controversial expression. It would unquestionably inhibit the presentation of controversy. So much for "balance."

I don't think we want to be among those who would intensify the chill an Unfairness Doctrine would induce. We either believe in the principle that broadcasting is entitled to the full freedom of the press that the First Amendment guarantees. Or we do not.

Governor Mario Cuomo continues to instruct us: "You can't get at bad taste and destructive communication through regulation. That's just substituting one evil for another. The ceding of authority, on a basic principle, has to come back to haunt us."

The great Cuomo (whom the *Boston Globe* calls "the pre-eminent philosopher-statesman of the American nation") is saying that maybe this generation of broadcasters, buffeted by new technology and competition (and consolidation), can survive by what I've called our "obsequious acquiescence" and by pulling our punches on free speech and content issues like an Unfairness Doctrine, but our kids won't—the people who will manage our stations and their programs when we leave.

I'm afraid broadcasters are not united in pushing for our long-overdue independence from content regulation. In every season, it seems, structural, so-called "pocketbook" issues take precedence among the speculators and investors, and even some broadcasters—those "market managers" who operate out of airport lounges with their Palm Pilots and BlackBerrys beholden to corporate masters a whole continent away. They'll beat their breasts about ownership caps, newspaper-broadcast cross-ownership, multicast–must carry, dual-carriage, retransmission consent, à la carte pricing, fin-sin rules, performance taxes, the DTV spectrum and those white spaces in the DTV band, low-power FM, satellite radio, SDARS repeaters, copyright royalties, main studio location, competition from telcos and iPods—all those pocketbook and structural issues that seem always to crowd out free speech matters.

But the broadcasting establishment and the NAB board, sadly, have always viewed the First Amendment as a stepchild among our priorities and even, occasionally, as a bargaining chip.

So before anyone attempts to bestow their imprimatur, it would be wise to give this some thought lest a lot of owners, people who make profits in this business (again, read: profession), sell freedom for fees or accommodation on structural, competitive issues. They will make deals with Speaker Pelosi and Congress. They will accept regulation we shouldn't be accepting—all in exchange for an opportunity to make more money, thus adding their weight to a destructive principle.

And what's more (and worse), they will flee from any controversial or meaningful programming and throw radio back to its "jukebox" era. That is the real danger. And I don't think we want to encourage that.

Why not, instead, use our resources and energy to revive our own flagging spirits and lack of attention to these fundamental issues? All aspects of today's modern media would be better served if broadcasters, podcasters, bloggers, Internet entrepreneurs, cable operators—all those now firmly fixed in, and those just entering, the Information Age—would come together to develop a consolidated, joint resolve against government intrusion into content and free expression.

Fairness? Balance? No matter how comforting it would be for Congress and the FCC to wrap themselves around "fairness," a concept not explicitly or penumbrally protected by the Constitution as free *speech* and free *press* expressly are, I am confident the Supreme Court will one day be compelled to concentrate on the clear, certain, elegant, unvarnished language in the First Amendment of the Bill of Rights should we ever again be confronted by the siren song of "fairness" by government fiat, decree, or doctrine.

No one disputes what has been called the "coarsening" of our culture. And yet the quest for "fairness" and "balance," while understandable and even commendable, is as much of a fool's errand as the crusade to install "decency" on the nation's airwaves. And perhaps even more dangerous.

Can't one just hear a Capitol Hill solon opining, "I *know* fairness when I *hear* it . . . and I also know *balance* when I *see* it"? Again, it's all in the eye of the beholder. And the same self-appointed censors who would seek to identify and define indecency, vulgarity, or obscenity should not be given the opportunity to determine fairness. Or balance. That should always be left to the journalist and his or her audience, which is the only permissible censor. Turn it off if you don't like it. Don't listen or watch if you find it offensive.

Programming should be based only on our judgment as journalists and the dictates of our audiences in whom we should ultimately place our trust. For the people, in their collective wisdom, are infinitely wiser than any government-appointed regulatory agency's idea of what the public should be allowed to hear and see.

Thirty-two years ago Eric Sevareid said, "The Washington intellectuals have always hated anything that the generality of people liked: They must, to preserve their distinctiveness, their eliteness, even (especially) those who claim they love humanity and who want to control the product of our labors. As Eric Hoffer once said, 'The businessman just wants your money; the military man wants you to obey. But the intellectual (and the censor) wants your soul. He wants people to get down on their knees and love what they hate and hate what they love.' "

And more than two hundred years ago the Founders saw to it that "*Congress shall make no law* respecting an establishment of religion, or prohibiting the free exercise thereof, or *abridging the freedom of speech; or the press,* or of the right of the people peaceably to assemble, and to petition the Government for a redress of grievances" (emphasis added).

Those forty-five simple words bound together in spare, unadorned prose are the wisest and most valuable design for democracy ever put to paper. Of all the clauses in the Constitution, it is the one passage that guarantees everything else in the greatest document ever struck off by the hand and mind of humankind.

In our world where ambiguity infects almost everything, this is the loveliest example of nonambiguity to be found anywhere. Concise, compact, marching in serried ranks, these "immortal" words have the taste of pure wisdom unsoiled by hesitancy.

What that glorious amendment means is that no matter how fiery the rhetoric, or frenzied the debate, or calamitous the cry, government cannot interrupt or intervene in the speech of its citizens.

It's not easy to be a First Amendment advocate. You must allow that which you may judge to be meretricious, squalid, smarmy, or without so-called redeeming value to enter the marketplace. Often we become irate ourselves at what is invading the culture of the community, particularly "awful" words and "terrible," even "dangerous" ideas from which we want to recoil.

Thankfully, not all regulators are immune to the lovely music and instruction of the First Amendment. Listen to these powerful (and courageous) findings announced some twenty years ago by the then-chairman and also the chief general counsel of the FCC as the commissioners struck a blow for freedom. Our freedom.

> The First Amendment does not guarantee a fair press, only a free press. The fairness doctrine chills free speech, is not narrowly tailored to achieve any substantial government interest, and therefore contravenes the First Amendment and the public interest. As a consequence, we can no longer impose fairness doctrine obligations on broadcasting and simultaneously honor our oath of office.
>
> FCC Chairman Dennis Patrick, August 4, 1987

> The framers had it right. No matter how good the intention, there is no way for government to restrict freedom of speech or the press and foster a robust and unfettered exchange of ideas. If we must choose whether editorial decisions are to be made in the free judgment of individual broadcasters *or* imposed by bureaucratic fiat, the choice must be for freedom.
>
> FCC General Counsel Diane Killory

Patrick Maines, the erudite president of the Media Institute, the prestigious Washington think tank, has been trying to drag us kicking and screaming onto the battlefield to confront government intrusion into our creative processes. Said the brainy and quite brave Mr. Maines,

> Politically speaking, freedom of speech in the United States is in tatters. Beleaguered by "progressives" on the Left, "social conservatives" on the Right, and policymakers and bureaucrats of all stripes, our ability to freely express ourselves would already be greatly diminished but for the Federal courts.
>
> Bad as the situation is within policymaking circles, it is little better in academia and even mainstream journalism, both of which, with a few exceptions, operate in the grip of a kind of political correctness that is the very antithesis of free speech, if not of freedom itself.
>
> The beginning of wisdom lies in understanding that free speech isn't imperiled because educated people don't know what it is. It's imperiled because educated people subordinate this knowledge to their political and cultural preferences.
>
> Whether you call it inconsistency, hypocrisy, or willfulness, it is at the heart of the present danger.
>
> As direct beneficiaries of the speech clause of the First Amendment, media companies have an obligation to act as the people's sentinels on this issue. As such they need to see that they [do not add] to the problem by acts of omission or commission, and to practice what they preach.
>
> Though it's not widely appreciated, the truth is that the First Amendment is indivisible. We don't have one First Amendment for newspapers and another for the Internet. Nor do we have one for the media and another for individuals, or one for news and one for entertainment, or one for Radio and another for Television.
>
> We have only *one* First Amendment and, such being the ways of precedent, if it is weakened anywhere it's weakened everywhere. Which is why it is incumbent on media companies to act rigorously and selflessly to protect it.
>
> Freedom of speech in the United States is at risk of dying a death of a thousand cuts. For the sake of the nation, as well as

the health of their profession, it is to be profoundly hoped that the media, old and new, will rethink and redouble their efforts to safeguard this cornerstone of our constitutional rights.

There are also *practical* reasons to oppose Pelosi and friends. A government doctrine would have an *opposite* effect by exerting a chilling restraint of speech because of the cost in time, money, and controversy on already beleaguered broadcasters, who as ordinary, practical business people, however privileged their calling and high estate, often prefer to pull their punches on free speech issues or stay out of the ring entirely on government intrusions into content.

They (the NAB Board) would rather save their gunpowder for assaults on the "bricks and mortar"—the structural integrity—of our "industry," assaults that threaten our purses and bottom lines. "Pocketbook" issues we can understand.

I'm afraid that station or network owners (or those market managers) unwilling to fight for full constitutional freedoms ought not to be in the business (read: profession).

During my service at the NAB, time and again I would remind our colleagues that we are not John Deere dealers or holders of a Budweiser franchise!

The minutes of the NAB's high councils for the last several decades contain thousands of references to our "industry." Mr. Sevareid, however, referred to what we do, our electronic journalism, as "a *profession* . . . a *trade* . . . or *calling*." I think that has a better ring to it.

As I finally and mercifully yield, let me point out that I'm not exactly alone in the general tone and tenor of my views. In an attempt to be glib, I said that they had Mrs. Pelosi, while I had only Mr. Madison.

But I'm reminded that opposition and revulsion to any so-called "fairness" doctrine can be found in the writings and pronouncements over the years of some of the brightest thinkers and public servants of our time: William Proxmire, Father Robert Drinan, Fred Friendly, Lionel Van Deerlin, Bob Packwood, Sol and Larry Taishoff, David Bazelon, Roman Hruska, Rush Limbaugh, Louis Boccardi, Nat Hentoff, Floyd Abrams, Jim Quello, Ward Quaal, Rick Kaplar,

Rachelle Chong, Dennis R. Patrick, Eric Sevareid, William S. Paley, Julian Goodman, Jacob K. Javits, Joe Reilly, Bob Grant, Mel Karmazin, Bill McElveen, David Hinckley, Eric Rhoads, Ronald Reagan, Dennis Jackson, John Harper, Walter Nelson Thayer, Ossie Davis, Ruby Dee, John Hay Whitney, A. M. Rosenthal, Neal Travis, Arthur O. Sulzberger, Ogden Rogers Reid, Dan Rather, Howard Stern, Sean Hannity, Jeffrey Bernbach, Michael Harrison, Bill Clark, Carl Marcucci, Les Brown, Steve Knoll, Jack Messmer, Fred Danzig, Daniel Patrick Moynihan, Martin Stone, Rainer K. Kraus, John Van Buren Sullivan, Lawrence Winer, Robin McNeil, Mimi Weyforth Dawson, George Carlin, Patricia Diaz Dennis, Charles Barton Castleberry, Potter Stewart, Diane Killory, Patrick Maines, Don West, Harry Jessell, John Eggerton, Jim Carnegie, Jay Mitchell, Bob Doll, Tom Taylor, Frank Saxe, Frank Stanton, Walter May, Don Stevens, Robert Corn-Revere, Erwin Krasnow, John Crigler, Walter Cronkite, Bruce Sanford, Patrick Leahy, John Wells King, Joseph Bellicossa, Justice William O. Douglas, and Mario Cuomo himself. And so many others who have stepped up for the First Amendment and broadcasters' rights and responsibilities.

The incomparable CBS founder William S. Paley, an iconic figure of our tribe, once said the Fairness Doctrine is like the Holy Roman Empire—only it is neither holy . . . nor Roman . . . and it's not an empire! This occurred at about the same time Mr. Paley took on the Honorable Harley O. Staggers, a right-of-way agent from Mineral County, West Virginia.

Mr. Staggers, who was also chairman of a powerful House subcommittee, wanted to find "contemptible" Paley's associates Frank Stanton and Walter Cronkite and slam their backsides right into a federal jail cell because of a most controversial television program of the day, "The Selling of the Pentagon."

Chairman Staggers, however, did not reckon with Bill Paley's vision and resolve or with the fierce opposition of a brilliant patrician congressman from Westchester named Ogden Rogers Reid, who raised holy hell about the issue on the floor of Congress—all in very gentlemanly fashion, of course.

"Brown" Reid, as he was known when he published the *New York Herald Tribune*, a newspaper of sainted memory founded by Horace

Greeley, was on his feet prowling the aisles to line up votes against the powerful chairman bent on censorship.

As the battle joined, Reid, who is now president of the Council of American Ambassadors (he had been our first ambassador to Israel), began to quote the legendary Tito Gainza Paz, the brave South American publisher of *La Prensa* who stood up to Juan Perón: "You either have a free press, Mr. Reid . . . or you don't."

And then Reid took to the well of the House to do a slow, steady recitation of those forty-five timeless words from the Founders of our Republic. Staggers was finished, and his motion for a contempt citation against the CBS elders was defeated.

It really happened not so long ago. And one wonders . . . where are all the Paleys of today who will stand up to coercion and intimidation? And where are the Reids who find no difference between print and broadcast journalism?

I thus hope those yearning for a new/old fairness doctrine will rethink their position regarding "fairness." If nothing else, the history of the doctrine, in its various manifestations, suggests that rather than protecting free speech, it has been used as a cudgel by both liberals and conservatives (and even a few presidents) to stem criticism and stifle dissent.

The Founding Fathers, in their wisdom, sought to ensure vigorous debate by guaranteeing free speech and a free press and by restraining the government from interfering. They had faith that the people could distinguish truth from fiction and that the people's interests would be best served by the unrestricted debate that would follow. Any policy or doctrine to regulate fairness assumes that the people's interests would be better served by a *restricted* debate in which the government would serve as a "papa knows best" referee.

Justice Potter Stewart wrote, "Fairness is far too fragile to be left for a government bureaucracy to accomplish."

I also pray that one day soon the courts will overturn *Pacifica*, which held that broadcasting was "uniquely pervasive," and *Red Lion v. FCC*, which upheld content regulation on the grounds that spectrum was a scarce commodity. Both need to fall to the First Amendment in the highest courts in our land, sooner rather than later. Until then we must hold grimly and tenaciously to every freedom the law now allows and fight for more.

Full disclosure: I have considerable regard for Nancy Pelosi. She and I were "unindicted co-conspirators" and collaborators in the effort to persuade Mario Cuomo to mount a bid for the presidency. We spent many hours on the phone discussing and framing the importunings that we hoped might persuade the governor to set aside his responsibilities in Albany and enter the presidential sweepstakes. She is one very bright woman. But she is ill advised on the fairness matter.

FURTHER NOTES ON THE FIRST AMENDMENT

I carry around these notes that have sustained me over the years—especially during those moments when I wonder why the hell my colleagues in the broadcasting profession always seem to let others speak for us on these fundamental issues.

Actually, Jack Valenti, the diminutive, brilliant advisor to President Lyndon Johnson, who for many years led the Motion Picture Association of America, had the loveliest paean to the First Amendment: "It's the greatest document ever struck off by the hand of man."

Of all the justices of the Supreme Court, the most persistent and stellar defenders of freedom of speech have been those three towering jurists Louis Brandeis, William Brennan, and William O. Douglas.

In 1973 Justice Douglass thundered, "The Fairness Doctrine has no place in our First Amendment regime. It puts the head of the camel inside the tent and enables administration after administration to toy with TV or radio in order to serve its sordid or its benevolent ends."

President Ronald Reagan, with urging from the great Midwestern broadcast legend Ward Quaal, vetoed a bill to restore the Fairness Doctrine in 1987 because, said the president, it was "antagonistic to the freedom of expression guaranteed by the First Amendment."

The brilliant writer Nat Hentoff in 2005 told a conference of media scholars at Hillsdale College, "The term 'Fairness Doctrine' exemplifies what George Orwell called 'Newspeak': it used language to mask the deleterious effects of its purported meaning."

James Madison did not have bifurcation of free speech in mind when he submitted his draft of the First Amendment.

Oliver Wendell Holmes Jr. wrote in 1929 (*United States of America v. Schwimmer*): "If there is any principle of the Constitution that more imperatively calls for attachment than any other it is the principle of free thought—not free thought for those who agree with us but freedom for the thought that we hate."

Just for a moment suppose the Brits had advised our impertinent New Rochelle neighbor Thomas Paine that he could go ahead and publish all his incendiary rants and ravings—but *only* if he also included, cheek by jowl, in the very same pamphlet, the views of the Royal Colonial Governor. I'm afraid that invitation to Mr. Paine (or, indeed, to another pesky, annoying neighbor of the day—John Peter Zenger), far from being an implementation of free speech, would have had just the opposite effect. It is surely a restriction of speech if, in order to have the privilege of expressing your own views, you have to accede to government dictums that you also have to drag up someone arguing an opposing view.

At its heart, the First Amendment is another of the checking mechanisms the Founders so intelligently promulgated to ensure that our worst instincts would be tempered by our better values. And speaking of "checking mechanisms," should the government take on that mantle, we've got a problem.

Despite the mounting evidence of the harm it causes, political correctness in our nation has so far escaped the opprobrium it deserves. Far from being the language of the enlightened, political correctness is the *lingua franca* of those who believe in control rather than debate. That control, of course, is the very essence of totalitarianism.

The First Amendment protects and serves rich and poor, liberals and conservatives, secularists and believers, and all those privileged to call themselves Americans.

Ambassador Ogden Rogers Reid said, "I don't like to see speech circumscribed in any way, shape or form. . . . I'd rather have free speech up or down with a little obscenity than lose free speech altogether."

"The security of the Nation is not at the ramparts alone. Security also lies in the value of our free institutions. A cantankerous press, an obstinate press, a ubiquitous press must be suffered by those in authority in order to preserve the even greater values of freedom of expression and the right of the people to know"—so intoned Federal Judge Murray Gurfein.

When James Madison wrote the phrase "Congress shall make no law . . ." across the foolscap in his quarters, he spoke for all Americans of every age. And for every broadcaster.

I call to mind others who have spoken out on behalf of the First Amendment principle. These wise men and philosophers and others, so much wiser, have spoken far more eloquently than I am able. Their counsel instructs us:

> No nation, ancient or modern, ever lost the liberty of speaking freely, writing, or publishing their sentiments, but forthwith lost their liberty in general and became slaves.
>
> John Peter Zenger

> A free press can of course be good or bad, but, most certainly, without freedom it will never be anything but bad. Freedom is nothing else but a chance to be better, whereas enslavement is a certainty of the worse.
>
> Albert Camus

> Censorship abroad was justified in euphemistic language. Terms like "responsibility" and "accountability," "values" and "honor" and even "democracy" itself were used to support the suppression of speech not only in ruthlessly totalitarian states such as Nazi Germany and the Soviet Union but in far less authoritarian nations as well.
>
> Floyd Abrams, *Speaking Freely*

Alexander Hamilton argued against adding a Bill of Rights to the new Constitution. It was Hamilton's view that it was "unnecessary," even "dangerous" even to suggest that the delegates at the Constitutional Convention in 1787 gave Congress the power to restrain the liberty of the press.

Mr. Jefferson, however, was deeply suspicious about the new powers being granted to the federal government by the Framers and made it known that he and his followers would not support any Constitution that did not include a crystal-clear Bill of Rights setting forth in direct, unadorned language those liberties upon which Congress could not impinge.

"What I do not like" about the new Constitution, the Virginian sent word to Madison from France, was "the omission of a bill of rights providing clearly and without the aid of sophisms for freedom of religion and freedom of the press."

As the Supreme Court later observed, adoption of the Bill of Rights was the *sine qua non* for the adoption of the Constitution itself.

As for the First Amendment, the extraordinary breadth of its language—"*no* law abridging"—is unmistakable.

In *New York Times Co. v. Sullivan,* the crown jewel of First Amendment law, Justice William J. Brennan's memorable voice gave support to the core First Amendment proposition "that debate on public issues should be uninhibited, robust and wide open and that it may well include vehement, caustic, and sometimes unpleasantly sharp attacks." Justice Brennan also found that "uninhibited, robust and wide open" speech should outweigh all but the most vital competing societal interests, and even then only in the narrowest of circumstances.

You don't have to be a First Amendment voluptuary to believe that the Framers would have extended First Amendment protections to the electronic press.

An unfettered marketplace of ideas is not only desirable, it's essential.

Floyd Abrams, the magnificent First Amendment champion and advocate, was described by Daniel Patrick Moynihan as "the most significant First Amendment lawyer of our age." He is a senior partner at Cahill Gordon and Reindel LLP and William J. Brennan Visiting Professor at the Columbia University Graduate School of Journalism. Here is what Abrams has written:

> While my work has led me to the view that sweeping First Amendment protections are essential to protect us against efforts—in bad faith or good—to limit speech, that does not mean that I believe that the institutional press or the multitude of speakers that now fill the Internet with information are free

> from error or that what is published, broadcast and otherwise communicated does no harm. *A free press is not necessarily an accurate or wise one*. Precisely because speech matters so much, it can do great harm, and in fact sometimes does so. Our approach under the First Amendment has wisely, I think, generally been to risk suffering the harm that speech may do in order to avoid the greater harm that suppression of speech has often caused.
>
> The First Amendment protects all who wish to speak—do I really have to say this?—from *governmental* decision-making about what and how much they may say. It is rooted in distrust of government, concern about historic misuse of governmental power. It is *not*—in fact, it is the *opposite* of—granting power to the government to decide who may speak about what.

Abrams has also written:

> The latest bunch of proponents of the fairness doctrine are totally unaware of its history of misuse by partisans on all sides ranging from President Kennedy to Accuracy in Media. Worse yet, they want it not because they want "fairness" but simply to stifle speech of which they disapprove—Fox and Rush today, heaven knows who tomorrow. And many of the folks on the "other side" urge the FCC to impose $500,000 fines on broadcasters for the broadcast of "fleeting expletives" only to discover the First Amendment when it's used against those with whom they agree.

And even back at the very dawn of our Republic, the graceful Virginian wrote:

> I know of no safe repository of the ultimate powers of our society but the people themselves; and if we think them not enlightened enough to exercise their control with a wholesome discretion, the remedy is not to take it from them, but to inform their discretion by education.
>
> The spirit of resistance to government is so valuable on certain occasions, that I wish it to be always kept alive. . . . The People are the only sure reliance for the preservation of our liberty.
>
> Thomas Jefferson

Throughout America's history, many have written or spoken about how the liberty to express our unfettered thoughts is the foundation of our very existence as a nation. Abraham Lincoln, for example, proclaimed these words at Edwardsville, Illinois, in 1858: "What constitutes the bulwark of our own liberty and independence? It is not our frowning battlements, our bristling sea coasts, our army and navy. These are not our reliance against tyranny. . . . Our reliance is the love of liberty. . . . Destroy this spirit and you have planted the seeds of despotism at your door."

Though we may never aspire to achieve the eloquence of a Jefferson or a Lincoln, they serve as shining examples of the stance we must take in order to preserve this fragile thing we call freedom. Thus we attempt to follow in their footsteps, supporting free expression in all media and, though we may run counter to the prevailing culture, opposing any abrogation of our First Amendment rights in the name of "fairness" or "political correctness."

U.S. COURT OF APPEALS RULING ON DECENCY

We were pleased to be able to air this statement on June 5, 2007.

The Founders of the Republic and, in particular, the framers of the First Amendment to the Constitution are smiling. So, too, is an itinerant printer named John Peter Zenger.

This is not about obscenity or indecency. It is about creative expression, the use of language, and, ultimately, the truth.

Government bureaucrats are unqualified to determine acceptable language.

This enlightened decision by the Second Circuit of the U.S. Court of Appeals invalidates Washington's flimsy rationale for defining the fine distinction between the profane and the obscene as summarized by that memorable phrase "I know it when I see it." This ridiculous notion has been exposed as a dangerous opportunity for censorship.

The remedy for vulgarity, grossness, and the coarsening of our culture should flow from loving parental instruction and example, not from the FCC.

REMARKS PREPARED FOR THE MEDIA INSTITUTE

The Media Institute is a highly regarded Washington think tank that has done brilliant work on free speech and First Amendment issues for many years. It is ably led by Patrick Maines and Rick Kaplar, who are our sentinels on the Potomac against government intrusion. Here are the remarks we prepared on February 1, 2005, for this valuable and influential entity.

I am a broadcaster and a businessman. So I quite understand the practical, political reasons why our fellow broadcasters are signing consent decrees with the FCC to settle indecency complaints: the cost of doing business.

But how high a price are we willing to pay?

Being about "the people's business," we should avoid consenting to censorship.

We are licensed to operate "in the public interest." The public should be primarily interested in a powerful electronic media, free to tell the truth, either through a news story or artistic expression.

Clearly, the government is neglecting the people's interest and the Constitution when it uses its vast life-and-death power to censor information, images, words, or expressions.

Such a climate is dangerously rampant today, and it breeds intolerance. And our profession has done nothing, collectively or individually, to stop it.

We await a savior, a statesman. "Where have you gone, Mr. Paley? Where have you gone, Dr. Stanton?"

We—all the disparate elements of our profession: radio, television, the networks, the independents and the groups—will one day regret our failure to check government regulation of indecent speech if we decide the next controversial category is worth fighting for.

If we wait until our own ox gets gored, it will be too late.

Because we didn't try to stop it now.

In controlling the electronic press, the people must be allowed to represent themselves by resorting to the remote control and the on/off button.

It's just that simple. And that essential. For all of us. As broadcasters. And as citizens.

For fans of James Madison, his message was clear: If you give up the First Amendment to save a buck, you could actually lose two bucks instead.

Satellite radio will embrace any popular programs broadcasters "self-censor" off the airwaves. And the cable, satellite, and phone companies, as well as the Internet and DVD producers, are all perfectly willing to program to their audiences.

We should avoid hunkering down or withdrawing into our shells to count our profits. This is a critical time to stand up for our freedom and compete in a multichannel marketplace!

Issues of indecency and obscenity should be handled by the courts, instead of by politically appointed bureaucrats with the power to deny licenses and franchises as well as impose must-carry obligations on cable and satellite operators, or decide how many media outlets broadcasters can own.

When a licensing body possesses life-or-death power over a business, the owner may sacrifice First Amendment values to please the regulators.

The courts are well equipped to address indecency and obscenity since local standards are the yardstick for enforcement. It does so for all other media: cable, film, the Internet, newspapers, and magazines.

Why should broadcasters be second-class citizens?

Everyone in this room knows about the petition to the Supreme Court by the *Tribune,* and the networks surely know about the *Red Lion* decision. In the intimacy of this room, the "dirty little secret," however, is that many broadcasters don't want to overturn *Red Lion*.

They are afraid of losing their status as a "scarce resource" operating "in the public interest," and thus "essential" for cable or satellite.

The networks are ready to abandon the "public trustee" concept and challenge the continued viability of *Red Lion*.

Now, this is not a plea for *Red Lion*. Because that decision lets the government march into our newsrooms and studios to intrude on our creative process.

Somehow, we must draw the distinction between "some" regulation and content controls.

Even as we seek to find a balance between political or economic considerations and the precious words of the First Amendment, we must agree that some things are not negotiable.

We should forget about tactics, strategy, and bickering over ownership caps and must-carry, and fight for the right to create our own programs.

We take this stand not as businessmen or broadcasters, but as Americans who love this country and believe in the people's right to decide.

RALLYING THE TROOPS: A LETTER TO BROADCASTING COLLEAGUES

August 7, 2006

Dear New York State Broadcaster:

I've been in touch with several lawyers, journalists, and First Amendment advocates, and we're trying to write a joint op-ed piece about censorship and the FCC's power to level draconian fines.

We know that community stations are vulnerable. We know that talk and sports radio is vulnerable. We know that any cutting-edge programming is vulnerable. We know that public radio is vulnerable. And so, ultimately, are our news broadcasts.

It is tempting to think this "Washington/FCC stuff" will be adjudicated in the federal courts, where the First Amendment resounds more powerfully than it does at the commission or in Congress.

But government bureaucrats, despite the acquiescence of a timid Congress, must be prevented from censuring your programming or the Voice of the People.

Please let me know your opinion during this "summer of our discontent."

I'm reminded of that haunting passage from Pastor Martin Niemoeller, the articulate Protestant clergyman in Nazi Germany:

"First they came for the Communists, but I was not a Communist so I did not speak out. Then they came for the Socialists and the Trade Unionists, but I was neither, so I did not speak out. Then they came for the Jews, but I was not a Jew so I did not speak out. And when they came for me, there was no one left to speak out for me." And then they came for us.

ONE TALL ORDER: A MEMO TO CENTRAL CASTING ABOUT THE CRITERIA FOR LEADERSHIP AT THE NAB

The National Association of Broadcasters (NAB) is our Washington-based national trade association. Over the years there has been a running battle: Do we need a politician-lobbyist or a broadcaster to represent American radio and television stations in the nation's capital? Former Senator Gordon Smith of Oregon is our new leader in 2010. He succeeded David Rehr, a brainy, dynamic Washington insider (and Bush loyalist), when Barack Obama was elected president. In this piece I tried to identify the qualities we should look for in a leader. (For many years I served as chairman of the NAB's Public Affairs Committee, which gave me a platform to advocate for First Amendment rights for our profession. So I had more than a passing interest in the direction of the NAB. Its record on free speech matters over the years has not always been so stellar.)

A daunting task awaits our new leader. The animus against broadcasting is growing each day, and it knows no ideological bounds. The Religious Right and the Intellectual Left are on the march against our most basic freedoms. And the single-issue "values" zealots are in full-throated control of the assault.

Many TV execs are intimidated by economic and legislative threats. And we radio broadcasters sail serenely by with our newfound wealth from consolidation . . . the buying up of small, regional community stations by absentee owners and speculators. (All this, of course, before the days of "penny" stocks.)

The First Amendment has become "trading" material, perhaps because we have brought much of this upon ourselves. The new NAB president must step up and initiate a frank discussion with the

American people about the vulgarity we have visited upon their homes.

Clearly, we require a diplomat who can still the partisan bickering, bind up our wounds, heal our divisions, and restore harmony among all the disparate elements of our profession: networks, independents, group owners, and local community broadcasters.

We will also need a potent lobbyist and shrewd strategist, as well as a leader with enough confidence to reach out to academics, scholars, liberals, and conservatives on matters like government intrusion and censorship. And we must respond to our critics and detractors.

We must reestablish a Public Affairs Department at the NAB and create an in-house "think tank" for societal issues. We must also reexamine the construction and composition of the NAB board. The "district" arrangement is ineffective and obsolete. These days, very few independent community broadcasters sit in the NAB's high councils, which are populated by group execs and their hired-gun itinerant "market managers."

The battle must be joined in Congress, at the FCC, with the Copyright Tribunal, which oversees performers' royalties, and those relentless and omnipresent "culture zealots."

But our most urgent task is to remain *relevant* in the face of technological change.

And now that the Radio Advertising Bureau (RAB) is in a weakened condition . . . a merger should be very high on the list of priorities. We've urged a takeover of the RAB for more than twenty years. There is no reason the NAB can't offer sales and marketing assistance to its members. Our proposals have always fallen on deaf ears because of those who fancy "Director of RAB" on their résumé.

To lead the NAB and all of us into an uncertain future . . . let's find someone as well rounded as *Dick Ferguson*; as collegial as *Bill McElveen, David Kennedy,* or *Bill Clark*; with the wisdom, eloquence, and articulation of *Mario Cuomo* (who would also make a great commissioner of baseball!); with the executive smarts of *Jeff Smulyan* or *Ed Christian*; someone wise enough to listen to *Don West, Harry Jessell,* and *John Eggerton*; with an unshakeable devotion to the First Amendment like *Patrick Maines* of the Media Institute and the great lawyers *Floyd Abrams*, *John Crigler,* and *Bruce Sanford*; with the flat-out honesty, fearlessness, and courage of *Phil Lombardo*; with the charm of the late *Tony Malara* or the shrewdness and rapier-sharp wit of *Nick Verbitsky* or the compassion of *Phil Beuth*; with the sheer, stunning brilliance of *Jerry Lee* and *Randy Michaels*; with the vivid, dashing demeanor of *Jack Valenti*; with the thoughtfulness, presence, and caring personas of *Erica Farber* and *Deborah Norville*; with the good genes of *Scott Knight* and *Stuart Beck,* or the scholarship and intellectual heft of *Dennis Jackson,* or the generosity of *Richard Foreman* and *Ed McLaughlin*; with the relentless drive of *Andy Fisher, Dennis Swanson,* or *Alan Frank*; with the understanding of the niceties of *Bob Bruno* and *Scott Herman*; with the savvy of *Marty Franks,* or the stature and carriage of *David Barrett*, or the graceful, cultured, natural demeanor of *William "Billy" Bush* (who will most certainly be the next Johnny Carson!); with the promotional instincts of *Hugh Panero*; with the good soul and shrewdness of *Eddie Fritts*; with the brainpower of *David Hinckley*, *Carl Marcucci,* or *Erwin Krasnow*; with the same relentless devotion to our tribe as exhibited by *Eric Rhoads*, *Frank Saxe, Mike Kinosian*, *Tom Taylor*, *Paul McLane, Jay Mitchell*, *Jim Carnegie*, *Bill Burton,* and *Michael Harrison*; with the grace and style of *Frances Preston*; with the great probity of *Bruce Reese,* or the salesmanship and chutzpah of *Mel Karmazin*; with the all-around bonhomie, good nature, and popularity of *Joe Reilly*; with the ability to massage the egos of media moguls possessed by *Louis Boccardi* (the soft-spoken, cerebral executive who ran the Associated Press with such skill); with the innate decency of *Stanley Hubbard*; and with the lobbying muscle and focus of *Jim May*. I suppose it also would be helpful if our candidate resembled *Peter Smyth* or *Peter Doyle.* And is as generous of soul and purse as *Dick Foreman*. (And he doesn't even have to fly his own plane!) Nor would I mind if our new leader traveled in a grand style like *Nick Verbitsky, Jeff Smulyan, Phil Lombardo,* or *Stan Hubbard.* I would also very much wish Central Casting would send someone with a sense of humor like *Paul Hedberg* or at least someone with a scratch handicap like his son and heir, *Mark*. Or how about just answering our prayers with a well-rounded, effective—and nice—guy like *Stu Olds.*

What we really require is a statesman with the carriage and dignity of a *Ward Quaal* who can tread the halls of Congress and even be welcomed into the Oval Office itself.

Even as I write this, I know it can't happen. Most of the individuals on this wish list are exactly that: *individuals* . . . who are unique and able to be defined only in their own terms. The Latin phrase for this is *sui generis*.

My personal preference, of course, is for someone who also eschews slogans, business-speak buzzwords, and catchphrases. Immediately disqualify anyone who utters the following exhortations: "Getting it done!" "Make it happen!" "Doin' what it takes!" "24/7!" "ASAP!" And avoid anyone who thinks broadcasting is an *industry*, instead of a *profession* or *craft*.

It's O.K., I suppose, for the candidate to be technologically astute and know how to handle a Palm Pilot and a BlackBerry in an airport lounge. But please send us someone who can write a letter like *Frank Boyle*. And for God's sake, send us a leader who believes the trade press can be an ally when the going gets tough. Forget that "Us" against "Them" stuff.

We need to bring sunshine, candor, and open discussion to the NAB's budget process with someone strong and wise enough to rein in and control the fiefdoms and archdukes of the NAB senior staff.

Because this is ultimately about our relationship with the American people, the new NAB chief must know his or her way around New York and Los Angeles, the centers of publishing, culture, entertainment, and influence, in addition to Washington, D.C.

It would help if our new leader could also imagine that we are about the people's business and that he or she represents a tribe that in its best moments can build up communities and make them stronger, better, even sweeter than they are.

Two unique individuals who could definitely lead us into the future: [Remember, I wrote this four years ago]: Andrew Cuomo, Clinton's HUD secretary, who, many think, would be a superb White House chief of staff. Problem: Andrew wants to run for Attorney

General of New York. [He did. He won. And, next, *another* Governor Cuomo?]

Or Rick Lazio, the attractive former congressman, who lost to Hillary Clinton. Problem: Rick just signed on as a highly paid government-relations executive for JP Morgan Chase. Neither may want to move to D.C., but both could lead the NAB right now. [It's now 2010 and Lazio also has his eye on Albany's Executive Mansion.]

Above all . . . and no pun intended: We need someone who is *on our wavelength* and hears the music of the Founders on free speech matters.

Who says all wisdom resides with us? Or that our new leader has to come from our own tribe?

THE "F-BOMB"

A polite conversation overheard on Madison Avenue:

LARRY KING (L.K.): Hey, O'Shaughnessy, how are the radio stations?

WILLIAM O'SHAUGHNESSY (W.O.): They're fine, Larry; we're keeping 'em going. Actually, we're hunkered down right now with this obscenity thing.

L.K.: What the hell does that mean?

W.O.: It means if somebody drops the "F-Bomb" on the air, it will cost about $200 thou!

L.K.: What's the "F-Bomb"?

W.O.: It means if somebody says "fuck," it will cost 200 big ones or more.

L.K.: Why the fuck would somebody want to say "fuck"?

REMARKS AT HOFSTRA UNIVERSITY

Whenever I present myself in an academic setting, I'm always struck by my own limitations. Confronting a few hundred bright, eager students in one of those amphitheater classrooms, I sometimes feel like retreating posthaste to a safe, secure broadcasting studio. Although I've made my way in my chosen profession armed only with a Jesuit high school education (I got a 28 in Chemistry), I have done lectures on radio and First Amendment issues at many institutions of higher learning, including Fordham, Manhattanville, Iona, New York University, Mount St. Mary College, SUNY New Paltz, Columbia, Purchase College, College of New Rochelle, Mercy College, Westchester Community College, and Hofstra University, where I made these remarks on November 12, 2003.

May it please you, Professor Evans . . . .

I'm grateful for the opportunity to present myself to so many of your marketing, advertising, communications, and journalism students.

As the permittee of WVOX and WVIP, I make my way as a local-yokel "townie" radio broadcaster up the road a piece in Westchester. My radio stations are endowed with very beguiling call letters: one is called WVOX, from the Latin *vox populi,* the "voice of the people"; and the other is called WVIP.

WVIP is a real powerhouse, with a big, strong FM signal. But WVOX, at 1460 on the AM dial, has less power than any other radio station in the metropolitan area. It has 500 vibrant, thrilling, relentless, pulsating, dynamic watts! (*laughter*) But they really resonate! And somehow, through hard work and sheer guile, we have managed to protect them from the speculators and absentee owners who have descended on radio.

Our profession is like everything else, I expect. It's been discovered in recent years by "investors." And most stations are now run out of airport lounges by guys working on Palm Pilots and beholden to corporate masters a continent away. They're run by what they call "market managers." And old-time local "townie" broadcasters like a Bill O'Shaughnessy have been replaced by these so-called brilliant "market managers." (*laughter*)

I'm going to give you a tip. Never sit next to one of these guys on an airplane. Because you'll want to jump right out of your skin. They talk in a strange dialect and use phrases like "Make it happen" and "Doing what it takes" and "Getting it done" and "24/7." And the mother of them all: "pro-active." And there is another wonderful locution they use: the exclamatory "Absolutely!"

Since we've had little success in getting rid of these business-speak words, we sent a memo to all our talk show hosts, and it was covered by the *New York Post, Daily News,* and *Forbes* magazine. "Effective immediately, there will be a $5.00 fine for any studio guest or talk show host who uses these words." (*applause*)

So I beg you, Professor Evans, if any of your students have to do term papers, flunk them immediately if any of those phrases occur. (*laughter*)

The great Mario Cuomo, whom I so admire, but who never misses a chance to stick it to me, sent a check for $156.00. He said, "I absolutely agree!" when we instituted the ban.

We've been very fortunate to keep these stations independent. And they're now practically the last locally owned and operated stations in the metropolitan region. I think there is one in Long Island owned by a fellow named Paul Sidney out in Sag Harbor. He's a Runyonesque character and still playing the Big Bands. He must be eighty years old—makes me seem like a young guy. But most of them have fallen to Clear Channel and Infinity and all the conglomerations.

But here comes the "However." Big is not necessarily bad. Jacob Javits, a New York senator back in the '60s and '70s and father of the War Powers Act—where are you now when we really need you!—once told me, "O'Shaughnessy, you either believe in the genius of the free enterprise system, or you don't." That's a nice Republican thought.

You know, I don't know what I am politically. But one thing has endured for many years, my admiration for Mario Cuomo. The great man was at Hofstra last week, and he told me just this morning, "Don't go there, O'Shaughnessy. You're not smart enough. Those Hofstra kids are very bright. They don't fool around!" (*applause*)

Governor Cuomo once told me, "I pray for sureness." And I said, "What do you mean by sureness?" He said, "It's very simple. You are on the road to Damascus. And the Lord appears in all His or Her refinements, accompanied by a hell of a lightning bolt to knock Saul off his horse. The Lord says, 'Your name is not Saul anymore. It's now Paul. And just one other thing—you're Saint Paul.' A lightning bolt in your tush! That's what I mean by 'sureness'!" (*laughter*)

So some things I'm not so sure of. But of this, I'm sure. I believe in the genius of the free enterprise system.

Despite my inclinations, I'm afraid I was accused recently—in a national magazine—of being something of a spokesperson for the independent, "down home," community broadcasters of America. I don't want to be anybody's spokesperson but my own. But now this wave of consolidation is sweeping over our "profession." I don't even want to call it an industry. On the board of the National Association of Broadcasters in Washington, D.C., where I served for a number of years, I insisted we always call it a profession. For in this high-tech, speeded-up, electronic day and age, radio is still the medium closest to the people. Radio is the Authentic Voice of the People, especially when you open up the phone lines as we do every day—without a seven-second delay.

I am one of those broadcasters who think you can be more than a performer or an entertainer, more than a disc jockey who spins records. You can sell more than diversion. And even you slick marketing guys can aspire—if you do it right—to preside over more than an instrument for conveying information about goods and products and services.

Because it's free, radio is still the medium closest to the people—to the poor, the lonely, the forgotten, the misunderstood, the disenfranchised. They don't spend any money for you future Madison Avenue moguls. They don't spend on the products or services you hucksters peddle. (*laughter*)

I've had television programs on United Artists Columbia and Cablevision. You had to pay the cable companies to see me in all my majesty. I've done some books. You have to buy the books.

But radio is available to everyone, anytime, anywhere—it's even on the Internet. George Plimpton called it a "nifty little slavey that goes everywhere with you." In the car. To the beach. It even accompanies your courting rites in the bedroom, or whatever the hell it is you're doing in there to the great consternation of your parents. *(laughter)*

I was in The Wiz, and this very good-looking guy—he looked like Tiki Barber—was showing me a pocket radio. He said, "We have one for $9.00." And I said, "That's perfect. Does it come with earphones? I'll buy one for everybody at the radio station." He asked, "Would you like to also buy an extended warranty? It's only $12.00." *(laughter)*

Although you have to buy the radio, it's then free and over the air. We call that the American system of broadcasting. That's my day job, ladies and gentlemen. I've been engaged in it for a long time. We've had a pretty good run with our independent radio stations for forty years.

As I reflect on all of this, I'm still persuaded that a radio station achieves its highest calling when it resembles a platform and forum where many different voices are heard in the land. It can aspire to be more than a jukebox. We endorse candidates. We editorialize. And our clients say, "If you're going to buy media in Westchester, you've got to do O'Shaughnessy's two radio stations." We're probably doing something right because we've been able to persuade more than five hundred advertisers to our cause, many of whom now use WVOX and WVIP exclusively.

While everyone else is chasing the kids, or the 18-to-34 demographic, we've attracted the older, more affluent adults in the spending cycle of their lives. We also offer multicultural programs for the great new Americans in the Bronx, Queens, Brooklyn, and the huge, growing cities of southern Westchester. "Where many different voices are heard in the land" is our motto.

We used to run our own ads: "America's Great Community Radio Stations" as quoted by the *Wall Street Journal,* which I don't even read. (*laughter*) And another one: "The Most Influential Stations in New York State," signed by George Pataki and Mario Cuomo, with a little line under it: "At least they agree on something!" (*laughter*) On the other hand, Jimmy Breslin, the best writer, the best columnist, the best reporter we've had in this country in fifty years, once said, "I love O'Shaughnessy because he does so much for Mamaroneck." (*laughter*) He's still writing wonderful stuff in *Newsday*; they pull it down for me off the Internet. We now say, "Only WVOX reaches the 'townies,' people with roots in the community." The folks who are firefighters, or schoolteachers, or crossing guards. "Townie" is not a very elegant term, but we know what it means. People with roots in the community. It isn't a pejorative term from me.

I asked Charles, who escorted me in here today, if he is a writer. It's clear he's going to be a star. He got us where we are supposed to go. He's going to be the president of an advertising agency. (*applause*) Charles asked me to recommend some good books to advance his studies and his career, so I suggested learning about writing by reading everything ever written by Breslin, Pete Hamill, Murray Kempton, Jimmy Cannon, Whitney Balliett, Wilfred Sheed, Robert Coles, David Hinckley, George Plimpton, Bill Saroyan, Will Durant, Walter "Red" Smith, James Brady, and Douglas Martin—even his beautiful obituaries in the *New York Times*. And this will almost instantly cause cardiac arrest among your professors, but you can also learn a hell of a lot by reading Richard Johnson, Cindy Adams, and Liz Smith in the *Post*!

If you really aspire to the world of broadcasting and communications, I recommend the brilliant books of Ken Auletta and my Westchester neighbor Gil Schwartz, aka Stanley Bing. You might even consider giving up your Springsteen front-row seats and trading them in for a one-year subscription to a magazine called *Broadcasting and Cable*. It is the "bible" of our profession, and I am partial to this particular weekly because, unlike other trade periodicals, it has a unique devotion to the First Amendment and serves as our sentinel on the Potomac against government intrusion. It's run by three brilliant fellows who are also great writers: Harry Jessell, John

Resurrection Church in Rye was packed for Ned Gerrity's funeral Mass as the great and the good came to bid farewell to a remarkable man who, with the legendary Harold Geneen, built ITT into America's first great conglomerate.

Shaking the money tree: Philip J. Lombardo of Bronxville has raised millions of dollars for the Broadcasters Foundation of America, one of the author's favorite charities.

Dandy Andys. Two recent Westchester County Executives: Republican Andy O'Rourke (left) and Democrat Andy Spano. Both nice guys and able leaders of the Golden Apple.

The Life of Reilly! Joe Reilly, with Governor Mario Cuomo, is one of my oldest friends. This charming Irishman, who is president of the New York State Broadcasters Association, has been the leader of our broadcasting tribe in the Empire State for more than three decades. The governor and I regard him highly.

From left: Phil Lombardo, chairman, Citadel Television, and head of the Broadcasters Foundation of America.; Richard Dimes Buckley, president, WOR; Governor Mario Cuomo; producer Rick Friedberg; Marvin Dames, superintendent, Royal Bahamas Police, at a Dutch Treat Club luncheon in Manhattan.

Above, from left: the author; Matilda Raffa Cuomo, chair, Mentoring USA; Ambassador Ogden Reid; Governor Mario Cuomo.

Below: Ambassador Reid, president, Council of American Ambassadors, and our first ambassador to Israel. "Brownie" Reid was also a superb congressman and staunch defender of the First Amendment. At right: Edward F. McLaughlin, former president, ABC Radio Network, was Paul Harvey's mentor and discovered Rush Limbaugh.

Above, from left: hero cop and former congressman Mario Biaggi; the great actress Ruby Dee, and her husband, actor and human rights activist Ossie Davis.

Below: Ossie Davis and the author in New York in 2005, moments before he delivered his last public address, included in this book. We lost this great man less than a month later (see highlights from the funeral service, page 577).

The "Queen of Gossip," Cindy Adams, killing the author softly with a great hug.

The author with the illustrious former New Jersey Governor Brendan Byrne.

Above: Cry Uncle! The author with legendary CBS anchor Walter Cronkite.

Right: Top Cop! New Rochelle police commissioner Patrick Carroll, who once headed NYPD's elite Critical Incident Unit.

Above: "Best Editorials in New York State."
ABC's Barbara Walters presents a prestigious
New York State Broadcasters Association
award to the author and his son
David Tucker O'Shaughnessy,
president, WVOX and WVIP.

Right: His business card reads:
"Just a little Italian lawyer from
Eastchester." Anthony J. Colavita is
also a former chairman of the New York
Republican Party and a powerbroker
known locally as "Mr. Westchester."

The author with "Inside Edition" host Deborah Norville and her husband, Karl Wellner. The beautiful and talented Deborah is a director of the Broadcasters Foundation of America, to which she assigns all her speaking fees.

The author and Dan Rather. We defended Rather against his corporate bosses at CBS.

Eggerton, and P. J. Bednarski. It won't really cost as much as a Springsteen ticket. (*laughter*)

I see you're writing this list down; here are a few more. Terry Golway of the *Observer*, Mark Twain and the brilliant critic Rex Reed. And there's a wonderful historian named Richard Norton Smith, who wrote a great biography of the Chicago press lord Colonel McCormick and is now working on the life of Nelson Rockefeller. There is also a fellow named Dick Wald who writes on journalism and communications. And after a great career as a top executive at newspapers, NBC News, and ABC News, he's now Fred W. Friendly Professor at the Columbia Journalism School. And you can find his thoughtful writings in their *Journalism Review*.

While I'm on the subject, there is another great book I should mention. It's about Marcus Aurelius, and it's called *The Emperor's Handbook*. Marcus Aurelius, with all his wisdom, couldn't save Rome, but maybe he could save us. It's a lovely little book put out by a graceful guy named David Hicks.

And there is one more I would presume to recommend. Mario Cuomo never made it as a baseball player, although he did get a bigger signing bonus than Mickey Mantle, but after serving for twelve years as governor, he finally found some time to write. One book is called *More Than Words*. Another is *Reason to Believe*. He's also got another one about Mr. Lincoln. Cuomo is a wonderful thinker and a masterful writer.

Now, Professor Evans suggested I might also provide—in the intimacy of this room—some practical advice and counsel. I think one of the surest ways to success is to venture forth accompanied by manners. Just plain, old-fashioned manners.

One of our interns who knows the importance of manners was William "Billy" Bush. His father is a friend of mine, a wonderful man named Jonathan Bush. Jonathan Bush is a brother of President George Herbert Walker Bush and uncle of the current president, George W. Bush. Billy Bush is going to become a big star not just because he has talent but also because he has manners. Even Scott Shannon, the great New York FM station WPLJ genius and a member of our Hall of Fame, called me up last week and said, "Isn't Billy Bush wonderful! Manners. Breeding. Genes."

I asked the president of Manhattanville College, Richard Berman, if the kids stand up when he walks into the room. He said, "Are you kidding?" I asked the president of Iona College, Brother Liguori, if the kids stand up when he walks into the room. He said, "Well now, you're talking about manners." So I asked, "Are you supposed to do something about that?" He said, "No. I educate them, but they get their manners at home."

So why am I so hung up on manners? Well, I got a call from a bank president whose daughter wanted to work for Miramax. My son David worked there, and then he went back and got two master's degrees. Now he's in the family business. Anyway, I sent this very bright, very attractive, very intelligent woman down for an interview at Miramax. Andrew Stengel set it up. He's the Senior Vice President of Public Affairs for Miramax. A big guy. And I was hoping they'd hire this girl.

After the interview, he told me, "She's bright. She's intelligent. She's good-looking." And I said, "But what?" He said, "She was interviewed by this executive vice president, a very tough woman, and she didn't stand up when the lady came in." So I asked, "What else?" He said, "Eleven days went by and no 'thank you' note."

Now, I don't know who teaches that, or where you develop a wonderful generosity of spirit. I've seen so many young people who want to get into radio and television, and mostly their focus is on themselves. I think I can give you an example. I had to buy a computer the other day, and I don't know anything about computers. So the first salesperson walks in. He's from IBM. So my eyes are glazing over, and I said, "Thank you very much, sir." And he walked out. The second was a very interesting woman. She was from Hewlett-Packard and dressed for business. So I said, "Thank you very much." And she walked out. The third one was a little Italian kid. He walks in and looks around in my office and asks, "You know Mario Cuomo?" (*laughter*) Forty-five minutes later, guess who walked out of there with a check for $75,000? Number three! (*applause*) Because the first two didn't sense my lack of interest in computers. But the third one was willing to step out of "himself" and make me feel my priorities were important.

Now, you didn't hear me say that flattery works. I did not presume on your generosity to say flattery works! (*laughter*) But I don't care if you're in the White House talking to the president or talking to a client, try it. David Ogilvy, the Madison Avenue legend, said, "If all else fails, all your marketing studies, all your focus groups, flatter somebody . . . even if you have to 'suggest' that the client should do the commercial himself!"

And incidentally, it drives me crazy when a young secretary has no telephone manners. You can have a hovel of an office, operating out of a basement. But telephone manners and presentation on the phone are so important. And you don't have to talk like Pia Lindstrom, daughter of Ingrid Bergman. A long-time TV anchor, Pia has a very cultured way of speaking.

Bill Paley, who lived up the road in Manhasset, ran CBS during its glory days. And twenty-some years ago, of the three networks—NBC, ABC, and CBS—a CBS station was worth about four times as much as an NBC station, and eight times as much as an ABC station. You know why? It wasn't because of their ratings. It was because of the style of William S. Paley. Somebody once said the reason for the preeminence of CBS is that their cufflinks are just a little smaller, a little more discreet, and thus a little classier than those of the other networks.

You should choose where you want to work. And you can do it. Years ago, when I started, WNEW was the New York Yankees of radio. I loved Stan Musial of the St. Louis Cardinals and Warren Spahn of the Braves, but I couldn't imagine anyone wanting to be in baseball and not dreaming of playing for the New York Yankees. Why? It's because of the style, the pinstripes, the lineage and heritage. WNEW, that legendary AM station of sainted memory, had the incomparable William B. Williams and "The Make Believe Ballroom" and a wonderful, charismatic leader named John Van Buren Sullivan. I just knew I had to be there. And one day I was.

I think your instincts will lead you to where you should work and what you want to do, if you will but listen to and follow them. Try to discern what corporate style suits you and what corporate philosophy makes sense to you.

If you want the comfort and structure and security of a big company with a lot of square guys with perfect razor haircuts and Palm Pilots, don't go to the Yankees. Because Steinbrenner is a character. He can be tough. But I have to admit I'm the first one to stand up and applaud when he walks into "21." Joe Torre said this morning in the *New York Times,* "The trick with George Steinbrenner is that you have to figure out what piece of him you want to keep." Maybe it's like in those days at CBS. Now, in corporate America, there's nobody with much style, because all the entrepreneurs and the pioneers are gone. But folks out there appreciate manners and sincerity and grace. And style.

Finally, after you've made all the money that's out there and after you've acquired three other agencies and own a mansion on the North Shore, with the Range Rovers and the BMWs, I would only plead with you to think about using your genius—the things you learn in these classrooms and in life—to build up the community where you grew up, to improve the neighborhood where you can and when you can.

Mario Cuomo was dirt-poor and lived behind a grocery store in Queens. And he went to St. John's Law School, where they had a big problem because no Italian had ever graduated at the head of the class. So they tied him with the Irishman. (*laughter*) He was governor of New York against all odds. Ed Koch ran against him. And Ed Koch had all the big New York Realtors with all the money in the primary. Then Lew Lehrman had Rite Aid drugstores and $10 million in the general election.

But I wish you could have heard him a few weeks ago on your campus because I know what he said. The governor said that every major religion started with what the Jews believe. They came up with this idea of *Tzedakah*; it means we're all alike. We're all in this together. We're all worthy of respect. We're all brothers and sisters. And then they came up with another crazy idea—*Tikkun Olam,* meaning God created the universe but didn't finish it. That's our job. To complete the universe. To be partners in creation. He also told about the guy who founded the Christian religion, who was walking down the street one day when this wise guy—probably a college professor—said, "Rabbi, I heard you were pretty good in the temple last night. What did you say to unsettle them so much?" He said, "Love your neighbor as yourself, for the love of Me because I am the Truth."

Finally, I'm reminded that a wise man named Walter Nelson Thayer, who was president of the *Herald Tribune* newspaper, founded by Horace Greeley, once said, "New York is littered with guys whose only goal was to make money. They almost never do."

They almost never do.

That, I think, is everything I know about advertising, marketing, communications, and broadcasting.

Also, about life.

INTERVIEW WITH DAVID REHR, OGDEN ROGERS REID, GOVERNOR MARIO CUOMO, AND GORDON HASTINGS ON FREE SPEECH ON THE AIRWAVES

We were pleased to receive a visit from National Association of Broadcasters (NAB) president David Rehr. His visit to Westchester was one of the first trips outside the Beltway for our new national leader. When David walked into the station, we almost immediately put him on the air via a four-way conference with some First Amendment advocates. The discussion, broadcast live on June 19, 2006, ranged far and wide, from the mores of Washington to the meaning of obscenity.

Also included were Ogden Rogers Reid, president, Council of American Ambassadors; Governor Mario Cuomo, Willkie, Farr & Gallagher; and Gordon Hastings, president, Broadcasters Foundation of America; on Free Speech on the Airwaves.

WILLIAM O'SHAUGHNESSY (W.O.): It's a pleasure once again to be invited into your hearth and home. This is a busy political season, and we have lined up a special guest from the nation's capital. He is president of the National Association of Broadcasters, the chief advocate for every radio and television station in America: David Rehr.

DAVID REHR (D.R.): Bill. I appreciate being here, and I am experiencing, in your station, the very best of local radio, and it's very inspiring.

W.O.: You represent . . .

D.R.: The National Association of Broadcasters and its 8,300 members, including 1,200 television affiliates and 7,000-plus radio stations all across America.

W.O.: You're gonna have 7,000 guys mad at you for saying those nice things about WVOX and WVIP. Not that the word would get out; I don't much like publicity. We won't tell anybody. (*laughter*)

D.R.: I'll read about it tomorrow, and I'll probably see it on all the major TV networks, if I know you, O'Shaughnessy! (*laughter*)

W.O.: President David Rehr, you have so much on your agenda. You're a big Washington-insider lobbyist. I hear you raised millions for George W. Bush.

D.R.: Well, that may be a little exaggerated. I raised a lot of money for the president in his last reelection because at the time I believed him to be very pro–small business.

W.O.: How do you think the president is doing now?

D.R.: I think he is doing better. I still believe there are a lot of issues troubling our country: our intervention in Iraq and Afghanistan on the international front and gas prices domestically. I think he has hit a low and is working his way back up in the polls.

W.O.: You talk to a lot of senators and congressional representatives. How would you rate George Bush as a president?

D.R.: He is very polarizing. You either like him, or you don't. I think we are living in a time, unfortunately, when our country is split between the blue and the red states on a bunch of issues. People are grasping for something to hold us together. If you look at the polls, it's like a mirror. Half the people want taxes cut; half the people don't.

W.O.: We are now joined by the president of the Broadcasters Foundation of America, Gordon Hastings. Listen to this voice; he's a real radio man.

GORDON HASTINGS (G.H.): What an introduction, Bill. It is always nice to see you. The last time was at another local radio station, my own WSRK in Oneonta.

W.O.: Well, you're one of us, Gordon. And you are doing the best work of your life with that Broadcasters Foundation of America. The chairman, Phil Lombardo, lives nearby in Bronxville. Gordon and David, we are joined by Ambassador Ogden Rogers Reid.

AMBASSADOR OGDEN REID (O.R.): I'm delighted to be with you, Bill.

W.O.: Ogden Reid needs no introduction to this audience. He represented this area in Congress and served as the first ambassador to Israel, and his family owned the *Herald Tribune*. He is now doing some of the best work of *his* life as president of the Council of American Ambassadors. He is a great defender of free speech and once took on a man named Harley O. Staggers on the floor of the House of Representatives when Frank Stanton and Walter Cronkite were in trouble. Ambassador Reid, you honor us.

O.R.: Well, I thank Bill O'Shaughnessy for his leadership of WVOX and the Broadcasters Foundation, and his defense of the First Amendment. I heard the earlier comments about John McCain, and in the current issue of the *Ambassadors Review,* McCain wrote an excellent piece on "earmarking," and the $15 billion in private pork projects. They go through the House and Senate without any committee action or even the knowledge of most members.

W.O.: Ogden Reid, what's wrong with bringing home the bacon? David Rehr, I ask you the same thing.

D.R.: I think it is important for people's taxes to be spent in their home districts. In Washington, people stand in line for the money. So historically, Congress would use committees to evaluate priorities and fund them. Over the years with this "earmarking" process, it's become very easy just to say, "Give me $4 million here and $6 million there." A lot of these programs, in my opinion, would be rejected by a committee of the member's peers.

W.O.: David Rehr, you are a lobbyist. That's not such an honorable title in this day and age.

D.R.: I remember my mother once asked me what I wanted to be, and I replied, "A lobbyist." She said, "Why don't you become a lawyer?" I said, "But Mom, you hate lawyers." She said, "Yeah, but at least I can tell my neighbors what you do!" (*laughter*)

Being a lobbyist in the Jack Abramoff era gets a lot of bad PR. But when you're standing in the halls of Congress next to a young person with diabetes, and you're asking the government for funds to cure him, you can say, "That's what's great about America." Everybody's opinion can be heard, and their member of Congress will listen.

W.O.: Ogden Reid, how long did you serve in Congress?

O.R.: I served for twelve years, Bill, and I was concerned with the "private" bills members would submit to bring in a nanny from Europe without consideration by the Immigration and Naturalization Service. A member of Congress can get five or ten thousand dollars for each one of those bills. I remember testifying before Charlie Halleck and telling him those communications should be a matter of public record. Halleck leaned over the bench and said "Reid, what are you trying to do, depopulate the place?" (*laughter*) I am all for bringing home the bacon with appropriate lobbying, but with scrutiny and transparency.

W.O.: Ambassador Reid, I haven't asked David Rehr about "indecency." My mind drifts back to those desperate times when Mr. Staggers, had you not prevailed, wanted to throw Walter Cronkite and Dr. Stanton into the slammer.

O.R.: This was all over outtakes, if you recall.

W.O.: David Rehr has his hands full because if someone drops the "F-bomb" on the airwaves, it's going to cost about $350,000. What advice would you, Ambassador Reid, glorious First Amendment champion that you are, give to President David Rehr on this matter?

O.R.: I don't like to see speech circumscribed at all. I suppose there are cases with blatant, repeated obscenity. But just because a play or show uses a word, that's a reflection of life. I spent a little bit of time in Paris with the *Herald Tribune,* and the French don't understand this obsession. I'd rather have free speech with a little obscenity than lose it altogether.

W.O.: David Rehr, I know you've thought a lot about this issue. You've got the FCC raising hell, parents raising hell, and Congress just rolling over.

D.R.: In fact, the Senate passed the Indecency Fines Bill by unanimous consent, and then the House passed it with only thirty-five members voting "no." It's an election year, and representatives want to "protect children." I think the ambassador makes a good point; it's a slippery slope when you control what people can say, when they can say it, and how they can say it.

W.O.: Ambassador Reid, I have advised David Rehr to seek your wisdom and counsel, and I'm sure you'll be hearing from him. Thank you, Ambassador, for joining us.

O.R.: I look forward to hearing from him. And it's great to be on the air with these distinguished gentlemen, President Rehr; and the president of the Broadcasters Foundation, Mr. Hastings; and you, Bill, whom I have admired for so long.

W.O.: It's 2:24 on this beautiful, summerlike day. Do you remember the "Fairness" Doctrine, David Rehr? We would have had a "Fairness" Doctrine; Rupert Murdoch wouldn't have had his Boston newspapers but for the intercession and great wisdom of our next guest. Please welcome to this important discussion the fifty-second governor of New York, Mario Matthew Cuomo. How are you, sir?

GOVERNOR MARIO CUOMO (M.C.): Well, I'm disbelieving at the moment, Bill. You've talked about my helping Rupert Murdoch keep his newspapers as "an act of wisdom." It turned me into a public citizen; that's what happened, actually. *(laughter)*

W.O.: Oh, that's right. Murdoch forgot. He studied Latin but was absent the day they taught *quid pro quo.*

M.C.: No, he remembered! He was nice enough to call up and say, "I'm sorry I'm going to have to beat you in this campaign, Mario, because you really did help me keep my papers aloft; any way I can help you in the private world, I will; good luck to you!" And I've been in the private world ever since! Mr. President Rehr, it's a privilege to say hello to you.

I'm in the "me too" category, having listened to Ambassador Reid and having spoken to him only days ago on this very subject. And you can just record my echo of his sentiments. The Fairness Doctrine sounded right—sounded "fair"—but in the long run, I thought it was far more dangerous.

And there is a certain degree of palpable hypocrisy by Congress when they pass moral judgments about obscenity. First of all, obscenity is an elusive subject to define. The Supreme Court could only say, "You know it when you see it." That's a hell of a thing to try to regulate.

Apart from that, if you want to talk about obscenity in communications, how about the billions of dollars they pass every year in invisible bills nobody gets a chance to see? We know how they tack on amendments for friends at the last moment.

So it comes with ill grace from any recent Congress to talk about concern for children. There are proliferating threats to children from all directions, and you must teach them morality at home or at school so they can define obscenity. And when they see it's wrong, they will stop listening to it. But to try to do it in a statute, it just doesn't work.

W.O.: Governor, a lot of people are still upset you didn't run for the presidency.

M.C.: Rupert's not! (*laughter*)

W.O.: A lot of people were also astonished you hung up on Bill Clinton and wouldn't let him put you on the Supreme Court. First of all, how would you decide this if you were a Supreme Court justice? Or a better question is, on this obscenity and indecency thing, would you have signed it like President Bush, our hero, if you were president?

M.C.: No, I wouldn't have. You can't do it that way, Bill. That's the whole point. That was Potter Stewart's point. You know it when you see it. How do you define obscenity? Different generations have defined it differently. But in the end, you can't define it with a law. You can't enforce it. It's not manageable.

These are cultural matters, not legislative. The issue must be self-imposed by your own culture. I gave a speech once in Los Angeles, and I said, "We desire what disgusts us. And we are disgusted by what we desire." If people didn't buy obscene or pornographic products, we would not have this problem. But we have this problem because the culture wants it, and you are not going to change the culture with a law, especially when the public believes the lawmakers are hypocritical.

W.O.: Governor, let me ask David Rehr, do you think your television and radio stations are entirely blameless? Remember the "Opie and Anthony" stunt in the cathedral?

D.R.: I think sometimes we are a little edgy.

W.O.: Is "edgy" a new word for vulgar?

D.R.: Yes, but we focus on the 1 or 2 percent that is edgy or vulgar instead of the 98 percent that is decent and wholesome.

G.H.: There is a term we have all grown up with in the broadcasting business, the responsibility of the local broadcaster as a "gatekeeper." Many broadcasters, general managers, and owners look at themselves as "gatekeepers" for their audience. A lot of those people would have "self-policed" Opie and Anthony. This is a republic, and when you represent the general population, you're not going to win with Howard Stern and Opie and Anthony as your poster boys.

W.O.: Governor, is there any way out of this "unholy" mess?

M.C.: If you mean, is there a perfect solution to perfectly define what society will find objectionable about sex, of course not. Society is constantly shifting and evolving.

Take the "F" word—I mean, I am still shocked at how freely that word is thrown around in movies, even "PG" movies! When I was hired by the Weinsteins for Michael Moore's movie, we had big discussions with the rule-makers.

The question was, "How do you determine a 'PG'?" Well, if you use a certain word twice, they drop it down a class. I said, "You're kidding!" These are basically arbitrary formulas. It's just the "F" word. Matilda and I were shocked. We had a movie, and it was "PG," and the language was just stunning.

W.O.: What did Matilda Cuomo say?

M.C.: "Tsk, tsk, change the channel, Mario. Stop sweating and change the channel." (*laughter*) Incidentally, that is the solution. Gordon says the broadcasters are "gatekeepers." But let's be candid. You appeal to a certain audience, and you know what they will tolerate. Some people will not stand for hip-hop language, and now, that's considered music. Yes, there are gatekeepers, but when you know you're not going to get enough people tuning in, you change your standard, or you go out of the business.

I'm willing to pay a big price for free speech, even if my sensitivities are offended from time to time.

W.O.: David Rehr, you have four children, ages three to seven, and Governor, you have how many granddaughters?

M.C.: Twelve, O'Shaughnessy. And I have a grandson, five months old. Incidentally, I'm working on standards for him. (*laughter*)

W.O.: Were you shocked when you heard it was a boy? What did your son Christopher Cuomo, who is with ABC News, say? "Dad, you're not going to believe this"?

M.C.: Well, since we are defining obscenity, this is a good example. Christopher is a television person. He is doing well, thank you, and his wife, Cristina, is very astute; so they asked Christopher, why did you name him Mario? I think it is easy enough to say, "I am very proud of my father." He didn't say that. He said the baby was born with an unusually large nose, and [he] saw it as soon as Cristina did. [They] looked at one another, and said, "This is a Mario if I ever saw one!" Now to me that is virtual obscenity! (*laughter*)

W.O.: Let me ask you, "Grandfather" Cuomo and "Father" Rehr, when you see this stuff come on television or hear it on the radio, do you get a little crazy?

M.C.: Let me jump in, Bill. We do that all the time. We are alone in the apartment in Manhattan, and the grandkids come over all the time, a nine-year-old, a ten-year-old; we won't count the twenty-one-year-old. We have this problem with them all the time.

W.O.: They don't watch cartoons?

M.C.: No, they do watch Disney, but they want to see movies, too. We go to the video store, and you have to be very careful. You can't just assume "PG" is okay. I agree with the Europeans who feel we don't rate violence. If we are going to overdo anything, we should overdo the restrictions on violence.

I'm offended when kids see so much violence, they take it for granted. In our tremendously violent society, American society, we still have the death penalty. That's violence. We still revere the gun, with people holding semi-automatic weapons over their heads, saying, "This is my flag." My God! Talk about violence. We were born in violence, in gunshot and flames; we expanded in violence; we invented the atom bomb. We are a violent people, and that bothers me. And so, I won't let my grandchildren look at that kind of stuff if I can prevent it.

W.O.: President David Rehr, do you wrestle with this?

D.R.: We do. I think every parent of young children wrestles about what's "age appropriate" for their kids, whether they are listening to the radio or watching television. Sometimes, we turn it off; sometimes, we switch channels or put in a DVD.

But I also want my children to understand how people can say and think what they want in America. When you believe there are things in America that should not be talked about, that is bad for our country. Very bad.

W.O.: Remember that line "sticks and stones"? Is there an eloquent way to say that, Mario Cuomo? "Sticks and stones may break my bones, but names will never hurt me"?

M.C.: I don't know, Bill. I have a book by A. J. Parkinson, my favorite philosopher and writer. I'll look at it and see what he says. (*laughter*)

D.R.: I think part of the problem we face as broadcasters is that the general culture?whether it be violent or sexual?has evolved and changed. A lot of people harken back to the good old days. But the good old days weren't all that good in many respects.

G.H.: The question is, "Are we over-the-air broadcasters going to have to carry the sword? Are we the ones who are going to be constantly forced to push the envelope?" These are public airwaves.

W.O.: And we are public trustees.

G.H.: Thank you for using that term. Because when you are a trustee, all these issues come into play. They come into play as a prudent business decision, as well as the concept of gatekeeper. I don't believe in censorship, and we all believe in the First Amendment, but we are also responsible for the maintenance of certain standards.

W.O.: David Rehr, you have been a lobbyist for a long time. Is it hard to talk to a congressional representative or a senator about this?

D.R.: It really isn't. I think a lot of people look at their members of Congress and think, "Wow, they're the brightest and smartest! They've been elected!" Many years ago, in the early '80s, I kind of felt the same way, until one day I woke up, and said, "You know what? They're kind of like America itself."

Congress represents America. We have tall people; we have short people; we have smart people, and maybe a group of people who aren't as smart. We have an eclectic group of people who all work really hard. New York is blessed to have some outstanding members of Congress representing them, but they are still regular people. We put them on these high pedestals, and after a while they start to believe it, and it changes their whole outlook on the world.

W.O.: Who are some of the good ones? I won't ask about the bad ones because we still have to deal with them. Take the Senate . . .

D.R.: I'll give you people who used to be in the Senate so I won't get into trouble. A person I always admired, at least on Social Security, Medicare, and Medicaid issues, was Daniel Patrick Moynihan. He was a brilliant man. I didn't agree with him all the time, but I always thought, "Here's a U.N. ambassador and a senator who really put the nation and his state first."

W.O.: He sat at that very microphone many times. You and Tim Russert and I should start a Pat Moynihan fan club. Who's another one? Give me a good member of the House.

D.R.: This will be somewhat controversial, but I think Newt Gingrich is one of the smartest people I have ever encountered in politics. He is on a book tour now and might run for president.

W.O.: Does he have a chance?

D.R.: Better than people think.

W.O.: Is it tough when you've got like 8,000 bosses? In the beer industry, you had the Busches and the Heinekens.

D.R.: I also had 1,850 distributors, family-owned and -operated, all across the country, plus the "Legacy" families. When I was interviewed for the NAB job, several of the people, including the great Phil Lombardo, said this is a rough-and-tumble business. I kind of looked at them and said, "Anyone here ever meet August Busch III?" He is one of the most intense people I have ever met in my life, a great businessman, a superb entrepreneur. I'll match up the intensity and competitive spirit of August III to anyone in television or radio.

G.H.: Isn't it interesting how the beer industry has taken the initiative on drinking responsibly and the problem of underage drinking? They have done a remarkable job in saying, "Hey, we are part of the issue, but we also want to be part of the solution."

W.O.: Before you leave, Mr. Rehr, is local radio going to be around for a while? We've got iPods and the damn "Star Wars" satellites you have to pay for. Is local-yokel radio going to survive?

D.R.: That's a very good question. When I'm out meeting with radio broadcasters, I remind them, in the case of satellite radio, both XM and Sirius have about 10 million subscribers. But every week between 260 and 280 million Americans listen to local radio!

W.O.: I've got twelve people in Mamaroneck myself! (*laughter*)

D.R.: I think local radio is all about community. Think of what the world would be like if we had no local radio.

G.H.: There would be only express trains! No local stops, you could take the train from here to Los Angeles and be unable to get off in Norwalk! (*laughter*)

D.R.: The *Wall Street Journal* said this radio station is "the quintessential local radio station in America."

W.O.: I don't even read the *Journal*!

D.R.: I read it religiously, but I needed to come and find out for myself. I have been so impressed with the diversity of viewpoints, the interesting people, and the interns who are getting an education here on what local radio is all about. It's a great testament to the ability of local radio to make the community vibrant.

W.O.: President Rehr, when he returns to D.C., will assemble his high council of advisors and say, "They don't pay me enough to listen to O'Shaughnessy!" (*laughter*)

D.R.: I think radio and television will adapt, and we will evolve. But that's what's great about our industry. We are fiercely entrepreneurial and tremendously competitive, and all of those juices and energy will serve the people who are listening to the station right now.

W.O.: I'm going to give you a new word for what we do: Profession.

D.R.: Profession. Yes, I agree.

W.O.: David Rehr, your presence honors us, and your intelligence inspires us.

D.R.: Thank you, Bill, and God bless you, and God bless all the people who listen to this remarkable radio station.

INTERVIEW WITH GOVERNOR MARIO M. CUOMO ABOUT INDECENCY IN BROADCASTING

Why must we broadcasters always leave it to others to make the case for us and remind us who we are and what we are about? Aired March 1, 2004.

WILLIAM O'SHAUGHNESSY (W.O.): We switch now, on this spring-like day, to Willkie, Farr & Gallagher, the decidedly white shoe (upstate elite), ivory-tower law firm high up in the canyons of Manhattan. And there in a spectacular corner office: Mario M. Cuomo, the former governor of New York, who was recently accused—by a college president—of being "the greatest thinker of the twentieth century." Can I ask you something that has to do with my own tribe, Governor?

GOVERNOR MARIO CUOMO (M.C.): Go for it, O'Shaughnessy.

W.O.: Indecency. Broadcasters have been rushing to "make nice" with Congress, particularly its Midwestern members, on obscenity and indecency and so on. You're a great defender of the First Amendment, and you've bailed broadcasters out over the years when government wanted to intrude in content. Howard Stern just got axed, knocked off five or six Clear Channel stations. And all the elders of broadcasting are afraid they're going to lose their licenses. Where is the First Amendment in all of this?

M.C.: Well, that's a really interesting question. Now you have to be very specific when you talk about the law. The First Amendment says you have a right in this country to a free press, thank God, and free speech, thank God. That is maybe the strongest of all the guarantees we have. And without it, we're not the United States of America.

W.O.: Does that right extend to the electronic press?

M.C.: It extends to *all* press, that right to free speech. Now, does that mean you can't be censured in any way? Justice Holmes made it clear: it doesn't mean you can falsely shout "Fire!" in a crowded theater. So there are some limitations, but very few. You can be stopped from publishing a story that would be a threat to the security of the United States of America. But the general proposition is to keep the government's hands off content. Remember the Fairness Doctrine, Bill?

W.O.: You helped torpedo the damned thing . . .

M.C.: Because you're an expert on this, just give us a simple definition of what the Fairness Doctrine meant to radio and television.

W.O.: I think it meant that if you take a stand you've got to go out and get somebody and give the other side a chance.

M.C.: It *sounded* reasonable, didn't it? It sounded fair. And our position was: Look, the government can't do that to Bill O'Shaughnessy's radio stations WVOX/WVIP—or anybody else's. You can't do it to them for the same reason you can't do it to the *New York Times*. You can't say to the *New York Times,* "You wrote an article on the Democrats, now you have to write an article on the Republicans that says approximately the same thing in the same number of words." And that's how we feel.

Incidentally, the Democrats disagreed with me when I argued against the Fairness Doctrine. So I'm still strong for "hands-off" by the government. Now, let's get to Howard Stern and what you say is the "caving in" to congressmen.

If the stations are caving in to congressmen, that's a bad thing. Why? I would rather trust the First Amendment than the congressmen. I would rather trust the insistence on freedom than the judgments of those congressmen.

I don't know who they are. And I don't know what they know about communication and about my soul and about my mind and about my welfare that would enable them to tell me what I can hear and what I can't, what I can see and what I can't. I don't think they would have that right.

Now, if they start censoring Stern, or anyone else on a television show, because she's about to tear the patch off her breast or on a radio show because he's going to start talking about things we would regard as filth, that's a different matter.

If you moved in on this because a *congressman* told you to, I would say that's bad and dangerous. If you did it because you thought it was bad *business* for yourself—if you thought your listeners didn't want that stuff and would be offended by it and wouldn't buy the products you're trying to sell them—or because you're public radio and you say, "Well, I don't have to worry about the products, but I do have to worry about the sensibilities of my people"—that's a big difference.

If you did it as a judgment that reflected what your people wanted, then I would have no objection to it. For the commercial stations, you pay a price for it. If you make the wrong judgment, you're going to lose money. If you make the right judgments, your audience will be pleased and you'll make money.

W.O.: But broadcasters today, Governor, seem to be interested only in protecting their licenses.

M.C.: Well, if they're doing it only in reaction to political pressure, then it's a dumb and bad thing. If they're making their own economic judgments—you do that every day, Bill, and you know it. You play classical music because you think you have people out there who want to hear it. And if I gave you some new super jet-jive group that has a new kind of sound in which they bang garbage can covers against old garbage cans and it was loud and that was regarded as virtuous, you wouldn't play it. Why? Because your people don't want to hear it.

Now, that's not a violation of the First Amendment. You don't have a Fairness Doctrine where you have to play all kinds of music. Or deliver all kinds of news. If you want to put Sean Hannity on and Rush Limbaugh, you can.

Look, what's Clear Channel doing now? Clear Channel has nothing but conservative talk show hosts. I don't see them putting any liberals on. Why not? Because they figure the talk show audience is mostly conservative. Is that what they want? Terrific! And they figure the conservative people are more entertaining. Whatever!

That's a judgment they make. I wouldn't object to that. And I don't.

W.O.: Governor, what about these draconian fines? $750,000 per incident.

M.C.: Well, I don't know. It's a draconian fine if it's against Bill O'Shaughnessy's stations, but it's not a draconian fine if it's against Clear Channel as a corporation.

W.O.: Senator John McCain—who admires you—says people are constantly redrawing the lines of social behavior and indecency and obscenity. It's constantly shifting and constantly changing. Who is to decide this? The FCC?

M.C.: The FCC shouldn't be the arbiter of taste. What qualifies them? Whom would you appoint? Religious leaders? Sailors? Baseball players? Smart lawyers? Mothers? Who would you put on the FCC and say, "You're in charge of telling us what is good for us to hear"?

W.O.: What about the U.S. Congress?

M.C.: No.

W.O.: But they're elected!

M.C.: So what? They elected *me* too! That doesn't always mean you're going to do everything right, O'Shaughnessy. I would rely on the *people,* basically. There is a thin, thin area where you make rules that involve domestic security or the security of the nation. But for the most part, you leave it up to the people.

Bill, let's face it: In the end, in this country, you get what you deserve as a public. We've said this over and over again in talking with broadcasters and everybody else about the First Amendment.

Frankly, I am shocked. If you get videocassettes—as Matilda and I do . . . we'll stay home and open a snack table, and Matilda will make a little meal, and we'll sit and talk and watch a movie. You call the guy and ask him, "What have you got?" You don't ask him what it's like. Some of them are shocking to us, old as we are and coming from middle-class Queens and Brooklyn. Some of the stuff is unbelievable. What the heck *is* this? People with no clothes making love in all kinds of ways.

W.O.: Are you disgusted by what you see?

M.C.: Yes, sometimes. And then we have the same conversation every time. But in the end I say, "Look, Matilda, if there's a lot of this, it's because America *wants* a lot of this. They won't say it—and some people will say they're *disgusted* by it. But they *desire* it. Or it wouldn't be up there, wouldn't be selling. And it's selling *big time*!

W.O.: Mario Cuomo once had an elegant but haunting line: "We are disgusted by what we crave . . ."

M.C.: We're *disgusted* by what we *desire,* but we *desire* what *disgusts* us. I think, in the end, Bill, it's the people who will determine what music they hear on your station, what talk shows they listen to on your station. Because if they don't like it in large numbers, they stop, and you have to replace your offering. We get what we deserve.

Some of us don't like the stuff we get, so we'll go to public radio or public television or go to the Knights of Columbus magazine or read *Commonweal* or *America,* instead of the other stuff because we just *prefer* it.

That's the way it ought to be. You ought to be able to pick from the menu *yourself*.

I don't want them telling me what to eat—not in a restaurant, and not in feeding my mind.

W.O.: Finally, are we a sick society? Your tormentor Bob Grant says it's sick out there and getting sicker. Is he right?

M.C.: Well, some people are more familiar with sickness than others. (*laughter*)

W.O.: Is he right?

M.C.: I don't know. Maybe he's more familiar with it than I am.

W.O.: Governor, what about the children? Aren't you concerned about children seeing some of this awful, vulgar stuff?

M.C.: The United States, with all its respect and reverence for the First Amendment and insistence on as much freedom as possible for the adult population, has always, at the same time, been mindful of the special needs of the children, who are not capable of this kind of discernment and judgment that most adults can be presumed to be capable of. And so, they make allowances—constitutionally—for children.

You can censor to help children. You can screen out to help children. You have more leeway in terms of departing from an absolute liberal free speech standard when you're talking about protecting children. So, an exception is made in the case of children.

W.O.: *Who* can censor, Governor? Who can "screen out"?

M.C.: The best and most effective censor is a parent. Or a person *in loco parentis*. But the government sometimes sees itself *in loco parentis,* in the place of the parent. And so the government is allowed more leeway in terms of censoring to protect children in special ways than they would be if they dealt only with an adult population. They have traditionally used different hours of the day and things that help deal with children to the exclusion of the adults.

W.O.: You don't like the notion of the government being a *babysitter*?

M.C.: Look, Aristotle said, "In all things, moderation." My mother said the same thing, and she couldn't read. But you have to be reasonable about these things, Bill. I don't mind government trying to help children by screening for them, as long as they don't overdo it, and in the process of screening for children, screen out the *adults* as well.

W.O.: So, you're not worried about "suffer the little children"?

M.C.: I *am* worried about the little children. And the government is worried about the little children. And for that reason I'm willing to accept limitations on expression and screening and monitoring of expression where *children* are concerned that I wouldn't accept for myself and other adults.

W.O.: Don't you think children are finding worse things on the Internet?

M.C.: Well, how do you handle that? You should start with the proposition that there are concessions we will make to protect our children that we would not make in dealing with the rest of the population.

W.O.: Wise words on a difficult subject, Governor. But one thing you've revealed, sir—and I'll mercifully yield—is that when you and Matilda Cuomo sit over a TV tray of an evening, you're watching regular movies. I really thought you were watching only old videotapes of your greatest speeches. (*laughter*)

M.C.: Are you kidding, O'Shaughnessy? They're *banned* in my house! The *last* place in the world you want to go for a Cuomo book or speech is in any of the Cuomo houses. A reporter was doing a column once on what kind of guy the governor is, and he asked what the governor was like at home. And Matilda said, "What do you mean, 'at home'?" So he said, "You know, when you're around the dinner table with just the family and you're talking. What does he sound like?" And she hesitated and said, "Sounds like an *affidavit*!" (*laughter*)

W.O.: Are you suggesting you're a prophet without honor in your own home?

M.C.: Well, I've done my share of prophesying. But, yeah, they may think of me as a *dishonorable* prophet. (*laughter*)

INTERVIEW WITH LOUIS BOCCARDI

Louis Boccardi is one of the most respected news executives in the nation. The low-key, self-effacing former president of the mighty Associated Press was called back into the limelight to investigate CBS News during the "Rathergate" contretemps. His brilliant counsel has also benefited our community radio stations over the years. Boccardi is an icon of the profession. We spoke with him on January 11, 2005.

WILLIAM O'SHAUGHNESSY (W.O.): CBS has just released his report. He's been on all the networks and cable shows, and he's been quoted this day in all the major journals of our nation. He's also one of our Westchester neighbors . . . Louis Boccardi. For a good, long time, he was president and CEO of the mighty Associated Press, one of the most respected news organizations in the world, and he is a director of the mighty Gannett Company. In recent months, he's been behind closed doors on an important assignment with Dick Thornburgh, the former U.S. attorney general, trying to figure out what the hell went wrong with CBS and Dan Rather. Lou Boccardi, was this one of your toughest assignments?

LOUIS BOCCARDI (L.B.): It was very difficult, Bill, because there were a large number of good people who thought they were doing the right thing—at least it seemed so to them at the moment they were doing it. Also, it's just a complicated story. So it was a tough assignment, yes.

W.O.: Louis Boccardi, three or four people lost their jobs. Do you feel bad about that?

L.B.: Well, that's a question you'd think would be awfully easy for me to answer, but we've made a pact with ourselves. CBS asked us to look at the story and both how it was done and the aftermath and didn't ask us to intervene in personnel issues, so I'm not commenting on anything they did in the way of personnel.

W.O.: What of Dan Rather, Mr. Boccardi? Did you talk to him in your investigation?

L.B.: Sure.

W.O.: What is your read, Lou Boccardi, as one of the best-known news executives in the country, on Dan Rather as a professional?

L.B.: Well, that's a question that, as you described it, transcends the report. I said, just this morning in a conversation, he's had an illustrious career, one that goes well beyond this issue, as attention-getting as this one event was. He's one of the largest figures in television news, one of the largest figures of his age in television news. Our report makes clear that some things went wrong on this story, and we called it as we saw it.

W.O.: Mario Cuomo said this Rather episode, was just that, an *episode* in a long career. A chapter.

L.B.: Well, call it an episode or an event, pick your own word for it—it's something that happened. It's clearly not going to be quickly forgotten. The fallout from it is extensive. Those are just the facts.

W.O.: Has the image of CBS News been tarnished?

L.B.: I think so. This isn't the first time a news organization has found itself confronted by something that represents a failure of some sort in its systems or in its people. You're always damaged when it happens. Now the challenge to them is to pick up and account for it openly, which it seems to me they've done—although I have inside perspective on that and may not be the best witness. But I think they've owned up to it in a very public way. They promised they would make our report public, and they did. They made that promise, of course, even before we started and had no idea what we'd say. I think they're doing what a news organization should do, which is to own up, be transparent in investigating what happened, have it investigated by outsiders, and then take steps to make sure it doesn't happen again. All those things are doable, and it seems to me that's the path CBS is on and that's the path I think helps you restore whatever damage an event might cause.

W.O.: Westchester neighbor Lou Boccardi, when you ran the mighty Associated Press, you had on your board all the moguls and press lords and barons. What of the *culture* of news gathering? What about the history, lineage, and tradition? CBS was once a proud organization. Is that all gone by the wayside?

L.B.: CBS is *still* a very proud news organization. And we saw that in the people whom we had to interrogate about what had happened. They spoke with great emotion about their loyalty to CBS and their sense of commitment. So I don't think it would be fair to say that this vision we have of another age would be all gone now. I think the reality is that a few things have changed in the business. And it's not just CBS.

Three broad ways things have changed: One is technology, in television news. When you look at the footage, you can see virtually instantly from virtually anywhere. Not very many years ago, you'd have to think about how you'd film something and fly it out and maybe if we're lucky get it on the network news tomorrow night or the night after that. All that is swept away with the enormous change in technology.

Another thing that's happened is something that you delve into, Bill, from time to time. This public issue of credibility and trust and the place of the media in this age and the great passions the press coverage stirs in the climate we're in now.

And the third thing that affects television news, as it does other media, is the economic pressures. In the days of the networks, when there were only three and no cable, and no twenty-four-hour broadcasts, the news audience was essentially a network audience. That's not the case anymore.

So, you have these enormous forces changing the nature of the business. And I don't think you can discuss the business without those forces in mind. It's a very long answer to a very short question, but I think those are factors you have to keep in mind when you're talking about whether this is different or whether this is an old glory from an old day that's shattered.

W.O.: Speaking of the glory from an old day . . . CBS was the house of legends: Lowell Thomas, Edward R. Murrow, Eric Sevareid, the great Cronkite. Anybody there today in that news organization who will one day be ranked among the immortals?

L.B.: There are certainly people who would say Dan is the heir. He's certainly and obviously Cronkite's direct heir. But go back to what I said a minute ago about a changed climate. The network was the center of everything, and that's shifted now. You have different places and different personalities, so it may not quite be that you can see a re-creation of this age that you're recalling because the environments are changing.

W.O.: Lou Boccardi, when you sit in your Westchester home with your wife, Joan, who is active in the civic life of our community, and you turn on the television, do you believe everything you see?

L.B.: I'm naïve enough to think everybody I see is trying to tell me the truth. Maybe that is a professional hazard or a professional weakness on my part. In the CBS thing, the people who put that story on the air believed every word of it. We didn't find the slightest hint that they put something on thinking it was wrong, or that they put it on knowing that there might be problems with it. They were anxious, for whatever reason, to get the story that might be damaging to the president on the air. So I think I would make the case that we, in the media, try very hard to get it right and want you to believe what we say. That is why it is so damaging when something goes awry. It damages all of us in its own way, in some way that gets into the bloodstream. If somebody listens to WVOX—now, obviously, that's not a short hop—that affects all of us. It affects how somebody will react when they read something on AP or hear something on ABC or CNN. These are not isolated events, and the public perception of what we do can be damaged when one of us gets so badly off the rail.

W.O.: Well, I hesitate to ask you, Lou Boccardi, if you believe everything you hear on WVOX.

L.B.: (*laughs*) Well, I'm tempted to say you're wise to hesitate to ask me, but you would think I was just being a smart-aleck neighbor from down the street . . .!

W.O.: Mr. Boccardi, was Dick Thornburgh, the former attorney general, good to work with, and did CBS cooperate with the two of you?

L.B.: Yes, on both counts. Dick brought, obviously, a many-decades-long legal career, including service as the attorney general and also as governor of Pennsylvania. And I brought four decades as a newsperson. I think we work together very effectively. We didn't have any ideological debates, which some of my friends predicted would happen. He was an even-handed investigator, as far as I could see, and I think he thought I was too.

W.O.: Are there any heroes left in the tribe, Lou Boccardi?

L.B.: I would nominate as heroes the people who are on the line in Baghdad, right now; amidst the squalor, the pain, and the suffering in Sri Lanka and Indonesia. I suspect that's not what you were thinking about in the question, but they are heroes, putting their lives on the line, putting themselves in jeopardy.

W.O.: Sir, I mercifully yield. What's next for Lou Boccardi, who once ran the mighty AP? You're a director of several entities. Do you miss the action?

L.B.: Well, I'd be lying if I said I didn't miss the action; of course I do. I'm going to re-retire and be happy about it.

INTERVIEW WITH FREDERIC DICKER, STATE EDITOR, *NEW YORK POST*

Fred Dicker has been the state editor and Albany bureau chief of the New York Post *for many, many years. I used to call him the "enfant terrible" of the Albany press corps. But he has too much seniority, longevity, and respect for that title. "Dean of the Albany Press Corps" is a more fitting appellation for this bespectacled and brilliant genius who is a frequent guest on "Imus in the Morning," MSNBC, Fox, and CNN. Fred also has his own daily radio show on "Talk 1300" in the Capital District. Other papers have a cadre of eager print and electronic journalists covering Albany. Nobody beats Dicker or the* Post. *Here is our interview with him broadcast on January 6, 2005.*

WILLIAM O'SHAUGHNESSY (W.O.): The national political action—the presidential election—is behind us. It's winter again in the land. And now the scene shifts to Albany, the capital city of our state, and we have on the line the "enfant terrible" of the press corps, which means he's one tough hombre. His name is Fred Dicker. He's the state editor of the *New York Post* daily newspaper. And another journal, the one that comes out on that funny salmon-colored stock, the *New York Observer,* also one of my favorites, called him the "King of Albany." Frederic Dicker, have you been getting kidded by your pals in the public press?

FRED DICKER (F.D.): Just a few, Bill. Let me just say it's a pleasure to be on with the King of Greater New York Media, Bill O'Shaughnessy, on his famous WVOX.

W.O.: Fred Dicker, what do you think about that article? They really gave it to you pretty good . . .

F.D.: Well, I *was* a little nervous. You have to be careful when you deal with the media, as we both know. (*laughter*) When I heard somebody was writing about me, I thought, "Oh my God!" But let me say it was a very nice piece, flattering—and frankly, without trying to blow my own horn, I thought it was an honest piece.

I've been at this game a long time. You've known me a long time, Bill. I think one of the first stories you told about me—in one of your books—is about when I tried to get some information out of *you* when I was working on a story. But you know I've always been the kind of person—and I think it comes across in the article—who tries to treat everybody the same, to pull back the curtain on the Wizard of Oz and let the public know what's really going on; and I think I've had a modicum of success. That has allowed me to feel good about what I've done over the years—and there have been a lot of years.

W.O.: I think that flattering profile called you "an equal opportunity ______"—I can't say it on the radio. Frederic Dicker, how long have you been sitting up there on your perch as state editor of my beloved *Post*?

F.D.: In one capacity or another, I've been with the *Post* since 1982. Before that, I was for a few years with the *Albany Times-Union*. So I've been watching the state capital scene lo these many years, going on—get this, Bill—*three* decades!

W.O.: Fred, we read in the public press—so it must be true—horrible things about the great Assembly of the state of New York and the state Senate. And you're no fan of the current governor—George Pataki—who just did his "State of the State" earlier this week. What kind of governor is George Elmer Pataki, in *your* eyes?

F.D.: That's the $64,000 question. He's certainly not the governor who took over the state in 1995, defeating your pal, Mario Cuomo, and promising to turn New York around. He came in with a $5 billion deficit, no death penalty on the books, a sense of an erosion of the state's economy, a hostile business climate . . . I could keep going on, but the point I'm making is: Here it is *ten* years later, he gives a "State of the State," and we have a $6 billion deficit, no death penalty, and the state's business climate, according to the business leaders themselves, is disastrous, on the brink of collapse. We've lost 2 million people as residents; the upstate New York area—as you know, as a guy who has his roots upstate—has been de-populated. So Governor Pataki is a governor who has disappointed not just his *critics* but his *fans*. And he is now widely seen as a governor on his way out, who has not accomplished what he set out to do.

W.O.: Fred Dicker, they say the foremost powerhouse players in Albany are the governor; the head of the Senate, Joe Bruno; and the Democrat who heads the Assembly, Sheldon Silver. They also say the *fourth* guy is Frederic Dicker. (*laughter*)

F.D.: I sort of wish I *had* that power, because if I did, I might be able to change things here. That was a nice compliment; sadly, it's totally hyperbolic. Those *three* are the power here, and those three are under criticism and attack, Bill, as you know, like never before—and let me just note, *deservingly so*.

W.O.: Everybody, Fred Dicker, says it doesn't *work*.

F.D.: It doesn't work the way it's *supposed* to, and it's been getting worse and worse. I have the advantage and unique perspective of somebody who has been here for so many years, that I can tell you, Bill, in the view of not just us journalists, but also of serious-minded professional administrators, serious lobbyists, and others who watch state government very carefully, that this state has devolved to a chaotic and incompetent level the likes of which nobody ever thought possible. Plus, now there is a "smell" of scandal around state government that was never here before, until just a few years ago. It's an ugly situation—people on the *inside* call it ugly—and it's all happened while Governor Pataki has been governor. So, rightly, some of the blame for this mess here has to reside with the state's chief executive.

W.O.: Is "ugly" a Fred Dicker word for corrupt?

F.D.: That could be. That's not Fred Dicker's word, though. But there's a widespread sense that this government is "for sale." You just take a look at who the leading lobbyists are. Who *are* they? Are they people of great accomplishment and skill, or are they people who have special, personal connections to the governor, Speaker Silver, and Majority Leader Bruno? The answer is the latter. You have people who are making *millions* of dollars trading on their personal access to the leaders of this state. That couldn't happen if the leaders of this state didn't *permit* and *encourage* it.

W.O.: Fred, wasn't it ever thus? Isn't there something in the Bible—"the lobbyists you will have with you always"?

F.D.: Lobbyists aren't necessarily bad. They *could* be very helpful. Ten years ago, when Mario Cuomo left office, $40 million a year was being spent on "reportable" lobbying. Today, it's *$120* million! That is major bucks. You've got people here who never went to college or achieved anything except moving their way up in the political world. All of a sudden, because of their connections, they're multi-millionaires. And that is *legal*. Beyond that, there is a widespread sense that it's a "Pay to Play" culture. If you want something done by this government, by this legislature, you've got to come up with *money,* via substantial contributions to their campaign committees. That *quid pro quo is* illegal. If I could prove it, I would write it. But there is a widespread sense that you have to do that now, and that hasn't been the case in the past.

W.O.: We're visiting on this January day with Frederic Dicker, the state editor of the *New York Post*. He wields a mighty pen, and also a mighty voice, with his own radio program in the Capital District.

F.D.: You should make "full disclosure" there, Bill, that you're really the "honorary" Westchester and Greater New York City chief correspondent of the show, "Live from the State Capitol, with Fred Dicker," on WROW (now WGDJ) in Albany.

W.O.: I proudly accept. Which do you like better, newspapers or radio? I've never asked you that, Dicker.

F.D.: I thought you were going to mention TV too, because for almost a year I worked at Channel 5 in New York, as the Investigative Producer. And frankly, I *hated* television. But I have to say, I tip my hat to you and WVOX and all your people. I *love* radio! Now, I like newspapering a great deal. Actually, I love it. But radio is wonderful. And for those of us, unlike yourself, who are "visually challenged"—you know, that "face made for radio" thing (*laughter*)—it's a place where you can have a lot of fun and create an image for yourself. I love it.

W.O.: Fred Dicker, you mentioned Mario Cuomo. I can remember when he was governor and you were giving him fits. He was tearing his hair out, and he asked me, "How do I get Dicker on my side? How do I 'enlighten' him?" Do you *miss* Mr. Cuomo?

F.D.: Well, it's true. I mean, I joked with the former governor one time, saying, "Let me tell you how bad it is. It's so bad I'm nostalgic for *you*!"—which he thought was very, very funny. Of course, it was half-joking. But when you see a contrast, when you see a new person, you come to appreciate things about the old person that you maybe took for granted. For instance, access to government and access to the governor; and a governor who was at the Capitol every day, working hard, and was actually living in the State Mansion. It's like night and day now. We have Governor Pataki, someone who *rarely* is at the state capitol; he's virtually *inaccessible* to journalists; he's *hostile* to the media, to a degree that, in my entire career as a journalist, I've never seen before. So in many ways, Mario Cuomo looks terrific. Plus, he's a very *engaging* guy. We *both* know—you better than I—Mario Cuomo is a guy who appreciates *ideas,* enjoys repartee with intelligent people, and is always *searching* for things. George Pataki does not enjoy that kind of repartee, from what we know. He doesn't *enjoy* intellectual discussions. He generally is a *secretive* person, so people don't have a sense of what he's about. Whereas, with Mario Cuomo, I think we always knew what he was about.

W.O.: Cuomo loves to mix it up with you, Fred Dicker. And in that article in the *New York Observer* he said, "Dicker is tough and fair." Let me put you to work now, and *be* tough and fair: Is Pataki going to run again for governor?

F.D.: I don't believe he is. I think his "State of the State" address this week was more of a farewell than a call to arms. The latest polls show him losing, even in upstate New York, to Eliot Spitzer, which is breathtaking for people who saw him win on the strength of his upstate support, over Mario Cuomo, back in 1994. Many of his top staffers have departed. The inside word is that George Pataki is in "exit mode," possibly for a private-sector job and a try at running for president, presumably as a Republican, in 2008.

W.O.: One of our Westchester neighbors, William Plunkett—you know him as a great power broker in the state—makes a pretty compelling case that Pataki might be the guy because they got nobody after Bush.

F.D.: Well, Plunkett is a booster for Governor Pataki. If Bill Plunkett says that, it's what he's *supposed* to say. But you point to some other serious Republicans around this country who think George Pataki has a chance, with his record here, which is not distinguished; with his very liberal stance on a whole range of issues; with his top political advisor, Arthur Finkelstein, telling an Israeli paper that President Bush's reelection means George Pataki *can't* run for president.

W.O.: Plunkett lives here in Westchester, and I have to tell you I admire the guy tremendously. I'm nuts about his wife, and I love his family. So does Nancy. *Even,* if you can believe it, Governor Cuomo thinks Plunkett is quite a good fellow, even after Plunkett did everything to try to beat Cuomo. They have great respect for each other.

F.D.: But you find me some Republicans *outside* the very tight-knit circle of people around Pataki who cashed in because of Pataki's stature. Find me someone other than those insiders who say he could be presidential timber, and I'll tip my hat to you.

W.O.: Fred Dicker, you're knowledgeable not only about the Empire State, our own New York, but we see you on Fox News and CNN talking about national stuff. Who else *have* we got after President Bush?

F.D.: Who's the "we"?

W.O.: The Republicans . . .

F.D.: Oh, the *Republicans* . . . *you* guys! There are a number of important "regional" figures, Bill. Jeb Bush, the governor of Florida; the Senate Majority Leader, Bill Frist, is interesting; John McCain is interesting. There are people on the national scene who are what I call "regional" forces. Rudy Giuliani, who clearly has an interest in the presidency and has obviously been damaged by the Bernard Kerik affair. Rudy may be in a unique position as a national figure because of his status: He was brought to a godlike stature in the wake of 9/11, and deservedly so. If Pataki thinks he can be as strong as those people, he ought to give it a try. People I know on the national scene—in the Republican Party—don't think he has a chance.

W.O.: If Pataki doesn't run again—you say he won't—then who runs?

F.D.: I know they'll talk to you, O'Shaughnessy, because they're looking for people with stature and wealth! But if you decide *not* to run, and Rudy Giuliani, as we suspect, decides not to run, then it's fair to say that if George Pataki doesn't run, then Eliot Spitzer will be the governor. I think it's not going to matter. I think they're going to have to find some Howard Mills–type, a throwaway candidate or a self-funding millionaire—or *billionaire*. But it's all over if Pataki and Giuliani say no. I think it's all over even if Pataki says *yes*. But I think Giuliani could certainly beat Eliot Spitzer, who's going to be the Democratic candidate.

W.O.: Attorney general? Right now, it's Spitzer. He wants to be governor; *Dicker* thinks he *will* be governor. Who is going to be the next *attorney general,* where once Spitzer sat?

F.D.: Well, that's a good question. It could conceivably be Jeanine Pirro as a Republican candidate, your own Westchester District Attorney. And on the Democratic side, they have a host of talented people: Andrew Cuomo, Mark Green, Richard Brodsky. Most of the people on the "inside" think it's between Andrew Cuomo, whom you know quite well, and Mark Green, the former public advocate for New York City.

W.O.: What about Mrs. Pirro? They say she has to get rid of that "baggage." Is it lingering, or has she gotten past that? I like the lady . . .

F.D.: Wait a minute! What "baggage" are you talking about?

W.O.: Her husband, Al, had some problems that were widely chronicled. He's a good friend of this radio station and one of our talk show hosts. He had his problem with the Feds.

F.D.: He's a convicted criminal, a tax evader! And *she* signed the tax returns as a DA and a lawyer, and said she didn't *read* them?

W.O.: He went away to "college," Fred. He paid for his omissions. He's a nice guy.

F.D.: Look, I don't doubt that at all. He's probably a terrific guy. He was a very effective lobbyist, very bright, but the facts are the facts, and that's a problem for Jeanine Pirro. On the other hand, she's very attractive, and as a DA, she's tough on crime. But she's going to be a "hampered" candidate. There's no question. With all her strengths, of course, on her side, is the fact that Mike Balboni, a senator from Long Island, might be the only alternative for the Republicans. And he's not that well known. The Republican Party—your beloved party—is a party, Bill, substantially without a "back bench" in this state, a party without a "talent pool." One of the reasons the Republican Party is going through a shakeup now—with Sandy Treadwell bounced out, with Kieran Mahoney and Arthur Finkelstein fired, with Stephen Minarik in there now, trying to do something to bring the party back to where Bill Powers and Al D'Amato and others had it ten or twelve or fourteen years ago—is because the Republican Party is in crisis in New York. And that, by the way, reflects on the governor as well. And right now, nobody within the GOP really knows what to do.

W.O.: Are you saying you miss Al D'Amato? I saw him at San Pietro a few nights ago and gave him a big, fat, wet kiss. Two, in fact. (*laughter*) I'm afraid I like him too.

F.D.: In many ways, Al D'Amato was the most important *political* figure in New York in the last twenty years. More important in some ways than even Mario Cuomo, because of his *legacy,* which is still with us. That's what George Pataki is and the Republican Party, in many ways, is. Of course, how could we *not* miss Al D'Amato or the great Mario Cuomo? These are larger-than-life political figures who were very exciting to cover.

W.O.: Final question. I've never asked you this before. You've been having your way with me and giving it to me for being a Republican. What the hell are *you,* Fred Dicker? A Republican? Or a Dem?

F.D.: I'm what's called "a *Blank.*" I'm un-enrolled, not in *any* political party. But I'm a registered voter. Personally, I'm a mix of views. I like Edmund Burke, Bill. I even like John Calvin. I'm a civil libertarian. I'm not easily defined or pinned down, as you may have noticed.

W.O.: That story in the *Observer* quoted you as saying Calvin may have been on to something, that you're doing the Lord's work at your profession, covering all the political nuts.

F.D.: What we do for a living should be a kind of "calling"; it has a certain religious quality to it; it's a commitment. By doing good work, you're serving God. That's always been attractive to me. I think that's a powerful message. I think that helped form America into what it is today, and I think it would be good if everybody had that sense with at least part of what they were doing. Whatever it is, whether they are gas pump jockeys, cleaners, hifalutin' politicians! To some degree, everyone can put a spiritual quality into what they're doing.

W.O.: You think God is pleased you're the best damn reporter in this state?

F.D.: Well, if there *is* a God, O'Shaughnessy, I don't think God would waste His—or Her—time on such trivialities.

W.O.: There you go—now you're messing with God, Dicker.

F.D.: Well, I *hope* there is one. Sometimes I have my doubts, but I'm a person who has some faith.

W.O.: Fred Dicker, thank you. You're also the best street reporter, and an editor with marvelous instincts. That's why you're bureau chief of the *New York Post* in our capital city. Thank you, sir.

F.D.: Coming from such an extraordinary figure, I thank you as well.

INTERVIEW WITH MATT DAVIES, 2004 PULITZER PRIZE–WINNING EDITORIAL CARTOONIST, *JOURNAL NEWS*

Matt Davies is the editorial cartoonist for the Journal News, *the powerful Gannett daily in the northern suburbs. He won a coveted Pulitzer Prize for his perceptive eye and deft, graceful pen. We interviewed him on April 12, 2004.*

WILLIAM O'SHAUGHNESSY (W.O.): Lightning struck the *Journal News* this week when the Pulitzer Prize Committee awarded a Pulitzer to the editorial cartoonist, Matt Davies. It's the first time in the long history of our hometown *Journal News* that we've ever received a Pulitzer. Matt Davies, when you got the news, how did you feel?

MATT DAVIES (M.D.): It was a big surprise, Bill. I knew I was a finalist, and the other finalists were Garry Trudeau and a fellow named Steve Sachs, a cartoonist for the *Minneapolis Star-Tribune*—and they're both *very* good cartoonists. Of course, Garry Trudeau is sort of the Nike of cartooning. I just assumed I wasn't going to win. And then when I found out, I was completely blown away because I prepared myself so well *not* to win.

W.O.: Doesn't Trudeau have a famous, beautiful wife?

M.D.: *Jane Pauley* is his wife; that's right, she's a broadcasting star.

W.O.: Well, it didn't help him. Did he call you to congratulate you, Matt Davies?

M.D.: Not yet.

W.O.: Pulitzer Prize–winner Matt Davies, I've been trying to get through to you for three days. How many calls have you had?

M.D.: I've had hundreds of calls and over a thousand e-mails so far. I think about 98 percent of them have been positive with only a couple of people saying not-so-nice things. But that's OK.

W.O.: Why would they say not-nice things?

M.D.: I think the best one I got was: "Congratulations on receiving the Liberal Arts Crapola Award!" (*laughter*)

W.O.: You've been pretty tough on President Bush, speaking of which.

M.D.: First of all, he's the president, and when Clinton was president, I was really tough on him too. I've got a bunch of cartoons here that got me in trouble for going after him as well. I just don't agree with the direction Bush is taking the country, and I think it's fair game to criticize. I don't go for the cheap shot. It's always a policy-based difference I have. Without getting into too many specifics, I just don't like pretty much anything he's done on the overseas front.

W.O.: I can hear in your voice that you churn and struggle with these things. Are you a journalist or an entertainer? What are you trying to do, make people laugh or think or cry? What are you doing with these cartoons that wowed the Pulitzer jury?

M.D.: Pretty much *all* of those. The job I have is an interesting one because it's in large part journalism. You have to have humor. You've got to be able to draw and write as well, and have an opinion on things. It's a unique combination.

W.O.: Matt Davies, there is a paper in Connecticut that was a finalist for a Pulitzer in 1937; it's on their masthead. They're still bragging about coming close. This is big stuff.

M.D.: I guess it really is a big deal if you put it on the masthead. (*laughter*)

W.O.: What about your colleagues at the *Journal News*? When they see you walking down the hall, do they make way for you?

M.D.: They've been great. I have a lot of friends here in the newsroom, and you should have heard the noise when I won. It was like the newsroom just erupted, like somebody scored a goal at a World Cup soccer match. It was just amazing. Everybody just stops me and tells me how thrilled they are and excited, and thrilled that the *paper* got the recognition as well.

W.O.: How many cartoons do you do every week for our hometown paper?

M.D.: I do five per week, one per day. I come in on Monday and do one for Tuesday, and then on Friday, I do one for Sunday's paper. And then they give me two days off, just to recharge the batteries.

W.O.: Matt, where do you get the *ideas*? How do you think these things up?

M.D.: A lot of staring out the window, Bill. I don't know . . . basically, I just read the newspaper like everybody else. I like to stay as informed as possible on every issue, and I just read and think at the same time. I have a sketch pad here next to me, and I just jot things down and do a lot of writing. And somehow, before 3:00 P.M., hopefully an idea pops into my head. I generally get an opinion on *something*. And, of course, there is nothing particularly clever about having an opinion—*everybody* has an opinion on *something*. I try to figure out a way to deliver it in as clever and humorous a way as possible, and as *visually* as possible. Going from the opinion to the visual—I don't know where that comes from. Like I said, it's just a lot of staring out the window, and it just comes.

W.O.: You did some good staring out the window this past week. You did a brilliant cartoon on the First Amendment. Could you describe it for us? I remember you had a guy sitting there with earphones on.

M.D.: That's the FCC. And I titled it "Shock Radio." I had the FCC as a DJ, tearing up a copy of the Constitution on the mike, which to me is as *shocking* as it can probably get. And it's referencing, of course, the recent upping of fines for indecency and unpleasant speech on air.

W.O.: You know what's shocking is that Matt Davies, editor and cartoonist, is worried about broadcasters. My own colleagues and fellows are nowhere to be seen. They're running for the hills. They're afraid of those *fines*.

M.D.: Exactly! God forbid they start fining editorial cartoonists. But I don't think that would shut me up either. (*laughter*) To me, the First Amendment is the life's blood of what we do. But of course, a political cartoonist is on the razor's edge of the First Amendment. I'm going after powerful people who could, if they wanted to, shut me down. But they don't. The idea of fining somebody that somebody *else* deems "indecent" is frightening, it's just un-American. And the idea of somebody trying to do that on a broader scale—that's where the grain of irritation about the whole thing is. Where do you *stop*? *What* is indecent? Where do you draw the line? Does somebody say, "Hey I don't like a cartoon, or I don't like that broadcaster's opinion"? If somebody doesn't like Rush Limbaugh's opinion, do they call the FCC and say that's indecent, I want him fined for that? It strikes me as dangerous territory.

W.O.: Didn't one of the government bureaucrats say, "I *know* it when I *see* it"?

M.D.: Absolutely, and I think that's very, very scary.

W.O.: Matt Davies, that's music to my ears, sir. You've picked on presidents, and I'm glad you're picking on the FCC and the weak-kneed broadcasters. Did any of your bosses, any of the elders at Gannett or the *Journal News,* ever come in and say, "Listen, Davies, pull your punch" or "I don't like this cartoon, we ain't running it"? Did Henry Freeman or Ron Patafio or the publisher ever do that?

M.D.: No, they just let me rip, they really do. I'm waiting for them to come in and stop me, but they haven't yet. The only thing they do is correct me if I have a spelling error or a typo. We've developed a bond of trust over the years I've been here, and they leave me completely alone.

W.O.: What do we hear in your voice? Where are you from?

M.D.: Originally, I'm from London, England. I moved here in 1983, when I was seventeen; I'm thirty-seven now. Actually, I've lived here longer than I lived in England, and I just can't seem to shake this accent.

W.O.: Doesn't your Mother England have a rich history of satire and biting political commentary?

M.D.: Absolutely. I grew up in a household which revered political cartoons and humor with the punch of all the great British cartoonists.

W.O.: Who is easier to draw, Bill Clinton or George W.?

M.D.: They're both very easy to draw.

W.O.: What about John Kerry?

M.D.: John Kerry is easy to draw too. In fact, I was being interviewed the other day on NPR, and the interviewer said, "You know, you draw George Bush to look like a monkey, and you draw John Kerry to look like a yak." And I thought, that sounds about right. (*laughter*)

W.O.: We'll let you get back to your Pulitzer Prize–winning drawing board. And congratulations. Incidentally, did you get any money with the Prize?

M.D.: They give you a $10,000 check.

W.O.: What are you going to do with it?

M.D.: I don't know, Bill. I'll probably give a whole lot of it to the tax man, and the rest I don't know yet. I figure I may go on vacation or something.

W.O.: We're very proud of you, Matt Davies. And you are as nice as your cartoons are brilliant.

M.D.: That's very kind of you. It's been a pleasure to be on.

W.O.: Congratulations from all of us to you and your wife, Lucy. And to your colleagues at the *Journal News*.

INTERVIEW WITH JOHN CRIGLER, WASHINGTON COMMUNICATIONS ATTORNEY

John Crigler is a Washington lawyer who specializes in First Amendment cases. Sadly, there are only a few others taken up in this noble work. Erwin Krasnow, Bruce Sanford, John Wells King, and the incomparable Floyd Abrams are some of the others. We broadcast this interview with Crigler on March 2, 2004.

WILLIAM O'SHAUGHNESSY (W.O.): The First Amendment is taking some haymaker punches from the Washington lawmakers. I guess it started with Janet Jackson's right breast during the Super Bowl. Now, they're picking on radio, just what you're listening to right now, here in the heart of the Eastern Establishment. There is a wise man in Washington named Crigler. John Crigler is a champion of the First Amendment, and he's worked on some notorious cases for the Pacifica Foundation and others. John Crigler, how do you feel when you see broadcasters go in and be so damned obsequious?

JOHN CRIGLER (J.C.): I feel embarrassed. The way things are going now, everyone is talking about regulating all the media on a broadcast model, and that's really a sea change. Until now, everyone has talked about broadcasting as a unique medium that will sustain these particularly intrusive governmental regulations. And now the tide is swinging the other way. And the mood on Capitol Hill is: Let's regulate *everything*.

W.O.: John Crigler, when you say "other" media, it seems like they're really picking on radio now.

J.C.: Well, they've been picking on radio since the beginning of the Indecency Standards. Until 1978, when the Supreme Court upheld the first Pacifica case, no one even knew whether indecency was a category of speech that could be regulated. And that was a radio case. From then until the standard was expanded in

1989, almost all the cases were radio cases. And that remained true through the '80s. So there is nothing new about applying it to radio. What *is* new is the severity of the fines and the threats of license revocation.

W.O.: The big money, of course, is in television. But even in this high-tech, speeded-up, electronic day and age I always thought radio, because it's free and over the air, is still the medium closest to the people. Would you agree?

J.C.: I would. And that may, in fact, be a partial explanation of why all the cases have been radio cases. People do, I think, feel closer to radio and to that voice that's right there in their ear. And that means they bond with it for good and evil. Most of the complaints have been radio complaints.

W.O.: We're talking with John Crigler, a senior partner at the famous Washington law firm Garvey, Schubert and Barber, home of the great Erwin Krasnow and John Wells King, two other great D.C. lawyers. John, what is *indecent*? I mean, is it the same as risqué or prurient or vulgar? What the hell does indecent *mean*?

J.C.: I used to be able to answer that question in seven words.

W.O.: What do you mean?

J.C.: The standard set by the FCC in the '70s was based on a George Carlin routine that was meant to be funny, and no one got the joke. The joke was what seven words you could never, ever say on radio or television. And stripped of its humor, it became the legal standard. What happened, really, beginning in 1986, was that the FCC decided to expand that standard to include not just seven words but anything that referred to sex or excretion and that, in the FCC's judgment, was offensive.

W.O.: Have you ever watched cable television late at night in Washington in your suburban home?

J.C.: I'm afraid I have.

W.O.: I mean, that's pretty strong stuff.

J.C.: That's what I meant with my earlier comment about which model we use to regulate. Until now, cable and satellite have been regulated as though they were print, and no one has ever had the nerve to suggest that some standard of decency could be applied to them by a censorship committee. That standard was unique to broadcasting. The anomaly, of course, is just the one you put your finger on, that meant that side by side it can be problematic to see the same content on an over-the-air radio or television station and not at all problematic to get the same material by satellite radio or satellite television or cable.

W.O.: But Counselor Crigler, why are they picking on Howard Stern's trash mouth? Why don't they trust the people to turn him off?

J.C.: Well, that's still the best argument. Who indeed knows what you want to see and hear better than the *people* themselves? I'm afraid Howard Stern is the latest sacrificial victim of the FCC.

W.O.: Are you saying the government ought to stay the hell out of content?

J.C.: That's the general principle of the First Amendment! The people have the first and best judgment about what's good for them to hear or see. And the only exception to that has been obscenity, which is something much different than indecency. It's not just risqué, it's not just trash, it's not just dirty jokes. Obscenity is, for the most part, outright pornography. And that's not speech. That's not protected under any medium. And the courts are pretty square about that. *Indecency* is a much looser, much vaguer, much broader standard.

W.O.: Who's to say which is which: which is obscene, which is indecent? Do you want some Midwestern congressmember to do that for you?

J.C.: No thanks, Bill. Right now, the only arbiters of what is indecent are the FCC commissioners and the FCC staff.

W.O.: Is that a good thing?

J.C.: Well, it's their job. It's now in the statute. What I think is particularly troubling about the times we're in now is the zealousness with which regulation is going to come. The commissioners are eager to regulate. Even the chairman who came in with a hands-off attitude is now saying: This is our chance, let's *do* something. The *fines* are going to get bigger. They're going to change the way they issue fines on a per-utterance basis, rather than a per-program basis. It's going to get easier to file complaints. And it's very hard to second-guess the FCC, since we're stuck with its making a judgment about what offends the average listener or viewer. And what that standard is at bottom is mighty hard to say.

W.O.: John Crigler, you've devoted your life and made a lot of pleadings on behalf of that document that Jack Valenti says is the finest struck off by the hand of man, the First Amendment to the Constitution. Are you about to be hit by a runaway freight train from Congress on this?

J.C.: Entirely possible. I don't know if you've heard the hearings going on in the House and Senate over the past several weeks . . . .

W.O.: I'm embarrassed by the broadcasters' rolling over on this.

J.C.: But that's exactly what's happening. I think the broadcasters are justifiably concerned that their licenses could be put at risk. And they're head-over-heels eager to please Congress to avoid that risk. The networks were almost in unison, saying we have no problem with a tenfold increase in fines!

W.O.: Let me ask you a question. Is this a political issue? Would a Kerry administration be a little more "sensitive"?

J.C.: I don't think it's escaped anyone who observes these things to note that this *is* an election year. Candidates are going to jump on this and wave the banner of protection of children. No one is in favor of indecency in an election year, so I think the short answer is, yes, this is very *much* a political issue.

W.O.: Do you have children, John Crigler?

J.C.: Yes.

W.O.: How old?

J.C.: The youngest is six.

W.O.: Who do you want deciding what that six-year-old youngster watches?

J.C.: Me.

W.O.: Thank you very much, sir. You are as bright as Erwin Krasnow, who is another brilliant Washington lawyer, told us you are. Thank you, and keep up the good work.

INTERVIEW WITH RALPH R. MARTINELLI

Ralph Martinelli, the conservative publisher who owned weekly newspapers in Westchester, was a fiery, feisty fellow who knew no fear. He was a royal pain to many smug politicians and a real "townie" newspaperman with whom I disagreed politically on almost every proposition, but I came to have great respect for the man. His passing left a void in the Golden Apple. For one thing, it's a lot quieter here in the Heart of the Eastern Establishment. Martinelli's papers are now in the care and keeping of Nick Sprayregan and his hard-working editor Dan Murphy. Our interview with Ralph Martinelli aired January 6, 2004.

WILLIAM O'SHAUGHNESSY (W.O.): We begin the New Year with a conversation with one of Westchester's most controversial citizens, the veteran publisher known as the "enfant terrible" of the public press. His name is Ralph Martinelli, and he runs all those Martinelli weekly newspapers, including the new "official" newspaper of Yonkers. It's a sweet victory for you, Mr. Martinelli.

RALPH MARTINELLI (R.M.): It certainly is. It was a long time coming.

W.O.: Ralph, you have taken on damn near everybody: Governor Pataki, Jeanine Pirro. How do you see your role as journalist and publisher?

R.M.: I believe newspapers should expose corruption in local government. There is plenty of it in Westchester County, as we've been pointing out. And the *Post,* the *Daily News,* and other papers are exposing it as well. But we're weekly publications. And the *Journal News* isn't inclined to expose corruption. They're only inclined to count their money.

W.O.: They call you Westchester's last angry man. But those who know you say, "That isn't the *real* Ralph Martinelli. He's a pussycat, a really nice guy."

R.M.: Thank you, Bill. But, by the same token, I am angry with public officials who steal and then put on this mask of integrity to the people. They are robbing us blind. And I'm out there to expose them whether they're Democrats or Republicans. Remember, most of the people I've been writing about belong to my own political party, the Republican Party. I'm a Ronald Reagan Republican and proud of it.

W.O.: How do you think George W. Bush is doing?

R.M.: I think he's doing fantastic. He reminds me of Ronald Reagan in many ways. There are a lot of people who criticize him, but they criticized Ronald Reagan for doing the right thing. And that's exactly what President Bush is doing.

W.O.: Ralph Martinelli, you've become famous in the last couple of years. The *New York Times* has even commended your front-page, signed editorials. When do you write those, in the middle of the night?

R.M.: No, I'm surprised myself. Every week, there seems to be an appealing subject. As a matter of fact, sometimes I'm doubled up with good ideas. But we've added a creative touch to these articles by using editorial cartoons.

W.O.: You sure don't pull any punches; you even whacked your friend, Governor Pataki.

R.M.: Well, George Pataki *was* my friend. But he had people around him, like Tom Doherty, who didn't represent the Republican Party. Tom Doherty was a bully from Eastchester who took it upon himself to try to destroy me and my newspapers with his friend, James Cavanaugh. Well, you know where they are now.

W.O.: Cavanaugh is out of Eastchester. Some think you had a little bit to do with that.

R.M.: I hope I had a lot to do with that. Because, frankly, I caught him cheating the taxpayers with a no-show job from Senator Nick Spano. He's never produced time sheets to justify $15,000 a year.

W.O.: But Jim Cavanaugh is also chairman of your Westchester Republican Party.

R.M.: You might call him chairman, but to me, he's a stooge for Nick Spano.

W.O.: Now, Nick Spano is someone else you're not crazy about. Tell us about him.

R.M.: Nick Spano professes to be a great Republican. But look what's happened to the Republican Party in Westchester County during his tenure. It's practically destroyed itself. Nick, right now, is a wounded animal. He's got no base or anchor because he's double-crossed so many people.

W.O.: He's a state senator. Isn't he a big muckety-muck in Albany?

R.M.: Sure, he's a big muckety-muck. But the bigger they are, the harder they fall.

W.O.: The Colavitas: the son and heir of Anthony Colavita, and our long-time friend, is back in Eastchester. Do you think your papers will get back in the good graces of that town?

R.M.: Well, I sure hope so. To me, Tony Colavita Sr. and now Tony Colavita Jr. are upstanding individuals, great politicians and leaders. No politician in Westchester County comes close to Anthony Colavita Sr., and I'm hoping Junior will follow in his footsteps.

W.O.: I want to ask you a question about Albert J. Pirro and also his wife, our District Attorney, Jeanine Pirro.

R.M.: My only comment on Al Pirro is that he's just not a decent human being. He cheated on his taxes; he cheated on his wife; and now, he's cheated on the public. And he's cheating on his illegitimate daughter. Here's a man who makes a lot of money, supposedly more than a million dollars a year, and yet he is cheating on his daughter, Jessica Marciano.

W.O.: Why don't you let God take care of that? Why do you have to straighten him out?

R.M.: Al and Jeanine pull these deals behind the public's back, and I am exposing them. You know, some people are afraid to do so. They're powerful people. In fact, they tried to sue me. And their lawyer sent me a nasty letter trying to dictate interview questions. The letter was supposed to be confidential. You know what I did? I put it on page one. I have nothing to hide. I'm not afraid of them. And as it turns out, that same attorney is being held for conflict of interest in Florida.

W.O.: Are you talking about the famous David Boies?

R.M.: Yes. The same attorney used by Al Gore [in *Bush v. Gore*]. The Florida Bar is bringing charges against him for conflict of interest.

W.O.: Do you think you could say something nice about Al Pirro?

R.M.: I would like to see him and his wife disappear from Westchester.

W.O.: Publisher Martinelli, what's your headline, sir, for the New Year, the first issue?

R.M.: We close one week in advance, but we had a headline about Anthony Mangone, the chief of staff for Senator Nick Spano. Mangone was almost convicted for voter fraud and then was appointed a special prosecutor in Putnam County. Now, how the hell does that happen?

W.O.: Ralph Martinelli, how old are you now?

R.M.: I'm seventy-seven, going on seventy-eight, and I'm strong.

W.O.: How long are you going to keep this up?

R.M.: Till God takes me away from here. I love what I do.

W.O.: You're a publisher. A muckraking, hell-raising publisher. What do you want on the tombstone?

R.M.: I haven't thought too much about it, Bill. I just want to be known as the person who did the right thing.

W.O.: Happy New Year, sir. I don't know if you're going to bring the governor down, or the Pirros, but clearly you're back in Yonkers and soon Eastchester as well. How about the guy who started this whole thing, who took some shots at your paper, Tom Doherty? He used to be a big shot with the governor. What about him?

R.M.: Tom Doherty is a jerk. You know, I gave him his first job out of college, and he paid me back by trying to put me out of business because I supported Colavita. Now, is that a reason to try to put me out of business? When you're a Republican, you should support Republicans. And I've been the only Republican voice in Westchester for many, many years.

W.O.: Doherty is a big-time lobbyist now and is still powerful in Eastchester, isn't he?

R.M.: He's not that powerful because he supported Cavanaugh, who lost. He's lost quite a bit of power, and his allies, such as Nick Spano, have lost some, too.

W.O.: Go back to your typewriter, Mr. Martinelli. Incidentally, do you use a word processor or a typewriter?

R.M.: I don't use either, Bill. I write my editorials on a pad, and my great editor, Louise Montclare, deciphers my terrible handwriting.

W.O.: I hear when you hand her those yellow legal sheets, there's usually smoke coming out of them!

R.M.: That's true. (*laughter*) Thank you, Bill. And thanks for the interview.

W.O.: Don't be a stranger, Ralph.

TODAY'S SUPREME COURT OPINION ON FLEETING EXPLETIVES

Here is our short but impassioned response to a Supreme Court ruling that still left open fundamental freedom of speech issues, broadcast April 28, 2009.

It appears that the Supreme Court is giving broadcasters "*Un*due Process."

Instead of a decision on the constitutionality of the First Amendment, the Court dwells on the intricacies of the Administrative Procedure Act.

Thus I'm afraid today's decision is *prologue* rather than epilogue, whose practical effect is to continue the dangerous status quo.

By focusing on the procedural issue of whether the FCC explained its new approach to "fleeting and isolated" words, the Court delayed the decision everyone should care passionately about: whether the FCC's Indecency Policy is constitutional.

As an opinion about what a government agency has to do to change a *prior* policy, the decision is primarily fodder for lawyers. It is far more interesting if read as a rehearsal for the main event.

Much more work has to be done on this free speech issue of fundamental importance for all Americans.

The FCC should stay out of the censorship business.

THE *POST* CARTOON

You're reading this commentary for the first time. I held this piece because I didn't want to add to the misunderstanding about a controversial cartoon in the New York Post *that many thought likened the president to a monkey. I'm absolutely convinced there was no malice involved. Fortunately, others agreed and cooler heads prevailed. The* Post *is a valuable and important voice in the lives of all New Yorkers. Its independence and irreverence are worthy of our respect, protection, and encouragement. Here is the commentary we broadcast on March 4, 2009.*

The contretemps over the Sean Delonas cartoon in the *New York Post* is winding down. It's about time.

The whole thing is bewildering to those who never actually saw the correlation between the poor, crazed ape who was put out of his misery last week up in Connecticut and the geniuses who hastily assembled the stimulus package in Washington.

It was suggested by one of our listeners that maybe, just maybe, the cartoonist was trying to illustrate the ancient concept of inevitability or "randomness," as reflected in the timeworn notion that if you put one thousand monkeys in a room and give them IBM typewriters, sooner or later they'll produce the entire works of Shakespeare.

I don't know who came up with that novel idea in the first place. But perhaps, just maybe, the illustrator had something akin to that in the back of his mind as he sat over his drawing board.

Anyway, it didn't work. Call it a misunderstanding. Call it a misfire. The cartoon was wide of the mark. *And it wasn't funny.*

It may even have been somewhat stupid. But it sure wasn't racist.

It is one hell of a stretch to suggest that it was an attack on President Obama, or designed to insult *any* African American, for that matter.

A cartoon is meant as social commentary to poke fun at our foibles, to tilt at windmills, and to illustrate our posturing and pretensions with wit and humor.

Bigotry is in the eyes of the creator or journalist. A cartoonist-humorist or print illustrator is not unlike a radio talk show host who doesn't make a hell of a lot of sense with *every* single pronouncement.

And clearly, the offending cartoon that endeavored to portray the framers of the so-called "bailout" as bumbling idiots certainly could have made the point without using a crazed primate.

(FYI: Another New York tabloid, just a few days later, published this lovely headline: "'Cretin' in Custody!" Provocative? Racist?)

When a grandfather calls a grandchild "a little monkey," is he a racist? When an exasperated parent advises a youngster, "I don't want any 'monkey business,'" is *that* racist?

Although the *New York Post* has been very good to me and mine (as have the *News* and the *Times*), we don't agree with everything it does or publishes. For example, I certainly *didn't* agree when the *Post* jettisoned Liz Smith, who is a glorious treasure of New York and has been a class act in every season of her life, just to save a few bucks.

But we sure *do* agree that the "cartoon controversy," as predicted by the *Post* itself, was used in a mean-spirited way by their tabloid competitors and all kinds of instigators of mayhem who have little respect for a daily newspaper or journal of opinion, which may one day become an endangered species. No pun intended.

We're especially disappointed that the NAACP and other responsible organizations would seek to punish the *Post* by threatening retaliation against their advertisers and broadcast holdings. Déjà vu Don Imus.

Newspapers are too precious and too few in this town for anyone to threaten their existence for financial leverage or political gain.

The *New York Post,* which is a vital, vibrant part of our city's life, is not exactly on life support. And I don't think they'll be running benefits for Rupert Murdoch any time soon. But the demise of a newspaper is a bad story we don't want to ever again have to cover.

We covered the death of the *New York Herald Tribune* of sainted memory on August 15, 1966, when John Hay Whitney and Walter Nelson Thayer folded the newspaper, which was founded by Horace Greeley. I remember Red Smith trying to steady his hand as he lit a cigarette and the great Jimmy Breslin screaming at the cleaning ladies on the sad day the *Trib* died, as the patrician Jock Whitney stood in the city room with glistening eyes.

John O'Hara, the author, wrote some lines that fit that strange, bitter afternoon in New York: "When a journalistic institution is threatened . . . every man and woman who has ever read a single word in that publication—in agreement or disagreement—is the loser. The loss to non-readers is incalculable. And the loss to freedom is absolute."

And Jack Gould, who wrote brilliantly of our own profession for my beloved *Times*, put it even better: "Every independent voice is a national asset."

You may think I'm talking about Al Sharpton, in all this. And I am.

An iconic figure of New York, beloved by many, hated by some, Sharpton, in his best moments, is a beguiling character, an authentic Runyonesque figure who could exist and flourish—I hope my neighbor Mrs. Adams will forgive me—"Only in New York."

But however provocative, colorful, or downright annoying he may be, *I like the guy*. For one thing, I never heard Ossie Davis say a bad word about the man.

We've already acknowledged that the damn *cartoon* was not funny. But what's *also* not funny is when someone threatens the livelihood of a reporter, a journalist, an editor, a cartoonist, a feature columnist, a printer, a deliveryman, or a vendor. Or the very life of a newspaper.

Corporate intimidation is just as evil as racism—real or imagined. Just as with Imus.

Rupert Murdoch's heartfelt and gracious apology, when he stepped right up and took responsibility for the misunderstanding last week, should more than satisfy our friend Reverend Sharpton and all his friends, including the new national president of the NAACP, Ben Jealous.

The whole thing has been a distraction from the essential and altogether necessary fight against authentic racism and bigotry that we must fight in every way in our personal lives and with the instruments of communication that have been entrusted to our care and keeping.

THE NEW YORK STATE BROADCASTERS HALL OF FAME INDUCTION CEREMONY, FIFTIETH-ANNIVERSARY CONFERENCE

Somebody once said that if you stick around long enough, they're bound to honor you for something. But it was a great honor to be among the very first inductees into the New York State Broadcasters Hall of Fame. Practically every single one of the other members has made greater contributions. But as the statewide organization, headed by Joe Reilly, is a great champion of free broadcasting, I was grateful for their wonderful, if undeserved, gesture. For more about NYSBA, we recommend Serving Their Communities *by Stephen Warley. It's a great fifty-year history of broadcasting in the Empire State. These are the remarks I prepared for delivery at The Sagamore in Bolton Landing, New York, on June 26, 2005.*

To be thought worthy of the company of your other twenty-four *really* worthy and altogether distinguished inductees, including William S. Paley, Walter Cronkite, the Gambling family, Sue Simmons, Thomas S. Murphy, Chuck Scarborough, and Frankie Crocker, is a great honor. You could poll our profession and find any number more worthy of this great honor. But you won't find anyone more grateful than Bill O'Shaughnessy.

This fraternity brings back memories and friendships of a lifetime: Tony Malara, Joe Reilly, Dick Novik, Marty Beck, Jim Champlin, Ed McLaughlin, Bob Bruno, Gordon Hastings, Phil Beuth, Dick Foreman, Ambassador Peter Straus, and my oldest friend, John Kelly.

I want to thank Ed Levine and Steve Baboulis, two great chairmen, for establishing a Hall of Fame in the first place and then commissioning the fifty-year history of the association. It's going to be a stunning and comprehensive retrospective. In fact, the staff at Fordham University Press, that great Jesuit institution in the City of New

York, told me they are dazzled by the sweep and scope of the early galleys turned in by our writer, Stephen Warley.

Please permit me to briefly thank only a few of those who have befriended me as a broadcaster, those generous souls who overlooked my many inadequacies and found merit in my erratic stewardship:

I'm grateful, first of all, to Ward Quaal, the gray eminence of our profession, for a thirty-year-plus running correspondence on the great issues of our society.

On the value of the First Amendment and free speech, I have been schooled by the genius of Don West, Harry Jessell, John Eggerton, Larry Taishoff, and his incomparable father, Sol, who indoctrinated me at an early age.

I must also thank my distinguished Westchester neighbor, Ambassador Ogden Rogers Reid, the great congressman, publisher, and First Amendment champion. And in recent years, Patrick Maines of the Media Institute; Erwin Krasnow, the Washington sage and lawyer; and David Hinckley of the *Daily News,* whom all of us should thank every day.

I also give my appreciation to Saverio Procario of Fordham University Press, who has indulged my enthusiasms and transformed my ravings into graceful, engaging books.

And, as always, the wonderful Cindy Hall Gallagher and the devoted Don Stevens of Whitney Radio.

As I look around this room tonight, my mind drifts back to early, gentle instruction from three extraordinary mentors: John Van Buren Sullivan of the original, magnificent WNEW, of sainted memory; Martin Stone of WVIP and the Herald Tribune Network; and a dear and distinguished former president of yours, C. Glover Delaney of Rochester.

Forgive them their encouragement of a young, awkward, untutored Bill O'Shaughnessy. They imbued our profession with a graceful, stylish music without ever considering it a business or industry.

I will mercifully yield, Tony, but please let me mention two others essential to my induction into the Hall of Fame:

Mario Cuomo, our fifty-second governor, called by the *Boston Globe* "the great philosopher-statesman of our nation," still finds time to reach down and lift me from frequent confusion, bewilderment, and error.

And the source of every good thing in my life, the epitome of wisdom and love, my wife, Nancy Curry O'Shaughnessy.

As I drove up the Northway to this idyllic spot on Lake George, I remembered the haunting verse of Sammy Cahn and Jule Styne's beautiful ballad "Time After Time":

> What good are words I say to you?
> They can't convey to you
> What's in my heart.
> If you could hear instead
> The things I've left unsaid . . .

I think the only thing I've left unsaid is to assure our newest members that you'll never ever regret anything you do for the New York State Broadcasters Association.

Or for our profession. And ultimately for our listeners and viewers.

Although I have already been fortunate in my already long professional and personal life beyond anything I deserve, this really means a lot.

To me. And mine.

To be thought worthy of being included in your first class of inductees along with some authentic legends of our tribe is a great honor.

DAN RATHER LAWSUIT

I've always liked Dan Rather. And as one of his many admirers, I was pained by his treatment at the hands of the elders of CBS. Dan and his wife, Jean, are gracious, lovely people, and they have been supporters of the Broadcasters Foundation of America. Dan's eloquent and heartfelt tribute to his CBS colleague Tony Malara will be found in this book's Part IV. This is the commentary I broadcast about Dan Rather's reporting controversy on September 26, 2007.

Dan Rather spent a lifetime reporting to the American people. During a long and illustrious career, no one ever accused the CBS anchor of a lack of sincerity or integrity. Why should we think otherwise when he has taken legal action against his former network? Mr. Rather may have been unintentionally inaccurate from time to time. But so have we all.

Dan Rather has always been innocent of deception. Thus, if he truly believes his network was unfair, unjust, or inaccurate in the aftermath of the Texas Air National Guard episode, then he has every right to speak out. He is, in effect, saying, "They're not telling the truth," a cause he has pursued his entire life and the basis of his reputation.

Mr. Rather is also implying that TV networks, as powerful instruments in our society, have an obligation to tell the truth. He believes his former employer lied about his role in the flawed exposé about the president's National Guard experience, and then exploited him as a scapegoat.

I think he wants more than personal vindication. Rather, this is just Rather being Rather, on a quest for the truth in whatever forum he can find.

On the other hand, Lou Boccardi, the co-chair of the CBS investigation with former Attorney General Richard Thornburgh, is a Westchester neighbor and an upstanding individual.

I am uncommitted on the legal merits of Dan's case, but it is admirable for him to seek redress in the courts. And in the court of public opinion.

THE DECLINE OF CBS

I was a great fan of William S. Paley, the legendary founder of CBS. When the Tiffany Network fell on hard times after Mr. Paley's demise, I penned this letter to Broadcasting *magazine about one of his successors. (I should add that Mr. Tisch, himself now departed, was a great philanthropist and friend of the infant State of Israel.) The Tisch family continues his philanthropic ways and is highly respected in New York. I have special regard for his nephew Jonathan Tisch, the president of Loews Hotels, who is a great civic leader and has been encouraged to enter the public arena and run for political office. Written on November 25, 2003, these are my thoughts on the decline of CBS.*

To properly draw the measure of Larry Tisch's time at CBS, you must look at his dazzling predecessor, William S. Paley. *Broadcasting & Cable*'s brilliant editorial "The House that Tisch Sold" and its sad conclusion, "He took a great company and made it small," really spoke for a lot of people who knew and admired Mr. Paley.

Despite all the encomiums in the New York papers last week, Larry Tisch will be remembered by our tribe for stripping the style, cachet, and tradition from the once-glorious CBS during his brief, but profitable, reign back in the '80s.

As has been so accurately pointed out, Tisch indeed made a lot of money in tobacco, movie theaters, insurance, and oil tankers. And then he enriched his own family-controlled business to the tune of $1 billion by diminishing the network and its divisions. But to him, CBS was just the means to an end, not a public trust or an instrument for community development.

Radio aficionados will remember a day in August 1988 when, without alerting either listeners or staff, Tisch shut down WCAU, the mighty Philadelphia radio station where CBS actually began in 1927.

Other memorable observations survive from the Tisch era to haunt us still. Sony chairman Akio Morita said, “Larry Tisch is breaking up the company and eating it himself.” And the devastating comment attributed to the great Frank Stanton, “CBS is now just another company with dirty carpets.”

To truly understand the damage Tisch wrought, one need only refer to Sally Bedell Smith’s definitive biography of Mr. Paley, *In All His Glory*.

At Mr. Paley’s eighty-sixth-birthday party at the St. Regis Hotel, Andy Rooney told the audience, “I went to work for CBS in 1949 and met William S. Paley maybe thirty times during those years, and tonight was the first time I ever called him Bill. Funny thing is I met Laurence Tisch only twice, and I called him Larry both times!”

Some years later, after Mr. Paley was gone, Rooney also said of CBS, “They’re just corporate initials now.” Larry Tisch made a lot of money. And, as has also been fairly reported, he gave away a lot of it. It’s regrettable, but very clear, that only statesmanship eluded him during his stewardship of CBS.

MISSING IN ACTION
BY PATRICK D. MAINES

I'm a great admirer of Patrick Maines, the gifted and brilliant president of the Media Institute, a respected Washington think tank. Maines and his associate Rick Kaplar have been great allies in our quest for freedom from government intrusion. This is just one of his intelligent commentaries.

Politically speaking, freedom of speech in the United States is in tatters. Beleaguered by "progressives" on the Left, "social conservatives" on the Right, and policymakers of all stripes, our ability to freely express ourselves would already be greatly diminished but for the federal courts.

Consider the landscape. The chairman of the FCC and large majorities in Congress favor content controls on indecent and/or violent TV programming. A leading candidate for president co-authored legislation that criminalizes even certain kinds of political speech when broadcast close to the date of federal elections. Left-leaning activist groups, unwilling to tolerate conservative opinion on talk radio and the Fox News Channel, openly advocate a return of the so-called Fairness Doctrine.

Bad as the situation is within policymaking circles, it is little better in academia and even mainstream journalism, both of which, with a few exceptions, operate in the grip of a kind of political correctness that is the very antithesis of free speech, if not of freedom itself.

Examples of both can be found on campuses in the preponderance of college speech "codes," and among journalists in the rush to abandon and fire Don Imus for what was, after all, a cruelly unfunny joke for which he apologized. Further evidence was recently provided by much of the media coverage, and the preposterous role of a large number of professors, in the Duke lacrosse farce.

Given the stakes, one might think that the media are working diligently to preserve at least that part of the First Amendment that guarantees freedom of the press. But in fact they are not.

From media and entertainment companies, and their related charitable and educational foundations, what passes for First Amendment advocacy is a mix of informational initiatives, like Sunshine Week, that are important in their own right but have little or nothing to do with the First Amendment; "education" programs, like the Illinois Press Association's First Amendment Center coloring book for grades K–4; and activities that amount to corporate brand promotion, like the purchase of "naming rights" to attractions at the new Newseum in Washington.

And this is the profile of those who are actually *doing* something! Most are doing *nothing,* either because (1) they don't have any real understanding of the issue; (2) they trust that, in the end, they'll be saved by the courts; or (3) they don't really care so long as whatever speech controls are enacted are applied to everyone.

The beginning of wisdom lies in understanding that free speech isn't imperiled because educated people don't know what it is. It's imperiled because educated people subordinate this knowledge to their political and cultural preferences. Whether you call it inconsistency, hypocrisy, or willfulness, it is at the heart of the present danger.

And what a danger it is! Perhaps because of factors like consolidation within elements of the "old media," the ubiquity of pornography, and the rise of conservative opinion within certain parts of the media, virtually every political and ideological group in the United States (save, perhaps, for libertarians) is now in favor of some kind of speech-controlling law or regulation. Taken together, and if enacted, they would amount to restrictions on nearly every kind of speech—from entertainment to news and print to electronic journalism.

That this has not happened, because of strong federal case law, is hardly a cause for complacency. Both parties in Congress have shown a knack for coercing "voluntarism" (and thereby steering clear of the case law) when they have media companies over any kind of barrel. And even the Supreme Court is by no means impervious to opinion in the larger society.

As direct beneficiaries of the speech clause of the First Amendment, media companies have an obligation to act as the people's sentinels on this issue. As such they need to see that they are not adding to the problem by acts of omission or commission, and to practice what they preach.

Though it's not widely appreciated, the truth is that the First Amendment is indivisible. We don't have one First Amendment for newspapers and another for the Internet. Nor do we have one for the media and another for individuals, or one for news and one for entertainment.

We have only *one* First Amendment and, such being the ways of precedent, if it is weakened anywhere it's weakened everywhere. Which is why it is incumbent on media companies to act rigorously and selflessly to protect it.

Freedom of speech in the United States is at risk of dying a death by a thousand cuts. For the sake of the nation, as well as the health of their profession, it is to be profoundly hoped that the media, old and new, will rethink and redouble their efforts to safeguard this cornerstone of our constitutional rights.

WHITNEY RADIO NO-NO'S: BANNED FROM THE AIRWAVES!

David Hinckley wrote about us in his column for the New York Daily News.

Whitney Radio, an industry-leading defender of free speech, and its president, Bill O'Shaughnessy, a passionate advocate for the First Amendment, have banned "business speak" buzzwords on their radio stations until further notice.

When O'Shaughnessy speaks on the college lecture circuit, he admonishes deans and professors, "If you encounter these drodsome phrases in any term paper or thesis, I hope you'll immediately flunk the offending student!"

Make it happen!
Be pro-active!
Absolutely!
Sounds like a plan!
Gettin' it done!
24/7
Doin' what it takes!
Change the paradigm!
Think outside the box!
The whole nine yards!
Maximizing assets
Multi-tasking
A new metric
Been there, done that!

BOB GRANT'S RETURN!

All of us in broadcasting were so pleased when Bob Grant decided to come back on the air.

He once called me a "stooge." And that's when he was in a really good mood! But I take special delight in Bob Grant's return to enliven New York's airwaves.

I know he's been lethal to Mario M. Cuomo, one of the most venerable figures in American history. But as a performer, social commentator, and radio talk show host, he is without peer.

And next Monday, when this seventy-nine-year-old walks into a WABC studio in New York City, adjusts his headphones, and leans into that microphone, the sparks will fly.

An icon is properly restored. We are all his students.

Welcome back, Mr. Grant.

M. PAUL REDD DIES SUDDENLY!

M. Paul Redd was a windmill-tilter—which automatically made him a friend of our radio stations. Here are our comments about his legacy and also Governor Mario Cuomo's January 9, 2009, thoughts on Paul Redd's passing.

One of Westchester's most prominent and durable African American leaders has died.

Word came from the office of New York state Assemblyman George Latimer that M. Paul Redd died suddenly last night of a massive heart attack. He was in his mid-eighties.

Paul Redd published the *Westchester County Press,* which only this year celebrated its eightieth anniversary as the county's only black-owned newspaper.

Paul Redd purchased the weekly many years ago from the late Dr. Alger Adams. In addition to his publishing activities, M. Paul Redd was very active in New York state and Westchester politics, serving as vice chairman of the state Democratic Party for many years. He was married to political activist Orial Redd, and their daughter Paula Redd Zeeman is the county's Director of Human Resources.

He was also a fixture at many WVOX broadcasts. For almost forty years, Mr. Redd attended this station's St. Patrick's Day salute broadcasts. (WVOX dedicated this year's broadcast to Mr. Redd.)

One of the features of his newspaper was the "Snoopy Allgood" column, which tweaked politicians in a good-natured, if occasionally pointed, way. Mr. Redd never revealed who actually wrote those Snoopy Allgood columns.

He was also a frequent guest on WVOX's radio and TV talk shows and discussion programs.

I remember that the paper announced my wedding thusly: "Automobile heiress NANCY CURRY is getting married to broadcaster WILLIAM O'SHAUGHNESSY . . . she must be *desperate*!" (I spent the last 20 years trying to persuade Nancy that it was a slam at *me,* not against *her.*)

The legendary publisher Roy Howard used to say: "You can't have a great newspaper unless you have *one* man or woman who has *something to say*."

Paul Redd had a *lot* of things to say, and he said them passionately, clearly, and with great eloquence.

His Westchester weekly had influence far beyond its circulation area, mostly because of that *one* man.

He went all the way back in this county to the time of Bill Luddy, Max Berking, Sam Fredman, Mario Cuomo, Al DelBello, Miriam Jackson, Andy O'Rourke, John Flynn, Edwin Gilbert Michaelian, Ossie Davis, Malcolm Wilson, Richard Ottinger, Joe Shannon, Napoleon Holmes, Milt Hoffmann, Paul Dennis, Whitney Young, Hugh Price, Guido Cribari, Nancy Q. Keefe, Ogden Reid, Vinnie Rippa, Tony Gioffre, Dennis Mehiel, Franklyn Richardson, Dr. Lester Cousin, Anthony J. Colavita, Bobby and Jack Kennedy, Ernie Davis, Ed Brady, Jack Javits, Vin Draddy, Bill Butcher, Fred Powers, Brother Jack Driscoll, Al Sulla, Tony Veteran, Francis X. O'Rourke, Wellington Mara, B. J. Harrington, William Congdon, Alvin Richard Ruskin, Angelo Martinelli, Bob Abplanalp, Kirby Scollon, Ed Hughes, Daniel Patrick Moynihan, Hugh Carey, and our magnificent neighbor Nelson Aldrich Rockefeller.

He amplified all their voices.

And we will miss *his.*

GOVERNOR MARIO M. CUOMO'S REMARKS ON THE PASSING OF M. PAUL REDD

I've just learned of Paul Redd's passing, and I am saddened by it.

Paul Redd had an awful lot of strength and a whole lot of strong opinions. He had a strong voice, and a strong will that inspired him to use that voice, speaking the truth, and spreading it, as he saw it, about politics, about politicians, and even beyond, whether politicians liked it or not.

He was a proud owner of the only black newspaper in the county, which has been around for eighty years.

And he spoke in that paper all he could on all these truths. And in doing it, the *color* of what he was saying was not black, it wasn't white, and it certainly wasn't yellow, as in "yellow journalism."

The color of what he was saying and writing and believing was red, white, and blue, as American as it could be.

It really was as basic as red, white, and blue, because what he was talking about, *all* the time, was equality and fairness, the same thing Lincoln talked about and the same thing the Declaration of Independence talks about.

We're going to miss him.

THE HELL-RAISER

We broadcast this encomium upon the occasion of the fiery publisher Ralph Martinelli's passing on September 13, 2004.

Ralph Martinelli was a muckraking hell-raiser, a scold, a crusading publisher, and a royal pain in the ass. He cut a vivid figure in an age of dullness and cookie-cutter journalism.

With his departure last week for what his late friend Governor Malcolm Wilson described as "another, and, we are sure, a better world," Westchester lost an independent voice, however harsh, however strident, however provocative.

At times, Martinelli could be vitriolic, unkind, and downright ornery. And he frequently stepped over the line of fairness and civility. Yet our colleagues in the press have covered Mr. Martinelli's passing with an extraordinary interest in his stewardship, despite the carping of his enemies and detractors.

Phil Reisman, the star columnist of the *Journal News,* weighed in with his rapier-sharp surgical wit to find the true value in Martinelli's life: "He was not exactly given to *subtlety,*" said the Gannett scribe mildly.

And the late Jack Gould, who wrote about WVOX for the *New York Times,* probably confirmed Reisman's analysis when he wrote, "Every independent voice is a national asset." Martinelli was an independent voice. And I don't care what the pipsqueak politicos in Eastchester or Yonkers say: Westchester is poorer with his demise.

His detractors claim Mr. Martinelli used his bully pulpit to secure the lucrative "official newspaper" designation from the towns and municipalities served by his weekly journals. However, I have always felt he was motivated by more than financial considerations. He firmly believed the local pols he had supported during a lifetime of advocacy should "do the right thing" by his papers. It is known to this day in the neighborhoods as Respect.

So, as we write "30" to his colorful, if tortured, life, I think that's what he was really all about: respect. And friendship. And loyalty.

Mr. Martinelli may have erred by denouncing politicos who betrayed and abandoned him. And maybe he never did learn to turn the other cheek. But I remain convinced he was a decent, if fragile, struggling soul. I believe he was of good heart in his best moments. And so, as the rain fell out of the Westchester sky when we dispatched him to meet his Maker, my prayer was different from the ones I uttered for Nancy Q. Keefe of Gannett and Neal Travis of the *New York Post* upon their passing.

For one thing, I prayed his widow, Francesca, a beautiful woman with an artistic soul, will let his devoted, long-time editor, Louise Montclare, and her crew keep Ralph's loud, raucous music playing.

For more than forty years, Martinelli kept his weekly papers rolling off antiquated presses, stirring up trouble and forcing people to think and react. He "rolled the hand grenade down the aisle" and made sure the papers were noticed. And read. And talked about.

He was a townie, a down-home newspaperman who kept the product of his labors on the newsstand week after week. And who's to say he was any worse—or any better—than William Randolph Hearst or Colonel [Robert] McCormick or even Rupert Murdoch?

Mario Cuomo once told me he prayed for "sureness." Ralph Martinelli was very sure of almost everything. He wasn't moved by the great, overarching issues of the day as much as the motivation of the public figures who addressed them. In other words, he was drawn to the heart and soul of those in public life.

Perhaps only God should judge those in government and politics in this way. But Martinelli never could resist throwing a few shots across the bow.

If he did nothing else, he helped return the wonderfully effective and estimable Colavitas to power in Eastchester. And he installed a good man named [Philip A.] Amicone in the mayor's office in Yonkers.

Over the years, I sat with Mr. Martinelli on various "good government" panels before League of Women Voters–type audiences. Invariably, after the "official" program was over, he would linger to engage a young student or an older, matronly type with bluing in her hair. Long after everyone else had drifted off into the night,

Mr. Martinelli would remain there to make another convert to his conservative cause.

As Reisman said, the man was a true believer.

And for those who maligned him in the public press and spoke ill of the departed: You never really got it.

It was never just about the money.

II ONE ON ONE: INTERVIEWS

JAMES BRADY: AUTHOR-COLUMNIST

James Brady had a colorful life: Marine hero, publisher of Women's Wear Daily, *one of the founders of "Page Six," author of many, many books. He was a regular at the Four Seasons, where he sat most days among the moguls whose lives he wrote about in many different publications, including* Ad Age *and* Crain's New York Business. *A familiar figure in the Hamptons, Brady had a modest house on one of the toniest streets in East Hampton. He left us in 2009. Here is our interview with him from December 2009.*

WILLIAM O'SHAUGHNESSY (W.O.): With snow predicted for Sunday, let's switch to the idyllic Hamptons before it arrives, to tony East Hampton and one of America's great writers and journalists: James Brady. Brady writes about press barons, beautiful women, and landed gentry, but best of all, about his beloved former colleagues, the Marines. Brady, you're in the middle of a national tour for your new book, *Why Marines Fight*. Why do Marines fight?

JAMES BRADY (J.B.): Bill, whether it's "good" wars like World War II or lousy wars like Vietnam and Iraq, the Marine Corps always seems to do very well. So I decided to plumb their motivation. Why do they fight and do it so well? I contacted about fifty combat Marines, and I asked them some very simple questions. Some were famous: Police Commissioner Ray Kelly in New York; Jerry Coleman, a second baseman for the New York Yankees; Peter Pace, the Chairman of the Joint Chiefs; Senator Jim Webb of Virginia. And others were just grunts. Machine-gunners seemed to be especially talkative.

I was on the *Today Show* with Matt Lauer, and this past Wednesday night I went to the Army and Navy Club in Washington, D.C., and spoke to a lot of old generals, admirals, and colonels. And as a former first lieutenant, it was wonderful to say,

"Alright, gentlemen, at ease," and see these guys follow my orders!

W.O.: You have a Bronze Star for your service, and you've been shot at lots of times. Is that pretty scary, Brady?

J.B.: Yeah, Bill, it was pretty scary. About a year and a half after college, at twenty-three, I was commanding forty Marines as a rifle platoon leader in North Korea in the winter. And the anticipation of combat scared me the most.

My company commander was John Chafee, a Yalie who graduated from Harvard Law, fought in the Marine Corps in two wars, and then later became a U.S. senator. He would say to me in the morning, "Okay, Brady, it's your turn to take out the night patrol." We would rotate that duty among three platoon leaders. I would become nervous in the afternoon, and at sunset, I'd really get uptight.

But it was weird, Bill, as soon as it got dark, I'd lead ten guys through the barbed wire and then became very calm. I knew exactly where we were going because I'd been studying the map and landmarks all day. Sometimes, we came back without a shot being fired, but either way, I felt fine.

And then a few days later, Chafee would say, "Hey, Brady, it's your turn in the barrel again tonight," and the cycle would repeat. I asked Ray Kelly down at Police Plaza about it, and he said, "You know, it's funny. I felt the same way."

W.O.: Your commanding officer, John Chafee, once stopped in New Rochelle near our main studios to ask directions. He was in a beat-up little Volkswagen, with Rhode Island 1 or 2 on it, and wanted to avoid a tie-up on the New England Thruway.

What do the Marines you talk to now think about Iraq?

J.B.: General Jim Conway, the new Marine commandant, said he thought the Marines should pull out of Iraq, stop all the police-keeping and nation-building stuff, and go back to Afghanistan because it's the kind of combat Marines are trained for: attacking hills and laying ambushes. But nothing has happened. I feel very strongly that way too. I was at Quantico just ten days ago, and the young Marines know it's a lousy war. But they're professional soldiers, warriors. You point them in the right direction, and they'll fight for the country. That's why they're paid.

I asked the late John Chafee—he passed away six or seven years ago—about his motivation for joining the Corps, and he replied, "Well, when Pearl Harbor was bombed, I was a nineteen-year-old sophomore at Yale and a middleweight star on the wrestling team. I was afraid we would defeat the Japanese so quickly, I'd miss all the fun." So he went to downtown New Haven and joined the Marine Corps as a private. And he fought during World War II in the South Pacific, was commissioned an officer, and fought on Guadalcanal and Okinawa. And then after Harvard Law and a marriage, and with a baby on the way, he was called back for Korea and commanded my rifle company.

He could have pulled a few strings. He came from a wealthy family, with a couple of grandfathers who had been governors of Rhode Island. But he just saluted and said, "Aye, aye, sir," and volunteered for war. That's the Marine spirit I've tried to capture in this book.

W.O.: Brady, you call Iraq a lousy war. Has there ever been a great one?

J.B.: I think wars for survival, like World War II, were great wars. Wellington fighting Napoleon was a great war. Yes, they're horrible, and they're ugly, and they're cruel. But there are "good wars." And I feel very strongly about that.

W.O.: We read your columns every Sunday in *Parade.* You interview celebrities and stars.

J.B.: For a living, Bill, but not quite as artfully as you.

W.O.: I don't even know your politics, Brady. Are you a Democrat or a Republican?

J.B.: I'm a liberal Democrat. But if I still lived in Manhattan, I'd vote for [Mayor Michael] Bloomberg. I voted for John Lindsay and Jack Javits. I always considered the man or the woman rather than the party. I'm not an ideologue at all. I grew up in the Great Depression, in an Irish Catholic family in Brooklyn. Bill, you won't remember this because you're so young, but if a Republican walked down the street, our mothers swooped in the kids from the stoop, lest they be kidnapped or assaulted.

W.O.: How old are you now, Brady?

J.B.: I was seventy-nine last week.

W.O.: I see you're still striding around Manhattan for various interviews. You're speaking to us from your redoubt in tony East Hampton. Is East Hampton still tony?

J.B.: Oh, absolutely. I live on Further Lane, the title of one of my novels. It was a screwball comedy, but people seemed to love it. Not to wax poetic, but it is one of the greatest places in the world. The ocean is four hundred yards from my back door. There's greenery all around me. Two deer ran around my back lawn this morning while I was making coffee. It's a lovely place to live, with an exotic cast of characters. I only keep an apartment in Manhattan for my interviews. But now I've achieved the American dream, the five-day weekend. And I always call my house on Further Lane "the low-rent district" because I think I'm the poorest man in the smallest house on the road.

W.O.: You got any poor folks out there?

J.B.: That's the sad part of it, Bill, because the soul of East Hampton is the blue-collar people, but they're being gradually priced out of existence. And you see them in the morning, commuting from the west, maybe thirty or forty miles away. That's where they live, most of them. The only ones who remain had families with their own potato farms or large stretches of property out here. They still have the houses where they were born, but they have to sell their possessions off gradually, I guess, to keep going.

W.O.: I think we know that song here in Westchester. There's an obit in this morning's *New York Times* about a saloonkeeper of great renown out there, Bobby Van. His name lingers to this day with some less-than-stellar steakhouses in Manhattan, but at one time, he ran a glorious saloon in Bridgehampton. Do you remember Bobby Van's? I think you were a regular.

J.B.: I remember it very well. It's about seven miles from my front door. And Bobby was a character. He was a very talented pianist, a professional, but he drank quite heavily. And he eventually lost the business; his marriage broke up; and he ended up driving a taxicab in Huntington. He was on dialysis at the V.A. hospital when he died the other day.

But that place was magical. Willie Morris wrote a wonderful piece for the *New York Times* about the magic of Bobby Van's in Bridgehampton, and how Truman Capote would line up outside the closed doors until noon, waiting to get in for his first drink, or, as the *New York Times* said, "for his first pour." James Jones, who wrote *From Here to Eternity,* and his wife, Gloria, were regulars. And George Plimpton, John Knowles, Shana Alexander, and Herb Schmertz, too. And Jack Whitaker, the golf announcer. It was very glamorous and a lot of fun.

But Bobby had these mood swings. Some nights, he'd be jovial, and other nights, he'd be scowling. And then way after midnight, we'd get him to sober up by saying, "Bobby, get to the damn piano will you, and shut up." And he'd just play this wonderful piano at no additional charge. It was heaven at Bobby Van's in those days, and we're going to miss him.

I sometimes saw John and Mary Lindsay there. And David Mahoney, who used to run Norton Simon. And a funny thing happened one night. Bill Flanagan, an editor at *Forbes* magazine, had written a rather hostile book about Dave Mahoney, and I had criticized John Lindsay for "Page Six" in the *New York Post*. Well, Flanagan and I are standing at the bar, and the waiter tells us, "Your table is ready, gentlemen." And when we sat down, we were right next to John and Mary Lindsay on one side, and Dave and Hillie Mahoney on the other. Mahoney got up to go to the men's room and never came back. And Lindsay, pointedly, looked in the other direction most of the evening. We all eventually made up after that.

Many marvelous things happened at Bobby Van's. It's like the Elaine Kaufman's of the East End.

W.O.: What makes for a great, legendary saloon?

J.B.: Well, I think, good booze. No, good bartenders, good service. And usually it has to exude the character and personality of the owner. Without a personality, there're always twelve other bars down the road.

Elaine Kaufman was once offered a lot of money to open a West Coast branch on Rodeo Drive, or Beverly Hills, and she turned it down. When I asked her why, she said, "I wasn't going to go flying out there every week, and without me, it wouldn't be the same thing."

W.O.: The *New York Times* said, "Brady knows war, the sound and the feel of war." And he's been called the "poet laureate" of the United States Marine Corps. You're still a Marine, aren't you, Brady?

J.B.: You're always a Marine, Bill. A sergeant once asked me, "You know, you really sound like you're still a Marine, and you miss it a lot. Do you ever wish you were back again?"

I said, "Sergeant, I never left." And I had been out of the Marine Corps thirty-five years at that point.

W.O.: You've been a class act in every season, in everything you've ever attempted. *Why Marines Fight* may be James Brady's best one yet. *Semper Fi*, Brady.

"THE SHINING CITY ON A HILL": AMERICA'S GREATEST ORATOR . . . TWENTY YEARS LATER

Many people remember with great vividness the brilliant speech that Governor Mario Cuomo delivered at the Democratic National Convention in 1984. On July 26, 2004, the twentieth anniversary of that keynote address, we asked Governor Cuomo about that speech, and about what has transpired in America since then.

WILLIAM O'SHAUGHNESSY (W.O.): The political season is here, and the national party conventions are upon us. The Democratic Party of Franklin Roosevelt, Harry Truman, and John F. Kennedy is meeting in the historic city of Boston. It's surely a busy place with hopeful Democrats gathering from all over the country. But let's switch now to New York City, and one of the most respected and revered Democrats of our time, the former governor of New York, Mario Cuomo. Governor, remember when you stood in the spotlight and gave that keynote in 1984?

GOVERNOR MARIO CUOMO (M.C.): I do remember, Bill. This is the twentieth anniversary.

W.O.: Were you nervous standing there? Do you remember that now-historic speech?

M.C.: I remember it extremely well. And I wasn't nervous because I resigned myself to utter failure! The speech wasn't something I wanted to do. As a matter of fact, I told Walter Mondale to get Ted Kennedy. And I had spoken to Kennedy about it, and he was willing to do it, but Mondale didn't want Kennedy. And when he asked me, I was shocked, and so was Tim Russert, who worked for me at the time, and my son Andrew. All three of us thought it was a bad idea. I resisted, but Fritz Mondale insisted.

And when we came to the podium, nobody appeared to be paying any attention, including John Forsythe, the actor; [former] President Carter; and even Ed Koch, the mayor of New York

City. And I remember John Forsythe saying, "Well, just look at the light; keep your eye on the red light; that's the television camera." So when I started the speech, I was prepared for the worst. I said a silent prayer, "Oh, Lord, please don't let me screw up too badly here."

W.O.: "There is another shining city on the hill, Mr. President." Did that line just fly into your head?

M.C.: Actually, when we reluctantly agreed to do the speech, I didn't know where to start. So I took my inaugural speech from the previous year in Albany. And then there was a story in the paper about President Ronald Reagan's referring to the country as a "shining city on a hill." And I got to thinking about that and the story of the shining city. And it just came naturally, the next line, yeah, it is a shining city on the hill, perhaps, but there are people in the gutter, where the glitter doesn't show. And there are people halfway up the hill who are sliding back down. So the allusions came very easily after the president himself painted the picture.

W.O.: After twenty years, Mario Cuomo, are they still sliding back down the hill?

M.C.: It's worse now than it was then, Bill. These days, it's easy for people to be swayed by partisanship, and I'm certainly biased. So let me quote somebody a lot closer to the Republican Party, Kevin Phillips. He is respected by both sides of the aisle but has been a Republican since Nixon's presidency. He's proud of his Republican credentials as a great writer, economist, and political analyst. In one of his books, titled *The Politics of Rich and Poor,* he wrote, "The country is fragmenting." There is a band of super wealthy people at the top, and it's growing thicker, and that's good.

But the center is becoming weaker. Only one out of four people [is a] highly skilled [worker]. Seven percent of the population earns $100,000; about 10 or 12 percent makes over $70,000; and the average income hovers around $42,000. What does that figure mean with a family to support, or when health care rises by 20 percent a year while wages go up by 1 percent?

And then there are 35 million poor people; 11 million of them are children.

The bottom two-thirds, at the very least, are in bad shape. Look, that's what Kevin Phillips says. That's what the *Wall Street Journal* pointed out earlier this week, in a major story on the front page.

To those who say the economy is good, ask the next question: For whom? It is good for large corporations and their investors, for a few highly skilled professionals in various industries. But for the middle and the bottom, it is a poor economy.

W.O.: Governor Mario Cuomo, why don't you just charge the hell up to Boston on a white horse and tell that to the Democrats, instead of hiding in your ivory-tower law firm?

M.C.: Well, they don't need me, O'Shaughnessy. John Edwards has been giving his stump speech on "two Americas," and we talked about my "City on the Hill" speech. He's saying essentially the same thing, and probably better than I did in 1984. So that view will be represented at the convention.

W.O.: We've listened to your inaugural speeches in Albany, and your "State of the State" addresses, as well as that memorable oration at Notre Dame about church and state. You really haven't changed your message very much in twenty years.

M.C.: No. We all learn new things, but I think the basic truths about our country have remained the same. You can say it a lot of different ways. This is certainly the greatest country in world history, with the most powerful army, the largest economy, and the best engine of opportunity. But we are not nearly as great as we could be. And that's a sin because we have so many resources. We shouldn't have all these poor people. We shouldn't have all these under-educated people. We shouldn't have over forty million people without health insurance. It just shouldn't be. It shouldn't be that our public school system is failing the children who need it the most. We're proud of Medicare, but it is hardly a health care policy for elderly people to face illness without worrying. That's nonsense. We're better than that! We're richer and stronger than that! We waste too much! We distribute our wealth unfairly. One trillion dollars, perhaps, in tax cuts to the top two million people over the next ten years. How does that make sense when we're running the largest federal deficit in our history? So, that's the story of two cities. It existed in Roosevelt's time, in Lincoln's time, and in Washington's time. And it's still around. But it shouldn't be as big a story as we've allowed it to become.

W.O.: Governor, are national political conventions anachronisms; are they all scripted?

M.C.: They are all scripted. I talked to Larry King the other night about this little book on Lincoln that's done amazingly well. . . .

W.O.: *Why Lincoln Matters*. You wrote it with Harold Holzer. It's on the *New York Times* bestseller list. Congrats.

M.C.: Well, not yet. It's on the "extended" bestseller list, and we're very pleased by that.

But I said to Larry, "So, Larry, you're going to the convention; what do you think?" And he said, "Listen, it's like a baseball game. Only with a baseball game, you don't know who's going to win. But with the convention, we know it's Kerry and Edwards." He said, "It will at least be fun. It's a party but without intrigue or excitement." I mean, he'll make it exciting. (*laughter*) But essentially, he's right.

To me, John Kerry's speech is the big story at the Democratic Convention. Kerry can make or break his candidacy. Everybody has been paying attention to President Bush until now because of our fight against terrorism. And now, for the first time, in a concerted way, the focus switches to John Kerry. And he must show what he's made of, and how much better he is than Bush, and what he will do differently. This is an essential moment for him, and that's the number one story.

The other story will be the keynote address. Barack Obama, the African American candidate for Senate from Illinois, will be the keynote speaker. And I'm telling you, Bill, after you hear him, you'll say, "Here comes a star."

W.O.: Governor, I've known and admired you for a very long time. You could have had your moment so many times. Are you sorry you never took it?

M.C.: Are you kidding? I have had wonderful moments.

W.O.: No, but you could have been in John Kerry's shoes.

M.C.: Listen, that's nice, wonderful fantasizing, and it's fun, I guess. I have had more than my share of moments, Bill. Twenty years in public service for New York state: secretary of state, lieutenant governor, governor. For twenty years, nobody has ever *seen* New York as I've seen it, not even Malcolm Wilson, the governor after Rockefeller, because he wouldn't fly. And so he never saw the Adirondacks because you have to fly over them to truly appreciate them. The same goes for the beaches in Long Island, or the rivers upstate, or the Great Lakes. For twenty years, I saw this state in a plane, in a helicopter, on the ground. I climbed its mountains. And with five kids, and eleven grandkids, and a professional baseball opportunity, and books and speeches, I've had my moments.

W.O.: Well, what about the cheers and the music, the adulation and applause, the balloons, the confetti?

M.C.: The applause and adulation is baloney. Anybody foolish enough to think, "Boy, that means I'm good" should know there are moments when people think you're better than you really are. And there are other times when people think you're worse than you really are. And so, people are often wrong about you in both directions.

In politics, you make many mistakes without any witnesses. And sometimes you do wonderful things no one knows about. But in the long run, it evens out. It's like baseball. You hit a line drive right at the third baseman. The next time up, you dribble the ball to the mound; it hits a pebble, jumps over the pitcher's glove, and you're on first base with a single. And you look at the box score, and nobody knows it was a miserable scratch hit.

W.O.: Are you disappointed when the elders of the Democratic Party avoid looking down the bench to say, "Cuomo, get a bat"?

M.C.: No. I'm delighted because it means we have a really strong lineup.

W.O.: Who is going to be the next president, sir?

M.C.: John Kerry. And that's not only because I want him to be. Why? Well, I could give you a dozen reasons, but I'll just focus on one for now. We have to get out of Iraq; everybody knows that. We're stuck there. It was a mistake. Even if you still think starting the war was a good idea, you have to agree we botched the occupation. We've lost one thousand people so far, and it's costing us a fortune. It's ruining the lives of reservists and National Guardsmen who never expected this kind of duty.

You can't get out if President Bush wins again because there will never be an international force to replace you. If Kerry defeats Bush, then a lot of countries will say, "Okay, now we'll put together an international force. We won't do it for Bush, not in France, Germany, or a lot of Arab nations, but we will do it for this next president." And I think that's only *one* reason. There are many others.

Like the economy. We went from the biggest surplus to the biggest deficit. How does that make any sense? We've produced no new jobs in four years. How does that make any sense? Use the Reagan test: "Are you better off four years ago than you are now?" Who in his right mind would say that we are better off than when Clinton left us, with 22 million new jobs, the largest surplus in history, the middle class growing stronger, fewer poor people? Who could say with any degree of fairness that we're better off now? And if you want to say President Reagan was wrong about this test for an incumbent president, ask yourself, "Am I better off four years ago than I am today?" You can't honestly answer that question yes.

W.O.: So, Mr. Kerry will have his turn this week.

M.C.: I think so.

W.O.: What are you going to be doing, America's greatest orator, when he's giving the speech?

M.C.: Talking to Bill O'Shaughnessy, probably.

W.O.: Dammit! You're still making us think, and I go to extraordinary lengths to avoid that, especially in the summer! (*laughter*) Thank you, Governor.

A CONVERSATION ABOUT CHRISTMAS . . . AND LIFE

We enjoy all of our conversations with Governor Mario Cuomo—and he tolerantly indulges our many intrusions into his busy schedule. We aired this interview in December 2007.

WILLIAM O'SHAUGHNESSY (W.O.): It's Christmas 2007 with a brand-new year hovering on the horizon. And who better to turn to for an inspiring vision of what's to come than the fifty-second governor of New York. Listeners to this radio station know of our great admiration for Governor Mario M. Cuomo.

GOVERNOR MARIO CUOMO (M.C.): Thank you, Bill. Merry Christmas. Happy New Year. Happy Hanukkah. Happy Holidays. Whatever your strain of belief, disbelief, anticipation, anxiety, or desire, I embrace it and extend my hope for a bright future.

W.O.: Governor, you used the word "happy" about five times. Are we happy?

M.C.: Well, as human beings, we can't be happy all the time because of our vulnerability, desires, and death. Saint Francis of Assisi prayed that he would lose all desires, except for the desire to give. But because we're vulnerable, we are beset by needs and disappointments.

But Christmas makes it easier to be happy because it reminds us of our blessings and the precious gift of Life.

W.O.: Governor Cuomo, someone once said, despite all Mario Cuomo's accomplishments, the guy should have been a priest.

M.C.: Oh, no. After recognizing my desire for women, I decided I probably wouldn't make a very good priest. But there are all kinds of priests. Anglican and Episcopal priests are allowed to have wives. I think they have it better than Catholics. It's easier to recruit new priests if you satisfy that part of life.

W.O.: Governor, you do seem relentlessly drawn to the great soulful, spiritual issues of the day. Everybody says, "What's Mario

Cuomo doing now?" And the answer is, "He's giving some of the greatest speeches of his life."

M.C.: Our circumstances, Bill, let us think about big issues: What is Life? When did it begin? What about God?

For most of us, for much of my life, and certainly for all of my parents' lives, they didn't have the time for that. They needed to put bread on the table and raise their kids. And so most people are driven by necessity and don't have the opportunity for conversations like this one.

I've been gifted with the time, and the situation, to think a lot about those issues. In politics, they come up all the time. A governor interacts with the private sector to help people lead fulfilling lives. But to do that, you must define a "full life" and determine how to distribute the resources of the society.

And yes, deep down inside me, even as a child, I had questions about life. And I think they derived from my early introduction to books.

My mother and father were never formally educated and only read a little bit. They ran a grocery store, and I was sheltered indoors during my early years because my older brother was hit by a car and badly injured.

So I listened to the radio and read books. My older brother brought them home from the junkyard in the war years because they were separated from the other paper due to their disproportionate weight.

And sometimes, it was an old Bible. Sometimes, it was an interesting book on lesbianism or homosexuality, an otherwise forbidden topic.

W.O.: In those days, that was really something.

M.C.: It was, in the 1940s. I read a lot, Bill. And I also became a Shabbos Goy. Our grocery store was on one corner, a synagogue on the other. And on the weekend, a Shabbos Goy performs tasks forbidden to Jews, such as taking out the garbage or other chores.

And you listen to their chants and witness their liturgies. And then on Sunday morning, you're an altar boy in the Catholic Church, and you compare the two. They both speak a foreign language: Hebrew and Latin. And you ask yourself, "Why?" And you conclude there's a "mystique." We can't know everything about God with our puny intelligence. God is indescribable, and that's what Christian encyclopedias say if you look for a definition.

With a start like that in life, those thoughts are constantly with you, and you can spend a lifetime mulling them over. And I have. And sometimes, you share your struggle with others, and they find it interesting.

W.O.: Governor, fast forward from your boyhood. You're now well into your seventies, your middle seventies. I'm reading a book by the late Arthur Schlesinger, the historian; and page after page, all the elders of the Democratic Party over the decades say, "Why doesn't he run? Cuomo's our best guy."

Even Richard Nixon, in his book, said as much. Do you now have any regrets that you never went for it? We're in a mess in Iowa and New Hampshire.

M.C.: There was a period, at least during the elections in '88 and '92, after I gave the 1984 keynote address at the convention, when people did talk about it, but in the beginning, I thought the very suggestion was foolish.

Because they didn't even know me. It was a little bit like Obama. I gave a good speech in 1984, and they immediately started talking about making me president.

My response was, "We have a great candidate in Mondale, and it's going to be hard to beat Reagan. I'm a young governor, and I just started at it. We've had a couple of pretty good years. But that doesn't mean I'm good enough to be president of the United States of America, the most powerful nation in world history."

But once you assume that kind of power, and with nuclear weapons, you think, "My God, just one really bad mistake can bring this place down." Especially if you think the president has the right to start a war by himself and can simply ignore the Constitution, as we did in Iraq. We've had presidents dropping bombs without ever going to the Congress as they're supposed to do. Not to mention all the other difficult problems. It always seemed there had to be better people than I.

W.O.: But, Governor, forgive me, a lot of very intelligent people thought you were the one. George Bush's father, the first President Bush, said the same thing. He didn't want to run against Mario Cuomo. Even Richard Nixon held you in awe. In fact, many Republicans did, except, I guess, for Ronald Reagan, who used to get you mixed up with Lee Iacocca. (*laughter*) But all your own tribe wanted you to go for it; Bill Clinton feared you more than anyone.

M.C.: Except for President Clinton, these are truly great and loyal Republicans. Perhaps, if a lot of Republicans felt I should be running for president as a Democrat, they thought I would be easier to beat. And that's how I thought when I was a politician.

W.O.: All right, here you are now. You spoke at the Waldorf-Astoria last week, in the grand ballroom, jam-packed into the triple tier, a thousand people or more, lawyers, members of the federal bar. You still have an amazing facility with words. Any regret you didn't do more with that?

M.C.: (*sigh*) I regret, the way many people do, that I wasn't better at what I did. Not in the first half of my life, where everything was trying to put bread on the table for five children, living in a furnished room, and then a walk-up apartment. But, then after that, you can write books, as you have, Bill, brilliant books, and give speeches, as you have, Bill. And you are probably unsatisfied as well.

You write the book because you think you have something to say. You give the speech because you think you have something to say. Look what is going on right now, an illegal war, and God forbid, the same thing might happen again in Iran. And you want to talk about it, and you're given the opportunity. And so you want to be effective.

Now, there's the rub. People don't listen. Yeah, they will applaud. But the purpose is to move people to a different level so they make different decisions.

After the election, when you had no impact, you're discouraged. And after my speech at the Waldorf-Astoria a few weeks ago, the Democrats still failed to respond.

When Bush chose to go to war, he made a mistake because he was misinformed by his intelligence people, because I don't believe he lied. The Founding Fathers knew that might happen if a single person had the power to wage war against another country.

And the Founding Fathers knew what happens with kings. They can become oppressive, stupid, mean, or sometimes just make a mistake. So they empowered Congress to declare war because there are many people in different parties, so a mistake is less likely.

That was what I was trying to convey. But the Democrats are unwilling to admit they were wrong when they sent that resolution to the president. So how do you feel after that? Disappointed. And what do you do? Well, you consider, "Is it worthwhile making another speech?"

W.O.: Governor, 140 federal judges were among the thousand or more people in the Waldorf just a few weeks ago, and they were applauding like crazy.

M.C.: That's because no one was taking their pictures. When they rule on a case, it's a different matter. Can I go back to Christmas, Brother Bill?

W.O.: Please, sir.

M.C.: See, at Christmas this kind of talk is a distant echo. Instead, you spend your time saying, "Thank you."

I mean, Christmas—whether you're a Christian, a Jew, or a nonbeliever—reminds people about the good life, honesty, generosity, loving one another, where there is a common understanding, whether you're educated or not.

And if you're human, you understand the value of love and helping one another. That's what the Christ Child represented.

That's the whole message of Christmas: "Love one another." And that's what the music says. That's what the prayers say. And that's what the words say. And for a while, we feel that way down deep.

And we feel kinder about the people we encounter. In the middle of the summer, we may look at the homeless with discomfort, but at Christmas we don't turn our back on them because we know they're hungry.

And it's a beautiful time of the year. Because you don't have to make a speech at all. You feel all the right and most beautiful things, whatever your beliefs.

W.O.: But, Governor, have you been to a shopping mall lately? Do you see people with a vacant, downtrodden look? How does your message penetrate their hardened hearts?

M.C.: I think the discomfort comes from wanting so much. And frankly, it's an uncomfortable way to shop, with people bumping up against one another and struggling to carry all the packages.

It's an uncomfortable experience but a superficial one. The real experience is the spirit that drove them to the mall. Because they were going to buy presents for others. And that spirit stays with them when they go home and celebrate Christmas.

And whether it's modest or lavish, if it's with people they love and who love them, then they have enjoyed Christmas fully.

W.O.: The *Boston Globe* called you "the great philosopher-statesman of the American nation." What, I wonder, would we do if we had a Christmas without Mario Cuomo?

M.C.: Well, first of all, I think that after they did that, their circulation and sales went down! So, we ought to check on that, Brother Bill.

W.O.: See, there you go again; you're always being humble.

M.C.: Bill, you could call almost anybody in my family, and you'd hear the same thing. And it would take them a lot less time to say it.

W.O.: I'm glad you're a friend of WVOX and WVIP, sir.

M.C.: How could I not be? They're wonderful, wonderful always to listen to. And so are you.

MARIO CUOMO, ESQ., TALKS ABOUT MARTHA STEWART, THE JUDICIAL SYSTEM, AND, ALWAYS, ABOUT MR. LINCOLN

We imposed upon Governor Cuomo's brilliant legal mind on March 16, 2004, to pose certain judicial questions that were in the headlines at the time.

WILLIAM O'SHAUGHNESSY (W.O.): The newspapers are filled with stories about Martha Stewart's legal troubles, and she may go to jail. Our guest today, Mario Cuomo, a former governor of New York, has appointed hundreds of judges to the Appellate Division and to the New York State Supreme Court, and could himself have been sitting this very day on the Supreme Court of the United States of America. Governor, did you follow the Martha Stewart trial?

GOVERNOR MARIO CUOMO (M.C.): I followed it every day. My son Christopher, as a matter of fact, is covering it for ABC. I haven't followed it the way I would if I were an attorney in the case and were going to handle an appeal. So I don't know all the details, but what I know has produced some strong feelings.

W.O.: Governor, do you know Robert Morvillo, her lawyer?

M.C.: I know him by reputation as an excellent attorney. From what I saw of the trial, he was a consummate professional. He's a very bright guy and knows what he's doing. Unfortunately, he didn't have enough material to work with to do well.

W.O.: Governor, Rosie O'Donnell and all those stars—Bill Cosby, et al.—do you think they helped or hurt her?

M.C.: They probably did a little of both. And this is a case, Bill, where lawyers must use common sense, because no one knows for sure how jurors think. Even when some of them come out later and speak about the case, who knows how much they tell you about what was in their hearts and minds while they sat in that box?

But I think she had to show some friends to the audience. Of course, some of the testimony implied she was rude on the telephone. At least by showing Cosby, Rosie O'Donnell, and others, it provides a kind of character witness.

W.O.: In almost every account, Governor, Martha Stewart is described as a tough lady. I observed her once in the foyer of a New York restaurant barking orders to her staffers, who were just standing there quaking in their boots as they hurriedly wrote things down on their yellow legal pads. Rosie O'Donnell called the whole trial a "bitch hunt." Do you think that's a crime, to be a "bitch"?

M.C.: Well, I'm not sure exactly what Rosie meant. Let's get back to your previous question instead. When you produce celebrities, you also remind jurors about Martha Stewart's celebrity, too. One juror came out and said after the trial, in effect, "Well, I'm a 'little' guy and this will show those 'big' people that they can't get away with that kind of arrogance."

I know who little people are. That's where I come from. They are strugglers; people who are working for a living; people who are good and raise families but don't have the advantages of rich people.

We know that syndrome well in this country. As a matter of fact, the gap between the very comfortable and the strugglers is increasing every day. So we all understand what that juror was saying. But that is no way to arrive at a conclusion in a jury. Because you're not there to show you can bring the big people down. You're there to show that justice works for everybody—whatever color, whatever sex, whatever size, and however much money they have in the bank.

W.O.: Governor Cuomo, some wise person once said—it may have been the philosopher "A. J. Parkinson," one of your nom de plumes—that prosecutors only move when they have the deck stacked. Does the defendant have a chance in the court system today?

M.C.: Absolutely. As a matter of fact, there are a lot of people who feel our constitutional principles provide the defense too many opportunities. "A. J. Parkinson" may have been talking about the grand jury level, where the prosecutor is there alone without a defendant's lawyer.

W.O.: Is that what they mean when they say you can indict a ham sandwich?

M.C.: Yes. And prosecutors are very good at knowing how a jury will react. But the law is designed to even that up. For example, it puts all the burden of proof on the prosecutor.

And, incidentally, the burden of proof for grand juries is beyond a reasonable doubt. If we had applied that standard to Iraq, we never would have been dropping bombs on Baghdad.

W.O.: Governor, two related questions. Steve Forbes, the magazine publisher and "libertarian Republican," says that when you get the IRS and Securities and Exchange Commission after you, you tend to panic.

M.C.: Well, I guess some people do. When you know that the government is against you, sure, you're going to be nervous. This is the era of Enron. And WorldCom. And the parade of manacled business executives in their dark blue suits.

W.O.: You've been pretty tough on all those guys yourself.

M.C.: Well, I hope not.

You're supposed to treat everybody fairly and apply the law without regard to economic status. You're supposed to divorce yourself from that and say, "Look, this is the burden of proof. And I must meet it beyond a reasonable doubt."

W.O.: Martha Stewart certainly will appeal, and I have been empowered to select her appeals lawyer. How much do you get an hour for doing this?

M.C.: Frankly, Bill, if any lawyers in America would answer that question for you right now, I would immediately discharge them. Because unless lawyers have been in the courtroom already and know the case intimately, they must first study and debate it with their colleagues.

And then after torturing themselves trying to find the right line of reasoning and argument, then they should be able to come to you and say, "Here's how I think it should be approached and how much it will cost."

Think of Bush against Gore. That was the big, big lawsuit in Florida. And the first trial was before this low-level judge. A very, very common court with common questions. And there was David Boies and these great lawyers on both sides. And both parties got badly hurt because their expert witnesses didn't testify correctly. Why? Because it was an election case and had to be decided immediately. The vote takes place one day. You're in court the next. You're in the Appellate Division the third day. You're in the Supreme Court the fifth day. And you never get a chance to sit down, study, and argue it out. And so it wasn't tried the way this Martha Stewart case will be tried. It wasn't argued the way this case will be argued. This one will be scrutinized closely.

But I do know that I would approach a plea for her on the failure of the people to present a case proven beyond a reasonable doubt. This is their only alternative. And I'm sure they'll spend a lot of time reminding the court what a reasonable doubt really is.

W.O.: Governor, again, respectfully, what would you say? You've been accused of being a pretty good lawyer, among other things. You're clearly uncomfortable with her conviction.

M.C.: I can't tell you what I would say. I really can't. The case is not what you and I think it is right now. The case is not what America thinks it is right now. Because none of us sat there with Morvillo; next to Cederbaum, the judge; next to the prosecutors; or watched and heard every witness, read every piece of evidence. That's the trouble with making a judgment on O. J. Simpson or any of these celebrity cases. Even if you watched it every day, you see only a part of it. So we are not privy to all the facts.

W.O.: And yet, are you not clearly "uncomfortable" with her conviction?

M.C.: I'm clearly "uncomfortable," as I said from the beginning. I won't address this as a lawyer; I can't. But when I heard a juror say, "This is a lesson to 'those' people, the big people," that should've been irrelevant.

W.O.: Can a judge order jurors not to talk to the press?

M.C.: I don't know, Bill. When we were younger, I don't remember jurors talking to the press. It's not a practice I'm pleased by. You could argue, however, that it's instructional to us and tells us what's going on in a jury. But if you have only snippets from one or two jurors, that's not the way to educate yourself about what really happened in that room.

W.O.: Governor Cuomo, do you think Wall Street will work better—and will you sleep better—if Martha Stewart is in jail someplace?

M.C.: I don't remember anyone saying that stock was in any way affected. One of the great ironies here is that ImClone really was approved eventually. So the thing they were all reacting to was that the Food and Drug Administration was not going to approve it. I don't know that her transaction had anything to do with the value of some small shareholder stocks. It was the fact she did not tell the truth. That was the problem.

W.O.: If Martha Stewart called you this week up at Willkie, Farr & Gallagher and said, "I want Mario Cuomo and Benito Romano, your partner and former federal prosecutor, to defend me," would you do it?

M.C.: Well, I certainly would recommend Benito Romano. I would not recommend myself. I do not believe I'm experienced on the subject matter. But that's academic. She has excellent attorneys right now in that courtroom—mainly Bob Morvillo.

W.O.: Governor Cuomo, to digress for a moment about your new book on Abraham Lincoln: I understand Barnes and Noble or Amazon just bought fifteen thousand copies, sight unseen. Is it finished?

M.C.: Yes. It'll be out in May. And I will only say some people have purchased the book in advance. It's called *Lincoln Matters: Today More Than Ever*. It looks at what Lincoln would say about contemporary issues such as preemptive war, stem cell research, and abortion.

What would Lincoln say about opportunity for workers in this country? What would he say about tax cuts for the rich? What would he say about multilateralism? What would he say about terrorism? And what would he say about race? Here's a key to understanding the importance of Lincoln: On the first memorial of 9/11, Governor George Pataki; the current mayor of New York City, Mike Bloomberg; and the former mayor, Rudolph Giuliani, were going to speak at the ceremony, and there was great anticipation as to what they would say. My God, how would they interpret it for us? How should we react to it? Their conclusion was not to speak about themselves. Instead, everyone used Lincoln for a comparison.

There's a great book by one of the top Lincoln scholars, James G. Randall, called *Lincoln: The Liberal Statesman*. On the other hand, Lew Lehrman and Jack Kemp and all the conservatives say he was a great Republican. That was technically his title. So everyone uses him.

And my question to myself was, after 9/11/2002: "Let's look again, Mario. Why do they all use him? Why is he an icon? Why have you studied him for all these years and written a book about him and referred to him when you were governor? Is it because he's a relic that you burn candles to?"

Well, he's no relic. He is a hero of the past. But he spoke to the ages. And to all of us everywhere. With large ideas. You look at the presidential campaign now. What is the difference between the candidates' two philosophical views? Can you answer that question?

Lincoln helps us answer it by telling us, "This is what I think it should be."

W.O.: Who'd have thunk it, Democrat Mario Cuomo bringing back Republican Abraham Lincoln. I just got an idea. Since you're bringing back Abe Lincoln, maybe he would defend Martha Stewart! I think I'd rather have him than you.

M.C.: (*laughter*) I would too, O'Shaughnessy! Lincoln was a fantastic lawyer. And you probably would have called him a "white shoe" lawyer at an "ivory tower" firm in the end. He wound up representing railroads at the end of his career. And real big guys. And getting good fees. (*laughter*)

W.O.: Sir, thank you for your visit.

M.C.: Any time, Brother Bill.

MARIO M. CUOMO ON THE DEATH PENALTY, SADDAM HUSSEIN, PRESIDENT BUSH, CHRISTMAS, AND GRANDCHILDREN

And once more into the "courtroom" with lawyer Cuomo, on December 16, 2003.

WILLIAM O'SHAUGHNESSY (W.O.): They found Saddam Hussein in a rat hole, and he will stand trial before some kind of tribunal. Would you represent him, lawyer Mario Cuomo?

GOVERNOR MARIO CUOMO (M.C.): Fortunately for him, Bill, that won't be necessary. There'll be other attorneys to represent him. I think a fair trial will conclude that he murdered many people. That much seems obvious from the evidence and his own confessions.

He painted the crimes as required by his position or justified by conflict. But there is no question he slaughtered human beings, so there will be no suspense with respect to the verdict.

I am intrigued by what he will say about weapons of mass destruction, about biological and chemical weapons, about his relationship with the United States. There are many unanswered questions.

W.O.: Do you think that tribunal will be effective and fair?

M.C.: The new Iraqi Constitution and laws are not written yet. Whether a defendant is entitled to a presumption of innocence or will be given the opportunity to investigate the evidence with his own lawyer is not known at the moment.

The first question will be: Where should he be tried? Some people suggest an international forum. But I think he should be tried in Iraq because he murdered his own people. He's guilty of international crimes as well, but it remains to be seen if he can be linked to 9/11.

W.O.: Governor, how does he defend himself? Does he say he didn't kill 1 million people, only 593,000?

M.C.: I think he will say all great nations have killed people, and many of them in dubious wars. His defenders will cite the United States. How did we take our land in the first place? And didn't we slaughter people in the process? And then they will raise all kinds of technical arguments. None of them will mean anything to the people of Iraq. What we know, Saddam, is that you took the lives of innocent people. You tortured people. You buried them alive.

You get some indication of the kind of defense he'll make from today's papers. They asked about the graves with all the bodies in them. And he said they were basically Iraqi soldiers who deserted their posts. In the Civil War, didn't we kill such people?

W.O.: Do you think there's a chance he might get off?

M.C.: No, there's no way. I think he will enhance President Bush's reasons for his preemptory attack. But we should remember that was the second rationale for going into Iraq, not the first.

The first was weapons of mass destruction and his imminent threat through Al Qaeda. The second was to liberate the Iraqis.

But I still think most Americans will support the president politically. However you dissolve it in the percolating cauldron of legal opinion, in the end, people will say the guy was terrible, and we're glad we got rid of him. And then they'll probably call for his decapitation or lethal injection, something I would regret.

W.O.: What about capital punishment for Saddam Hussein?

M.C.: Either you believe in taking the life of a killer, or you don't. I don't believe in that. There should be no exception, whether it's Saddam Hussein or Adolf Hitler. Life imprisonment without parole is much more severe than capital punishment.

W.O.: You've been called "America's greatest orator." How do you feel about President George Bush as a speaker?

M.C.: Some of the best speeches I've ever heard were delivered by this president in the last three years, his first address to the nation and his first budget address. He gave one about two weeks ago—wonderful material. I didn't agree with all of it, but it was beautiful to listen to.

W.O.: You're praising George Bush?

M.C.: I'm praising the speeches, and how he delivered them. Maybe somebody else wrote them, but so what? How many presidents wrote their own speeches?

W.O.: Christmas is starting to overwhelm us again. A college president in Westchester got up one day and called you the greatest thinker of the twentieth century. What about this Christmas thing?

M.C.: We never needed it more than now.

W.O.: But what if you don't quite feel Christmas yet?

M.C.: That's why we need it, Bill. For the people who don't feel it and must be urged to do so. That's why the Scrooge story plays over and over again. The most hardened hearts should be softened by Christmas.

That's what Christianity is supposed to be. I'm not sure why they pronounce it Christianity instead of *Christ*ianity. But Jesus should evoke love instead of anxiety, uncertainty, alienation, and anger.

We have the wonderful gift of life, O'Shaughnessy. We can do beautiful things and share beautiful moments. That's what Christmas reminds us.

W.O.: Did you ever think about becoming Father Cuomo, a priest?

M.C.: I became Grandfather Cuomo instead. My grandchildren make it very easy. No matter how many elections I lost, strikeouts I suffered when I played baseball, and bad moments I endured, I contributed to the birth of eleven new beautiful creatures, grand*daughters*, and before them, five others who produced the eleven.

It's a good feeling. I know you have a grand*son*, O'Shaughnessy. When we decide to have grand*sons*, we are going to have twelve!

MURRAY RICHMAN, ESQ., ON GUY VELELLA

Murray Richman, the famed criminal lawyer based in the Bronx, has represented a lot of "wise guys." And even some failed politicians, like former state Senator Guy Velella. Here's our interview from December 23, 2004.

WILLIAM O'SHAUGHNESSY (W.O.): 'Tis the Christmas season, but not for disgraced former state Senator Guy Velella, who goes back to jail on Monday.

Joining us here in our studio is the famous criminal lawyer from New York state who was profiled in a seventeen-page article in *The New Yorker*. His name is Murray Richman, and he knows Guy Velella well. Mr. Richman, what do you think about this decision by the Appellate Division to send Guy Velella back to the slammer?

MURRAY RICHMAN (M.R.): I think it's a travesty of justice. I was very active in the Velella case and even represented his father during the trial. This man is being punished for who he is. When you attract unwanted attention, the nail sticking up gets beaten down. Guy Velella is that nail. This man was released from jail through an early release program enacted by the mayor. And when the newspapers got wind of it, they criticized the mayor, who responded, "What program are you talking about? I know nothing about it." In fact, he had just appointed two people to serve on the panel. Then, instead of following due process in the courts to challenge the agency's decision, he changed the agency to send Velella back to jail.

W.O.: We're talking about Guy Velella, who used to represent part of Westchester.

Murray Richman, power lawyer, knows Guy Velella well. As a matter of fact, we saw you on television by his side. What kind of guy is he?

M.R.: He was a state senator who was there for everyone. Whenever something had to get done in Westchester County or the Bronx, you went to Guy Velella. Now he's been shamed; he's disgraced; he's lost his seat; he's lost his license; he's lost his good name; and they sent him to jail. Now what else do you want to take from him?

W.O.: You have argued cases and persuaded thousands of juries. What about Velella? First of all, did he take the damn money?

M.R.: That I don't know. Some say he copped a plea to protect his father, who was ninety-one at the time. I became involved in that facet of the case. But that is not the issue. He was granted a reduced sentence, and it was taken away because the press created a *cause célèbre*.

W.O.: Counselor, would this chain of events have occurred to Guy Velella if he were a great liberal icon?

M.R.: Bill, to be honest with you, I don't think it would have made any difference. He was sent back to jail because he was well known. We live in a society where the name of the game is to get someone famous.

W.O.: You claim he didn't get "due process." What exactly do you mean by that?

M.R.: It's very simple. Due process means you have to follow the rules, and it is mandated by the Constitution.

W.O.: You mean in court you have to follow the rules?

M.R.: Well, not just in court; in administrative proceedings as well. If an administrative agency takes an action and you don't like the decision, you can't just change the administrative agency. You must appeal under Article 78, a writ for review of administrative actions. The government just bypassed that; they changed the agency instead and added somebody who had previously voiced opposition to Mr. Velella.

W.O.: Murray Richman, you know a lot of people. What about Mayor Bloomberg?

M.R.: He's a disappointment! I like Mayor Bloomberg. I still like him for what he's done for the city. I'm just disappointed he became merely a "mouth."

W.O.: You say Bloomberg is "merely a mouth"; why?

M.R.: In this particular instance, I felt he was rather two-faced when he said a person who is out of jail shouldn't get credit for time served. Why is he becoming involved? Because the case grabbed the attention of the public, so he gets his name out there.

W.O.: Counselor, Governor Pataki has run for the hills. Seems like Guy Velella has been abandoned by all his so-called friends. What does this say about politics; what does this say about us?

M.R.: That the morals of a politician are about a quarter of an inch above those of a child molester. Our politicians become so accustomed to currying good favor with the public that when it comes time to show courage, they're afraid to do so. Years ago, President Kennedy wrote a book called *Profiles in Courage*. These times require courageous people, and they're in short supply.

W.O.: You've represented some "bad" guys, even murderers. How does Guy Velella compare?

M.R.: Let me tell you something, Mr. O'Shaughnessy, if they were all like Guy Velella, we'd be a lot better off. He's a good man, a good human being. A person who is charged with a crime is often measured by his worst act. If his crime represents his worst act, then he is still a good guy in my opinion.

W.O.: What do you think will happen to Guy Velella? He'll do his time, and he'll come out. . . .

M.R.: He'll come out, and he'll be stronger for it. But it's so disappointing to see fair-weather friends abandon him.

W.O.: Mr. Stillman, your colleague, was the lead lawyer, but you were also advising Guy Velella. You got shut down by the highest court in the state, five to nothing. Do you still have faith in the system you've served for so long?

M.R.: You've got to have faith, Bill. If I lost faith, I wouldn't be able to go on. I'm very disappointed. I know the judges in question. But they make the law. I don't.

W.O.: What did you just say to Guy Velella? I heard you talked to him a few moments ago on the phone.

M.R.: I told him to stay strong. We were discussing this recent decision and the mayor's reaction. And I said, "I'm going to the radio station right now, Guy, and I'm going to make a statement."

DICK GIDRON: LEGENDARY CAR DEALER BACK IN ACTION, SUING GENERAL MOTORS FOR $150 MILLION!

We aired this interview on August 17, 2006.

WILLIAM O'SHAUGHNESSY (W.O.): This is Bill O'Shaughnessy in Studio 1A at One Broadcast Forum in New Rochelle. We are interviewing a special guest today. Dick Gidron, one of the most famous car dealers in America, epitomizes the Horatio Alger story. He's joining us from his beautiful home in Scarsdale, where he entertains power brokers and celebrities. He called me earlier this week and said, "Listen, I have a story to tell. People have read a lot of stuff about me in the press, and some of it ain't true."

Dick Gidron, what are you doing now? I understand you served time. You were away at "college" for a spell.

DICK GIDRON (D.G.): Yes, I did, Mr. O. I was incarcerated for a year.

W.O.: That must be pretty hard for a famous guy with a healthy ego. Was that tough on you, being in the slammer?

D.G.: It was very, very tough. I never even had a speeding violation before. But it was especially tough since General Motors refused to keep their commitment.

W.O.: Are you totally free?

D.G.: Yes, I am. I am home and trying to recoup funds lost because General Motors let me down.

W.O.: Are you wearing any electronic ankle bracelets or tracking device?

D.G.: Oh, no, nothing like that. I am free to go where I please.

W.O.: Do you report to a parole officer?

D.G.: Yes, I do.

W.O.: Is that pretty humbling for you?

D.G.: That's extremely humbling, especially because I don't think I deserved it.

W.O.: You were head of the Bronx Chamber of Commerce. You were chairman of the powerful Bronx Democratic Party. How the hell did it all come unglued for you?

D.G.: Here's exactly what happened. We had a fire in June of 2000. After the fire, Mr. O'Shaughnessy, we found there was no insurance. But the building was owned by General Motors and still is!

W.O.: Was this your original dealership? Let me just go back a minute. You started as a car hop, I'm told, in Chicago. By the age of twenty-five, you were earning $140,000 a year, and that was forty years ago!

D.G.: Yes, that's all true.

W.O.: Then General Motors approached you about a dealership they sold in New Rochelle to the late Jim Heaphy. And they asked this attractive, beguiling guy with a dazzling personality, Dick Gidron, to expand into the Bronx. So this fire you were talking about, was that at the dealership near Fordham University?

D.G.: We moved from the Bronx site in 1998 to the Yonkers location. The fire was in Yonkers in 2000. I worked there for two years, and we were doing extremely well. When we had the fire and found there was no insurance, GM asked me to renovate the building to meet Yonkers Fire Department codes and then promised to sell it to me for X amount of dollars.

W.O.: This was Gidron Cadillac on Central Avenue in Yonkers?

D.G.: Exactly. I renovated the building for about $1.5 million. But GM never acquired a certificate of occupancy to sell the building. So I ended up losing about $2.5 million in profits from the dealership. As a result, I fell behind in some sales taxes, and that was the reason for my demise.

W.O.: That's why they put you in jail for a year? Just for falling behind on your taxes? Didn't the newspaper say you embezzled some funds?

D.G.: Uh, no, no, I never did that.

W.O.: They gave you a year in jail just for falling behind in your taxes? You think that was fair?

D.G.: No, I don't, but again, we live in a society where we abide by the laws and by the decisions of the courts.

W.O.: Dick Gidron, I heard former mayors of New York, and even several elders of the New York Yankees, and everybody around here went to bat for you. Anybody who was anybody testified, "He's a good guy. Cut him a break."

D.G.: That is true. I didn't catch a break. I had judges come, New York Yankees, Mayor [David] Dinkins. . . .

W.O.: You "made" a few judges when you were Democratic chairman, didn't you?

D.G.: Yes, I did. One of my greatest thrills was helping to elect the first African American district attorney in New York State.

W.O.: He's a good one. You know why I like Robert Johnson? He is against the damn death penalty.

D.G.: Yeah, he is a good district attorney. George Freeman was the county leader at the time, and we worked diligently to get him elected.

W.O.: So who the hell prosecuted you? If you picked the D.A., who was left?

D.G.: The prosecution had Mr. Morgenthau.

W.O.: Robert Morgenthau is an icon of his profession. Why do you think he went after you?

D.G.: Good question! When the case first came to court, the judge threw it out because he didn't have any jurisdiction in Westchester or the Bronx. Somehow, Robert Morgenthau acquired jurisdiction in Westchester County and pursued me until I was incarcerated.

W.O.: You are blaming your financial problems on General Motors?

D.G.: No question! If General Motors had sold me the building, I could have mortgaged it and recouped my expenditures for renovation. I would have added over $2 million to my cash flow, and I would not have had any of these problems.

W.O.: You are now suing General Motors?

D.G.: $150 million!

W.O.: $150 million? You know General Motors is having its own problems now?

D.G.: I know, but so am I! General Motors created them for me!

W.O.: You think they did it on purpose?

D.G.: I can't say. We had many conversations, and I wrote to two or three vice presidents of General Motors for assistance before this happened. The building was completed in 1999, and I hired a lawyer, personally, to get the certificate of occupancy for General Motors. By the time I got all that done, it was too late. They are 100 percent responsible for this situation, and I think they should come to the table and settle it.

W.O.: You were once their "Golden Boy," perhaps their most famous dealer. What happened? They made you!

D.G.: Well, that's true. I worked seven days a week and served 45,000 customers. I think we helped each other, and I appreciate what they did. They even sent me to Harvard.

W.O.: You graduated from Harvard?

D.G.: Harvard Business School: an MBA.

W.O.: In your trial, if people said he's a great guy but not a great businessman, you should have blamed it on Harvard! (*laughter*)

D.G.: No, Harvard's a great school. I would never blame anything on Harvard.

W.O.: How old are you now, Dick Gidron?

D.G.: I am sixty-five.

W.O.: As you look back, do you think life has treated you fairly?

D.G.: You know, there are good times and bad times. Overall, God has been very good to me. I work very hard. I am fortunate to have a good education and a nice family. I met many people and have lived in the New York metropolitan area for over thirty years. I always try to give something back to the community. As I look at it, I would say life has been good to me even though things could be better now.

W.O.: Are you broke now?

D.G.: No.

W.O.: I mean, do you have "walking around" money? (*laughter*)

D.G.: Yes, Mr. O'Shaughnessy, I have "walking around" money. If I didn't, I would come to see you.

W.O.: We've talked over the years to your wife. Was this tough on her?

D.G.: It's been tougher on my family than on me.

W.O.: Your parties in Scarsdale are legendary. You used to invite A-list celebrities. Did some of these people abandon you in your time of need?

D.G.: Yes, they did. When you do time, you separate your real friends from your associates.

W.O.: You had some neighbors in the Bronx with similar "entanglements": Mario Biaggi and Guy Velella, who was a state senator.

D.G.: They are both dear friends of mine.

W.O.: You guys can almost start a club.

D.G.: Guy Velella is a dear, dear friend. The district attorney wanted me to testify against him, and when I refused, they came after me like a ton of bricks.

W.O.: Now, wait a minute, are you saying that if you had turned on Velella, you wouldn't have gone to jail?

D.G.: Yes.

W.O.: Mr. Morgenthau, or Dan Castleman, at the Criminal Division, said, "Give us Velella, and you walk?"

D.G.: Yes.

W.O.: Have you ever told this to anyone?

D.G.: No.

W.O.: Do you regret not turning on Guy Velella?

D.G.: No, I don't. I wouldn't lie about anybody. I didn't know anything about Mr. Velella's situation. Therefore, I refused to raise my right hand and perjure myself for personal gain.

W.O.: Mr. Morgenthau is an icon of his profession. He's the most famous, beloved prosecutor in America. What are you saying?

D.G.: Well, maybe he is. I met him on social occasions. Still, I don't think I got a fair deal.

W.O.: So, you are suing General Motors for $150 million. What are you going to do with it?

D.G.: I don't know. I have to get it first! I know people who have worked with me for over thirty years, and I have an obligation to them and their families.

W.O.: Where is this lawsuit, "Richard Gidron v. General Motors"?

D.G.: It's in White Plains federal court.

W.O.: Didn't you hear the old wives' tale, "Don't take on General Motors"?

D.G.: Oh, I've heard that. I don't want to take on anybody, but sometimes in life you have to do the right thing. I can show you the letters I wrote to them in vain. I can't afford to shell out $1.5 million to repair General Motors' property.

W.O.: What do you think the elders of General Motors think now about Dick Gidron, their former star? Has he become a pain in the neck? Is he "trouble"?

D.G.: Not me, I would never be a pain in the neck to anybody, Mr. O'Shaughnessy. But I think General Motors is a large bureaucracy, and the upper echelons don't always know what's going on.

W.O.: It's 12:34 in Westchester. Since this is live radio, let's see if we can get some callers. We are on the open line with Dick Gidron, one of the most famous auto dealers in America. He is suing General Motors for $150 million. He just came out of "college," as we call it. Where were you being held?

D.G.: In Buffalo, New York, at Collinsville Correctional Facility.

W.O.: Was that a hard life for you?

D.G.: It was a hard life, but I was held in "private protection," so I didn't socialize with many inmates. I was escorted everywhere by a guard.

W.O.: What do you mean, "private protection"?

D.G.: Private protection is the department for high-profile cases. They don't put you in a regular prison, and they protect you.

W.O.: Well, you're a big guy. How tall are you?

D.G.: I'm six feet three inches.

W.O.: How much do you weigh?

D.G.: About 215 to 218.

W.O.: I don't think anyone would fool with you. It's not like what we see on TV with "Oz," is it?

D.G.: No, but it was devastating. I survived through tenacity and prayer.

W.O.: You have sons. Isn't there a Dick Gidron Jr.?

D.G.: Yes.

W.O.: Do you think there are lessons in your life for your son and heir?

D.G.: Definitely. I hope he would be extremely careful in business transactions. I want to emphasize, Mr. O'Shaughnessy, prior to my agreement with General Motors, the contract was read and approved by my lawyer.

W.O.: Well, now, can General Motors use that against you? That your lawyer read it, and there was no insurance?

D.G.: I'm talking about after the fire when they signed the failed agreement to buy the building.

W.O.: Will you be selling cars any time soon?

D.G.: I have a loyal customer base and certainly hope so.

W.O.: So, you might be back in action soon?

D.G.: Not necessarily soon, but sooner or later.

W.O.: Let's bring in a caller. You are on the air!

CALLER 1: Do you have a realistic chance of reopening your dealerships?

D.G.: On a scale of 1 to 10, hopefully, it would be a 7 or an 8.

CALLER 2: Mr. Gidron, would you ever consider hosting a show on WVOX?

D.G.: Well, that's Mr. O'Shaughnessy's decision. I appreciate your question, but I would rather be in the automobile business.

W.O.: You want to do your own program? The *New York Times* said the way to get on isn't very difficult. You just have to ask! (*laughter*)

D.G.: Well, let's see what happens with the lawsuit first.

W.O.: Dick Gidron, you are nice to share these thoughts with your local community radio station. You have a lot of friends who believe in you. The hearing against General Motors is in October 2006. Welcome home and welcome back.

D.G.: Thank you, Mr. O'Shaughnessy. God bless you and your family.

BARBARA TAYLOR BRADFORD: "A WOMAN OF SUBSTANCE"

We have been most fortunate to enjoy a friendship with a number of today's greatest writers (every one of them more accomplished and gifted of pen than Yours Truly!). Though we can't hold a candle to her ability to craft a story, Barbara Taylor Bradford graciously includes my family in her circle. This warm, wonderful writer spoke candidly with us about her career on August 17, 2006.

WILLIAM O'SHAUGHNESSY (W.O.): Today, we are visiting one of the great legends of publishing at her spectacular abode overlooking the East River in Manhattan, the great journalist, author, and writer Barbara Taylor Bradford. Mrs. Bradford, my wife, Nancy O'Shaughnessy, is crazy about you, and I am an admirer of your famous husband, Robert Bradford, the movie producer. Will you trust me to conduct myself fairly and properly? (*laughter*)

BARBARA TAYLOR BRADFORD (B.T.B.): Of course I will, Bill! But, please, call me Barbara, as you do when the four of us are together of an evening. "Mrs. Bradford" makes me sound like an old lady.

W.O.: Okay, have it as you will, Barbara, I'm not trying to embarrass you, but you are published in over ninety countries in forty languages, and have sold 75 million books! You're a damned industry!

B.T.B.: That's right, more or less. (*laughter*) Worldwide, of course, not just in America or England. It's probably gone up a bit actually—hopefully. (*laughter*)

W.O.: Has it made you rich?

B.T.B.: Of course it has. It would be silly to say otherwise. That's not why I do the work, though. We all want to have money, of course. But I simply like to write.

W.O.: You just started writing books, your novels, in a mid-life "correction," after an illustrious career as a reporter in Great Britain?

B.T.B.: I actually sold my first short story when I was ten years old, Bill. My mother didn't intend to sell it; she wasn't looking to make money. But she was my great encourager, the person who knew I would be a writer. She taught me to read when I was four years old and encouraged me to write my little stories, and I wrote a special one when I was ten, and she thought it was great. She had me recopy it because there were ink blots everywhere, and then sent it to a children's magazine. They didn't respond initially, but about three months later, we received a letter saying they were going to publish it and were sending me ten shillings and six "spoons" in a money order!

W.O.: Even then they knew—at least your mother did.

B.T.B.: Well, my mother thought I was talented, yes, even as a child. I did become a cub reporter at the *Yorkshire Evening Post* when I was sixteen. At eighteen, I became women's page editor of a big daily paper, and then when I was twenty, I went to work in Fleet Street. I didn't became a novelist until I was forty.

W.O.: That was an historic first book, *A Woman of Substance*.

B.T.B.: You know, I never believed my editor when she told me, "Oh, Barbara, you've written a bestseller." It was a very long book, Bill. It was originally 1,520 pages long and weighed fifteen and a half pounds! I actually took it to the local D'Agostino's and weighed it. But we cut it to 700 pages.

W.O.: Do you remember walking down Fifth Avenue, looking in the bookstore windows and saying, "Oh my God, that's me"?

B.T.B.: Well, it's funny, because I didn't know they were going to pile up this book in a display mountain. It became an instant bestseller, which is very unusual for an unknown artist.

W.O.: Well, you ain't anymore, Barbara Taylor Bradford!

B.T.B.: Oh no, I know! (*laughter*)

W.O.: Now, you've done twenty-one novels, and your newest is *Just Rewards*. What's that about?

B.T.B.: Well, you know, after *A Woman of Substance*, I wrote a book called *Voice of the Heart*. There was such a demand for Emma Harte again, and her family, so I wrote *Hold a Dream*. Later, I made it a trilogy with *To Be the Best*. Then I left the Hartes alone to write quite a lot of other books, but a peculiar thing happened.

Young women who were children when their mothers read *A Woman of Substance* read the book themselves, and they sent me e-mails saying, "Why did you stop?" So one day I said to my publisher, "I think I'll write some more Emma Harte books." And she replied, "But all of the family is dead!"

W.O.: You killed them all off?

B.T.B.: I know, that was rather stupid, especially to kill Emma off. So what I did was create the great-granddaughters of Emma Harte. Twice, in two of the books, I succeeded in bringing her back in flashbacks, and that series began with *Emma's Secret, Unexpected Blessings*, and now *Just Rewards*. It came out in hardcover a year ago and should be out in paperback soon.

W.O.: Where do you get your ideas? Your books are so richly textured. Do you know the plot when you start to write?

B.T.B.: Well, yes. I think out a book first, Bill. I am not one of those writers who sit down at a typewriter or a computer and say, "Okay, I'll let it take me where it leads me."

W.O.: Liz Smith, the famous columnist, calls you one of the most generous women in New York. You work for a lot of charities, the Police Athletic League, the New York Pops, and you have been wonderful to the Broadcasters Foundation of America. You are often seen about town with Robert Bradford. How many years have you been hitched to him?

B.T.B.: We will be married forty-one years at Christmas. We got married on December 24.

W.O.: Are you still in love with the guy?

B.T.B.: Well, the other day I told him, "Don't count on forty-two!" (*laughter*) But, yes, of course. He makes a lot of my movies.

W.O.: He has also turned your stories into miniseries for television.

B.T.B.: Nine out of ten, actually.

W.O.: You are such a romantic; you only have to read your books to know that. What's the secret of a happy marriage?

B.T.B.: Well, he travels a lot! (*laughter*) He used to travel a lot because he was always away making movies. No, I think the secret of a happy marriage is liking each other as well as being in love and having a shared interest. You know, he has a European background too. He was born in Germany, raised in France. I was born and raised in England. The British won't let me go, Bill!

W.O.: They have given you lots of honors and awards, Barbara.

B.T.B.: Yes, but so have the Americans. About that shared background, we agree about the past and what's happening today. We were both very little in the Second World War, but we were very much aware of it. America was never invaded on its own ground until 9/11.

W.O.: Someone told me once that you have nicknames for each other.

B.T.B.: Well, he is very bossy; so one day I started to call him "Bismarck" since he is German born; and he calls me "Napoleon." We have a cushion that says, "Napoleon lives! I married him." He crossed out "him" and put in "her." (*laughter*)

W.O.: Barbara, do you write on a schedule? Do you decide at eight o'clock every morning, I am going to sit at that damn word processor?

B.T.B.: You only see me at night, Bill, at dinner and at charity functions. Very few people see me during the day. I guess I am like a vampire. (*laughter*)

W.O.: A lovely vampire! My wife thinks you're a knockout, an altogether glamorous dame.

B.T.B.: Aw, well, your Nancy is sweet. I love her, too, and she is a knockout herself.

W.O.: What are your days like?

B.T.B.: I just finished a 902-page manuscript of my twenty-second book. It will come out in England in October and here in January. In the last three months, I was working eighteen hours a day.

My days are like this: In the beginning, I go to my desk at six in the morning. Then I feed the dogs and go back to my desk with coffee. I work until about 5:00 P.M. with a break for lunch. But as the deadline approaches, I get up at 4:00, 4:30, 5:00; I've even been known to get up at 3:00 A.M. I put in a good ten to twelve hours every day.

W.O.: Do you ever just sit there, and it just doesn't fly out of your bright, fine mind? I guess it is called "writer's block." Do you ever have it?

B.T.B.: Only momentarily, because I don't really believe in it, and I'll tell you why. There will be days when I can't get something right, and then I stop and pack it in, even in the morning. But I always make sure I have a semblance of what I am trying to say on a piece of paper. That way, the next day, there is something to rewrite. I had a great mentor who taught me, "Barbara, I don't care if it takes you four days to write one page; you must put something down so you have something to rewrite."

W.O.: Who was that?

B.T.B.: Well, he is dead now. His name was Cornelius Ryan. He wrote *The Longest Day*, *The Last Battle*, *A Bridge Too Far*; *The Longest Day* was also a movie. He said, "You have a gift for storytelling, and you cannot remain a journalist."

W.O.: Seventy-five million books later, apparently, readers all over the world agree with him. Barbara, you mentioned your European background. Share your knowledge of the world as you know it. You go all over the planet for book signings and honorary degrees; is there any way out of this mess in the Middle East? Is this a "holy war" we are in?

B.T.B.: In a sense, it is. It is the rise to power of Islamic fundamentalism, but it started a thousand years ago.

It all began with the Crusades when British and French knights traveled to Jerusalem to drive out the Islamic Saracens. Also the Battle of Poitiers [the Battle of Tours] in the 500s, when Charles Martel was a Frankish king, was about the same issue, driving out the Islamic hordes. Islam has fought Western democracies for centuries because they think we are materialistic and secular.

W.O.: Is this about more than oil?

B.T.B.: You know, Bill, I think I told you about a book I read that got an extraordinary review; it is called *The Looming Tower*. It discusses how the West seems to have it all, and Third World countries have very little. The subtitle is *Al Qaeda and the Road to 9/11*, and the writer, Lawrence Wright, shows how Islamic fundamentalism revived from the seventh century because a man named Sayyid Qutb, an Egyptian scholar, came to America in 1948 and was horrified by our materialism and secular way of life. Anyway, Qutb lived in America for several years, and when he went home became a part of the Muslim Brotherhood in Egypt.

W.O.: So you read books other than your own?

B.T.B.: I read a lot of history books. Somebody said to me recently, "Why are there always wars; why haven't we learned anything?" My answer to that is we are no different now from the knights of the Crusades. Humanity has not changed, and we have not learned anything.

W.O.: Was there really a Richard the Lionheart?

B.T.B.: There was, and he was the first son of Henry II and Eleanor of Aquitaine. He went out on the Crusades and was the king of England after his son had died. Remember that wonderful play, and movie too, called *The Lion in Winter*? That was the father and mother of Richard Cour-de-Lion, who happened to be married and also a homosexual.

W.O.: That's more than we ever wanted to know about Richard the Lionheart! (*laughter*) Those days when this conflict all began, the Saracens went someplace where they didn't belong. Today, are the Jews in a place where they don't belong?

B.T.B.: Well, no, why? I mean Jews lived in Palestine. Look, I don't know what was going on in their minds in 1917 and 1918, when General [Edmund] Allenby and Winston Churchill carved out that whole area of land. Saudi Arabia became part of it, and another part became Jordan.

Lawrence of Arabia said, "Find a tribe that has a good leader, and let's make them rulers of this land called Jordan." They chose Sheik Faisal, who was a Hashemite, and now we have the Hashemite Empire in Jordan. I would say that the Jews are entitled to live in Israel. Let us remember one thing, Bill: Israel is a bulwark for America and the West in the Middle East.

W.O.: You are a romance novelist, a journalist, and you seem to be an historian as well. Is it ever going to stop in the Middle East?

B.T.B.: It is all a question of how many extremist presidents and leaders are going to stay in power over there. Unless they can come to their senses, it will continue for a long time.

W.O.: Unless they can be made to see what?

B.T.B.: To see the sense! In all wars, it is innocent people who get killed! Eight million people died in the World War! Eight million people! Is that going to happen again? Look, I have just finished a 902-page manuscript called *The Ravenscar Dynasty*. It's a modern story about two families fighting each other for a business empire. I took a medieval king and his cousin and based the book on real history. To me, the world hasn't changed since medieval times.

W.O.: You talk about other presidents, what about our president? I think you like George W. Bush.

B.T.B.: Well, any president or prime minister has a really tough job, Bill, whatever country he is running today. George Bush did not invent all this. It's a thousand years old, for God's sake! I try to understand the difficulties he faces.

W.O.: Since you are of dual citizenship, I should also ask you for an opinion on Tony Blair, your prime minister.

B.T.B.: I think he is facing the same kind of thing. It is like walking on the tightrope. At one time, I would have liked to have been a politician because I am a great fan of Margaret Thatcher, and of course, you know very well, Tony Blair bases his politics on hers.

W.O.: In all the books, twenty in all, and 75 million of them sold, what's the loveliest line you ever wrote?

B.T.B.: I think the end of *A Woman of Substance*, if it is not perhaps the loveliest, I think it is the truth. It is often quoted back to me: "You are the author of your own life. You write the script and you play the part." At the end of the book, Blackie O'Neil, who was played by Liam Neeson in the movie, says to Deborah Kerr, who played the older Emma, "What is the secret of life? What have you learned? What is the secret, Emma?" She says, "It is to endure."

W.O.: Someone has even written a book about you called, *THE Woman of Substance*. Was that an "approved" book? Did you cooperate with the author?

B.T.B.: Yes, I did. Piers Dudgeon did a wonderful job. It was mostly about my childhood, my writing, and my books, but it touched on my marriage as well. Of course, I was really shocked, Bill, when he discovered that my grandmother had a romantic liaison with the Marquis of Ripon for many years and had bore him three children, including my mother! It is a good book; it's an interesting book; and it is coming over here in November.

W.O.: *The Woman of Substance* about a woman of substance, Barbara Taylor Bradford. You should see the look on the faces in our control room.

B.T.B.: Why?

W.O.: You have just shared so much good stuff with us today, and we are so grateful. You really are a woman of substance.

B.T.B.: Thanks, Bill. Best home to your dazzling Nancy.

LOUIS CAPPELLI AT THE JACEE LYNN CAPPELLI DIABETES CENTER OF SOUND SHORE MEDICAL CENTER

Louis Cappelli came out of Yonkers, New York, and changed the skyline of several Westchester cities. This conversation with the mega-developer took place on November 13, 2007, at the dedication of a diabetes center named for his niece.

WILLIAM O'SHAUGHNESSY (W.O.): Louis Cappelli, you're successful, in every telling and by every account, as a developer. You could get a lot done and still be as successful as you are, without putting all this money back.

LOUIS CAPPELLI (L.C.): Well, I think maybe I'm superstitious, first of all, and second, I do believe that if you make money—and it's a privilege to make money—you have to *give* money. And in New Rochelle, White Plains, and other places where we are successful, I think it's incumbent on every developer and successful businessman also to give back to the community in one fashion or another. It makes *you* feel good. I think it makes *God* feel good. It makes us *all* feel good. And I think you do better, and I think the people you give the money to, and the ones you help, do better. *Everybody* gets a benefit from a successful development in a community, and *all* of us benefit. And then all of us are winners, and I think that's really good.

W.O.: Well, what I'm trying to say, Louis Cappelli, is that you don't *have* to do this. . . .

L.C.: Oh, but I do. I feel like I do. I feel like it's my obligation, to my family in this instance, particularly. But I have an obligation anyway. I do think that I and other successful businessmen have an absolute *obligation* to give back to the communities because what else are we doing it for?

W.O.: You mention God. Usually rich, successful businessmen, mega-developers, don't mention the Almighty. Are you pretty religious?

L.C.: I *believe*. I believe in God—*and* Ben Bernanke right now! I hope *Ben Bernanke* is going to do the right thing. I know *God* has been doing the right thing for a long time.

I'm just thrilled to be part of the strength and fortitude my niece has shown. When you get to meet her, or if others out there in the listening audience get to meet Jacee Lynn Cappelli, they would see a poised ten-year-old who has been through so much in the last seven years, more than I've been through. She's been through *way* more. And she's just come out of this thing, and she's fighting and she's beautiful and she's vibrant. She's just an inspiration to me.

W.O.: You mention God *and* Bernanke: Who better to ask? Is the economy going to tank?

L.C.: Well, everything I say usually goes the opposite way, so I'm debating right now whether to say something the opposite way. But I'm hoping that, at least through the Christmas season, they hold things together because everybody wants to be buoyant through *Christmas*, everybody wants to be upbeat. What happens *after* that, in the first quarter, I don't really know. But we are positioned for, and expecting, a downturn. If it happens, hopefully we've insulated ourselves as best as possible. Our buyers are closing, they're happy, and the good news is they're purchasing, not on speculation, as in Miami and Las Vegas. They are purchasing here in New Rochelle and White Plains because it's their *homes*. That's very good news for us and our developments.

W.O.: Those spectacular luxury apartments in New Rochelle and White Plains that bear your name and Donald Trump's are selling?

L.C.: Oh, yes, Bill. We are closing now, and 70 percent of the people who purchased have moved into New Rochelle's Trump Tower, Trump Plaza. And in White Plains, the Ritz Carlton will be closed by Christmastime. In a lot of regions, these purchases are speculative, and those speculators don't close in bad times. But people who are buying from our jobs are people who are actually *locating* here or selling their homes to live in a high-rise complex, and they're all closing because the stock market and economy don't affect them as much. This is their *home*; it's not a "speculative" play for them.

W.O.: You've changed the skyline, Louis Cappelli, with bricks and mortar—and you also put something back into the social fabric. Which are you proudest of at the end of the day?

L.C.: You know, Bill, you can't put very much back into the social fabric unless you are successful on the bricks-and-mortar side because the bricks and mortar generate the cash flow—the money. Then you can say: We've done very well here, we're very successful, let's give something back. I think they go hand in hand. That doesn't mean if the project isn't successful, we wouldn't step up and do *something* here, especially with my niece being the common denominator, but it certainly makes the *size* of the gift easier. It makes the size of *future* gifts easier, as you build these large projects and they are successful.

W.O.: A million bucks is still a lot of money, Louis.

L.C.: Not when it comes to the health and welfare of your niece, or of others who need help and assistance. It's just a piece of the pie, and you just have to spend what you have to spend.

And all of you guys out there listening to me now who make a lot of money, I think *you* should *spend* some of that money, and I know most of you already do, on these important causes, because they are very important.

W.O.: Thank you, sir. Well done.

GOVERNOR MARIO M. CUOMO ON A GRIM ELECTION DAY, 2004

Governor Mario Cuomo remains one of our most astute political observers, and we often solicit his analyses so that we can better understand the great issues of the day.

WILLIAM O'SHAUGHNESSY (W.O.): It's Election Day 2004, with Bush against Kerry. Let's switch now to Manhattan, to the wise Conscience of the Democratic Party. We had to wait in line because everyone in the country is calling him today: Governor Mario Cuomo. Thank you, sir. Did you vote?

GOVERNOR MARIO CUOMO (M.C.): I did, very early this morning, Bill, in the midst of a very large crowd, at six o'clock.

W.O.: Governor, I hear you vote with a lot of Republicans!

M.C.: It *looked* like there were a lot of Republicans there this morning. And they seemed quite confident, probably because the president said this morning he was going to win. And we all know the president has the True Word being delivered to him at all times. So that was enough to give these people a good day—at least until the exit polls come out.

W.O.: Governor, didn't you tell another interviewer today—you have been everywhere on radio and television—there was kind of an "intensity" to it all?

M.C.: Normally, when you stand on line on Election Day, there is conversation and chitchat back and forth and a kind of gentility, a kind of fun aspect to it, no matter what side you're on. I didn't detect that. This morning there was a kind of grim intensity to it—not hostility by any means, but intensity. People were not bantering like they normally would, and I think that's a reflection of the issues that have made this such a compelling election: 9/11 and Iraq. There are plenty of domestic problems as well, and since the Bush Administration took over, a lot of things have gone wrong and there are a lot of things to complain about. I think, basically, the memory of 9/11, the existence of the war in Iraq—

losing men and women every day, not being sure what the future holds—have us in an extremely serious mood, and that's what is driving this vote.

It's coming out because we're worried about what is happening to us, and what we are going to be able to do about it immediately. That seriousness is probably a very good thing, whoever the next president is. We desperately need to bring people closer to solidarity in this country. We're nowhere near as strong as we need to be to fight this terrorist threat and solve the domestic problems. Today, I sensed the "urgency" that will exist, no matter *who* is elected. If President Bush gets another opportunity or if John Kerry gets it, they will be able to use that commitment to seriousness to help mend people closer together.

W.O.: Governor Mario Cuomo, didn't you also tell someone as you stood in line to vote in Manhattan this morning that beyond the seriousness there was almost a sense of grimness?

M.C.: Yes, because the nature of the problems are grim. People are dying: innocent people on the other side of this war. And certainly there are innocent people dying on our side, and others coming back without body parts. There doesn't appear to be any end to it, and if you could say, "Well, okay, this is the *price* we are paying"—we're certainly getting our money's worth.

You can't say that. What are you going to get in return, for all the people we have wounded, injured, scarred, and killed? Of course, there is a grimness here. I did sense it this morning, and I will continue to sense it until it is over.

W.O.: Everyone listening in Westchester, Long Island, and the Bronx knows I admire you and have for years. I can't con them about this. You could have been voting for *yourself* to be president. You didn't do it, and a lot of people are still damned unhappy you didn't run.

M.C.: Bill, I think it's hard for any sane person to think he or she is qualified to be president of the United States. I will give both Kerry and Bush the benefit of the doubt, that they are sane. They both obviously think they can do it. It is an awful lot to ask of a human being. It has to be a person with very special gifts, ones I do not believe I ever had. It's nice of you to say those kind things.

But nobody can do the job of president unless this country comes together behind them.

Coming together means you have to give up a little bit of your position sometimes to make a deal with the other side. That's what we're going to have to do in order to end this war. We are all going to have to give a little bit, especially in Congress. We should be pushing our representatives in Congress, whatever party they're in, to work as hard as they can to support the president, whoever he is. That is the only way we're going to end this mess we are in.

W.O.: Governor, the *Boston Globe* called you the "great philosopher-statesman" of the whole bloody American nation. You're a Democrat. When we look at the stellar guys the Democrats have put up—Mondale, Dukakis, Gore, and George McGovern—we have to ask why the hell didn't you ever . . .?

M.C.: Forget me, Bill. The interesting thing is to ask what is *really* powerful in this country? It's *not* the presidents. The presidents don't make us powerful. It's wonderful to have a Lincoln, a George Washington to get us launched, and it's marvelous to be inspired by a John Kennedy or a Ronald Reagan. All that is lovely. But what makes this country strong is the genius of the Constitution. And the generations of tough, ambitious, eager people who have come from all over the globe to find their life here. What they have left us is a *heritage*.

It's the *country* that is powerful, and all we have to do is have enough *leadership* with *intelligence* to recognize that strength, and to cooperate with it, to help it realize itself. We the People, with all our 290 million members, *we're* the strength of this place. We are the ones who have to come together and assert ourselves. That is the best thing about this election. If we set a new record of 70 percent turnout, then we are beginning to realize our strength and to put it at the disposal of the next president. That's the important thing. Even more important than who the president is.

W.O.: It is Election Day, so I can presume to ask you these dumb questions! Half the people *love* Bush, half the people *hate* him.

Almost the same could be said for Kerry. Why this division and hatred?

M.C.: I will tell you the irony there. And it is a sad irony. The president was made president by the Supreme Court vote, as we all know, in 2000. We all know there was resentment about that, and unhappiness. We know we were good enough as a country, however, to come together behind him, although he did not win the popular vote.

So he got off to a weak start. Then came 9/11. He performed brilliantly. Maybe it was an obvious choice, but he made it. He made it intelligently and dramatically. He won us all when he said, "We, you, I, us, the rest of the world with us, are going to go to Afghanistan and get Osama bin Laden and Al Qaeda because we know they're the bad guys. They are the terrorists; they sum up this terrorist threat. They have admitted it to us, so let's go get them." Our hearts, minds, and prayers went with the president. This country was united the way it has not been since the Second World War.

W.O.: And . . .?

M.C.: Three months later, he started, for whatever reason, preparing to attack Iraq. Tommy Franks—I know he supports him, but he never denies having said to [Senator] Bob Graham in February of 2002, as he was leading the troops in Afghanistan, that planning Iraq action is a mistake. "We're not ready to go to Iraq; our intelligence on the weapons of mass destruction is not good." You can read it, on pages 125, 126, and 127 of Bob Graham's book *Intelligence Matters*.

Franks said we should finish the job with Osama and Al Qaeda. This is February 2002, fourteen months before Baghdad. Then, he says, we should go to Somalia where Al Qaeda is, then Yemen, before we go to Saddam. Despite all that, the president went to Iraq, and at that point the solidarity ended. At that point, the *argument* started. Now the country is divided in half over Iraq. Right after 9/11, the president had us all. "We're all with you, Mr. President." And most of the world was with you. You gave up that solidarity, and you lost three-quarters of the world's support. And half of your own country's support at least. Now you're in Iraq because you chose to be. Choosing three reasons you said were wrong but have now justified by saying, "Even if I was wrong for going in, it was a good result because he is a bad dictator and he would have hurt us."

There are a lot of bad dictators, Bill. They *all* can hurt us. If you make him president again, he can use that logic to fight anybody he wants who is a dictator and a bad guy. That is the problem. It's not hate.

I do not know a lot of people who hate the president. How are you going to hate a man, who is obviously a man of faith, who, yes, comes to different conclusions than you do, but is doing it for his country and makes the sacrifice of taking this beating day after day. It is kind of hard to hate him. Disapprove of his choices? Yes, absolutely. Want him to step aside? Yes, absolutely. Pray for something better than he and John Kerry? Yes, absolutely. But I don't think it's hate; I think it is a disapproval of the second judgment he made. Our war in Afghanistan was terrific. His war in Iraq is not as popular.

W.O.: Governor Cuomo, as I listen, I have to wonder, when you talk to Matilda Raffa Cuomo, your wife of so many years, if you ever say, of an evening, "You know, *I* could have been running this whirlwind, I could have been directing this storm, instead of just talking about it."

Last time I will ever ask you that!

M.C.: No, Bill, I don't think about that. I think a lot about how *lucky* I am. And the older and closer I get to the ultimate accounting, the more I think about how good this country has been to us, to our family. I think about how I can make my contribution. I am all over the country; I do give speeches—and they are not all for money, incidentally, O'Shaughnessy. But I do give as many as I can. I do speak my piece and try to make my case in the hope that it will help a little to advance the dialogue in this country, and be a contribution. I want desperately to be as useful as I can be.

I don't think I had the stuff to be a president. I really don't. I know what I am good at, and I know what I can do. The notion that you are smart enough, wise enough, and strong enough to run the whole place, to do the most powerful job in the world. . . . George Bush had the confidence for that position. John Kerry certainly did. But not all of us feel that way about our own abilities.

W.O.: Is there some "missing gene" that held you back?

M.C.: No, but I'll tell you this. Unless you end this interview now, you're going to be missing a very important appointment—and perhaps something else, O'Shaughnessy!

W.O.: Who is going to win? Here we are, late afternoon on Election Day, as the shadows lengthen over Westchester. Prediction, Governor Mario Cuomo?

M.C.: You know who *my* choice is.

W.O.: And you know who *mine* is!

M.C.: I do know. And we can *both* win, Bill. It would depend on how America responds to the leadership of the next president. If we're willing to work to come together, then we will all win. Whether it is Bush or Kerry. And that is what we should be praying for.

W.O.: You're picking Kerry. I am picking Bush. Do you want to make a bet right now?

M.C.: What do you want to bet, O'Shaughnessy?

W.O.: Well, I don't know. . . .

M.C.: If *I* win, I want to interview *you*! And I want you to answer all my questions the way you expect me to answer all your questions. How is that?

W.O.: All right, sir.

M.C.: Prepare yourself for some real shots, O'Shaughnessy!

W.O.: The good part is that no matter who wins, you will still be there, to remind us, to urge us forward.

M.C.: With all willingness!

W.O.: Thank you, Governor.

MEETING STEVE FORBES AND GOVERNOR MARIO M. CUOMO FOR "BREAKFAST AT '21'"

To get two different views on the economic situation of the time and the state of the presidency, we interviewed Steve Forbes, one-time presidential candidate, and Governor Mario Cuomo, who we continue to hope will run for the highest office in the land. These interviews were broadcast from the "21" Club in New York on February 11, 2004.

WILLIAM O'SHAUGHNESSY (W.O.): Steve Forbes, as we listen to you at "21" this morning, we have to say that "President Forbes" has a nice ring to it. Have you gotten that out of your system yet?

STEVE FORBES (S.F.): The *voters* got it out of my system! And I'm not going to run for president again, but I am in a happy position now of being an "outside agitator," pushing things like tax reform and the like.

W.O.: But you were almost president, Steve Forbes. You took a good run at it four years ago. Are you sorry you didn't make it to the Oval Office?

S.F.: Well, it's much more fun, Bill, to win elections than to lose them. But the one thing I've learned and my siblings have learned from my father is that you always put the past behind you and look to the future. Life is a short trip. Don't get caught up in regrets, and always look toward tomorrow.

W.O.: Steve Forbes, I saw you talking to Mario Cuomo before your speech at "21" this morning. What the hell were you two talking about?

S.F.: We were plotting a takeover of the government! only kidding! But seriously, we were exchanging notes on the political scene. He obviously has been a major player in politics. I was very interested in what he had to say about the Democratic race.

W.O.: Mr. Forbes, does *Forbes* magazine endorse candidates for president?

S.F.: We make our favorites known. I endorsed President Bush when he ran four years ago and expect to again this year.

W.O.: How do you think he did with Tim Russert on *Meet the Press*?

S.F.: I was delighted that he realized he's got to get out there and get his case across. And I think the president is going to be even more effective in the future. If you read the transcript of the interview, you'll see it wasn't bad. But if you watch the visuals, he was obviously very uncomfortable. He's not accustomed to doing that. But on the following Monday, when he went out to talk about the tax issue, he was like Harry Truman, feisty and on fire. So I think he knows he's got to get out there, get the message out, go on offense, and set the agenda.

W.O.: Steve Forbes, you said you were a "libertarian Republican." Your father used to call himself a Rockefeller Republican. What kind of Republican is President Bush?

S.F.: I think he's a "conservative Republican." He's more in the Reagan mold. I'm a great admirer of Ronald Reagan. Bush has got to convince people his policies and principles are the best way to move ahead. It's not a negative approach. It's the "Reaganesque," positive approach.

W.O.: Steve, I guess nobody knows the economy like you and your magazine. Do you think the economy can save President Bush?

S.F.: I think the economy will be a major factor in helping President Bush. As the year goes on and people begin to feel that the recovery has legs and is for real, I think that will be a big plus for him.

W.O.: I would be stupid if I had the opportunity and didn't ask you: What are some good stock tips, some categories, at least for this day and age?

S.F.: We've got some very good recommendations in the new issue of *Forbes* magazine, Bill. And I'll give you a special discount on a subscription! (*laughter*)

WILLIAM O'SHAUGHNESSY (W.O.): Governor Cuomo, I saw you talking with Steve Forbes earlier before his speech. What would Steve Forbes and Mario Cuomo be talking about?

GOVERNOR MARIO CUOMO (M.C.): Well, Steve Forbes was doing the talking, and I came to listen. And what he was talking about was the economy. And whether you're a Democrat or if you think of yourself as progressive—as I do—or Republican or conservative, the economy has to be one of the top three issues you always have to deal with. I know a lot about Forbes and where he stands. He is marvelously clear in what he has to say. And he is a good representative of the conservative economic doctrine. If I had to express a bit of a disappointment about the presentation, it would be the tendency of the conservatives to talk about the *system*, dominantly, and not so much about its effect on the *people*. They'll talk about how well businesses are doing, but they won't talk about how well 160 million workers in this country are doing when your business is thriving because it's sending work overseas. *My* emphasis is just the other way around. Of course, the economy is important. But the purpose of the economy should be to serve people.

W.O.: Governor, Steve Forbes says the economy is coming back.

M.C.: Let's remember what the economy is. The economy literally is the production of goods and services, distributing them and getting them consumed. People buying tickets on airlines, people buying clothes, etc. The economy is good when you do a lot of that. When you produce a lot of goods and services, you sell a lot of it, and you make a profit doing it. When that's happening, businesses are doing better. Shareholders in those businesses, therefore, are doing better.

Now the *question* is: What about the *workers*? What about the poor people? What about the people who don't own businesses and don't own a whole lot of shares? People say half or more of the American public now have shares. That's a false number. You can have a terrific economy, but all the jobs are going to Malaysia, Mexico, China, India. Even high-skilled jobs. And your people can be poor—35 million of them. The average wage is only $42,000, and it goes up 1 percent a year. And the costs go up in multiples of that. That's the part of the case I emphasize. Any help for the workers has to be sound economically. But to say the economy is doing well without saying whom it is benefiting and whom it is leaving out is an incomplete argument.

W.O.: Governor, he ran for president as a Republican. You were begged to run as a Democrat. They were knocking at your door and beating it down. Are you sorry you didn't run?

M.C.: No, Bill. There are a lot of big differences between Steve Forbes and Mario Cuomo. One of the biggest was he didn't have a legislature and a job as governor at the time he was being asked to run. He didn't have that commitment. If I had been free at the time, then they wouldn't have been asking me. But Steve decided to run. Of course, he was free to. He was running a company that could run itself. I was running a state. I couldn't run unless I left the job, quit and turned it all over to the lieutenant governor—which is a violation of the implicit commitment I made when I won the election. That was the difference between me and him.

Do I have any regrets? No. Let me tell you how easy it is not to have a regret. That election was 1992. We wound up with Bill Clinton. And we got eight years of the finest economy in our history. *And* a lot of "entertainment"! (*laughter*)

W.O.: Governor, what about the Democratic nominee? It looks like it could be John Kerry.

M.C.: John Kerry has a very good chance of becoming president, in my opinion. But we have to add, with what has happened so far, that we now have to come with a positive case. The fire in the Democratic Party now is the enthusiasm about getting rid of Bush. They just don't like this president. That will motivate them. But we are not entitled to win on that alone. Nor *should* we win without coming with a *positive* case to show how we're going to bring a different kind of government. And to show whom it's going to benefit, the old-fashioned way. And that's what we have to do now. Right now, Kerry is winning on the basis of the appearance of his "winnability" over Bush, but without reference specifically to what his issues are and how he's going to describe them. That's what we have to do. The *positive* case.

W.O.: "President Cuomo": Have you gotten that out of your system yet?

M.C.: I never had it in my system, O'Shaughnessy. I never even once considered it until they told me to give it a good look in 1992. For all those years it was an issue—and it was a long time—I said the same thing: "I have no plans to run for president. And I have no plans to *make* plans." And then the reporters said to me, "Then why don't you just say, 'I absolutely won't run'?" I said, "If I say that, you will then start asking, 'Why won't you run?' And I will tell you the truth. And you won't believe it. And you'll make up stories, which—you'll recall—is precisely what happened when I finally said, 'I cannot run.'" But I never once teased them or said I might or that I was looking at it until October 1991.

I then said, "I'll take a good look." I took a good look. It took five weeks. I came back and said, "I can't do it because the Republicans will not give me a budget. And that means I'd leave here, and the next day we'd be in trouble economically and the *New York Times* would run a headline and my campaign would be over."

W.O.: You know, in this day and age, not too many people believe that story: that you would keep your commitment, stay at your post, and not seek the presidency because of a cockamamie budget.

M.C.: A cockamamie budget? And then 18 million New Yorkers whom you swore to help as governor would be left with schools closed, with no money to pay the police department, etc. No, it's not a cockamamie thing, Bill.

It's easy to think, "Well, what the heck! We're talking about the presidency." And what could be more important than the presidency is your job that you swore to do as governor of the state of New York. And incidentally, unless you say to yourself, "Look, there's nobody out there as good as I am to run this country," then you shouldn't even give it a second thought.

W.O.: You know, a lot of people tried to tell you that.

M.C.: And if I believed it, you should have put me in an institution. And I have some bad news for you, O'Shaughnessy. Don't *you* start thinking *you're* the guy either!

W.O.: You're impossible. It's too early to try arguing with Mario Cuomo at this hour of the morning. But seriously, don't you have a website up there that's being bombarded with pleadings and importunings that you run for president right now in 2004?

M.C.: I did until recently, but then I ended it. I took down the website.

W.O.: Why?

M.C.: Because unless I kept up with it every day, it would get stale. And that started happening. And I just don't have the time to update it all the time. And I don't want a website that has speeches in it that I gave three months ago when so many different things have happened since then.

W.O.: Once more, I didn't lay a glove on you.

CHRIS MATTHEWS, "BREAKFAST AT '21'"

Known for his no-nonsense approach and MSNBC political commentary, Chris Matthews has been the host of "The Chris Matthews Show" on NBC since 2002. He spoke at the "21" Club on October 2, 2007.

BRIAN MCGUIRE: Welcome to "21." It's October in New York, and that means post-season baseball in the Bronx and "wait until next year" in Queens. (*laughter*) This is another in our series of breakfasts at "21." What began as a VIP program ushering in the millennium is now in its tenth year. Many of our distinguished speakers return as guests, and our special guest today is Chris Matthews, host of "Hardball with Chris Matthews," which just celebrated its tenth anniversary on MSNBC. In addition to "Hardball," he also hosts "The Chris Matthews Show" and is a contributor to NBC's "Today" show. One of America's most acclaimed journalists, Chris has covered American presidential election campaigns since 1988.

CHRIS MATTHEWS: Is this on the radio? I see Bill O'Shaughnessy here. I have to be somewhat careful. Thank you, everybody. Thank you, Your Honor. Thank you, Governor. Hey, didn't Jay Kriegel run this place once? Anyway, I want to talk about what is happening right now in the presidential election of 2008, the particular moment we are in on October 2, 2007. And I won't give you what I did on television.

It seems to me every presidential election we all grew up with had one fundamental reality you could see in your rearview mirror as you got further away from it. But you had a hard time realizing it at the time. It's the kernel, the core, the nut of the campaign.

In 1952, for example, the first election of which I have any recollection, all the Catholic kids were starting to go Republican. Everybody had "I like Ike" buttons on the school bus, except for poor Mike Matthews, my friend, who was the son of the Democratic Committee leader. He stuck with [Adlai] Stevenson. But that election was about an era, about the Korean War, in which we were stuck. We were not exactly losing it. We're slogging our way up the peninsula—and some of the guys here this morning were there—and we're winning. But boy, what a bloody campaign. Nobody liked the war. And they hoped to forget it as fast as they could.

So we wanted to get out of that frozen place, where everyone was wearing earmuffs and their guns were freezing. And Ike said, "I will go to Korea." He's the guy who received a Nazi surrender, and whose grandson, David, once said, "Once you receive the Nazi surrender, even being president is no big deal." We had a problem, and we had a solution. We had Korea, and we had Ike. And when you look back, it's simple. There are a couple of campaigns that stand out that way. Very clear problems and clear solutions. Not that the solutions were permanent. But they were good at the time, for the era.

In 1960, it looked like Ike was losing a few steps, and we kids thought he definitely lost a few steps during the U-2 situation. Because of that, because of *Sputnik*, and because of Cuba, it looked like we were losing a few steps in the Cold War. In fact, the great American movie *North by Northwest* captured that feeling with Leo G. Carroll, who plays a CIA agent, saying, "Why do we have to have women like this play undercover agents, to become mistresses of bad guys like the Communist" played by James Mason? Someone says, "Well, maybe we should be losing the Cold War." And Leo G. Carroll, the agent, says, "Well, I'm afraid we are doing a good job doing that." At the time, there was a sense of drift, of losing place, of losing the Cold War.

So we brought in John Kennedy, a smart Cold Warrior, the youngest president ever elected. We solved the problem of age with youth. That's what we do. We are professional democrats, lower case. We solve problems with presidential elections. So try if you might, I am not getting into the war issue. I can fight with it all day. We can all fight about the war in Iraq. But what is the problem now?

Certainly in 1976 it was the corruption of Watergate. Jimmy Carter had never been to Washington, and he did not know anybody. That's what we wanted: absolute virginity. And he was a great guy—not a great executive, but a great guy. I worked for him. By the time it was 1980, we wanted strength and brought in Reagan with his ideological certitude.

In 2000, although we will argue about this the rest of our lives, we saw a problem: Monica! From the day this president we have now started in New Hampshire—I was there under a tent for every speech he gave—he was the solution to a problem, which was Monica. He says when a man takes an oath to the office of the presidency, to the Constitution, he must also promise to uphold the dignity of the Oval Office.

Every single American knew exactly what he meant when George W. Bush said I go to bed with my wife at 9:30 every night. It seems informal now, stupid perhaps, but he was offering himself as a direct *solution* to a *direct* problem.

So now we get to the year 2008: What is the *problem*? And what do we see happening in this campaign?

The press people, like me—bored, cynical reporters covering this campaign—form our attitude about whether this is wrong or right. Now what seems to me to be the problem with America today—and I'll be very non-ideological about this—is that we feel *stuck*. That's my word for it. We are stuck without any exit strategy from any of our problems. We feel we're in a quagmire, stuck in the desert; the wheels are spinning; we are getting deeper into the sand. The more effort we give, the deeper we get. That's what we feel like.

It's in the polling out today about the president, about the direction of the country. We feel stuck. Stuck in Iraq. We do not imagine getting out under any circumstances for years to come. Iran seems inevitable. We are going go to war with that country, and it is going to be a mess.

No matter which way we go with it—whether we pull back, go forward, or hit them tactically—it's a mess. We will go after their weaponry, if we can even find it. Then Israel gets involved. We are stuck in that track right now.

The American people feel *stuck* now. That is a *problem* that requires a *solution*. It requires not improvement, not modification, not caution, not more bravado—I can't tell Rudy enough times, not more bravado! What we need is deliverance to a new way of looking at the future, a new way of getting through our problems with the Third World, with Islam, with radical Islam, with terror Islam. All we have to deal with is massive, and we never had to deal with something so complicated. Certainly the Soviet Union and the '40s, '50s, and '60s were complicated, but not as complicated as this. The problem today requires a mind, it requires street smarts, it requires moxie, someone who listens, and someone who does not live on a ranch! (*laughter*)

I want to get to what's going on and why I set it up in terms of a problem looking for a solution, and how the definition of the solution comes right out of the problem itself and why this election will find clarity by next November. First of all, what is happening the last couple of days is fascinating. Watch the press when it gets bored. It's like a herd of cattle. Remember old cowboy movies like *Red River*. The herd is restless and spooked. The men were careful going for the sugar for fear of making the tin pans drop and scaring the cattle. MOO!! You know they are going crazy out there! So the herd is the restless press right now. Mario Cuomo knows what I'm talking about. The mood of boredom is the most dangerous state the press can be in.

We've just gotten to what Churchill would call the end of the beginning of this campaign. A couple of days ago it came with Hillary and her five-star performance on Sunday. If she had gone on TV against Tim Russert, he would have held her even. He's loaded for bear; she's loaded for bear. They go at each other three or four times with follow-up questions. I've learned in this business I can go four times. Tim can go three times. You can only go at it three or four times. And if you don't get the answer, she slips by and you have to live with it. But if Tim held her to a tie, he would have won.

But when she ties five guys on a panel, she wins. It reminds me of Groucho Marx in *Horse Feathers*: When he could not sell his Tootsie Fruitsie Ice Cream, he said, "Okay, I'll fight any man in the house for a dollar!" It's like what Hillary was doing. I'll fight any man for a dollar. All five guys draw, but she wins. But something came out of that: the "cackle." Just write *this* down. This is the press, and this is what's going on with this campaign: the cackle!

Rudy Giuliani has been able to wow a lot of these cultural conservative groups; in fact, I have been hearing good stuff about Rudy for years from down South in places like Jackson, Mississippi; Atlanta, Georgia; anywhere businessmen meet. Businesspeople meet at lunchtime, and they're for Rudy. Not the church-bus crowd. The business-lunch crowd. Downtown, they love Rudy. They do not even know how to spell his name, but they love him. I'm not sure if I know how to spell his name. By the way, he's not Italian. He's a Yankee. That's how they look at things down there. You're a Yankee or a Southerner. But they love him because he's tough, and they love the street smarts and the crime record. They don't know about Bernie Kerik. So what did Rudy get in trouble for? He does the NRA, and they look at him like tissue rejection. Who is this guy? This city mouse talking to the country mice. They all got guns. Imagine going in the room where everyone in the room was armed. I mean, everybody! Someone on my show said I love guys who stick their necks out because it gets them fired, and they go out with a good metaphor. Remember in *Animal House* the white kids went to the black bar, and they realize they are in strange territory and scared to death. This was like what happened to Rudy: "God, these guys are different," you know? So he takes a cell phone call from his wife! (*laughter*)

When I went out covering campaigns with my New York friends, I would say, get rid of that goddamn phone! Don't let anybody in this local restaurant see you with that phone! They see you as the enemy. That's like the instrument of death. Don't do that to people. Attend to them. I used to say to my wife, I call you to get your attention, because you will take the call. Rudy takes the call: I'm Gotham, and you're nothing! I get the message.

Hillary promises a softer, maybe a Hubert Humphrey approach to the Vietnam War; not a McGovern, not a hawk, not a [Henry] Scoop [Jackson], but something comfortable, vaguely in the middle, that won't offend anybody. She reminds me of Archie Andrews in the comics. It's always Betty and Veronica. I can't decide if in every one of her speeches she is the hawk. Yeah, I'm not going to talk with Ahmadinejad. Yeah, I'm going to sign on to the latest petition, I'm going to bring the troops home. I can't figure her out. Is she a hawk? A dove? What is she?

She's *smart* because she is keeping everyone vaguely happy. She is keeping the interest groups all vaguely happy. Nobody's thrilled. Nobody is *inspired* by Hillary Clinton. Everybody is *impressed* with her. She is a professional pol, and she's good at it. That's one scene the press does not like, because it's good. It's too good.

Rudy, on the other hand, promises more bravado, and we had a lot of that in the last seven years. Rudy promises a lot more of it, but no real change in policy. He hired Norm Podhoretz, the kid. I like the old guy. He is definitely with the hawks, with the John Bolton mustache. This guy is staying the course with More Bush Policy. So you have to wonder what's going on here.

The cackle is interesting. When Hillary cackled to Chris Wallace, I said great! Because when Chris Wallace from Fox Television asked, "Why you are so partisan?" the only answer is a cackle! This was the only appropriate response I can think of: a *cackle*! A few weeks before, he had nailed Bill Clinton. Remember Bill ended up, which he rarely does, showing his attitude toward someone, and he was pointing that finger into his knee. He was really coming back on that guy, so that was an appropriate cackle. But then I found out that she cackled to Bob Schieffer, which made no sense at all!

And then I found out that Rudy has intruded forty times on major meetings or speeches to take a call from Judith! Forty times! I think Judith likes it, like I think nobody else does. Nobody else does it like one of the guys on Broadway in a theater.

I want to kill these people: They just let their phone ring because they think nobody notices it, as if to say if I reach for it and they'll know it's me. They know it's you! So they just let those actors die out there. F. Murray Abraham finally had to work it into his act the other day. I'm with the actors, but I'm not with Rudy on this one. I do not know if he is going to stop or not. If she stops cackling, you will know it. If she keeps cackling, we will keep attacking her. She can't win on this point. She can't win on the cackle. And he better stop taking the calls.

The American people are behind the press on this without thinking very much about it. Because they want these campaigns to contest the issue of who will deliver us to a better future. The way Ike did in '52, the way Jack Kennedy did with the New Frontier, the way Reagan did with the Reagan Revolution. Every great presidency has begun with promise of deliverance, some new hope. Jack Kennedy's theme song was "High Hopes," the Sinatra song. Roosevelt's was "Happy Days Are Here Again"; Clinton's was "Don't Stop Thinking About Tomorrow" by Fleetwood Mac. Every presidential campaign had a *tune* of hope. Al Smith's was the "Happy Warrior."

We know how complicated it is. But we want a leader with a well-founded optimism about changing the direction of where we are, so we don't have one war after another. Some *solutions*, some *vision*. That's what we are looking for. Neither of the front-runners is offering it right now. That's because they are both playing it cautious.

Rudy has beat the odds, he's beat the spread, he has been very successful. Although if you look at his numbers over the years, they've gone down. Fred Thompson, who has shown nothing, had gone up because they are still out there looking for someone who might offer something different. [Mitt] Romney's not doing much. Although he got the front cover of *Newsweek*, I predict it will be their lowest-selling issue ever. I don't want to know more about Mitt Romney. I'm not interested in the "Mormon Journey."

Thompson is fascinating only because here's a guy that has nothing to show, really. He was a senator with no record. The only thing he did was hold investigations on Clinton fundraising.

He's the only guy in the world that could make nothing of something. He had everything, the Lincoln Bedroom. He had Motel 6, the money coming in and out. He managed to get nothing out of it. John Glenn beat him. (*laughter*)

When I think about Fred Thompson, I think about those cowboy westerns where they have the storefronts along Main Street with the saloon on one side, and the general store on the other, but they are just propped up with two-by-fours when you see a long camera shot. I keep thinking, if I walk through the saloon doors of Fred Thompson, I am going to end up in the desert. (*laughter*) Wow! Ain't nothin' back here! But I don't know, because we have not bothered to go through the saloon doors yet. He's not grabbing us to do it. Maybe he should keep the doors up through December. We all say it looks good because he is on television and the stupid Democrats always say yeah, he's a movie star—like that's a put-down—while we are politicians. You know they don't get it. People like movie stars more than they like politicians!

Have you read the papers lately? People know more about Britney than they do about any of the politicians. Rudy has not grabbed people because Rudy is playing it too bravado, too tough. I think he has shown some street smarts and brains. I think his politics here in New York on crime in the beginning was breathtaking. I come up here with my kids. Rudy made it safe for everybody, and he did a great job on the subways. I think he was right with Crown Heights, and he handled himself very well on 9/11.

I'm on Jon Stewart's show tonight. I am going to rave about Rudy. Jon Stewart says he suffers from 9/11 Tourette's. (*laughter*) 9/11 falls into all of his sentences now. How come you have been taking phone calls from your wife on your cell phone? "Because ever since 9/11 we have been staying in very close touch." Rudy is sort of stuck there. But nobody is catching Rudy right now. If you poll people, the Christian Right people like Rudy because they consider security the number one issue right now. So Rudy can pull it off; he can surprise everybody. Hillary is playing it safe, very impressively. She's very likeable. I've met few politicians as good as she, remembering a lot about you when you meet. I think the parts of my new book *Life's a Campaign* you might find fascinating are the parts about the strengths and traits of politicians. Really good politicians have a couple of strengths in common. They really have an interest in people. They are not faking it. Hillary was there yesterday raving about my daughter at Penn.

Both these front runners are playing it too safe. One is just too bravado, the other one is just too slick. Hillary, all of a sudden, is going from the word "flawless" to the word "slick." This is the transfer you just don't want to make. She's morphing from the flawless candidate to the slick candidate. That is what I think she was trying to do with the cackle, showing she is not too diligent, not doing too much in all this. But she's fighting the problem of being the frontrunner right now.

I want to talk about the candidate I have always been fascinated with since day one, and why I think he needs to get his act together. He can still win this thing. And that's Barack. If you look at the papers today, he leads the well-educated people, he leads the liberals, and he leads with people further left from the Democratic Party. He leads the young people. I can tell from my family. When I was in Springfield [Illinois], it was the most inspiring moment in politics. Three degrees below zero, and there were seventeen thousand white people standing there cheering this guy in the frigid cold. And he comes in looking like the young John Kennedy, short hair on the sides, a skinny guy. He looked every inch the American hero. It just stunned me. I said, this was magical. And that was between where Lincoln was a young legislator, in that old capitol building, and where he was a law partner across the street in the second or third floor. This young guy, Obama, is the reality Lincoln wanted. This is America moving ahead. This is the opportunity. This is the African American guy with the interesting background. He is probably the best-read, most articulate candidate; He's smart, "textured right" to run for president, not a ghostwriter's candidate.

People went crazy for him, and then he did not do anything. He went to Oakland, went to Austin, went to all the liberal places, and got big crowds. He got a big crowd at Washington Square the other day. My own kid was down there.

Barack can do that. But he has not translated that into a real political movement. I was on with Joe Scarborough this morning, yelling to these twenty thousand people to start blog pieces. How come neoconservatives dominate our blog pages? Start writing articles, start calling up, and start working with campaigns. T-shirts don't win elections. Just go out and *do* something! Bloggers don't win elections. They cause trouble.

Obama has not been able to transfer that enthusiasm into an army, and I don't know why he hasn't. He has raised all this money. My recommendation to him is: Go after it.

If [John] Edwards wins in New Hampshire, and he can pull off Iowa, he can change this campaign from Hillary probably winning it. If you check Intrade.com, it's the Irish betting on Hillary. She is where the money is going. You have to bet a dollar to win 66 cents. The only other person close is Barack.

I don't know who is giving Obama advice. This guy has David Axelrod. He's got a gear loose. When he is on television he looks crazy, but I don't know how he is in the room. Hillary has got the best and brightest around her. She's got Mandy Grunwald, she's got Mark Penn. This guy Howard Wolfson is a fighter. The minute Obama says he is going to speak with Ahmadinejad, this guy is on my show the next day saying, "He wants to talk with a Holocaust denier?" This is hardball. He is dealing with the pros. These people make you pay, like Israel used to do; ten for one! You mess with me, we make you pay for it. Hillary runs a really tough campaign. Barack is up against a tough warrior. He has got to get in the ring with her. That's what he has not done.

On the other side is Rudy. I think Rudy still has the odds with him in this campaign. I have been predicting Rudy to my liberal friends in the media for two years, those who did not grow up in Republican families.

The difference between a Republican and a Democrat is something Democrats need to be taught, especially media people. Republicans like leaders. Democrats like meetings. Democrats need someone to be the "chair." They want a chair; they don't say chairmen, of course, rather, who's going to be chair? Hillary's always in a lunchtime meeting. And everybody's clapping at each other; I don't know what's going on at these meetings, but everybody is applauding about something. They are celebrating something really very good, and I'm not in on the party. She knows what she's doing.

Republicans are different. Somebody once said Democrats fall in love, but Republicans fall in line. Republicans like John Wayne. They like leaders, they like Ike. They like Reagan. Tell us what to do. Republicans, we do not want to read the papers, just tell us what to do. We do not want complications. I want to play golf on Saturday and Sunday, vote Republican on Tuesday, and go to church on Sunday. What else am I suppose to do? The Republicans do not want to engage in an intellectual process.

Maybe from Hillary the public senses more caution. From Rudy they sense a little more street smarts, a little more toughness. Rudy would have been in [New Orleans after Hurricane] Katrina. He would have been *there*. He may have been booed, but Rudy would have shown up at the convention center in New Orleans. Hillary would have been there; LBJ would have been there. All our great presidents would have been. And I think a lot of the public unease started with Katrina, with the sense that this guy [Bush] is on his ranch somewhere and somebody is giving him DVDs to tell him what he missed. (*laughter*)

I would like to ask you: Who was the chief of staff who did not walk in to say, "Mr. President, put down the near beer; we need to get on the road! There are people dying down there, and all they want you to do is show up and pass out water bottles and you will be a hero." Instead, they said: Maybe Thursday, we'll get down there. Just remember, when this president, with all his weaknesses today, showed up on September 14, that Friday at

Ground Zero, he was magical—he was King Arthur. He was capable of doing what a president should do.

He could *deliver* us from a *problem*.

And today we are looking for a president who can do the same thing. Show up at the site of a disaster and stand in rubble and say he can deliver us, or she can deliver us. When that moment of inspiration comes, we'll know this campaign is going places.

JOSEPH A. CALIFANO JR.

Our interview with Joseph Califano, broadcast on March 29, 2004, ranged widely over a long and illustrious career and the important work he's now doing to prevent addiction and substance abuse.

WILLIAM O'SHAUGHNESSY (W.O.): We're going to switch now to Morningside Heights, the National Center on Addiction and Substance Abuse at Columbia University. The man who runs that has done a lot of things in his time on this planet. He ran the White House for President Lyndon Johnson. I didn't know this, but they tried to get him to run for the U.S. Senate, after Senator Javits, of sainted memory. Jacob K. Javits left, and this man could have spared us Al D'Amato had he been persuaded to do that. They also wanted to run him for governor of New York.

He came out of Brooklyn and went right to the highest councils of this nation. His name is Joseph A. Califano. I should tell you he was also Secretary of Health, Education and Welfare (HEW).

He's written a new book called *Inside: A Public and Private Life*. You finally did it!

JOSEPH CALIFANO (J.C.): (*laughs*) Well, I spent four and a half years, and I really wrote this book for my kids. I wanted them to know what an incredible country this is. I knew nobody when I went to Washington—I was just a young lawyer in the Pentagon. I also wanted them to understand how important it is to have a moral compass, especially when you're exercising public power.

My moral compass was my Catholic faith. It's very important for people with enormous public power to have moral standards.

W.O.: Joe Califano, you run your own law firm, you were with some of the legendary Washington firms after you left the White House and Lyndon Johnson: Arnold and Porter and Edward Bennett Williams. You write a lot about it, you were like brothers.

J.C.: Well, we were. Ed and I became partners in 1971 and were partners for most of the '70s, until I went to become Secretary of

HEW, and we had a wonderful time. During that time I was counsel for the Democratic Party. I was also the counsel for the *Washington Post* during Watergate. As counsel of the Democratic Party, on the Tuesday after that Saturday break-in, I filed a lawsuit against the Committee to Re-Elect the President, accusing them of the break-in, of financing the break-in, and that lawsuit really produced the depositions and the information that helped Woodward and Bernstein enormously in finding out what was going on.

W.O.: So, you deposed a president. Early on, Joe Califano, did you know what you had?

J.C.: No. When I announced the lawsuit, Larry O'Brien, the chairman of the Democratic National Committee, was standing next to me and said, "This leads right to the White House." I said, "My Lord, Larry, how do you know that?" He said, "I know Nixon."

We found out that somebody had been bugging the National Committee long before the break-in. In the beginning Ed Williams said, "This is your lawsuit." And he was worried that it might have been a frivolous lawsuit. He used to tease me about it, and I wanted to get him interested in it. So I made an offer he couldn't refuse. I said, "Do you want to question John Mitchell in his deposition?"—the attorney general at that time. Ed just couldn't wait. He had three big black binders labeled Mitchell 1, Mitchell 2, and Mitchell 3, and he started questioning Mitchell. What Mitchell didn't know was that the black binders had nothing but blank sheets of paper in them, but [Ed] kept looking as though he had information and data. And the next day he said to me, "Boy, have we got ourselves a lawsuit." He said, "I don't know much about politics, but I know when somebody is lying, and John Mitchell had to hold his sides together to avoid wetting his pants."

Washington was a different place in those days.

W.O.: How so?

J.C.: I hired Al Haig when I was in the Pentagon to work with me on Cuban problems, and he talked to me all throughout Watergate and asked me if he should go over and be chief of staff because he was then Vice Chief of Staff of the Army. Of course, the question was: should he become Nixon's chief of staff? And we both said, "The presidency is important, and you can help save it."

W.O.: Joe Califano, didn't John Mitchell say something pretty colorful about one of your clients, Mrs. Graham, at the *Washington Post*?

J.C: Mitchell sure did. He said she would get her breast—that's not the word he used—[caught] in a wringer over this issue.

W.O.: What did you really think of Richard Nixon, whom you helped bring down?

J.C.: Well, I ultimately concluded that he really was a threat to the Constitution. When you think about what happened, the break-in to the psychiatrist office of Daniel Ellsberg, the break-in of the Democratic National Committee, turning the FBI off and using the CIA to follow reporters and other people, he really was violating constitutional principles. And remember, when the impeachment process began and they voted on a couple of counts of impeachment, it was Barry Goldwater and a couple of the Republican leaders who went over to Nixon and said, "Mr. President, you have to get out. You've got to resign for the sake of the country." And he did the next day.

I think the country was much better off because he was removed from office. Not just for him, but for other presidents. The temptation to use power is just enormous when you're in the White House.

W.O.: You've been around power, Mr. Secretary. Why weren't you ever persuaded to run yourself? You came close. I read that in your book, *Inside: A Public and Private Life*. I think you announced for the first time that you were damn near close to it.

J.C.: Well, you think about it a little bit, and friends of mine were urging me to run for the Senate from New York and use that as a stepping stone to run for the White House. But I didn't have it in my stomach. What you need to do is go out and raise all that money. All the pandering that is involved in all of that.

And the other thing was, at that time in my life, I was separated from my first wife and I was worried about my kids, because there is nothing you can do that will ease the pain for children of going through a divorce. I wanted to make sure I was there for them, and politics is too consuming. All you have to do is look at these people today. They have no lives. They start early in the morning and they go late into the evening, meeting people and raising money. The elected life was not a life I wanted.

W.O.: Mr. Secretary, in your book you write *your* life is really *our* life. How old are you now?

J.C.: Seventy-two. I'll be 73 on May 15.

W.O.: It's in the book, but who are some of the good guys? Who are some of your heroes?

J.C.: I think Kay Graham is clearly a hero. During Watergate, when the *Washington Post* was hanging out there alone, before any of the other media got interested, she stayed with it. She put her whole family and the family's fortune and paper on the line. If the reporters were wrong, they would have gone and gotten another job. If I had been wrong, I would have gotten another client. But if the *Post* were wrong, it was over for her. So I think she's one of the great heroes of this country, in all of its history.

I thought Edward Bennett Williams was a hero. One of our clients was the Teamsters, and Frank Fitzsimmons was the head of the Teamsters. Probably a quarter of our law firm worked for the Teamsters. Fitzsimmons came over to see Ed Williams, who had won every single case for the Teamsters, and said, "I don't think we could be represented by a firm that has a partner in it that is so frivolous that he'd file a lawsuit against the Republicans and the Nixon campaign committee." He left, and Ed called me down to tell me what happened. I didn't know what he was going to do. Ed said, "Years ago, Morris Sterns, the great constitutional lawyer, brought Frank Costello, the mobster, in to see me and asked me to argue his case to the Supreme Court to prevent him from being thrown out of the country. At one point Costello said, 'Are you Ed Williams, the guy that represented Senator Joe McCarthy?' 'Yes, I am.' And he said, 'I don't want to be represented by the guy who represented Joe McCarthy.'" And Ed told me he said, "Nobody picks my clients." Costello ultimately let Ed represent him, and Ed saved him. Then Ed turned to me and said, "That rule still goes; nobody tells us what to do."

The Democrats had no money to pay us, and in many cases they couldn't even meet our expenses. The Teamsters were a quarter of the income we made. When Ed told Fitzsimmons that, the next day Fitzsimmons ordered us to send all the files over to Chuck Colson, who had been a former Nixon counsel, and said that he was taking all the business away from us. Just think about where you would find a lawyer in a major law firm today who would do something like that if a quarter of their business was going to walk out the door. So I think he was a hero.

And Ben Bradlee.

W.O.: He was the big editor?

J.C.: He was the editor of the *Washington Post*, and he hung tough. There were some very tough nights.

And I think LBJ was a hero. People forget Lyndon Johnson was a revolutionary. He saved this country as much as [Franklin] Roosevelt did. When you stop and think about it, it was Lyndon Johnson who proposed and passed all the civil rights laws: the 1964 Law on Public Accommodations; the 1967 Voting Rights Act, which he said was to get people off the streets and into the voting booth; and the 1968 Fair Housing Act.

W.O.: He had you whispering in his ear, Joe Califano.

J.C.: Those pictures in the book. (*laughs*)

W.O.: Joe Califano, you worked very closely with him. Was Lyndon Johnson a coarse, crude guy?

J.C.: I think that's exaggerated. I think he was very dramatic. He really wanted to dramatize things. And he wanted to use every single minute of his presidency, so he worked all the time. He was tough, but he had a marvelous sense of humor. I'll give you an example. Do you remember Stokely Carmichael, the great firebrand black leader? After Dr. Martin Luther King was assassinated, I would bring reports to the president every couple hours from the FBI. We had violence; we had riots in one hundred cities that April. One report I brought to him said Stokely Carmichael was organizing a mob at the corner of 14th and U Street in Washington to march on Georgetown and burn it down. And Georgetown, as you know, is the section of Washington where all the TV anchormen and TV reporters and the liberal columnists lived.

And Johnson read that and said, "Damn, I've waited thirty-five years for this night." (*laughter*)

W.O.: You wrote a book on Lyndon Johnson. You've written ten books, at least nine.

J.C.: Ten.

W.O.: It's one of my favorite biographies. I think it's still in print, called the *The Triumph and Tragedy of Lyndon Johnson*. You have a wonderful vignette in there. You guys, the staffers, even cabinet secretaries, used to go down to his ranch, down by the Pedernales River, or whatever it was called. There were a lot of short guys, and he would move down to the deep end of the pool.

J.C.: Oh, the first weekend Lyndon Johnson asked me to be his assistant for domestic matters, I flew down to the ranch, and he was in the pool. He said, "Come on in the water." I get in the pool, we swim down to the deep end of the pool, he's 6 foot 3 and I'm 5 foot 10. He's got me in a place where I'm treading water and he's standing. And he starts poking on my shoulder and he says, "Now, the transportation system in this country is a mess. I want a new Department of Transportation. Can you get that done?" And then he says, "The cities, we need to show that we can rebuild the cities. I want a Model Cities Program." And then he says, "I want a Fair Housing Bill. I want it so the people, whether they're white, black, yellow, green, purple, or red can live wherever they want to live, every color." He jabs me in the shoulder and pushes me down and I hang on with everything I have. And he says, "Now, can you do that?" And I say, "Yes," having no idea how and hoping he won't push me down again.

W.O.: You were just trying not to drown.

J.C.: Right. As I got to know him, I knew he had intentionally picked that part of the pool, where he could stand and I had to tread water.

W.O.: Secretary Joe Califano, in your new book you write about how you left Washington and came up to New York. You took a new wife, and you write very movingly about Hillary Califano. Was it love at first sight?

J.C.: No, actually I got divorced. I was happy living alone; I thought I'd never marry again. I had a wonderful little house in Georgetown. I was practicing law, writing, still involved in politics and public policy. I met Hillary having dinner with her and Governor Carey and a bunch of other people.

W.O.: Hugh Carey.

J.C.: Hugh Carey, the former governor of New York, on the night of Reagan's inauguration. And then I saw her again in New York a few months later, and we had a wonderful dinner, and from that day on we talked to each other every day and then eventually decided to get married. I also tried to write in the book in more detail than I think anyone would like to read what it was like to get a Catholic annulment, and how important that was.

W.O.: Well, why didn't you just go ahead and marry her?

J.C.: Well, I did marry her in the Episcopal Church. I talked to several priests. I wanted to be able to receive communion because to me, Mass and communion were a very central part of my life.

W.O.: Did you go today?

J.C.: No, but I go every Sunday.

W.O.: Hillary is your new love interest, and I should say she came from a very well-founded family. Her father was the legendary William S. Paley, the titan of CBS. You're from Brooklyn. Did you ever meet Bill Paley, the father-in-law?

J.C.: Well, sure, of course. I went to see him to ask for his daughter's hand. I actually represented somebody he didn't like, Daniel Schorr, the CBS reporter, and he had to pay the bill because under Schorr's contract, CBS had to pay the bill. But I went over to see Bill Paley at his apartment. He has an incredible apartment at 820 Park Avenue. You walk in and the first thing that greets you when you get off the elevator is an enormous Picasso of a boy and a horse.

W.O.: Did you know what it was?

J.C.: I think I did know what that was. But then I went into the den, which was full of these Impressionist paintings, and I didn't know what most of them were, but they were Monets and Picassos, and they were incredible. We had breakfast. It was a very moving morning because his wife, the legendary Babe Paley, had died. She was clearly the love of his life, and when I told him I wanted to marry his daughter, he started talking about how much Babe had meant to him and how important it was to have a woman by your side. It was a very, very moving morning.

W.O.: Bill Paley was a titan, a legend. We still call him Mr. Paley. Even his best friends called him Mr. Paley. What did you call him, "Dad"?

J.C.: No, I called him Bill. (*laughs*) He was very happy about our getting together.

W.O.: You talk about having to go before the people who do annulments for the Roman Catholic Church. You seemed as nervous as if you were appearing before the Supreme Court or even the president.

J.C.: More nervous. It was interesting that it never occurred to me to get an annulment. I was comfortable in my conscience. I was married in the Episcopal Church. We were married happily. I was going to Mass and receiving communion, and then the pastor at Saint Ignatius Loyola Church in New York, a Jesuit Father, William Madres—he's still the pastor there—said to me, "You know, you mentioned to me a few times about being a divorced Catholic. You ought to get an annulment." I said, "That's ridiculous. I was married twenty-two years, I had three kids." He said, "Don't be so sure." And he said, "The Church really wants to find a way to heal in these situations." So he sent me down to see an incredible nun, Sister Amadeus McKevett, who worked at the Metropolitan Tribunal here on Third Avenue in the archdiocese. I went to see her, Sister Amadeus, and I'll never forget her. She was seventy-five years old and was very sprightly. She said, "Look, the Church wants to make you whole, the Church wants you to be married in the Church, and we're going to work on this." And she said, "What your view was, what your ability to understand all the rights and obligations of married life at the time you got married has nothing to do with what happened after you got married. We'll work on that." I was very skeptical when I first started. At one point she took me through the whole process and how it would work, and I laid it all out in the book. At one point she said to me, "The administrative cost you have to pay is $600.00," and I was surprised because I thought people paid thousands and thousands of dollars for a Catholic annulment.

W.O.: You thought it was sort of a payoff?

J.C.: Yes. And then she looked at me and misunderstood my surprise. She said to me, "If you don't have $600.00, you can pay it off in installments, or you can get your parish priest to write a letter. And if he says you can't pay, there is no charge." And I said, "No, Sister, I can pay the 600 bucks. I was just surprised that it was so little." And I went through the process of meeting with her, filing the papers, being interviewed by Monsignor Vella, who was then the head of the tribunal.

W.O.: Desmond Vella?

J.C.: Yes, Desmond Vella. It was really a beautiful experience. I am convinced that whole experience was very healing, not only for Hillary and me, but for my first wife and me and for my children, and indeed for Hillary's children. Everything changed.

W.O.: Joe Califano, did William S. Paley toast you at the wedding?

J.C.: I had represented Daniel Schorr, the CBS reporter who got his hands on the Pike Commission intelligence report. It was a report about the dirty tricks of the CIA and their illegal activities. CBS wouldn't run it, so Schorr gave it to the *Village Voice*, and Congress wanted to cite him for contempt. And Paley hated Schorr because Schorr had done a report out of Germany that was incorrect that said Barry Goldwater was going to meet with Nazis and neo-Nazis, and Paley wanted to do nothing to help Schorr.

W.O.: His own newsman.

J.C.: Right, he was a famous newsman. But in Schorr's contract, he had the right to pick his own lawyer, and he asked me to represent him before Congress. Everyone thought Schorr would be cited for contempt, for failure to reveal who the source of this secret report was. When we went before the committee—because it was on live television—all the committee members were there. And as we started to make the case as to why a confidential reporter's source should be protected, I detected the committee members changing their minds. Ultimately the committee voted 4–3 not to cite Schorr for contempt, and that was a major victory.

As we began to win, Dick Salant—who, if you recall, was the head of CBS News in those days—and Bill Paley issued statements about the First Amendment. They had been no help to us at all, and now [that] we were beginning to win, they jumped on the bandwagon.

I came back to my office the day after and there was a note from Ben Bradlee saying I was great, and right. So I said, because Paley was no help, I'm going to send him a hell of a bill. And I sent [Paley] a bill for $150,000.00, which was a lot of money for a couple of weeks' work in those days. And he was furious, but he had to pay the bill. But he never stopped complaining about it. And when he toasted me at the wedding, he said some nice things about me, but he started by mentioning that bill again! (*laughs*)

W.O.: You came up to New York, and instead of being a big powerful lawyer—you had lots of offers—you've been at Columbia University, Morningside Heights, at something called the National Center on Addiction and Substance Abuse. You've been there for ten years. Why? What are you doing there?

J.C.: I made money as a lawyer and I enjoyed practicing law, but I really wasn't fulfilled. And I thought to myself, "What should I do? Why did God give me this talent or celebrity or this Rolodex of people?" I looked around; addiction is a killer problem for this country and for our young people. I think it's implicated in every social problem we have. It's filling our prisons. . . .

W.O.: Alcohol or drugs?

J.C.: Alcohol and drugs and tobacco and prescription drugs and performance-enhancing drugs, all of them. The issue is addiction, not the substance. But alcohol is the most implicated in crime; drugs are too, to a large degree. Our prisons are full of people who have drug and alcohol problems that have committed violent crimes. In 90 percent of the rapes that take place on college campuses, alcohol or drugs are implicated. Tobacco and alcohol and drugs are responsible for filling more than half the hospital beds in this country, when you take into account cancer, respiratory diseases, kidney problems, accidents, broken backs, crushed heads, auto accidents. Seventy percent of the children in the child-welfare system are there because of drug- and alcohol-abusing parents. Most teens who get pregnant are high, one or both of them, when the act of conception takes place. One of the fastest growing parts of the AIDS population is intravenous drug users and their sexual partners.

I saw it at HEW when I started the anti-smoking campaign in 1978, and I was out there alone in those days.

W.O.: Mr. Secretary, how do you fix it? You've been dealing with this for ten years, so who would know better than you?

J.C.: We are seeing some progress. There is a decline in teen drug use and a significant decline in teen smoking. If you ask me, the most important thing we've learned in ten or twelve years is, first, this is all about kids. It's all about a child who gets through age twenty-one without smoking, without using illegal drugs, and without abusing alcohol. The child who gets through age twenty-one is virtually certain to never become an addict or an abuser.

And second, we understand the importance of parental engagement. Parent power is the most important and under-utilized weapon in this battle. This problem is going to be solved in the living room, in the dining room, across the kitchen table, and in the home, but not in the congressional hearing rooms and the jury rooms and the rooms of the executive offices of the governors and the president. This is a problem to be dealt with in the family.

W.O.: The kid says, "Leave me alone, you don't understand. Bug off."

J.C.: Yes, and you have to say, "I'm not bugging off, you're my kid." We started something, Bill, called Family Day, a day to have dinner with your children, the fourth Monday in September. Why? Because we survey teens every year, and what we found consistently is that the more often a teen has dinner with their parents, the less likely that child is to smoke, drink, or use drugs. Why? We do "focuses" with these kids. In this day and age, with two parents working and everything going on, they say, "My parents care enough to have dinner with me every night." They may gripe, "I don't want to have dinner tonight, I want to stay in my room," but it's important to do it because the kids know they're going to be seen every night. It's a wonderful opportunity to communicate. On every level, this is very important. We got President Bush to proclaim it, we got thirty-five governors to proclaim it, a couple of hundred cities and counties too, and we're going to really try and push it this year, as a symbol, like the Great American Smokeout. This is a symbol to remind parents of how important it is to have dinner with their kids. And believe me, it is important.

W.O.: You have all those governors and the president. Who is going to turn you down, Joe Califano? So you haven't given up on a whole generation. You still hope for young people?

J.C.: Oh, there is a lot of hope for young people. Remember, most young people don't use this stuff. You've got about 20 percent who smoke pot—and pot is more dangerous than it's ever been, it's stronger, it's more addictive—and in all the work we've done, we see it's a gateway drug: Kids who smoke marijuana are more likely to start using other drugs like heroin and cocaine and ecstasy.

I grew up in Brooklyn, in Crown Heights, right by Bedford-Stuyvesant; as I wrote in the book about the neighborhood in those days, there were no drugs there. We have to get back to that way, the way this country was. And we will. I believe we work hard here at the National Center on Addiction and Substance Abuse at Columbia to get information out. I believe we have the brightest group of people that ever worked on this problem, but there are thousands of Americans that will have even better ideas. If Americans get the information, they'll do something about it.

W.O.: The book is called *Inside: A Public and Private Life* by Joseph A. Califano Jr., and it's got a red and black cover and is put out by a brand-new publishing house called Public Affairs. I saw people fighting over it at Borders, and it's a great book. It's a history of our time, I think, and a very touching, revealing memoir by someone whose career we followed in every season of his life.

Joe Califano, what do you want to be remembered for? This is a very personal, moving book. You were a power lawyer, an advisor, counselor to a president, a cabinet officer. What do you want on the stone?

J.C.: I want somebody to say he did the best he could with the gifts God gave him. That's what I want to be remembered for.

COMPOSER–SONGWRITER–SALOON SINGER: MURRAY GRAND AT EIGHTY-FIVE

I've always had a great affinity for saloon singers, those minstrels of the night who sit in a pencil spotlight astride an out-of-tune piano, whispering sweet importunings into the barroom gloom. Billy Joel described this dwindling breed quite brilliantly in his classic "Piano Man." They are different from grand cabaret singers who emote and perform for well-heeled swells in the few remaining upscale venues like the Carlyle and Michael Feinstein's at Tisch's Regency. Out of town, of course, these bards of loneliness and longing are called lounge singers. By any name, they're very special—all who croon the blues in near-empty rooms on lonely boulevards of broken dreams in busted-out cities.

My favorites of the genre include Matt Dennis, the composer and Sinatra pal ("Angel Eyes," "Let's Get Away from It All," "Violets for Your Furs"), and the regal, incomparable Mabel Mercer. Even the great Sir Richard Rodney Bennett loved to set aside his laurels and adopt the mantle of a saloon singer of an evening. His own composition "I Never Went Away from You" is a haunting and lovely ballad, perfect for a nocturnal audience. And some years ago I gave the eulogy at St. Monica's Church in Manhattan for wonderful, classy Hugh Shannon, who, in his smoking jacket and velvet slippers, was best described by the "ladies who lunch" and the international set as a "society" singer. However, his last album was called, appropriately and simply, "Saloon Singer." Hugh knew who he was, and so did more than a thousand tony admirers who came to his funeral.

As I said, it's a dying breed. But I'm glad Darryl Sherman and Ronnie Whyte and Christyne Andreas and Marlene VerPlanck and Peter Mintun and diva-like K. T. Sullivan are still around. And Danny Nye at Bruno Selimaj's Club A Steakhouse on East 58th Street in the great city can still light up the night. The magnificent Bobby Short left the stage a few years back, and society dames and their walkers still mourn his passing. But Tony Bennett is still around to sing the classic American songbook. Murray Grand played in this league too. And although he now plays celestial melodies too, I interviewed him late in his career, on October 13, 2004.

Murray Grand looked like Ed Koch. His eyes had a mischievous twinkle to them, and he delivered his witty and mournful ballads in a breathy croak.

But you got the point as he sang of our lost loves and the diminishments we all suffer.

WILLIAM O'SHAUGHNESSY (W.O.): We're going to switch now to Fort Lauderdale. First of all, is it sunny?

MURRAY GRAND (M.G.): It is today, which is rare. During the last three weeks, it was mostly rain and hurricanes. It was terrible, but today is beautiful.

W.O.: The voice we're hearing is the voice of one of the great composers, one of the great men of the theater—and I think of him as my favorite saloon singer: Murray Grand.

"Guess Who I Saw Today?" Does that sound familiar?

M.G.: I think so. I think somebody called Murray Grand wrote it.

I was going to Julliard when I wrote that. I literally wrote that song for a class. They were very impressed. I wrote that and "Thursday's Child" during those days.

"So I thought I'd stop and have a bite when I was through/I looked around for someplace near/when it occurred to me where I had parked the car/with the most attractive French café and bar/a little place not very far/and then, guess who I saw today?"

W.O.: Eydie Gormé made that a big hit.

M.G.: Actually, in truth, Nancy Wilson outsold Eydie, by far.

W.O.: Are you still making money on that, Murray Grand?

M.G.: Oh, yes! (*laughter*)

W.O.: You get a little check every month?

M.G.: Yes. Unfortunately, it *is* a little check. Sony sends the bigger checks; ASCAP sends the small ones; but Sony owns it now.

W.O.: When did you move to Florida?

M.G.: Seventeen years ago.

W.O.: Why? You're a New York guy.

M.G.: I had friends that moved down here. And I wanted to retire—in my head. I'm mad about animals and wanted to open a pet food store, which did not do so well because I'm not a businessman. I opened like a Ma and Pa store with my friend and his wife, and it failed after three years. It was a bad location. And that was it.

After I was down here for a while, I ran into June Taylor, who knew me indirectly through "The Jackie Gleason Show" and through Jimmy Shelton, the writer. And she said, "You've got to start doing the society shows." So I started helping her put together shows to raise money—a society-foundation thing. And that's how I got back in the business, playing down here.

W.O.: Murray Grand, can I be so bold? How old you are, sir?

M.G.: Eighty-five.

W.O.: Do you *feel* eighty-five?

M.G.: Unfortunately, most of the time I do, but I'm still getting around. I don't drive much anymore. Listen, eighty-five is eighty-five. I have a sister who's ninety-six, believe it or not.

W.O.: And you still *sit* at your piano of an evening?

M.G.: Well, I only do that one day a week. But I *have* to do that, I have to keep a finger in—and it gets me out of the house. And I enjoy it, because it's the one thing I do that's "social."

W.O.: You have thousands of fans in the New York area who remember back to the '70s and '80s when you used to play all over Manhattan at only swell bistros. Do you remember the New York days?

M.G.: Oh, I do, Bill. I've never forgotten; how could I? That was the best period of my life—that, and a short time in Paris and Rome, when I was very friendly with Bobby Short and Blossom Dearie.

W.O.: How many songs have you written, Murray Grand?

M.G.: Conservatively, I would say, to my knowledge, over three hundred. Maybe close to four hundred, but I'm not sure. I never sat down and figured it out. But I have written about five unproduced shows, minimum. I've written two with Patrick Dennis that never got on, and I wrote one with Gus Schirmer, *Don't Rush the Love*, that didn't get on. And I wrote one with Bob Elson called *Murder at the Gaiety*. And then I wrote a thing with Teddy Frings called *Fountain of Youth*. Unfortunately, none of those shows made it. The only shows that really went on were the ones with "New Faces," from '52 to '56. And I had some stuff in '68 and '72.

W.O.: You wrote "Guess Who I Saw Today?" What are some other Murray Grand songs we love?

M.G.: The most popular, I think, is "Thursday's Child"; and "After Time" had a lot of recordings.

W.O.: "Thursday's Child"?

M.G.: It was Eartha Kitt's signature number at that time, and she wrote a book called *Thursday's Child*, taking the title from the song. And, at that time, there was "Come by Sunday," which was getting played a lot. Jerry Southern had a big thing on it. And then "April in Fairbanks" has been done an awful lot. In fact, Mandy Patinkin recorded it about two years ago.

W.O.: "April in Fairbanks": How does that go?

M.G.: (*sings*) "April in Fairbanks/there's nothing more appealing/ you'll feel your blood congealing/it's April in Fairbanks." It's a comedy song, a takeoff on "April in Paris" and all the other April songs.

W.O.: Murray Grand, a friend of yours is playing right now in Manhattan, at Feinstein's: Cy Coleman. Remember him?

M.G.: Very well. I wrote many songs with Cy.

W.O.: Now, like the old line, did you write the *words* or the *lyrics*?

M.G.: (*laughter*) Yes, I wrote *both*. With Cy, when we collaborated, I always wrote lyrics. My favorite thing that we wrote together—and Sinatra was going to record—was a song called "Boozers and Losers."

It's the title of an album that was sung by Claire Hogan, who was a great jazz singer and a friend of Cy's and mine. And they did an album at MGM, I believe, in the old days. The whole thing was interesting because one side had loser songs and the other side had boozer songs; and I wrote the title song.

W.O.: You say it's a "social" thing for you to sit at a piano in the spotlight and whisper those songs. Nobody ever accused you of having the greatest voice.

M.G.: No way! But I *do* get the message across, which is the lyric. I think if you're doing songs, which have words, you have to tell the story. And if you have a great voice, sometimes you have a tendency to listen to yourself and forget about the message.

W.O.: Murray Grand, man of the theater, man of music, who are some of the great singers still around today? There's Tony Bennett. Who else?

M.G.: Tony's great. And k.d. lang, whom I've become a fan of recently—only when she began singing with Tony in his commercials. And I love Natalie Cole; I think she's just great.

W.O.: Is she as good as her old man?

M.G.: No one is as good as her old man. He's one of my favorite singers of all time, along with Sinatra.

W.O.: Who are the greatest crooners? You've got to give the first spot to Sinatra, right?

M.G.: Absolutely, no doubt about it. Sinatra is number one.

W.O.: And who else?

M.G.: Nat Cole. After that, I even like Julius La Rosa, if you remember him.

W.O.: He lives down the street apiece from us in Westchester.

M.G.: He does? I wasn't even sure he was alive.

W.O.: Yes, in Dobbs Ferry.

M.G.: As for women, it goes without saying: Ella [Fitzgerald] and Sarah [Vaughan]. But I think Mabel Mercer, in her own way, had more effect on people than anybody knew because singers would love to go hear her. Frank Sinatra learned so much from Mabel, as did Tony Bennett. So did many others who sat in the room entranced, even though her voice was gone completely by the time they got around to hearing her.

W.O.: It's almost like a cult following; she's been gone for years. And there's a guy in New York, Donald Smith, who tries to keep her legacy alive. Tell us about Mabel Mercer.

M.G.: Well, strangely enough, she was the one who recommended me for my first major job in New York, which was Spivey's Roof at 57th and Lexington. Liberace had been playing there, but he had gotten an offer at the Waldorf, and off he went to pursue a legendary career. Spivey had called her friend Mabel and asked if she would audition the piano players because she wasn't sure what she wanted and how good one could be. And Mabel selected me, which is how I got my first job. She was charming.

I had heard Mabel earlier, before I went overseas as a soldier, and she was a high soprano in those days. But she developed a cancerous situation in her throat, and she had an operation. After that, she was no longer a soprano; she would just practically speak the words. But she developed a style of drama that related the story. It was very engrossing—and most singers don't do that. A lot of singers just listen to themselves.

W.O.: Murray Grand, in her last years, didn't Mabel Mercer used to sit up there in a big wingback chair?

M.G.: Yes. As a matter of fact, my memory of her is going to her eighty-fifth-birthday party, given at the Guggenheim Museum; and I'll tell you, every celebrity in the world was there. It was just amazing.

W.O.: She used to live alone in a house up in the Hudson Valley area, near Chatham, New York. She was a very religious woman.

M.G.: I don't think she was entirely alone. I mean that, in a sense, she was with Sam Beard,who was alive for a while and was her manager. It was strictly a platonic relationship, a business relationship. And he spent a lot of time up there. I don't know if he officially lived there, but he was there most of the time.

W.O.: Murray Grand, what about some of those guys who appeared of an evening when you were in Manhattan? My mind goes back to Hugh Shannon . . . .

M.G.: Oh, yes, he was fabulous. He was what we called a "society" player, and he worked on the Riviera and at the Bricktops in Rome. When he left, I replaced him, and Hubbel Pierce replaced me. Hugh worked very fancy jobs in New York and in the Hamptons. And I know you gave the gorgeous eulogy for him, Bill, at St. Monica's in New York.

W.O.: What's the difference, Murray Grand, between a society singer and a saloon singer?

M.G.: Well, there is no difference, basically, except society people worked in the upper class—like Bobby Short made sure he only worked in specific locations. A saloon singer will sing anywhere people are drinking.

W.O.: Bobby Short is still around. He'll be opening again—for about the hundredth year—at the Carlyle Hotel.

M.G.: As a matter of fact, his last performance will be January 1. I believe he's quitting. And they gave a big party for him at the Rainbow Room for his eightieth birthday about two weeks ago.

W.O.: Can you believe Bobby Short is eighty? He still has those beamish boy looks.

M.G.: And he's remarkable in that he doesn't read a note of music. But if you play something for him. . . . I remember I found a copy of a song called "That's Love" by Rodgers and Hart that Larry Hart's nephew brought to me; I had never heard of it—we didn't even know it was in print. And the song was never published in America. It was published in England. So I told Bobby about it and he said, "Oh my God, I want to learn it." He came to my apartment, and I played it for ten or fifteen minutes. After that he played it and sang it. He's amazing: He mostly plays on black keys, meaning he's in the key of G flat, which is a lulu to play in anyway.

W.O.: But they call him a New York treasure.

M.G.: Well, he is, absolutely; there is nobody else like him. He defined what he wanted to do and he found a market for it—he's great at marketing. And he only attached himself to the best-dressed, well-heeled people in town and that's where he went. And by God, he made it.

W.O.: And did you know Sylvia Syms?

M.G.: Oh yes. Sylvia and I were friends for quite a long time. As she got older, she got more desperate and more impossible. And I'll tell you about that. Cy Coleman went to see her when she was appearing at the Algonquin—and I forget who was playing, but it wasn't Mike Rienzi. Do you know Mike Rienzi?

W.O.: Sure I do.

M.G.: He's fabulous—one of my best friends. I talk to him every night. And he writes for "Sesame Street" and won awards for it.

At any rate, Cy went to see Sylvia, and he sent a note with the waiter, saying, "After the first set, drop by the table." And she got through and came down. When she got through talking to Cy, she said, "Cy, why don't you come up on stage and do a couple of numbers with me?" Suddenly, she started to heave, and she dropped on the floor and she never came back. They had to call the paramedics. And she died right there.

W.O.: On the stage?

M.G.: Right there at the table! At Cy Coleman's table. And irreverently he said later, "I asked her to drop *by* at the table. I didn't say drop *dead* at the table!" And that's a fact. (*laughter*)

W.O.: She was a pretty good singer, wasn't she?

M.G.: She was a marvelous singer, but an impossible person. As she got older, she got worse.

W.O.: She was built like a battleship.

M.G.: I went to Boston to play *Storyville* with her, and after that engagement she was really terrible. She made a mistake or forgot the lyrics, and she turned around and stared at the piano player like it was his fault. It didn't matter which piano player it was.

I went to see Mike Rienzi at the 92nd Street Y, and they were doing a big program with Rex Reed. I forget who it was dedicated to, maybe Rodgers and Hart. Well, by God, I went back to congratulate them on the show and I hear this screaming and yelling, and I opened the door to their dressing room. Mike Rienzi had broken a chair; he had the leg in his hand and was about to hit her over the head with it. (*laughter*)

W.O.: You know whom I talk to once in a while? Rex Reed. He lives in Roxbury.

M.G.: Well, I'm in touch with him because of Linda Levinson.

W.O.: Murray, why don't you do a book?

M.G.: I did do a book. But I didn't mention these names. It's called *Guess Who I Saw Today?* but it was never in print.

W.O.: Where is it now?

M.G.: Right here in my apartment. A lot of people have copies that I made for them. I'll send you a copy. I don't care about the money. I would just like to see it get published.

W.O.: We talked about Mabel Mercer's cult following. . . . I don't want to embarrass you, but you have a cult following too, whether you know it or not. Do you do know that?

M.G.: Well, sure. It's been so long since I've worked in New York that a lot of the people I knew are gone.

W.O.: Would you ever be persuaded to come up and do a few nights?

M.G.: It would seem unlikely because I don't travel well by plane, you know, with emphysema. Don Smith is forever asking me to do the Mabel Mercer shows every year. He does the cabaret shows at the theater. And I did the very first one at Town Hall; Don Smith had organized it.

W.O.: But you still play one night a week in Fort Lauderdale.

M.G.: Just three hours.

W.O.: Those lucky people. Murray Grand, are Florida audiences different from New York audiences?

M.G.: Yes.

W.O.: How so?

M.G.: They're not as informed. You have to remember, when I was playing in New York in the '50s and '60s, it was the center of show music. Show music as we knew it has changed so much. You can't compare the score of *Hairspray* with anything that Rodgers and Hammerstein wrote; it doesn't wash. . . .

W.O.: No pun intended. (*laughter*)

M.G.: Also, *Urinetown* or *Rent*—scores like that, which rarely have songs in them that you can play or perform outside of the show. But they are commercial to a younger audience, and that's where the trend has been going. I think it's turning around a little bit. For a long time, most clubs in New York didn't hire people who did the kind of material I do.

W.O.: When you write a song, Murray Grand, do you start with the music or with the lyric?

M.G.: Lyric. Always.

W.O.: The words come first?

M.G.: Yes. I get an idea for the words, and then I find a melody almost instantly that will fit it.

W.O.: Where do you get the ideas for the lyrics?

M.G.: Well, it varies. One song I wrote, "I Was Beautiful," I wrote sitting on a park bench in Central Park after I came out of my therapist's office, who was trying to convince me to like myself. Alice Ghostley sang it.

W.O.: How does it go?

M.G.: "I woke up this morning and, lo and behold/I was beautiful. My face was the face of a twenty-year-old/and I was beautiful." This goes on and on, and at the end she's under arrest because she forgot to get dressed. (*laughter*) She's so beautiful that she didn't put any clothes on!

W.O.: Then you go to the music. Where do you find the music, still on the park bench?

M.G.: That comes naturally. A lot of times I almost write the lyrics and the music simultaneously. With "Boozers and Losers," I wrote a complete lyric for Cy, and in order to feel my way through it, I gave it a fake melody because I knew he wasn't going to use it. And when I went in to see him, I did not sing it. I just gave him the lyric. It was a very long lyric and a long song, and he set it to music.

A lot of times it's neck and neck, but a lot of times, I write the complete lyric first.

W.O.: It's a wonderful visit with a legendary man of music. We've almost been sitting on a park bench—do they have such a thing in Fort Lauderdale?

M.G.: Yes, they do, strangely enough. But one park I know is filled with drug dealers, so I don't sit there.

W.O.: Do you walk along the beach?

M.G.: Yes, the beach is fabulous.

W.O.: Do you get ideas?

M.G.: Not necessarily. Most of my ideas come in the middle of the night or at home when I'm cloistered.

W.O.: What do you do, jump up and write them down?

M.G.: I wrote this for Harry Warren—I was so crazy about his melody; as a matter of fact, you can hear the tune on the Harry Warren website if they open the show with it. There are no lyrics with it; there never were, until I wrote them. It's in the process of finding someone to record it. It's called "There's One Love in My Life."

W.O.: How does that go?

M.G.: (*sings*) "There's one love in my life/and that love is you. / You're my love, you're my life. /No one else will do. /From the moment we met I can never forget/the most wonderful dreams started to come true. /You're the heart of my life I have waited for. /You're my reason to live and more. /You're all that I desire, my partner and my friend. /There's one love in my life. /You're the love of my life until the end." That's it.

W.O.: Murray Grand, you're a love of our life. I have one more question. When you're sitting there facing the audience—the ice cubes are tinkling and the whirlymixer is going at the bar—what's the killer song you sing if you feel you're not getting to some of the idiots out there?

M.G.: Generally speaking, my comedy songs. The romantic songs, I don't have the voice to do, ballads particularly. So if they're not a very hip audience and they don't figure out the ballads, I do comedy, which I'm known for. Songs like "Too Old to Die Young."

W.O.: It's a classic. "I'm Too Old to Die Young." How does that go?

M.G.: (*sings*) "Let me run in front of trucks, /smash the mirror on my wall. /Let me puff away and choke, /sniff a little coke and have myself a ball. /After all, I'm too old to die young." And it goes on from there. It's—you know—laugh, laugh, laugh, supposedly. It's been very successful and has been performed by a lot of people. And those songs seem to be lasting in the clubs in New York. I hear people doing them all the time.

Strangely enough, there's a man named Tom Keogh—he's Irish and very bulky—who's like Dame Edna. He gets into women's clothing and does an act called Ruth Canal, which is a play on the words "root canal." And he has a website www.rootcanal.com. He did a CD with all Murray Grand on it. It's called *Mostly Murray*. And he does mostly my comedy things that were done before by

Alice Ghostley, Bea Arthur, Dodie Goodman, Nancy Walker, Phyllis Diller—comedy people, the ladies. And those songs are still being performed a lot.

W.O.: Murray Grand, we're so glad we tracked you down, and thank you for letting us intrude on your sojourn. I'm going to do a CD about you called "I Feel Like a Jewish Grandmother With You . . . He Never Calls Me."

M.G.: Well, there you go, O'Shaughnessy.

W.O.: Stay in touch, will you, sir?

M.G.: I certainly will, and I hope you hear a lot about the Harry Warren tune. I hope it goes somewhere.

GOVERNOR MARIO M. CUOMO TALKS ABOUT JOHN EDWARDS AND HOW TO BRING PEACE TO IRAQ

This interview aired on July 8, 2004.

WILLIAM O'SHAUGHNESSY (W.O.): The political season has begun, almost officially. John Kerry isn't yet the nominee, but he's said he would like to run with John Edwards, a senator from North Carolina.

Let's switch now to Willkie, Farr & Gallagher, the famous law firm in Manhattan, and its most illustrious partner, Mario Matthew Cuomo, the former governor of New York. Governor, what do you think of Kerry's choice?

GOVERNOR MARIO CUOMO (M.C.): It's a good one, for a lot of reasons. Edwards is obviously an excellent spokesperson, and that's always useful. And of the four people in this race, he's undoubtedly the most charming and most persuasive. He's young. He has a young family. And he's politically correct. He gets along with Kerry. And the polls indicate 64–65 percent of everybody—Democrats, Republicans—thinks it's a good choice. I think it's been better received than I expected it to be. I don't see much to the negatives being hurled at him by the Republicans.

W.O.: Governor Mario Cuomo, before you came on the radio with us on this summer day, you were with your old staffer Tim Russert, who has done pretty well since he left your service in the Executive Chamber in Albany. What did you tell Russert? Did you give him all your good stuff?

M.C.: (*laughter*) No. He was talking about my book *Why Lincoln Matters: Today More Than Ever*, and he asked about Edwards. And I said to him about Edwards what I just said to you.

He also spent a lot of time on the *attacks* on Edwards: Republicans saying he has no experience. Well, that's ridiculous. I'm not going to use the obvious contrast, and that is the contrast with

Bush's own experience. Bush's lack of experience when he took the job is a good argument against Edwards because Bush has done so poorly as president. So I'm not going to make that argument. I will say this: If you compare him to Jack Kennedy, if you compare him to Franklin Roosevelt, if you compare him to Abraham Lincoln exclusively on the basis of what their preparation was for the job of president, he fares very well.

W.O.: You're talking about Edwards?

M.C.: Yes. So the experience argument doesn't work. As a matter of fact, experience is the weakest suit for the Republicans. Their "experience" is what got them in trouble. They've been there for four years, and now they've taken 22 million new jobs created by the previous administration and have produced the worst record since Hoover. We'll be lucky if they break even, not having lost jobs over the past four years, let alone not having produced any new ones. They took the largest surplus we ever had and left us with a deficit. They took a middle class that was moving upward and are sinking it. The only people who have done well over the past four years are people who are at the top. The Republicans took what could have been a very successful effort in Afghanistan, which we were all cheering, and walked away from it to start an optional war that most of the world didn't want, in Iraq, which was a debacle.

W.O.: You're talking about President Bush?

M.C.: Sure. The Republicans' experience is the worst thing they have to offer. Not to mention what the president said yesterday: "Well, the best thing about Cheney is he could be president." God forbid he could be president! Are you kidding? He was the principal "movant" to get us into the war in Iraq, which you confessed, Mr. President, was wrong, at least on the basis of the predicates they gave you. Wrong about weapons of mass destruction, wrong about complicity, wrong about imminence—and now you're saying he should be president? Well, Cheney as president—the slogan would be "Cheney for President: Wars as Far as the Eye Can See!"

W.O.: *Democrat* Mario Cuomo. . . .

M.C.: Right. Now, they're making me more of a Democrat than I ever was.

W.O.: Let's say that somebody *likes* George W. Bush. Like me.

M.C.: A lot of people do.

W.O.: Do you know that his father likes you, Mario Cuomo?

M.C.: *I* like his *father*! And I don't *dislike* George Bush. I don't like his *policies*. I don't know George Bush. From the outside, he looks like a fine fellow. I know friends of his, like Fred Wilpon, who owns the Mets; he told me a long time ago, "This is a really good man. You ought to get to know him." I never did. But Fred knew him and said people underestimate his abilities. This has nothing to do with the president personally. I don't have the privilege or the pleasure of knowing him. I *do* know his policies, and that's what I disagree with.

W.O.: Governor Cuomo, every time the Democrats put up somebody, whether it's Mondale or Dukakis or Al Gore or this eager John Kerry, a lot of people who admire you get mad at you because . . . why the hell wouldn't you go for it? I've never been so tough on you. But please answer that question, sir.

M.C.: It's easy to say, Bill, "Well, we could have done better with this, we could've done better with that." You'll never know. It's possible, if I became a candidate, I would've been an atrocious candidate and gotten wiped out. You'll just never know. But it's irrelevant. What *is* relevant is what we should do to get this nation back on the course we were on before. How do we deal with terrorism?

Two things with how we deal with terrorism. Right now, I don't see any real solutions to terrorism other than military power, which we're using to get Osama bin Laden, which I approve of 100 percent—using military power in Afghanistan, which we all approve of 100 percent. The war in Iraq—I don't know how that relates to terrorism. I do know it relates to freeing the people of Iraq, and I know that's a good thing. Taking down a dictator is a good thing. But what else are we going to do to fight terrorism? It's obvious that terrorism is everywhere around the world. What are we going to do beyond the war in Iraq? The president says Iraq is the new theater of the war against terrorism. Well, when you're finished in Iraq, what theater will you move to then? Are you going to start another war? And what are you doing besides using military power? Aren't there other things we can do to dissuade these people? Aren't there other things we can do to get the Palestinians and the Israelis to make a deal? Isn't there anything else we can do? That's number one.

Number two, why are the Republicans beginning to tell us every day, "Well, Bush saw to it that there were no attacks on the United States"? Every time I hear that, I get a chill. What, are we daring them to try and attack? Why would we say that every day? As if it's an argument for Bush that there has been no attack. That's the same as standing up and looking at the Muslims that hate us the most, the Jihadists, the terrorists, and saying, "I dare you." What do you think of that, Bill?

W.O.: Governor, everybody says they want to be tough on terrorism. Kerry says it, and now Edwards is saying it. The president's big thing is "steadfast and resolute."

M.C.: "Steadfast and resolute" in what?

W.O.: In being tough on the damn terrorists.

M.C.: How is he being tough?

W.O.: Well, he's chasing them all over. . . .

M.C.: Where? There were no terrorists in Iraq until he went in there and attracted them to Iraq. They're coming in now. If he wanted to follow the terrorists, why didn't he stay in Afghanistan where Osama was? And what is he doing in Iran to be tough? And what is he doing in Syria to be tough? And what is he doing in Saudi Arabia—most of all, where he has so many friends—to be tough?

W.O.: Once you're tough, as Kerry wants to be tough—as I think Bush is tough—how does Mario Cuomo get them to confront the ancient tribal rivalries and the ancient hatred and the religious thing?

M.C.: There are a lot of things you have to do in addition to flexing your military muscle.

W.O.: Give me Mario Cuomo words.

M.C.: Well, first of all, you have to be more aggressive—and the whole world has to join you—in making peace in Israel so that nobody uses that as an excuse for terrorist activity—and we know that people do that. We have to make that a number two priority after protecting this nation, which is number one. We're a long way from being secure. You've got your bureaucracy now. On the trains, on the buses, on the planes, you've made some progress.

INTERVIEW WITH MARIAN B. JAVITS ON THE 100TH ANNIVERSARY OF THE BIRTH OF SENATOR JACOB K. JAVITS

The widow of Senator Jacob K. Javits, Marian Javits is a whirlwind force in her own right and a great supporter of the arts. We aired this interview with her on May 17, 2004.

WILLIAM O'SHAUGHNESSY (W.O.): There has been a relentlessly familiar and recurring theme in all my rants, raves, and preaching: "Where are the *giants* who once strode across our political landscape and walked the land?" On these two radio stations we have talked so often about Nelson Aldrich Rockefeller, Dwight David Eisenhower, Mario Cuomo, Jack Kennedy, Adlai Stevenson, Pat Moynihan. We've looked at the current crop of politicians and politicos, and so often they come up short. They certainly don't measure up to those mythic figures of a few decades ago, where once giants walked the land.

This is the month of May, in the springtime of the year 2004. And on the 17th of May, one of those giants would have been one hundred years old. It's the hundredth birthday of a towering New Yorker, a great United States senator from the state of New York: Jacob K. Javits. With us from New York City is his wife, Marian Borros Javits. Marian Javits is today chair of the Jacob Javits Foundation. Marian Javits, you still miss him, don't you?

MARIAN JAVITS (M.J.): Oh, yes, I miss him. And what a delight it is to talk to you, Bill O'Shaughnessy. You were one of the early compatriots, despite perhaps your occasional allegiance to Democrats like Mario Cuomo, whom you adore. And you've always respected and understood Jock Whitney, Walter Thayer, Nelson Rockefeller, and Jack Javits. They were all the same *kind* of Republicans. And they *really* mattered because they were moderates about fiscal policy. They were also more interested in solving the problems of the poor. Therefore, on social issues they always took the helm and leadership and tried to make things work and give balance to what is known as politics.

W.O.: Marian, Jack Javits, your late husband, was part of the progressive wing of the Republican Party.

M.J.: They were all moderates.

W.O.: Is there anything left of that today?

M.J.: No, it's really not there anymore. The people I admire seem to be Democrats. I love Joe Biden. I wish he'd run for president. I enjoy John McCain. I'd certainly be first on board to support a ticket with Kerry and McCain because, to me, it makes great sense. This man [McCain] represents all the fallacies that have been happening in our world during this war: the torture and upset in jails, as well as coming through as a very intelligent and progressive and, if you will, *moderate* leader in the Republican Party. It is being whispered aloud that Kerry might turn to McCain. So that would please us. There are other areas of politics I won't get into at this time, because I do have very passionate feelings as to where we are and where we are not. But the leadership I look for, that *you're* asking for, is not prevalent. There are some, but they're a little more silent than they ought to be. We need some people to come forward with ideas and dedication.

W.O.: Marian Javits, let's go back to the days when Jacob K. Javits was on his feet in the Senate. He was the "father" of the War Powers Act and an awesome intellect. Do you remember those days?

M.J.: Indeed I do, Bill, because the Javits Foundation has followed that for the last seventeen years. When Jack died, he left me in charge, and I took the helm. I went from a dancing darling enjoying New York for all it's worth. I *am* a New Yorker, even though I was born in Detroit, Michigan, but I've enjoyed New York since I was six months old. And I love all its manifestations. The arts, particularly, where I did the research for the National Endowment for the Arts and the Humanities, and Jack Javits sponsored the bill we developed. It took *sixteen years* to get that passed. During the Reagan administration, they began to question what *is* the arts. And it remains, the denial of support for it. But we did go forward with War Powers because we have a distinguished scholar-in-residence with New York University. And my first accommodation was to a very brilliant scholar: Jeffrey Stone. He dealt with the War Powers legislation. We're doing it again this year, possibly with Gary Hart at the helm and one of their own scholars at the school. We have a debate and a seminar in which the scholar follows. It is a very prestigious and respected program.

W.O.: Marian, Jacob Javits of sainted memory stood out as a great debater, and he was enormously respected. Senator Robert Byrd comes to mind as perhaps the only one who could stand up to Javits in a debate. Or the great Moynihan. Did you ever argue at home?

M.J.: Oh, yes, but the only area we ever had difficulty with was the Vietnam War. I was definitely opposed as it continued, and Lyndon took the rap for it, but he shouldn't have because this Vietnam thing all started before *Truman's* time. Jack did a very wonderful thing. I had a group come in to see me—Norman Mailer, Warren Beatty, and others—about a little march against the war.

I said to Jack, "I'm here because I must go with this little group." And he said, "No, you really shouldn't, Marian. It's a little dangerous." And I said, "Well, I must." And he said, "Well, I must go *with* you." I said, "Jack, it'll only be a scandal." And he said, "No, I will go with you." And he followed me, and he was brave and he was wonderful. He took a chance to get into a muck-a-muck with the politicians. But that was Jack Javits. He always stood strong and forthright for what he believed. And he believed in *me* as his wife.

He wasn't with me at that time on Vietnam, because it took him a while after Bobby Kennedy came forward supporting that war, after he went with Senator [Claiborne] Pell to Vietnam to see how he felt about it and what he could learn. But he was more my *husband* than he was the politician. He proved it, certainly, at that time. Those were the times of love, commitment, devotion. I always revered Jack Javits's big brain. He was called the most brilliant man in the Senate by the administrative assistants for years—the "number one mind." And he was that. He was also a very *fair* man. Nancy Kassebaum, the former senator, now Mrs. Howard Baker, once said, "I would always have to pass his desk in the well of the Senate when I didn't vote the way he did and *explain* to him that I had a constituency but that I really *agreed* with him." And she would always apologize to him for not being on his side.

W.O.: Mrs. Javits, I'm not talking now about Marian Javits, the *public* woman. You've *always* been formidable, and most say you *match* Javits in terms of brain power. But what about on the home front? I mean, you were both very *strong* people. If you wanted potatoes and he wanted tomatoes, which did you have for dinner?

M.J.: Whatever *he* wanted, Bill, because I was still a little housewife at the time. Today we might have to split the idea. Today we would have potatoes and tomorrow we would have tomatoes because he was always fair. We would always split the ideas we had. But not much. We really were pretty much in agreement. I've always been an independent voter. Some of the people didn't appreciate that at the time. But I really vote for the man and what I believe he is capable of. And I am a *believer*.

And by the way, Mario Cuomo, who is your dearest friend, gave us the greatest honor when he said, "Would you ask Jack if we can name the convention center for him?" I said, "He turned down a few things like schools and streets and bridges because he didn't think it was right. But he's in the hospital in intensive care, Mario; may I call you back?" So there Jack was, stretched out with all the needles in him, and I said, "Jack, the governor called and he's asking about using your name on the big, new, modern convention center in New York City." And his eyes teared up—those blue, blue eyes danced a bit—and he said, "That's for me."

Jack loved the show-biz part of being a senator. He liked the press. He liked always being heard from. In fact, they would quote him on issues more than anybody else because he was so forceful and so clear about what the issues were, whether he was on that side or not. And that's what Jack liked, a little applause. He was a good man.

W.O.: He came off the Lower East Side and became one of the strongest, most cerebral ever to serve in the United States Senate. Did you ever have any *fun*?

M.J.: When we met, I just knew we were going to be a together team. One, he had those blue, blue eyes, and he was always a giving person. Two, as soon as we had our first date, we went dancing, and he was one of the most terrific dancers around. He knew every dance, and if he didn't, he'd ask his daughter, Joy, who is a choreographer in North Carolina. She would teach it to both of us. He *loved* to dance. We would go down to El Morocco. There was no Club 54. But he did enter the portals of Studio 54 before the end, I can tell you. And we had great times.

He loved entertaining. He loved when we'd have a brunch or a few people over. He would give me short notice, and I would suddenly have a few *dozen* people because he needed it, or wanted it, and was available. I guess that's my training with Jack Javits. And you know what? I loved *every* minute of it.

W.O.: But you didn't love every minute of *Washington*. You were famously absent from Washington. You're a New Yorker, and you've always been. You didn't run right down to Washington to get into the social swing down there, as I recall.

M.J.: No, but remember, Bill, you're talking about the early '50s, and it wasn't the same social thing then. There were a lot of conservative people left over from before World War II. It was after World War II and when the Kennedys showed up that the social life became acknowledged. And when Senator [Arthur] Vandenberg was around, it was very quiet and only gossipy things went on. But they weren't the social kind. Kay Graham tried to do it. And she would have her brunches or her little dinners with all the heavyweights. And no, I didn't feel part of it. One, because of my politics; and two, because they gave short shrift to anybody who wasn't a "big" get. A senator was like Frank Sinatra, a superstar they had to kind of attack. And I felt in the way. So I went back to New York after trying to live in Washington. And I studied at Columbia University. I studied acting with Gertrude Lawrence. I studied languages; I studied English literature; I studied

Russian. I had a great time, because we lived near Columbia University at the time. And now, if you want to know what I'm doing, I'm going to work with Columbia University, developing a great Center for the Arts. That will be up on the West Side, in Harlem. I'm very excited about that because they really do understand what the future might bring. The arts and technology have got to move their understanding together because this is a very special time.

W.O.: Marian Javits, did you ever think of running for office yourself?

M.J.: No, not really, because I had this great man, and if I had any great line it came from him, although neither of us had graduated from college. I always took courses, and he got his law degree. In those years, Bill, people didn't need to have a bachelor's degree in order to get the law degree. Jack Javits never got his bachelor's degree. He got a law degree going two years at night. And then he became the great senator. So, you see, the most brilliant man in the Senate never graduated from college.

W.O.: I can remember an event at the Jacob K. Javits Center, by the Hudson River in Manhattan. And you, head of the Javits Foundation, had about four United States senators and a lot of ambassadors you were pushing around—running the show. Are you sure you never thought of saying, "I'll run myself"?

M.J.: No. But once we gave Bob Dole a Javits Award. We still continue to give the Javits Senator Award to senators who are doing provocative and interesting and rather complicated legislation. The first were given to Senator Byrd and Senator Dole. Bob Dole stood up and said, "You know, this is a first, but when Marian Javits calls, you better answer the phone." I never gave up trying to get him to attend my meetings.

I just don't give up; that's what it's about. Jack ran the last time [in 1980] and thought he'd be setting the course for me to be able to get the appointment from the Republicans and the Democrats for the remaining year if he died while in office. But of course, as we know, he didn't. He could have served a few years and been valid to his time. I was always disappointed that didn't happen. But as a family, we all voted—the children and I—and we all said, "Jack, *don't* run." We told him we thought time had passed him by a bit.

And while he was still sufficient in his brain, which never left him, he thought they might anoint me senator.

W.O.: He was replaced by Alfonse D'Amato.

M.J.: Lordy, Lord, Lord, *please*. That was one of the most unpleasant campaigns we've ever had. The others were pretty fair. I was never happy about that; it was a sadness to us, not just that he lost, but the way the campaign had been conducted.

W.O.: What do you mean?

M.J.: He really was able to carry out his duties and he would have been able to stay firm.

The ALS, Amyotrophic Lateral Sclerosis, which he suddenly had for a year and a half. . . . Nobody was able to tell us what was wrong with him. He was gripping his tennis racquet too hard, and we thought that was the problem. But it took us a year and a half at the Johns Hopkins Hospital. And then Doctor Posner at Memorial became his ardent doctor and saw him every week for the four or five years he was ill at home.

We had a hospital bed at home. When David Niven got ALS, he had nobody there with him. I said we'll just put up another hospital bed alongside Jack. And Jack and David, who were friends, had an exchange. But David died too soon. He had the attack on his tongue, which was terrible. Jack's was in the stomach. It's an attack upon all the muscles in the body. We're most fortunate it never hit his brain. Sometimes that "muscle" gets hit too.

ALS needs more consideration. Senator [Arlen] Specter is one of the leaders on trying to get more funding for each of these particular neurological diseases. And it would be helpful and useful if they began to separate all of them, so the funding could go to the right researchers. That's among the things I'm "busy" with.

W.O.: Marian Javits, was it hard for you, as Jacob Javits lay dying in your East Side apartment?

M.J.: I'm afraid he died suddenly. As a matter of fact, he was in Florida in a small apartment, which he rented from his sister-in-law. He would go there from time to time with his "trache" and his nurse. I sold a couple of paintings to make that work because it got very expensive, that illness. It was lucky I was in the art world; that's why I could live as luxuriously as I do now, Bill. I'm in a lucky place because my devotion to the arts paid off and I never knew it would, because I did it for love, and I still do.

I made chicken soup when he had pneumonia, and I said, "You have to *have* it." And he said, "Oh, all right." Then I said, "I got to go do a little exercise now, Jack." And the last words I ever heard from him were, "Have a good time, dear." That was the way it always was between us.

W.O.: Marian Javits, did you ever forgive Alfonse D'Amato for pushing the great Javits out of the Senate?

M.J.: I think this is too sweet a time for us to talk about negative things, Bill. I'm pleased with what [Senator] Chuck Schumer tries to do. He's a very first-rate guy. And he's involved with all the issues I really care about. And Hillary speaks so well that I'm watching her too. I don't think I need worry about something that wasn't.

W.O.: You mentioned your admiration for Joe Biden. You give the Javits Award to worthy senators.

M.J.: Yes, Pete Domenici got one because he was doing something on economics. We select them carefully.

W.O.: Who else is good down there now, Marian Javits?

M.J.: Well, it's difficult for me, because I don't watch the new names as much as I watch the people that have been on my board: Senator Dole, Senator Moynihan, Senator [Charles] Percy. Remember, it's a little past my time for being active.

But I do watch and listen all day long to CNN and Fox News to get both sides of what's going on. I don't think there are really outstanding voices, but it's better than I presumed it was recently. This war has brought people about to articulate in interesting ways. Many previously were playing both sides a little more than they should. It seems to me they're finally coming together. Biden said that yesterday. This isn't a time for politics, it's a time for trying to really rectify our dignity, the best place Americans have always had, with great respect. People still want to come here with all the ugliness we have seen in recent days. I'm just hoping for any voice that speaks *well* of our country. That's what McCain is doing; he speaks so well, and he's always fair; he's not coy, he's genuine. I am a great admirer of his. And with Biden, they'd make a good team. But if you've got Kerry and McCain and Biden as secretary of state, then that's my ticket. I've liked George Bush Sr.—loved him—I thought he was a good man, substantial; he rewarded us with his great service, and he was right for his time. And now it's time for some other thoughts, and whatever direction the country will go, I will stand and watch privately.

Jack Javits always said: Your vote is *yours*. "It's private and it belongs to you, Marian." And I said to him, "What if I don't vote the way *you* do? *You* are going to vote, and the whole country, the world, will know." And he said, "You are a *citizen*, and if *you're* voting, then you must do what your thought and heart tells you."

W.O.: You said it's a little past your time and there aren't too many strong, independent voices. I believe we're listening to a strong, independent voice right now on the radio.

Incidentally, how the hell old are you, Marian Javits?

M.J.: (*laughter*) Oh, Bill O'Shaughnessy, aren't you ashamed of yourself? Never, never, *never* will I say! Much, much younger than Jack Javits! I'm afraid I'm still that coy woman. You can look it up, and you'd probably find it. But I'd tell you that you're wrong. My children are in their forties and a few in their fifties, so I've got to be a big girl, huh? But I'm not telling the number. I was born in Detroit, Michigan—look me up. (*laughter*)

W.O.: Marian Javits, why can't a Joe Biden get elected president? I like the Delaware guy too.

M.J.: Well, Joe decided he didn't want to run. That was the key. Remember, there was a problem about a speech he wrote and said this or that, and he lowered his profile.

His wife and child were also in a horrible car accident. And that put him in a terribly emotional place, not wanting to give more time than was necessary: His devotion was to his wife and family. He just figures he can do the big job from where he now sits. In fact, there is no more powerful job than being a senator. Because remember, if we're going to be for the War Powers legislation—which Jack put in place and the Constitution originated—

the president can declare war for forty-eight hours, but the Senate can say nay.

And that was why there was a confusion about Kerry also, because he was *against* it and then he was *for* it. It's never been made clear because the press always convolutes what happens with someone, and they say he's a two-headed monster, which is untrue.

Kerry has spoken truth and people aren't paying attention to each line. They get a headline and they think they know what they're considering. In any event, I once said to Joe Biden, "Hey, this is *your* time." And it must be, because he's the right age for it—I forget what he is, late fifties or early sixties—and it is a perfect time for him. But they're now talking about him as secretary of state, and I think he might be able to handle that because he's married and has another family now. He is somebody to watch.

Joe was in China with us when we went in 1975; we were the first group to go in after Nixon. We went twice, as a matter of fact, with the Foreign Relations Committee, to see what it was like, and it is amazing. It is a country to watch and to be concerned about because they are going to be quite intrusive unless we get stronger about protecting our own country.

W.O.: Marian Javits, on this, the hundredth anniversary of the natal day of Jacob K. Javits, you mentioned the Foreign Relations Committee. What would your late husband do about Iraq? Would he say, let's cut and run and get the hell out of there?

M.J.: Well, I think you're asking the question that should have been answered previously. The problem of this nice President Bush is that he did not really concern himself with precisely the question you're asking. He should have had that in mind. If we win, if we've made a dent, if we've made ourselves heard properly, if we get rid of the ogres that are there, if we can help them create, if they wish, a democracy, we've got to make a *plan*. I think you have a few of these people we hear from now and again who are not as sure-minded as they should be about the big plan.

I believe Jack Javits would say we have to be quite concerned with what we've done and therefore *protect* what we've done.

We've got to help them restore the place to some kind of democratic country with leadership that can be respected, to help their people. I think there ought to be a plan, and that has not come forward, and I'm surprised there are so many leaders who, while they talk, criticize and negate and have not put forward a *plan*. The Big Plan ought not to give Halliburton the big contracts, nor the oil interests. They need to have an economy they can consider to be trustworthy. *Then* you'll find leaders, you'll find intelligent people who *really* want in earnest to be a part of growth for their country.

Every country isn't *all* bad. Sometimes it's the leadership and sometimes it's stagnation because of so many years of trying to negate the growth of their country. But in Iraq, Jack Javits would say: Let's make a *plan*. You ought to talk to the big minds in the economy, get the *business* going. But not focus on the oil interests alone and not make deals with other countries that are really much more involved in their *own* interests and raising oil prices, which is what can happen if you don't have strong voices.

But I'm going back to Washington. We had stopped our Javits Fellows Program, but I'm going back to it because I believe so strongly that we were helping young and brilliant people in their master's program. They had to satisfy us they were going to stay in Washington and be dedicated to just the kinds of questions you've been asking me. So I'm going to go back and try to do that again for a while. I'm a volunteer. I don't need to raise any money for it. I just have to get the sanction of the Senate, and they have all shown they appreciated it. I used to get letters from Secretary [of Defense William S.] Cohen and Ted Kennedy and Pete Domenici, and they all said: Please send those young people to us that you've selected so well. So I'm proud of the little contribution I can make with our Javits Fellows Program.

Anyway, it's too late for me to run for office. Bill, *you* run for office. You're a good, bright, and intelligent man, and you're the right number. I've seen your family, your wife—you're both beautiful. I'd vote for you.

W.O.: I'm going to cut you off on that, Mrs. Javits. Marian Javits, you were—until a few seconds ago—a pretty keen political observer. Give me a quick fifteen or twenty seconds on some of today's people out there: George Elmer Pataki, the Republican governor of your state.

M.J.: I don't follow him well enough. I know he tries, but I don't understand his leadership. I know there have not been sufficient voices in the legislature up in Albany that came forward to help him. They deal with these things in a rather untidy way. You never really know who is on what side and what the issue *should* be, rather than what it is. There's not any clarity given to it, and I think if I miss anything with the governor, when he's heard from, it should be that sense of clarity. He should be more in charge of perhaps different things than the president. A governor needs to declare: *These* are the issues, this is what *I* stand for, these are my allies, and we have to rearrange whatever has been to give this recognition and support. And that, of course, has to do with where the *money* comes from. Jack Javits once taught me that too. He said, "No matter what, our country is a wealthy enough country, and if you look hard in the right places, everything can get the support it needs—if it's done with integrity and with devotion."

W.O.: Mrs. Javits, you said you like the job Chuck Schumer is doing. What about Hillary Rodham Clinton?

M.J.: I heard her the other day. Gabe Pressman had her on Channel 4. I'm a news junkie, and all my news is on different channels throughout the day. There wasn't a bleep out of her that missed the target. You've been kind in asking *me* questions I have answers to. She's exactly that, not just because she's smart or clever. She's an intelligent woman. Our problem here in America is we don't forgive *money* and we don't forgive *sex*. She made a deal early on. Maybe it was wrong—Whitewater or whatever. But we've got to consider that this woman has *grown* over the past twenty years they've been in public life. We've got to think about what she's saying about the *issues*. She's speaking well to the issues. She doesn't get in anybody's way.

We have to take another think about Hillary Clinton and what she is thinking about doing because maybe it's time for us to take a look at the other voices we don't necessarily go for and find out what are they thinking. I don't know how the Senate operates on that level anymore, so forgive me, I'm flubbing on this one. But I did like what she said. I don't think she's as involved with foreign relations and foreign affairs. I think the more local issues are hers, but maybe that's because it's the way she developed her reputation. Schumer, on the other hand, really has a larger overview of what it is he's trying and hoping to do.

W.O.: I'm reminded that Jack Javits, before he became a towering icon of the Senate, was the attorney general of New York. Eliot Spitzer seems to have a bright future. What do you know about him?

M.J.: I think he is busy exposing things that are pretty bad. I would like to hear from him, just as I said about the legislature and Hillary, telling me more about how he's going to build and have answers to the issues that are in his office. We ought to have more clarity than this. I'm not sure if the press handles someone like Spitzer well, someone who doesn't make friends with them. I used to be that front runner making friends with the press and gathering them at my Sunday brunches—having people come in and meld so that then they would understand about Javits. The press grew up with us because we were a team and we worked well together on that basis.

We have to get to know each other. You *know* me, and you're asking every question you think I'm capable of handling. That's what happens when we get to know the people who are running for office. Too often, we accept a little headline, or they bleeped wrong, or they condescended to something that didn't belong to them or made a wrong turn, and we don't forgive. We've got to begin to understand that everybody makes mistakes, unless it's really ratchety and it goes too far like giving out contracts—which I understand is happening now in Iraq.

I think that what really bothers me most of all is what's going to happen to the *oil*. Who's getting the *contracts*? I understand there are things we have to take a big, hard look at. I would love to hear from Mario Cuomo—I wish *he'd* run for office—if anyone is first class. . . . He's probably one of those people who could sit down and write out some very interesting ideas that should be consumed by certain people that he referred to when he was governor.

W.O.: But he is a *Democrat*. You, Marian Javits, are a *Republican*.

M.J.: I'm an Independent, though. I'm for Biden. He's a Democrat. I gave Domenici an award because he did brilliant things for the economy when they were trying to decide how and what to give you a tax for, Bill.

We've got to be a little more forgiving and understanding of what the other is about and not divide our country because it is Democrat or Republican. I think Biden and McCain are saying *that* more than anything. We don't have to be as concerned as we once were about the division. How many *jobs* can you get, and how many contracts do you want to take a look at? The press is going to watch over you in any event. Let's make it *work*. Let's get some solid people. Bush *thinks* he has them, but I think they're kind of used up.

I think we need the new faces that I've been naming. McCain is a Republican. He's a good, solid Republican who comes out of the Navy, and his father and his grandfather were part of the Navy. My grandson seems to think he wants to go to West Point. I'm worried; he's fourteen, and here I am, this radical and liberal grandmother, and he's going to go into the conservative profession, the Army. But I do respect that we have an Army that protects us and the world and has been so respected all over the world for so long.

W.O.: Marian Javits, we've kept you too long from your busy and productive life. And I know you have, from all over the country, relatives of your beloved Jacob Javits coming in to town to help you remember him on what would be his hundredth birthday.

As I mercifully yield, I'm reminded we had a man here on our Westchester radio station, Dr. Thomas Fogarty, who once threw out a pretty sobering observation. He said, "One hundred years from today, *few* people will ever know you *existed*." It seems to me like you are hell bent and determined to make sure that doesn't happen to Jacob K. Javits.

M.J.: Correct. Because there were issues he left that weren't finished. And one is the War Powers legislation. We need leadership to back it.

And the pension plans: Corporations have overlooked people who have worked for them for many, many years; these workers without a pension plan don't know which way to turn. People should get their pensions after working fifteen or twenty years at a corporation, and not be fired or be given "deals" to get them to leave.

And then, my love above all, the National Endowment for the Arts and Humanities. They are wonderful people. They're really the way the world is to be because they contemplate the problems without any holes and contracts. There are not offices they want to hold. They just want to explore our generation thoughtfully and with no malice. I think scientists and architects are the people I would want to lean on heavily to make our world a better place than it already is, right now.

We have to reconsider how we live. The architects are redesigning buildings, and the technologists and scientists are finding answers to those devastating medical illnesses. Those three issues are the big ones—and of course, *education*, but that's a little more complicated.

But now, most of all, I'm looking forward to seeing Joshua, Joy, and Carla, who are coming into town to help me reminisce and remember their father, a great, great American. I'm so proud of the children, each one bright and accomplished.

W.O.: Marian, I don't think I laid a glove on you. You wouldn't even tell me how old you are. I intend no disrespect, but you still have all your marbles, Widow Javits.

M.J.: Well, the marbles aren't going to leave me, Bill. They didn't leave Javits; we didn't let that happen. We just have to keep moving forward and understand our world and try to make it a little better, however we can. My love of the arts world is because of no claim, just intelligence that's trying to find out how we can be motivated and how to make things work.

W.O.: Thank you for sharing this anniversary of a great American, maybe the smartest senator we ever had in this country.

Above: Partners in good government: Lieutenant Governor Malcolm Wilson and the great Governor (and later Vice President) Nelson Aldrich Rockefeller. When "Rocky" resigned as governor, Wilson succeeded him. He later lost to Hugh L. Carey.

Below: "The Donald" and the author. The author emcees many of Trump's events and openings. The master builder is also a generous contributor to the Broadcasters Foundation of America.

Above: "Out on the hustings." Governor Mario Cuomo, visiting Elmira, greets Tom Flynn (far right), a former mayor of that upstate city. The author, who put aside his press pass to do a little "advance" work, spread the word that "everybody will be fed"—almost five thousand showed up.

Below: the late Tony Malara (left), president of the CBS Television Network, and Ralph Baruch, founder of Viacom, at a reception for the Broadcasters Foundation of America. Malara was a great raconteur who emceed many broadcasters' events.

Above: Julian Niccolini (left) and Alex Von Bidder (right), co-partners of Manhattan's fabled Four Seasons restaurant. The author (center) emceed their 35th anniversary gala in 2010.

Below: *Mama Mia!* Mama Rose Bochino Migliucci (center) with (from left) Barbara, Mario, and Joseph Migliucci, proprietor of Mario's, the landmark Arthur Avenue restaurant in the Little Italy section of the Bronx. The author eulogized both "Mama Rose" and her husband, Mario Sr.

Above: "I'm glad somebody here can act!" Sirio Maccioni, the Le Cirque ringmaster; Robert De Niro and his wife, Grace Hightower; the author.

Right: Egidiana Palmieri Maccioni was a famous up-and-coming songstress in Italy when she gave up a huge signing bonus to marry the legendary restaurateur.

Below, from left: Arthur Hill Diedrick, chairman, Communications International; novelist Barbara Taylor Bradford; Sirio Maccioni; Tara Stacom Diedrick; movie producer Robert Bradford.

Governor Mario M. Cuomo and the late Bernard F. Curry Jr., one of the pioneering car dealers in America, talk politics at a dinner event hosted by the author.

Grand Dames (from left) Kitty Carlisle Hart, widow of the legendary playwright Moss Hart; "Mama" Rose Bocchino Migliucci, "First Lady of Arthur Avenue"; Matilda Raffa Cuomo, chair, Mentoring USA; and Barbara Migliucci.

The luminous Kitty Carlisle Hart sang “I’ll Be Loving You Always” at a birthday party for the author. The widow of legendary producer Moss Hart was a familiar and beloved presence around New York well into her nineties. She also chaired the New York State Council of the Arts under four governors. She called them all “Darling”!

The author with communications broker Richard Foreman, who flies his own jet up and down the Eastern seaboard doing nice things for lots of people. His most recent errand of mercy was to airlift medical supplies into quake-torn Haiti. The author and Foreman serve on the board and the executive committee of the Broadcasters Foundation of America.

Beloved New York Giants co-owner Wellington Mara. "Mr. Mara" had a lively correspondence and wonderful friendship with the author, whom he called "Coach."

Ann (Mrs. Wellington) Mara receives the author's attentions as her daughter Susan Mara McDonnell looks on.

"I've got your number!" Beloved New York Mayor Ed Koch joking with his old rival Governor Mario Cuomo at an early breakfast at "21." Photo by the author.

M.J.: I think that's true. They always quoted Javits. They would ask all those questions of everybody, but the quote always came down to what Javits said. Some of that has been recognized, but not enough. I'm still looking for that big beautiful book that would explain why Javits was in conflict with parts of his own party or the presidents. He was a man who was always fair-minded, as I said about Kassebaum. If they had problems with legislation, even the Democrats would say, could you please help us write this so it makes *sense*. They could always ask Javits because the *mind* was able to accommodate the need for fairness and what needed to be done. Mario Cuomo is like that. He should get back into the race. He should not be out of it. And I know how devoted you are to him. He's a *very* good man.

W.O.: Jack Javits was pretty lucky to have you, lady.

M.J.: It's been a good ride and I've been lucky, Bill. And to have friends like you too. You were so spontaneous when I mentioned this. And your own books are pretty damn good. I have your latest right in front of me; I'm reading *More Riffs, Rants, and Raves*, and I'm loving it. It's a big book, like Mr. Cuomo said, but you really know how to tell stories, and I really enjoy what you're into. You've always been that kind of person I enjoyed. And it's a pleasure, as always, Bill.

W.O.: Thank you, Mrs. Javits. I hope to see you soon.

"TRUE LOVE": WARD QUAAL TALKS ABOUT PRESIDENT REAGAN

We spoke with Ward Quaal, the legendary Chicago broadcaster, on June 10, 2004, just a few days after the passing of President Ronald Reagan, whom Quaal had served as an advisor and friend.

WILLIAM O'SHAUGHNESSY (W.O.): The flags are at half-staff all over the nation on this warm day because we have lost a president. And, it appears, a great one. Let's go to Chicago, Illinois—the great Midwest, the heartland—to talk with a man who was an advisor to President Ronald Wilson Reagan, and also to Gerald Ford and Richard Nixon.

His name is Ward Quaal. Mr. Quaal ran the legendary WGN, one of the mighty radio stations of this nation, for many years. He's now an advisor to the powerful Tribune Company, which owns a lot of newspapers and television stations.

Ward Quaal, it seems like a lot of people really *loved* Ronald Reagan.

WARD QUAAL (W.Q.): A lot of people did love him, Bill. And the outpouring of support from coast to coast is just tremendous, even more enormous, I believe, than his dear Nancy anticipated. He was an outstanding American in every way.

I actually got to know him years ago, when I was a very young announcer. And, of course, later on, when I had Tribune Radio and Television and helped the growth of the company go beyond Chicago, was a time when I saw quite a bit of Ronald Reagan because he was in Washington at the time serving as one of our great presidents. We also saw one another on other matters, on a more personal basis, in Chicago and Washington and on the West Coast.

W.O.: I hope I'm not violating any confidences, but I've seen handwritten notes from President Reagan to you, Ward Quaal. He was a pretty nice man.

W.Q.: He was a wonderful man and a person you could trust. And if he was your friend, then he was *really* your friend. He was a very fine human being. There was nothing at all shallow about him.

He wasn't a Republican, or anything else, primarily. Yes, he headed the Republican Party for that period of time, but he was an authentic American and proud to be an American. Proud of his heritage from little Dixon, Illinois, and before that, the tiny town of Tampico, Illinois. He never forgot his roots in that small community. And he was the same man as one of our greatest presidents as he was as a mere youngster and as a Sunday school teacher in the little church in Dixon, Illinois. Ronald Reagan was genuine.

W.O.: Mr. Quaal, as you sit there in the great midwestern part of our country today and reflect on your friendship with President Reagan, tell us about Nancy. Was that really a storybook romance?

W.Q.: It was a *great* romance. And I'll have to tell you this story. In the early days of television, I had to step into a studio one night at WGN Television. I was assistant to the general manager, who was no longer on the air, and I had to do the news show that night because this individual was ill. When I finished the news program at 10:00 that night, an usher came up to me with a note to call Mrs. Loyal Davis. So I called and she said, "Ward, I want to have you and Dorothy for dinner." Dr. Loyal Davis was a celebrated neurosurgeon.

W.O.: Nancy Reagan's parents?

W.Q.: Yes. Loyal was very upset that Nancy was interested in a fellow named Ronald Reagan, an actor. Mrs. Davis said, "You know Ronald so well, and it would be helpful if you folks would come to dinner and calm down Loyal. He doesn't like the idea of Nancy marrying anybody in Hollywood." So I said, "Here's our phone number. Call Dorothy at home, and if she agrees, you have a date."

To make a long story short, we get together that evening at the home of Dr. and Mrs. Loyal Davis: she, the mother of Nancy; and Loyal Davis, her stepfather. After we finished dinner, Loyal said, "Ward, let's go into the library so we can talk a little bit."

He told me this Reagan guy might be all right but said, "I just don't want Nancy marrying anybody in Hollywood. I just don't like that idea." And I said, "Well, I'll tell you, I've known Reagan for quite a while, both personally and professionally. We're very good friends. I don't think there is a finer person out there, in Hollywood or anywhere, than Ronald Reagan."

And I said, "Let me tell you something. *You* married an actress. Your wife was Spencer Tracy's first leading lady. How can you be married to her and then tell your stepdaughter she shouldn't marry an actor or anybody on the Hollywood scene?" He said, "Ward, I know that doesn't sound consistent, but I'd prefer she didn't do it."

I said, "Well, if she loves Ronald, and Ronald loves Nancy, why don't we just leave it at that? And you and I can call it a successful dinner and a nice evening, and both of us can rejoice in their happiness and love for one another."

And that's the way it ended.

W.O.: Ward Quaal, there have been thousands of vignettes told about Ronald and Nancy Reagan in recent days. I never heard *that* story. But for your advice to his father-in-law, they may have never gotten together.

W.Q.: (*laughter*) Well, I don't know about that. I guess Loyal believed in me, and Ronald did, and Nancy did too; and they lived happily ever after. So we have to look at it that way. It was a great match.

W.O.: Mr. Quaal, you've been a great mentor to me as chairman of our Broadcasters Foundation of America in so many ways over the years. I don't want to take too much time away from your busy consulting practice. You advise not only presidents but also the big television and radio broadcasters in this nation. How old are you now?

W.Q.: I'm eighty-five.

W.O.: Well, let me ask you one more question, sir. As you know—without apologies—I'm a Rockefeller Republican. In my younger days, I thought Ronald Reagan was the devil incarnate. But it seems that even though he was a conservative, he was a pretty good guy. A lot of conservatives are just yahoos, if you know what I mean. What was different about Reagan?

W.Q.: I think he was genuine, Bill. He was conservative, but not as a matter of philosophy. He just was a person who believed in the word "conservative." The typical conservative today has carried it too far. I grew up in a very conservative family in northern Michigan. My people were "conservative" in that they loved the Almighty God and were loyal to their church.

We also had a limited income, and it was very difficult for a small-town merchant to keep going during the Depression years. So they conserved their money and also helped conserve nature. The typical conservative today—the right-wing variety—doesn't give a hoot about keeping our beautiful countryside in its current state. There is no interest in fighting pollution, no interest in preserving our national parks—all that is secondary. I'd say the typical conservative of today—the right-wing conservative—is working counter to the conservatism in which I grew up, and for which the great Ronald Reagan stood.

W.O.: Ward Quaal, you've counseled presidents—three of them—and today on the radio, you've counseled all of us. It appears we've lost not only a president, but a nice man.

W.Q.: We've lost a very fine man, a truly great American. He was loved all over the world because he stood on principle and he was decent and honorable.

STATE SENATOR JOE PISANI TALKS ABOUT JEANINE PIRRO, POLITICS, AND HIS NEW LIFE

Joe Pisani was a vivid and beguiling fellow who almost went all the way to the top in New York state—until he ran afoul of one Rudy Giuliani. After a colorful and turbulent political career, he finally found some peace out of the spotlight up in the Hudson Valley. We interviewed him on August 19, 2005.

WILLIAM O'SHAUGHNESSY (W.O.): The summer is winding down, and maybe it's a good thing, for this has been a mean political season. We're talking with one of New York state's most beloved and best-known political figures, Joseph Raymond Pisani. We caught up with Senator Joe in the Hudson Valley, and we switch now to his redoubt high above the mighty river. Senator Joe, what are you doing these days?

SENATOR JOE PISANI (J.P.): I'm practicing law. And, thank God, I still have a lot of energy. I'm working hard every day, trying to right the wrongs and correct the injustices that come to my door.

W.O.: Joe Pisani, how old are you now?

J.P.: I'll be seventy-six on August 31.

W.O.: Are you any the wiser for being seventy-six?

J.P.: Well, there is some truth to the statement that when you get a little older, you get a little wiser. But, I'm probably capable of making the same mistakes I've made in the past. (*laughs*)

W.O.: Joe Pisani, you've had your ups and downs in politics. You were a New Rochelle city councilman, a New York state senator; you were being touted in a lot of circles even for governor of New York, and you almost ran for Westchester County executive. Joe, do you know Jeanine Pirro?

J.P.: Oh, I know her very well, Bill. I have high regard for her. I've known her since she was up at Albany Law School.

W.O.: What do you think of Madam D.A.? We still call her "Judge" Pirro.

J.P.: I think she's an extremely capable person. I think she's as sharp as can be, as far as a lawyer is concerned. I think she's got a lot of charisma, and she's got an enviable record of having been a judge, an assistant district attorney, and district attorney of Westchester for some time now. I think she is someone to be reckoned with in politics today.

W.O.: Joseph Pisani, you're a smart politician. Do you think she can beat Hillary Clinton [in 2006]?

J.P.: Oh, boy, if I could predict races in politics, I'd probably be a rich man today! Anyone can beat anyone on any given day if they have the right resources, if the ducks all fall in line, if the climate is right. Is she a shoe-in winner? No. She's got a tough row to hoe. I don't think Hillary is unbeatable; I think Hillary *can* be beaten. Of all the available candidates in the Republican Party, quite frankly, I think Pirro's the only one with a chance of beating Hillary. However, if she had come to me and asked me if she should run against Hillary, I probably would have advised her to run for attorney general.

W.O.: Senator Joe Pisani, politics is a mean business. Nobody, I expect, knows that more than you. You ran afoul of a U.S. Attorney named Rudy Giuliani.

J.P.: I sure did.

W.O.: Have you forgiven him yet?

J.P.: (*laughs*) It's not for me to forgive. I mean, there is not a question of forgiving anyone. What happened, happened. I'm living with it. I'm back on my feet, in spite of his efforts, and I'm practicing law. As I said the day I was convicted, my friends are still my friends, and my enemies just have more to talk about.

W.O.: What do you mean?

J.P.: I mean that I feel I've survived and I still have my true friends from when I was riding on top of the political crest, and those who were not favorable to my candidacies just had more to talk about.

W.O.: So it's fair to say that politics, Joe Pisani, is a mean business.

J.P.: Oh, it can be *very* mean. I think politics brings out the best in people and also the worst. It depends on who you are and on the circumstances. I've seen some good people do some mean things; I've seen some pretty ugly people doing some nice things. It just depends on the circumstances.

W.O.: What about the press, Joe Pisani? Any regrets? Did the press treat you fairly?

J.P.: I think the press gave me a fair shake. I had some quarrels during my campaign when I ran for county executive. I know the Gannett chain received information they shouldn't have received from the grand jury. And any reputable news organization would not have printed it. But they had to answer to what they did, and I had to answer to what I did. But basically, and honestly, I have received good treatment from the press. There is no one in the press corps with whom I have any bones to pick. I do look back with some regret because I made some mistakes—there's no question about that. But I think I accomplished a lot, and I think they gave me a fair shake.

W.O.: Joe Pisani, you're established now—kind of like a second act—up in the Hudson Valley, in a place called West Park over the Hudson. Do you miss New Rochelle? You were a townie guy.

J.P.: Let me put it this way, Bill: I miss the action because most of my action now is in the courtroom. I'm not involved in politics, although I have been dragged into some of the local political fights as an attorney, but I haven't gotten involved in the actual political process. But I'm back in New Rochelle; I was there this morning, as a matter of fact. I still represent some clients in New Rochelle; I still go to the City Court of New Rochelle on occasion. I'm not completely removed from the city; I haven't turned my back on the city by any means.

W.O.: How about Judge Sandy Scher, Preston "Sandy" Scher, the chief city judge; do you know him?

J.P.: I know him. I think Sandy Scher is a marvelous judge. Since he took over the City Court of New Rochelle, he has run it in a professional and very judicious way. He is a wonderful judge with a wonderful temperament. He was a good lawyer before. On many occasions, when I would be called upon to make a speech confirming a judge, I would always start off by saying, "In order to be a good lawyer, you have to be a good person; in order to be a good judge, you've got to be a good lawyer." Sandy is all of that, and he has been a good judge. I think he deserves the wholehearted recognition of all the people of New Rochelle and should be given this opportunity to continue to serve.

W.O.: Senator Joe Pisani, the politicians usually cross-endorse when a judge is doing a good job, but the New Rochelle Democrats didn't do that.

J.P.: Well, it's not a question of whether a judge has done a good job, or whether a judge has not done a good job. There are many political factors involved; there are ambitions involved. There are a lot of things that go on in the undercurrent of politics that have nothing to do with whether anyone is a good candidate or a good judge. I've seen bad judges cross-endorsed, and I've seen bad candidates cross-endorsed. The fact that Sandy Scher is not being endorsed by the Democrats has nothing to do with his ability. I'm sure it has to do with internal politics.

W.O.: It's wonderful to talk to you, sir. Who is going to be the next governor of New York, when Pataki leaves?

J.P.: Right now, I know they're talking about some candidates, but I don't see anyone on the horizon who has the wherewithall to beat the system.

W.O.: What about William Weld? He was governor of Massachusetts; everybody seemed to like the guy.

J.P.: Well, what can I tell you? Sometimes things happen. We're in August, and it's close to November, but it's not that close. I honestly feel you can't get a feel of the political battlefields until you get into the beginning of October; then things start getting hot and heavy. People take the summer off and don't really think about politics. While I would advise candidates to get out and shake hands, you don't bring the big guns out until you start approaching October, when the people start seeing and hearing the candidates and concentrating on candidacies. They know Jeanine is running against Hillary, but they're not really paying that much attention to it. Hillary has got to do her thing; and Jeanine, I'm sure, will do her thing—she's got a lot of energy and she's going to attract a lot of attention, and I think she's going to make a good run of it. But nothing is really happening until the middle of September, beginning of October.

W.O.: Senator Pisani, as I listen to you, I don't hear much enthusiasm for the current crop, except for Jeanine Pirro and Judge Sandy Scher. But my mind drifts back, remembering the Rocco Bellantonis, the Frank Garitos, the Hughey Doyles, the Alvin Ruskins . . . and Teddy Greens. . . .

J.P.: These were real people in politics, and New Rochelle has had the benefit of the Rocco Bellantonis and the Frank Garitos. These were not people who were politicians, per se; they were local citizens who were tapped on the shoulder and asked to come into the fray, and they did. They gave of themselves. Sometimes small towns are lucky that way, to have the benefit of ordinary citizens, the nonprofessional politicians. My problem with politicians today is that there are too many "professionals." You don't have a "common man" politician any more. I think if you look at the legislature, everybody is a full-time politician; I think you could count on the fingers of one hand the number of people up there who are independently involved in another profession, other than politics. I think that's not good; the pendulum has swung too much in the other direction, and we're going in the wrong direction in politics today. Everything is too professional, everything is too slick, everything is controlled by polls and professional advisors. You never have anyone getting up to say exactly what they think. Most politicians today get up and say what they think you want them to say. That unfortunately is the state of politics today, and I'm not particularly happy with it.

W.O.: I saw Guy Velella—another state senator, powerful, like you—who had some problems with the courts. Do you think he could put his life back together? They're beating him up pretty good.

J.P.: I know. I haven't spoken to him since he got into some difficulty. But you have to step away from it, you have to get out of it to stop being a target. Because of what happened to us, lightning keeps striking in the same place, and you've got to remove yourself from the fray and get out and gather yourself together and take care of your own life first.

W.O.: So you're saying there is life after politics?

J.P.: There is life after politics, Bill. Whether you retire from politics on a high note or you go out on a low note, there is still life after politics; it's what you make of it. And I am happy where I am. I'm practicing law; I have a great reputation in the community and in the courts; and I enjoy it. People come to my door asking for help, and I'm there to help them. Life could not be better for me. I've still got a good tennis game too.

W.O.: Do you still row on the river?

J.P.: I don't row anymore because I don't have any opportunities.

W.O.: Are you still a big hunter?

J.P.: Oh, I'm a big hunter though. As soon as you get up in the north country, the first day of hunting season is just as important as Thanksgiving, Christmas, or Easter, in terms of holidays. (*laughs*) Nobody works; everybody is in the woods; and I'm one of them.

W.O.: Senator, when you were in Albany, you were famous for your Wednesday night suppers with a big pot of spaghetti, and you used to feed about fifty homeless senators. Do you still cook spaghetti?

J.P.: I still cook everything. I cook spaghetti; I cook wild game; and I still have my parties, only there are different people attending my parties now.

W.O.: One of a kind: Joseph Raymond Pisani. Thank you, Senator Joe.

J.P.: Thank you, Bill. Good talking to you on my old hometown radio station.

ANDY SPANO TALKS ABOUT WESTCHESTER MEDICAL CENTER, HOMELESS SHELTERS, HIS HAIR, AND HIS WIFE

In recent years many commentators and critics have questioned the need for county government. We've covered Westchester County executives all the way back to the legendary Edwin Gilbert Michaelian ("Mr. Westchester") and all through the administrations of Andrew P. O'Rourke, Alfred B. DelBello, and Andy Spano, who presided over the Golden Apple until 2010 when Rob Astorino, a radio producer and former member of the County Board, upset the likeable Spano. We did this interview with Spano five years earlier, on July 28, 2005, when he was still riding high.

WILLIAM O'SHAUGHNESSY (W.O.): Ladies and gentlemen, how nice to be with you. This is Bill O'Shaughnessy. You may remember me. It's been a time since I've enjoyed the privilege of your hearth and home and your good, fine, bright minds. This is what the Brits would call a "brilliant" day; it may be one of the ten nicest days of the year!

This is a special edition of "Westchester with O'Shaughnessy." We were able today—thanks to Susan Tolchin—to beg a few moments of his schedule. He's very busy, as you've read in the public press. Our guest for the next twenty-five minutes on WVOX is the County Executive of Westchester, the Golden Apple: Andy Spano.

ANDY SPANO (A.S.): It's always a pleasure to be here with you, Bill.

W.O.: Why are you running again? Why the hell are you doing it?

A.S.: I think this a fantastic county. I've been in office eight years now. I think we've done a number of things that have improved the county and led to the enhancement of our quality of life in Westchester. I still have some unfinished business. I love the job.

I think I do it well, and I want a "verification" of that on Election Day.

W.O.: These are difficult times for the county. First of all, Mr. County Executive, the Westchester Medical Center: Is it ever going to heal? Is it ever going to get better?

A.S.: If you had asked me that a couple of years ago, I would have been less optimistic than I am right now. But at this particular point, I think we've bought them enough time with the county's investment in this hospital. I think there's a bright sign in Albany in terms of assisting the hospital. There are some nuances we differ with Albany on, but I think we can work those out.

W.O.: Is that another word for money?

A.S.: Yes. They're interested in putting it in. It's more the governance that's a problem. Before I get into this discussion, I would just like to say this: This hospital does not belong to the county government of Westchester. This is a public-benefit corporation that stands on its own, created by the previous administration. And every effort we're making to keep it is related to the importance of the hospital and the people of Westchester County.

W.O.: Who set it up? Are you talking about Andy O'Rourke?

A.S.: Andy O'Rourke and the previous administration and the Board of Legislators at the time.

W.O.: Is it a good system? What's up there now?

A.S.: I think what's in there now is good. What happened when they let it go and put it on its own was that they did not instill in the management that they were now private and away from the county. They had to create a whole new culture at the hospital, new management procedures to operate entrepreneurially, like a regular hospital does, in order to make money. In the old days, what happened was very simple. At the end of the year, whatever loss there was, the county would pay. The year before I came in, 1997, it was costing the county $34 million a year to run the hospital. It was spun off for legitimate reasons. It's hard for hospitals to exist in this environment, as a government entity. Governments operate too slowly. Hospitals today need to react to the market.

W.O.: So, Mr. County Executive, you're saying the government is back in there now? You've got a grip on it?

A.S.: We have a group made up of the county government, hospital personnel, and the board of the hospital that meets on an ongoing basis and goes over all the finances of the hospital and makes recommendations to the board of directors.

W.O.: And you're starting to see a little light at the end of the tunnel?

A.S.: Well, the county is putting $37 million in to help with the cash flow so they can keep going as we negotiate other things. Now, a couple of things have happened. One, the professional management team that is in there now has saved over $20 million one year and a projected $20 million this year, by reducing costs. The county has come in with what basically amounts to a subsidy, and we will—on an ongoing basis—give them a subsidy.

W.O.: How much are you giving them now?

A.S.: We gave them $37 million this year, which involves a $27 million direct grant and a $10 million "forgiveness" of services.

W.O.: How big is your county budget?

A.S.: One billion, four hundred million dollars.

W.O.: Didn't somebody say that's larger than many states in the union?

A.S.: The County of Westchester budget is larger than the budgets of seven states.

W.O.: If you could get rid of the Medical Center, would you?

A.S.: No, absolutely not. We would love to get rid of the *problem* of the medical center, but it would be totally irresponsible to get rid of the Medical Center. This is not just a hospital. It is a unique medical center, the only tertiary care institution between New York and Albany.

W.O.: Which means . . .

A.S.: Which means it handles medical procedures that are different from all the other hospitals.

W.O.: Should they have been doing this "world-class" medical thing? It used to be Grasslands. It was where they put you if you were a little crazy.

A.S.: Yes. But that goes way back before the DelBello administration. This new hospital was set up during the DelBello administration, in the mid-'70s, and continued through the O'Rourke administration.

W.O.: They may be the big tertiary site for the whole region. But Senator Nick Spano—no relation to you—said nobody but us seems to want to keep the damned thing afloat. The upstate counties don't want it.

A.S.: Well, someone didn't make the effort, at one time, to get these people roped in. Forty percent of the patients come to the hospital from outside Westchester County. It serves the entire Hudson Valley region.

W.O.: Do you ever talk to your fellow county executives? Even your worst critics would say Andy is a good politician.

A.S.: The answer to your question is yes. And we're still doing it. I organized all the county executives in the region. We talked about sharing half of the one-quarter percent sales tax that goes to those counties.

W.O.: Do they hear your music on that?

A.S.: The county executives basically hear my music. The assembly members and senators that represent those districts do not hear it at this point.

There are short-term problems at the hospital and long-term problems. So we solve the short-term problems right now, and we're working on the long-term problems. I have not only gone to see them, but I've put together the chambers of commerce from various regions and have them talking to one another. I've involved the County Association, which is doing a whole evaluation and study of the process.

W.O.: Mr. County Executive Andy Spano, you've got two very bright guys in your service: Richard Berman, president of Manhattanville College, and John Spicer. They know what the hell they're talking about.

A.S.: Correct.

W.O.: So do you think things are going to get better up there?

A.S.: Well, I think they're getting better now, but the entire payroll of that institution was handled *manually*! Now, trying to handle the payroll of a 24/7 institution with 3,500 to 4,000 workers is an extremely difficult thing to do manually. They may have been paying dead people, for all we know!

W.O.: But is this the classic case where *private* enterprise can do it better than government?

A.S.: No. There are a lot of hospitals in trouble right now that aren't public hospitals. This hospital is unique, and it has to do unique things. It doesn't belong to the county of Westchester, but we're in there trying to help them.

W.O.: But you *can* put some of your guys on the board.

A.S.: I have put Dick Berman on the board, and he is the chair right now. Not only is he president of Manhattanville College, but he was also the administrator of New York Medical Center before he became president of Manhattanville.

W.O.: Wasn't he one of Hugh Carey's health commissioners?

A.S.: He was the health commissioner under Hugh Carey. We also have a person who just retired from MBIA, who was in charge of all the evaluation of bonding for medical institutions. We're trying to get professional help in there. We're more optimistic now than we have been before.

W.O.: Our guest is the County Executive of the Golden Apple, Andy Spano, the husband of Brenda Resnick Spano.

A.S.: I'm glad you defined that because that's very important. (*laughs*)

W.O.: Are you two still together?

A.S.: We're together now *and* forever, O'Shaughnessy.

W.O.: You and I have married well, I have to tell you.

A.S.: Everyone tells me that. Everywhere I go by myself, everyone says, "Where's Brenda?" I say, "What am I? Chopped liver?"

W.O.: Didn't you get introduced at the Mount Vernon Kiwanis Club as a self-made man through *marriage*?

A.S.: (*laughs*) Do you know Charlie King at all?

W.O.: Yes, sir.

A.S.: Charlie King is running for attorney general. And I am backing Richard Brodsky for attorney general, but my wife is backing Charlie King. My wife and Charlie King have a good relationship. So she drags me to a Charlie King fundraiser in Manhattan. I said,

"I just can't go there." She said, "Just go there. You know Charlie. Just tell him not to make a big deal that you're there." I said, "Fine." So we go, and Charlie comes out. I said, "Charlie, don't even mention my name. Don't say a word." So he gets up and says to this group, "I want to thank some of my supporters who are here." And he announces this guy and that guy. And then he says, "I have the First Lady of Westchester County, Brenda Resnick Spano, and her spouse, who came here kicking and moaning." (*laughter*)

W.O.: She's a wonderful woman. Please give her our best. You're a smart guy in politics. Who is going to be the next governor?

A.S.: That's a no-brainer. Eliot Spitzer is going to be the next governor.

W.O.: OK, who's going to be the next attorney general?

A.S.: That's going to be Richard Brodsky.

W.O.: You think so?

A.S.: That's who I'm supporting.

W.O.: Listen, if I were a betting man, I would find out whom *Brenda* is for and put my chips there. (*laughter*)

Mr. County Executive, let me ask you something about that homeless shelter near the airport. Some things never change. I did editorials twenty years ago about the "families of the night." Endowed as Westchester is with all the money, all the influence, all the reputation, we still have some tremendous poverty and the disenfranchised. The elders in White Plains, the county seat, are raging and raging. The district attorney is involved. The mayor of White Plains is actually *suing* you to close the damn thing down. Joseph Delfino is on a roll right now. But these people have to stay someplace!

A.S.: Well, that's the point. We have over *fifteen* centers for the homeless in Westchester County. We have two kinds of facilities. We have shelters, where they actually live, and we have *programs* for them, jobs programs, mental health programs, and so on. And then we have *drop-in centers*. It's important to know the distinction. The drop-in centers are for people who don't want to be in the shelters or, for one reason or another, are not eligible for the shelters.

W.O.: How would you not be eligible for a roof over your head?

A.S.: Here's how you're not eligible, like this guy that killed a woman in White Plains.

W.O.: Who lived in a shelter . . .

A.S.: No, he didn't live there. He was living there last year. You must go through the program of the shelter. You must go where they send you, go through the evaluation, get the therapy they send you for, abide by the rules. He just refused. When you refuse, you just can't stay in the shelter anymore. So he left the shelter, or was thrown out of the shelter. That puts him, along with others who have no ties to any system, free to do anything they want.

W.O.: He fell through the cracks.

A.S.: That's correct. He served his sentence. He met his responsibility to the state for whatever it was—twenty-three years—and then they let him out. And when you serve your sentence, there are no ties after that. There is no parole, no probation, no anything. You're just out. He was a state prisoner who was brought here without a home. And they said to us, "Here he is; he is in *your* domain." And we have him and a number of others like that. There are, in all our towns and cities, homeless who wander around and do not want to go to the shelter. We don't have any responsibility, legally, for doing anything with them. We try to help them. We try to encourage them to go into programs, but we don't have any direct *legal* responsibility.

However, years ago, when my predecessors were in office, everyone realized that it was not a humane thing to do to just leave people wandering around the streets. So they decided, along with the Board of Legislators, to have what they call "drop-in centers" so that people, in the winter and other times during the year, would have a place to sleep. We have one in Yonkers and one at the airport. But you can't ask people without resources to get themselves to the airport, so we have a pickup area in White Plains, where, at 10:00 at night, anybody who wants a place to sleep can get a ride to the shelter. We try to encourage them to go to the shelter, but if they don't want to go . . . these are free people. Our only choices with them are not to pick them up at all and just leave them in White Plains.

W.O.: Let them wander around?

A.S.: Yes. We don't have any responsibility to shelter them. I'd get it off my back just by leaving them on the streets, but that would be totally irresponsible.

W.O.: Mr. County Executive Andy Spano, you're a Democrat. Do Democrats look at this homeless problem differently than Republicans?

A.S.: No, actually not.

W.O.: You preside over a county of a million people. We have incredible wealth in Bronxville, and Bedford, and Rye. But we've got people wandering the streets. . . .

A.S.: You should know one thing though, Bill. We have one of the best programs for the homeless in the entire region. We're the only place in the region where the homeless population isn't rising.

W.O.: What is the homeless population?

A.S.: I don't know the exact numbers. But we used to have the largest homeless population in the country percentage-wise, at the tail end of the O'Rourke administration. O'Rourke worked on it also. It had nothing to do with him. He worked on the same kinds of programs we're talking about now; he and his predecessor, Al DelBello, instituted them. And they're good programs. We've been able to maintain them and enhance them and keep the homeless population down in Westchester. For instance, we have half the people on welfare that we used to have when I came into office. We could say, "If you don't follow the rules we can let you go," but we don't do that anymore. When they go off welfare, we follow them up with jobs and housing and other help so they don't come back into the homeless population.

W.O.: Andy Spano, maybe you can't fix this. It's in the Bible: "the poor you shall have with you always. . . ."

A.S.: Look, you can fix *some* of it. Johns Hopkins did a study years ago that said even if you built all the housing in the world, you will still have homeless. There are people who have other kinds of problems, who just are not going to respond to the fact that there is affordable housing around.

The fact is, we don't have legal tools that allow us to take people who obviously have problems and take them off the street and put them in programs. Well, if we can't do that without their permission, we've got problems.

W.O.: Nice guy that he is, isn't Delfino saying, "Not in *my* back yard"?

A.S.: Well, these are White Plains people we're picking up. These are not Westchester County people.

W.O.: Have you called up Joseph Delfino, the White Plains mayor, and said, "*Where* the hell do you want me to *put* them?"

A.S.: I've asked that of everybody who has criticized our system: "Where do you want us to put them?" We have an excellent shelter system and an excellent system to help the homeless, and we're trying to do more. This problem of location is not about the homeless; it has come up about sex offenders. Joe Delfino, by the way, knows about all of these programs because he was part of the legislature that instituted some of them.

W.O.: Andy Spano, you slipped right by, very modestly, the fact that you cut the welfare rolls in half. I understand that you get high marks—even from critics—for that and for westchestergov.com. Now, I wouldn't know a computer if it hit me. Why are you so famous for this cockamamie westchestergov.com?

A.S.: (*laughter*) We've won many awards for the website. The reason that it was instituted was because it's easy to inform people through it. Seventy percent of the people in Westchester get on the Internet. Let me give you just a simple way the government helps the people. They have constant information they can look up. Let's look at the old way: *no* website. If someone wanted information, they would dial a phone number and get an operator. They would say to the operator, "I'm so and so and I want . . .," and the operator would say, "I think the person you want is . . .," and the operator transfers the call. It may be the right person, or if it's the wrong person, that person would say, "That's not me, but I know who it is"—and the call would be transferred again. When you finally get to the right person, you'd ask him the question. That person would say, "Let me look up the information and

I'll call you back." In that process, the productivity of every worker is compromised a bit.

W.O.: So you brought it into high tech.

A.S.: Yes. Now you get on the website and get your answer while my guy is working on something else.

W.O.: How old are you, Andy Spano?

A.S.: I'm sixty-nine years old.

W.O.: How long have you been county executive?

A.S.: This is my eighth year.

W.O.: Are you sure you want to do this?

A.S.: I love this job. This is a great job. Being county executive of Westchester County is probably one of the greatest satisfactions you can have. You can talk to DelBello about it, or O'Rourke. For *two* reasons. One, you live in this incredible county and you have an opportunity to enhance the quality of life. And two: You have the resources in its people and its workers and its other tangible financial resources to really make a difference. That's why I like the job: I want to make that difference.

W.O.: You have, some say, "no opponent," but you do have a Republican running against you.

A.S.: I have an opponent. I see him running. He's bringing up interesting questions. We do have a campaign.

W.O.: Do you like it when Phil Reisman and the elders at Gannett bang you around? They hit everybody; every incumbent is fair game.

A.S.: In this business, on its best day, you feel a little comfortable, you do some good things, and everyone tells you you're a great guy. Most of the days, someone hits you over the head. You have opponents who really don't like you and don't tell the truth. You have media that latch onto little things that you're not even thinking about and bring them out to the forefront and you have to answer them. Most of the time, you have real problems. You have the Medical Center; you have the homeless; you have drunk people flying into the airport; you've got security problems. But I'm staying in office as long as I don't *cause* the problems. The minute I begin *causing* the problems, then it's time for me to leave.

W.O.: One of our colorful journalists abroad in the field, Phil Reisman, is going on the radio today at noon. . . .

A.S.: Double trouble; now I have to read him in the newspaper *and* listen to him on the *radio*! (*laughter*) He's a great guy, a funny guy, very smart, good writer. I certainly don't always agree with him.

W.O.: He picks on you sometimes.

A.S.: He picks on my *hair*.

W.O.: He does?

A.S.: Yes, he thinks my hair is phony. Like you, I have this great hair. Of course, it's a different color, but he thinks it's a wig.

W.O.: Are you having a good hair day?

A.S.: Every day is a good hair day for *me*!

W.O.: You know who your hair looks like? Dan Rather's.

A.S.: Is that right?

W.O.: You and Rather have the same hairdo. Why don't you let it grow out a little?

A.S.: To some people that's a negative. In this business it's about minimizing the negative. If I want to communicate with people and have clarity, I can't have them looking at my hair.

W.O.: (*laughter*) Our guest has been the county executive of Westchester, Andy Spano.

Do you think Gannett will endorse you this time?

A.S.: I have no idea. It's up to Gannett. Look, I treat every campaign like it's the last one. I've got the most awesome opponent, and I have to prove myself to the people, and the press, and everybody else; and that's what I'm trying to do.

W.O.: I think you're one of the nicest men in public life.

A.S.: Thank you for that. Thank you very much.

W.O.: Brenda . . .

A.S.: Brenda's better. I know. (*laughter*)

W.O.: Our guest has been Andy Spano. Governor Cuomo calls you "Spahno."

A.S.: "Spahno" is correct. "Spahno" is the Italian pronunciation. In Italian, every vowel only has one sound; it's not like English. And "a" is always "ah."

W.O.: So the senator you're not related to, he's a "Spahno" too?

A.S.: He's a "Spahno" too.

W.O.: What about Domenic Procopio? Are you still close with him?

A.S.: Very close. Only he's what we call Calabrese; he comes from Calabria. My people are from Puglia, which is different.

W.O.: Where is Puglia?

A.S.: Puglia is the heel of Italy. The other Spanos and myself are all from the same town.

W.O.: Aren't you from Bari?

A.S.: We're from Provincia de Bari, which is like a state, or like a county; and in that province is the city of Bari and a number of other little cities. And one of those little towns in the province of Bari is called Grumo—and that's where we're from.

W.O.: Do you still have family there?

A.S.: Not in that town, but in another town; they moved.

W.O.: I heard when you go over there with your beautiful American wife, Brenda Spano, you're treated like a king.

A.S.: They treat me well. They like to see Italian Americans who have made it over here. And I have a pride in where I came from, and they feel that too. So we have a wonderful time. Once a year, I try to get back. On vacation—I want to make that clear—on vacation.

W.O.: County Executive, thank you. Can we do it again? Sometimes I feel like a Jewish grandmother with you. "He never calls me. . . ."

A.S.: Yes, of course we can do it again, Bill.

ROBERT J. GREY JR., PRESIDENT, AMERICAN BAR ASSOCIATION

Frank Trotta, a former New Rochellean who is now based in Greenwich, where he serves as an advisor to Lewis Lehrman (the Rite Aid founder who ran for governor of New York but lost to Mario Cuomo), called me up one day and said, "You gotta get this guy Robert Grey in. Among other things, he's president of the American Bar Association." Upon our interviewing him on September 21, 2004, I found Grey to be not only a great lawyer but also a great American with an inspiring story.

WILLIAM O'SHAUGHNESSY (W.O.): It's a perfectly splendid Indian Summer day, what the Brits would call a quite "brilliant" day.

And for the next forty-five minutes or so, while we're in your care and keeping, we're going to present a very attractive man. I wish we had a damned television camera operating today. He's sent from Central Casting, I'm afraid. He is president of the American Bar Association, the number one lawyer in the whole damn republic. His name is Robert Grey Jr. He hails from Richmond, Virginia, and he is in the Golden Apple to talk to some folks from the Gannett Editorial Board and tell them what *lawyers* think about the great issues of the day. Then he's going to address the Greenwich Bar Association, a very tony group, up the line a piece. Mr. President Grey, welcome to Westchester.

ROBERT GREY (R.G.): Thank you, Bill. I'm delighted to be here.

W.O.: Is that how courtly lawyers dress in the South? You have a pinstriped suit, a pink shirt, and a pink tie.

R.G.: Well, it's a beautiful day, and I thought I would look the way I feel. Pink. (*laughter*)

W.O.: Have you ever been to Westchester before, Mr. Grey?

R.G.: I have not. But I'm delighted to be here. The hospitality is fabulous, and I'm looking forward to the interview. Your reputation precedes you.

W.O.: Sooner or later, everyone peddling a book idea or a candidacy comes through Westchester because the influence and the money reside here. You don't want to run for anything, do you?

R.G.: I'm not running for anything or from anything. Thank goodness my election is over and I am now serving that term.

W.O.: How did you get to be president of the American Bar Association? That's heavy stuff.

R.G.: Well, you have to have a little bit of luck, some pretty good timing, and a lot of friends. Because it is an election and requires some "time on turf"—like twenty years—within the Bar Association. I started when I was a young lawyer in my thirties. I'm now in my fifties and have had a wonderful run of experiences within the Bar Association, practicing law in Virginia. And I felt very strongly about the importance of lawyers' work in society. The American Bar Association is the largest association of professionals in the world: 405,000 members.

W.O.: Do you know them all by their first names?

R.G.: Most, but not all. (*laughter*)

W.O.: Are there some bad apples there among the 400,000?

R.G.: It's a little hard not to find bad apples in a barrel that big.

W.O.: But what do you do about it? Someone once said radio is the last turf on which an "entrepreneur" can run. And my wife is a car dealer. So we've all taken our shots. Are you glad to be a lawyer? Can you look at yourself in the mirror?

R.G.: Oh, absolutely. I wake up every morning and feel blessed someone was out there to provide guidance for me in choosing law as a profession.

I had a unique upbringing because I saw the legal profession provide leadership in a very troubled time in our society. That was during integration and segregation in a country that professed to be one with liberty, freedom, and individual rights. Growing up, I was in segregated schools. But during my adolescence I went to integrated schools as part of the generation of *Brown v. Board of Education*, which we celebrated last year on its fiftieth anniversary.

I grew up around the corner from Doug Wilder, who is a lawyer and the first person of color elected governor in the United

States. Down the street was Oliver Hill, who graduated second in his class from the Howard [University] Law School in 1933. The number one graduate that year was Thurgood Marshall. And the two were very dear friends and colleagues. They were the team that provided the background and advocacy for *Brown v. Board of Education* before the Supreme Court. Across the park from me was Arthur Ashe. His dad was superintendent of the park where we played. His dad had X-ray vision and could see behind walls. So when we were cutting up, he'd say, "Son, you need to straighten up or I'm going to take you to see your parents."

W.O.: Did the white guys play?

R.G.: No. This was a very segregated community I grew up in. I wouldn't trade what I experienced as a young person for anything. But I recognize the value of what we've done in this country since that time. There was a very strong community spirit in Richmond, with tremendous support for each others' families. So if somebody needed help, it was an open-door policy in our community that others would come to their aid. That's hard to knock.

W.O.: You referred to Douglas Wilder as a "person of color." Now, I asked a neighbor of ours, the former president of the National Urban League, Hugh Price, what is the "term du jour": Is it "African American"? Ossie Davis lives two blocks from here, and he watches me closely on all matters of faith and correctness. So do we refer to Governor Wilder or yourself as "African Americans" or as "persons of color"?

R.G.: I have resisted this idea of limiting the description because I think people say what they are used to saying and what they heard as most descriptive of people. I think the important thing is that you respect the other person. I am resistant to labels. I try to be very careful about trying not to suggest that somebody needs to call me black or African American or anything else. And if they say something that in their mind was not meant to offend me, then that's the most important thing—that people are honest with each other and that we have some tolerance with each other regarding these labels.

W.O.: You know what Hugh Price said? He said, "Bill, it doesn't matter anymore. I've been called five different things in my lifetime."

R.G.: That's true, we have. And if you've lived as long as we have, you understand that we went from "Negro" to "colored" to "black" to "African American" to "persons of color." That is five different labels. I think what's most important, and what I tell people, is that I'm proud to be an American. This is my country as much as it is anybody else's. I don't know that I look like any particular anything other than who I am. I'm pretty comfortable in my skin and very comfortable telling people that I'm an American.

W.O.: I believe we're listening to the voice of quite a *great* American at this precise moment. He's president of the 400,000-member American Bar Association. We're honored to have Robert J. Grey Jr. And we'll even put you on the radio with Mr. Grey. Counselor, do you want to take a few calls?

R.G.: I'd be delighted.

CALLER 1: Yes, good morning, Bill, my name is Ken. I'd like to cover two areas if I may. Now, you have the call letters of the NAACP. If I would say, "I know a friend of mine who is colored," would you be offended?

R.G.: As I said before, I think we have used labels before. "Colored" was a label that was used, sometimes, to be derogatory.

CALLER 1: Well, sir, can I interrupt you by saying, why do you go under the heading NAACP, which is the National Association for the Advancement for Colored People? Now, would you be offended if I say I have a friend of mine who is colored?

R.G.: As I said before, I think it wasn't the term itself as much as it was the context in which we say it.

CALLER 1: I'm looking at this high-profile case of O. J. Simpson. We're talking about justice. He was involved in a double murder and the evidence was all there. He had the blood on his shoes, on his property. . . .

W.O.: Mr. Grey is shaking his head. I think he agrees with you. What's your point?

CALLER I: The point is, he got off a double murder because Johnnie Cochran used theatrics in the courtroom, which enabled him to beat the law.

W.O.: Hold it. You're the top lawyer in the country. Do you agree with what Ken just said?

R.G.: I don't. I think everyone is entitled to a defense lawyer. O. J. Simpson picked Johnnie Cochran. But our system of justice says prosecutors have a job. And their job is to prove people's guilt beyond reasonable doubt.

CALLER I: He was certainly guilty. Nobody else did it!

R.G.: That is an opinion you have, and if you were on the jury, you could have expressed that. But you were not on the jury.

CALLER I: Listen, he had blood on his shoes! He was leaving with ten thousand in his Jeep when he was trying to take off. . . .

W.O.: Ken . . . Ken . . . Ken . . . I would not want you sitting on my jury, but I like you in our audience. Thank you very much.

Ladies and gentlemen, it is four minutes before eleven o'clock here in the Golden Apple. Our guest on this special edition of "Westchester Open Line" is Robert Grey Jr. He's president of the American Bar Association. We're very grateful to a child of New Rochelle, who's also done very well himself. He's an associate of Lewis Lehrman, the financier and philanthropist. I'm talking about Frank Trotta Jr. Thanks to Frank, Mr. Grey is here, and he's agreed to suffer my presence and take some calls.

You're talking about defendants. I always root for the defendant, and Mario Cuomo said he does too. What about you?

R.G.: Well, we have a system of justice better than anything else anywhere in the world. And the reason it is the best is because people come into our system of justice *presumed* innocent. They must be *proven* guilty. As a defense lawyer, you don't prove your client's innocence; you defend your client. It's the prosecution's responsibility to prove the guilt. That is a very important distinction. As I guess Ken would describe it, they were up there having sort of a "free for all" in the courtroom. But the responsibility in our system of justice is that you have to prove guilt. And not only prove it, but prove it beyond a reasonable doubt. Not every scintilla of doubt, but a *reasonable* doubt. It is a very high standard, but a very fair standard that we have enjoyed all these many years. And by and large it works. Some guilty people go free, and unfortunately, some innocent people are convicted.

W.O.: Mr. President Grey, I'd like to tell you something—I hope you don't lose all respect for me—but I was at a very swell luncheon club in Manhattan, the Dutch Treat Club. I was the only one who cheered when that verdict was announced. I didn't care if he was guilty or not. I didn't particularly like Marcia Clark. (*laughter*) Is that a terrible thing to admit?

R.G.: No, I think that was an interesting trial. It was the first to receive the publicity and attention of the public focusing on our American justice system. And many of us cheered because justice was served and O. J. Simpson got a fair trial. The prosecution failed in its responsibility to prove his guilt beyond a reasonable doubt. And the jury agreed.

W.O.: Let's go again to the lines—they're all backed up—I've been rattling on.

CALLER 2: Good morning, gentlemen. This is Bob Schaefer. I just want to say we are entitled to as much justice as we can afford. O. J. Simpson has proven that affirmative action works. What's your position on affirmative action, and has it helped you?

R.G.: Affirmative action has been a very positive development in our society. It is and has gone through several forms. We started out with this idea that in order to achieve some racial balance within departments of police and fire we had to establish quotas. We did that for a while and focused on the *number* and not on the *quality*. And we said that's not really helping us, and it's not helping those who are being hired. Let's focus on quality with an emphasis on ethnicity. So we modified affirmative action, and then we started to look at quality with an emphasis on ethnicity, and we got better results.

W.O.: Where did you graduate in your law class, at Washington and Lee? How high in the class?

R.G.: In the middle.

W.O.: How about in high school?

R.G.: In the middle.

W.O.: And now you're president of the Bar Association.

R.G.: At the top. (*laughter*)

W.O.: You're on the air. . . .

CALLER 3: Good morning, Bill, and good morning, Mr. Grey. I would like to ask you a question concerning jurors. If you find a juror was left to preside over a trial and then found out this individual went in deliberately trying to overturn the jurors with respect to his or her point of view and then went in and said the individual was guilty before a verdict was received, what would you do?

R.G.: We have a process in what ends up being an examination of jurors before we impanel them. And we try very hard to keep that from happening. You know and I know . . .

CALLER 3: They lie, some of them.

R.G.: You can't stop people from telling a lie. But our system promotes truth, and it promotes justice. I am convinced our jury system works, and 99 percent of those who serve on the jury do it with a high calling of citizenship. They do it with honor and integrity. Our system of justice is the envy around the world.

CALLER 3: Also, is an individual required to have a jury or can they request no jury?

R.G.: You are absolutely right: They have a choice. They can have a jury trial, or they can have a trial by a judge.

W.O.: In any court?

R.G.: In any court.

CALLER 3: Which is beneficial to the individual?

R.G.: Well, that's a great question. We took a survey because your question is a very important question that all of us thought about as well. Seventy-five percent of those surveyed said if they had their matter in court, they'd prefer to have a jury decide it as opposed to a judge.

W.O.: I want to ask you, sir: If you do nothing else, Mr. President, can you and your group kill off the death penalty in this country, which demeans us? I haven't even asked you where you stand on this.

R.G.: I wear the hat today as president of the American Bar Association. The Bar Association has not taken a position on the death penalty. We have debated the merits of the death penalty in terms of how it is applied. And after a very heated debate we decided a moratorium needed to be declared on the death penalty, until and unless states could be assured they were applying the standard required to take someone's life with the greatest of care, with the highest of excellence toward defense counsel—investigatory opportunities for the defendant and great care in the prosecution of the case. Unless states could assure themselves that those standards were being met, we suggested they declare a moratorium and determine how they were applying the death penalty.

W.O.: Do you have lobbyists at the American Bar Association like any other group?

R.G.: We have a government relations department in Washington, D.C., that advocates for the resolutions that are passed by the House of Delegates of the American Bar Association, which passed the resolution on the moratorium.

W.O.: How do you, Robert Grey—child of Richmond, now very successful lawyer—stand on this?

R.G.: I can't tell you how I stand on this because I wear a hat right now, and I am the spokesperson for the American Bar Association. I prefer to tell you as that representative what our position is and how we're advocating in support of it. I believe, however, we have a responsibility in this country. We have a responsibility to be fair, to be just, and to respect the wishes of those we elect and the work they do. And until such time as that work is proven to be contrary to the public good, then that's the law, and we must uphold it.

W.O.: Mr. Grey, we have some calls backed up, but what about Martha Stewart? Do you feel one damn bit safer with her behind bars?

R.G.: Martha Stewart represents what has been an issue in our society: that the privileged have special consideration attached to their conduct. And as a result of her conduct, as a result of those in charge of Enron, WorldCom, and other institutions, we are saying that the confidence in our corporate society must be respected by those who are running corporate America. And if they don't do it, well, then we are unable to have confidence in our economic system. If they lie, if they cheat, they must be brought to justice. Martha Stewart represents bringing corporate America to justice.

W.O.: My position on her case is: She's guilty of being a bitch. But is that what she went down for, being a rich bitch?

R.G.: You have to understand, Mr. O'Shaughnessy, that one makes a decision. In deciding to move forward in a trial and take whatever the jury decides, one is rolling the dice to a certain extent. I am sure at some point there was some discussion about a plea bargain. Defendants have the opportunity to accept or reject plea bargains. Obviously, there was no meeting of the minds with her, and she decided to take her case to the jury. And in taking that case to the jury, there was a certain amount of risk involved. She took the risk and she lost. And now she stands accused, and convicted, of having broken the law. And now she must pay the price.

W.O.: So do you think she's where she deserves to be, about one foot away from jail?

R.G.: Well, justice was served in her case.

W.O.: Let's go again to the phones. This is a very bright man and I'm making little headway trying to persuade Robert Grey Jr., president of the American Bar Association, to my point of view on damn near anything. You're on the air.

CALLER 4: It's Marty Rochelle, Bill.

W.O.: Colonel Marty Rochelle: This is the largest bail bondsman in the entire northeastern United States. He's also the king of Yonkers, where true love conquers. Go ahead, Colonel Rochelle.

CALLER 4: Mr. Grey, what do you think of the American bail system, excluding the federal system?

R.G.: I may be treading on territory that I'm not an expert in. I did practice some criminal law for a while, but my experience is limited to the state in which I practiced. As far as I was able to discern, our system has worked well, and a great deal is based on what prosecutors are able to convey, in terms of setting bail. People find that the opportunity to be free, pending their trial, allows them to prepare for their defense. One problem is that some people who are on bail take that opportunity to leave the jurisdiction—that's not a good thing. But, on balance, I think the system has worked pretty well.

W.O.: What do you think about that, Colonel?

CALLER 4: I think one of the best parts of criminal justice is that you're entitled to bail, whereas in many other countries, you languish in jail, pending trial. I'd like to ask a second question. Do you think the criminal [justice] system should abolish plea bargaining and have you stand trial as charged?

R.G.: No. I think plea bargaining is an important part of our process, just as alternative dispute resolution in civil cases is an important part of the trial process. I think there are times and situations where the opportunity to work out a compromise supports the system and allows for a more effective administration of justice.

CALLER 4: Even though the district attorney can overcharge because he knows you're going to take a plea?

R.G.: Well, everybody has to come to the table with a certain degree of good faith. You can't always determine whether that's the case or not. But I'm pretty confident our criminal defense lawyers understand the difference between a prosecutor who is loading up on the charges and one trying to be fair and zero in on a particular charge against a person. Prosecutors have to be careful because juries know when somebody is being not prosecuted but persecuted. Therein lies a great deal of the confidence I think we have in the American jury system.

W.O.: I should tell you that these proceedings are greatly enhanced by the presence in our studio at this moment by the Chief City Judge of New Rochelle, Judge Preston "Sandy" Scher. And also by the man who runs our courthouse, James Generoso.

I want to ask you, President Grey, about the Supreme Court. You and I spoke earlier about one Mario Cuomo, our former governor. I, at one point in time, tried to talk him out of going on the Supreme Court. He said, "It's a great job—you don't even have to wear underwear!"

I think if I were the president of the United States, I'd be knocking on *your* door. I think you'd make a great Supreme Court justice.

R.G.: You're very kind. I think I'm enjoying being a practicing lawyer too much.

W.O.: Have you ever appeared before the Supreme Court?

R.G.: I have appeared before the Supreme Court, but it was to move the admission of the lawyers to the court. I have not argued a case before the United States Supreme Court.

W.O.: Do you know those guys? The justices?

R.G.: I know some of them, and I'm actually going to make an effort during my tenure to meet each and every one of them. Because I think it's important to listen to their thoughts and comments, and to let them know what we're doing as the representative for all the lawyers and judges in the country.

W.O.: Doesn't every lawyer look in the mirror and see a judge? Don't they dream of one day being a judge?

R.G.: Being a judge is a very special job, and it takes a very special person. Not every lawyer can be a judge. But every judge is a lawyer, thank goodness. It's a temperament, a manner, a sense of wholeness at representing the system of justice that we have built in this country. The demeanor and temperament of a judge is extremely important to the proper administration of justice and the confidence that we as lawyers have in our judicial system, and the confidence citizens have. Judges mean more to our system and serve as the nucleus around which all of us meet to administer justice. Their thoughtfulness, their integrity, their willingness to, in a sense, separate themselves to some degree from society is important so they can be beyond reproach based on conflict of interest. Not everyone wants to live that kind of life. There is some isolation in being a judge. And I take my hat off to those who serve as judges because it's an important and essential responsibility in our justice system.

W.O.: But if the president called you and said, "I'd like to appoint you a Supreme Court justice," what would you say?

R.G.: How could I say no about that? (*laughter*)

W.O.: Robert Grey, speaking of great judges, we have one in the studio at the moment. I'll tell you just how good Judge Scher is, if Mr. Generoso doesn't beat me to the punch.

JAMES GENEROSO (J.G.): I have to tell you, I've been at the court for more than thirty years. Mr. Grey's answer was absolutely right on target. Temperament and fairness—especially in a local court, more than the Supreme Court—and a way of dealing with people and knowledge of the law are so important. And one thing I'm sure he'll agree with me on: A lot of great attorneys like Judge Scher and Mr. Grey are out there in private practice, and when it comes time to take the bench, they have to give up a lot of financial reward in order to pay back the community. It's tough to find good judges who are willing to give up those dollars to serve the community. Judge Scher is one of them, and I've had the pleasure of serving with a lot of good judges here in Westchester, including Judge Ken Rudolph and Judge Ben Mermelstein and it's an honor to serve with them.

W.O.: And this is a local-yokel court, a tough court.

J.G.: Five thousand criminal cases a year.

R.G.: Local courts are where justice is done, where the rubber meets the road. This is where the respect for our system is developed in the first instance.

W.O.: Judge Scher, do you agree?

PRESTON "SANDY" SCHER: Not only do I agree . . . one of your great people here in New Rochelle, Mayor Alvin Ruskin, who was a judge, once observed that the local city court was the people's court. And that's true. I love my job. It's completely different from "practicing law," which I did for over thirty years. Let me just say that Mr. O'Shaughnessy is doing a great service to the community by inviting a gentleman of your stature and ability to articulate views that are very difficult to present in a coherent and cogent manner. And you've done that. I appreciate that, and I know the people do.

W.O.: Are you backing somebody for president, Mr. Grey?

R.G.: I'm going to vote.

W.O.: But is the Bar Association going to endorse somebody?

R.G.: Our association does not endorse anybody.

W.O.: Why won't you endorse?

R.G.: Because the Bar Association has, as one of its fundamental functions, the responsibility to review the candidates for the federal bench. And we do that in an impartial, bipartisan manner: We will review those candidates proposed by Democratic and Republican presidents. In doing so, it's important for us not to be affiliated with the party of our background at the time we are serving.

W.O.: So if someone listening right now wants to be a federal judge, he or she would be well advised to make nice with your group.

R.G.: Well, he's got to make nice with the president of the United States! (*laughter*) Because the president is the one who makes the nomination. When we get the nomination, we look at demeanor, at the person's skill at writing opinions, and at the person's temperament, and then we advise the president based on a rating of well-qualified, qualified, or not qualified. Our investigation is based on talking to judges, talking to court officials, talking to lawyers, even talking to radio talk show hosts, like Bill O'Shaughnessy. (*laughter*)

W.O.: President Grey, what is tort reform? Everybody seems to think we need it. Does that mean lawyers get rich? And isn't there a guy [Senator John Edwards] running for vice president who made a lot of money? So what is tort reform, and where do you stand on that?

R.G.: That's a very tough issue. We are all wrestling with it. But I will tell you this: We have many moving parts in this concept, this idea of tort reform.

W.O.: My *doctor* wanted me to ask you.

R.G.: Your doctor is one of the moving parts. The medical profession is a moving part. The legal profession is a moving part. Insurance companies are a moving part. Legislatures are a moving part. To determine a doctor's insurability, for example, insurance companies do a "risk assessment" based on a doctor's activities. We have to, I think, have a very frank discussion based on the facts. And I don't know that we have had that.

W.O.: Is it out of control now, sir?

R.G.: No, it's not out of control.

W.O.: These outrageous gifts that juries are giving?

R.G.: How many outrageous gifts can you identify? When you have 80,000 trials but can point to one or two examples a year, how is that outrageous?

W.O.: Well, why are the doctors screaming, the guys who keep us alive?

R.G.: Because their premiums are going through the roof. I'd be screaming too.

W.O.: And whose fault is that?

R.G.: Well, I think what is not fair is to lay blame at the feet of lawyers for the entire predicament we find ourselves in, in this society. I mean, there are a lot of moving parts, and the moving parts have to sit down and have a discussion based on the facts. And if we have that, I suggest we can come up with a solution. Until that happens, we are finger pointing, and finger pointing never got us anywhere.

W.O.: One argument, I guess, against tort reform is that you don't trust the jury.

R.G.: Oh, I think doctors trust juries. When a case goes to a jury, we have found, most of the cases are decided for the defense, in America. So I don't buy the argument that people are afraid to take their case to a jury.

W.O.: What if the guy running for vice president with John Kerry—John Edwards—gets in? Is he going to help his lawyers, his former colleagues?

R.G.: You know what? As a lawyer, I hope he is fair, considerate, looks at the facts, and does what is right for America. And if that means lawyers have to take a hit, lawyers have to take a hit.

W.O.: You are so thoughtful and focused, sir. Thank you for not letting me distract you.

We have one more call: I always get in trouble with the last call.

CALLER 5: Good morning, Mr. O'. Mr. Grey, it's Bruce on this side. It's a great show and an honor to be on with both of you today. Mr. Grey, you started off by saying this nation was founded on individual liberty and personal responsibility. As I get older and my hair goes from blond to gray, I cherish that more and more.

But I see this trend rapidly changing. It seems like there is always another law protecting citizens from themselves. A perfect example: I was in the middle of Hurricane Frances; I live right by the ocean and I was in a number one evacuation, and they insisted I go to a shelter. Fortunately, I didn't. The idea of a shelter seems wonderful, but once you enter the shelter, you lose autonomy over your own life. They tell you when you can leave. You can't use your individual liberty or your personal responsibility anymore. And the same thing goes for arresting people for being out after 10:00 at night—curfews. I was wondering what you thought about this trend.

W.O.: Good question. Individual freedom and liberty.

R.G.: Laws are passed by legislatures, not by the Bar Association. So what we have to do is elect people we believe are going to do the right thing by us. And they campaign based on that. We sometimes find ourselves in situations where society or the state is trying to protect most of the people in a very difficult situation. And the one you described is most difficult. The enforcement side is where I think you have raised the issue of what we call "discretion." Discretion is used to make sure the law is presented in a fair manner. If done so, usually we end up with the protection of individual property and individual life.

W.O.: Are you concerned about [U.S. Attorney General] John Ashcroft and Guantánamo?

R.G.: I am. This is a great nation. We are maybe one of the greatest civilizations in history. Why? Because of our military might, because of our economic success; but it's not just those things that define great civilizations. Ours is great not only because of those two things, but because it's blended with freedom, liberty, and the right to pursue one's destiny free of intervention. We have a civilization that provides the greatest opportunity for an individual to succeed and be free to enjoy that freedom. We are a beacon of hope to the rest of the world in providing that opportunity. And we have also said to the rest of the world that there are certain standards that go with this democracy. People are entitled to due process; they are entitled to representation; and there are certain commitments important to our essence that must be adhered to. When we fail to adhere to the laws we subscribe to in signing treaties and agreeing to conventions against torture, we hurt the reputation of this country, and we have to guard against that. Lawyers have a particular responsibility to bring such failures to the attention to those enforcing the law, passing the law, and observing the law.

W.O.: Are you for or against the PATRIOT Act?

R.G.: The PATRIOT Act as a set of laws is something that has to be examined by Congress in light of how it's used. The law itself is not a bad thing. Any law is not necessarily bad; it is how it's used.

W.O.: Does John Ashcroft make you a little nervous?

R.G.: The attorney general has a responsibility to us and to the country. He believes he is executing his job in a way that supports the president and supports this country. Do I agree with everything he has done? No. But that's his job. And to the extent I find I disagree with the way he performs that job, then I am going to stand up and say I don't think that's the way it ought to be done. But he is the attorney general, and to that extent, he has the responsibility of doing what the lawyer for the country has to do. And he believed what he did was something that was important to do.

W.O.: Robert Grey, September 11 three years ago was a day not unlike this day. We sat at these very microphones in this very radio studio and listened to it all. Everybody thought it was a television story, but as the awful day wore on it became a radio story. People called—thousands of phone calls. I still walk down the street and think about it, and I say, "Those bastards." And I sort of am where Ashcroft is.

R.G.: That was one of the most horrific acts this country ever faced, or the world has ever faced. And as horrific as it was . . .

W.O.: Where were you when it happened?

R.G.: I was in Richmond.

W.O.: What were you doing?

R.G.: I was actually getting ready to leave for work, and I was looking at the news. I saw the first tower in flames, and the thought was that we didn't know exactly what had happened, and we were wondering how this "error" could have happened. When the next plane appeared on the horizon and impacted the second tower, it was clear what had happened and what was going on. And it sent the most wicked chill through my spine that I have ever felt. It was a sobering experience, frightful. After all that was over, I was angry, I was upset, and I wanted revenge for the devastation that was forced on us. But I'll tell you this: This country is resilient. This country stands for justice, for freedom, and for liberty. And above all we are going to continue our stand for that. And the protection and adherence to the laws that we pass and to the way we enforce our laws must comport with the ideals of the Framers of the Constitution and the attitude of this country in being a leader of the free world.

W.O.: His name is Robert Grey Jr., and he's a good, bright, wise, decent, and intelligent man. And I'm grateful to Frank Trotta for sending him to our door, also to Chief Judge "Sandy" Scher and Jim Generoso of our court for this wonderful program.

The American Bar Association is based in Chicago, Illinois. Their phone number is (312) 988–5109. And Mr. Grey's personal office is at Riverfront Plaza in Richmond, Virginia. 951 East Byrd Street. Is that named after Robert Byrd?

R.G.: Not *Robert* Byrd, but it is named for Senator Harry Byrd.

W.O.: Sir, when are you coming back to Westchester? You're welcome here any old time.

R.G.: Let me tell you something, Bill. This is what it is all about to me: talking about the most important part of the democracy we have established in this country, our system of justice. And I'd merely like to close with this, if you don't mind. We are a society built on the Rule of Law. And as such, we have been able to sustain the growth of this democracy over a century. And the reason it is continuing is because others look at us and say this great experiment that America has engaged in is what we want to engage in. And as I travel around the world, I meet many lawyers, many judges, many politicians who admire us for the way we stand up independently as citizens. And the support we have, not only for our government, but for our country, because of our willingness to criticize it when it's wrong.

W.O.: When you ran for president of the American Bar Association, was anybody dumb enough to run against you?

R.G.: No, sir.

JOHN SPICER

John Spicer is a highly respected hospital administrator with a national reputation. He presides ably, to this day, over Sound Shore Medical Center based in New Rochelle and also sits on the board of the Westchester Medical Center. We interviewed him on September 30, 2004.

WILLIAM O'SHAUGHNESSY (W.O.): This is Bill O'Shaughnessy with a special edition of "Westchester Open Line." We're here live in our Westchester studios, flying airborne at 1460 on the right side of the dial and also at 93.5 on the FM.

For our guests today, we do a double hit. For the next forty-five minutes while we are in your care and keeping, we're going to be visiting with an individual I think is the essential—I can't think of a better word—person in the entire southern Westchester region. He's the president and CEO of the entity known as the Sound Shore Medical Center, John Spicer. Welcome, sir.

JOHN SPICER (J.S.): Thank you, Bill, it's good to be here.

W.O.: My wife, Nancy Curry O'Shaughnessy, is crazy about your wife, Kathy Spicer. Will you thus trust me to conduct myself fairly and properly and objectively?

J.S.: Yes, but I have a little leverage, I think, so you better be nice.

W.O.: I have to go home tonight.

J.S.: You're right.

W.O.: John Spicer, this is such a—I almost said a perilous time—maybe that's not misapplied for health care and hospitals.

Do you remember Alec Norton?

J.S.: Oh, sure.

W.O.: He was your predecessor. A colorful, Runyonesque guy. When did you take over our hospital?

J.S.: I came aboard in July of 1988. And I really followed George Vecchione, but Alec was the man that both George and I had to live up to. His reputation (*laughing*) went far beyond the borders of New Rochelle.

W.O.: He was a pretty colorful guy, Alec Norton.

J.S.: I remember the first tour of the city, and every restaurant in New Rochelle that we went into, Alec Norton had his own seat. I felt a little intimidated that this man had connections with everyone.

W.O.: He had a lot of stamina too!

J.S.: (*laughing*) Yes, I think that was widely known also. (*laughing*)

W.O.: John Spicer, I still call it New Rochelle Hospital, is that . . . all right?

J.S.: Yeah.

W.O.: I remember when you changed the name. Did you get a lot of flak on that?

J.S.: Actually, Bill, most of the people were very, very supportive because they welcomed the fact that the City of New Rochelle was the host to a regional medical center. That, in fact, Sound Shore was drawing patients from Rye and from Larchmont, and from Mamaroneck, Eastchester, and the Bronx.

When we made the name change, more than half of our patients were coming from outside New Rochelle proper. I remember sitting with our wonderful Mayor Tim Idoni and talking to him about the fact that we were growing to become a regional center, and he was remarkably supportive and felt that as long as it was 16 Guion Place, New Rochelle, that this would only enhance the reputation of the city. And I think it has worked that way.

W.O.: But you're also the big muckety-muck over at Mt. Vernon Hospital.

J.S.: That relationship happened about five years ago. Mt. Vernon Hospital was struggling financially, and they were looking to develop a relationship with another institution.

I was concerned that one of the big New York City hospitals would plop down in our back yard. So we began to talk to the Mt. Vernon board of trustees and felt that it would be much better for the residents in southern Westchester if we could develop a community-based health system, which essentially would be run by board members who come from our local communities, not from some entity in New York City.

And the Mt. Vernon board and the Sound Shore board were very supportive of the concept, and we brought the two institutions together. I think the results have been terrific: Mt. Vernon Hospital for the last four years has operated in the black. We are hopeful that by this time next year, we'll be well on our way to opening a brand-new emergency room—which is critical for that town; they have the largest wound care hyperbaric oxygen treatment program in the county and get patients from as far away as upstate New York and Connecticut.

W.O.: There are so many things we want to ask John Spicer, the president and CEO of Sound Shore and also Mt. Vernon Hospital; and in every telling he is also the brightest guy on the board of our troubled Westchester County Medical Center.

These proceedings are greatly enhanced by the presence of Jim Link, a former top executive at Iona College. Jim, how long have you been at this medical center?

JIM LINK (J.L.): Just over a year, Bill.

W.O.: You're the director of development. Is it easy raising money these days?

J.L.: That's an interesting question! I think it is easy when you have a great product like Sound Shore. People feel strongly about the mission of the institution and are very actively involved in supporting the medical center.

W.O.: You know, I don't like the word "product," because what you do is almost a calling, I think.

Mr. Spicer mentioned the emergency room. (*laughing*) My kids have set a record in that emergency room; they have their initials carved on the wall over there. You must feel pretty good about this, don't you?

J.L.: Yes, absolutely, we've got a terrific staff. People come to us at all points in their life when they have serious needs, and because they have a positive experience, it then makes my job easier to solicit support for the medical center.

W.O.: Call—it's very easy to get on the air with us. And I shouldn't tell you this, but we're the only radio station in the country that flies without a net: no seven-second delay. You could hurt me a lot, if you wanted to.

John Spicer, we see in the public press, all is not well at Westchester County Medical Center. What's going on, sir?

J.S.: Ah, Bill, I believe frankly that this has been a tough period of time for them; however, I think we are all seeing the light at the end of the tunnel.

W.O.: Is it a good light?

J.S.: Yes, it is. Westchester Medical Center is absolutely essential for the health care of the people in the Hudson Valley; it is the only institution that does what it does: high-end tertiary-level care.

W.O.: What is tertiary?

J.S.: Well, that's about as sophisticated care as you can possibly get, so when you're talking about that level of care, you're talking about high-end open-heart surgery, liver transplants, kidney transplants, heart transplants, very intricate neurosurgery, the most sophisticated neonatal nursery in the metropolitan area. Those are the services that they provide that the community-based institutions really don't have the wherewithall to do.

W.O.: You say "essential to the Hudson Valley"; does that mean the Sound Shore?

J.S.: That means the Sound Shore also. We refer our open-heart work to Westchester, some of the very difficult neurosurgical cases go to Westchester, and certainly all the transplant work goes there.

W.O.: But you got some good doctors at your place. I know a few of them, and they're world class. Right in our back yard.

J.S.: For what we do, which is really 99 percent of the diagnoses that are made around the country, Sound Shore does very well.

We have a very sophisticated medical staff; you know we are a teaching hospital. A lot of people don't understand what that means, but it means that we train medical students and residents to become doctors. It takes a certain kind of physician to want to work in that environment because they are constantly questioned by the interns, and I think actually that provides and develops a much stronger medical staff.

W.O.: You mean it makes the doctors sharper?

J.S.: That's right. They need to be on the cutting edge of medicine, because they're training new doctors.

W.O.: And they're all at Sound Shore?

J.S.: They are all at Sound Shore.

You know, New York state is highly regulated, but we have gotten approval to be what is termed a level-three nursery. We deliver about seventeen to eighteen hundred babies a year.

W.O.: You smile when you say that; it makes you feel good.

J.S.: Well, yeah, it's a nice thing.

What is also nice is that we knew we didn't want to have to transfer many babies out of the community. So we can handle all but the very critically ill children. We transfer virtually no babies out of the hospital because we have a very sophisticated nursery.

We're also the only community hospital in Westchester that has a cardiac cath lab, which means that about 99 percent of all cardiac problems other than open-heart surgery are handled in Sound Shore.

W.O.: You got a guy over there who is one of the smartest men I have ever met: Richard "Rocco" Pisano. Thanks to him I have a pacemaker. He told me I have a state-of-the-art device, a better pacemaker than Dick Cheney. I said, "Oh, that's reassuring; thank you." (*laughing*) They honored him last week.

J.S.: Right now, he is the president of the medical staff. He is an internist, but . . .

W.O.: What does that mean?

J.S.: Internal medicine: He is your front-line doctor, and he's got a wonderful practice. But as important as his medical skills are, Bill, this is a fellow that grew up in this area. He knows New Rochelle, came out of the Bronx—it's not only his medical skills, it's his loyalty to his patients and to the institution that makes him important to the medical center.

W.O.: You have a brother in the business, don't you? What's his name?

J.S.: My younger brother Michael; he's a president and CEO at St. Joseph's in Yonkers.

W.O.: Does it run in the family?

J.S.: (*laughing*) We don't know how this happened, but actually we are very happy about it.

W.O.: You are on the radio; good morning!

CALLER I: Good morning!

J.S.: Hello, how are you?

CALLER I: I am fine, thank you. Mr. Spicer, I would like to ask you a question concerning the medical center. I found that when it was the New Rochelle Hospital, we had more care than we have now. We have so much going on now that we really don't know what to do; we have a general practitioner who will send you to every different medical expert there—so if you have a toe that's bothering you, they won't look at it unless it's actually the toe. I don't know how we could afford that.

W.O.: Do you have a good toe doctor there?

CALLER I: No, you know what I'm trying to say? Because I find that unless you specify that you want your blood pressure taken and all that, they don't even bother with it. They require another visit, which I think is obscene.

J.S.: Obviously, you know that medicine continues to change and evolve; there are so many things that we now know about the human body that it almost requires a specialist to deal with certain problems.

I think the key to all of this is to make sure you have a good primary-care physician, a good internist or family practitioner, who can essentially help you through the system. Because you're right, it is very difficult if you're trying to navigate your health on your own. And you really need to rely on your family doctor to help you through that.

CALLER I: Well, I have an excellent one, and I have an excellent heart doctor, which I'm very grateful for. The only thing that bothers me is the exorbitant cost of medical services; it's getting to the point where you either have to die before you can get care or you can't afford it; or you determine if you're going to pay for your fuel, your health care, or your food. It's getting very difficult to live.

J.S.: Listen, you are just echoing what is I think a national debate right now. The fact is, health care is expensive; it's not just the doctor in the hospital but the drug costs, the technology costs.

W.O.: Now what about the lawsuits, John Spicer?

CALLER I: That's right, that's there too.

J.S.: Well, that is another issue. We don't have any caps on our lawsuits. I can tell you that almost all the obstetricians in Westchester are spending at least $100,000 a year in malpractice insurance, and that's after taxes.

W.O.: Can you thank [Senator] John Edwards for that? Is that a low blow?

J.S.: (*laughing*)Yeah, that's a low blow.

CALLER 1: Well, let me get off, gentlemen, with saying this: Today you're a "drive thru" patient—you go in one door and before you know it you're finished, you go out the other door, and that goes for giving birth to a child too. It's gotten to the point that unless you're desperately ill, you're thrown out of the hospital quicker than you should be if you require aftercare.

Thank you kindly, and Bill, I'm sorry I'm annoying.

W.O.: No, you stick around; you're one of our favorite listeners.

Let me ask a question: Do doctors get a commission when they send somebody to another doctor, to a specialist?

J.S.: Oh, no, no, no; in fact, that is illegal.

W.O.: But they always ask, "Who referred you?"

J.S.: The specialists like to know who they have relationships with, and they do talk amongst one another about whether they are providing the right service. It's like any other business. If an internist refers to a cardiologist, that cardiologist wants to know why: What about his practice does the internist like? I think that dialogue makes for better patient care.

W.O.: Are some of these guys more into accounting and business than the practice of medicine? Do you see any of that?

J.S.: That's the dilemma of modern medicine: 99.9 percent of these physicians would love it if you would just let them practice medicine. I frequently refer to the days after 9/11, when those physicians and nurses at St. Vincent's in Manhattan worked with no paperwork requirements and no fear of malpractice; it was marvelous just to watch them take care of those patients. And that's what every doctor and nurse wants to do, but we have this overlay of, as you said, "defensive medicine." The billing process with the HMOs, the fact that there is overhead just to handle billing of two hundred different insurance companies, who all have a different process—it all means that doctors have to hire three or four different clerks.

W.O.: Are you saying they have to spend too much time protecting their ass?

J.S.: Yes, that's part of the issue. The other part of the issue is to actually submit a bill and get paid: It costs a fortune.

W.O.: You want a Hillary Clinton! Is she on to anything?

J.S.: Listen, I think we need a discussion about a single payer, or I would refer to it more as a single process. There is no reason why Aetna and Oxford and UnitedHealthcare cannot have similar payment processes, so that we don't have a different form for each insurer. It doesn't mean you need one insurer, and there could be different products.

W.O.: Who is responsible? Who is the bad guy? Is it the unions? Is it the insurance company? Or is it the selfish doctors? Who's at fault for the cost of health care?

J.S.: I think we have to acknowledge that a big piece of the cost, Bill, is the evolution of technology and drugs. You do see the ads on television now by the drug companies; the fact of the matter is that we need to accept as a society that it does cost a lot of money for these guys to develop these drugs.

As these costs have exploded, the complexity of the system needs to be simplified. We just have too much of an administrative overlay, and I think that's the real issue. We have got to get those people together to say, we can't be spending thirty-five cents on a dollar on the administration of the process.

W.O.: Are the drug companies spending too much on erectile dysfunction and not enough on things that keep you alive?

J.S.: No, I don't believe that's the major driving dilemma. I think you actually want them to spend time on quality-of-life drugs, as well as the absolutely essential lifesaving drugs. I really do believe that it is the administrative overlay of all of this stuff that costs us too much money.

W.O.: Let's go again to the phones: You're on the air; good morning!

CALLER 2: Hi, good morning!

W.O.: Sir, go ahead.

CALLER 2: Yes, I just wanted to say there should be a way to collect money from the community. In other words, for argument's sake, if everybody in Mamaroneck put in a thousand dollars a year, we become a special customer whereby anything that isn't covered by the insurance would then be picked up by the hospital. Like sub-insurance. It would provide a lot of funds for the hospital.

W.O.: You are shaking your head, Mr. Spicer.

J.S.: That concept is actually popping up around the country; it's not a bad idea.

CALLER 2: I had a hernia operation, and I had to go out of the hospital on the same day. If I had this special card I could stay overnight!

And also it gives the people motivation that they can actually benefit from it, and then they become committed; you know them, and they become a quality patient. And they could make additional donations too.

W.O.: Why do you want to stay an extra night? Everybody I know wants to get the hell out of there!

CALLER 2: Well, you have a hernia operation, you have terrific pain when you are leaving. Believe me, and I am telling you it's important.

I just want to say one more thing. I know you have a board of directors and watchers, but you should have local committees to interview the patients, see how the hospital is running, and make suggestions. Every patient that comes out of the hospital should be able to give you an opinion, and these private people on the committees, just volunteers, would be able to talk with them.

W.O.: What about that, Mr. Spicer?

J.S.: We do get feedback from about 60 percent of the patients that come through Sound Shore, and we do use those surveys and those reports to try to change and improve the way we do business. In fact, as a result of that feedback we have hired three or four people we now call patient navigators.

And they're available on the floors and in the emergency room to talk to patients and families, and help them understand what's going on.

CALLER 2: They are wonderful people.

J.S.: In the emergency room, the person who is getting treated is in the back room; it is the family that is sitting on the edge of the seat and just doesn't really know what's happening. It's the anxiety that creates the frustration. So we've tried to improve the situation by bringing these people in, and knock on wood, the complaints have dropped in half.

W.O.: Thanks for your call, sir.

The biggest complaint has got to be about the food, right?

J.S.: That's exactly right

W.O.: The Jell-O!

J.S.: That's why getting the patients out quickly is important—because they only get one meal, and then they go.

W.O.: You're kidding!

J.S.: We try to pay attention to the specific diet that a patient is on, so if you come to the hospital and your food has no salt, it's because many patients are on salt-free diets. It's an industry-wide issue. The food is something we constantly work on.

W.O.: You are on the radio; good morning!

CALLER 3: Good morning, it's Mr. Cam from New Rochelle.

You are kind of shifting the chairs on the *Titanic* here, gentlemen. There is no way to reinvent the wheel or make the system work. Everyone works, and everyone that earns in this country is going down the hole of medical expenses. Sixteen percent of the GNP.

W.O.: Is that true, Mr. Spicer?

J.S.: Yeah, he's on target.

CALLER 3: Okay, so this colossal amount of money is also twice as much as what other countries are paying, and of course, we have the only private system. So they're paying 8 percent of GNP, we are paying 16, and we have the lowest life expectancy of any developed country; the Swedes and the Japanese are tied for fifth place, and they're at about 8 percent GNP.

The question is: Where is the money going? Obviously, there is an enormous amount of fraud and bad medicine and waste. Hillary Clinton wrote an article recently on medical care; she said about half the procedures are worthless or injurious. The third leading cause of death is operations.

W.O.: Sir, how do you get all this information; are you in the medical business?

CALLER 3: I'm an elite liberal intellectual, and I follow all this stuff because I'm retired; and I've been overseas so I have a cosmopolitan view of things.

W.O.: Is he right, John Spicer?

J.S.: I think the point he is making has some validity to it. I would argue on the other hand though that the hospitals in Buffalo and Rochester are more than 30 percent filled with Canadians who cannot get care when they want it. That's where some of the money goes.

CALLER 3: I don't think that's true; I can tell you that the Canadians just had a discussion about the health care system, and they are perfectly happy with their national health care system; not to say that it's perfect, but it's working: Canadians live a good deal longer than we do, and their costs are running around 8–9 percent GNP.

One other figure I can tell you: The government in this country has a 3 percent overhead in Medicare and Medicaid in transferring money from one place to another.

W.O.: Let me ask you both a question, Mr. Elite Liberal Listener and Mr. John Spicer, Hospital Administrator. Aren't a great deal of these costs because of us—because we drink too much, we use illegal drugs? Doesn't a lot of the action in an emergency room proceed from drug use and alcoholism?

J.S.: Yeah, Bill, I think that's true.

W.O.: Or we eat the wrong stuff or we smoke.

J.S.: Some of those problems are not unique to us; for example, in Britain they have the same issues now about obesity that we are dealing with. It creates an enormous strain on the system, because everybody now has diabetes and wants the "fat surgery," and that creates a new expense for everybody.

I still believe to a great extent that [the reason] our costs are high is that our service is exceptional. You know, you can get a hip replacement here in a week and you cannot do that in either Canada or Great Britain. I was called about two weeks ago from the National Health Service in England, and they are identifying about twenty-five centers here that do bariatric surgery because the National Health Service in England cannot handle it.

W.O.: Are you one of them?

J.S.: Yep, we are one of them, and they are looking to recommend us to their population as a place where this care can be delivered.

W.O.: Let's go again to the phones:go ahead; good morning!

CALLER 4: Hey, how are you doing. I work in a hospital. Don't you think some of the high prices or the high cost of insurance [is] due to the fact that some of the practitioners make silly mistakes that change the life of a patient forever?

J.S.: I think that's a national issue, and the Institute of Medicine put out a report a couple of years ago that essentially documented that medical errors do have a considerable impact on the cost and level of care. There is a big move nationwide—and I think New York is looking to lead the way—to support the institutions as we move more into the area of information technology. Things like having the physician directly interact with the information system as he orders his test, so that the human error factor begins to get eliminated.

CALLER 4: I'm all for speeding up the process, but I think speeding up the process creates more mistakes sometimes.

W.O.: What about that, Mr. Spicer?

J.S.: I don't disagree with you. The pressure on everyone now to move patients through the system quickly certainly has not helped the whole process.

But I think right now there is a tremendous focus on patient safety; I can tell you that all the accrediting bodies and all the local institutions are focused primarily on patient safety, and we have put in a whole series of new procedures that in many ways do slow the process down because there are checks and double-checks and triple-checks on what we do and how we do it.

W.O.: Isn't there a big move now, not to go blindly into that operating room, to ask questions, to talk up: Don't leave it to your doctor; pummel him with questions?

J.S.: Bill, I think that is absolutely right, and I tell you [that] the process now before surgery is done—particularly whether it's to be done on the right hip or the left hip, for example—is very similar to watching a pilot and a co-pilot in an airplane. We call it a timeout: Before an incision is made on a patient in the operating room, the surgeon has to call a timeout, and everybody in that room has got to agree exactly where that incision is to be placed. The nurse, the anesthesiologist, the surgeon—left side, left hip. Nationwide, hospitals are doing this.

W.O.: Do you have to crack down on your doctors; you got any sloppy ones?

J.S.: I would say that we have an extraordinarily good medical staff.

W.O.: If a doctor is a little casual, who calls him in? The medical board or you?

J.S.: We provide the medical board with the data. We track every case, every physician, and every outcome.

The medical board has what they call a Quality Care Committee that reviews that data on a regular basis. If any physician is not up to the standard of care, that physician is called in by their director, and there is a discussion about what's going on. I think the oversight is very good.

W.O.: Thank you for your call.

John Spicer, you say they're going to see a brighter light at Westchester Medical Center!

J.S.: I think there were a couple of problems that existed in Westchester; one, the spin-off from the county was a unique and very difficult process. In retrospect, in many areas of that spin-off the Medical Center was underfunded: in their malpractice pools and in their workman's comp pools, which three years down the road began to put a financial strain on the organization.

Two, there was tremendous emphasis put on improving the sophistication of the care. Everybody was focused on growing the business . . .

W.O.: This is up in Valhalla?

J.S.: Valhalla. Bringing in new transplant surgeons, building the open-heart program. As that was happening, there was not a clear understanding that some of the infrastructure really wasn't up to snuff. So the billing system, the purchasing system, the payroll system were relatively dysfunctional.

And we only discovered the problems when we began to notice that even with the increase in activity, the bottom line was going the wrong way.

W.O.: Did you have any political interference?

J.S.: When I said that I would step in on an interim basis, the situation there was so critical that most of the politics was now out of the way and everybody was focused on "We better figure out how to fix this thing."

While I was there, there were a couple of things that really jumped out at me. First and foremost is that the quality of medicine up there is spectacular, and my role was to ensure that those physicians would not leave the medical center, to give them some reassurance that we were beginning to develop a plan that would keep the institution at the level it was at.

W.O.: What about all those stories in the Gannett [newspapers] day after day? They have taken a lot of shots the last five years.

J.S.: The way the Gannett reported some of those things was very disturbing. As with any major hospital, they did have some incidents, they had a problem with their MRI, but by and large their outcomes, their statistics match up favorably with those of any hospital in the metropolitan area. The quality of care up there is good, so one incident would be blown out of proportion and you would think, "Oh, boy, the place is in total disarray." The patient experience up there is still very good.

W.O.: It used to be called the Old Grasslands Hospital, like a county hospital. And wasn't it the loony bin for a while?

J.S.: Twenty years ago it was Grasslands, and it was an afterthought—it was the hospital of the poor, patients who couldn't get into the private hospitals.

W.O.: So it has come a long way!

J.S.: Oh, yes, in no shape or form is it like that now.

W.O.: This is a hot subject right now in the local papers, so I have to ask you: The Board of Legislators and the county executive still have some oversight up there, right?

J.S.: Yes, the Board of Legislators [has] a responsibility for appointing five or six of the board members; five or six board members are appointed by the governor, and then a couple by the county executive.

W.O.: You are up for reappointment; do you want to be reappointed?

J.S.: Yes, I would like very much to be reappointed.

W.O.: Why?

J.S.: First, I could be helpful in making sure that the changes being made are good. Also, fifteen years ago Sound Shore Medical Center decided to affiliate both academically and clinically with the Westchester Medical Center, the premise being that if Westchester Medical Center was competitive with the major academic centers in the city, people in Westchester would prefer staying in Westchester.

W.O.: You still believe that?

J.S.: I still believe that! Now one of the reasons I want to stay on is to ensure that Westchester Medical Center stays at that level, so that all the time investment and effort that we at Sound Shore and the entire New Rochelle community put into making sure that this relationship is strong isn't wasted.

W.O.: So if you can keep Westchester Medical Center propped up, it helps Sound Shore, it helps Mt. Vernon?

J.S.: Yes, and it helps St. John's in Yonkers.

W.O.: One of the New York hospitals took a run at you a few years ago. You don't hear about them anymore; Montefiore was doing all these satellite offices, and they have retreated from the field. How did you beat them back?

J.S.: The edge that Montefiore didn't really see, the edge that we have at Sound Shore, is that our doctors are local. People like to be able to walk down the street, see their doctor, and say, "Hi, Doc." You would like to go to the Little League field and see the doctor coaching or watching his kids because that develops confidence: You say, "I know this person." Montefiore was bringing physicians in from out of our area; people didn't know who they were; there was no relationship. Once they saw that, our physician community got a little more active. I told them, "You guys better start going back to church and synagogue so people can see you." Because that's the edge.

W.O.: It works, because they have closed most of those satellite offices.

J.S.: Sure, because if people have confidence in the local community, they want to stay local.

W.O.: You are on the air with John Spicer; go ahead!

CALLER 5: First of all, Mr. O'Shaughnessy, you seem to be chiding Mr. Cam for his knowledge.

W.O.: Listen, I was dazzled by his intelligence.

CALLER 5: He is so intelligent; he calls all the time, and I love to hear him.

W.O.: This is the Elite Liberal.

CALLER 5: I don't care what he is! Mr. Spicer, I would like to know how do you run the Medical Center and the New Rochelle Hospital together?

J.S.: Well, I only did that for a couple of months.

CALLER 5: Oh, you are not running it now?

J.S.: No, they went out and hired a management company.

W.O.: I remember at this very microphone one of the greatest brain surgeons in the world, now retired from Rye, Dr. Richard A.R. Fraser, was the head of one of the great New York hospitals, with a worldwide reputation; he operated on the Rockefellers and the Whitneys. He once told me at this very microphone, "You know, I've killed people; I have made mistakes with my hands."

So it's an inexact science. Do you think God has anything to do with the practice of medicine, John Spicer?

J.S.: That's a personal issue. I happen to believe that, yes. We try the best we can, Bill, to do the most good for as many people. But it is still an inexact science with human beings interacting, so there are errors and mistakes. People need to understand and hopefully believe that we all do as much as possible to ensure that we minimize the errors that happen.

One of the things we don't talk about enough at Sound Shore is that last year, between the hospitals and the physicians, we gave $18 million of free care to the people in this community. We get about thirty cents on the dollar from the state government, and that's a commitment by a lot of people who are very dedicated to the preservation of human life. It doesn't mean we are perfect.

W.O.: A lot of people express their gratitude with grants, and a lot of people leave you money before they depart this planet: Do you think that is well spent?

J.S.: I think we are very careful about what we do with that. Most of it goes to support the community. One of our trustees this past week set up a fund and gave a gift of $200,000 to provide care to the uninsured in the emergency room.

W.O.: John, let me just thank you as we let you go back to all your many duties. On behalf of every parent and every grandparent in the Sound Shore, because if we didn't have you there, it's a long way to Valhalla, baby!

And it's a long way under that George Washington Bridge, so I hope you keep going forever.

MILT HOFFMAN

The veteran reporter—dean of the Westchester press corps—talked with us about politics and politicians on December 28, 2009.

WILLIAM O'SHAUGHNESSY (W.O.): The week between Christmas and New Year's is supposed to be quiet. Well, it's anything *but* quiet at WVOX and WVIP, and this morning in our studios we are graced by the presence of the dean of Westchester journalists, Milton Hoffman.

You will remember Mr. Hoffman, who was, for years and years, the political editor of Gannett Westchester and the *Journal News* and before that the Macy–Westchester Group. Milt was also editorial director of our good old reliable local-yokel newspapers.

Milt Hoffman, I heard you on the radio with our Mike Dandry, and you were talking about "They don't make 'em like they used to." You were talking about politicians in this day and age.

MILT HOFFMAN (M.H.): Everybody who gets into politics wants to do a good job when they are elected. But sometimes they are "deterred" for different reasons. Most of the time they face reelection and have to answer to certain special groups, the vested interests they need for their reelection campaigns—money and stuff like that—so they have to vote a certain way. Another problem they have here in Westchester politics they did not have in the old days is the multiplicity of political parties. At one time it was just Democrat, and Republican. And if you go way back, you had the Liberals, but basically it was Democrat and Republican. Then the Conservatives came along, and at least *they* had an agenda.

W.O.: That was to beat [Nelson] Rockefeller.

M.H.: Well, whatever, at least they had a *platform*. And now you have different groups coming in as parties. Basically, they are there to just stir up the pot, and that means jobs for themselves. Look at, for example, the so-called Independence Party of Westchester. They are not "independent." If you're running for office, they put a lot of pressure on you to get their endorsements, and you have to buy tickets to their events, and things like that. Politics is a whole lot different today.

W.O.: What about the Working Families Party?

M.H.: Some of their endorsements are very strange to me; I don't have a very high regard for them at all.

W.O.: Milton Hoffman, legendary journalist, you go all the way back here in the Golden Apple, our beloved county of Westchester, to the days of Nelson Aldrich Rockefeller. On the radio today, you seemed to suggest there was once a day when "giants walked the land." But they don't make 'em anymore.

M.H.: I wouldn't say they were "giants," Bill. They were just really good people. There still are good people. At the County Board of Legislators we had Herman Geist, Audrey Hochberg, Sandy Galef, and Richard Brodsky—people like that. Ed Brady did a lot of good things for the county. Andy O'Rourke was a member of the County Board of Legislators and went on to become county executive. So there *were* people dedicated to the job and who got things done. They get things done *today* at the County Board, but they are not necessarily things that deal with the county infrastructure. They pass laws—you can't smoke, you can't drive drunk—which are important things, but these are *state* responsibilities. They pass other laws: You have to post the amount of fat in menus and so forth. They get involved in these issues, and I am not so sure these are the kinds of issues county government should be involved with.

W.O.: Milton Hoffman, iconic journalist of our home heath, should we *abolish* county government, just say the hell with it?

M.H.: Absolutely not! The county government is the one main government that keeps us going. Everybody says Westchester County is the highest-taxed county government in the nation. They forget that's because county governments in New York state have to pay for Medicaid; other states' counties don't have to pay that. Everyone forgets that Westchester is among the top seven communities in the world in intellect. I am not big on technology, but they put in high-tech lines—fiber optics, etc.—so that the entire county would have high-speed communications [that] businesses can tap into.

W.O.: Is that good or bad?

M.H.: That's good, *very* good. We have a good parks system. We still have good roads. We still have a pretty good quality of life here. A part of it has to be attributed to the fact that we had, over the years, *county* government. The problem is not the *structure* of county government. The problem has been the *people* who are in there. We had an election this year for the County Board of Legislators. There are seventeen members, and only seven of them were opposed. We had ten members who were reelected without any opposition. It's the people's fault because they don't get involved themselves.

W.O.: Wouldn't you agree, Milt, that men and women of quality and ability and of good heart are not drawn to public life? They won't subject themselves to scrutiny anymore or to the rigors of public service. Isn't that the big problem, that good people will not go into public life?

M.H.: Well, we don't have as many of these people today as we used to have.

W.O.: Why?

M.H.: We don't have as many people *voting* today as we used to. We had an election here in Westchester. Everyone was supposedly mad at all the high taxes and what's going on and practically everything. And we had the second-lowest turnout in county history! In seventy-one years of county executives, the second-lowest turnout, even with the fact that we have more voters now! The only time we had a lower turnout was in 1945, during the war, when people were still at war, away from home, and not voting.

W.O.: What does that say?

M.H.: It says the people are lazy, that they are not involved. I don't know where they are getting their information from. Maybe they don't listen to the radio, or read newspapers. But if they think they are gonna get their information from the Internet, they are mistaken, because they don't get any local news from the Internet.

W.O.: Milt Hoffman, you go back a long way.

M.H.: I started with the newspapers in 1951. I was there for fifty years. Now I am still active in the community. I belong to the Historical Society, the Campaign Fair Practices Committee; I'm also on a committee to build a new Tappan Zee Bridge. I am still involved because I really love this community, and I just didn't want to retire and go on the golf course.

W.O.: Here comes a curve ball: How old are you now?

M.H.: I am eighty-one years old and proud of it.

W.O.: Milt, I hear you talk about the Westchester you covered so well. You still love the damn place, don't you?

M.H.: This is the greatest county in the state. I have not been to many states, but this a great *county* to live in and work in; and the county government itself has a great *structure*. Sometimes you might want to get rid of a few of the legislators and get some back that you used to have. And maybe we would improve.

W.O.: Do you miss Ed Michaelian and Nelson Rockefeller and Malcolm Wilson?

M.H.: Oh. Michaelian was great! You know what? We have had good county executives—Judge Bleakley, Herb Gerlach, Jim Hopkins, Ed Michaelian, Al DelBello, Andy O'Rourke, Andy Spano—and they all did a good job.

W.O.: Who was the greatest county executive of those you just mentioned?

M.H.: I only covered five of them; I don't want to pick one. They all did good. They all did something, including Spano, who is now leaving government. I have an article running this week in the *Journal News*, and it recounts some of the things that happened on his watch.

W.O.: So you think there are still a few good ones out there?

M.H.: Oh, yeah, there are a lot of good people out there. I was just with Sandy Galef. She is an assemblywoman from the Ossining area, and she is terrific. There are a lot of good people out there, Bill.

W.O.: You honor us, Milton Hoffman, with your writing, your longevity, and your presence. The microphone is always yours at any time.

M.H.: Bill, thank you for having me.

SY SYMS

Sy Syms was one of America's most successful retailers: "An educated consumer is our best customer." He loved a microphone and often indulged his love of sports with cameo appearances on our broadcasts. We spoke with him on the air about his business on May 24, 1990.

WILLIAM O'SHAUGHNESSY (W.O.): Live in our Westchester studios we have Sy Syms, one of the preeminent merchant princes and retailers of America. With him is his daughter Marcy Syms, the president and chief operating officer of Syms stores. We're very glad to have you both here. First of all, we're trying to get you back, Sy, to your original career.

SY SYMS (S.S.): Yes, my original career was to become a play-by-play broadcaster anywhere in the United States. When I went to school they didn't call it communications; it was called radio broadcasting and production. My ultimate goal was to broadcast for any of the sixteen major league teams. But now I'm very happy to be doing my first golf tournament for WVOX this weekend. I've done basketball, football, and baseball for you, so I'm thrilled to be announcing golf as well.

W.O.: Sy Syms is going to do the Seniors Tournament live from the Sleepy Hollow Club here in Westchester, and he is going to be our celebrity show host. Who's in the tournament: Lee Trevino, . . . ?

S.S.: Yes, and Bob Charles. There's several of the greats—Trevino probably the most well known.

W.O.: Marcy, did you arrange this to get your dad the hell out of the executive suite? Is this a Marcy Syms strategy?

MARCY SYMS (M.S.): No, this was actually at the creative graces of your own stations and Judy Fremont. Your people came up with it, and I thought it was a great idea, and I knew Sy would love it. But we promise not to conduct any official business at Syms while he's gone.

W.O.: You know you gave a talk for me once for the Advertising Club of Westchester. We had a string of speakers that year—the late Nelson Rockefeller, Arthur Goldberg, and Toots Shor. But they all remembered you! You didn't talk about clothes or clothing . . . .

S.S.: I talked about advertising . . . .

W.O.: No, you talked about *sports*!

S.S.: Oh, yeah, that's right. You know there are subliminal effects in advertising that are very important.

W.O.: What do you mean?

S.S.: In conscious advertising, the message you're giving is what you want to give—presented in that light. Psychological or subliminal advertising is double messages. You think of the double-entendre of Johnny Carson as a claim to fame now, for over twenty-five years.

W.O.: You are a multi-millionaire. You've opened these Syms clothing stores in faraway places like Texas. I've seen them locally in Long Island and White Plains.

S.S.: That's very romantic: You call Texas a "faraway" place. Texas is a humming, bustling, citified, beautiful community, whether it's Dallas, Austin, or Houston.

W.O.: What's the farthest, most remote place you've hung the Syms banner?

S.S.: We're in Chicago, St. Louis, Detroit, Pittsburgh, and I guess maybe Dallas and Houston.

W.O.: That's pretty good for a haberdasher from New York City. Why don't you run for office?

S.S.: I *did* run for office, in the city of Yonkers in 1963 for City Council. I lost the election by two to one to Eddie O'Neil, who was the councilman as well as a *Daily News* City Hall reporter. I spent ten years in politics.

W.O.: Do you buy your clothes at Syms?

S.S.: Of course! Well, I shouldn't say that arrogantly, but yes, I do. And I'm very satisfied with everything I buy.

W.O.: Marcy Syms, we're going to talk about fathers and daughters. When did you decide to follow in your father's footsteps in the clothing industry?

M.S.: I guess I've been following him for a long time because I was also educated and pursued a career in broadcasting and was also involved in TV and radio production. As you know, there's a lot of unemployment and layoffs right now, and such was the case with me when my father first spoke of Syms going into the Washington, D.C., market. It was really the first time Syms had done any market research to find out where the Syms customer was outside the metro area.

W.O.: What do you call your father?

M.S.: Dad, and Sy. When we're alone I just call him Dad.

W.O.: Sy Syms, how did you feel when your daughter told you she wanted to get into the business?

S.S.: I'm not sure I remember exactly what I felt. It was always a comfortable feeling to have your own child in the business. When she started, she was actually a freelance worker for the company. Then, when we opened in Washington, she said, "You know, Dad, I forgot how exciting this is." She looked at me and said, "I really would like to get into retail." I have six children, and the days when I worked in lower Manhattan and lived in Westchester, I used to take the kids in occasionally on Saturdays to help out. Marcy had a taste of that maybe as early as five, and she remembers the days of working in the stores along with the rest of my kids. I remember my sons used to hate to sort hangers. We'd throw all different kinds of hangers in a cart and they'd get to sort them out for hours!

W.O.: How about you, Marcy?

M.S.: What I hated doing was *socks*. My first real job at Syms was when I was thirteen. There were a lot of young men coming in from Fordham University, and that was very exciting for me. I had my first date during that summer!

W.O.: Sy, doesn't Marcy have other siblings currently in the business?

S.S.: Yes, Robert, Steven, and my youngest daughter, Adrienne, who just started this summer.

W.O.: Sy, in the intimacy of this conversation—do you ever have to come out of the chairman's office because "Marcy and the boys are at it again"?

S.S.: No fights of recent vintage. Remember, they have been with the company for twelve or thirteen years. We've had our "moments," and there *were* tough times. It's very hard for an employer to [dissociate] himself from his child. You *can't* treat them like an employee.

W.O.: But Marcy is sitting here in the office as your CEO. Is it ever tough for the boys reporting to you, Marcy?

M.S.: The way the company has evolved, there really isn't that direct report. As president, there are people in between to whom they are reporting, and I speak with them. But we get together also on an informal basis and talk about good things that are happening, say, for instance, in the St. Louis store, or about brand-new advertisers, and things like that.

W.O.: Do you ever have a hell of a row with your father?

M.S.: No. I think what makes it very easy to work together is that philosophically, we're in harmony. We have the same philosophical attitude about what Syms is and where we're going as a company. Having that harmony has seen us through the little disagreements because it's the big picture we're in agreement about.

S.S.: Yeah. There were "steamy" sessions in the past. I'm not saying they involved Marcy and the boys, but the sibling rivalry does permeate a business relationship. I would say the relationship is great now.

W.O.: But, Mr. Syms, do you ever have to go into your CEO's office—who also happens to be your daughter—and say, "Honey, um, I don't agree with what you're doing"?

S.S.: Oh, sure. But I'm very accustomed to having my children in the business with me making decisions. I'm not the type to "rip somebody up," so even if it wasn't my child, I've never had a rough style of management; I'm not the type to bawl someone out either. Very rarely do I have to say, "I'm the chairman. I'm the largest stockholder, and that's that!"

W.O.: Which are some of the hip towns? Is St. Louis more hip than Houston?

M.S.: I think Houston is a *very* hip town, and Dallas as well. They're very fashion-conscious, and they have a lot of European boutiques. You get a sense of how far the fashion dollar goes in an area by visiting the stores there.

W.O.: Sy, I know you follow sports. Are there any great heroes left?

S.S.: There's a young man out in Los Angeles named Magic Johnson. There's a man who might be the greatest basketball player of my lifetime—Michael Jordan of Chicago. There couldn't be bigger stars than that.

W.O.: I don't see today the Joe DiMaggios or the Ted Williamses. There are stars with huge contracts, but they don't seem to have what *they* had.

S.S.: With all due respect, you have to take the Ted Williamses and the Joe DiMaggios in the time frame in which they lived. We look back to the last generation. Things were much simpler then, in the "golden years." So the DiMaggios and the Williamses were living with a different social aura in those days.

W.O.: Do you mean to tell me that what happens at Yankee Stadium is the same as what happened when Gehrig was on first base or Allie Reynolds was on the mound?

S.S.: Well, if I'm a die-hard Yankee fan in 1928, and I'm a die-hard fan in 1990, what takes place in either time is just as important.

W.O.: Sy, if you had the chance to do it all over again, what would you be—a sportscaster or a businessman?

S.S.: If you're asking me the question today, I'd rather be a businessman. If you asked me that question within five years of when I made the decision, I would have said, "No, I'm very happy with the events of my life and career." I must admit I enjoy being in a store today as much I enjoy being in front of the microphone today talking to you, Bill.

W.O.: We were talking about fathers and daughters earlier. I had lunch in town yesterday with a young man named Nelson Aldrich Rockefeller Jr. He has family. He has his uncles and wealth and fame, but he has no father. Do you think you could keep this thing going if Sy just suddenly went off the reservation or went to the great sports microphone in the sky?

M.S.: Bill, I sure hope so. The way in which my father mentored me and allowed me in the beginning to shadow him around from store to store—I hope I've been a good student. I have been in a position to make mistakes and to learn from those mistakes myself. It has always been my intent and his that I could carry on the business.

S.S.: Bill, I would like to add that if I were to retire tomorrow, in my opinion, the company wouldn't have hardly any loss whatsoever. It would be extremely minor. Things are in place organizationally. Marcy has just about been in charge for five years now, so we're not talking about a big transition.

W.O.: Governor Mario Cuomo has spoken often about his relationship with his son-and-heir Andrew. They talk twelve times a day, and I think the governor trusts him more than anyone. Do you trust Marcy more than anyone?

S.S.: Well, more than anyone in business, yes. I trust my sons and my other daughter in business as well, but Marcy is the head of the company, so I have complete trust in her.

W.O.: Sy, why do some retailers make it? Didn't your own brother just go out of business?

S.S.: There's one reason and it's pretty precise in my mind: respect for your customer. When I broke into the business and worked in my father's store many years ago, a merchant's greatest profitability was how he could put it over on his customer. Look, I know much more about clothing than my customer, much more. I could really rip 'em off pretty good in many respects if I wanted to and have a good run for a while. I could get certain items in and price them at $199 rather than $159. Never be motivated by profit. Profit will be there if you are doing the right things.

W.O.: You mean to say, Marcy doesn't come in and say, "Houston is up and St. Louis is down"?

S.S.: Yes, that's gross receipts. We watch that, but that's not profitability. You know, I've respected everyone who's come in our front door and told them about our products. I wouldn't sell you; I'd let you make that decision on your own whether or not to buy.

W.O.: I would buy anything from Marcy—I would even invest in a Broadway show! How do you find people to work behind the counter who have that same respect as you?

S.S.: There's an old adage in retail: When the founder of a company opens his second unit, it has to run on 50 percent efficiency because that human being can't be in both places at the same time. We're in seventeen different television markets today. We try to lead, to teach, but you can't teach a person to have respect for a customer. That has to be something inherent, inborn in a person.

W.O.: Do you have to fire people? Who's your "heavy" whom you send in for that?

S.S.: That depends on who hires him.

W.O.: Who's tougher, you or your daughter?

S.S.: Oh, Marcy's tougher—no question.

M.S.: That's the worst part of the job. We usually don't handle that aspect of the business, but I don't think anyone relishes the thought of having to let someone go.

W.O.: What do you tell people when a new class of employees enters the business?

M.S.: We try and give them some background on what Sy was talking about. We've stayed in business and have grown over the years—it's not hard work alone, but that *respect* for the consumer. It's the little things, like not to chew gum, to have proper body language, and to look people in the eye when you talk to them.

W.O.: Sy Syms, one final question: Do you ever think about retiring?

S.S.: No. I may cut back a few days during the week, but I won't retire—not me!

III AT THE PODIUM

DR. RICHARD ROCCO PISANO

Like everything else, the medical profession has changed a lot in recent years. But there are still some dedicated practitioners—healers—like Richard Pisano. We spoke about him on September 24, 2004, at the Beckwithe Point Club.

Ladies and gentlemen, welcome to the sixtieth-birthday celebration of a very special individual.

First of all, thank you to his remarkable and indispensable wife, Kathy Pisano, for this lovely party. She is essential to his practice, his career, and his life. He knows it, and so do we all!

There are all kinds of people here tonight: other doctors—his colleagues—city officials, relatives, in-laws, and even a few outlaws. So please humor me as I recount some things you may not know about Kathy's husband.

He was born August 16, 1944, on the Feast of Saint Rocco.

Saint Rocco, a Frenchman, traveled to Italy to win eternal glory through miraculous healings of people afflicted by the plague. Thus, the Church of Rome venerates his birthday for protection against disease. Dr. Richard Rocco Pisano is aptly named—for a healer and a saint.

Some of you first encountered him as a young man at Xavier, the famous Jesuit high school in Manhattan. After graduation, he returned to the Jesuits at Fordham when it was truly a great university, before they began publishing my books! He trained at the prestigious University of Bologna in Italy and interned at Fordham Hospital, St. Barnabas in New Jersey, and New Rochelle Hospital.

And the rest is history. In twenty-four years, he became the most respected general practitioner in southern Westchester and rose to president of the Medical Board of Sound Shore Medical Center, whose great president, John Spicer, is here and will confirm Dr. Pisano's genius and dedication. But there's more.

He's essentially an ontologist. Now I know that's a high-sounding word that doesn't quite fit into all the disciplines, specialties, and categories by which practitioners of modern medicine cast themselves. That's what Mario Cuomo called him at one of my book parties. He's into Being. He's into Life. Like his namesake from the thirteenth century, he has dedicated the past two and a half decades to encouraging Life, to prolonging Life, to enhancing Life, to protecting Life, to sustaining it.

He's also a diplomat and a role model for his profession. Sometimes you can size up a doctor by the shingle outside his office. [If he's a dermatologist, you can size him up by the shingles *in* his office.] If there's a "P.C." after the name, it stands for Professional Corporation. If there's an "LLC" after the name, it means Limited Liability Corporation. And if you see that, you know you're in trouble!

Some of these guys practice business instead of medicine. But not this man. He examines, diagnoses, recommends, prescribes, lectures, treats, heals, ministers, counsels, and loves. He's at his second-floor office on Memorial Highway day after day or at our great Medical Center, making rounds, visiting, evaluating, inspiring, and teaching.

His patients include the young, the old and infirm, our families, our parents, and those we love.

Even a sixty-six-year-old white-haired broadcaster with a pacemaker! You know, when I got my pacemaker, he said, "You have a better device than Dick Cheney." I replied, "Oh, that's reassuring!"

Finally, think back to the 1970s in our city. Three top doctors in the region—Ira Gelb, a kindly white-haired man named Dan Sherber, and the pediatrician Irv Samuels—all retired the same year.

And when I asked them for recommendations, these wonderful, beloved icons of years gone by all said the same thing. There's a wonderfully bright, dedicated, and hard-working general practitioner we recommend very highly. His name is Pisano. Dr. Richard Pisano.

And so, he's healed and comforted us for the last twenty-four years. We trust him with our very lives.

Please welcome our great friend, counselor, and physician, who was so aptly named sixty years ago on that August day, the Feast of Saint Rocco.

Dr. Richard Rocco Pisano! Physician and healer who was named for a saint.

REMARKS ON THE NEW ROCHELLE POLICE FOUNDATION

An original speech delivered June 16, 2004, at the American Yacht Club, Milton Point, Rye.

Nancy and I are glad you came.

We share your admiration for our wonderful low-key but every effective Chairman Charlie McCabe; our great police commissioner of national renown, Pat Carroll; City Manager Chuck Strome; Chief Judge Sandy Scher; my fellow directors, who work so much harder at the foundation's business than I do; and our next New York state assemblyman, Domenico Procopio! (*laughter*) (*applause*)

In just a few short years, our Police Foundation has transformed law enforcement in our city. Thanks to your dedication and generosity, the lives of our officers have been enhanced, and their mission made easier. We have all been grateful for the privilege of supporting and backstopping the service of the New Rochelle Police Department.

The first requirement of any society is public safety. Before you can have a just society, or a compassionate and caring one, you have to ensure domestic tranquility. And only then can you make the community stronger, sweeter, and more agreeable for all our citizens. Only then. All our other aspirations are held together by this notion.

And also by the reputation and stature of our great police commissioner, Pat Carroll. (*applause*)

He and Chairman Charlie preside over a frugal board of directors, so you can be sure your money is well invested. The New Rochelle Police Foundation is a tightly run ship, an effective entity with a relevant, focused sense of mission.

So, I guess it remains for me only to thank Nancy Curry O'Shaughnessy for having this nice party. (*applause*)

And also Commodore Everett, Vice Commodore Furnary, and Mr. Tim McCormick for providing this spectacular venue to celebrate your generosity.

FRÉDÉRIC FEKKAI AT LITTLE FLOWER CHILDREN AND FAMILY SERVICES

Frédéric Fekkai is the most famous hair stylist in America. This dazzlingly handsome New Yorker is also a highly successful entrepreneur and businessman. Frédéric has mentored and encouraged hundreds of talented young stylists and designers over the years. He's also making his mark as a philanthropist who seeks out obscure but worthy charities for his blessing and imprimatur. Frédéric and his spectacular wife, Shirin, are treasures of New York. Here is how I introduced him at the Humanitarian Award Dinner on June 8, 2005.

Ladies and gentlemen, welcome to the Metropolitan Club and the Humanitarian Award Dinner of Little Flower Children and Family Services.

On behalf of Cornelia Guest and Carla Lawhon, our chairs; and Sigourney Weaver, Lorraine Bracco, and Heidi Klum, our honorary elders; we thank you for the generosity of your purse and the gift of your presence.

Little Flower Children and Family Services was founded seventy-five years ago in a small, obscure Brooklyn parish in the Bed-Stuy section, and Herb Stupp, its gifted CEO, is an old friend, a colleague, a TV journalist and producer. We welcome you on his behalf as well as the wonderful Grace LoGrande, our executive director; the chairman of the board, Father Patrick West; and your president, Doug Singer.

Little Flower operates a haven in Wading River for over a hundred youngsters from third to tenth grade who are ineligible for foster care. Most are from broken homes; some suffered from fetal alcohol syndrome; and all of them struggle with emotional problems. "Children who know the sound of gunfire before they ever hear the sound of an orchestra," as former Governor Mario Cuomo once remarked. And for them, for these children no one wanted,

Little Flower offers shelter, treatment, and education. Caring. And love. It started as a Catholic enterprise but is now fully nonsectarian for the benefit of all God's children.

And they do get better, many of them. The "graduates" from Little Flower include a boxer, a judge, an attorney, and you'll meet tonight an extraordinary and inspiring young woman, Natalie Whittingham.

Little Flower also runs four homes, called the McSherry Residences, in Queens, Brooklyn, and Wading River for the mentally disabled of all ages.

Now about our honoree.

We all know Frédéric Fekkai professionally, as a designer, stylist, and very successful corporate business executive. He has established his imprimatur in Beverly Hills, Palm Beach, and every upscale department store in America!

For a guy lacking in charm, without good looks, he's done O.K.!

Imagine, will you just imagine, how far he could go if somehow he could overcome his terrible shyness and lack of confidence? If only he had an engaging smile, a better personality, and just a little bit of charisma!

I mean the guy is so damn good-looking. Frédéric, I intend no disrespect or insult to you profession. But before you came to this town, if our wives said, "Honey, I'm having dinner tonight with my hair stylist," we didn't really worry. It was O.K. Now, Frédéric, you've changed the entire dynamic. Now we *worry*—a little!

So, there's a Frédéric Fekkai the world knows. We read about him in the columns of Liz Smith and Cindy Adams, of *Women's Wear Daily* and Richard Johnson. And we see him in the magazines and on "Oprah."

But there's another Frédéric. And that's the one we honor tonight. Because once you get past the glamour, celebrity, and style, you find a magnificent, generous, and relentlessly loving soul.

There are a lot of smart people in the room tonight. And you all know the phonies, the hustlers, the takers, those who grab and put nothing back. They are all around us and everywhere apparent in this tough town.

But every once in awhile, Central Casting sends us someone who's got it all, a quiet philanthropist relentlessly drawn to good works away from the glare of publicity.

And you should know, ladies and gentlemen, that this extraordinary and worthwhile organization alone, a personal favorite of Frédéric's, has raised thousands of dollars on his "salon nights" and tens of thousands in donated auction prizes, all given quietly, almost stealthily, by Frédéric and his chief of staff, Kimberly Callet.

And he takes his philanthropy very seriously, like his business. You won't see him hanging out at the big, established, tony charities; his enthusiasm is reserved for smaller, more effective and deserving projects like Little Flower, which last year alone placed 184 kids into adoption and helped 315 children return to their families.

He's also done so much for hospice care and breast cancer research. But he picks his spots. He does it thoughtfully and with great care.

He specializes, really, in the hurting, the disabled, the disenfranchised, the misunderstood, the lonely, and the misbegotten.

Frédéric, you have a lot to answer for! Because of how you are, and who you are.

And we love you for it.

We're glad you're our friend. All four hundred of us.

THE ROBERT MERRILL POSTAL STATION

Robert Merrill was a familiar and beloved figure in our home heath. The famous Metropolitan Opera baritone loved New Rochelle. And his neighbors adored him—so much so that they persuaded the U.S. Postal Service to name the Wykagyl Branch Post Office in his honor. Mr. Merrill made thousands of concert appearances all over the world and countless television appearances. He also found time to give Frank Sinatra "tune-up" voice lessons over the long-distance telephone.

Among his proudest possessions was a Yankees jersey #1½ given to him by Billy Martin.

These are my remarks at the dedication of the post office on June 2, 2008.

Marion Merrill: Bob's accompanist, his partner, his muse, his beloved.

And Nita Lowey, our superb and inexhaustible congresswoman. She has become a ranking "cardinal" in the House and one of its most powerful and effective members through her dynamism and keen intelligence. All of us here also know of her goodness.

We thank Mrs. Lowey for exerting her influence and stature to unanimously enact Public Law 110–102: the renaming of the Wykagyl Post Office for Robert Merrill.

And so we gather today on this dazzling spring morning with Marion, Congresswoman Lowey, and our brilliant young mayor, Noam Bramson.

We thank the officials of the U.S. Postal Service: our own Postmaster General, Jerry Shapiro; and the District Chief, Mr. Joseph Lubrano, who oversees hundreds of post offices.

We are also joined by Yankees greats Roy White and Mike Torrez; Mr. George Steinbrenner's personal representative, Deborah Tyman; and her associate, Greg King. Bob Merrill reveled in his long association with our beloved Yankees. He often wore his World Series rings and, sometimes, even his pinstriped uniform, emblazoned with his "official" number 1½, awarded to him by Billy Martin.

We've had *three* illustrious Yankees in these precincts. The great Mariano Rivera favored New Rochelle with his own restaurant. And for many, many years, this was the home of a Yankees immortal: Lou Gehrig. So Bob Merrill wasn't the only guy around here entitled to wear pinstripes.

Though I never heard Robert Merrill sing at the Met, I knew him as a neighbor and a cherished friend. He always complied with my requests to appear at various charitable events, for both local and national organizations, such as the Broadcasters Foundation of America. He and Marion also graced the Sound Shore Medical Center benefits and visited many Westchester opera groups.

This was his neighborhood, with his trees, and his sidewalks, and his shopping center with his bagel store, and his A&P, and his deli, and his newspaper store. All shared with his neighbors.

I often wondered why he spent so many years with us, especially his last ones. This highly successful individual of international fame and personal wealth made over fifty albums. And like Ossie Davis, another famous resident, Bob could have easily settled in a more tony, upscale neighborhood in Rye, Greenwich, or Scarsdale.

And you know why he chose New Rochelle? He gave the same response as Ossie Davis: "These are my people."

And when the glory years faded away, and he aged well into his eighties, Mr. Merrill would stroll around this neighborhood, on lovely spring days like today or in the dead of winter. In every season of the year, this was his.

He would roam into Manhattan for meetings of the fabled Dutch Treat Luncheon Club. All the writers, artists, and publishers belong to Dutch Treat, founded about eighty years ago by James Montgomery Flagg, a New Rochelle resident and one of the most famous illustrators from the 1920s, when Norman Rockwell also lived here. Bob was an elder of Dutch Treat and the Friars Club as well.

Bob would call me at the radio station at about this time of the morning to urgently request my presence at Dutch Treat, and then, afterward, we would discuss cosmic issues of the day at Pete's Tavern or, occasionally, at "21."

Marion would graciously receive us when we made it back to New Rochelle by nightfall. Or at least in time for dinner!

During these delightful sessions, I heard some wonderful stories, and I will share just two of them now:

I once asked the famous baritone, "Bob, who was the greatest tenor: Pavarotti or Domingo?" Without missing a beat, Merrill said, "That's easy: FRANK SINATRA!"

We know he often gave Sinatra singing lessons—on the phone! One day, when I came to pick him up, Marion said, "He'll just be another minute; he's giving Frank a little 'vocal tune up.' But you can go in." Even I wouldn't dare intrude on that! After his telephonic lesson with the great Sinatra, I asked if Sinatra said anything. "Yes, he called me a showoff!"

There's also a baseball story about the day Bob was "managing" the Yankees' "Old Timers' Day" squad. When the great Joe DiMaggio himself came to the plate, the infield dropped back, and the outfield went deep. Everybody in the stadium waited to see the graceful DiMaggio swing.

However, "Manager" Merrill then flashed the bunt sign. That was like asking Sinatra to sing in the chorus! Well, the Yankee Clipper, Bob loved to recall, laid down a perfect sacrifice!

Speaking of which: I'd like to respectfully ask Deborah Tymon to petition Mr. Steinbrenner about playing Bob's stirring rendition of "God Bless America" during the seventh-inning stretch! Enough with Kate Smith already! You can hear Bob's tribute to our country every evening at 6:00 P.M. when our colleague, the great Bill Mazer, ends his WVOX program with the song.

His voice thrilled millions all over the world. And as Mrs. Lowey pointed out, he sang for every president since Ronald Reagan. During his brilliant career, he performed in opera halls, in movies, on television, on radio, and in almost sixty albums. And during his lifetime, he received every award for the arts our presidents could bestow.

Robert Merrill had a glorious voice and a glorious life and shared them with the world. But after all the applause and the curtain calls, and all the encomiums, he came back to this neighborhood, where he loved us and was loved back.

He and Marion are glad you came to dedicate "his" post office.

ANDY ALBANESE: AN ICON PROPERLY RESTORED (WITH A LITTLE HELP FROM FOUR GOVERNORS!)

Delivered on the occasion of the Italian-American Citizen Club Dinner-Dance held at Alex & Henry's in Eastchester, New York, on October 13, 1995.

County Executive Andy O'Rourke; Assemblywoman Audrey Hochberg; Supervisor Jim Cavanaugh; Legislator Joe Delfino; Commissioner Ray Albanese; Supervisor Jim Doody; Council members Vicky Ford and Vito Pinto; Judge Dominick Porco; and Anthony J. Colavita Jr., the spitting image of his father. Also my pal Dave DiRubba.

With a few exceptions, this is a very strong Republican group. And so I hesitate to remind you about the night in 1982 when I came home from Andy's restaurant with a pizza and a thousand-dollar check for Mario Cuomo's campaign! (*laughter*)

Ladies and gentlemen, for you to allow an O'Shaughnessy to present himself at your Italian-American dinner-dance speaks volumes about your legendary forbearance, understanding, and generosity. I won't intrude for very long.

I come to honor a longtime and valued friend. You have left your hearth and home on this splendid Indian summer night for the same reason.

It is fitting to appropriate this brilliant day to pay tribute to Andy Albanese. He is a child of your neighborhood, of you and yours. I can't tell you anything about him you don't already know.

The Supreme Court Judge Alvin Richard Ruskin once told me, when he was a youngster in this fabled town, there was no one poorer, or richer, than Andy Albanese. I suppose he was referring to Andy's dedication, fortitude, and devotion, to both this town and region, as well as his service as chairman of the Board of Legislators.

Today, the Albanese family name is synonymous with Eastchester, just like those of Francis X. O'Rourke, Tony Colavita, Nick Colabella, and Vin Bellew, of sainted memory.

Anyone who loves Andy is here tonight. His incomparable Linda. And Ray and John and Greg and their wives and their children.

We honor them all as we pay tribute to one of New York state's most endearing and enduring public servants. Milton Hoffman, the dean of the press corps in these parts, calls him "venerable." We call him only "ours."

In White Plains, the county seat, in the corridors of power, he is known as "Legislator Albanese" or "Mr. Chairman." In his family restaurant, he is the gracious, colorful, outgoing impresario who hosted Frank Gifford, Y. A. Tittle, Robert Merrill, Larry Tisch, and a motley crew of failed priests, monsignors, rabbis, and rogue cops! (*laughter*)

In everything, Andy Albanese radiates a vivid, zestful, beguiling presence. Even in adversity, when confronted with not one but three life-threatening illnesses. And Andy, you didn't have to burden us with all this for the last two years! All those wheelchairs with jet propulsion! And the Kojak look! We'd have given you the damn "Man of the Year" Award anyway! (*applause*)

But through it all, you never changed. I remember the race for governor last fall. A friend whose words we will hear shortly flew in to the Westchester County Airport and was accosted by my colleagues in the press, when someone from the crowd yelled to the governor of New York: "Mario, why don't you just tell them to go to hell!" (*laughter*)

Nancy and I have attended a lot of events over the years. We remember so many right here at Mario Faustini's Alex & Henry's, which used to be Schrafft's. And at the Rye Town Hilton, the Waldorf, and many other venues.

But I cannot recall an occasion when four governors of the Empire State praised an honoree.

You have already heard the sentiments of His Excellency Governor George Pataki, who spoke of Andy's "immeasurable" contributions to our state. And we thank the governor for his gracious words and his citation. I'm sure it will receive a place of honor in Andy's den.

Now, Governor Pataki's three living predecessors also requested equal time.

First, from the graceful and articulate fiftieth governor of New York, Malcolm Wilson, a beloved figure in these precincts:

> We have shared countless evenings at political and civic dinners—many of them at Alex & Henry's in the town which you have distinguished for so long.
>
> It is fitting and proper then that you are receiving the Eastchester Italian-American Club's "Man of the Year" Award at this particular venue in your home heath.
>
> The Award, which is given for service to your community, speaks volumes of your dedication as well as your longevity. Please know also that a neighbor and friend who was privileged to serve as the fiftieth governor of New York has valued your counsel as I treasure your friendship.
>
> You are truly *sui generis*.

Thank you, Governor Wilson. Now a note from Governor Hugh Leo Carey:

> I join with all your Westchester neighbors in saluting one of New York state's best-known public servants.
>
> As you gather this night with your family and friends, please know that all of us are grateful for your public service and inspired by your dedication and perseverance. You truly are one of New York's most vivid and respected figures.
>
> Forgive me only for using a rogue like O'Shaughnessy to convey my very best wishes to you, Linda, your children, and grandchildren.

Thank you, Governor Carey. Except for the last line!

Here's one more message from a former chief executive, dispatched this day from the New York law firm Willkie, Farr & Gallagher:

> Your designation as "Man of the Year," Andy, by this great charitable and civic organization pleases all your many admirers throughout New York state. And Matilda and I are among them. We will never forget your wise counsel and your friendship. You taught us something about courage, too.

There has never been any question about where Andy Albanese stood on the great issues of the day whether his position was popular or not. You are one of New York's treasures.

Matilda and I continue to receive good reports on your remarkable progress. We send prayers, our congratulations, and our love to you and your beloved Linda.

Signed: Mario (*applause*)

Thank you, ladies and gentlemen. As I gaze across the room, I see my beautiful Nancy Curry and a man who served yet another governor. Joseph Wood Canzeri requested I share some wonderful stories of you, Andy, and our marvelous, zestful neighbor Nelson Aldrich Rockefeller.

You were one of the very few entitled to call him "Rocky" when you visited him at Pocantico. (*laughter*) He loved you, Andy.

And I remember Nelson's memorial service at Riverside Church when you and your spectacular Linda strode right up to the third row to pray with all the dignitaries and sat with the Rockefeller family! (*laughter*)

I felt privileged to sit in row ninety-three with Perry Duryea, our candidate for governor that year [1978]. And Barry Goldwater sat in the last row of that great church. But our shy, modest, retiring Andy was in row three. (*applause*) I think Canzeri had to dislodge the Spanish ambassador to make room for you!

But you deserved to honor Nelson there. And we deserve to honor you here tonight.

We love you, Andy, and are so grateful you're back among us. An icon is properly restored. And frankly, and somewhat selfishly, we could not imagine Westchester without you.

And so, tonight we express our feelings of love and admiration. And our great relief you have prevailed in all your recent travails and struggles.

The old Jesuits used to say the word *finite* is the strongest in any language. In Latin, it's *esse*. To be. Andy, you are.

And we are all so damn glad.

BRUCE SNYDER AT "21"

Bruce Snyder was the classy, stylish dining-room manager for many years at the fabled "21" Club. I was privileged to speak at his retirement party on April 17, 2005, which was held on all three floors of the venerable watering hole with closed circuit television screens in every room. More than one thousand patrons came to see off "Mr. Bruce."

Ladies and gentlemen, I won't intrude for very long on your evening. For one thing, I've got Bryan McGuire hovering over me. And for another, Nancy is on full battle alert whenever I approach a microphone.

First of all, we want to thank you, Mr. McGuire, for this brilliant party as we honor an icon of our beloved "21" Club, Bruce Snyder. "21" is packed this night with your fans, and our remarks are being carried by closed circuit on every floor of this legendary saloon.

We must also thank Mr. James Sherwood, Dr. Shirley Sherwood, and your colleagues at Orient-Express, Dean Andrews and Jack Landry.

We are grateful for the gift of your presence. Seven hundred folks on a Sunday night, and they even have closed circuit monitors downstairs at the bar!

Bruce, I think you should know you are loved!

I see somebody brought Bruce a tie tonight. That's a great gift, just what he needs, another tie!

I was thinking of something a little more substantial for his new home in Virginia, something more on the order of a garage! Or a swimming pool!

Tonight is also a great tribute to "21," an altogether unique institution—read: saloon—renowned for its hospitality, because it has sustained and encouraged Bruce Snyder's genius and dedication for all these years. It's also a tribute that Bruce found this marvelous place worthy of his industry, his integrity, and his love. "21" was always the perfect turf for a thoroughbred like Bruce to run. It's truly an ideal venue, a forum for his special genius and graceful talents.

You have been the keeper of the flame in these precincts, Mr. Bruce, and the protector of "21's" heritage, lineage, and traditions. And for many of us, Bruce, you are "21." And you are a treasure of New York.

This place brings back fond memories for all of us. Of so many glorious nights. So much camaraderie, good food, and too much booze!

And always, through all of it, there, presiding over the dining room, was this elegant, splendidly attired, graceful guy, Bruce Snyder.

There have been other dining-room dazzlers during your time in our city, Bruce: the great Sirio Maccioni of Le Cirque; those two mad but charming Italians Julian Niccolini at the Four Seasons and Gerardo Bruno at San Pietro; and, of course, the incomparable Toots Shor, your next-door neighbor of sainted memory. Also wonderful Oreste Carnevale, who continues to hold down the fort; your own colleague, Dottore Natale Rusconi, who presides over the glorious Cipriani in Venice; and Bruno Dussin, of the original LeCirque and now at Circo. There is also Nino Selimaj and his brother Bruno. Also Franco Lazzari of Vice Versa, Giuliano Zuliani of Primola, Dino Arpaia of Cellini, and Mario Wainer, also of Le Cirque.

But you are truly unique, Bruce. There ain't nobody like you in this city or this profession. And they know it. And we know it.

And tonight on this lovely spring night, we remember some of the other "21" legends: Mr. Pete, and Sheldon, and Mac, and Bob Kriendler, and the wonderful Jerry Berns.

We can also discern, through the mist of time, the marvelous characters who whiled away their time at this beguiling New York institution. Seventy-year-old Mr. Paley coming down the stairs with his dazzling energy and beamish boy eyes. Or Nelson Rockefeller and the great Sinatra making a grand entrance. Mr. Robert Benchley, of course, sat at his own table. Even Toots Shor would lurch through the front door of an evening to pay you a backhanded compliment, "What a dump! What is this, a saloon? Or a toy store?" And five presidents of the United States repaired to this joint to escape the confines of the White House and the burdens of their high office, and be greeted by you.

I saw the brilliant Mario Cuomo sitting in a corner one day with the late Neal Travis, talking about their souls and the great issues of the day. And over at the bar, as my mind drifts back, there was Paul Screvane with some of the Skeeters. Also John Hennessey, Jerry Cummins, Bill Plunkett, Mike Letis, Bill Flynn, Tom Moran, Peter Maas, Jack Landry, and Gay Talese. And who will ever forget George Plimpton holding forth after chaining his bicycle to the iron gate outside?

I also remember a most agreeable afternoon after a Dutch Treat Club luncheon when Robert Merrill announced he wanted to drop by for "high tea." It was another glorious spring day, much like this one, at about three o'clock, the slack time between lunch and dinner.

"Hell-lowe."

And Bruce, who knows even less about opera than I do, inquired, "Mr. Merrill, are you a baritone?"

Bob Merrill said, "I hope so!"

And then Bruce posed this query: "Who in your opinion is the greatest tenor today? Luciano Pavarotti? Or Placido Domingo?"

Without missing a beat, Robert Merrill shot back, "Sinatra, who else?!"

We changed the subject. To girls. Or baseball.

And on another occasion, I heard Bernard Curry—"Papa" Curry, Nancy's father—bellowing out, "What do you say, Bruce?"

And Libby and George Pataki sitting alone in the bay window near the fireplace. And, Bruce, you will surely remember, I know, the night Ed McLaughlin sold Rush Limbaugh for $75 million! You and I are still waiting for the commission on that one!

And always, it seems, Gianni Agnelli would walk through the foyer propped up by two blondes.

Who could forget the classy women who were always welcome here—Marietta Tree, Laura Bush, Happy Rockefeller, Jackie Kennedy, Kitty Carlisle Hart, Liz Smith, and my shy, modest, retiring neighbor Cindy Adams? They would all listen to Hugh Carey and Lanny Ross sing "Danny Boy" at the bar.

And leaning against that same glorious bar one night, I remember Mary Higgins Clark, Barbara Taylor Bradford, and William Kennedy, all standing right under my book while it dangled precariously from the ceiling, quite undeserving of that distinguished company!

Over the years, Bruce, we've entrusted ourselves to your care at the tables you presided over with such elegance and style.

We've come to share our victories, brag about our grandchildren, and seek consolation in sadness and rejection, when you inevitably cheered us up and restored our sanity by your wonderfully generous and agreeable persona.

And also, Bruce, by some of the worst—and cleanest—jokes we've ever heard!

And the one thing we all really came to hear, that magical Mr. Bruce greeting, "Hell-lowe."

Bruce, does everyone talk like that down in Oklahoma? Because, I'll tell you, when all the elders and trustees of Oklahoma State University came here last month to announce the scholarship in your name, this one guy, T. Boone Pickens, the richest trustee, got up, and he sure didn't talk like you, Mr. Bruce!

Mr. Cuomo, the fifty-second governor of New York, who honors us with his presence, said you have a name like a Prussian general and a voice like a British poet. "Hell-lowe." So I can't understand why the Irish love you most of all!

You have been a class act in every season of your life. And in every season of our lives.

And as I mercifully yield the microphone, let me just say it's fitting for you to locate your new redoubt close to Williamsburg, a bastion of Americana. However, despite all its charms, I'm also certain you and Marcia will class up the place just by strolling arm-in-arm on those cobblestone streets amid all that glorious colonial architecture. I also know the tour guides down there will soon be greeting visitors with the immortal utterance, "Hell-lowe!"

In conclusion, we especially thank you, Bruce, for sharing the dazzling and luminous Marcia with us. Though we had to tolerate your jokes for many years, it was all worthwhile when Marcia indulged us by dropping in for supper.

So please know, Bruce and Marcia, as you take your leave, that we go with you.

And although your new domicile is located in the Commonwealth of Virginia, please be very certain that you always have a home here, in our thoughts, in our hearts, in our love. And in this hallowed place we call "The Numbers."

Thank you again, Bruce, for so many agreeable nights, so much fun, and for your classic, stylish, timeless hospitality. We are all your students and your friends.

JOE MACARILLO AND THE SUN VALLEY TRIO

Sun Valley, Idaho, was America's first great ski resort. Founded by Averell Harriman and his Union Pacific pals, Sun Valley still draws a moneyed crowd. There are several glorious saloons in the town, including my favorite, the Pioneer and Michel Rudigoz's Cristiania, where you can rub elbows with Supreme Court justices and throw down a drink with the crooner Jack Jones of an evening. But by far, the most welcoming venue in this upscale town is the Lodge Dining Room in the Sun Valley Lodge, presided over by Claude Guignon. It's the most spectacular dining room in North America, with lovely "society" music every night provided by an old smoothie named Joe Macarillo. After he played sweet music for the swells for about fifty years, they decided to honor him. These are my remarks upon that occasion on September 20, 2003.

Ladies and gentlemen, I won't intrude for very long on your evening or on Joe's beautiful music.

Nancy and I just flew in from New York, and on our first night in town we usually head straight for the Pio, Duffy Witmer's Pioneer Saloon, saving this legendary Lodge Dining Room until later in the week. But this is a very special occasion.

We're here tonight, Joe, because we love you. And we love your sweet music.

Thank you for all the memorable nights you've bestowed upon us, and for all the lovely songs.

For fifty years you and the Sun Valley Trio have accompanied our courting rites on this very dance floor, with a lot more grace than our earnest but clumsy moves to the strains of your wonderful melodies.

You've also witnessed thousands of young couples taking their first tenuous steps and moving across this fabled dance floor in each other's arms to the graceful melodies of your songs.

And all those old guys—like me; and Nancy's father, Bernie Curry; and Bob Mitchell—who try to make people think we can still dance! Or at least "sway" a little, impelled and emboldened by your graceful rhythms.

We should also thank Earl Holding, Wally Huffman, and Claude Guignon for maintaining and sustaining this spectacular venue as a suitable setting for your genius. It is surely one of the most beautiful dining rooms in North America.

You've kept the music playing in our lives, Joe, by modest calculation, for 15,000 evenings! For all the parties, all the events, all the celebrations, all the anniversaries, all the birthdays, all the first dates.

And how many times, Joe, did we make you play "Feelings," "My Way," "I Gotta Be Me," and "New York, New York"!

You always indulged and accommodated us, smiling throughout, insisting only that we have fun on your dance floor, and have a good time while you kept time.

And so as we salute you, we must also acknowledge some of the colleagues who've accompanied your genius over the years: Jim Watkinson on piano and Bart Bailey on drums tonight on this anniversary evening.

And permit us also to thank Jane for sharing you with us on all those nights, waiting up until you came home after making so many people happy with your music.

Tonight, we must also commend you for keeping alive the classic songs of the great American composers: Cole Porter, Rodgers and Hart, the Gershwins, Johnny Mercer, and Johnny Burke, to name a few. For fifty years, we've associated you with the allure of their melodies and the exquisite insight of their lyrics.

So how can we thank you enough, Joe, for the many years of lovely night music? Well, I guess we can just keep showing up to hear you play at the Lodge here in Sun Valley and to see if Bob Mitchell can still move on the dance floor! And we'll do that as long as you'll permit us.

But we also wanted to commemorate this anniversary with a token of our love. And the nice folks at Towne and Parke Jewelers have created something I hope you'll appreciate. Dean Newman has had them under siege for three months designing this!

So please—from all your fans—accept this gold watch and promise us another fifty years of joy and celebration.

We really love you, Joe.

MAESTRO SIRIO: THE RINGMASTER

"Maestro" Sirio Maccioni is America's greatest restaurateur. He and his wife, Egidiana, and his sons, Mario, Marco, and Mauro, have been our friends for more than thirty years. One of the smartest men I've ever met, Sirio is also one of the most generous I've encountered. I bless the day we met. I broadcast this token of my esteem on May 15, 2006.

On Thursday, glamour and style return to the New York dining scene. The great Sirio Maccioni, America's quintessential restaurateur, returns to center stage with the third incarnation of his legendary Le Cirque, a New York institution.

Sirio Maccioni is seventy-three. He may yet do something in Paris or Dubai. But even he knows this will be one of his last high-wire acts in the center ring of the great city where he has been a featured performer for so long. He begins this week on East 58th Street.

The relentless clock reminds us it is 2006, and we are all mortal. But for at least this one special night, in Sirio's honor, I hope Joe DiMaggio roams centerfield once more at Yankee Stadium. Frank Sinatra should be on stage at Carnegie Hall crooning a Cole Porter song. William S. Paley again heads the Tiffany network where the cufflinks are just a little smaller and more discreet than those of NBC and ABC.

It requires a time when the sportswriter Jimmy Cannon wrote pure poetry in a lonely room near Times Square. Mario Cuomo is standing on a flatbed truck in the Garment District screaming at elderly Jewish women hanging out the window. Ossie Davis is speaking pure truth to an audience at a church in Harlem. Gay Talese is coming down Lexington Avenue with his fine clothes and a very good cigar. Robert Merrill is singing the national anthem at Yankee Stadium for George M. Steinbrenner III. And Kitty Carlisle Hart is at Feinstein's every night.

I know, I know, it is now 2006. But Sirio Maccioni, with roots in the glory days of our town, is still in the game. He is to his profession what each of these spectacular luminaries was to their own. All of them—and Sirio—are not merely among the gifted and elite. They are simply the best and have earned the right to the majestic Latin appellation *sui generis*. It means "unique and able to be defined only in its own terms." Sirio belongs to that exclusive, rarefied fraternity.

I know I can't turn back the tick-tock of the stately clock to the days when he started in this town, but for just this one night, opening night, let all politicians everywhere look like John Lindsay, walk into a room like Nelson Rockefeller, carry themselves like Jacob Javits, and think and speak like Mario Cuomo.

I know we are living, as Jimmy Breslin reminds us, in a "between you and I" age. And all these magnificent and dazzling personages have been replaced by media creations such as Paris Hilton and Anna Nicole Smith.

But this is still a tough, unforgiving town, and Sirio will have to impress Frank Bruni of the *Times*, Steve Cuozzo of the *Post*, Adam Platt of *New York* magazine, Bob Lape of *Crain's*, Gail Greene, and John Mariani. But his legion of admirers pray the music from the new joint will last for a good, long time. Even his competitors, who were stunned when the Italian was honored by the French government a few years back, hope he makes it. It will be the greatest score for the gifted, graceful Tuscan impresario who walks with kings and prime ministers but still remembers the Germans sweeping through his town and breaking down his grandfather's door.

There is something quite special about the man. It was to Sirio's table the magnificent Mayor Rudy repaired in the desperate days following 9/11. An exhausted Giuliani would drop by late at night and have supper in the kitchen with the dust and soot and the horrible stench of vaporized death on his clothes. The two sons of Montecatini would talk over a bowl of pasta late into the night, and Giuliani would then go home to catch a few hours of sleep before rallying the indomitable spirit of a city where Sirio Maccioni is the greatest restaurateur. Then. And now.

The Italians have a word it for it: *convivio*, which means you tarry over food and wine to talk about life, love, politics, and everything else. But mostly it's about a celebration of life. And that, too, is Sirio: *Convivio!*

The Tuscan knows he exists alone in a changing profession now run by lawyers, speculators, bookkeepers, and accountants. To be sure, there are other restaurants of standing and reputation in our town. Many are temples to culinary greatness and the fussy skill of the chef, some with international reputations. But nobody is having any fun at their serious tables. I prefer to pay homage and do my praying in a church, not in restaurants. There's no magic, no music in these gastronomic cathedrals, and absolutely, to be sure, no one is having any fun on their hard, slick banquettes.

There *are* a few exceptions to the formulaic, programmed, and predictable venues of ambition and greed in the restaurant business. Gerardo Bruno, an authentic dining-room dazzler, weaves his magic nightly at San Pietro. And David Burke can be exhilarating. It is a "downtown" place, uptown, and the manager, Teddy, is terrific. The glorious "21" still has a lot of lineage and cachet if you can score a table with Milan, Joseph, or Oreste. The estimable Four Seasons, run by zany Julian Niccolini and sedate, serene Alex Von Bidder, still makes each visit special. But when the great Sirio beckons from the center ring in the great city, even these accommodating joints must yield to his considerable genius.

There are many other highly successful eateries where all is programmed and computerized. Some entrepreneurial business types own ten or more venues. These humorless souls like Danny Meyer talk of "synergy" and "return on investment" and charge outrageous markups on water and wine. Some even bill for bread and butter. Sirio, however, is all about people enjoying themselves, having fun during an evening away from the pressures of a world spinning out of control. He is happy just to provide a stage for our courting rites. To others, the whole thing is a business. To Sirio, a profession. And he is the most sensitive, generous man in the field where glamour and style still carry the day.

In upstate New York, at the Cornell University Hotel School, where they teach hospitality and management for spas, restaurants, and resorts, they don't teach Sirio's methods, because what he brings to a restaurant cannot be taught in a classroom by even the most gifted of instructors. It is called "intuition" and a generosity of spirit. They teach Danny Meyer, Drew Nieporent, Steve Hansen, Alan Stillman, and Nick Valenti. But the smartest graduates always head straight for Sirio's employ. And it is the same way with the best and brightest from the Culinary Institute of America at Hyde Park. He is the Winston Churchill of his profession.

At other restaurants, you encounter three Debbies, two Jennifers, one Chad, a Lance, a Tiffany, and "Hi guys! So what do you folks feel like for dinner tonight?" At Le Cirque you are greeted by the graceful, attractive proprietor and his savvy deputies, Mario Wainer, Bruno Dussin, and Benito Sevarin. And if you are lucky enough to dine with a good-looking woman like Nancy Curry O'Shaughnessy, on the way out Sirio will whisper to her, "Why don't you come for lunch tomorrow—without him?"

And when he opens this Thursday to the applause of 2,000 of his admirers, he will be attended by Egidiana Palmieri, the talented and earthy beauty who gave up a singing career many years ago to cast her lot with a dashing Tuscan on a fast Vespa from the hill town of Montecatini. Egi and Sirio Maccioni will bask in the spotlight with their three sons, Mario, Marco, and Mauro. And so will Stella Sofia Maccioni, who is not yet nine months but has made the *Times*'s society page twice and Liz Smith four times!

Adam Tihany, another certifiable genius, and Costas Kondylis, the charismatic architect, have created a spectacular new venue with a circus theme, with monkeys and elephants suspended Calder-like from the ceilings, to complement Maccioni's genius. Together with Sirio, they have spent millions of dollars, and taken several years off the life of Steven Roth, the head of Vornado, one of the smartest and most successful developers in New York. But he never saw anything like the Tuscan showman.

But they did it. And Liz Smith; Cindy Adams; Judith and Rudy Giuliani; Michael Bloomberg; Silvio Berlusconi; King Juan Carlos of Spain; Bill Cosby; Tony Bennett; Barbara Taylor Bradford and her husband, Bob; Steve Forbes; Matilda and Mario Cuomo; and Archbishop Edward Egan will be there to herald his return.

New York becomes New York again when Sirio steps forward, once more into the spotlight, greeting people, loving them and being loved in return, at his Le Cirque. An icon is properly restored. He has been a class act in every season of his life. And in every season of *our* lives. Sirio Maccioni is a marvelous New York story. It's 2006. But he's still here. In the center ring.

SIRIO: THE BRIGHTEST STAR

And we broadcast this "review" of Le Cirque on February 7, 2008.

New York is crammed with eateries employing a bevy of bimbos flanked by a dour, self-important maître d' standing imperiously behind a lectern punching numbers into a computer. Think BLT Steak on 57th owned by moneyman Jimmy Haber, or Quality Meats on 58th Street, and its cousin, The Post House, where the venerable Quo Vadis once shined.

But this town still offers cozy restaurants with beckoning proprietors unaffected by "investors." The permittees of these agreeable havens have names such as Arpaia, Burke, Niccolini, Carravagi, Von Bidder, Zuliani, Selimaj, Cipriani, Lomonaco, Masson, Tong, Dussin, McGuire, Viterale, Suric, Bruno, and, up in the Bronx, Migliucci. One of these old-school purveyors of food and hospitality, Sirio Maccioni, is the best of all of them.

The great Sirio was ensconced this recent winter night at a small round table near the coat room of his dazzling enterprise, Le Cirque, off 58th Street on the East Side of Manhattan. The unobtrusive table is known to every busboy, waiter, captain, bartender, and sommelier as "Maestro Sirio's table."

The out-of-the-way location, however, does offer a strategic vantage point of any shapely legs or low-cut dresses coming through the revolving front door. At age seventy-five, the Ringmaster of Le Cirque misses nothing.

For most of this dreary February day, the handsome Tuscan waits like an angry lion for the latest review by the *Times*'s gifted food critic, Frank Bruni, who, two years ago, denied Maccioni three stars.

The brilliant Bruni, who served as Houston bureau chief for the *Times* when George W. Bush was governor, and as Rome bureau chief in the Eternal City, is now the most powerful food critic in America.

On this winter night, no one approached the man in the elegant velvet dinner jacket at the round table near the coat room. Even his comely wife, Egidiana, and his attractive sons Marco and Mauro gave Sirio a wide berth on this tense night. The only member of the Maccioni family oblivious to the suspense was two-and-a-half-year-old Stella Sofia Maccioni, who was using all her wiles to distract "Nonno Sirio."

Wednesday's *New York Times* daily newspaper would slap sidewalks all over the world at dawn the next day. But at precisely 8:45 P.M., Christophe Bellanca, Le Cirque's new head chef, burst from the kitchen, exclaiming, "Maestro, *three* stars!"

And then all over this fancy place, imagined by Adam Tihany to resemble a circus, the corks started popping, and the champagne flowed. As the excitement encompassed the man in the velvet jacket, the two-and-a-half-year-old little girl with bright eyes pushed through the crowd, clenching a single red rose plucked from one of the tables. Stella Maccioni held it high and proffered it to her grandfather, "Bravo, Nonno!" And then she kissed the world's greatest restaurateur, whose weathered face was moistened with tears of gratitude.

The seventy-five-year-old man embraced his granddaughter and shook hands with Marta, the coat check girl, and Mario Wainer, the cordial and very correct maître d'. Both were smiling for the first time all day. Sirio then composed himself and entered the dining room to perform his nightly magic.

He once fed Sinatra, DiMaggio, and a pope, not to mention "the ladies who lunch." Some of the dazzlers like Marietta Tree, Brooke Astor, and Kitty Hart are gone. And Gianni Agnelli, Bill Paley, and Nelson (you have to ask?) are only memories of this town's splendor. But the great Maccioni is still in the game.

Tomorrow, Mr. Maccioni will receive congratulatory messages from Silvio Berlusconi, King Juan Carlos of Spain, Rudy Giuliani, Edward Cardinal Egan, Liz Smith, Tony Bennett, Cindy Adams, John Fairchild, Barbara Walters, Mario Cuomo, Donald Trump, Ron Perelman, Barbara Taylor Bradford, David Patrick Columbia, Carl Icahn, Woody Allen, and Robert De Niro.

He will even accept calls from colleagues and competitors such as Julian Niccolini of the Four Seasons, Gerardo Bruno of San Pietro, Bruce Snyder and Bryan McGuire of "21," and Michael

Lomonaco of Porter House, praising the Italian who elevated their calling with a restaurant with a French name.

In a rather glib headline for such a glowing review, the *Times* labeled Sirio's service "decadence." His patrons call it grace, style, glamour, class, and a relentless generosity of spirit.

As Sirio flitted from table to table this happy night, Egidiana Palmieri, who left Montecatini so long ago and sacrificed a singing career to become his supportive wife during the early years at the Colony, La Foret, and Delmonico's, was explaining, "Sirio means 'star' in Italian; he was named after the brightest star, the North Star."

ON THE GRILL

Readers of my three previous volumes will know something of my enthusiasm for saloons. I've written often of my admiration for such disreputable Manhattan watering holes as "21," the Four Seasons, Primola, San Pietro, Vice Versa, Club A Steakhouse, Porter House, Circo, Cellini, and all three incarnations of Sirio Maccioni's Le Cirque. And just to prove I'm not a snob, I've celebrated such far-flung joints as Bernie Murray's and Tommy Moretti's way upstate in Elmira. And lest I forget, my beloved Mario's on Arthur Avenue in the Little Italy section of the Bronx.

In all of these disparate venues there's usually some news and, often, a good story to be had just by listening to the fascinating cast of characters assembled at their tables of an evening.

One of my all-time favorites is the West Street Grill, a marvelous restaurant owned by two endearing characters, Charlie Kafferman and James O'Shea, in historic Litchfield, Connecticut. Over the years the Grill has also won the favor of Rose and Bill Styron, Rex Reed, Jim Hoge, Bill vanden Heuvel, Richard Gere, Caryl and Bill Plunkett, Sirio Maccioni, Danny Meyer, Richard Widmark, Phillip Roth, and Jonathan Bush. I did this piece in April 2010, when O'Shea and Kafferman celebrated the Grill's first twenty years.

Foodies from all over New England patronize this pristine jewel of an eatery for the superb cuisine.

I go for O'Shea and Kafferman.

Twenty years is a pretty damn good run for an upscale, quality restaurant—or for any endeavor—in this turbulent day and age.

Litchfield's West Street Grill has survived the two tumultuous decades since its founding with grace and considerable style. Great style, in fact.

The Grill has an enviable reputation among the proprietors' colleagues in the hospitality profession and among our neighbors, most of whom love the bloody place.

Its name and fame extend far beyond the Grill's perfect and welcoming perch astride the historic Green in Litchfield.

Charlie Kafferman is surely one of the nicest souls most of us have ever encountered in this crazy, speeded-up world. We eagerly and confidently repair to his benevolent and warm care and keeping in moments of elation, celebration, and good fortune. And also when life turns sad and difficult. His irresistible charm, of course, is accompanied, and not diminished at all, by those terrible, entirely risqué jokes appropriated of an evening from Arthur Diedrick or Ray Oneglia.

And the relentless, impatient, uncompromising—and irresistible—genius of James O'Shea and the cadre of young chefs and waitstaff he's mentored and inspired over the years have actually raised culinary standards in the entire New England area.

I make my living with words (usually inartfully and awkwardly). But how in hell does one fashion the phrases and sentences to properly describe the Grill's worth and merit and importance in our lives?

I mean, this estimable joint is simply *sui generis*, unique and able to be defined only in its own terms.

So they've made it to 2010. And the grand anniversary is coming up this May. As I said, the West Street Grill has been special to all of us townies for a very long time. And its influence in the restaurant profession is considerable. Just ask O'Shea. He'll tell you. And tell you. And tell you.

Long may they ever.

W.O. AS SPEECHWRITER

I ghosted this for my pal Gerardo Bruno, the hard-working and colorful owner of San Pietro (where all the Wall Street guys and moguls hang out), to deliver upon receipt of the Italian Ministry of Foreign Affairs (Istituto Di Cultura Italiana) Young Entrepreneurs Award on December 15, 2007.

Your Excellencies, fellow honorees, and distinguished guests.

You honor me. You honor my family. You honor my brothers, Cosimo, Giuseppe, and Antonio, and you honor all my associates at San Pietro and Sistina. And I am grateful for your kindness and generosity.

I'm a child of Italy, with a father who, to this very day, produces olive oil and grows his own tomatoes in the hill town of Monte Corvino Rovella.

My friends in New York have sustained us at San Pietro for fifteen years and at Sistina for twenty-five years. In my profession, that's a pretty good run!

I learned my trade at the famous Culinary Institute of Italy in 1976. But I believe my father's instruction, at his table and in his vineyards, led to our remarkable success here in America.

Our first distinguished guest, His Majesty Juan Carlos of Spain, was followed by captains of industry, cardinals, archbishops, cabinet officers, and ambassadors. Indeed, I think we've fed most of the Roman Curia during their visits to the great city!

We also entertained my shy, modest, retiring friend Mr. Donald Trump. And the honorable Mario Cuomo.

Tonight, as we are surrounded by great art and the genius of centuries, I'm reminded that we came to this country as seekers. Most of us started as busboys or dishwashers. The other honorees and I were young men, and our only baggage was the integrity of our artistic souls.

Our stewardship here in America has been graced by an innate sense of hospitality and our Old World manners. From the very beginning, we knew thousands of restaurants and private clubs existed for the business world.

But we sought to provide more than an agreeable "watering spot" for tycoons and titans. Italian restaurateurs offered more—a courtliness, a dignity, a style.

The New World yearns for our values, integrity, quality, and endurance. And through it all, we remembered who we were and where we came from.

My name is Gerardo Bruno. I am a son of Monte Corvino Rovella. And I'm immensely grateful to all of you.

JUDGE YE NOT

It's so difficult to persuade men and women of real quality to submit to the rigors of public life. And thus government, at almost every level, is populated by hacks. However, as you will note throughout this volume, there are exceptions. One such exception is Judge Preston "Sandy" Scher, who serves, with distinction, in the relatively thankless job of New Rochelle City Judge. Because he is not a "politician," Judge Scher has often had to scramble to get reelected. In the end, however, real quality prevailed. I spoke on the radio about the fine work of Judge Scher in March 2005.

On the façade of the Federal Courthouse at Foley Square in lower Manhattan are chiseled these words: "The True Administration of Justice Is the Firmest Pillar of Good Government."

It's a long way away from New Rochelle. But the majestic words of that noble pronouncement apply to our home heath as well.

In our city, we are blessed with eminent institutions, including a great regional medical center; three colleges, College of New Rochelle, Iona College, and Monroe College; and three extraordinary prep schools, Ursuline, Iona, and Thornton-Donovan. Our great school system and enlightened city government are unsurpassed in New York state.

Phil Reisman, the brilliant writer for Gannett, describes these assets as "the third sector." And we got it pretty good.

New Rochelle has also won the favor of Louis Cappelli, the great visionary mega-developer and philanthropist who is transforming our skyline. We're also home to another individual of great generosity and achievement, Sidney Frank, the wine and spirits baron.

And yet these illustrious residents and third-sector institutions are only some of the reasons for our civic pride. There is yet another essential entity, and it ensures public safety and domestic tranquility. And without it, we have no community.

Though New Rochelle's stellar police department and its dedicated commissioner, Patrick Carroll, with his national reputation, deserve our admiration, I'm referring to another organization.

The "firm pillar" holding our community together is the City Court of New Rochelle, and its very able and extraordinary chief city judge, Preston Scher.

Judge Scher has presided over our City Court for the past ten years and will hopefully run for another term to give New Rochelle five more years of his wisdom, judgment, fairness, and integrity.

Often called the "Court of First Resort," the municipal court is located on the second floor of the criminal justice building right above the police department. And here, justice—or at least fairness—is dispensed day in and day out by the judge's staff of thirty, led by the able and dedicated James Generoso. There are other associate judges as well. But Preston Scher, the chief city judge, presides over them all.

Consider the numbers. The court handles 5,600 criminal cases each year, misdemeanors, felonies, and mundane acts including violations of city codes; 14,000 moving-traffic violations; contentious landlord–tenant disputes; 4,000 civil cases; and 500 small-claims suits.

The court also collects over $5 million a year in fees and fines. But when you dig beneath the statistics, you somehow transcend the minutiae of local governance and peacekeeping, the rendering of fines, and the resolution of domestic and economic conflicts. It goes beyond money.

And for a perfect example, look at the New Rochelle Drug Court, started by Judge Scher and Mr. Generoso three years ago.

Three hundred youngsters have participated in the Drug Court Program, without entering the criminal justice system or jail. There are seventy-five active participants, and thirty-eight have recently "graduated" by remaining drug free for at least twelve months. If these youngsters were jailed for a year, it would have cost taxpayers $1 million, at $32,000 annually per incarceration.

It's enlightening to visit the courthouse and see this Drug Court in action. Sit, watch, and marvel at the exchanges between the judge and the addicted, struggling kids. All Scher's fancy, formal legal training, all his degrees are useless as he dispenses positive reinforcement, compassion, encouragement, and understanding.

"I like your haircut, very good; you look good."

To another: "That's a nice shirt and tie. I'm proud of you for being on the right track for three months. Keep it up."

And another: "Mr. Generoso and I are going to start an 'alumni association' to keep track of you and see how well you're doing when you graduate."

To a beaming youngster: "That's a nice sweater."

A young girl in a party dress to the judge: "I want to thank you and the New Rochelle Police Department for arresting me. I was going downhill, Judge. Thank you for believin' in me."

Judge: "Not only do I believe in you, I know you can make it."

A young girl: "Judge, can I show you a picture of my baby?"

Judge: "Let me see that beautiful child. Step up here while the entire court sings happy birthday to you."

A woman: "I've been before a lot of judges. Recovering is difficult. But I'm fighting my addiction. I signed your contract, Judge."

Judge: "I'm proud of you."

A man: "I got baptized yesterday. I didn't exactly join a church. But I gave myself to Jesus. I just needed a little help to quit drinkin'."

Judge: "Keep going; you're better than you think you are; don't give up."

It is truly an epiphany to behold Sandy Scher interacting with these fragile souls, one step away from jail. Or death from addiction.

So what's the problem? Why are we raising this now?

Well, certain local lawyers in the town are attempting to persuade the Democratic City Committee to overlook all the good done by this court and its leader.

WVOX has covered New Rochelle's chief judges for the last thirty years, but Preston Scher is the finest and fairest judge to ever sit in a black robe and wield a gavel. Sandy Scher isn't a political "hail fellow well met" backslapping jurist, looking to trade up to the next judicial level, Family Court or County Court or the State Supreme Court.

Here, in our own back yard, he's made his stand, using only his patience, his fairness, his judgment, and his superior brainpower to ensure the domestic tranquility of the neighborhood.

Here's what the Fund for Modern Courts, a statewide judicial monitoring group, says about Preston Scher. He's "fair, helpful, compassionate and efficient." He "took the time to be sure defendants' rights were 'protected'" and "carefully explained court proceedings." He "moves quickly and decisively." And yet is "polite" and "non-threatening."

Firm but fair, in my opinion. And you can ask the cops and county prosecutors if they agree. And they do. You might also contact the chief administrative judge of the entire 9th Judicial District—Mr. Justice Frank Nicolai—to solicit his professional view.

New Rochelle Democrats will meet on the fourteenth to select a candidate for judge. So we call on the great elders of the New Rochelle Democratic Party; its brilliant chairman, Arnie Klugman; and its sure bet for mayor, the estimable Noam Bramson, to keep politics out of the courthouse.

Astute observers believe the Democratic Party's "reluctance" to "cross-endorse" an outstanding judge like Mr. Scher stems from the harshness and stridency injected by the Republican Party in recent years. But even if that be the case, it is no excuse to dump this very superior and highly regarded jurist.

"Payback time" and politics do not belong in the courtroom or the halls of justice.

SEPTEMBER SONG: WITH A LITTLE HELP FROM HER "FRIENDS"

I had the biggest crush on Kitty Carlisle Hart for the longest time. But so did every other guy who ever met the woman. She was one classy dame. You may remember her from television. But the widow of the legendary producer Moss Hart also chaired the New York State Council on the Arts for Governors Nelson Rockefeller, Hugh Carey, Mario Cuomo, and George Pataki. She once sang "I'll Be Loving You Always" at a birthday party in my honor. I now return the favor. I broadcast this "appreciation" of Mrs. Hart on September 22, 2004.

Kitty Carlisle Hart, age ninety-four-and-a-half, stood in the spotlight last night at Feinstein's in the Regency Hotel on Park Avenue in Manhattan, a most fitting venue for this particular, spectacular dame. The New York newspapers call her an "uber diva." And Liz Smith says she's got the best pair of legs in New York.

For her opening number, Mrs. Hart proclaimed to her adoring fans, "Hello, old friends. Are you O.K., old friends? Who's like us? Damn few!"

Her "old friends" being Cole Porter, Richard Rodgers, Lorenz Hart, George Gershwin, Oscar Hammerstein, Harold Arlen, Alan Jay Lerner, Arthur Schwartz, and Irving Berlin.

Mrs. Hart dedicated her show—she calls it a "gig"—to "the giants of the American musical theater" she knew and entertained as a young leading lady, and later as the wife of a towering legend, Moss Hart, the playwright and producer. She was brilliantly accompanied at the piano by David Lewis, whose thin, reedy voice evokes memories of the great singer-songwriter Matt Dennis.

Kitty Hart looked out into the New York audience and with clear, perfect diction, said, "I began my career seventy years ago. And I'm thrilled to return to my beginnings."

Some of the songs she sang were achingly tender. Others were witty and sophisticated. All were incurably romantic:

From Jerome Kern: "They asked me how I knew when your heart's on fire/They must realize smoke gets in your eyes."

From Cole Porter: "It was just one of those things/A trip to the moon on gossamer wings."

From Irving Berlin: "All alone, by the telephone."

Mrs. Hart enraptured the smart, well-heeled audience with marvelous stories about the times she sang at parties for icons of the theater and Hollywood.

"When I was young, I got good reviews on my legs!" she exclaimed, and proceeded to show them, ever so discreetly. Liz Smith was right.

In addition to her gams, Kitty Carlisle Hart showed off her voice, her charisma, her spectacularly lovely hands, her posture, her presence, and a radiantly beautiful, ageless face.

Nancy Curry, no slouch herself in the physical-attraction department, once said of the woman in the spotlight, "She's always the prettiest girl in the room."

Though time seemed to stand still for Kitty Hart, she informed the Park Avenue crowd, "When you're very young, time passes so slowly. But my mother once said, 'When you get to be fifty, every fifteen minutes, it seems like breakfast!'"

The ninety-four-and-a-half-year-old diva also threw in a sly reference to the choreographer George Abbott, "who lived to be 107, which is not very much these days, darling!" Her remark brought the house down.

As the evening progressed, Kitty's voice grew richer, stronger, and lovelier, and she only paused for a brief libation after about fifty minutes, observing, "I believe I need a glass of water."

Preston Robert Tisch, the former Postmaster General of the United States, who also happens to own the Regency, stepped forward and proffered his own glass.

"Thank you, darling," said a grateful Mrs. Hart.

And then, without further delay, she resumed with a stunning version of the old classic "Something Wonderful," a hauntingly beautiful love song by Rodgers and Hammerstein. It has never been treated better than it was by Kitty Hart last night.

Interspersed among all her lovely songs was the very personal story of a young girl who would, at a very early age, become a leading lady.

"George Gershwin, when I knew him, used to invite me to come up to his place and sing 'Summertime' while he sat at the piano and fiddled with the arrangements. After doing this a few times, I finally figured out that this was a ploy, something akin to 'Would you like to come up and see my etchings sometime?' George was a bachelor, and handsome. The ladies loved him. And he returned the compliment!"

Again and again, she praised her musical "friends," singing, "Why was I born? Why am I living? Why was I born? To love you" and, "Ah yes, I remember it well."

For her penultimate number Mrs. Hart chose "September Song": "As the days dwindle down to September/And these few precious days/I spend with you."

And then to Mr. Berlin: "I'll be loving you, always, always," and the audience sang it right back to Mrs. Hart.

For an encore, the woman chose a fairly new song, "Here's to Life": "I still believe in chasing dreams/As long as I'm in the game, I want to play/For life, for love."

And then the ageless diva retired to an adjoining room to receive her fans, including the Tisch family; songwriter Hal David; Ambassador William vanden Heuvel; Betsy Von Furstenberg; Democratic bigwig Bill Rollnick; and impresario and keeper of the Mabel Mercer flame Donald Smith. Also Joan Rivers, and Matilda and Mario Cuomo.

The flashbulbs popped, and the camera shutters clicked as the leading lady thanked those who came to celebrate her ninety-fourth-and-a-half "birthday."

They were among the lucky ones. Carlo Mariani, the Feinstein's maître d', had turned away more than two hundred for this first performance of her three-night stand. Supposedly, even Walter Cronkite couldn't snag a table.

But take heart, Walter. The girl with the great legs will perform again tonight. And she may again bring along a few of her "friends."

On the way out, Mario Cuomo, interviewed by a waiting reporter, said, “She is an ontologist, someone who is into being, someone who loves life. This whole night, her performance was like a sermon, a homily on life.”

At ninety-four-and-a-half, Kitty Hart is still a leading lady of New York. She is still something wonderful. And every guy in the room would still like to invite her to come up and see their etchings.

But Gershwin thought of it first.

THE "UBER DIVA"

After Mrs. Hart's ninety-fifth birthday, I shared these remarks with the Whitney Media audience via WVOX and WVIP on March 2, 2006.

The columnist Liz Smith, no slouch in the glamour girl department, says Kitty Carlisle Hart has the best pair of legs in New York.

And last night, the ninety-five-year-old woman stood in the spotlight with a spectacular figure and those exquisite hands, just some of the equipment she uses to define and weave magic into the classic, timeless songs she learned from George Gershwin, Cole Porter, Irving Berlin, and Jerome Kern. What she said charmed audiences, as she has done throughout her career and life:

> I've just celebrated my birthday, darlings. I'm ninety-five. George Abbott lived to be 107—which doesn't really seem very old at all, now does it?
>
> The Great Depression and I arrived in New York at about the same time. . . .
>
> Frankly, darlings, I got somewhat greater notices on my *legs* than on my voice or my acting.
>
> I auditioned for Moss Hart. I didn't get the job. But, some years later, I got the man. . . .

In addition to her glamorous persona and charisma, Mrs. Hart was also accompanied last night by a lovely voice and flawless phrasing—which enabled her to pack more class and style into her presentation than any of today's "leading ladies" and wannabe divas could ever muster.

She used to call Nelson Rockefeller and Mario Cuomo "Governor, darling" when she ran the New York State Council for the Arts. Neither governor ever had to think twice about reappointing "Commissioner" Hart to her high post as chief patronage dispenser in the world of art back in the '70s and '80s.

She is the *ultimate* anti-bimbo dame.

And when she walks onto the stage and stands in the spotlight at Michael Feinstein's club in the Regency, Kitty Hart wipes out Mariah Carey, Beyoncé Knowles, Lindsay Lohan, Jennifer Lopez, Angelina Jolie, Britney Spears, and Paris Hilton every time.

Smoke gets in your eyes . . . they asked me how I knew . . . and yet today . . . I am without my love. . . .

Here's to us . . . Old Friends. Who's like us? Damn *few*!

What is this thing called Love . . . this mystery . . .?

It was just one of those things . . . if we thought a bit . . . about the end of it. . . .

All alone . . . by the telephone . . . wondering how you are and if you are . . . all alone too.

For it's a long, long time from May to December . . . these precious days I spend with you.

No complaints and no regrets. I still believe in chasing dreams. So here's to life . . . and every joy it brings.

I'll be loving you . . . always . . . always. . . .

Nancy Curry O'Shaughnessy says Kitty Hart has always been the prettiest girl in the room in every season of her life.

She still is.

Class reigns on Park Avenue until Saturday night.

TALESE THE WRITER

I've always admired all those wordsmiths who write so much more gracefully than I am able. That long list includes Jimmy Breslin, Pete Hamill, Jimmy Cannon, Bill Saroyan, Ken Auletta, David Hinckley, Nancy Q. Keefe, Mario Cuomo, Phil Reisman, Wilfred Sheed, Whitney Balliett, and Gay Talese. Here is a review of Gay Talese's memoir A Writer's Life, *broadcast April 14, 2006.*

Maybe you think you've got a budding author in the family? A condition that never threatened my old man.

Well, O.K., it only costs around $50,000 a year—just for the tuition—at the Columbia School of Journalism. If your kid is so inclined, you could always contact the "J" School and pay off the tab for the next five years.

Or you could just shell out twenty-six bucks and buy the kid a copy of *A Writer's Life* by Gay Talese, the great New York journalist, reporter, and author.

Mr. Talese, whose earlier magazine pieces on Frank Sinatra, Joe DiMaggio, and Floyd Patterson are the stuff of legend, has finally written about himself.

The son and heir of a master tailor from Calabria, Gay Talese once created exquisite haberdashery, but he now uses graceful words and elegant sentences to create exquisite books.

He's written several bestsellers, such as *The Kingdom and the Power* about the *New York Times*, *Honor Thy Father* about the Mafia, and *Unto the Sons* about immigrants in America. Also, a dazzling collection of magazine and newspaper gems, *The Gay Talese Reader*.

The highbrow *Atlantic Monthly* opined, "Gay Talese has written some of the best American prose of the second half of the twentieth century." And David Halberstam, in the *Boston Globe*, pegged Talese as "the most important nonfiction writer of his generation."

Forget all that stuff. After you save yourself $49,974.00 in college tuition for your gifted kid, buy another copy of *A Writer's Life* for yourself and stay up for two nights as I did reading it.

As usual in Talese's books, colorful characters abound. But this time, Talese is the star. A meticulous craftsman, he is famous for taking years to complete a manuscript. And this one is no exception; it required sixty years of his life to assemble, but it was well worth the wait.

Much research occurred over his preferred dry gin martinis at the tables of Elaine Kaufman of Elaine's, Frank Pellegrino of Rao's, Bruce Snyder and Bryan McGuire of "21," and Maestro Sirio Maccioni of Le Cirque. He has also known the haze of an evening at a marvelous kind of threadbare place near Bloomingdale's called Gino's that is not long for this world.

Talese also logged many hours with a rather nefarious group known as "The Skeeters," a drinking society founded by the late Ted Husing that, according to its by-laws, "exists for no good or useful purpose." Current members in good standing include Hugh Leo Carey; Brendan Byrne; Jerry Cummins; Mike Letis; John Hennessy; Jack Landry; insurance moguls Bill Flynn and Tom Moran; William Plunkett, Esq.; Nelson Doubleday; Bill Barry of the FBI; and Tom, the son of Sonny Werblin. There is also a Mara, a Quick, and Tony Rolfe. With the possible exceptions of Carey and Byrne, the ex-governors, not one of the Skeeters has ever written a coherent sentence. Most have never even read a book from cover to cover except for maybe the *Daily Racing Form*. And thus Talese's talent is barely tolerated in this august fraternity.

Talese is a relentless researcher, voracious gatherer of facts, and explorer of nuances, and his brilliance derives from his role as an observer and expert interviewer. Indeed, he credits his remarkable ability to "my natural, though at times misguided, affinity for people and places that exist in the shadows and side streets of the city and other overlooked places in which there are untold stories awaiting my discovery and development!" He doesn't miss much in this wonderful book.

You've no doubt seen Gay Talese painting the town red. His dazzling wife, the former Nan Ahearn, also works with words as a prominent publisher with her own imprint. She comes from Westchester originally and attended Rye Country Day School, Convent of the Sacred Heart, and Manhattanville College.

Like all great books, as you amble through *A Writer's Life*, you never want the thing to end. You never want Gay Talese to end. Now, at last, we know who he is.

Alfred A. Knopf is the publisher. It goes right on the shelf next to Breslin, Hamill, Mario Cuomo, Saroyan, Jimmy Cannon, and Gay Talese's other books. But this is the best one he's ever done.

MOUNT ST. MARY COLLEGE 46TH COMMENCEMENT CEREMONY

I never went to a single day of college. It is one of my greatest regrets. Then again, I never learned to play the piano either. And, at seventy-two, I'm still not able to boot up a computer. "Computer illiterate," I think they call me.

Thus, it was with some astonishment I learned that a marvelous college in the Hudson Valley thought me worthy of a "Doctor of Humane Letters" honorary degree.

When I learned that Mount St. Mary College had recently installed Father Kevin Mackin as its new president, I understood. Mackin is a Franciscan. They forgive us gently and generously. He's also an educator of national reputation, the same one who moved Siena College into the big time in a few short years.

This is what I told the graduates and their families—2,000 in all—on that spring day, May 16, 2009.

I'm pleased to report that Mount St. Mary College in Newburgh, New York, survived the day. It's now one of the "hottest" colleges in the region. Father Kevin's magic appears to be working again.

Mr. Chairman John Donoghue;

Father President Kevin Mackin, a great educator, a magnificent priest, a Franciscan, which says it all . . . ;

Sister Ann, who served this Hudson Valley treasure so well and with such dedication . . . ;

Mr. Jack Abernethy of Fox Television, a statesman of our profession of national reputation, a child of the Hudson Valley in whom we are all so well pleased by his high estate at Fox Television and Broadcasting . . . ;

Distinguished *Faculty* of Mount Saint Mary . . . ;

Influential *Trustees*, the guardians and sustainers of this great institution . . . ;

And *Graduates*, those who really *earned* your degrees . . . ;

And also your *Parents*, whose sacrifices and support during your years at the Mount were only the most recent manifestation of their love for each of you—

As it appears that I am the only one that stands between you and your own degree—a position from which I propose to extricate myself expeditiously, if not deftly—I will be mercifully brief.

I thank you all for this honor.

I never thought I would have the privilege of standing here, especially after the Jesuits gave me a 28 in that Chemistry exam in high school!

Did anybody ever sink so low as to get a *28* on a test? (We should start a club!)

And Algebra and Trigonometry: fuhgeddaboudit!

Somehow, despite that, I've been asked, over the years, to lecture at some seventeen colleges. But none ever stuck a cap on my gray head or offered me a degree! A *real* one like yours. Or "honorary" like mine.

So I won't forget this day. Or your kindness.

You know, "Doctor of Humane Letters" has a majestic, almost noble ring to it; but I was hoping, if you must know, for something I could relate to. Don't you have something like "Doctor of Humane *Chemistry*" or "Doctor of Computer Software"? How about "Doctor of Intergalactic Trigonometry"! I'm *really* good at that! And it would enable me to get back at those wonderful Jesuits who get even with me by publishing my books, revealing my shortcomings to an even wider audience.

During a luncheon at Mr. Maccioni's in New York City with Father Kevin and Joe Reilly (as the leader of all the broadcasters in this state, the president of our entire tribe) and my friend for life, my old Army buddy John Kelly, whose presence blesses the day, this honorary degree was under some "discussion," I can tell you, at that glorious sit-down with Father Kevin. Actually it was a pretty "memorable" lunch (I think we stumbled out of there rather late in the afternoon—as the sun was setting over Manhattan, in fact).

But *not* before Father Kevin said, "I'll give you three or four minutes to sum up *everything* you've learned in seventy-one years." I told the president of the Mount, "I'm not a scholar. Let this cup pass." It did not.

And so I'll tell you what I've learned: *Plagiarism*! *That's* what I've learned!

The *two* best ideas I've ever encountered came from a failed baseball player with too many vowels in his name known as Mario Cuomo who served this state as governor when most of you here assembled were but in grammar school, I imagine.

He was—he *is*—the son of a man who came here from Italy to dig trenches. And his *son* became governor. (That man—Andrea Cuomo—also had a *grandson* named *Andrew* who, many believe, might also have the makings of a fine governor.)

I want to tell you that this *Mario* Cuomo, Andrew's old man, told me everything I think we need to know about life issues. So here it is; and I hope you won't pull my honorary degree for plagiarism!

Mr. Cuomo said on the radio one day down in Westchester: *All* the major religions—Judaism, Christianity, Islam, Buddhism—have only *two* ideas at their foundation. Just *two*.

And you don't need a guy who came down from the mountain with tablets to instruct you on these fundamental ideas. Or an O'Shaughnessy. Even an ethical humanist or an atheist should be able to figure this out as a smart, sensible, practical way of living.

It started—this one *basic* notion—with the Jewish people, the ancient Hebrews, four or five thousand years ago.

They called this instinct *Tzedakah*, which means we're *all* brothers and sisters, we're *all* alike, and we're *all* in this together as children of the *same*, one God.

Then they added the *second* part—a concept known as *Tikkun Olam*, which means: God *created* the world but didn't *finish* it. That's *our* job: to *finish* it. To *complete* it.

And guess what—speaking of plagiarism—the *Christians* stole it whole from the *Jews* with the teaching of the Nazarene—the carpenter's son.

Now, I'm a reporter, a broadcaster, so I can tell you *exactly* how it happened—with *great* certainty.

The Lord, you see, was striding down the street one day, hanging out with some followers; and a wise guy, a scoffer (probably a professor of Chemistry), said, "I heard you were sensational in the temple last night, Rabbi!"

The Lord replied, with a smile, "Yeah, I had a pretty good night!"

And then the scoffer said, "So, give it to me in a *headline*, something I can understand. But do it in a *twenty-second* headline . . . or a sixty-second sound bite (for Mr. Abernethy). I'm a little busy."

The Lord said, "I'll do it for you in *ten* seconds: Love your neighbor as you love yourself, for the love of Me; for I am Truth."

"So that's it?" I inquired of Mr. Cuomo.

"That's the *Whole Law*," said the governor.

God *created*, but didn't *complete* or *finish*, the world in which we live and to which you now go forth.

And *we* are thus called to be "*collaborators* in Creation" as the philosopher Teilhard de Chardin put it. (Another Jesuit!)

And with the essential confirmation from the Lord to love your neighbor, that really *is* the *whole* law.

Here's another example to carry with you as you go forth this day. Jimmy Breslin, one of our greatest writers and a journalist who makes his living with words—even more gracefully than Mr. Cuomo, and much more artfully than *I* am able—had to get up the other day for the sad task of burying a daughter.

Kelly Breslin was forty-four.

Her father got up, looked out at the church, and said simply, "In her forty-four years, she never hurt anybody." And then he sat down.

He'd said it all.

Over the years, I've heard only a few pieces of counsel worth bringing to your attention. I remember something President Kennedy said: "When the dust of centuries has fallen on our cities . . .

we will be remembered . . . not for the battles we have won (and Mr. Abernethy, I would add: not for the *ratings* we have won) . . . but for our contributions to the human spirit."

I also recall an observation from another wise man in the public arena. Walter Nelson Thayer was a New York investor and publisher (of the *New York Herald Tribune*, of sainted memory) back in the '70s and '80s. (He was also the grandfather of my own son and heir David, who brought my granddaughter Lily here today). Mr. Thayer, a partner of John Hay Whitney, and a pillar of the Eastern Establishment and moderate-progressive Republicanism, once said, "New York is littered with guys whose only *goal* is to make *money*; they almost *never* do." I take that to mean you've got to have *something else* to carry you, something else to inspire you, something else to feel passionate about, something else to strive for.

So that's *everything I've* learned, in fifty years as a broadcaster, Father Kevin. And in seventy-one years as Bill O'Shaughnessy.

The young pitcher for the Yankees Joba Chamberlain told my friend John Sterling on the radio just last week about his struggles to become a starter with a place in the rotation: "I don't think you ever really 'get it,' or achieve perfection, or get to be perfect on the mound," said Joba.

So I guess the *test* is not really what you *achieve*, although we all *strive* to achieve; the *test* is really how hard you *try*.

As I said in front—I am not a scholar. (As you and your parents have readily perceived and instantly recognized.)

But I do have the wisdom to also repair occasionally to Father Mackin's brother friars at St. Francis of Assisi Church on 31st Street in Manhattan to confess some of the times *I* didn't try. (That's where all the suburban Catholics go when they're loaded with guilt.)

Those wonderful Franciscans who forgive us gently and generously (I'm talking here of priests who dispense three Hail Marys for a homicide!), they *know* all my failings.

Father President—I hope they won't drum you out of the Order of Friars Minor for your great kindness to me on this spring day.

And finally, to each of the 755 graduates here assembled, 250 of you with master's degrees: I hope when you go off to build up the community, as the ancient teachings say we must—to make it stronger, better, sweeter than it is—I hope you will remember and hold a good thought, when you come into your kingdom, for this magnificent college by the Hudson, and do what you can to help it continue to grow in wisdom and age and stature.

Because grow it will in the enlightened care and keeping of its talented and enlightened new president.

I'm immensely grateful to all of you for this honor and for indulging my enthusiasms.

"THE FUTURE IS HERE . . . BEHOLD THE FUTURE!"

The City of New Rochelle, rich in history, was a late bloomer economically. The Queen City of Long Island Sound finally got its act together a few years ago, encouraged by the vision of mega-developer Louis Cappelli and a brilliant young mayor, Noam Bramson. I gave this talk high up in one of New Rochelle's towering new skyscrapers at a breakfast for the merchant princes, industrialists, and the elders of the town, at the Avalon East on September 15, 2008.

THE HON. NITA LOWEY: This is a real honor for me. Never before in the twenty years I have been your congressperson have I been asked to be the "warm-up band" for the great Bill O'Shaughnessy. I have to tell you it's an impossible task because Bill O'Shaughnessy *is* New Rochelle. He has been involved in New Rochelle, loving New Rochelle, committed to New Rochelle for as long as I can remember. So I did want to thank him for all he has done to create such excitement. It also takes a team to do all this, and I'm glad to see that most of city hall and all the business leaders are here to hear Bill O'Shaughnessy's keynote remarks. He is my friend.

JOHN SPICER (PRESIDENT & CEO, SOUND SHORE MEDICAL CENTER): Being in New Rochelle for twenty years, it is very exciting for me too. It is a positive reflection on the city to see all of you here today. I've been given the responsibility of introducing someone who really doesn't need an introduction. When I first came to New Rochelle from NYU Medical Center, any number of people told me: "John, if you want to have half a chance when you get up there, you better get to know Bill O'Shaughnessy, and you better like him!" And in the last twenty years, Bill has taken me—and the medical center—under his wing and helped guide us through so many different issues, and through his willingness to give us his time—and in some cases, if we can get his knockout wife, Nancy, engaged—even his money, to keep the hospital moving forward.

He has done all this and so much more for the city. All of you know that Bill plays a variety of different roles in our community. For the City of New Rochelle itself, he has watched carefully and encouraged growth and development. He's not afraid to comment on how he sees us moving. In many ways, he serves as the "conscience of the community." He certainly is its historian, with his elegant prose and his books, because he can bring you back to how we got to where we are. But, most important, Bill is this city's cheerleader. He gives us the confidence, which I think this whole *country* needs right now. He gives us the confidence that we have the wherewithal and the potential to move forward directly, that we can develop into one of the key cities in the New York metropolitan area. We are seeing that happen right now.

But through all the good times and the bad, Bill has served as *the* cheerleader for this town. He has been out there pushing development and telling people we have one of the most beautiful shorelines in the region, that we have a downtown with a lot of potential, a disparate, multicultural suburban community, and a school district second to none. He has been saying that for more than twenty years, and now I think we're right about there, where he always said we should be and where we deserve to be. It is my pleasure to introduce New Rochelle's historian, cheerleader, and one of the best creative minds in the area: Bill O'Shaughnessy!

WILLIAM O'SHAUGHNESSY: Ladies and gentlemen, I'm grateful for your invitation, and for John Spicer's friendship of so many years. His introductions are getting better. He used to introduce me as a "self-made man . . . through *marriage*!" (*laughter*) And it's *true*! (*applause*)

In the moments you've given to me this morning I do want to invoke a little history and perhaps do a little reminiscing. I'm not an historian. I'll leave that to Tom Hoctor and Barbara Davis. But the portfolio you've allowed me to carry has enabled me to observe some wonderful and colorful characters who have populated this city over the years. I'll get to that in a moment.

I'm certainly glad to be here and away from the harsh, unpleasant news of the day. I've listened to WVOX and WVIP, and I've read five newspapers this morning. It's like "Roller Derby Day" on Wall Street. And I don't think anyone knows what the answer is, except to do what Mrs. Lowey suggested. You do the best you can on your own block, in your own community, and in your own neighborhood. You build it up, as Mr. Cuomo instructs us always. You try to make it stronger, better, even sweeter than it was. That's all we can do. That's everything we can do. And I hate to get biblical at this hour of the morning, but we could even resort to the ancient wisdom and "love our neighbor . . ." . You know the rest.

The image of New Rochelle as a popular and agreeable residential haven has endured over the years burnished by the presence of Norman Rockwell; Lou Gehrig; Whitney Young; James Montgomery Flagg; the Big Band crooner David Allyn; Hugh Price; Teresa Brewer; Eddie Foy; E. L. Doctorow; Cynthia Ozick; the fiftieth governor of New York, Malcolm Wilson; Frankie Frisch; Katherine and Ken Chenault; and, for a while, the dazzling Maria Cuomo, now Mrs. Kenneth Cole, Frances Sternhagen, Robert Merrill, Lou Boccardi, Kenneth Raske, Mariano Rivera, Ossie Davis, Ruby Dee, and those endearing characters Rob and Laura Petrie, played by Dick Van Dyke and Mary Tyler Moore. It is also home, one must acknowledge, to that great Shakespearean actor Vincent Pastore who, as you recall, was that memorable figure "Big Pussy" in "The Sopranos." I would call him a thespian, but I don't want any problems. (*laughter*)

So much for the glamorous *image* this suburban city has enjoyed over the years in the tabloids and among celebrity journalists. *You*, however, deal with *reality*, with the sinew and heart and soul and pulse of the city. And that's what I'd like to talk about today.

They—the civic boosters over the years—used to call this "A City Alive!" Remember that campaign? But it was only a flicker, an empty slogan, until Mr. Cappelli invested his money and his vision. And there were others—like the Avalon folks.

You know of our stations' high regard for shy, modest, retiring Mr. Cappelli, and for his vision and dynamism, as well as my admiration for him personally. I'm glad to note that the Chamber of Commerce has always stood in his corner and encouraged this extraordinary developer's Herculean and really, I think, quite noble efforts to reinvigorate our city.

I *am* pleased, and tremendously proud, to have been the permittee with a fiduciary relationship to your community radio stations for almost forty years, and I am glad to be here today high among the clouds with a spectacular view of the entire metropolitan area as you begin the business week here in our home heath.

I surely want to tell you of my admiration for Noam Bramson, the brilliant young mayor who serves us so well. Also for our terrific city manager, Chuck Strome, my former colleague on the airwaves. I've known a lot of mayors in my day, and city managers, and right now in 2008, at this precise moment, we have the two best individuals we've ever had leading our city. In Craig King we also have an excellent commissioner of development. Their genius is everywhere apparent all around us.

Senator "Suzi" is here. She goes on forever, and long may she ever. You could not have a better friend at 3:00 in the morning than Assemblyman George Latimer or Legislator Vito Pinto. And, of course, the absolutely essential individual in our community is John Spicer. I wanted to also remember to tell you of my gratitude to the great Cindy Hall Gallagher and our chief of staff Don Stevens and my son and heir David O'Shaughnessy.

And Nita Lowey, who elevates and honors us with her remarkable service in Westchester. Her House colleagues made her a "cardinal" and a chair of a powerful committee (I wanted to make her a *senator*!). They know how smart she is, how dynamic she is. We know how *good* she is. Mrs. Lowey is already on her way back to Washington, but I hope she (or her husband, Steven) won't mind me telling you I'm just crazy about the lady! (*applause*)

Most radio stations today have fallen to speculators and absentee owners, ladies and gentlemen. And they are run by what they call "market managers" or "asset managers" who operate out of airport lounges on their Palm Pilots and BlackBerrys, beholden to corporate masters a whole continent away. It's a sad truth—and I guess the same is true for delicatessens or banks or car dealers or oil companies—that radio stations are worth more "in play" among speculators than they are being operated as radio stations.

When the *Wall Street Journal* called WVOX "America's Quintessential Community Station," that is an appellation in which you, as our patrons, sponsors, and benefactors, must share. So I'm proud WVOX and WVIP are perhaps the last locally owned and locally operated independent radio stations in the land.

I wanted to tell you, as you go through this week—and you've got some really good programs planned—that as you perhaps know from the public press, I'm more than a little interested in First Amendment matters. I'm afraid I'm often the one they drag out when Howard Stern goes too far! He calls me the "white-haired mogul from Westchester who sometimes gets it right." (*laughter*)

We lost a great friend of the First Amendment in George Carlin. You remember his "Seven Dirty Words"! I can't say those seven dirty words even here. But I beg you, as you go through this week, please don't let any of your panelists say the following—which, I believe, are even far worse than George Carlin's seven dirty words. I refer to the business-speak *buzzwords* of our professions. If you hear any speakers say, "Make it happen!" or "Doin' what it takes!" or "Gettin' it done!" or "24/7" or "The whole nine yards!" throw them the hell out! For I think these utterances are even more dangerous and vulgar than the seven dirty words. To hell with the First Amendment! I just had to tell you that. (*laughter*)

In every endeavor there are the *takers* and there are the *givers*. And here assembled in this room are obviously the givers. By your presence early on a Monday morning you are firmly among *this* generation of givers.

But I want to remember, for just a moment, those who came before us, those business leaders who got us where we are. I arrived in this town in 1967. And I never dreamed we would one day be sitting assembled in high council above the clouds like this in a thirty-two-story skyscraper. We started out, after all, in the subterranean basement of George Kaufman's Pershing Square Building! (*laughter*)

We've come a long way together. I remember the battles we fought along with Alvin Richard Ruskin, a former mayor (one of the great ones) now in his eighties living in a retirement home in Connecticut, to get the first mall built; with Ossie Davis confronting the bulldozer operators threatening to run over the black street people. A lot has happened since then. And you are the inheritors of the example and vision of all those marvelous leaders in the business community in years gone by.

The Chamber of Commerce has always been a magnet. I want to congratulate you not only on Denise's service but on having the wisdom to elect the *first* woman president of the New Rochelle Chamber of Commerce: Rita Mabli.

Now, as promised, the history. I'm going to try out some names on you, and I bet you haven't heard these in a good, long time. In my books, I've mentioned some of them. I read a chapter about John Brophy this morning. Remember John Brophy? He led every parade in this town for many decades. He was also a big American Legion guy. And he would send off our servicemen and -women with a Bible and a comb-and-brush set; he would see them off by dawn at the train station. But he always hung out at the Chamber of Commerce.

And on this brilliant morning in 2008 those marvelous townie characters come back to us through the mist of time: Alex Norton, the flamboyant and endearing administrator of the old New Rochelle Hospital; Jack Cesario of the restaurant family; Mayor Stanley W. Church (all the widows in town loved Stanley Church) (*laughter*); one of my personal all-time favorites: Rocco Bellantoni Jr., who owned several businesses in this town and even became a member of the City Council; and old Charlie Librett and his son Arthur. Also Charlie Wendelkin of Blessed Sacrament. And Lou Saporito before he split with Loretta. All your Chamber of Commerce and civic dinners were held at the fabled Glen Island Casino, which was presided over by Angelo Badolatto. All of these people were active in Chamber of Commerce affairs. It's in your minutes. And in our memories and in our hearts.

Here's another name: Jack Kornsweet, with his thatch of white hair, ran Better Built Bedding, and he had an opinion on everything. Another of my favorites was always Marvin Goldfluss. He ran the Camera Craft store. He too knew damn near everything about everything, and he let you know about it. (I'm reminded that we need a good *camera store* in this town. And a *bookstore*.) Murray Mendelson. I'm going to write a novel: *Whatever Happened to Murray Mendelson?* (*laughter*) Milton Gould of Gould Buick down the street. I sat next to his daughter at a dinner in New York the other night. She's now married to the chairman of the MTA, Dale Hemmerdinger. And Lenny DeMarco; he was a big Chamber of Commerce guy. And Alex Scott. Where do you buy appliances now? In the old days you would call him—"My washing machine broke down"—and he would send you a new one. And send you a bill three weeks later. I don't know how you do that now.

A great hangout for Chamber of Commerce types, especially on Saturday mornings, was The Mannerly Shop, a men's store presided over by Sal Generoso. He was haberdasher to the townie establishment. And even the mayors of the day called him "Goombah Sal," for he was also Republican chairman of the city. His estimable son Jim Generoso now runs the busy New Rochelle City Court, which has often been accused of being one of the very best in all of New York State. I think the Chief City Judge, Preston Scher, gets some credit for that too. A lot, in fact.

An especially vivid and much beloved figure during the city's struggles was Israel Streger. They called him "Murph," but his real name was Israel. And his two sons: David went into politics, served on the Council, and ran for mayor a few times; Bobby served as your president.

The bankers of the day: Arthur Geoghegan, who walked about twenty-seven blocks down North Avenue every morning—this is where he picked up most of the business for First Westchester National Bank. And Keith Fulsher. And Jack Dowling of Westchester Federal Savings; he was a great contrarian who even founded his own Presbyterian Church! That building that looks like Ventura Boulevard is still there. Now I think it's HSBC. I had to repair to Dowling every time I would defend the city manager of the day. Dowling would cancel his advertising. I would say, "Jack, you don't have to do this just to get me in here; you're a 'patron!'" (*laughter*)

I think it's wonderful you have a cooperative, working relationship with the Business Improvement District. The BID is led so ably by Ralph DiBart and Steven Jerome's brilliant young son Marc. It wasn't always thus in this town because they had a Chamber of Commerce *and* they also had a Downtown Association led by Sidney Mudd and the Joyce Beverage people and Mike Risavi who ran Bloomingdale's. And there was an attractive, educated man named Hubert Horan who ran People's Bank. And speaking of bankers, there were also two bachelor girls: Mary O'Leary and Evie Haas. Rosemary remembers them. As I recall, they enjoyed a cocktail or two of an evening. And they were great dames.

And Hughie Doyle: He was a great Chamber of Commerce guy, like a Tip O'Neill of his day. Some other endearing characters: Remember Bill Scollon and David Kendig, a very smart guy? And Paddy O'Neil? All the elders of the town met at Paddy O'Neil's saloon for lunch right nearby. He would not recognize this fancy, swell place. He would not believe it! O'Neill presided over a wonderful saloon and everybody would eat there on paper plates. Arthur Geoghegan and Owen Mandeville from Larchmont. And Bill Scott with his magnificent clothes. And J. Ray McGovern and Frank Connelly. And if they didn't eat at Paddy O'Neil's they would eat at Schrafft's where Paul Scott was. And the lure of Schrafft's was a ninety-nine-cent cranberry sandwich and a whiskey sour that always came with a small pitcher for the overflow!

And Brother Darby Ruane. And Del Olan, who loved the microphone. And Bob Feinman, maybe the brightest guy who ever walked these streets. And he let you know it. Jimmy Stillman and Gene Palazzo of Liebman's and Hector Hyacynthe and Steve Tenore. And—he's not here because he's probably at the radio station—Peter Mustich. (*applause*)

J. Addison Young, Jack Gardner, Les Albertson, the Fanellis, Charlie Seidenstein, and Frank Connelly Sr. were the prominent lawyers of the day, just as John Vasile, Bill McKenna, Bob Mancuso, and Frank Connelly Jr. are of this day and age. Ira Gelb, Dan Sherber, and Irv Samuels were the outstanding physicians then, as Rich Pisano is today.

And, my God, how did we get through this litany without even a mention of the Honorable Theodore R. "Teddy" Greene (*applause*), the beguiling and absolutely irresistible city councilman who was also a merchant prince? He owned an art gallery. But he was always running for mayor, and he drove Alvin Ruskin nuts with his antics. (*laughter*) Remember when Teddy stuck the "Up with People" troupe of fresh-faced kids from the heartland out on David's Island for an entire summer and tens of thousands came from all over the Eastern seaboard to hear them sing patriotic anthems and ballads with great resolve and sureness? With all of this going on, still finding time to flirt with everything that moved! (*laughter*) Teddy was also constantly inserting himself into the affairs of the Chamber of Commerce. And we loved him for it.

Over the years, my associates at the radio station often partnered with these great characters and the Chamber of Commerce on the great issues of the day. When we tried to save Bloomingdale's, we went down to plead with the elegant and very grand Lawrence Lachman, the Bloomies chairman, and a representative of the Chamber of Commerce was with us in those desperate days.

When we stopped that shopping center across from Iona College, the Chamber of Commerce was there.

We did that for Brother Jack Driscoll, a great friend of ours. Some other administrators of that great college in our midst perhaps studied Latin—but were maybe absent and went missing the day they taught *quid pro quo* because there would have been a shopping center there if we didn't stop it. But that was long ago, Brother Liguori, and you forgot. (*laughter*)

When Nita Lowey and Mayor Bramson persuaded the U.S. Congress and the U.S. Postal Service to honor the memory of our beloved Robert Merrill, the Chamber of Commerce was there.

And I want to tell you about David's Island. This is an absolutely true story, and City Manager Strome will remember. The City was interested in selling David's Island to Con Edison, also known as the Edison Company. (I always let on to the old-timers that I was "connected" because we didn't call it Con Edison, we called it "the Edison Company.") So we told Alvin Ruskin, the mayor, to call them up and tell them we've got an island for sale, right out there rotting, sitting in the noonday sun.

He said, "You don't do it that way, O'Shaughnessy."

At this time, there was a new chairman of The Edison Company; he came from Walla Walla, Washington, from the Bonneville Power Authority. His name was Chuck Luce, a very distinguished man. I called him up and said, "I need to talk to you, sir. I am a Very Important Person from Westchester, with my 500 throbbing watts of power."

He said, "Mr. O'Shaughnessy, do you ever do dinner?"

I said, "You mean, like a *business* dinner? Maybe my wife would let me do that!" I told Alvin, the mayor, we're going to dinner, and I took them to Toots Shor. And Toots was having a good time that night with about five brandy and sodas under his belt. (*laughter*)

He took right away to Charles Luce and immediately punched the chairman in the gut and told him he looked like Johnny Carson, and the great barroom philosopher right then and there predicted he would go far in this town. (*laughter*)

Then we went next door to "21," and I thought maybe I'm in a little over my head and maybe I shouldn't have done this. We had a few more cocktails and, as we were leaving, I sheared off my bumper on a mail truck! Ruskin, the mayor, said, "Luce didn't see it; he's already in his limousine. We'll go around the block and pick up your damn bumper." (*laughter*)

The next day W. Dunham Crawford of Con Ed was in the Office of the Mayor negotiating the biggest land deal in the history of Westchester County: $10 million. And I'm feeling real good about this! Ten million bucks! And the councilmen of the day, they couldn't wait to spend that $10 million.

And then some people with many vowels in their names down in the south end of town, and a few Irishmen too, heard the word "*nuclear*." "You want to build a *what* out there?" (Forget that nuclear energy is the cheapest and cleanest.) "Not in *my* back yard!" I'm afraid we had to reluctantly cover that story in some detail. And, guess what? They sold it back for $10! $10 million to $10! (*laughter*)

Wait! Some years later, I'm walking into the American Yacht Club with Alvin Ruskin, now a Supreme Court justice, thanks to Nelson Rockefeller. Charles Luce is there with his daughter. He said, "Come over here, gentlemen." He said, "Honey, these are two very important gentlemen. You should get to know Mr. O'Shaughnessy, the head of the radio station, and Judge Ruskin. You should really know them if you ever want to *lose* money in a real estate deal!" (*applause*) (*laughter*) So although we were not always successful, the Chamber of Commerce *was* there to support our efforts.

We salute as well the leaders and visionaries of *today*, those who have been so active in Chamber of Commerce affairs: your past president Frank Dursi, Louis Iacopetta, Gary Terrigian, Joe Simone, Bob Young, Charles DePasquale. Someday one of my sons will be up here telling you just how great they were. And all of you.

Valerie Moore O'Keefe, the highly respected supervisor of the Town of Mamaroneck, once said, "As New Rochelle goes, so goes the entire Sound Shore area." She is one bright lady. And the recent rebirth and renaissance of New Rochelle has lifted all boats, and also the fortunes and well-being of the residents of Pelham, Larchmont, Eastchester, Harrison, and Rye as well, our neighbors.

I remember when this city was trying to get UNICEF. We took the guy down to Le Cirque and got him loaded, but he was already wired by Phyllis Wagner, who wanted to keep this huge UN organization in the Big Apple. Mrs. Wagner was a powerful woman and a widow times two. She had been married to Bennett Cerf and New York Mayor Robert Wagner. *Plus*, she was Frank Sinatra's best friend. Who was going to mess with *Sinatra*? (*laughter*) So we were outgunned in our efforts to attract UNICEF. But the head guy—I remember he had a ponytail—pulled me aside and said, "You have a fabulous 'organic city'; it's got waterfront, parkways, top-notch schools, a great police department, two superior colleges, a magnificent medical center, everything!"

The Chamber of Commerce has always put aside parochial interests to look beyond the demands of its purse, the imperatives of commerce, and beyond your own narrow interests. And through an inclination to statesmanship, you have always been stalwart and reliable champions for the greater good of the community. Actually, you are almost misnamed. Your organization is very much more than a mere "Chamber of *Commerce*."

I can only leave you with this thought. David's grandfather Walter Nelson Thayer, who was president of the *Herald Tribune*, a great newspaper of sainted memory, was quoted in the *New York Times*: "New York is littered with guys whose only goal is to make money; they almost never do." I think he meant you've got to have something else to drive you, to guide you—something else to inspire you. You've go be the best tile-setter. You've got to make the best salad at the deli. You've got to be the most caring and compassionate banker of the day or the most dedicated hospital administrator. And always, as Mario Cuomo constantly instructs us, you've got to build up the community and make it stronger, better, and sweeter than it was.

But I expect, as your presence indicates, you know all of these things.

Thomas Carlyle once said, "The glory of a workman, *still more* of a *master* workman—that he does his work well—ought to be his most precious possession—and like the honor of a soldier—dearer to him than life."

So thank you for indulging my enthusiasms for so many years in this extraordinary city, which has been so good to me and mine.

And congratulations to Madame President Rita Mabli. You're in very good and capable hands. . . .

But it was ever thus!

FOUR SEASONS ROAST: 50TH ANNIVERSARY

The Four Seasons Restaurant in the Seagram's Building in Manhattan is one of America's most famous and enduring dining venues. And its interior is an actual New York City landmark. (My remarks at the Landmark Designation Hearing can be found in one of my earlier books.) On May 5, 2009, this venerable institution celebrated its fiftieth anniversary with a charity "roast" for the benefit of "Meals on Wheels." It was a glittering and fun evening, even by the standards of this fabled restaurant.

Welcome to a very special New York evening.

We gather on this spring night to celebrate the spectacular fifty-year run of this glorious high-class saloon.

How wonderful it is to be here, and for a good cause: Citymeals-on-Wheels.

So permit me to thank you for the gift of your presence and the generosity of your purse.

We thank our hosts: Julian Niccolini and Alex Von Bidder, who've rounded up 250 of their nearest and dearest for this sold-out historic evening.

We eagerly anticipate their comeuppance at the hands of some of the most vivid and powerful among our well-founded neighbors in New York.

Your presence also honors those wonderful Four Seasons hands who have bestowed their loyalty and devotion on this fabled landmark venue over so many years: Tradeep, Lawrence, Pedro, Italo, Giuseppe, Charlie, John the Artist, George—all of them who make us feel special and welcome, the marvelous characters whose industry and dedication bless the joint.

Our roasters are surrogates for those same Four Seasons staffers who have been waiting for this moment when Alex and Julian will be put on the rack.

Some ground rules: You may not use the word "certifiable" when referring to one of the partners. (Julian!)

And I would ask you to welcome the two long-suffering, saintly, forgiving individuals who will enjoy this evening the most; please welcome Sondra Von Bidder and Lisa Niccolini.

These proceedings are greatly enhanced by many of my colleagues in the public press. Fred Ferretti of the *Times*. Peter Elliot of Bloomberg. Pamela Fiori, the editor of *Town and Country*. "R. J." Richard Johnson of the *Post*'s "Page Six." Bob Lape of WCBS. George Rush of the *News*. Glenn Collins, who writes like an angel for our beloved *New York Times*.

As I look around this marvelous room I see Joe Armstrong, Richard Maier—the legendary architect—Dr. Iris Love, Joan Ganz Cooney, Mauro Maccioni, Jonathan Tisch, Liz Smith, Sirio Maccioni, Joe Migliucci—the King of Arthur Avenue, Little Italy. And we could not enjoy the evening without thinking of Mr. Secretary Pete Peterson; Edgar Bronfman, the international philanthropist and patron-protector of the Four Seasons; and Jack Rudin, patriarch of the Rudin family, who gets the best table in the house.

All week, Julian has been a nervous wreck. He called me ten times a day. "Pete Peterson is really going to hurt me; he's taking this much too seriously." And in the middle of one night: "Don't forget it's *Mr.* Bronfman; without him I wouldn't exist!" And on and on.

Alex, as taciturn and Swiss as ever, sailed serenely through all the preparations for this evening.

Until this morning. He said to Tradeep: "Should we have done this?" Too late, Alex!

And then, after all the blood-letting, we'll let Julian and Alex defend themselves.

Will Julian pull a stunt to make the papers tomorrow? He's already tried the "walking on water" bit here in the Pool Room (he failed!). You'll also recall the day he posed all those people in the "nutty" (that's high church for "nude," Julian).

And here comes a very serious problem: What happens if Alex comes across tonight as *funnier* than Julian? That would be beautiful.

Alex is a sailor, as we know; he's quite an accomplished helmsman at the Larchmont Yacht Club.

Julian, of course, would have us believe that *he* is a swordsman! In your dreams, Julian!

Anyway, with all due deference to Alex, I will suggest we celebrate where we are at this point in time, having savored and enjoyed fifty wonderful years here in this Meisian space enveloped by Philip Johnson's genius. I will put it in nautical terms for Alex. But it is meant for Julian as well. Pay attention, Julian.

As we celebrate the fiftieth anniversary of this brilliant and welcoming place, amidst these uncertain times that have really descended on the whole world, we are confident—nay, we're *sure*—you will both continue to sail against the winds of convention that blow toward mediocrity in the restaurant and hospitality profession. We are altogether confident you won't let this world-class venue—an American institution—drift into ordinariness or lie at the anchor of complacency. Mr. Sokolov in the *Wall Street Journal* says the wind is blowing in another direction. Everywhere we look we are faced with a lowering of standards, a cheapening, a coarsening of the culture. But we are sure that you two fellows—as permittees and stewards of this lovely treasure, which is *sui generis* in your profession (Julian: That means the place is altogether unique and able to be defined only in its own terms!)—hear the music of all those marvelous souls who have repaired to your care and keeping. At any rate, we're *certain*, all of us here assembled, that you'll *never* heed the siren call of those tempted to say it is time to furl the sail of this landmark restaurant that has resided in your devotion and passion for a good part of those fifty years.

It came to your stewardship with the faith, confidence, and patronage of the Bronfman family, accompanied over the years by the industry and labor of the late Paul Kovi and Tom Margittai, the great Squire of Sante Fe, and the legendary Joe Baum. You are the beneficiaries of their vision.

So tonight, Alex and Julian, we re-dedicate the Four Seasons to your continued stewardship and care and keeping. Our charge to you—with great affection, with admiration for your considerable talents, and with gratitude for your friendship *in every season*—our charge to you is to keep on doing what you're doing so well. And don't change a God-damn thing!

There are so many restaurants in the land that take themselves altogether much too seriously or where you are confronted by a Debby, a Jennifer, a Candy, a Lance, or Trevor standing behind a lectern, and then you are led to a table where the food is sometimes good, sometimes not. But nobody is having any fun at those serious tables.

We come here to have some fun of an evening. Now let's get started. . . .

ELIOT SPITZER, ONCE AND FORMER GOVERNOR

We spoke about the fallen governor's troubles on March 12, 2008.

It is an excruciating personal tragedy for the Governor, his family and the rest of our society to whom he has meant so much.

Governor Mario Cuomo

Once again Mario Cuomo got it exactly right. The great philosopher-statesman who once occupied the high office Eliot Spitzer [is relinquishing] framed this bizarre episode with precision and his usual compassion.

All the editorial writers and every journal in the land have relentlessly denounced Eliot Spitzer in recent days. But as he who held so much promise steps down in disgrace, my mind drifts back to a conversation we had some years ago in this very same radio studio with then–Attorney General Spitzer. It was during the very worst time for Al and Jeanine Pirro. (You remember them, shy, modest, and retiring as they were!)

As Spitzer sat in our Westchester radio studio on that day long ago taking calls from our listeners, Albert J. Pirro was fighting for his own freedom and reputation in a U.S. District Federal Court up the road a piece in White Plains.

As the program went on, it may be recalled, I gave him several opportunities to jump on the Pirros. However, and despite his "steamroller" rep, he refused to hit Al or Jeanine Pirro when they were down. I remember that.

Now, on this sad day, who, I wonder, will cut Eliot Spitzer a break?

For all his character deficits, obvious failings, and all-too-human weaknesses—those we know about and those we have not yet identified—some goodness must still reside in the man.

For one thing, he was able to win the favor and devotion of a remarkable woman—Silda Spitzer. And together, they have three wonderful daughters. We've also been impressed that Eliot Spitzer was found worthy of the friendship of the estimable William Mulrow of Bronxville, who was recently named to preside over Mr. Spitzer's "Kitchen Cabinet" of informal advisors and friends.

We're not alone in our tremendous admiration for Mr. Mulrow, who, in every telling, is one of *the* most thoughtful, decent, ethical individuals ever to aspire to public service or civic leadership in this state. There is no finer individual in these precincts than Bill Mulrow.

And it should be fairly acknowledged that during his controversial service as attorney general and governor, Mr. Spitzer did throw several well-deserved shots across the bow of some selfish, grubby Wall Street moguls and corporate types whose greed knew no bounds.

He presided where Nelson Rockefeller, Alfred E. Smith, Tom Dewey, Charles Evans Hughes, Malcolm Wilson, Hugh Carey, Averell Harriman, and the great Mario Cuomo once sat. And now Eliot Spitzer becomes an asterisk in the long history of New York.

But it is to be hoped, as he struggles to return to private life, that he be given an unfettered chance to atone for his failings, first to his wife and daughters and then to himself as he confronts his demons through therapy and honest introspection.

The man has important personal work to do without being hounded by the U.S. Justice Department or any "on the make" federal or state prosecutor who may be tempted to visit what is known as "selective prosecution" on the fallen governor.

In other words, the people of New York will probably not look kindly on anyone who wants to burnish their reputation by dragging out and adding any more sad chapters to this tawdry and ultimately tragic tale.

As Chris Matthews said last night, "We're sick of this story . . . let's move on and talk about something else."

LOWEY FOR CONGRESS: WHERE ONCE GIANTS WALKED THE LAND

We are longtime supporters of Nita Lowey. Here's a commentary from way back on October 31, 1988, when this now-powerful member of Congress was just getting started.

The 20th Congressional District of Westchester always did have a proud, consistent *tradition* of designating superior and enlightened individuals as our federal representatives: Ogden Rogers Reid, publisher of the *Herald Tribune* and our first ambassador to a brave, growing nation called Israel. And Richard Ottinger, a relentless environmental champion, law professor, and tilter at Establishment windmills. Both came to our service from great families with long histories of public service.

And our country squire neighbors to the north had the good sense to designate Hamilton Fish, a moderate Republican and a respected hero of Watergate, who is enormously popular among his House colleagues. It is very much to your lasting credit that the incomparable Nelson Rockefeller was first propelled to the national stage by our Westchester neighbors.

In other words, we have had a pretty good record. Almost without exception, when someone rose to speak for Westchester in the high councils of our nation, that individual was possessed of extraordinary ability, grace, and stature. It is, as we've noted, a tradition among our people.

Until four years ago, that is, when one Joseph DioGuardi burst on the scene to presume to speak for the enlightened residents of our county. Actually, he didn't exactly come out of left field. DioGuardi had been appearing on "Page Six" as the marketer and promoter of a pop fad item called a "mood ring." And he came to our attention when our local station uncovered a scheme by New Rochelle politicians and members of the Board of Education to install DioGuardi's New York accounting firm as auditor for the city school district, a position long held by the venerable and highly respected Bennett Kielsen firm.

And then—he always bounces back—Accountant DioGuardi aspired to a seat in Congress. *Your* seat in Congress. So we gave him the benefit of the doubt against one Oren Teicher, a rather cerebral staff-type, lacking in dynamism. And DioGuardi was surely to be *much preferred* against fiery, controversial Bella Abzug, that flamboyant remnant of the sixties, who trooped all over the county trying to impress us with her New York celebrity friends and Hollywood stars. You weren't buying any of it. And so DioGuardi was returned to Congress.

But now, it is 1988. And the Honorable Joseph DioGuardi—now Congressman DioGuardi—has himself a real horse race, for perhaps the first time. It's about time.

At long last the Democratic Party has fielded a candidate of great substance and conviction. Her name is Nita Lowey, and we endorse her with enthusiasm and strong admiration.

Mrs. Lowey is strong on the issues. She is bright, concerned, and caring, and she brings to this contest a vision and sophistication totally lacking in the incumbent. We don't agree with her on every issue. But the Democratic candidate, to her credit, has not tailored her position to fit the fashion of the season, neither ours nor anyone else's.

Nita Lowey, during her exemplary service as Governor Mario Cuomo's Assistant Secretary of State, has been a relentless champion of the poor and the homeless and has earned very high marks for her creative initiatives in child care.

Mr. DioGuardi, the Republican-Conservative, has shown absolutely no leadership on the Yonkers housing case and its attendant anarchy, which was everywhere apparent. It took him fully six months even to acknowledge that, yes, maybe Yonkers should at least obey the law of the land. Our colleagues in the public press will confirm that DioGuardi had to be dragged, kicking and screaming, into that volatile issue so in need of diplomacy and statesmanship. Or perhaps merely a little courage.

His record on the *homeless* is *abysmal*. When County Executive Andy O'Rourke and Andrew Cuomo began their innovative campaign to build housing for the homeless, this station urged Mr. DioGuardi, in our offices, to get behind the effort in a true nonpartisan fashion and help O'Rourke and Cuomo. He broke a promise even to meet with WestHELP officials, and nothing more was heard from the congressman on this vital matter, which the Gannett papers have correctly identified as the number one issue facing Westchester today.

His one "claim to fame" seems to be a feigned, almost transparent interest in Long Island Sound. But the League of Conservation Voters and Environmental Action have endorsed Nita Lowey, suggesting that her opponent was only "masquerading" as an environmentalist.

In one area, however, Mr. DioGuardi takes a back seat to no one. He is the most prolific and relentless political fundraiser we've ever seen in these parts. Possessed of seemingly inexhaustible energy, DioGuardi has identified and descended on every fat cat in the district with his persuasive charm.

Incredibly, the energetic Republican is now favored to win over the gifted and more able Mrs. Lowey. For he wears the mantle of an incumbent, symbolized by that red Congressional Members pin he displays too prominently on his lapel when he saunters into the main dining room of the Winged Foot Golf Club. We can't resist the observation, however, that it's merely *pinned* on Mr. DioGuardi and not at all part of the fabric of the man.

We've told you what we think about some of his predecessors: Reid and Ottinger, Edwin B. Dooley and Peter Peyser—talented heavyweights who gave Westchester so many reasons to be proud of their representation in the House.

Despite four years of trying, DioGuardi has never quite succeeded in ingratiating himself with the House leadership, despite going so far as to write those obsequious memos identifying "loopholes" on outside income for the benefit of his colleagues.

Our *main* finding against the Republican candidate, then, is that the redoubtable and irrepressible Mr. DioGuardi spends an entirely inordinate amount of time raising money for Mr. DioGuardi, rather than putting that energy to the service of the people of the 20th District.

We really have a right, once more, to expect better performance from a more enlightened representative in the halls of Congress.

And so we're *for* Nita Lowey, who has her priorities right.
We regret having to be so harsh with her opponent.
Let's put it this way: There are no *bad* guys in this race.
Only *one terrific woman*.

LATIMER FOR ASSEMBLY

George Latimer is a politician the way those of my father's time imagined them to be. Broadcast on October 29, 2004.

In the thirty-five years we've presumed to endorse and recommend candidates for public office, this is the easiest choice we've ever had to make: George Latimer is one of the finest political figures we've encountered in almost four decades.

Mr. Latimer served with distinction as chairman of the Westchester County Legislature and, briefly, as County Democratic chairman. This wonderfully appealing and good-natured man is almost the *complete opposite* of the greedy, selfish, upwardly mobile politicos who populate the body politic in this day and age. Especially at the local level.

George Latimer is a master of constituent service. It comes naturally to him. He is a man of infinite patience and a coalition builder of great resourcefulness. He is also a keen student of local governance who will, from the first day—the minute he is sworn in—almost instantly become a star in the Assembly of our state.

We've watched this fellow grow in wisdom and age for many years, and we're delighted the voters of the Sound Shore Assembly District will finally have a chance to elevate a very savvy and superior public servant. And *you*, ladies and gentlemen, will be the beneficiaries of George Latimer's remarkable dedication and commitment.

Indeed, this recognition of his extraordinary quality and many talents is long overdue. In the past, he's been mentioned for lieutenant governor and the U.S. Congress. But Latimer, as gifted as he is, has always been reluctant to advance himself. But he sure knows how to advance the causes of his constituents.

This time, it appears, the *people* have spoken, and he has the solid support of Democrats in our area, as well as many of the Conservative supporters of Assemblyman Ron Tocci, who is stepping down after a long, distinguished career in Albany. Latimer will be a more than worthy successor.

He is so good, so decent, and so committed, we have absolutely *no hesitation* in commending him to your favorable judgment.

Would that *all* the choices we'll confront on Election Day were as easy as *Latimer for New York State Assembly*!

WVOX and WVIP endorse *George Latimer*.

It was a long time coming. But we're *very* fortunate to have him.

THE LAST PUBLIC REMARKS OF OSSIE DAVIS

Ossie Davis, the great American actor, was a New Rochelle neighbor. He was also a citizen-activist with whom we collaborated on many civil rights and community issues over the years. He would often appear in our lobby to "enlighten" us. I was honored to introduce him at his last public appearance, upon the occasion of Lincoln Hall's annual dinner at The Water Club, New York City, on January 7, 2005.

WILLIAM O'SHAUGHNESSY: Welcome to the Lincoln Hall Annual Dinner. Thank you for the generosity of your purse and your willingness to leave hearth and home for a noble purpose. I'm reminded—as the late New York Governor Malcolm Wilson once observed—that I am, as the program indicates, the only one standing between you and your dinner (*laughter*), and I plan to extricate myself from that position promptly and expeditiously, if not deftly. (*applause*)

We're here tonight, ladies and gentlemen, because no one in my home can resist a summons from Nancy Curry O'Shaughnessy, our dinner chair. (*applause*)

The towering reputation of your president, Jim Nugent, also compels our presence. For thirty years, he has served Lincoln Hall with relentless devotion, a personality flaw also shared by your vice president, Douglas Wyatt. (*applause*)

In the last few years, Lincoln Hall has raised over $100,000 for the McCooey Scholarship Fund, an organization providing grants to deserving young men after they leave your care and keeping.

Lincoln Hall, named for our greatest president, was founded some 139 years ago and has quietly compiled a remarkable record. Except for a small group of family judges, youth counselors, social workers, and Catholic officials, no one really knew anything about Lincoln Hall until just a few years ago. Of course, the chairman of the board today is Edward Cardinal Egan, the archbishop of New York. Monsignor Kevin Sullivan, the head of Catholic Charities; Terence Cardinal Cooke and his protégé Monsignor Terry Attridge; and our beloved John Cardinal O'Connor have always known of Lincoln Hall and its wonderful work. Over time, however, Lincoln Hall has built a national reputation as a haven for the restoration and renewal of troubled young boys aged twelve to seventeen.

So the Abraham Lincoln Spirit Award commemorates our greatest president. In his first inaugural address, Mr. Lincoln called for "a new birth of freedom," precisely the meaning of Lincoln Hall for thousands of young people. Today, Lincoln Hall eschews the punitive measures currently so popular and focuses on rehabilitative strategies to achieve lasting change.

Most of Lincoln Hall's boys come from turbulent neighborhoods teeming with squalor, drugs, poverty, and illiteracy, and from streets filled with prostitution, degradation, and little hope. Most of them, as the great Mario Cuomo once so stunningly observed, "knew the sound of gunfire before they ever heard the sound of an orchestra."

Your presence here tonight and your generosity directly benefit the 232 boys who are now putting their lives together at Lincoln Hall's spectacular campus in Lincolndale. So on behalf of these young men, I thank you.

Allow me a moment to tell you about this year's honoree. He's an actor, a star of stage, screen, and television; he's a playwright; an author of children's books; a director; a churchgoer; a lecturer. He's best described as a citizen-activist, probably the greatest and most succinct appellation I can give him. Malcolm X sat in his living room and sought his counsel. Governors and presidents did the same.

He has been bestowed with many titles and roles in his long, illustrious life. A former New Rochelle police commissioner once labeled him a "subversive" during the sixties because he hung out with Pete Seeger. (*laughter*) And Paul Zuber. And I. Philip Sipser. And Paul O'Dwyer. In fact, the New Rochelle Police Department had a special file on him, and it omitted any mention of his priceless gifts to the theater or how he inspired the nation with his plays, writing, acting, directing, and books, in addition to his civic activism. He is, by all accounts, one of the most versatile and valuable citizens in our country.

I tell my grandchildren there are still some heroes around. And ladies and gentlemen, here is one of them, the recipient of your Abraham Lincoln Spirit Award, Mr. Ossie Davis. (*applause*)

OSSIE DAVIS: Ladies and gentlemen, friends, fellow citizens of the world, I'm thankful for this opportunity to meet with you once again because we bear a close kinship and serious responsibility. We are "citizens," a very serious category, and one of the most important aspirations in our beloved country.

My heart is light because I have the great pleasure of bringing with me tonight my partner, and the one who made it possible for me to attain the Abraham Lincoln Award. And she is Miss Ruby Dee. (*applause*)

The last year was tumultuous for us because my mother passed away in June. Mama was 105, but as I stood over her body giving her eulogy, it was not an easy thing. And it was a serious responsibility to assume. As is my message to you tonight.

Ladies and gentlemen, we, in our world, in our time, in our universe, are confronted by the face of horror, of death, of pain; by the blood of young folks and children. What is our response?

Certainly, one part is merely "good manners" and charity.

But just as certainly, you cannot respond to what's happening in the world today without considering the whole nature of existence and what our responsibility must be when faced with such overwhelming tragedies. I often don't know where to begin.

Of course, we understand the meaning of charity and the obligation of filling the helpless hand with whatever bread we can spare, of rushing in with all our resources to bind up wounds caused by natural disasters. I thank God for His mercy and for the reputation of this country over the years. And yet, we look; we pause; we wonder. And we ask ourselves the deepest questions of all.

What is this life? Where do brotherhood and sisterhood begin and end? "And by this, ye know that ye are My disciples." What is the true nature of love?

I'm honored you think of me as someone who's been responsive to the needs of ordinary citizens, problems solved by Lincoln Hall and other charitable, front-line institutions that understand the true meaning of America.

As I look beyond the horizon, I try to perceive what the future will hold. I say to myself, surely there must be much more we can offer as human beings during times of trouble, besides giving bread to beggars and soothing those who need comfort. Is there not something else in our ability? Is there not something else in our gifts? Is there not something else beyond the technical capacity to respond?

Who more than we are capable of feeding the hungry? Who more than we are capable of flying from one tragedy to another? Who more than America should the world look to in a crisis? And yet, is that our only assignment? Is it our responsibility to interrupt our joyous occasions only when tragedy calls? Is there any other way we can, as Americans, prepare ourselves?

We have not yet escaped our bondage to nature. Has America a special responsibility? Look you, America, and be prepared! Is it enough that we are able to send money, food, clothing, and shelter only after the disaster has struck? Can we not somehow detect when it is on the way toward us? Is there no way we can bring this wonderful gift we call America and say, "It is for this that God put you in this world"?

I don't know. I have no answers. I ask you because you are my friends. I ask you because you are my neighbors. I have lived for a long time here with my wife and my family and have been granted God's gift to end my citizenship on this prosperous ground.

I am pleased to accept this honor and further the mission of Lincoln Hall. I speak with particular gratitude because I know some of the young boys Lincoln Hall has helped. It's also my privilege, at least once a year, to visit the young prisoners at Sing Sing. So I know the feelings of young boys, young black boys in particular, for whom the world has no hope, no helping hand, no meaning to discern.

Sometimes, perhaps, they might perceive us as the last hope, the last chance. So I'm glad to support your generosity and your heart. And when I meet struggling young men in the future, I will tell them about you.

And they will respond; they care; they love you; they still want you to succeed. And you want all of this. For them.

I'm glad to participate in that opportunity. And I will continue to do so for as long as I am able. But it seems to me that the time has come to think wiser and deeper thoughts about all of this and about our world.

What should we do in the future, Oh Lord, to face the hammer nature can wield? How can we avoid, by our greed and selfishness, adding to her destruction?

We must look; we must think; we must relate to all that is human within us. Perhaps what we need now is a new definition of "human being."

Maybe we already are too small for the world we have created. Perhaps our own technology has reduced us to the verge of insignificance. Maybe we need a new vision, a new model, a new Lincoln, to remind us of our deeper obligations. If that is the case, then I would like, at the end of my days, to be among those who responded. (*applause*)

You honor me tonight; you honor yourselves. God bless you. God bless us all. And let us never forget our capabilities are greater than we imagine.

Sometimes, if we search again, the little gift we overlooked might be the very one that, if called upon, might help save humankind!

Thank you very much. (*applause*)

WILLIAM O'SHAUGHNESSY: Ladies and gentlemen, these microphones rarely convey a more meaningful talk than we've heard this winter night. I was looking over Mr. Davis's shoulder, and it was almost as if the roiling, swirling tide in the East River turned and started running upstream. We're very grateful to you, Ossie

Davis, our neighbor and friend, for your insights and graceful heart.

You've given us a special gift. With your life. With your example. With your wisdom. With your friendship. (*applause*)

BROADCASTERS FOUNDATION OF AMERICA REMARKS OF BARBARA TAYLOR BRADFORD, AMBASSADOR OGDEN ROGERS REID, AND CHAIRMAN PHIL LOMBARDO

We emceed the Broadcasters Foundation of America annual dinner at the American Yacht Club, Milton Point, Rye, New York, on September 20, 2005.

WILLIAM O'SHAUGHNESSY: Welcome to the American Yacht Club. Here, tonight, at the country's most hallowed and revered sailing venue, we honor the Broadcasters Foundation and those directors and benefactors who have done so much, in so many generous and tangible ways, for the Broadcasters Foundation of America.

First of all, be assured this is *not* a fundraiser but only a wonderful and becoming gesture by Nancy O'Shaughnessy, who, five years ago, put together some of our New York, Westchester, and Connecticut friends to spend a delightful evening here in the Golden Apple with some of America's leading broadcasters. We're grateful to Nancy for this evening of wonderful food, friendship, good conversation, and Joe Claffey with Michael Carney's wonderful society music!

And we're glad you could join us.

I'll introduce some of my colleagues and members of our board, and our chairman, Phil Lombardo, a little later. But first, permit me to welcome some of our other special guests, most of them known to you and yours:

The president and CEO of New York & Company, in charge of all tourism and visitors for the Big Apple: Cristyne Nicholas!

A director of the Gannett Company who co-chaired the recent CBS investigation, the former CEO of the Associated Press: Lou Boccardi and his wife, Joan.

Two great and generous philanthropists: Emily and Eugene Grant of the Grant Foundation!

The president of Sound Shore Medical Center and a director of Westchester Medical Center: John Spicer and his wife, Kathy.

The stylish proprietor of the famous Shun Lee and Shun Lee Palace in Manhattan: Mr. Michael Tong!

Author—actor—boxer—biker—and now radio star: Chuck Zito!

Last year we had Jonathan Bush and some of his "Yalie" classmates singing Whiffenpoof songs for us. And this year, we're honored to have a Yale Fellow who in *real* life is superintendent of the Royal Bahamas Police and an old friend of Nancy and Bill's: Superintendent Marvin Dames! And his wife, Stacey.

The author of *Ireland: The Novel* and *James Joyce's Odyssey* who wrote the screenplay for *Goodbye, Mr. Chips*. He also *logged* thirty-two years with the BBC: Frank Delaney!

And speaking of writers: the author of *My Life and Le Cirque: America's Greatest Restaurateur*, the ringmaster himself: Maestro Sirio Maccioni! And his wonderful Egidiana, herself the author of *The Maccioni Family Cookbook*.

Please welcome our colleagues from the public press:

Elsa Brenner of the *New York Times*!

Howard Sturman of Hometown Media!

The great editor and journalist Harry Jessell!

And *his* mentor and colleague of many years and our friend: Don West, the newly elected president of the Library of American Broadcasting at the University of Maryland!

Also the star feature columnist of Gannett: Phil Reisman!

The chairman of RNN: Dick French and his wife, Cristina!

The head of *Publishers Weekly* and a longtime friend and director of the Foundation: Bill McCorry!

The National Democratic Committeeman for New York (you read about him damn near every morning in Cindy Adams and Liz Smith): Bob Zimmerman!

And, just to make sure we've got all the bases covered, we're pleased to welcome the dynamic district attorney of Westchester, who, in case you haven't noticed, is running for the U.S. Senate against one Hillary Rodham Clinton! Judge Jeanine Pirro! And her husband, Al Pirro!

Just a few more:

An individual who absolutely *hates* it when we call him "the most powerful man in New York state": William Plunkett and his wife, Caryl! (Now *that's* powerful!)

And finally, if you ever get in a *jam*—a man who was recently featured in a twenty-four-page profile in *The New Yorker:* the famed criminal lawyer Murray Richman!

We've gone a *long way* from Jonathan Bush!

We're also honored, ladies and gentlemen, by the presence of the distinguished *president* of the Council of American Ambassadors, the former publisher of the *Herald Tribune,* ambassador to Israel, and a *great* champion of the First Amendment: Ambassador Ogden Rogers Reid, and Mrs. Reid! When Mr. Chairman Harley O. Staggers of Mineral County, West Virginia, was threatening to put Frank Stanton and Walter Cronkite behind bars, Ambassador Reid led a valiant fight against government censorship! Ambassador, would you honor us with a few words, sir?

ODGEN ROGERS REID: President Hastings, Nancy and Bill O'Shaughnessy, it's a treat to be with you and with the Broadcasters Foundation of America. Some time ago, a matter came up involving a very able columnist of the *Herald Tribune,* Marie Torre. She had written in her column that it was quite likely Judy Garland would not have her contract renewed because she had put on a little weight. Sid Luft took some exception to that, and we ended up in court on the grounds that we had to reveal the *source.* We declined that "privilege," and I visited Marie Torre in jail. She was valiant and stood her ground.

Fast forward a little: A question came up recently with regard to Mr. Justice Potter Stewart, who handled the case. Originally conservatively inclined, interestingly enough, when he got on the Supreme Court he became a strong and articulate defender of

First Amendment rights. Today a friend of mine—and I'm sure of many in this room—who is one of our ablest correspondents, Judy Miller, is in jail.

What most of you know, but I'm not sure the American public does completely, was that earlier there was an attempt by the federal government to subpoena *all*—not some, but *all*—of her telephone records. Of course, as you know, she was asked to reveal the *source*—not of something she wrote, because she didn't put pen to paper, but whom she had been *talking* with, and she declined the privilege.

She went to jail and was not even given a bed the first night. The point of all this is to say the First Amendment is something each generation, and the leadership that exists in this room, has always got to tackle.

I think there should be a "federal shield law." Most of you know—but I'm not sure all of us are doing enough—there are forty-nine states that protect the privilege of a reporter, similar to the privilege afforded a doctor or a lawyer. Not so the federal government. And I think it's vital if the press is to be able, regardless of politics, to report accurately and fully, with an appropriate sense of national security, what the facts are in any given case. And this Judy Miller case, of course, involved Ambassador Joseph Wilson and his wife, Valerie Plame.

There are at least *three* bills in Congress, one by [Senator] Dick Lugar [of Indiana], another by Hillary Clinton, as Bill mentioned with great affection earlier. What this would do is give reasonable protection—mindful of national security questions when it's clear and very much to the point—under federal law to reporters in fifty states. I think that today, one thing we must always do is protect the rights of the press.

I had something to do with a little matter that came up in the Congress—Frank Stanton—and Bill O'Shaughnessy was very interested and involved in that because they wanted to give him some grief with regard to certain outtakes. And I said even though radio was not invented at the time the First Amendment was written, it was just as important that radio, TV, *broadcast* media, as well as the press, have reasonable protection.

So I hope with the leadership here in this room that we can do a little bit more to get Congress to pass the legislation, which isn't exactly moving with lightning speed on this fundamental matter. Chris Dodd [of Connecticut] is another senator who has put in legislation. And I think it's quite carefully drawn, and I'm going to talk—as Bill has—with the great Floyd Abrams to make sure the language is appropriate and consistent. But I think what we're faced with is an attempt to make sure that *all* of you—and *all* the members of the press—can stand up fearlessly and report the truth. And I know you will stand up always for the precious First Amendment.

WILLIAM O'SHAUGHNESSY: Thank you, Ambassador Reid, president of the Council of American Ambassadors.

Do I need to say any more about Barbara Taylor Bradford? She is a remarkable and legendary woman of letters, the author of twenty memorable books, including the unforgettable *A Woman of Substance*! She has sold over 75 *million* copies, in over forty languages, in more than ninety countries! The only person that I know who has sold more books than that is Bill O'Shaughnessy! (*laughter*) She is here tonight with her *husband*, the distinguished movie and television producer, who made ten of Barbara's novels into miniseries for television: Robert Bradford! Barbara . . .

BARBARA TAYLOR BRADFORD: Good evening. I don't know about the other women here, but I've never been able to resist an Irishman. (*laughter*) Now you know as well as I do, they've all kissed the Blarney stone—and certainly, Bill O'Shaughnessy has. (*laughter*) I didn't know I was going to speak tonight until I was sitting down to dinner and Bill said, "You *will* say a few words, won't you?" And I said, "What about? I can't talk about one of my books; I'm not here to promote a book." So he explained about the Foundation, and told me more than I knew already. So here I am. And it will be only a few words.

You know, we live in a world today when we like thinking about the terms and longevity of "superstars," whether it's Christopher Plummer on Broadway or Nicole Kidman in a movie, David McCullough with a book about 1776, or John Grisham, or Dan Brown.

And then we have, of course, television and broadcasters. There's my great friend that I love and my husband loves: Chuck Scarborough, whom we watch every night on television. And there's the Tom Brokaws of this world and the late Peter Jennings and Dan Rather; and what about that wonderful gentleman we see around New York, Walter Cronkite?

So we hear about the "superstars" in every field, whether it's books or broadcasting or theater, music, the law. Think about it. There is a world out there where the *superstar* dominates. What about those people who have been "superstars" but have slipped? Maybe because of no other reason than tastes change and people want a different face or a different voice.

What about people who get sick or have unfortunate things happen in their lives and suddenly they're down on their luck and need help? Bill told me tonight this is what the Foundation is all about: giving back.

And so I wanted to thank you all for coming and giving back something to those people who are not as fortunate as we are today. All of us here today are very successful. And I forgot to mention my great friend Sirio Maccioni: *He* is a "superstar"—and how we miss Le Cirque! When are you coming back? (*applause*)

So, thank you for coming. I would like to tell you one thing, which I didn't know, and perhaps you don't. The Foundation will be helping 250 broadcasters who have lost everything and are down on their luck and have been wiped out, all because of the hurricane [Katrina]. Isn't it wonderful that you all are helping those people in Mississippi and Louisiana?

Thank you for your generosity. And thank you all for coming. And thank you for having me.

WILLIAM O'SHAUGHNESSY: Ladies and gentlemen, it is a pleasure to introduce with his wife, Kim, at his side, the dynamic and able Chairman of the Board of the Broadcasters Foundation, Phil Lombardo.

PHIL LOMBARDO: Trust me, after listening to O'Shaughnessy drone on forever, this will be brief. (*laughter*)

Number one: Barbara, you are *truly* "a woman of substance." I could not have said as well what you did tonight. (*applause*) You were able to crystallize the *reason* why we are here this evening, and I appreciate that greatly.

Gordon was kind enough to introduce the Board of Directors. That Board of Directors is what makes this Foundation as good as it is, and it gets better every year. And I appreciate all of them. They are of enormous support, and they are hardworking people. They believe in this mission, and they deserve *my* round of applause. (*applause*)

I thank you all for coming tonight. We appreciate your friendship; we appreciate your generosity; and we hope you will all keep us uppermost in your thoughts when you think of charity.

The Broadcasters Foundation really appreciates it.

JEANINE PIRRO AT THE DUTCH TREAT CLUB

Judge Jeanine Pirro was a vivid and colorful presence in Westchester before she became a television star. In the many different seasons of her life, the comely politician has never resembled a shrinking violet. She appeared before the Dutch Treat Club in Manhattan on January 20, 2004, to talk about her life and career. The well-founded members of the prestigious luncheon club were dazzled by Pirro's presentation.

WILLIAM O'SHAUGHNESSY: Ladies and gentlemen, I have to tread carefully here. Because I was asked to introduce the district attorney since our estimable Ralph Graves, the president of the Dutch Treat Club, is in Florida. So I initially agreed, but after hanging up, I thought, "Don't go there, O'Shaughnessy. You should call in sick that day."

Because, you see, I had previously introduced Gloria Steinem to a thousand broadcasters in Cooperstown, near the Baseball Hall of Fame. And I blithely said, "She is as beautiful and attractive as she is bright and able." And Ms. Steinem fixed me with a most malevolent stare. And all the upstate papers, including the AP, called it a "withering glance." (*laughter*)

So I don't call people beautiful or attractive any more. Only bright and able. (*laughter*) I'm not going to call you ugly, Jeanine, so you don't have to worry! (*laughter*) Our star feature columnist, Phil Reisman, calls her "comely" in his graceful Gannett columns. But I've learned my lesson.

In Westchester County, the Golden Apple—or the "Outback" as our late president Lowell Thomas called it—there is no presence more dazzling than Jeanine Pirro's. You see her on "Geraldo," and I saw her on "Larry King" last week. Incidentally, I don't want to stir up trouble with your husband, but from the way Larry King was looking at you, I think he was measuring you up for wife number eight! (*laughter*) She is a serious, purposeful woman who was one of the very best judges in Westchester. Even perpetrators think she's one tough, no-nonsense lady.

Cindy Adams and Liz Smith are crazy about the woman. And so is my Nancy. Some say I could be introducing the next attorney general of New York state. But for now, we like her right where she is, as the chief law enforcement officer of the Golden Apple: Judge Jeanine Pirro, Madame District Attorney. (*applause*)

JEANINE PIRRO: Thank you very much, Bill. I'm always grateful to receive one of your legendary introductions. And, by the way, I didn't realize how influential you are. Now you can even name attorneys general, O'Shaughnessy!

First of all, congratulations to Georgia Osborne. Your musical performance was just delightful. Everyone was thinking, "I wish I could get up there and belt one out like that." It really is a tribute to talent and hard work and discipline. And our hats go off to you.

And speaking of hats off—I walked up to Tim Sullivan and asked, "Might you be a country music singer?" He's literally from Oklahoma and did a one-man play called *The Diary of a Songwriter*. And he's someone I think we need to keep our eye on in the near future.

I am delighted to be here. And, by the way, Bill introduced Jim Generoso, the chief City Court clerk of New Rochelle; he introduced me as the DA; he introduced Marty Rochelle as the largest bail bondsman in the country. We could literally arraign someone today! Any suggestions, Bill? (*laughter*)

I'm here today to talk about my book, *To Punish and Protect*, and I'm going to start by discussing my passion for working in the criminal justice system.

A very good friend of mine repeatedly encouraged me to write about my experiences as a prosecutor and judge. And one day, I took her seriously and said, "You know, it really is time to step back and evaluate my life's work." After twenty-nine years, as a prosecutor, as a judge, as someone with strong feelings about justice in America, I decided to detach myself from my role and reexamine the system. And fortunately, my editor, who is with us today, Diane Reverand from St. Martin's Press, and a phenomenal writer, Catherine Whitney, helped put my thoughts on the page. But, in reflecting on the criminal justice system, I found serious flaws. We say we punish the criminal and protect the victim when it's just the opposite.

I started my career as a young prosecutor in the mid-seventies with one of the first domestic-violence units in the country. At that time, battered women were considered inconsequential. Domestic violence was treated as a social problem instead of a criminal justice problem. So I became an advocate and a fighter in a system that essentially condoned crime in the home. But after my election to the county court bench, I was expected to be dispassionate and detached about the cases in my courtroom. And I realized this wasn't my character. So I decided to leave the bench and run for DA.

Every day in criminal courts, judges suppress evidence. They suppress identification. They suppress statements of criminal defendants. They suppress photographs and lineups and prior criminal history. And so, when we believe our society seeks the truth in the courtroom, we are absolutely mistaken.

Criminal justice in our country has become an exercise in making the criminal look as good as possible. And so my book, *To Punish and Protect*, is really a tribute to forgotten victims, the unheard voices, the silent witnesses who surround us every day, the ones in memory, the victims I met who were ultimately killed by the people who said they would do so.

The book chronicles various stories throughout my career. And although we live in the greatest country in the world, with the most incredible Constitution to protect our individual rights, we also live in one of the most violent societies. We're the most technologically advanced, and yet we are the most violent in the Western world. Our murder rate is eleven times that of England. Our rape rate is twenty-three times that of Italy. Every five seconds, someone becomes a victim, someone like you or me, going about their lives, dealing with inconsequential, mundane matters.

And then, like a thunderbolt, their lives are forever changed. And they enter "the system." That's where I meet them. And my office is a battleground. Every day, we fight for good against evil. Every day, we fight for the victim, whose life becomes an open book, who is dissected and trashed by a society that sympathizes with the criminal.

Why do we glorify criminals? Why did *People* magazine include O. J. Simpson, Susan Smith, and the Unabomber among "the most intriguing people of 1994"? Why do we apologize for and excuse criminals? It's almost like a national therapy session. "Where did we go wrong?" "Did we lose them as children?" "Were they abused?" "What happened?" Well, I don't care if they were abused. I care about the person in my office who has been abused or, in a homicide, the members of the family who are suffering from the agony of their loss.

As a society, we've got to stop this retrospective and become prospective. Have you ever heard of a study tracking victims? Have you ever heard about the lost and forgotten who, through no fault of their own, became statistics?

During the twenty minutes I'll speak here today, 240 people will become victims of violent crimes. We don't hear about them. We don't heal them. We don't protect them.

In my office, we don't just pay lip service to victims. We track them to see if they're healed. Sometimes, the victim becomes a criminal. In 59 percent of juvenile cases, the defendants had been victimized as a child. They are the lost and the despairing, the suicidal. We lose them.

And then I see another route, where the victims heal themselves. And I ask myself why. What's the difference?

In New Rochelle, an eighty-year-old woman opened the door because there were workmen in her building, and someone asked for a glass of water. She was a trusting, caring individual who was raised to be polite. And she opened the door and gave him water. He was nineteen. And he raped her.

It took days for her to come forward, and then only when her daughter saw the bruises and convinced her to visit my office.

Understand that she was eighty. She wasn't used to describing sexual matters.

And if that wasn't bad enough, the defense attorney sent investigators to interrogate her neighbors about men leaving her apartment late at night. They inferred she was a promiscuous woman who maybe deserved what she got.

She was re-victimized by the investigation. And when she took the stand, she was re-victimized again. But ultimately, he was convicted and sent to prison. Whatever happened to her? I don't know.

I do know what happened to Judy and Jimmy. Judy was eight and Jimmy was seven when they were raped and sodomized by the babysitter and her boyfriend. The children testified and were courageous. And the defendants, Hickey and Moore, went to prison. I think the judge gave them seventy-five years when the maximum was twenty-five!

When I was a county judge ten years later, the hairs on the back of my neck stood up. I saw Judy's blue eyes and cherubic face. She had tried to commit suicide. Jimmy was a male prostitute. We lost them. Their lives were shattered forever by that one traumatic event. We shouldn't be surprised since we did nothing for them after the trial. You can rest assured the convicts got education, medication, therapy, treatment, and three square meals. But we just threw Jimmy and Judy away.

And finally, Michael. Michael was nine when his father shot his mother thirteen times and put her in an oven. Michael said he didn't see anything, but when we got to trial, he recounted the whole thing. Michael became the star witness, and we convicted his father. We said goodbye to Michael, and that was it.

But thirteen years later, when I was DA, Michael was the defendant in a shooting. He's now serving twenty-five years in prison.

As a society, when we make excuses for criminal behavior, we gloss over the victim's tragedy. Yes, defendants are presumed innocent. But that's not why prosecutors drag them into court. Grand juries indict when there's sufficient evidence to charge a person with a crime. And yet, it then becomes open season on the victims for everything they've ever done in their lives. Why is that? Perhaps, if we can blame the victim, we can insulate ourselves from the pain and believe it could never happen to us.

There are three ways to improve this situation. Number one: Use "preventative" bail. Preventative bail keeps a defendant in custody to stop another crime. Bail today is set to ensure the defendant will return to court. In the Michael Linton case, we arrested the father before he killed the mother. And he said to the police, "Is that bitch crazy? I'll be out of here in thirty minutes, and I'm going to kill her." She was dead about three weeks later! But the father's statement could not be used in determining bail. That's only allowed in the federal system and one state, Arizona, for sex offenders.

Let's talk about pedophiles. They are the largest recidivist population in the criminal justice system. You can rest assured pedophiles are not home praying for redemption when they're out on bail. They're enticing new victims. A classic example from my Internet pedophile sting operation. We picked up a guy soliciting sex with my undercover investigator, who he believed was a fourteen-year-old boy, the night before he was scheduled to be sentenced in Rockland County for sodomizing another fifteen-year-old boy!

Secondly, the insanity defense is insane! It has absolutely no place in the criminal justice system. (*applause*) How do you tell the victim's family, when their son or daughter was killed, they will be denied their day in court because the murderer is suffering from a mental disease. There's no blood test. There's no objective criteria. It is a subjective analysis by a psychiatrist based on what the defendant says about himself.

My office prosecuted Paul Harnish, a former assistant DA, who ran over a newlywed rollerblading with his wife. The family, as in every homicide case, came into that conference room numb with shock. And I had to tell them this former assistant district attorney, who handled insanity cases himself, told a psychiatrist he was hearing voices. And it was pulled out of the criminal justice system.

If our justice system is about fact and truth, we should be ashamed of ourselves. Because we're not trying to decide if someone did it or didn't do it. We're letting a psychiatrist explain why he did it. I'm not saying they shouldn't get treatment or therapy. But give the victims their day in court. (*applause*)

And the third thing is the statute of limitations. You become the victim of a robbery. The defendant videotapes it. Five years and one day later, he plays that videotape on cable access. I can't prosecute him because the law says, after a certain amount of time, for anything other than a homicide, they get away with it. Why? What's that about? Sometimes, if a defendant can abscond long enough, he can outrun the clock.

And what about the pedophile priests? My office did a grand jury report on that. They had the aura of God but were sexually molesting children. You think those kids are going to come forward? We should definitely eliminate the statute of limitations for child sexual abuse. If the passage of time hurts the case, trust the jury to render that verdict.

That's pretty much my life. I deal every day with people who never expect to see me and never expect to know me. But I want to live in a society where every criminal trial reinforces our core values. And unless we become vocal about the victims, like Jimmy and Judy and Michael, our cycle of violence will never end.

Let me end on a positive note. Danny was tied to a radiator when he was eight years old. The police broke into the apartment and found him emaciated and so small, everyone thought he was five. And even though he had a sister, no one in the apartment building even knew he lived there.

Danny and I had a good relationship, and we worked with Danny for years. When I asked Danny what should happen to his mother, he replied, "What she did to me was wrong. She should go to jail." The social thinking at the time encouraged keeping kids with their parents. Sometimes, they're better off without their parents. Danny stayed in touch with me over the years, but even more so with his social worker at Child Protective Services.

Danny became a social worker himself. His real father came back. He interacted with other people in the system. And Danny is out there now healing other kids.

My last story is about Connie. She was fourteen when her father dressed her up in her deceased stepmother's clothing and forced her to go out with him to clubs, and raped and sodomized her, and made her little sisters and brothers call her "Mommy."

Connie was impregnated by her father, but she endured. We went to trial, and I convicted Connie's father for the rape. But the cause of death for Connie's stepmother had been ruled "undetermined." That is, not a homicide, suicide, or an accident. I reviewed the autopsy. The report suggested depression and an overdose of cocaine. But the pictures showed otherwise. Her eyebrows were perfectly tweezed. Her nails were manicured. When they found her, she was wearing a blinking reindeer on her sweatshirt and wrapping presents for her kids. I took Connie's father to trial for the murder of her stepmother and convicted him.

Connie became an assistant DA. She worked for me. And she is one of those shining lights in the system for other victims to emulate.

Thank you, Bill, and thank you very much, ladies and gentlemen, for your invitation to this prestigious club.

MARIO CUOMO AT THE DUTCH TREAT CLUB, 100TH ANNIVERSARY

Mario Cuomo spoke at the one-hundredth-anniversary luncheon of the Dutch Treat Club, held at the National Arts Club, Gramercy Park, New York, on October 5, 2004.

WILLIAM O'SHAUGHNESSY: Our great E. Nobles Lowe, John Donnelly, and Ted Crane met at Sardi's last summer to find a worthy keynote speaker for this historic occasion. The governor was their first, second, and third choice. So they didn't leave us too much running room!

He is a unique public figure who wasn't enticed by the Supreme Court of the land or the presidency itself. But he is by our invitation. And we're so glad he's here.

The *Boston Globe* calls him "our foremost philosopher-statesman." A college president labeled him "the greatest thinker of the twentieth century." I can't beat that. Everyone knows he served for three terms with great distinction as the fifty-second governor of New York. And among this sophisticated gathering of journalists, academics, and artists, many can quote verbatim from his brilliant speeches at Notre Dame and at the Democratic Convention in San Francisco in 1984, when he electrified a nation.

He's written ten books, including his newest, on the *New York Times* "extended" bestseller list, *Why Lincoln Matters: Now More Than Ever*. It's not the first time he's written about President Lincoln. His *Lincoln on Democracy* was translated into many languages and read avidly around the world.

By day, he practices law at the uptown firm founded by Wendell Willkie. He hates it when I call it an "ivory tower/white shoe" law firm.

When I'm feeling brave, I introduce him as a "failed baseball player with too many vowels in his name"! And he actually did get a bigger signing bonus than Mickey Mantle, who later called that scout "the dumbest guy on the planet"!

But I think, at heart, he's a teacher with great and rare gifts.

Kenneth Woodward, in *Commonweal*, writes, "He never gave a speech that didn't glisten with the sweat of moral conviction."

This week, I received the best referral in a note from a Westchester neighbor: "We have admired and trusted him for many years."

Here to begin our one-hundredth year: Governor Mario Matthew Cuomo.

MARIO CUOMO: Thank you.

Happy birthday to the Dutch Treat Club! One hundred years is a long time for anything created by mere mortals to live. When it's art then the creation is usually deemed classical and becomes a treasure. You have become a treasure as well, a classical congregation of creative talents and lovers of creativity, who have gathered at regular intervals with a sense of conviviality to share your joy of living, continuously for a century.

The roster of members sparkles with illustrious names: James Montgomery Flagg, Lowell Thomas, William Morris, Walter Cronkite, Isaac Asimov, the great George Plimpton whom we lost last year, President Ford, and, of course, contemporary distinguished members Ralph Graves, Roy Rowan, and Nobles Lowe. I congratulate all of the members and wish you continuing success at least for a century more!

I thank you for the privilege of addressing you on this auspicious occasion despite the fact that I have no credential that would earn me the honor. I am a lawyer and—I admit—an unreformed politician, at a time in our history when it would be hard to boast that either of those professions is considered conspicuously creative. I'm not even sure we can say of ourselves that we have helped make the most of our extraordinary resources.

The United States is the virtually unrivaled global hegemon with the richest, most powerful economy and the most devastating array of military forces and weapons in history.

We have been the greatest engine of opportunity ever, giving ten generations of people from other lands a chance to succeed in life that they would not have had in their lands of origin.

But even with analysts saying that technical economic indicators are improving, most of America is struggling not to slide back down the mountain: and many Americans are already there.

Today, we have more billionaires, millionaires, and people earning over $200,000 a year than ever. That's an emphatic affirmation of the potential of American free enterprise. But only about 2 percent of all American taxpayers are doing that well in this increasingly fragmented society. We have about 160 million workers, of which only one in four or five is high-skilled, in a world that every day demands high skills more insistently. The rest, their personal productivity hobbled by a lack of adequate education and training, earn modest wages, and their living conditions are worsening. About 15 million American workers are out of work, working part-time when they need more work, or have given up looking for work. The average income of all American households is down more than $1,500, and it goes up about only 1 percent a year, unless someone finds extra work. But the costs of health care, education, gasoline, and housing are increasing much faster than that, and most workers are already up to their ears in credit card debt, with last year setting another record for personal bankruptcies. Forty-three million Americans don't qualify for Medicaid, are not old enough for Medicare, or not lucky enough to have a health insurance plan, with health care costs soaring out of reach. Nearly 35 million Americans live in poverty, 11 million of them children at risk of inadequate education, joblessness, and abuse of all kinds. Many of them grow up in neighborhoods surrounded by pimps, prostitutes, drugs, and violence. Some grow up familiar with the sound of gunfire before they've ever heard an orchestra play. Without better schools, housing, and more and better jobs, they will probably wind up tragic human failures, and their lack of productivity will continue to be a drag on the economy.

Government has made it more difficult to deal with these problems today by creating a huge and growing federal deficit and debt?the largest in our history?hanging like a great albatross around Uncle Sam's neck. Much of the deficit is attributable to the huge tax cuts.

The first tax cut was given in 2001 on the presidential assurance that "we don't need the money."

Notwithstanding that the Clinton administration had left us the largest budget surplus in history, the tax cut was criticized as fiscally and economically unwise by *The Economist*, the *Wall Street Journal*, and most experts who could count but weren't politicians. They were all apparently correct.

Then, on 9/11/2001, all these domestic concerns were temporarily eclipsed.

At first we were stunned, almost disbelieving. Then, as more and more of the grotesque details were revealed, the nation was wracked with anguish, rage, and fear caused by the frightening revelation that there are in this world people—perhaps many people—who hate or fear *us* so much that they would eagerly give up their lives to take ours. President Bush reacted by declaring the beginning of what he continues to call a war against terrorism. The whole nation joined in supporting our attacks in Afghanistan against the Taliban, Al Qaeda, and Osama bin Laden, who boasted of leading the terrorists' "victory" over the United States, which he called "The Great Satan."

Gradually, as the battle lagged in Afghanistan and bin Laden continued to elude our forces, uncertainty began to replace sureness in the minds of the nation's people. It grew into real doubt as the result of a series of decisions by our president.

Telling us he was sure it was necessary because Saddam Hussein was complicit with Al Qaeda, had weapons of mass destruction, and was threatening to use them against us, the president suddenly redirected our forces from the fight against the Al Qaeda terrorists in Afghanistan to Iraq, where there were no Al Qaeda terrorists. He said we would defeat Saddam and our troops would be hailed as conquering heroes.

From then on, when the president used the words "the war against terrorism," he equated it with the war in Iraq. It was a decision Tommy Franks, the general in charge, had earlier warned would be a mistake. Now more and more Americans and intelligence sources are inclined to agree.

We bombed Baghdad; killed perhaps 20,000 innocent Iraqis; lost hundreds of our troops; and captured Saddam Hussein. But we never found any weapons of mass destruction, evidence of complicity with bin Laden, or imminent threat.

Since then we have lost hundreds more of our men and women in Iraq and hundreds of others have come back without body parts. Thousands of innocent Iraqis have also been injured or killed.

We continue to be stuck in Iraq with more than 100,000 of our troops on constant guard against further guerrilla attacks, and more Americans and Iraqis die almost every day. New separate insurgencies by both the Shia and Sunni Muslims remind us that while many Iraqis may have loved us as liberators, many more hate us as occupiers. It is not clear when the occupation will end or if it is possible for the Iraqis to govern themselves with some form of democracy. John McCain says we will be there for ten years. Other analysts say a civil war—instead of stabilization—is increasingly likely.

What *is* clear is that we must do better than we are doing now—*at home and abroad*. What is not as clear is how. We appear not to have created for ourselves a comprehensive and comprehensible overarching vision and plan of exactly what we want to be as a nation and how we will get there.

Since before 9/11 we've been tempted to see ourselves as fifty separate states—or worse, 280 million disassociated individuals struggling for survival or dominance in a dog-eat-dog world—instead of members of a fully integrated society, here in the United States and in the world, interconnected, interdependent, growing stronger together by sharing benefits and burdens. That's what we have been in the past when we were at our very best.

In the Great Depression that nearly destroyed us, Franklin Delano Roosevelt helped save us by marshaling the strength that was left in America, lifting himself from his wheelchair to lift us from our knees, by bringing America together, not by replacing the market system, but by supplementing it. Not by "stealing from the hard working and successful Americans their honestly earned resources and wasting it on failed programs conceived by mushy headed do-gooders" but by using our wealth to create more wealth—by investing in people, helping them to help themselves, through the WPA, Unemployment Insurance, Workmen's Compensation, Home Relief, Social Security.

And public schools.

He provided those who were able with the chance to work and provide for themselves, and the disabled with the sustenance they could not provide for themselves. Then later, Democratic and Republican presidents put aside narrow partisanship to strengthen us further with the G.I. Bill, the Interstate Highway System, Medicare, Medicaid, civil rights, and the space program, with its avalanche of dividends in research and technology.

More recently, we demonstrated our ability to make progress through the sharing of our strengths, redistributing our wealth dramatically to pay penance for the sins of a market system that needed more discipline than it had received—when we created the Resolution Trust Corporation and bailed out the savings and loan depositors, as we had bailed out Chrysler.

These exercises in mutuality weren't conservative or liberal or even ideological—they were simply good and useful things to do—not just because they were compassionate, but because they were intelligently pragmatic.

Perhaps the clearest example of all was the Marshall Plan with which—despite the Holocaust and the murderous history of the Nazis and the Japanese warriors—we brought both their nations back to life with billions of our dollars.

There were many in my old neighborhood whose brothers, husbands, or fathers never came back from the Second World War—or came back invalids—who weren't terribly happy about what we were doing. But we did it because we needed Europe and Japan as trading partners and to avoid the chaos that their postwar desperation might have created. So too, today with Russia.

What did we learn from this history of succeeding by sharing?

After 9/11, the principal thing we did was to give up still another huge portion of what the president called our "newly liberated wealth"—making it approximately $2.5 trillion in tax cuts. The largest part—as much as a trillion dollars by some estimates—will go to the tiniest segment of our taxpayers and the least needy—the top 2 percent of them, some 2 million taxpayers—instead of directing that wealth to our many domestic needs.

Instead, we could have taken as our inspiration the lesson taught by our history—and by the stunning contrast that came out of the horror of 9/11: the ugly and frightening reality of people who hated us so much they were willing to give up their own lives to take ours; responded to by the magnificent valor of hundreds of first responders, firefighters, police emergency workers, and volunteers who loved humanity so much they were willing to charge into the smoke and flames unhesitatingly, in the hope that they might be able to save someone they did not even know. That was a dramatic and ineffably beautiful illustration of a simple idea—big enough and strong enough to serve as the foundation of all our policies of self-governance: the *willingness to share our strengths to deal with our weaknesses and overcome challenges.*

We've seen the good effects of acting on that idea over and over again for three-quarters of a century beginning in the Depression. We should have acted on it in 2001—and 2002—but failed to.

We mustn't fail again.

We should share our resources to strengthen our whole nation, not just the already strong, at the same time increasing our capacity to do more for the rest of the planet.

We should *educate more of our people* to the high skills needed in this increasingly competitive world economy. It's totally unacceptable that only one of four or five Americans is highly skilled. One hundred fifty years ago we decided all Americans should have at least a secondary education, so we made education to that level free in our great system of public schools. *Isn't it clear that the same logic today should guarantee a college education to as many as possible?*

And shouldn't everyone be able to afford *health care*?

We must beef up Homeland Security that is today more a political promise than a comforting reality. Our ports, and the cargoes they receive, need to be monitored. There must be more effective scrutiny of passengers and baggage on trains. We need to deal with the threat of shoulder-held missile launchers bringing down airliners, the way they brought down helicopters in Iraq; the lack of Arab-speaking intelligence agents; and a host of other obvious weaknesses, including the lack of adequate equipment, training, and compensation for our first responders.

There's no doubt we have the capacity to do it. Think of it: We are going to give perhaps a trillion dollars back to fewer than 2 million taxpayers, the richest in America who already have all that hundreds of millions of other Americans desperately need. We could use some of that money to help reduce the deficit, or to create another stimulus to the economy by giving more tax relief to the middle-class consumers who are most likely to spend it because they have to.

An intelligent, vigorous sense of community should also guide us in using our power as a global hegemon. We should stop pretending we can do what must be done without the help of much of the rest of the industrial world!

Most disconcerting is the admission by Secretary of Defense Donald Rumsfeld a few months ago that there appears to be no real strategy to fight terrorism. Think about it. What *is* our plan to fight terrorists? The president makes it sound as though the war in Iraq *is* the war against terrorism. If that is true, what happens once the war in Iraq ends? Have we then won the war against terrorism—or will it then move to Iran, or South Korea, or Syria, with more bombing, more death of innocents and Americans, more $200 billion in expenditures?

God forbid!

Of course, we should use all the force needed to get rid of Saddam Hussein, Osama bin Laden, Al Qaeda, and the other known groups of terrorists around the world because they are lethal tumors on the body of humankind and must be destroyed.

But this is not a war of our great army against their less formidable armies. We can't win this struggle against terrorism *with force alone*: Bullets and bombs alone will not cure the cancer of hatred that produces the terrorists. Indeed, as demonstrated in Israel, killing suicidal terrorists just produces more suicidal terrorists eager to give their lives to take ours. In order to cure the disease, we need to stop what causes it.

With the significant assistance of as many partners as we can recruit, we need to complete our missions in Afghanistan and, now that we are there, Iraq—helping those millions of people to build—if it is possible—their own free societies with strong economies providing them the kind of opportunity we take for granted in the United States.

Then we must get our American occupying troops out of Iraq as soon as the Iraqis are prepared to take over. Iraq has become a gathering and festering place for all sorts of belligerent haters of the United States and terrorists whose anger is fed by the struggle with us as occupiers. We must—if possible—share the task with the United Nations, NATO, and the Arab nations.

We must also discourage the Saudi Arabians and others from supporting *madrassas* teaching Muslim youths to hate and kill the Western "infidels."

And the United States needs to show the same kind of energy in promoting the two-states solution that it demonstrated in helping create Israel more than a half century ago because the continuance of hostilities there is one of the principal excuses used by terrorists.

We have made ourselves the greatest nation in world history by following, in our best moments, a vision that we need to bring back into focus.

We did it by being bold, courageous, open to innovation and by overcoming our worst impulses toward a crude and harsh elitism. *By understanding that our ability to increase our productivity and strength depends on how we will reconcile our profound instinct for individualism with the inescapable need for a sense of community.*

Most of all we must remember we became more together than any of us could have been alone, by recognizing that neither here, in our own beloved nation, nor in the wide world beyond, can we reach the levels of strength and civility we should, with only a small part of our people striding up the mountain with perfect confidence, and with most of our people laboring not to slide back down the mountain and the rest desperate in the ditches by the side of the trail.

We should continue to help the world to choose cooperation and integration, recognizing that our nation and the world are both growing up toward greater democracy and civility through integration and not fragmentation.

And one last thing: We should show a little creativity in selecting a president this year. Let's choose, not a Hawk or a Dove—but an Owl who is strong enough to fight but wise enough to know when it's necessary.

Thank you for listening.

MARIO CUOMO AT THE DUTCH TREAT CLUB, 104TH ANNIVERSARY

The governor spoke again to this prestigious group four years later, on October 7, 2008.

WILLIAM O'SHAUGHNESSY: Our altogether distinguished speaker is known and admired for many things. That the *Boston Globe* accused him of being "the great philosopher-statesman of the American nation" is known to everyone here assembled. I mean, you just *know* these things! (*laughter*) He is also, I should tell you, a famous *father* and an illustrious *husband*. He's the *father* of the star of ABC's "Good Morning, America," Chris Cuomo. He's the *father* of Maria Cuomo, the dazzling head of Housing Enterprise for the Less Privileged (H.E.L.P.), the largest provider of homeless housing in the world. He's the *husband* of the incomparable Matilda Cuomo, the founder of Mentoring, USA.

He has an adoring son-in-law, a rich designer and philanthropist named Kenneth Cole. *And* he has yet another son and heir, named Andrew, whom John McCain wants to use to straighten out Washington, even though he's a Democrat! Andrew is also quite gainfully employed at the people's business as the attorney general of New York in whom we are all so well pleased. (*applause*)

Along the way, our keynote speaker *has* done some things on his very own as well, and I have a list of *his* accomplishments. I have it right here . . . someplace. (*laughter*) Actually, he's had time to write nine beautifully graceful books which should commend him to the favorable judgment of all the authors and writers in the room like James Brady, Sidney Offit, and Ralph Graves. (*applause*) But I must tell you, this is the time—every four years—when I get good and mad at him for denying us the opportunity to put him in the damn White House or on the Supreme Court. (*applause*) For that you applaud? (*laughter*)

But he *was* governor of New York for twelve years, as you know. And every time he sits down to think or write, every time he speaks into a microphone and approaches a lectern, he elevates the public discourse.

Please, as we begin our 104th year, welcome quite a great man: Governor Mario M. Cuomo. Governor, with all that's going on, you've got a *lot* of explaining to do. . . . (*applause*)

GOVERNOR MARIO M. CUOMO: Thank you, Bill, for that "lovely" introduction. I think we're about to go from the rhapsodic and inspiring to the ruggedly real and disappointing facts about what is going on in America today.

As I said to you four years ago at your centennial celebration, I think of the Dutch Treat Club as a classical congregation of creative talents and lovers of creativity who share your joy of living—always with conviviality and serious intelligence.

Both those qualities, I believe, are especially needed today as we struggle to understand the condition of our great nation in this presidential election year.

All modern presidential elections have raised significant issues, but few have presented as many vital and difficult questions as the election to be held a month from now.

My suggestion was that I'd be free to answer any questions you have. Walking into the room, I met at least a dozen people, and they all had different things they wanted to hear about the campaign and the debate tonight: Can Obama lose? Can McCain come back at this point? A *lot* of people want to hear about the *economy*.

I'd prefer to deal with your questions because that way I'd be sure I'm answering with something you feel is relevant. If I have to go through all of this myself, I'll make all my own judgments about what's relevant.

I tried this on Bill, but he said, "No, you have to give a speech!" (*laughter*)

I'm going to try to compromise and rush through some remarks and then take your questions. So please, think up some good questions.

DEBATE THE ISSUES

I'm here with distinguished lecturer and professor Flos Frucher at my table. She and I and a man named Doug Muzzio are giving a course at Baruch College: fourteen Wednesday nights in which we talk all about the issues of the campaign. How did I get into a situation like that one? Early on in this campaign, it appeared to me there would be more important big issues in this presidential campaign than in any political campaign in modern history—and that's absolutely the case.

Just look at it. Start with the *domestic*. Start with the economy. Start with the health care problem. Start with all those things that affect us every day. And then get to foreign policy—my God, with Iran and North Korea, not to mention Israel and Iraq and the war in Afghanistan we're now getting into. My hope was we could have real debates and intelligent discussions. Newt Gingrich, on a television show, says I agree with you. But how are we going to get them to debate the issues? I said, let's put on a debate at Cooper Union that shows the way we would want the debates to occur.

Incidentally, I don't think debates are the best way to do it, frankly. I think the best way to do it is to put her or him up there in a chair and give them a "Tim Russert" workout for an hour and a half or so. Ask them every tough question you can. Give them all the time they need to answer. Don't give them the excuse to say they only had ninety seconds. Don't give them the excuse to say, "Well, the red light went on." Find out where they stand. Where *do* you stand on abortion? Where do you *stand* on stem cell research? Before you answer that question, answer the *ultimate* question: How do you define human life? And where is it said that human life begins here or there? Is that a scientific position? Or is that a religious position? Questions like that haven't been answered. Or asked.

And I'm disappointed to tell you that, having gone all these weeks and months in this campaign, I don't think any of the really big issues have been treated in depth. Now there are a lot of reasons for that. One is the mechanical, superficial one that we don't have the time, and another is that people aren't really interested. That's a lot of nonsense. People are desperate to know the truth. Those accidental arguments don't work. The real argument is that a lot of the candidates don't want to commit themselves on these issues because they are by definition contentious. It means there are people on both sides. And so if a candidate takes a clear position for the war in Iraq, he or she might lose a lot of people. So the heck with that. Let's try to win anyway by avoiding contention, and then we'll tackle the issues later on.

There are two things wrong with doing that. Number one, you're dishonest to me. I'm a voter. And if you have a position on abortion or Afghanistan, if you have it and are not revealing it, then you're lying to me. And number two, if you don't have it, then you shouldn't be running. So either you have a position or you don't. If you have it, you should tell me about it. And so we waited and got aggravated by the lack of response by the candidates.

In my college classes, we invited the students to debate. We're now into the seventh week, and we've taken one issue at a time. We have twenty-five really bright students at Baruch. The three of us—three professors—spend two-and-a-half hours with them every Wednesday night. It's wonderful. The bright minds of these young people—and not-so-young people in some cases—wonderful students. All with a point of view. All eager for this information. And then by the time we're finished, these students will all be better informed than all of their neighbors because we're reading the books. We're arguing about the issues. And we get very precise and specific about all this.

That's how I feel about the *issues*.

Now I'm going to disappoint myself by doing the same thing that the candidates are doing, which is shrinking to the point where you're not getting the full story. But because O'Shaughnessy wouldn't do it my way, I'm going to have to do it this imperfect way. (*laughter*)

So let's start with the *economy*. We're still the greatest country in the world—probably. We have been the greatest country in the world for a long time. Why? It's poetry? It's really *prose*. And that's another thing. I wrote a line in a speech at Yale in 1985 that became very real in the last campaign. You campaign in poetry. But you govern in prose. It's very easy in the campaigns to be "large": to be philosophical, to be general, to be a lot of things. But when you get to the governance, you have to be *precise*. You have to be specific and objective. You campaign in poetry. But you govern in prose.

MY PARENTS

We're the greatest nation in the world because we have the biggest economy. And because we have the strongest military forces. Because we have been the most generous nation in world history. We have taken eleven or twelve generations of immigrants from all over the world and allowed them to come here like my family from Salerno, Italy. Allowed them to come here uneducated, unrespected, unfairly treated. Allowed them to come here with a lack of skills, a lack of education. And an absolute commitment to working hard.

This country allowed [my parents] to come here and raise four children. And to go on to lead a fairly comfortable middle-class life. I remember being interviewed for the Statue of Liberty story, which was done by the very great person who does those documentaries, Ken Burns. He asked, What about your own family? What about your mother coming from Italy and your father before her? How do you feel about all of that, Governor?

I'm just imagining my mother coming to Ellis Island and being interviewed by somebody like Mike Wallace, and what that interview would be like if you could imagine it:

What is your name?

My name is Immaculata Cuomo.

That's a beautiful name. It's immaculate, beautiful. And who is that?

That's my son, Francesco.

And what are you doing here?

Well, my husband is here already. He's a ditch digger. He's a laborer. He can use a shovel, a wheelbarrow. He can't do bricks, but he's working on being a bricklayer.

And so where are you living?

Well, we're in trouble because they tell me we've got nothing after 1929. They don't have money. So he has no more work. But he says they have room for me in Jersey City, New Jersey, and for Frank.

My God, you have no money, no skills. Do you have people here?

No, no friends here because we had to lie to come. We had to lie to our parents because they came before us and failed. They

> were told the streets were paved with gold. And they discovered that streets weren't paved with gold. They weren't even paved! And you were expected to pave them. And they didn't give you any gold. So they went back. And made their children promise to never come here.

So my mother was one of them, with my father, both of them having lied. Both of them left without resources, without friends, without skills.

The interviewer asks, "What do you expect of this country, Immaculata Cuomo?" Well, she says not too much, just, some day, I would like one of my children to be governor of the state of New York! (*laughter*) (*applause*)

I can't get over that, O'Shaughnessy! I could have done things like that all night here. Do you know what I mean? (*applause*)

THE ECONOMY

So we were really a great nation. Go back eight years to 2000. Go back and think about what happened in the Clinton years. We had 22 million new jobs. You had a shrinking poor population. You had the four best market years in history. You had a balanced budget. And a projected surplus of $5.4 trillion. You had an ascending middle class—which is very good because most of America is middle class. One percent of the people make a million dollars. Thirty-six percent are poor. All the rest are middle class. You had all of that. *And* we were at peace. That's how great we are. That's how great we were. What the heck happened to us?

In the first days of the new millennium we were beset by two great calamities that a fragmented and ideologically driven political system has been unable to prevent or correct: *war* and a *seriously wounded economy*.

It was one of our nation's most regrettable and costly blunders. Nearly 5,000 of our men and women have been killed, 30,000 more have been seriously wounded, and some 300,000 innocent Iraqis and others have also been killed and many more wounded.

Since then, what's happened to us? All those 2000 numbers are *reversed*. Instead of a balanced budget, you have a $500 billion deficit. Instead of an ascending middle class, you have a stifled middle class holding on not to slip down to the despairing poor that don't even get mentioned in this campaign. Try to think of one person after John Edwards—Obama or McCain or any of them—who have said one word about 30 or 35 million poor people.

CHILDREN AT RISK

One time, would somebody in this campaign step up and say, in addition to all the foreclosures and problems, that we have 13 million children at risk? What are they at risk of? A child at risk is a child who usually doesn't have enough support behind him or her in the family to have a fair chance at reasonable development. That chance that this kid will get into a good school or get a good education is probably very thin.

And *that's* the person that needs help. And there *are* some people that are willing to help them. But there are 13 million of them. And some of them are the ones I've lived near in South Jamaica, Queens—very, very poor. Not too far from here, it's a miserably poor neighborhood. I went back after years and years; I brought some of my own kids there so they could see where we came from.

You could see children in the streets in the summertime, some two-and three-year-olds. Some of them alone! In the *streets*, believe it or not. And some of them would grow up confident that they understood the sound of gunfire and could describe it before ever having heard an orchestra play.

Before they are introduced to music, good music, they are introduced to horrors. That's South Jamaica, Queens. That still happens in ghettos all over the United States. But rule it out. Why? Because we have *other* problems. We have *bigger* problems than that. We have the problems of the "street." We have the problems of Wall Street. We have the problems of the millionaires, the billionaires, and all of their problems. And what are those problems? This one is even harder to explain.

TRICKLE DOWN

Ronald Reagan was a wonderful human being—I loved him, even though I disagreed with him on almost everything, most certainly his big ideas. And his big idea was basically an old conservative idea called "trickle-down," now called "supply-side." The "invisible hand"—theoretically, the hand of Adam Smith—just let them do their thing in the market and everything would be fine. That's what Reagan believed. He was against regulation of all kind by government. That caught on as an attitude. And to be candid with you, a lot of Democrats participated. I won't name them because I'm a Democrat. (*laughter*)

So there was this period of deregulation. Let them do what they wanted to do; and what did they do? They put their wonderful, bright minds to work at creating *new* kinds of securities. What's a security? A piece of *paper* that's supposed to be worth a lot of money? And they created new kinds that were so complicated. A "credit swap"—what is that? I never heard of that before! It's a *derivative*. What's a derivative?

Have some fun when you get home; go to your computer and look up "derivative." But if you find a real definition, it will give you a headache. You can't understand it. Warren Buffett said, "*Nobody* understands what these things are."

Sub-prime mortgages! Look up "sub-prime mortgage." Do you know what a sub-prime mortgage is? Do you know what "sub-prime" means? Are you sure? With all that's happened, shouldn't we all know? Shouldn't it have been debated with us by Obama and McCain? Shouldn't they have said, "This is what a sub-prime mortgage is"? "This is *what* is happening there. This is *why* it's happening." "Sub-prime" means less than good. It means it's such a lousy deal that they now call it "junk"! The people who dealt with it, they made it a derivative. What type of derivative? A municipal bond.

MUNICIPAL BONDS

A municipal bond is a very simple thing. The state of New York needs money to build roads, so it promises you it will pay "x" dollars with this interest rate and will pay you back in a number of years. These municipal bonds are gold. Why? Because New York has never, never walked away from its obligations. A municipal bond is like a beautiful country girl. Really, this isn't sexist. This is what it was: beautiful teeth, wonderful face, nice bosom, sweet dress on, beneath the knee (*laughter*), with the blond hair and the perfect skin. That was the municipal bond.

Next to federal paper it was the best investment you could make. But then they made it a *derivative*! What's a derivative? They spritzed it with some perfume, they frizzed up all the hair, they gave it some very wild lipstick, they pulled the blouse down (*laughter*) and pulled [the dress] up, and they had a derivative. And that's what the derivatives are. (*applause*)

THE MORTGAGE MESS

They did this over and over. And then what happened with the derivatives? Here's what happened. Somebody said we give mortgages all the time. What's a mortgage? A mortgage is what in the old days I tried to get my father to take, and he wouldn't because he would only buy things with cash.

I said, "Pop, instead of living behind the store or on top of the store, I can go to Jamaica Savings Bank, buy a house for $15,000."

"Really?" he said. "How?"

I said, "Pop, they will give you $15,000, maybe even $16,000 or $17,000! And you have to promise to pay them back over twenty-five years at a certain rate."

He said, "Nope! Nope! It's not *mine,* and then I have to wait twenty-five years before it's mine! No!"

And so we didn't have a house for twenty-five years because it took him that long to make the money. But that's what a mortgage was.

But here's what they did to the mortgage in recent years. They put it together with all the other mortgages and made them a big bundle and securitized them. And then we had all these big bundles of mortgages, and nobody really knows what the bundle is worth because you are no longer relating to an individual house. It's a whole lot of houses that we invested in.

And they did that over and over. Except if they had picked all good houses, and all honest brokers were making the judgments and honest appraisers were making the appraisals, it wouldn't be so bad. Everything would have worked out fairly well. But what they did was sub-prime—less than quality. This guy has no income. This guy has no track record. He has no real credit. We want to make the deal. Why do we want to make the deal? Because if we make the deal, we could put this into a *bundle*, and it gets lost in the bundle. And we all make money. We do this with a lot of people. So we don't care so much about the true value. But don't you care about this guy's ability to pay it off? No, we won't worry about it. We'll just make our money first.

So they sold junk. And they lied about it. The broker lied about it. The appraiser lied about it. The investor lied about it. Everyone lied down the line. They lied about it by letting it happen. They encouraged it. They openly dealt with what they call "liars' mortgages"! Do you think I'm kidding? Look it up! It's not like the Jamaica Savings Bank where you have the same relationship with the same person for twenty-five years. It's going to disappear into the matrix, into the ether, into the mix, into the confusion! And we're all going to make a lot of money. But if anyone had taken a close look at it, they would have known it was a phony!

THE $700 BILLION BAILOUT

The worst thing of all! Look at the *New York Times* last weekend. Christopher Cox is [chairman of the] SEC [Securities and Exchange Commission]. Cox is very important. He meets with Henry Paulson, Secretary of the Treasury, and also four other investment bankers. They say to Cox: Right now you're insisting we keep a certain margin of money, or capital, behind our thing because we're leveraging. Leveraging means that you have $1 behind you but you use it as though it's $50 or $30. It's magic! So if you can reduce the amount of capital we have to keep in our bank as security, then we should be able to pay our bills.

We want to buy *more* of those sub-prime mortgages because everyone is making money on them. What happened? Paulson gave them permission. He just made the new plan. He set up a watch guard, an office, because he said this was dangerous stuff. But it was never implemented! That was 2004. This is 2008. And now Paulson has given us a plan for $700 billion! Let me say this about the plan. Nobody in this room can describe it to me, and I can't describe it to you because it's not done yet. And I don't think it will ever be done.

You can write this down. I'm so sure of this, I'm thinking of making it a security. Not really! I don't think we'll ever have to spend the $700 billion because the theory of it is as follows, if I can understand it and communicate it properly: The government wants $700 billion to go to the banks that are *holding* the junk, that *bought* the junk. Not because somebody came in with a gun and said, "Here, take this junk and sit there with it"! They made mistakes.

So they have a lapful of junk and they are going to take *our* money—the taxpayers' money—to stay in business and give credit to other people. For what? To give them junk? No. The theory is that if we can scrub the balance sheet clean now of all the junk, the banks will be free to go back to business. But when they go back to business: no derivatives, absolute prudence, absolute integrity, absolute honesty. They're going to have to promise that, because last time we did this, look what happened!

Who in this room would bet that they would suddenly be transformed into little altar boys and little altar girls? (*laughter*) How is it going to work? Here's how: You're going to have this army of people out there who are going to have to go to the banks and say, "We are going to buy this from you, the junk, on behalf of the government."

How do we value it? What do you think it's worth? It's junk! Nada! Nothing! *That's* what it's worth. That's why we're here. It doesn't have any value. We have to give it a *value*. Why? Because we're going to give you taxpayers' money for it. So let's argue: $12? $15? Let's get an arbitrary number and buy all these things. You sit there and wait for the value to come back because there is a house out there somewhere that has some kind of value. And somehow, by magic, the value is going to come back.

Was this ever done before? No! Is there any reason to believe this will work? No! Is there any *guarantee*? Of course not. And incidentally, who is going to be doing the business again? Well, the people we're going to hire and give a lot of money to represent us as the taxpayer are all from *Wall Street*. You're kidding! Yeah. Some of them from companies that have just been killed. Or died from ignorance. So they're going to be representing us? Yes! With whom are they dealing? Their buddies on Wall Street! Oh! In my neighborhood we wouldn't allow something like that. We would say that's what we call incestuous, and everyone would understand that.

You don't do business that way! So I don't think it is ever going to work. The theory of it is, if it works at least we'll have *credit*. And we need credit. And you can buy a car. You can't go to school without it. You can't buy a house without it. You can't pay your bills in some cases without it. You need the credit back. You must have the credit. The theory is, when we get it back they won't do it again, and second, that's the beginning of the good economy.

You're right to say that *availability* of *credit* is an essential for a good economy. You're wrong to imply that it is sufficient to create a good *economy*. So what do you have to do to create a good economy? Now I'm being very simplistic. I know and I apologize. And it's all O'Shaughnessy's fault (*laughter*), and I get more and more angry at him as I go along.

A LITTLE HISTORY

Here's what you need. You can study all the books; the professor and I have read all about it, and Kevin Phillips and all the bright people will all say the same thing about an economy. Right now 20 percent of our economy is *finances*. "Finances" is what? People *making* loans on Wall Street. We make a lot of money from it: 20 percent of our economy.

Thirteen percent is *making* things that we can sell for money: manufacturing. All the books will tell you that no nation survives with that little. Certainly no great nation. In order to survive you must be able to make a *profit*. That's what does it. Look at Switzerland, China, Germany: They *make* things and *sell* them.

Look at us. What made us great after the Second World War? In 1945 we were making everything; we were making the cars, we were making the refrigerators, we were making all the things that really mattered. We were *The* Maker. The *Manufacturer* in the world—because nothing was left in Europe. Japan was coming

Above: The author signs one of his previous books for Federal Judge Charles Brieant. His Honor was an enlightened jurist and champion of the First Amendment and freedom of speech.

Left: “A Colonel of Truth”! Runyonesque Yonkers power-broker “Col.” Marty Rochelle is the largest bail-bondsman in the northeast. He also presides over his own radio program on WVOX.

Below: An Extraordinary Woman: the author and Governor Mario M. Cuomo hold Cindy Hall Gallagher in high regard. She is a senior executive at Whitney Media and the author’s oldest confidante and advisor.

Above: Mr. Mayor: The author interviews Ernie Davis, popular mayor of Mount Vernon, New York. The soft-spoken and courtly Davis has his own weekly radio program on WVOX.

Below: Former HUD Secretary (now New York Attorney General) Andrew Cuomo (left) and former Congressman Rick Lazio (right), now rival contenders for the governorship, teamed up between public-service gigs for a trial-run radio program produced at our studios by Ian Rae, the former head of Fox News.

Above, left: "Mr. Bruce." Bruce Snyder, seen here with his wife, Marcia, was the classy dining room manager for many years at the "21" Club in Manhattan. The author spoke at his going-away party.

Right: the great Metropolitan Opera baritone Robert Merrill was a New Rochelle neighbor. The author was instrumental in persuading the U.S. Postal Service to name the local post office in his honor. To this day, WVOX signs on every morning with his rendition of "The Star Spangled Banner."

Below: "Good Hair Daze": the author with cable TV contributor Robert Zimmerman, who heads one of New York's premier PR agencies.

"Seeing Redd": the late M. Paul Redd, publisher of Westchester's only black-owned newspaper, *The Westchester County Press,* and a frequent guest on WVOX's community programs.

William Kirby Scollon was a "townie" writer and broadcaster who used to pal with President Kennedy on his visits to New York. Scollon was also a gray eminence of the Democratic Party. In his spare time he designed crossword puzzles for the *New York Times.*

Legal Eagles: from left: Donna Slotnick; the author; Caryl Plunkett; William Plunkett, Jr., New York power broker and advisor to the Archdiocese of New York; and famed defense attorney Barry Slotnick.

Above: "World Champion"! The author is a great Yankees fan and often sports this World Series ring. Left: one of the author's previous books had the whole front window at the Barnes & Noble flagship store on Fifth Avenue.

Captain Rob Taishoff, USN, seen here with his wife, Laurie, is chairman of the Taishoff Family Foundation, which supports a number of good causes, including the Broadcasters Foundation of America and the National Down Syndrome Foundation. Rob's father, Larry, and his grandfather Sol were Washington-based publishers of *Broadcasting* magazine, which, for many years, served as our sentinel on the Potomac protecting broadcasters' First Amendment rights.

1 W 81
NYC 10024
23 Aug 98

724-2432

Dear Bill,

I was too stimulated to go right to sleep last night so I looked back over an irrgular journal I keep—occasional thoughts and came across some eschatalogical musings on acting that I'm prsuptuous enough to suppose you might find interesting.

The best acting I'vw ever seen: Ralph Richardson as Mercutiom with Miss Cornell in Tulsa in 1935, Maurice Evans as Richard II and Falstaff in Chicago in 1937, Pa ul Lukas as Dr. Rank in A Doll's House, also Chicagon 1937, Morris Carnovsky and Luther Adler in Awake and Sing, about 1938, Laurettle Taylor in Outward Bound -I saw it twice--and TheGlass Menagerie. Ethel Waters in Mamba's Daughters, Paul Lukas in Watch on the Rhine, Lee Cobb in Clash by Night (his best)--also in The Gentle People (one of the funniest perfonrmances of a lifetime, Like Alastair Sim in The Magistrate), Ethel Waters in Cabin in the Sky and Memmberf the Wedding,Paul Lukas in Flight out of Egypt, Olivier in Oedipus, Olivier as Othello(the greatestascting I have seen), also in Dance of Death and Long Day's Journey, Gribov of the Moscow Art Theatre in 3 Sisters, Cherry Orchard and Dead Souls, Aaron Meskin of the Habima in The Dybuk, David's Crown and The Golem, John Neville as Aguecheek, Brando in Streetcar.

Some who have come close are Karl Malden in All My Sons and Streetcar and Desire Under the Elms, Lee Cobb in Salesman, Colin Blakely in The Crucible—also Joyce Redmond, Maggie Smith in Hay Fever, Vanessa Redgrave in The Prime of Miss Jean Brodie, Edw. Petherbridge as Don Armado, Monty Clift in Our Town, Michael Redgrave as Vanya.

That's it for a liftetime.

In the best acting there is no acting, no performing—just being and behaving. We all believe in it but you seldom s ee it. Many are brilliant performers, even super-brilliant. But this is not acting. No one ever was more brilliant than Olivier. He was magnetic on stage and could get away with anything. But really, it's only showing off. At the same time he was deep and true. It seems the contradiction would fatally dilute the good work and it did but in Othello it was as if all his life he had only been rehearsing, waiting for this role.

The only one I've seen do it with perfect purity was Laurette Taylor. She gave no performance--she didn't know an audienace was there. She didn't project (The ruination of most acting). The audience came to her. They sat forward, mesmerized--as she was--hanging on every word. She could imagine a new human being and simply become that person and for two hours live a different life. In Outward Bound she was a bent little Cockney charwoman, inThe Glass Menagerie a faded Southern Belle, two more dissimilar people couldn't be, each with a strange accent, not at zall authentic, just the way She heard the person. I suppose it's all in the imagination--and having the courage to obey it and nothing else. I don't know. It's always been beyond my grasp.

Why do I go on like this--I can't even type.

Great meeting you lst night. When I got home I called Heatther in NC and she remembered you from Le Cirque. Hope to see you soon again.

Best,

Tony Randall

Midnight Missive: Tony Randall was a great man of the theater. The Broadway and movie legend sent this letter to the author one night after dinner. His comments about the legends of the theater are priceless.

The Fred Astaire of Madison Avenue. The author and Edward Noonan Ney, chairman emeritus of Young & Rubicam, who also served as U.S. ambassador to Canada. Ed Ney is one classy guy.

Jonathan Bush, the Connecticut investor, is a brother of President George H.W. Bush, uncle of President George W. Bush, and father of William "Billy" Bush, star of "Access Hollywood," who began his career at WVOX. He and his talented son and heir never let us forget it.

back. We were the sellers. We were the lenders. People came to us to borrow money.

And what's happened? We don't *make* anything anymore. We're the buyers. Not the sellers. Not the makers. China is the principal maker, and now we have to buy from China and give them what? Our money. Terrific! And then what? We have to borrow it back. Why? Because we have deficits.

Mario, let's slow down here; I'm getting a headache. (*laughter*)

We used to be the manufacturer who made the things; they gave us money; then they borrowed from us. And now we buy everything and they have our money. We're overspending, and we have a $500 billion deficit and don't know how to govern, and because of those reasons we have to borrow the money. Well, our principal export is *debt*. It is not cars, it is *debt*. How long can we go this way? Not forever.

AN INFRASTRUCTURE BANK

We have to get back to making things. How do you do that, Mario? One good idea: *infrastructure*. Roads, bridges. We want $80 billion for an Infrastructure Bank. What would you do with an infrastructure bank? The government would take $80 billion, and state governments would be able to use that money to build roads, bridges, etc. Private people who wanted to do the building would make deals.

Part of it also is to build high-tech machinery that relates to energy alternatives. Take wind. For wind you need those things with the big propellers on them; $60,000 apiece for those things. But you could make them in various ways. This would advance our high-tech, which is really the only way we're ever really going to sell things to the rest of the world because anything that depends on cheap labor they are going to beat us with, because everyone has cheaper labor than we do. And our high technology has to be better than their high technology. The infrastructure bank will help us do that. That's a great idea.

But what's happening? It's on Obama's list, and he will start pushing this. It's a good idea, and it's a start. It will give us jobs here. You need jobs that pay well. *Infrastructure* creates jobs. The designer, the manager, the guy who digs, the guy who pushes the wheelbarrow. All of these people will be working. But then they'll say, "Where are you going to get the $80 billion?" Now this is my favorite line. *Here's* where you *get* the $80 billion. First of all, there's a lot of money you can get right away. In 1998 we had a balanced budget. *Balancing the budget is a good way to make money. Because if your economy is working, money is coming into the Treasury.*

TAXES

But now you're putting the cart before the horse. We're starting now to build a good economy. But here's one place to "make" money: waste. There's a lot of waste. Get the money from the earmarks legislators love to argue about. And get the money from the billionaires: Bill Gates and Warren Buffett and all the really big guys say, "It's ridiculous not to tax us, it's ridiculous to give us Social Security. Yes, we're entitled to it. Yes we paid the bill. But what the hell are you giving us Social Security for? We're billionaires! You're broke. You need an economy. You need to go to work. We'd rather invest it, because if you build an economy, we're the ones who are going to make the most in a good economy." Who makes the most when you have a roaring economy? The people at the top, the big investors, the banks. That's the irony of it.

And here's another thing: Raise taxes on the rich people. Now listen to this one, and I'm going to say it fast. It's the God's honest truth! Reagan gave you the biggest tax cut in history. But it was too good. And he was told it was too good. He said, "No, it's the magic of supply-side. When you give these tax cuts to the people who are the investors and the people who have the most money and the most experience, the business people, they invest it right away. And if you give them a tax cut that is really rich they say, 'Oh boy! This is terrific!' And they invest more and more and the wheels of the economy are spinning, and before you know it you get all the money back that you lost by cutting their taxes. You get it all back." Well, Mr. President, why don't we do *this?* Cut all the taxes to zero, then we'll be the richest people in the world. What you're telling me is that if you cut the taxes, this makes you wealthy? Cut them to zero? You can't do that. You have to be reasonable. What happened?

Reagan had a deficit and debt so big he had to raise taxes at the end of his term. He raised taxes $100 billion, and the person after him who was his vice president and became president came in and said, "Read my lips: no new taxes." But because the deficit was so big, he *had* to raise taxes $99 billion. And then Bill Clinton followed them, and instead of doing the infrastructure program, he followed the advice of Bob Rubin, who told him, "One more tax increase at the top the way Reagan and Bush did it, and we'll nail this deficit. We'll have a balanced budget." And he raised taxes by $100 billion. Now that's three big tax increases on the people at the top, the richest people.

Now, what do some elements of our society say? "Oh, you can't raise the taxes, that will kill the economy." This *made* the economy. I started by telling you how good those eight years were. We had the best economic eight years. We had eight years of growth. Four years of terrific markets. Balanced budgets. $5.4 trillion surplus.

A PLAN

So *raise* taxes on the richest people. Build the infrastructure. Put people to work. That is the only salvation to our economy. I give it to you in shorthand.

Mario, we understand all of that; you went very fast, but we can understand it more or less. But we're still not clear. You're asking me where we're going to get $80 billion. You just gave $700 billion! Now let me ask you a question. Where are we going to get the $700 billion? And let me ask you another question: In the Second World War, which we won, we spent $3 trillion! And that was right in the middle of the remains of the Great Depression! Where did you get $3 trillion? And with deficits in your budget, you just spent nearly a trillion in Iraq.

Everyone is talking about taking the troops out of Iraq. McCain agrees, but they're arguing about how fast. So they should come home, right? No, they are going to Afghanistan. Why? Because the war is now in Afghanistan, and that's the "good" war that we started right after 9/11 because Osama bin Laden was there. And the Taliban was there, and Al Qaeda was there! And they were the ones who attacked on 9/11! Are they still there? And will they stay there if you send in 20,000 troops? Well, we didn't get to that yet. And how much is it going to cost us?

Where are you going to get $80 billion? From the same place you got all that other money: They make dollar bills. (*laughter*) Don't laugh! That is the process. The state can't do it. The city can't do it. You can do it, but you would go to jail. (*laughter*) The federal government can do it! There is no need for a balanced budget. So what does it come down to? You know what it comes down to? In the old neighborhood, in South Jamaica, we did horses. In Harlem, you did numbers, it was part of the culture; you sold numbers and people bought numbers all the time. Everyone was poor and needy, so they would bet and pray for a winner.

COMMON SENSE

In South Jamaica, there was a bookmaker right in the back yard behind the store. Tony Buffalo. I never asked why his name was Tony Buffalo, because his nickname was not Buffalo! You could go to Tony Buffalo if you were a guy who was out of work, if you were a laborer and they were going to kick you out of the apartment above the store on Rockaway Road. You could go to him and say, "Tony, I've got to have $50. I've got to pay the rent." He would give you five for six! You've heard that expression. He'll give you $5 and you give him back $6 on this date. And this is how they did business. And they continued to do business this way as long as Tony Buffalo felt you were good for it. And we will be able to make dollar bills as long as the world thinks we're good for it.

And only two Sundays ago, Wen Jiabao, who is the premier of China, met with Fareed Zakaria, who is this brilliant guy on foreign policy, and said to him, "Look, they're going crazy in the United States of America. Look at what's happened to our economy here. Look at all the bankruptcies here. All the foreclosures, etc. And you are our biggest lender!" Yes we are.

Zakaria said, "Aren't you concerned about it?"

"No, I'm not."

"Why?"

"You're still the biggest economy in the world. You still have the biggest armed forces. You still have a legacy of being generous to ages of immigrants. You're still a great, great country. Not only that, you're our best customer. And the way you saved Europe after the Second World War with the Marshall Plan, the way you brought back Japan, the way you brought back Germany, the way you brought back Italy."

It wasn't that you had told the people in my neighborhood in South Jamaica what you were doing with our money—bringing those countries back—they would have screamed at you! Because they weren't educated enough to know why Truman and you were doing it. Number one, to avoid all sorts of catastrophe and all sorts of unsettlement in that part of the world. But also to create *customers* for our trading. You have to have somebody to deal with. And, incidentally, we did create new customers, and they did so well with our assistance that after a while they started making things better than we did because we sat down on the job—but that's another story.

JOBS

So we are still trusted. There is no good argument against using the $80 billion! *If you want a real economy, you have to make things.*

Another thing, you have to have workers with high skills. Only one of four workers in this country has high skills. One out of four. Only 75 percent of our children are graduating from high school. To have high skills, you have to have four years after high school. That costs money. Kids can't get into college. They do not have money. We need money for that. We need skilled workers. We need infrastructure. We need jobs. And also we need health care and a lot of other things. And the money is there. Once you are operating with a real economy and learn how not to overspend as a people—that's a whole other thing too—then we'll be on our way back.

Do you really believe everything I've said to you? Obviously I believe this profoundly, and we've thought about it, and we've studied it, and we teach it. I also believe it will be a sin for us to be so frightened we'd lose strength and we'd lose focus.

WHERE WE CAME FROM

Just remember where we came from. We had to beat an empire even to have a chance for freedom and liberty and a democracy. The

British Empire couldn't defeat us. And after we won, we put together these thirteen states, trying to organize with the Articles of Confederation. But that was a very important lesson because it didn't work. Why? Because they weren't close enough. They weren't interrelated enough! We have to stay interrelated. We have to work like a family at all times. And we did that with the Constitution. We tied ourselves all together and were a little stronger.

But then we had the Civil War and lost 650,000 people and almost lost our nation. But we kept at it and won!

And then we went on to win two world wars. And to deal with recessions and the Great Depression. And we succeeded.

There is no reason now to feel that we're any less able to deal with these problems. These are big problems. *Very* big problems. These are problems that shouldn't have occurred.

This is not a God-sent catastrophe. This is not a natural disaster. This is from our foolishness. This is our greed. Our inadvertence allowed this to happen.

THE FUTURE

There is no question in the world that we can be as strong as we were and go back to the way we were, and be much, much stronger with the lessons we've learned here.

And nobody should know that better than the Dutch Treat Club because you've been around for 104 years!

THOUGHTS IN THE SUMMER OF 2006, BY MARIO M. CUOMO

His admirers, and I am certainly among them, persuaded Mario Cuomo to reflect on all the great, pressing issues in the summer of 2006. This amazing man produced this wide-ranging essay. Many of the issues he addressed linger to this day.

INTRODUCTION

For the last six years, and for most of the last quarter of a century, a Republican president and conservative politics have dominated the nation's government.

They have created a bonanza for the top 1 percent of our taxpayers while the overwhelming majority of our workers struggle to avoid sliding backward. The number of poor Americans has grown to 37 million, more than one out of ten, and 13 million of them are children. That's four times the number of all the children in Illinois.

They have squandered the nation's wealth, burdening us with the highest debt and trade deficits in our history.

They have demonstrated an appalling incompetence in handling the machinery of government, a callousness toward people in need, and a shocking disrespect for the Bill of Rights and balance of powers enumerated in our Constitution.

At the same time, they have distracted us from the war on terror and the savage brutality of 9/11 by starting a conflagration in Iraq, preemptively and without adequate planning or resources. That catastrophic blunder has cost us thousands of lives and billions of dollars with no apparent strategy for egress. It has also squandered hard-won respect and cooperation around the globe and increased the hostility of many who were already our enemies.

To win the next election, some Democrats believe these blatant failures should be proclaimed repeatedly without proposing policy alternatives. Even if that were true, Democrats would then lack a specific mandate once in office.

Therefore, I offer the following policy suggestions to answer the voters' inquiry, "So, Democrats, what would you do instead?"

WHERE WE ARE TODAY

We live in the strongest nation in world history, where ten generations of immigrants have enjoyed unparalleled opportunities. However, we could be even stronger, for ourselves and for the rest of the world, if we managed our resources more wisely and adopted prudent policies.

The failure to do so has become particularly apparent in the past six years. Before then, we were moving boldly up the ladder as a richer, stronger, and more inclusive Union. When George W. Bush was elected in 2000, he inherited eight years of economic growth, the four strongest stock market years in our history, the creation of 22 million new jobs, a balanced budget, an upwardly mobile middle class, fewer poor, and a projected surplus of over $5 trillion.

Since then, 9/11, terrorism, the war in Afghanistan, our invasion and occupation of Iraq, [Hurricane] Katrina, huge and gratuitous tax cuts, and exorbitant spending have left us indebted and dependent on financing from China, Japan, and the rest of the world. Meanwhile, we are stuck in a quagmire in Iraq with more than 180,000 people killed or seriously wounded, more than 20,000 of them American, and no end in sight.

Measured by traditional econometrics, the current economy is said to be "growing." In fact, however, the economy has been wonderfully rewarding for high-level corporate executives and big stockholders at the expense of most other Americans. Growth over the past few years was actually fueled by increased consumer spending, personal debt, and depleted savings. A large part of the spending was driven by residential real estate purchased through mortgage financing. Most working Americans are awash in red ink; consumer debt is soaring; and personal bankruptcy filings are increasing dramatically.

In the last four years, many of the middle-class majority, about 80 percent of our workforce, are sliding downward economically while beneath them on the ladder, the number of Americans living below the poverty line has grown.

Only the very top of our "Shining City on the Hill" glows more brightly. In a column titled "Rich Man, Poor Man," published in *U.S. News & World Report* on June 6, 2006, Mortimer Zuckerman writes,

> The generation that emerged from World War II enjoyed income growth fairly evenly spread throughout our entire population. The past 25 years tell an utterly different story. Median family incomes have risen by less than one percent a year—for a total of 18 percent overall—but median incomes for the top one percent have gone up more than 10 times faster—by an astounding 200 percent! As a nation, America has experienced extraordinary growth. From 1980 to 2004, our gross domestic product rose by almost two-thirds, but when you factor in inflation, the wages of the typical earner actually fell—not a lot, but compare that with the top American earners, and the widening gap between the richest and the poorest Americans becomes starkly clear: Among the top 20 percent of American earners, real incomes increased 59 percent. . . .

Most American workers are falling behind, in part because only one in four is "highly skilled" (four years of education beyond high school), and only about two-thirds of American teenagers graduate from high school.

Our elementary and secondary public schools in disadvantaged areas are failing, and a college education is out of reach for many qualified students. As a result, we have lost our competitive advantage in science and engineering, and American employers are importing thousands of skilled workers, or they are outsourcing jobs to Ireland, India, and China.

At the same time, the costs of health care, education, retirement security, transportation, housing, and energy are growing far faster than the incomes of most working Americans. For the first time in our recorded history, household incomes, after inflation, have failed to increase for five years in a row while personal debt has grown.

And further down the ladder, 37 million Americans are mired in poverty. That's more than [there were] five years ago, but it's ignored because the poor don't vote very much. That's especially regrettable because 13 million of them are children vulnerable to abuse, drugs, and violence. Many learn the sound of gunfire before they've ever heard an orchestra. Without adequate education, their chance for economic self-sufficiency as adults is virtually nil.

In addition, we have corrupted the flow of immigrant workers into our nation. As legal immigrants are forced to wait for years to become citizens, 12 or more million illegal ones usurp low-level jobs, depressing wages for unskilled American citizens.

Our fiscal situation has impaired our ability to strengthen our weakened social programs. Together with our huge record trade deficits, $201.6 billion with China alone, budget deficits and debt affect the value of the dollar and magnify our need to borrow huge amounts from China, Japan, and other foreign interests. In November 2005, the Goldman Sachs Group predicted $5 trillion in deficits over the next decade. The president responded by proposing huge reductions in programs for the great majority of Americans, the middle class and the poor, including Medicaid, mentoring for at-risk children, food stamps, police for urban areas, child support, and job training.

At the same time, the president asked for tax cuts of more than $70 billion annually for the wealthy, even though their taxes today are lower than they have been in sixty years!

When combined with that terrible tangle of foreign policy issues, this apparent unfairness has confused, frightened, and angered many Americans. We need—and deserve—honest, clear, and sensible answers from our political leaders to unite us as a people instead of tearing us apart.

HOW TO REDIRECT THE NATION'S ECONOMY

We Democrats are demonstrating it's easier to criticize than to be constructive, especially when the Republicans' failures are so numerous and blatant. We recount the costs of Iraq military action in lives, dollars, and allies; the president's disregard for the Constitution; the neglect of American workers in favor of tax cuts for the wealthy; the mismanagement of Katrina; and the policy failures on oil prices and immigration while wedge issues such as religion and marriage are used to divide us.

On the other hand, we have so far failed to offer significant alternatives, especially when faced with political risk, particularly regarding the need to increase taxes and cut popular programs to avoid plunging us further into debt. But unless we deal effectively with both sides of the balance sheet, our country will remain saddled with the unfortunate status quo. To fulfill our mission, we must talk to the American people directly, bluntly and plainly.

We should start by addressing the expectations of our citizens for the twenty-first century. These include the value of education, hard work, integrity, and risk-taking in economic success:

1. **Education:** Many leaders in the business community resort to importing skilled workers at lower prices from overseas. Still, most Americans would prefer to hire U.S. citizens. To meet the growing need, we must produce more skilled workers through college education, technological literacy, and lifelong training. Our efforts should be supplemented by a reduction in the number of visas for those willing to accept significantly lower wages, thereby depressing remuneration for American workers.

To improve public elementary and secondary schools, we must offer special assistance to poor children in unstable families. Mentors, after-school programs, smaller classes, and, most important, a good job for the head of the household will give them a better chance to succeed.

2. **Health care:** The current system for financing health care is dysfunctional. Today, some 45 million Americans are uninsured, and that increases the cost of health care for everyone, including industries already providing health care to their employees.

Our current health care system produces massive profits for insurance companies, pharmaceutical companies, and other private health care businesses, and, therefore, we should consider a single-payer system. But meanwhile, a series of incrementally beneficial steps is more likely to be adopted. These include increasing child-health coverage, a program pioneered by New York state while I was governor; reorienting Medicaid and Medicare for home care and community-based services; increased use of communications and information technology to computerize record keeping; safe and legal registration of prescription drugs; and increased attention to preventive practices such as hygiene and nutrition, education about illicit drugs and alcohol abuse, and redesign of efficient emergency rooms. Meanwhile, some states, like Massachusetts, are already finding their own solutions. Democrats at the state level should encourage that trend as well.

3. **Trade:** Our trade barriers are among the most permissive in the world, but partly because of our growing unpopularity, other nations are reluctant to reciprocate. One remedy? Better relations with the rest of the world instead of the arrogance we demonstrated in the invasion of Iraq.

We also need balanced trade to complement "free trade." With China and Japan, we have given more than we have received. Our best deals involve Canada, Australia, and other economies comparable to our own. All of our trading partners must ensure basic human rights and enforce labor and environmental standards.

4. **Energy and the environment:** The energy crisis presents one of our greatest challenges. We must vigorously improve conservation techniques and find alternative sources of energy to avoid dependence on oil from the Middle East. That would simultaneously reduce economic and military threats and address the "inconvenient truth" of global warming. We should explore alternative fuels such as ethanol and hydrogen and pursue technological advances to "sanitize" the use of coal.

And we should take a fresh look at nuclear energy because uranium is readily available, inexpensive, and a good replacement for fossil fuels and their dangerous carbon dioxide emissions. Until now, new nuclear power plants in the United States have been stalled because of imperfect construction technology, careless site locations, and the problem with storage of nuclear waste.

If we can find a way to travel to the moon and back, we can solve all these technological problems as well. France has been doing so for years. We should approach conservation and new forms of energy with the same commitment we adopted to put a man on the moon.

5. **Homeland security:** We are way behind in the race to protect ourselves, even from the type of attacks we have envisioned. The bureaucratic Homeland Security goliath has jammed together a bevy of smaller bureaucracies and made things worse instead of better, as demonstrated in the Katrina disaster. In fact, Homeland Security has mainly succeeded in lining the pockets of favored private contractors and former federal officials. FEMA and many other units should be severed from this mega-bureaucracy.

Our borders are frighteningly porous, as evidenced by 12 million undocumented aliens. Container ships from all over the world must be scrutinized. Our energy and water supply systems, trains, and subways must be protected. We must adopt new security technologies already available, including three-dimensional face detection, facial fingerprinting, voice identification, "smart" videos, surveillance cameras, and faster cargo scanners.

6. **Immigration:** Without immigrants, there would be no United States of America. People came here from all over the world for a better life, and in the process, they built us into the most diverse and powerful nation in the world.

Because we enacted laws to regulate immigration but then failed to enforce them, we created about 12 million technically illegal aliens. We couldn't send them home if we wanted to, and many American businesses and households have become dependent on them.

The Democrats should promote a practical, humane policy with both a path to citizenship and an effective deterrence of illegals crossing our porous borders. A failure to do so after the amnesty program of 1986 produced the current situation. That deterrence must include serious sanctions on employers who exploit illegal aliens.

Simultaneously, we should raise the federal minimum wage from the current paltry $5.15 level to at least $7.15; require mandatory instruction in the English language; and prioritize the few million with legal applications, who have been awaiting their opportunity for years.

Democrats should push all these changes vigorously.

7. **Privacy and protection of constitutional rights:** We should prohibit excessive government intervention into and intrusion upon our private lives, such as the president's order scrutinizing millions of American phone calls. President Bush's clumsiness, jurisprudential insensitivity, and naïvely greedy attempt to seize power is well known and documented. Our next president must respect the Constitution.

PAYING FOR WHAT WE NEED

Some Republicans and Democrats say it is impossible to improve our domestic programs, reduce the debt, and balance the budget. Perhaps, if we had the $5.4 trillion potential surplus President Bill Clinton bequeathed us in 2000, it would have been easier; nevertheless, it can still be done today.

One solution to our national poverty was attempted in the 1980s and 1990s. Tax cuts for the investor class, labeled "supply-side economics," could produce so much new income that the federal Treasury would recoup the cost of the cuts plus much more. Similarly, any increase of taxes on the investor class would lead to economic decline.

Certainly, in some situations, this tax policy can stimulate or retard economic growth. But the supply-siders have extended those simple truths to absurd extremes. That's what happened in the Reagan and Bush eras and is occurring again with Bush II. Only recently, he claimed America was on the right track economically because of his tax cuts for the rich. But the wealthiest 10 percent of the taxpayers benefited and hardly anyone else. According to government predictions, the temporary reduction of the deficit will be supplanted by a substantial shortfall next year.

President Ronald Reagan started his administration in 1981 with the biggest tax cut in history by reducing rates for the highest earners. At the same time, he added massive new expenditures, particularly in the military budget. He then promised the tax cuts would speed the economy's growth so dramatically, it would balance his swollen budget in three years. He miscalculated badly. The cuts helped produce the recession of 1982 as well as the largest deficit and debt in American history, at that time.

How did President Reagan then resolve the situation? By doing the exact opposite, raising taxes, mostly on wealthy corporations and individuals. His first tax increase was the largest in American history.

President George H.W. Bush followed suit with nearly $100 billion in tax increases, despite his "Read my lips" vow. Then President Clinton imposed another tax increase of about $100 billion, mostly on the top corporate and personal earners. This history is verified in an admirably candid book, *Who's in Control? Polar Politics and the Sensible Center*, by a major figure in both the Reagan and Bush [I] administrations, Richard Darman. It is also confirmed in David Stockman's book *Triumph of Politics: Why the Reagan Revolution Failed.*

What happened after all those tax increases on our richest taxpayers? Eight years of economic growth, the four best stock market years in our history, 22 million new jobs, a $5 trillion projected budget surplus, an upwardly mobile middle class, fewer poor, and the discrediting of "supply-side magic." In the long run, the increased taxes on the rich helped all Americans and produced more billionaires and millionaires than ever before.

This should have come as no surprise. America thrived for half a century under a level of federal taxes higher than today. In Bush's second term, we will levy the lowest tax as a percentage of GDP (gross domestic product) since Truman, 16.5 percent.

The inescapable conclusion: Our current deficit and debt crisis is even worse than before. To learn from our history, we should reverse President Bush's huge tax cuts for the 1 or 2 million wealthiest taxpayers.

At the same time, we should either limit our entitlement programs by reducing Social Security and Medicare benefits for those rich enough [not to need them] or, alternatively, apply Social Security and Medicare taxes to all income, including nonsalary. Even Bill Gates Sr., Warren Buffett, and several hundred other billionaires and millionaires have publicly approved this approach.

After discontinuing tax cuts for the wealthy and reducing entitlements, we should reenact Robert Rubin's successful pay-as-you-go budgeting and reduce wasteful spending, including what John

McCain calls "corporate welfare," so that we can finance much-needed programs for the American people.

OUR FOREIGN POLICY

While making ourselves stronger and safer at home, we must also become more realistic and flexible in conducting our foreign policy. We must recognize the folly of both isolationism and forcing democracy on other societies.

In the past few years, the plague of terrorism unleashed by 9/11 has continued to preoccupy us. Our inability to apprehend Osama bin Laden for more than five years has been underscored by President Bush's vow to get him "dead or alive." Recently, bin Laden taunted us for boasting about our prevention of a terrorist attack since 9/11, promising a surprise in the near future. The optimism after the death of Abu Musab al-Zarqawi only demonstrated the volatility of public opinion and failed to abate attacks by either the Al Qaeda network or insurgents.

We must find an intelligent way to climb out of the snake pit we have entered in Iraq. Our occupation pins down more than 140,000 of our troops in a battle without a perceivable end and prevents us from fighting the real "war against terrorism." It also distracts us from the proliferation of nuclear weapons in North Korea and Iran as well as the escalating violence in Israel and Lebanon.

Before President Bush's tragic decision to preemptively attack Iraq, he declared war against the Taliban in Afghanistan with the full support of this nation and most of the world. Four years later, the Taliban remain, despite our presence and backup from NATO forces.

The preemptive attack on Iraq was based on the threat that Saddam Hussein would work with Al Qaeda to attack us with weapons of mass destruction. The president has been forced to admit his mistake. Nevertheless, he says he's pleased we went forward anyway, despite the aftermath of the attack and our predicament in a lethal quagmire.

Hussein has been ousted, and an election provided Iraq's first taste of representative government, but insurgents and Al Qaeda strike with regularity. After three years of occupation, sectarian violence has erupted into a virtual civil war, with both sides regarding the United States as their common enemy. The Iraqi police force is ineffective, and we are loath to insert our forces between the fiercely hostile Shiites and Sunnis. The president presides over a no-win disaster, much like the last phases of Vietnam.

Meanwhile, Iraq's infrastructure is in shambles, and oil production, the key to Iraq's economy, is still depressed below prewar levels. Moreover, despite some progress in forming an all-Iraqi government, we are unsure what kind of representative government it will become or its effect on terrorism.

Without a permanent tripartite, the current violent unrest and killing of Americans will continue until the president has had enough. In fact, Republican strategy commits us to remain in Iraq indefinitely, hoping the irreconcilable differences among three competing cultures will melt away.

As long as the president pursues his impossible dream of a truly united Iraq, our continued occupation is inevitable. Some analysts are now suggesting the partition of Iraq into an independent Kurdistan, a Shiite state, and a Sunni state. In fact, the current Iraqi constitution resembles our early Articles of Confederation more than our Constitution. [During the period when the news was reporting that "the Iraqis are writing a constitution," I heard someone say, "Why don't we give them ours? It's not like we're using it."] Separating the three areas and sharing the profits from oil should be pursued.

Otherwise, the Democrats should demand an exit plan beyond the glib "We'll step down when they step up." A number of Democrats have suggested a private arrangement with Iraqi leaders to redeploy our troops over six to twelve months while enlisting assistance from other Muslim countries. Turkey will probably help Kurdistan; Iran will help the Shia; and Sunni nations will help Sunni Iraqis. Meanwhile, some American troops can remain in Kuwait, Bahrain, and other Persian Gulf locations, as suggested by Congressman John Murtha.

Once we have departed Iraq, we can intensify our struggle against jihadist terrorists in Afghanistan and other parts of the world. That struggle, unlike our clumsy efforts in Iraq, has virtually total bipartisan support.

We also must discourage Saudi Arabia and others from supporting *madrassas* because they teach impressionable Muslim youths to hate the Western "infidels." And we must join with our allies to fight economic oppression and its exploitation by terrorists. President Bush's "Millennium Challenge" and "Arab Partnership" programs should be fully funded.

In short, we must combine military force, intelligence, and police power with concerted, collaborative economic and social aid, instead of precipitous, preemptive, poorly prepared, rash, and pointless wars, such as the president's attack on Iraq.

That has become even more obvious in light of Hezbollah's startlingly effective military effort against Israel. The ugly conflict in Lebanon has roiled the entire Arab world and derailed any peace plan for Israel and the Palestinians. At the moment [early August 2006], we are closer to a regional war than we have been in decades. The Hezbollah rationale is particularly distressing: "Israel has no right to exist as a nation and must, therefore, be destroyed." As long as Hezbollah and others in the Arab world insist on that radical rejection of Israel's legitimacy, no peace plan is possible.

It would be unfair to blame all our problems in the Mideast on our current president. But the cynicism, naïveté, and arrogance behind the attack on Iraq has contributed to the intensification of other grievances. We need an inspired and gifted new president, less bellicose, with a competent foreign policy team to untie the knots we have created. Regrettably, we must wait until 2008 to find one.

VALUES CAN DIVIDE OR UNITE US

America is faced with a choice for its national identity: 300 million dissociated individuals struggling in a dog-eat-dog society or a grand coalition of workers including the poor and a growing class of enlightened affluent benefactors with a profound commitment to sharing their benefits for the common good.

In the last five-and-a-half years, instead of working aggressively to bring the people of this nation together in our journey to a "Shining City on a Hill," our leaders have allowed us to become fragmented and weak.

Many now see us as two Americas, the "Red States" and the "Blue States," standing on opposite sides of a cultural canyon, glaring at one another suspiciously, unwilling to start building a bridge from either side.

We have always been a nation challenged by our great diversity of cultures and values, particularly religious ones. The thirteen colonies joined a new union with a high degree of independence, as did the varied populations in each. Over the decades, we added to our melting pot with free men and women, black slaves, wealthy landowners, entrepreneurs, workers, farmers, shopkeepers, and seekers of opportunity from all over the world.

Our Founding Fathers accommodated that diversity in the Constitution, protecting individual rights and independence. They assumed we would strengthen our nation by becoming a sharing community. And for two hundred years, we have done so, removing walls and developing new synergisms. For most of our first century, our population grew to fill the vast new expanse from ocean to ocean, and the federal government stayed on the sidelines. But after that, we found the market system and philanthropy were insufficient to build a strong society, and our government responded with programs and other solutions.

The nation's sense of community has withered during the second Bush administration. In addition to economic fragmentation, we have been split by a clash of religious values, caused, in part, by a conservative political constituency. The president and every other citizen may advocate values of religious origin as part of an American consensus. But they must be based on something more than an act of faith. Our citizens will demand a rationale acceptable to most Americans whatever their religious disposition, especially since the Constitution instructs us to avoid an establishment of religion by government mandate.

The president's position with respect to embryonic stem cells provides a case in point. He forbids their use because human life starts at conception, and the research destroys the embryo, tantamount to killing a human being. But the president's science advisor, Dr. John Marburger, admitted the question was a "sacred" one and not scientific. Thus, the president is ordering America to conform to his religious belief. He also explained one reason for selecting Harriet Miers as a nominee for the Supreme Court: her conversion from

Roman Catholicism to Evangelicalism. This occurred at the same time he was warning Iraqis about creating a "theocracy" in their new government. Many Americans reject the president's faith-based argument about embryonic stem cells because of the potential for curing disease and improving the lives of millions of human beings. Most Americans would also avoid selecting a Supreme Court justice on the basis of his or her religion.

Thus, deeply rooted cultural biases have been calcified into rock-hard impediments to civility and fairness. That's the case with opposition to "same-sex" marriage. Both President Bush and John Kerry understood the propriety of "civil unions" to provide same-sex partners with all the legal privileges of marriage. But they reserved the word "marriage" for heterosexuals. Why? For religious reasons, cultural traditions, and political cover. In the process, civil unions became a divisive issue as well.

On the other hand, some religious values are compellingly rational to believers and nonbelievers alike. For example, two principles are fundamental to virtually all our religions and social policy. The first, respect for one another as kindred spirits, and the second, to share our strengths to create a better society, help us protect the weak and innocent, resist evil aggression, provide opportunity for seekers, and care for the disabled.

In effect, these fundamental religious beliefs promote a strong, effective, and caring community. The Hebrews called them *Tzedakah* and *Tikkun Olam*. Christians say, "We should love one another as we love ourselves." And the Koran agrees through the lovely symbolism of the Islamic *Ashira* or "Noah's Pudding," a thousand-year-old tradition shared by Muslims, Christians, and Jews in the Middle East to celebrate the landing of Noah's ark. The pudding consists of forty different ingredients: almonds, figs, berries, and many delicacies mixed into one pot. It symbolizes synergism, collaboration, and harmony.

That simple but profound message resonates with millions of human beings of all nationalities and value systems. It should be leveraged to avoid war, fight poverty, work for social justice, preserve the environment, provide economic opportunity, and aid the disabled. It should rally us to help impoverished people in undeveloped nations as well as the victims of the tsunami, Katrina, and 9/11. Adam Smith wrote about it in *Theory of Moral Sentiments*, and President Abraham Lincoln used it to infuse the natural law of the Declaration of Independence into the Constitution. Lincoln believed the market system anchors our nation, but we need more to thrive as a society. So he called upon people to use our common government, in addition to the private sector, for housing, education, and infrastructure. That's exactly what we've done with public education, Medicare and Medicaid, Social Security, and the Marshall Plan. Together, we've built highways, intervened in the market, and landed a man on the moon.

Lincoln understood what today's Republican leaders forget: Our progress as a nation depends upon combining our individuality with a commitment to community. He believed in integration instead of fragmentation. Although globalization was at least a hundred years away, Lincoln's vision incorporated all the nations of the world because he believed they were interdependent. He repeatedly said his principles could affect all humanity for generations to come. A far cry from the narrow unilateralism of the Bush administration.

Today, on this ever-shrinking globe, we must collaborate and cooperate with other world powers. Even the mighty United States needs the rest of the world to protect and promote its interests. Just think about going it alone in a preemptive war against North Korea or Iran.

SUMMARY

The long list of blunders and omissions by the current Republican administration has forced American voters to seek change. But victories by Democrats in 2006 and 2008 will lack a mandate for real change unless we offer our own promising alternatives now.

Twenty-five years ago, a political "Tale of Two Cities" was spun by the Reagan–Bush crowd with governing principles, particularly supply-side economics, very similar to those followed by President Bush for the last six years. At the 1984 Democratic Convention, we warned about the danger of those policies, and the possibility of creating a weak, poor, and fragmented America. Eight years later, when President Clinton was elected in 1992, it became clear the Democrats were right.

In a chilling reprise, the Republicans have done it again. Only six years ago, George W. Bush inherited leadership of a nation with eight years of economic growth, 22 million new jobs, a balanced budget, a $5.4 trillion potential surplus, an upwardly mobile middle class, fewer poor, and more billionaires and millionaires than ever. President Bush sustained only the growth of billionaires and millionaires. We now have the largest annual deficits and debt in our history, an eroding middle class, and a growing number of families below the poverty line, the most badly fragmented population in our nation's modern history, and our lowest global approval rating, a major factor in our trade relations and military power.

Our president's most significant foreign policy decision, his preemptive invasion of Iraq, has killed or seriously wounded more than 180,000 human beings with no end in sight.

The suggestions in these pages are humbly offered as possible solutions to our predicament.

MARIO CUOMO'S OMEGA SOCIETY SPEECH: A MEDITATION ON ULTIMATE VALUES

So many readers and listeners who have indulged my enthusiasms over the years know of my great admiration for Mario M. Cuomo. Thus I'm often greeted with an inquiry about his present activities.

I answer them this way. He practices law at the prestigious New York law firm of Willkie, Farr & Gallagher. He continues to write and takes more than a passing interest in the career of his son and heir Andrew M. Cuomo, who presently serves as New York attorney general and who many of us believe would make a pretty good governor himself.

Meanwhile, the gifted man the Boston Globe *called "the great philosopher-statesman of the American nation" often departs from the confines of his ivory tower law firm in midtown Manhattan to give the thought-provoking speeches for which he is known.*

This one before The Omega Society, a group of "thinkers and seekers," is one of Cuomo's best, delivered in April 2005 at the Sheraton New York.

When I was asked to give the closing remarks tonight, I hesitated because of the intelligent, distinguished, and articulate individuals slated to appear before me.

The representative of Omega insisted, "Your input as a three-term governor could be especially relevant given the frightening implications of 9/11."

So I agreed to try.

Actually, I once offered similar observations at a conference titled "Who or What Is God?"

I addressed the question then, as I do now, as an ordinary New Yorker from Queens, who grew up in a poor and middle-class neighborhood with asphalt streets and stickball, and earned a living, somewhat improbably, in the demanding world of politics.

I struggle to maintain my belief in God as a Catholic raised with simple Sunday Mass practitioners, far from the high intellectual traditions of Talmudic scholars, elegant Episcopalian homilists, or abstruse Jesuit teachers.

The simple folk of South Jamaica, Queens, came from tenements and attached houses and perceived the world as a cosmic basic-training course, filled by God with obstacles and traps for the unworthy. The prevailing moral standard was easily learned: "If you liked it, it was probably a sin; if you liked it a lot, it was probably a mortal sin."

The believers saw themselves as "the poor, banished children of Eve, mourning and weeping in this vale of tears," until by some combination of grace and good works, and luck, they escaped final damnation.

For many, their sense of God was reflected in their own collective experience as the poor and wounded.

God seemed to have a cold voice when—on Beaver Road, next to a cemetery across the street from St. Monica's Catholic Church—a famous ex-jockey, one of the homeless winos, froze to death while sleeping in a large wooden crate.

Maybe others in America felt content with their world. But for most of the people in my old neighborhood, it was hard to see God's goodness in the pathetic faces pleading with my father for bread at our small grocery store, until the next relief check came in.

It grew harder still during the Second World War, when a gold star in a window announced the death of someone's son.

It was hard to believe in God after Hiroshima, too.

Others reveled in the cultural liberation of the sixties, but for most of our neighborhood, the sadness of that time was memorialized by Simon and Garfunkel: "Where have you gone, Joe DiMaggio?/Our nation turns its lonely eyes to you/What's that you say, Mrs. Robinson?/Joltin' Joe has left and gone away."

No more John F. Kennedy, no more Martin Luther King. No more Bobby Kennedy. Nothing to believe in. Nothing to grab hold of. Nothing to uplift us.

People weren't asking, "*Who* is God?" They were asking, "Is there a God?"

Many asked the same question after 9/11, after a preemptive war in Iraq killed more than 40,000 human beings, most of them innocent civilians; after Rwanda; after the grotesquely lethal tsunami.

Many ask the same question today when a child dies in a crib. Many resign themselves to a world with no answers to the biggest questions.

For some of us, however, the burden becomes intolerable; the absurdity of a world without explanation pushes us to find a rationale, an excuse, anything to escape the despair, something larger than ourselves to believe in.

We yearn for more than a God of prohibition, guilt, and punishment. More than John Calvin's chilling conclusion that God loves Jacob but hates Esau. For us, it must be a God of the New Testament, of mercy, peace, and hope. In the end, to make any sense, it must be a God of love!

Mostly, we want a God because the accumulation of material goods and the constant seeking to satisfy our petty appetites, for a flash of ecstasy or popularity or even temporary fame, is just a desperate, frantic attempt to fill the shrinking interval between birth and death!

In my old neighborhood, despite the doubts, the simple and sincere theology of the pre–Vatican II Catholic Church and the prodding of uneducated parents were still respected. Probably because there was no viable alternative.

In the fifties, some of us were presented with the enlightened vision and profound wisdom of an extraordinary man. A scientist, a paleontologist. A person who understood evolution. A soldier who knew the inexplicable evil of the battlefield. A scholar who studied the ages. A philosopher, a theologian, a believer. And a great priest. Teilhard de Chardin heard our lament, and he answered us. He reoriented our theology and rewrote its language, linking it, inseparably, with science. His wonderful book, *The Divine Milieu*, dedicated to "those who love the world," made negativism a sin.

Teilhard glorified the world and everything in it. He taught us to love and respect ourselves as the pinnacle of God's creation. He taught us how the whole universe, even the pain and imperfection, is sacred. He taught us in powerful, cogent, and persuasive prose, and in soaring poetry.

He integrated his extensive knowledge of evolution with his religious understanding of the "divine milieu." He envisioned a vibrant human future, "We are all foot soldiers in the struggle to unify the human spirit. . . ."

"Faith," he said, "is not a call to escape the world but to embrace it." Creation is not an elaborate testing ground with moral obstacles but an invitation to join in the work of restoration; his was a voice urging us to improve the world by our individual and collective efforts, making it kinder, safer, and more loving. Repairing the wounded world helps it move upward to the "pleroma," St. Paul's word for the consummation of human life. The Omega Point, when the level of consciousness and civility eventually converge, elevates us to the highest level of morality. A new universe, a peerless one; one we could help create by our own behavior. Teilhard's vision challenges the imagination, but it has achieved sufficient plausibility among celebrated intellectuals like Robert Wright, a scientist and declared agnostic.

Some of Teilhard's fundamental principles are clear to all rational human beings whatever their level of formal education. They are called "natural theology" or "natural law" because they can be ascertained solely through observing the world around us.

Without books, instruction, or revelation, three things should strike us about our place in the world.

First, the greatest gift is our very existence.

Second, we are each unique elements of creation, deserving respect and dignity.

Third, we work together to protect and enhance the life we share.

The Hebrews spread these ideas as the foundation of their monotheistic belief. The principle of *Tzedakah* involves treating one another as brothers and sisters from the same great source of life. And the tenet of *Tikkun Olam* instructs us to join together in repairing the world.

Rabbi Hillel merged these two ideas as the foundation of the whole law. "All the rest," he said, "is commentary."

Jesus did likewise for Christians, saying essentially, "The whole law is that you should love one another as you love yourself for the love of truth, and the truth is God made the world but did not complete it; you are to be collaborators in creation."

I don't know any religion that rejects these ideals.

If politicians today are looking for guidance from religion, they must apply the ancient truth used by primitive people to ward off their enemies and wild beasts, to find food and shelter, to raise their children in safety, and eventually to raise up a civilization: We're all in this together, like a family, interconnected and interdependent, and we cannot afford to revert to a world of Us against Them.

It is the one indispensable idea to realizing our full potential as a people; to sharing the wealth of our economy; to relieving the economic and political oppression all over the world; and to rescuing millions of Africans from the ravages of AIDS and the barbarism of warlords.

Each of us must choose whether we will change the world for the better. The brilliant, agnostic Justice Oliver Wendell Holmes echoed Teilhard's call for vigorous involvement but added a warning. He said, "As life is action and passion, we are required to share the passion and action of our time, at the peril of being judged not to have lived."

Teilhard would have augmented Holmes's remarks with his promise of glory: "The day will come when, after harnessing the wind, the mind, the tides and gravity, we shall harness for God the energies of love, and on that day, for the second time in the history of man, we will have discovered fire."

I wish I could record people's favorite music. In Teilhard's vision, I hear Beethoven's wonderful message in his Ninth Symphony, with its unforgettable ending.

Beethoven saw the world as a family. Listen to the symphony again. It begins dark and threatening; disaster and confusion loom from clashes of the will, misunderstanding, and alienation. It then moves into the frenetic hunt for meaning, seeking an answer to comfort and reassure humanity. Then, in the final movement, it swiftly presents again the initial picture of disunity and discord, only to dissolve into the "Ode to Joy," using the words of Friedrich von Schiller's poem, ending in "ecstatic jubilation," the chorus rejoicing at the convergence of the world's people through maturity, brotherhood, and love!

Simple, and simply wonderful!

So, "Who or what is God?"

I have grown old enough to understand the vanity of trying to define the infinite and eternal. But I'm not required to eliminate any possibilities by the limits of my intellect either. In the end, I can choose to believe and call it "faith" if I must, if that promises me meaningfulness.

So it may not be easy to understand Teilhard or why God commits us to the endless task of improving the world around us, with fulfillment an eternity away.

But it's better than the anguish of futility. Better than the emptiness of despair.

And capable of bringing meaning to our most modest and clumsy efforts.

That's a useful consolation for any of us still struggling to believe.

LESLEY STAHL INTERVIEWS GOVERNOR MARIO M. CUOMO FOR "BREAKFAST AT '21'"

Original interview, January 21, 2004, at the "21" Club, New York City.

LESLEY STAHL (L.S.): Governor Cuomo, let's start off with the State of the Union address. Give us your analysis of how you think President Bush did last night. The president really had his spinach!

GOVERNOR MARIO CUOMO (M.C.): Well, if he did well in your opinion because he had his spinach, I would suggest next time he try escarole! (*laughter*) There are two Republicans I think we should consider when judging this campaign: Abe Lincoln and Ronald Reagan.

And Ronald Reagan may be the most relevant because he gave us a test when he said [in 1980], "Ask yourself whether you are better off now than you were four years ago." And I think that's a valid test for an incumbent president. And I don't think President Bush passed.

We were much better off four years ago, obviously: 22 million new jobs, the largest surplus in American history, the middle class moving up, the poor moving up. By every measurement, we were doing better.

The president tried very hard to convince us we are safer now. How dare he even suggest it! Having lost a thousand of our young men and women already in Iraq. Losing another one every day. Having abandoned the war against terrorism in Afghanistan when he knew where Osama bin Laden was—the true terrorist—and Al Qaeda, and fighting a vicious, brutal tyrant who he knew was a pushover. And it has enraged much of the Muslim world as well as many of our own former allies.

As to the economy, it's a travesty to suggest it is good for 160 million workers or retirees. It's good for large corporations; it's good for large shareholders; it's good for people who are invested heavily overseas; it's good for people who are betting against the dollar. It is not good for 160 million workers whose average wage has fallen. Fifteen million of them—not eight million—fifteen million of them are unemployed, part-time, or out of the market altogether. To suggest the economy is good! So, escarole next time! (*laughter*) (*applause*)

L.S.: Governor, what did you think of the Howard Dean performance last night?

M.C.: Actually, I didn't see it. I heard it on the radio. It didn't sound hysterical but perhaps "super energetic." It was a little bit like the stock market when your shares are doing really well. There's that same kind of behavior by lucky people. I wouldn't rule him out by any means. He's still leading in New Hampshire. He still has a lot of money. He still has a lot of young people. The irony is that his strength initially came from that kind of feistiness, and now it threatens to make him weak.

I don't think he can beat Bush, however. I think if he wins in New Hampshire or even runs a strong second, you won't be covering that story anymore. And he'll be back in the race.

L.S.: And what about a constitutional amendment on marriage, Governor?

M.C.: Once again, I think the president last night attempted to distract the American people from the main issues. And that's why you get into these questions. He has no intention of proposing an amendment to the Constitution on marriage.

Because then you'd have to define your position. You'd have to say marriage must be taken as the basis of all relationships because that's the way you produce children. And then people would say, "Well, how about people who want to get married and not have children?" or "What about people who want to get married and are not capable of having children?"

What is his rationale for this position? He is no more going to submit a constitutional amendment on marriage than he will on abortion. Why? Because they can't make their case to the people of this country. And so, that's a distraction. It divides this country terribly at a time when we don't need it.

We are now more polarized than we have ever been, certainly more than during the Clinton years. Did we Democrats create this class division? No way! We the Democrats gave you Bill Clinton. And Clinton gave you the richest four years in American history. And Clinton gave you the largest surplus in history. And Clinton gave you the Army and Navy that defeated the Taliban and won the war in Iraq by a general he appointed. Clinton gave you an economy with a recession in 2001 that ended in November of the same year, but it's been downhill ever since. Then, there's all this foolishness claiming, "We're improving on our failures." You'd have to grow 275,000 jobs every month to win back the 3 million you've lost. That's going to give Bush the record as the worst job-producing and -losing administration since the Depression. Last month, he created one thousand jobs. Congratulations! So he wants to distract us from the two biggest issues.

What about the war on terrorism? Donald Rumsfeld is the Secretary of Defense, and he says he can't tell whether we're winning or not. Tom Ridge is in charge of Homeland Security. He gives us an orange signal, a yellow signal. What does that mean? We're winning the war on terrorism? Who's winning the war on terrorism?

The whole world is mad at us. Who are the people who are killing our soldiers in Iraq other than terrorists? Are we defeating them? We killed 60,000 Iraqis, most of them innocent. We lost 1,000 American men and women to start that war in Iraq—when the real war on terrorism was against Osama bin Laden, whom you [Bush] knew well, whose family you [Bush] knew well, and with whom you [Bush] dealt in Saudi Arabia.

L.S.: But how, Governor, are the Democrats going to win?

M.C.: Right now, there is a great deal of anger. And the Democrats cannot win with just anger. They need a positive approach. We have a terrible problem with trade, and unless you sit down and re-rationalize trade altogether, then it's ridiculous now to pretend you're where Abraham Lincoln was or where we were twenty years ago.

It's a whole new ballgame. Now they're producing skilled workers in China who are taking skilled jobs away from us. What are you going to do about that? Well, there's a lot you can do. You have only one high-skilled worker out of five in this country. We gave away $3 trillion in tax cuts; 60 percent of it went to the middle class. And that money was spent by the middle class, and it did boost the economy. And the middle class spent it because their average wage is under $43,000 a year. Their debt is way up. They've set a record for individual bankruptcies every year. That tax cut was useful. And if you could give another one, it would be useful, too. It's only a stimulus, but it's useful.

The $1 trillion you gave to me and my clients at Willkie, Farr & Gallagher; fewer than 3 million taxpayers in the United States get $1 trillion. How do you rationalize that? We're not short of investor money. We're short of consumption money. The economy is 70 percent consumption. Instead of giving me those tax cuts, take that money and direct it to the middle class, where it will be spent. Direct some of it toward deficit reduction. Direct some of it to George Pataki and the other governors, and Michael Bloomberg and the other mayors, who have to raise taxes at the local level while you're cutting the progressive tax. That's a positive thing. Redirect that money. Reinvest it in education, in health care, and in training, especially if you don't have an answer to the trade problem.

As for terrorism, it's very simple. Terrorism is unlike any other war. If it were army against army, or nation against nation, we would have won the way we did in Iraq, and it would be all over. But it is not like that. There are millions of people who hate us so much they'll give up their lives to take ours. What do you do about that?

The president mentioned it yesterday and in his defense strategy in 2002. He said you can no more stop this terrorism from the Middle East with an army than you can stop crime in New York City with police. Well, then, what do you have to do? Use your influence with the Saudi Arabians. Take the president's good program that Colin Powell is running—whose theory was that we must invest in the Arab economy and create opportunity.

L.S.: Governor, you stated before, in reference to President Bush and Osama bin Laden: "whose family he dealt with in Saudi Arabia." Would you expand on that statement?

M.C.: Well, I think it's well known that the bin Laden family and the Carlyle Corporation were connected in Saudi Arabia. Nobody ever accused them of illegality. And I refer you to the *New York Times* and other publications that ran the story. It astonished me when it never went anywhere. But there was no question that Osama bin Laden's family was invested in Carlyle, and Carlyle was invested in Middle Eastern oil, doing business in Saudi Arabia.

L.S.: Governor, can the Democrats win by isolating their base?

M.C.: I don't like that emphasis. Especially on these "quasi" or totally religious issues. Marriage—like abortion—is either a religious issue or a civil issue. And I think it can be reconciled with everybody. And I think the Founding Fathers put their finger on it.

If you have a religious belief, you should be protected in your right to pursue it. And if you think, in your religion, that only certain people should be married, then only certain people are married in your religion. But don't force your religious belief on me.

That's what the First Amendment says. First, it says you can practice your own religion, whatever it is. If you believe life begins at conception, then you don't have to deal in embryonic stem cells. And we will protect you against it. On the other hand, don't insist that everyone else believe the same thing.

We should do that with all the issues. There is a way to please everybody on the economy. By enhancing your work force—your 160 million workers—by making them more highly skilled and making them more secure, by taking that money back from the wealthy people who don't need it and who wouldn't stimulate the economy, by redistributing that to the workers, everybody will profit. By being better at multilateralism internationally, by winning back the old friends, by doing whatever the heck you have to do to get France and Germany to help you in Iraq, you'll save us money. And you'll save lives.

I have to mention Abraham Lincoln again. He was a great Republican, but he was really a progressive liberal. He believed in two things: equality and unity. Give everybody a chance, and the whole country becomes stronger. You can do that in foreign policy. You can do that in domestic policy. You don't have to win by dividing people.

L.S.: One final question, Governor. Can you predict who the Democratic nominee will be and who will win the election?

M.C.: Two white males! (*laughter*) (*applause*)

ADVICE FOR PRESIDENT OBAMA FROM PRESIDENT LINCOLN VIA GOVERNOR CUOMO

Mario Cuomo once told me that he finds President Obama to be one of the most articulate of our presidents. With all the daunting challenges facing our young president, the governor was reminded of the trials and tribulations of Mr. Lincoln. These are Governor Cuomo's thoughts, delivered on Inauguration Day, January 20, 2009.

On February 12, three weeks into the administration of our forty-fourth president, Barack Obama, America will mark the two hundredth birthday of our sixteenth president, Abraham Lincoln—considered by most historians to be our greatest president ever.

The competition by presidents and presidential candidates to claim the mantle of Lincoln in ways big and small has come to embrace all political faiths. Obama is no exception. He will be the first president to be sworn in on the same Bible used by Lincoln in 1861, having arrived in Washington from Philadelphia by train as Lincoln had, and he has mentioned several times that he is studying Lincoln's speeches for help in preparing his own inaugural address.

Obama's inauguration started what will be the most challenge-ridden presidential term since Lincoln's. Only history will eventually tell us how it compares with Lincoln's, but there are already apparent similarities and differences in their personalities, positions, and situations that indicate the kind of leadership we can expect from Obama.

Obama, like Lincoln, has superb personal gifts: a brilliant analytical mind, riveting oratorical and writing abilities, and the capability to remain calm under fire. Both were born and raised in modest circumstances. Neither had significant executive experience before becoming president, and both were considered underdogs at the outset of their campaigns.

Obama, like Lincoln, rejects rigid ideology in policymaking, relying instead on common sense, benign pragmatism, and an overarching grand concept designed to inspire and unify us. Lincoln grasped that single most important concept that would sustain and provoke him for the rest of his days: the Declaration of Independence's achievable goal of equality and opportunity.

To Lincoln—and now to Obama—this is not only a lofty dream or sweet poetry to soothe the soul by wrapping it in high aspiration. It was and is the attainable goal of flesh-and-blood humans who would have to find ways to provide fairly rewarded work, education, health care, security in our older years, and, most of all, equality of opportunity and the right to be treated with dignity.

Lincoln respected the indispensable need for a market-system economy in achieving these goals, but he also realized that while the market is essential to a successful economy, it is not by itself sufficient to assure it. For that reason Lincoln urged that government be used aggressively to meet the needs the market economy failed to satisfy. Obama has already demonstrated clearly that he, like Lincoln, will not hesitate to call for substantial governmental assistance in the effort to right the ship of state in today's troubled waters. Obama also shares Lincoln's extraordinary vision. Lincoln looked beyond the superficial differences that God or history had imposed on us to see the essential truths that unite us. He sympathized vigorously with the cause of democracy in other lands, in Hungary and South America and Greece. He understood that a respect for individual dignity and the equality of all people was the essential foundation, not just for his American family, but for the whole human race.

Lincoln knew, as Obama surely does, that we cannot end terror here, in the Middle East or anywhere in the world, just by having the world's most powerful weapons and the best fighting force. We have to add to this force whatever is needed to provide the realistic hope for opportunity and dignity that quiets people's rage and produces peace here at home and across the globe.

Because Obama shares much of Abraham Lincoln's personality and many of his fundamental beliefs, his leadership could give our nation the chance to live the American dream as Lincoln perceived it, an opportunity that Lincoln himself was denied by an assassin's bullet.

But Obama's leadership could mean much more. While there are significant similarities between Obama and Lincoln, there's a vast and important difference between the circumstances faced by the two in their first term as president. Lincoln focused his 1861 inaugural address on the one issue that eventually dominated his political career—slavery in the United States and how it would affect the Union. In the first moments of his inaugural address, Lincoln dismissed the other issues facing him as creating neither excitement nor anxiety.

Obama, on the other hand, has literally scores of daunting global issues to deal with, and his success or failure will have an impact worldwide. Obama will be the president and commander-in-chief of the dominant superpower in a world that has more than 6 billion human beings, many of whom depend to one extent or another on the nation Obama will lead.

Never before has there been a nation with such tremendous influence on the entire planet—a planet infested with weapons of mass destruction possessed by dozens of nations, many of them hostile to one another, some already at war and others poised at the brink. Further menacing the planet is the inconvenient truth of global warming, terrorism, pandemics of various kinds, regular episodes of genocide, hunger threatening millions of human beings, and now a badly wounded world economy, ailing in part because of a serious recession in the United States.

One hundred forty-eight years of globalization with its benefits and burdens make this a very different world from the one Lincoln lived and served in and one that will make Obama's presidency much more consequential. Lincoln's failure would have scarred the face of America, extending the cruel tragedy of slavery and perhaps fracturing the Union. His success helped keep the American dream alive.

On the other hand, Obama's failure would heighten the threat of unprecedented global damage—but his success could help lead our great nation and this entire threatened world into a new period of enlightenment and progress never before achieved.

And so, Obama's moment in history is a unique one. There seldom has been more to concern us, but neither has there ever been more to hope for.

We should choose hope.

MARIO CUOMO'S REMARKS ON THE OCCASION OF JIMMY BRESLIN'S 70TH BIRTHDAY

Mario Cuomo and the great writer-reporter Jimmy Breslin both came out of Queens to become stalwarts of their professions. They've also been great friends for many decades. Cuomo and Breslin are both struggling Roman Catholic seekers. Each is a great interpreter of the other—and of the world around us. The governor prepared these remarks on December 7, 2009.

I'm not eager to go out to events at night. Like a lot of other people, my day's work is sufficiently challenging to make me look forward to quiet evenings at home. It takes a really good reason to get me out, so when Pete Hamill called and told me that on December 7 there would be an event at night to honor Jimmy for his sixty years as a writer, I wanted to be sure it was real.

I asked Pete, "Does Jimmy know?"

And he said, "Yeah, he's all for it."

At first it didn't sound right to me. Jimmy didn't even celebrate sixty years of *being alive*, so why would he be eager to celebrate sixty years as a writer?

Logic gave me a quick answer. "Just being alive meant a lot less to Jimmy than being alive and *writing*."

That's the way it is with truly gifted people like him. Writers will remind you this evening of his Pulitzer and a wall full of other significant honors over the years acknowledging his unique and vibrant writing skills. As a reporter he became the uncommon voice of the common person with his uncanny ability to find in newsworthy events details that made the events more meaningful to the people of New York's boroughs and millions of other people like them. Interviewing the gravedigger at John F. Kennedy's burial is a good example. The writers will remind you how he could make people smile or laugh out loud when they bring back some of Jimmy's inimitable descriptions of hapless ballplayers, second-rate mobsters, and third-rate politicians, or reintroduce you to "Fat Thomas" and "Robert J. Allen."

There may even be a tear or two if someone chooses to read from *The Short Sweet Dream of Eduardo Gutierrez* or parts of *World without End, Amen.*

But no matter how many bits of Breslin inspiration are shared this evening, they will amount to only light hints of the immense amount of great writing he has done in his uniquely long, productive, and heralded career. Think of it: He still works every day, writing or thinking about writing, and he has done it for sixty years—nearly 22,000 days and nights—except for the short hiatus when doctors were forced to drill a hole in his head to let out of his congested brain some of his unused lines. Then he wrote a book about it!

That's a lot of "Jim Breslin Writing" to cover in a single night of celebration. And the challenge is even greater because, as Pete has pointed out, there are really "at least two Jim Breslins." One "Breslin" is the public person, writer, raconteur, and celebrity figure.

The other is the private guy from Queens when he's not on the stage or on the screen but is himself, on the phone or having an otherwise quiet dinner, explaining to you the world and its various dysfunctionalities. And excoriating those who are responsible for the disorder, by creating it or by not doing enough to fix it—that often includes the people he's talking to at the moment. That's when he's just "Jimmy," and that's the way I know him best and have for more than forty years.

I met him when I was a youngish lawyer trying to help sixty-nine barely middle-class homeowners in Corona, Queens, save their homes from a mayor who was about to condemn them to accommodate the builder of a huge housing complex.

They couldn't afford a big law firm, and I was neither prestigious nor politically influential, so the sixty-nine would probably have lost their homes if Jimmy hadn't gotten involved. He came to a meeting of the group, did some research, then wrote a long story and some short ones and talked to some influential people at City Hall. He convinced them the mayor was wrong, and the sixty-nine stayed in their homes. That was Jimmy at his best, and it led to a friendship that has survived all the years since then. Good days and hard days. Days when we enjoyed some lucky breaks and other days when we got hit by tragedies.

And most of the real tragedies were on Jimmy's side of the relationship. Heavy, heavy blows that would have left me and most people crippled and helpless.

But not Jimmy.

It had to be hard for him for sure, but Jimmy just kept writing. He had to! His world was too big, too complex, too filled with great characters. There were too many great stories that needed telling and retelling. And there were too many big problems that needed solving!

There still are! As there have been for sixty years: nearly 22,000 nights and days!

Almost every morning before he goes to his typewriter, he'll call one of his many friends to describe some of the problems: a war we should be ending, a health care bill we need to pass. I can hear him now: "Did you see the first page of the *Times*? Food stamps are back! Food stamps—and they say the recession is over! What are you doing about it? Write a damn letter! Call somebody—some big shot. You must know someone! Tell them about the abused immigrants and the abusive landlords, the crooked politicians and the bad priests."

Every morning Jimmy has a bowl of oatmeal *and* his outrage. And I suspect that's the way it will always be. He won't ever stop thinking about the world he lives in and writing about it. Why? Because way down deep "Jimmy" is a believer. He will argue with the priests of his church, but he knows the God they are supposed to be working for has given him a personal gift. A gift that is given to only a few. And he will not offend his God by not using that gift. And he *will* use it until there are no more stories to tell or problems to solve.

Thank you, Jimmy. Keep going!

"REASON TO BELIEVE": LIFE LESSONS—MARIO M. CUOMO AT THE 92ND STREET Y

Delivered in New York on January 25, 2010.

When Susan Engel suggested that I share with you what I have learned about life and politics that I believe is most relevant, I told her I wasn't convinced I could add significantly to the already considerable wisdom of a 92nd Street Y audience.

Susan handled that concern by pointing out that she was reserving a block of time for questions and observations from the *audience*—and they, *the audience*, would assure we would hear at least *some* stimulating intelligence before the night was over.

And so I agreed to talk about some of the things I have learned over the years in my own search for truth and efficacy in life. I will try my best to do so as swiftly as I can to save most of our time for discussion with you.

I suspect a lot of what I have to say will sound familiar to some of you.

I offer these thoughts not as a seer, or scholar, or philosopher, or politician, but as an ordinary New Yorker, from South Jamaica in Queens, raised on asphalt streets with brick stoops and stickball games, who was lucky enough to become a lawyer, make a living, marry a wonderful woman, Matilda—who has always been much more than I deserve—help raise a family, and then find my way, somewhat improbably, into the complicated world of politics.

Throughout my youth I was only *mildly interested* in politics.

The things I came to believe in most deeply I learned from the sweaty example of my immigrant parents' struggle to build a life for themselves and their children; from the nuns at St. Monica's Church in Jamaica, Queens, the priests at St. John's University, the great rabbis like Israel Mowshowitz, whom I met during the Second Vatican Council; and from the enlightened vision and profound wisdom of an extraordinary man, Pierre Teilhard de Chardin—a French paleontologist who participated in the discovery of "Peking man" and who understood evolution, a soldier who knew the inexplicable evil of the battlefield, a scholar who studied the ages, a philosopher, a Catholic theologian, and a teacher.

Teilhard reoriented our theology, rewrote its language, and linked it, inseparably, with science. His wonderful books *The Phenomenon of Man* and *The Divine Milieu*, dedicated to "those who love the world," made negativism a sin. Teilhard glorified the world and everything in it. He taught us to love and respect ourselves as the pinnacle of God's creation to this point in evolution. He taught us how the whole universe—even the pain and imperfection we see—is sacred. He taught us in powerful, cogent, and persuasive prose and in soaring poetry. He envisioned a viable and vibrant human future: "We are all foot soldiers in the struggle to unify the human spirit despite all the disruptions of conflict, war and natural calamities." "Faith," he said, "is not a call to escape the world, but to embrace it." Creation is not an elaborate testing ground with nothing but moral obstacles to surmount, but an invitation to join in the work of *restoration*; a voice urging us to be involved in actively *working to improve the world we were born to—by our individual and collective efforts* making it kinder, safer, and more loving.

If one looks closely, some of the most fundamental of Teilhard's principles were then and are now equally available to me and to you and to *all* rational humans.

They can be ascertained by using evidence that is there for all of us to see and feel with nothing more than the gift of reason, and exposure to the world around us.

Without books or history, without saints or sermons, without instruction or revelation, *two things* about our place in the world should occur to us as human beings.

The first is that the greatest gift we have been given is *our existence, our life*.

The second is that since we all share the same principal needs and desires, our intelligence naturally inclines us to treat one another with respect and dignity.

The Hebrews, who gave us probably the first of our monotheistic religions, made these ideas the foundation of their beliefs. *Tzedakah* is the principle that we should treat one another as brother and sister, children of the same great source of life. And *Tikkun Olam* is the principle that instructs us to join together in repairing the world. Rabbi Hillel pointed out that these two radiantly logical principles together make up the whole law. "All the rest," he said, "is commentary."

Jesus agreed it was also the whole law for Christians. "The whole law is that you should love one another as you love yourself for the love of truth and the truth is, God made the world but did not complete it; you are to be collaborators in creation."

Teilhard confirmed for me the intelligence and efficacy of the words of both Hillel and Jesus.

From all these sources—my struggling immigrant parents and neighbors, the nuns and priests and rabbis, Hillel and Jesus and Teilhard, Our Lady of the Law, with whom I fell profoundly and irretrievably in love, and my own other life experiences—by the mid-seventies I felt I had all the simple, basic values I needed to build a life for myself and my family.

All these values were based ultimately on the two precepts described so elegantly by Teilhard: "a love of life, and a life of love" for oneself and one another. In the home, in the community, and in the world.

And all together, these values seemed right and useful, not only for me and for my family, but for society and *the governments* society creates to rule and guide us all.

I did not think I needed a course in political science to teach me what the role of our government should be. It seemed to me that all we needed from our government, in addition to all the values I've mentioned, was a lot of common sense.

I didn't fret over whether we should be for *big government* or *small government*: It seemed clear to me then—and does now—that Lincoln had it right when he said, "We should have *only* the government we need, but we should insist on *all* the government we need."

And with respect to political ideologies, I believed there should be a place for ideology in political policymaking, but it shouldn't be *first place*. *First place* should go to common sense and benign pragmatism; the policy would have to be good for the community being governed.

It seemed to me clear that government should work to assure us opportunity while insisting we bear individual responsibility for providing all we can for ourselves.

And that government should protect our liberty—our right to live securely and to express ourselves freely so long as we deny no one else the same right. And government should see to it that the productive remain productive and, indeed, grow stronger.

It also seemed apparent that there are two major groups that deserve more of government's efforts than they are receiving. The first consists of those who work for a living because they have to, people not poor enough to be desperate but not rich enough to be worry-free.

The second is those people who are struggling to make it but, for whatever reason, cannot.

For my first two decades as a lawyer, I tried applying these basic principles to the small circle of my family and, beyond that, to the larger community through a series of confrontations with government in court and outside of it on behalf of individuals and small groups who, I believed, had been dealt with wrongly by government. I had some success that brought me some public notice, but with *only* partial satisfaction.

I became convinced that the only way I could help change things significantly was if I became part of the political system and pushed for my values from inside government.

And that's what I did for twenty years as secretary of state, lieutenant governor with Governor Hugh Carey, and governor for twelve years.

In serving, I tried always to remember that all the values I had been taught by my parents, priests, nuns, and Teilhard are not just fodder for lofty theological contemplation: They are practical—even vital—rules that should be part of any political system.

And I did everything I could to make them a vital part of my public service—especially as governor—whether it was creating campaigns to fight AIDS, crack cocaine, and homelessness in 1983; preventing the death penalty from becoming law for twelve years;

creating the Decade of the Child led by the First Lady that produced dozens of ways to protect our children; signing the first seat belt law in the United States that has saved so many lives from serious injury or even death; or creating the 1985 Task Force on Life and the Law that dealt with a determination of death, do-not-resuscitate orders, organ and tissue transplantation, health care proxy, surrogate parenting, abortion. The work of the task force was also cited by the United States Supreme Court in decisions on assisted suicide. Or visiting Europe and Israel, trying to help improve trade with the one and the chances for peace in the other.

I believe with all my *heart* and my *mind* that the principles of *Tzedakah* and *Tikkun Olam* and the teachings so elegantly elaborated by Teilhard remain compelling today. Indeed, the *need* for the strong sense of community they demand is stronger today than it has been in years. We are more fragmented. We have more superwealthy people than ever, but they make up less than 1.5 percent of our population. A majority of Americans are working hard and sliding backward economically because their income is not growing as fast as the costs of health care, education, transportation, housing, and all the other things they need most. More than 10 percent of our people are unemployed. Nearly 40 million Americans go without health care insurance. Only one of four or five of our workers has been able to get educated to the high skills level required by our ever more competitive economy. And struggling to survive are 35 million poor people. Eleven million of them are children at risk of poverty, ignorance, and abuse of all kinds. Many of them in urban areas—like South Jamaica—grow up familiar with the sound of gunfire before they've ever heard an orchestra play.

We have more incarcerated Americans, more handguns per capita, and more executions than *any other industrialized nation*. And all of this while we struggle to find ways to end a war in Afghanistan and Pakistan and find help for the victims of the horrendous earthquake in Haiti. And find a path to peace in the Middle East.

If it were clear that our nation lacked the capacity to improve our current conditions significantly, we could settle for self-pity. But we don't have that luxury.

Only a decade ago this great nation produced 22 million new jobs, regularly balanced budgets, a rising middle class, a shrinking number of poor citizens, and a potential surplus of $5.4 trillion. And we were at peace, except for the short war in Kuwait.

It's clear, therefore, that we *can* do what we *must* do to make ourselves a more "perfect union"—if we *choose* to!

If we do *not,* we risk further dividing our nation into the lucky and the left-out. A nation that is squandering its opportunity to lead our people and the rest of the world to a better life.

As to whether as individuals we should become involved in meeting that challenge, we should keep in mind the words of the brilliant, agnostic Justice Oliver Wendell Holmes, who echoed Teilhard's call for the vigorous involvement of all of us in the management of the world around us but added a warning. He said, "As life is action and passion we are required to share the passion and action of our time at the peril of being judged not to have lived."

So what do I think I have learned in my life that's worth sharing? I have learned the vanity of trying to know and to define fully the infinite and the eternal.

But I have also learned that in the end, even if my intelligence is too limited for me to *know absolutely the truth of things,* I can nevertheless choose to believe—and call it "faith" if I must—if that promises me meaningfulness.

I can respond to the ancient summons of *Tzedakah* and *Tikkun Olam,* knowing my own religion's faith rests solidly on those same two pillars.

And on a more materialistic and practical level, dealing with politics, I can choose to recall the many times our nation has faltered only to rise again stronger than ever.

And recalling that, I can choose to believe that—despite Massachusetts—with our help, President Barack Obama and our government will soon produce a health care bill that improves our situation to some extent, albeit without satisfying everyone.

I can choose to believe that, with our urging, our leaders will help our economy to bounce back as it has from other recessions, and unemployment will be reduced dramatically as it has been before.

I can also reasonably choose to believe that *with our help*, this greatest nation in world history with the world's biggest economy, most powerful military, and unique Rule of Law can deal with its challenges and ultimately take its place as the global leader that helps lead the whole world to a higher level of peace and civility.

It may not be easy to understand Teilhard de Chardin or believe that God and nature commit us to the endless task of seeking improvement of the world around us, knowing that fulfillment is an eternity away. But for me, I'd rather be committed to those propositions than not. I'd rather believe, because it's better than the anguish of fearing futility. And better than the bitterness of despair. And because it brings meaning to our most modest and clumsy efforts.

That's a useful consolation for many of us, including a guy from Queens who has seen a lot of the world and has found more and more "reason to believe."

INTERVIEW WITH GOVERNOR MARIO M. CUOMO RE: THE SUPREME COURT, SENATOR ROBERT BYRD, LARRY KING, ANDREW CUOMO, AND THE BP OIL SPILL

July 2, 2010

WILLIAM O'SHAUGHNESSY (W.O.): Before we all go off to see the rockets' red glare and fireworks on the Fourth of July, let's switch to Willkie, Farr & Gallagher, the prestigious New York law firm, and its most illustrious partner, the fifty-second governor of New York, Mario Matthew Cuomo. Governor Cuomo, there's much we want to seek your wisdom on this Fourth of July weekend. First of all, the people in Washington are wrestling with the question of another Supreme Court justice: Elena Kagan. Will she be a good justice?

GOVERNOR MARIO CUOMO (M.C.): That's a really complicated question, Bill, because you have to define a lot of things. The first is, what is a good justice? What is a good justice supposed to do? And believe it or not, that simple-sounding question is a very difficult one to answer because people have different views of the Constitution. People have different views of the role of the Supreme Court. For me, the Supreme Court is supposed to be—or at least was *intended* to be by the Founding Fathers—totally free of politics. The way the government was established there would be a political branch—meaning the people selected their leaders, with remote authority at least. You pick congresspeople, you pick a president, etc. And you have an expectation that that person will do what you selected them to do. That's the *political* side of our government. But the judicial side, the Supreme Court, has nothing to do—or should have nothing to do—with the politics. Except it's the politicians who grill them and the politicians who nominate them to begin with. The president nominates them and then the Senate has to approve that person. But that should be the end of the influence. You simply make that choice. It's not worked out that way. I believe people have made the Supreme Court more and more political. More and more it acts as though it were a congressional body.

W.O.: Who has made it more political, Governor? The presidents who appoint?

M.C.: The presidents have appointed the members of the Supreme Court from the very beginning, including my favorite president, Abraham Lincoln. The presidents who appointed people invariably have tried to get *their* political view reflected by the person they select.

W.O.: Is that good or bad?

M.C.: It's bad. The most outrageous of the attempts was by Franklin Roosevelt, who wanted people who would be absolutely certain to give him the decisions he wanted to establish a new America—at least economically. OK, so that is the complication. They act like politicians too often. Here's a very good modern example. What happened in the presidential election between Bush and Gore? What happened when the Supreme Court had a virtual tie and if you counted every vote it would have been a win for the Democrat, Al Gore? What happened? The Court decided they wanted not Al Gore, but George W. Bush.

W.O.: You don't think they found on the merits?

M.C.: They describe what they believe to be the merits. But very few people would say there's a question that they selected him *politically*. Incidentally, when asked how he justified the vote, Justice Antonin Scalia responded, "Get over it. Period!" It's too *political* a process. . . .

W.O.: Governor Mario Cuomo, *you* could have been there. You turned the damn thing down. You once glibly said it's a great job, you don't even have to wear underwear!

M.C.: No, I didn't say that! Please, O'Shaughnessy. I said: Look, you don't have to buy any real suit. They give you a gown, in effect. They call it a robe that goes from your neck to your toes. You could come in sneakers and shorts, for God's sake, and be ready to play a basketball game.

W.O.: Do you think Ruth Bader Ginsburg comes in sneakers?

M.C.: No, I don't. I think they are all very discreet. But the point I was trying to make is it can be a very comfortable place if you are suited to it. It's a wonderfully important place. And that's why I make the point about politics. It is very important that it not be utterly political. That the president will do for us. That the Congress will do for us. It was not expected that the Supreme Court would do that for us. The Supreme Court should be a law court.

W.O.: Governor Cuomo, do I hear that you're less than enthusiastic about Elena Kagan, the Solicitor General?

M.C.: No, you don't hear that at all. I don't know what she's going to be like. Neither do you; neither do the senators; neither does the president! You may have expectations that arise from the answers she gives, but nobody knows what she might be like. And in a way, that is a saving feature because the president usually picks somebody whose politics they like. And if the people they selected reflected those politics all the time, consistently, it would mean they were being political. But what's happened is often the person the president selected because of what he thought his or her politics was going to be surprised them. David Souter surprised [George H.W.] Bush. Bush was told that Souter was a conservative Republican, lived up in the woods, and would act like a conservative. And he didn't behave that way at all. Hugo Black was a member of the Ku Klux Klan and it was thought that he was going to bring those politics into the courtroom; but he did nothing like that. He decided on the merits of the case, doing what a judge should do. So very often people who are selected because of their politics by a president disappointed the president and chose to be proper Supreme Court justices. That's what may happen with Kagan.

W.O.: Why did Bill Clinton think Mario Cuomo would be a good Supreme Court justice?

M.C.: I'm not sure what the president thought. You would have to ask the president. I was overly flattered, but I thought they didn't need me for the Supreme Court. They had plenty of good choices, and they found a good choice, Ruth Bader Ginsburg—who, regrettably, just lost her husband. They were both wonderful lawyers. She is a great justice. But she is going to be leaving the Court. She took the spot that President Clinton had been talking about with me. Some people thought that I would run for president in 1992, and I said no to that; and whom did we get as president instead? Bill Clinton! So because of the judgments I made, I participated in giving the country Bill Clinton as a president and Justice Ginsburg as a Supreme Court justice. So I say, *my* two rejections produced much better people than you would have gotten if I had said yes to either of those two positions.

W.O.: Governor, you can sell me damn near anything. But I don't buy that argument. Not for a minute.

M.C.: But at least you have to accept it as *logical*, O'Shaughnessy!

W.O.: Why *did* you shake off the Supreme Court? I never asked you this. You left a lot of Mario Cuomo admirers—thousands of them—disappointed. Why?

M.C.: I didn't think that was the best way I could serve. I spent over twenty years learning about the issues of being secretary of state and then being a lieutenant governor and watching and working with Hugh Carey, who I think was the greatest governor of our modern history. I think he saved the state when he saved the city in 1975, '76, '77. And I learned a whole lot, and I feel very strongly on a lot of issues. *Very* strongly on the role of Supreme Court justices and how they should be conducting themselves. On how we should deal with our people. On how we should deal with government. On how we should deal with foreign policy. I have very strong opinions on all of this.

If you become a Supreme Court justice, you have to swallow all your political positions. You have to stop speaking publicly on all of them. You can never have an argument in public or give a speech on whether or not Israel should behave this way or that way. Or whether or not Iran should behave this way or that way. And what we should do about it. I didn't want to give up all those many things that concern all of us as citizens and concern me in a special way because of being in government for over twenty years. I didn't want to give that up. Otherwise, being a Supreme Court justice would be ideal for a guy like me. I don't like cocktail parties. I hate raising money. I hate doing a lot of the things politicians have to do. It's a wonderful position, and I was honored to be considered, but I wanted to be free to make the case on *other* issues.

The response to that was: "Look, you're probably going to lose in 1994." And I did, by a couple of points, I think. And so the suggestion was made to me more than once: "See, if you had gone on the Supreme Court, you could have been very influential, and now you have no influence at all." And I said, "No, you're making a mistake. Now I'm free to argue. I'm free to go on the radio with Bill O'Shaughnessy and answer his questions and offer what I think is the truth and the wisdom of it. I'm free to do that." I believe the story about the Arab and the sparrow. The Arab was riding on the camel in the desert, looked down and saw the sparrow lying with its claws extended looking toward the heavens. The Arab says, "What are you doing down there in the sand lying on your back?" The sparrow said, "I was told to disguise my fall, and I thought I would do what I can to help hold them up." The Arab laughed and said, "You foolish sparrow. You're only a tiny thing." And the sparrow responded by saying, "One does what one can." And ultimately, Bill, that's the end of your responsibility as a human being. *Doing what you can.* And as long as you do everything you can to make a difference, then you have succeeded. No matter what results you get.

W.O.: Wisdom from Mario Cuomo on this summer day. Governor, you've also been accused of being America's greatest orator. In the Senate, this week, we lost a giant. Perhaps one of the greatest orators ever in that legislative body. Senator Robert Byrd [of West Virginia]. Did you know him? He sure could talk.

M.C.: I had the great pleasure and honor of meeting him, shaking his hand and telling him how good I thought he was as a senator. And he was great. And when you talk about eloquence and you talk about great speakers, like President Obama—and I don't know if there has been any president who has spoken better than Obama—or like Byrd as a senator or a congressman, there are *two* things you can measure them by. Their eloquence. That's their choice of *words*. The use of *images*. Even the sound of their voice and how it affects you. Yes, that's all part of how we come to judge speakers. But the other thing and the more important is what is she saying? What is he saying, and is it *truthful*? And does it move you as being honest? And so the eloquence of manner and selection of words is one thing. But the power of the *message* is the thing that is most important in a great speech. It would be a great speech if it were *wise* and moved you in a significant way—in a correct way—toward the truth.

That's the way you should be judging speakers. Do they move you properly? Do they move you strongly? Do they move you in the right direction? Do you learn something from them? Are you moved by them? I have heard speeches that bring me to tears and make me think again about things that I thought were right or maybe were wrong. That's the mark of a great speech. A lot of people are able to make the *music* without delivering the *message*.

W.O.: Governor Cuomo, speaking of speech-making, a very scholarly journal suggested that the product of your tongue and your good mind—everything that proceeds from you—glistens with the sweat of moral conviction. They said that about you, every time you open your damn mouth. . . .

M.C.: You see, there's a very good example of what I'm talking about. That was nothing but *words*. Those are good words. But I'm not going to give that an "A," I'll tell you that.

W.O.: Sir, I've got to ask you about a friend of yours, a great friend who is stepping down from his perch at CNN: Larry King. I know you're pals. I know you counsel often with him. Did you tell him to give it up?

M.C.: No, he's *not* giving it up! I was on the radio the night after he started [his cutting back] by saying, "My first guest is Mario Cuomo." The next morning, they interviewed me and I said, "He's *not* all through. You didn't listen to the man. He's just beginning." He's going to take 50,000 interviews—that's the number they gave; it's hard to believe. But you've got to learn something from 50,000 interviews of important people. Now that's the knowledge base he has. That's what he's learned. And he's going to have four or five or six big interviews in the days ahead of very important people on very important subjects. And he can do it with an intelligence and an effectiveness that you can have only if you've had 50,000 interviews to practice with.

W.O.: We know you've been on Larry King a lot, but what do you two guys talk about off the camera?

M.C.: That's very interesting, Bill. Larry is a wonderful human being with a great sense of humor. There is a restaurant somewhere down in New York City, and it has a menu that has large amounts of offensive food if you have a bad heart. It's a lot of fat. . . .

W.O.: Could this be a Jewish delicatessen?

M.C.: Well, it's that kind of thing. He has a birthday party, and he invites Matilda and me. It's one of his seventies birthday parties. And we are astonished to learn that it is at this little restaurant that is a wonderful place with a great name. It starts with somebody's first name, just to give you a hint. We thought that's a strange place to go for a birthday party; and at that party was the doctor who operated on his heart. And he was sitting next to me and eating this food, and so was Larry, and I was waiting for bread. I wouldn't touch the stuff. I was scared to death that then and there I would be taken with a stroke. That's how offensive this food appeared to be. I said, "Larry, how can you be eating this stuff?" He said, "Ask the doctor!"

W.O.: Governor, do you ever give him marriage counseling? You failed if you did. Has he ever asked your advice on affairs of the heart?

M.C.: No, it's too bad that I wasn't in the position to counsel his wives! I had no responsibility for those numerous unions.

W.O.: Governor Cuomo, let me beg just a few seconds on a subject you seem somewhat reluctant to discuss. Everybody is talking about *another* Governor Cuomo. And when we spoke about Robert Byrd, you talked about speeches that bring you to tears. I watched you when Andrew Mark Cuomo gave his acceptance speech at the Democratic State Convention here in Westchester. First of all, only a Cuomo would ad-lib such an important speech. Were you tearing up a little as you watched him?

M.C.: No, I don't think so. Was I *moved* by his speech? Yes. Was his mother moved by his speech? Yes. That's to be expected. But what's more important is that everybody in the place was moved by his speech. And moved in an intelligent way, and what they were saying in effect is that we agree with what you propose to do. We're supportive of what you propose to do. And that was a wonderful way to start a campaign.

People ask if you're proud of your son for becoming a candidate for the governorship. We answer it usually this way—and here I can speak for Matilda. You can say you're proud. But what we really feel is that we know how gifted he has been from the beginning. God just elected to make him strong physically. He is very strong physically, and he has manifested that in many way. And intelligently. He has a wonderful mind. But these are *gifts*. These are strengths, yes. But they're *gifts*. And what you have to say is "Thank you, Lord, for the *gift*." What you can say about Andrew is "Thank you, Andrew, for the way you are choosing to *use* them. We are proud of you. You could have gone and made a whole lot of money in the private world. We know that. With your intelligence, strength, and experience, having worked with President Clinton, you could go and raise a whole lot of money, and you and your family could live comfortably ever after. Instead, you've chosen to try to get to be governor at a time that will present the next governor with maybe the hardest challenge in the modern history of our state because the budget is in such horrible condition. The problems are so large. The need for reform is so great. And you've undertaken to say, 'I will accept the *responsibility* of trying to make a change. A big change.' That's a gutsy call. And that's one we're proud of . . .".

W.O.: Governor, when you were shooting hoops *togethe*r with Andrew as a youngster, and even when you roomed together when you were lieutenant governor up in Albany at the Hotel DeWitt, did you ever look over at him at the breakfast table and think, "You know, this kid could become governor"?

M.C.: Not specifically. But if the question had been raised, I would have said, Yes, he could. Once I was taking the family all to Far Rockaway, the beach; he was sitting next to me, and we were talking about automobiles. I'd seen Andrew with his sets of toys we'd given him: these parts to automobiles made in plastic. They give you pages and pages of plans and instructions, but he would put them together without the instructions. He would "feel" it; he had a wonderful ability to create things with his hands. He was a great carpenter as a kid. He still is. He works on automobile engines now, just to relax. He has these old cars in his garage, and when he's really looking to get away from the problems of the moment and to think about nothing else, he dives under the hood of his vehicle and starts polishing and switching. And during that drive to Far Rockaway, I said to his mother, he would make a great engineer; he has an engineer's mind. And I see that engineer's mind now in his work as a lawyer and in his work with President Clinton, doing housing and the other things he did on the federal level as a member of the president's cabinet. He's very, very logical. He has a wonderful, wonderful mind. And a capacity to see things clearly that other people don't see at all.

And so yes, it's a *gift*. This is not something you can praise him for. It's something the *use* of which you can praise him for. And so yes, did I think he would be a good lawyer? Of course. But he could have been a good engineer. He could have been a lot of good things. And he can certainly be a good—maybe even a *great*—governor of this state. I think he has that *capacity*.

W.O.: But has he got the "vision" thing?

M.C.: He has the vision, Bill. He has the *experience*. He has the *heart*. And he has the *mind*. And he has a *family* that will do everything to help him.

W.O.: He had a line in his acceptance speech: that in one section of the city, first-graders are on the Internet; while in *other* sections—the poor sections—they don't even have a *basketball* net. That had echoes of *another* Governor Cuomo. And he spoke about the "Family of New York." Does that sound familiar?

M.C.: Look, the idea of family is fundamental. Just think about it. People argue now about big government and little government and what kind of government you should have. Well, then the first question that should be asked is What is government? What do you *mean* by government? Abraham Lincoln took care of that for us. Government is the coming together of people to do for one another collectively what they couldn't do as well at all privately.

OK. So government is people coming together to get done something they need to have done for their own welfare that they can't get done alone. Just multiply that, and government is people getting together in large numbers to create a society where, if you can't get things done through the market system or philanthropy—and we tried to give everybody health care through philanthropy and the private sector for 176 years, and we found out that people were dying because they were sick and poor—you have to come up with Medicaid and Medicare. The whole thing starts from the idea of family. Andrew has had that *instinct* from the very beginning. With his siblings, his wonderful brother, Christopher, and his three beautiful and bright daughters. And with Matilda. There's no match for Matilda. That family meant something to Andrew.

W.O.: He was raised at your knee. He gets a lot of this from you, doesn't he?

M.C.: But the whole idea of family, Bill—that's the way he was with the people in the neighborhood. We have to *help* one another. We have to *work* with one another. What he knew as a rugby player you need in order to be a great political leader: You have to learn how to bring people together for their own good and to get things done through the government that you couldn't get done privately.

If you could get it done privately—well, that's wonderful. Make government the last resort. But in the end, did the private sector get us to the moon? Why didn't all those companies that make ships and make airplanes do it on their own? Well, because they couldn't make enough money at it. So, the government had to do it. And we spent $19–20 billion a year on space. Andrew understands that. Andrew *understands* that what the government should do is the things that cannot get done well without the government. And so that's the answer to big government and little government. All the government you need, but *only* the government you need.

W.O.: Governor, you talk about big government and private enterprise. Who the hell can fix that oil spill? Obama is getting belted around about it.

M.C.: Why? Why are they belting him around? Did he make the mistake? Or did BP make the mistake?

W.O.: Aren't there stories that other countries have offered to send help but the bureaucracy says "No, you can't come and help us"?

M.C.: That's politics. It's a joke. He did what can be done. He's doing everything that he can do. If anybody can come up with a better idea, would he say no to it? Of course not. He's doing everything that can be done. He's done some things that most people thought couldn't be done. He went into a meeting with BP and he said, "Look, I want money. And I want money put aside. I want it put aside notwithstanding. There's nothing in a law book that says you should be forced to do it as a matter of law. I don't care. I want you to put $20 billion aside because I'm telling you that you have that obligation. And I'm telling you I'll be *very* unhappy if you don't do it." And so they did it. Now that was something not even the law could have enforced. And he got it done. And so the notion that he's not doing the right thing is an absurdity. Pure politics, superficial *politics*. And to me, not impressive politics.

W.O.: Governor Mario Cuomo, thank you for the gift of your wisdom on this summer day. Maybe you make me glad you didn't go on the Supreme Court and thus would not be able to talk about these issues with us. You've given me one unsettling bit of news though: that Andrew was a *rugby* player as a youngster. Is that a sport that young Italian guys from Queens take up? Rugby?

M.C.: I don't even know how you say "rugby" in Italian, O'Shaughnessy!

W.O.: Wonderful stuff. Thank you, sir.

SIR LAURENCE OLIVIER

Sir Laurence Olivier was, in every telling, one of the world's greatest actors. During a long, illustrious career, Lord Olivier received hundreds of awards, tributes, and encomiums for his brilliant work in the theater and cinema.

During one such occasion some twenty-five years ago, the great Olivier accepted an award with much grace and style.

In the multiplicity of your nation's goodnesses, this demonstration of it must make it seem that at times such prodigality must surely be in danger of overlapping itself. But never, it seems, does it fall or falter.

This new star in its firmament must outshine the suns of all men's days and render the one thus shone upon quite dumb, jaw-droppedly mute in the face of its blaze.

My heart is indeed so full as to be in danger of overflowing and causing my desperate struggle for expression to drown itself in dismal helplessness and drown you in most painful embarrassment.

I can only say thank you for the amplitude of your kindness to one who is a foreigner, though not perhaps a stranger; for the glowing generosity that prompts you to give to me the totally undeserved but nonetheless wondrous glory of such an occasion.

30: WHEN ALL IS SAID AND DONE

FOR MICHAEL

This one was personal, very personal. Michael was twenty-two.

First of all, thank you for coming.

Many of you have canceled plans; some have cut short vacations; and others have completely rearranged your schedules on this winter weekend. And we appreciate it.

You've come to comfort Nancy. And because you loved Michael. And he is glad you came.

I want to also thank two great priests of our Roman Catholic Church: the beloved pastor of St. Pius, who meant so much in Papa's life and who was the first to call Mr. Curry "Lazarus" after that remarkable comeback three years ago. Father John O'Brien's intercessions and prayers helped then, as they do now on this sad Saturday morning. We should thank also another great priest, Father Joseph Cavoto. He's a family friend—and a longtime friend of Michael's. He's also a Franciscan. So to call him "great" is redundant.

I'll be mercifully brief. I've done this for all kinds of people—relatives, acquaintances, friends of the station, politicians, in-laws, even some out-laws. I've also spoken for my brother, my mother, my father.

But never for a son.

We gather here today because we need to. We cannot bear so great a grief without sharing it.

We are comforted by embraces and tears and sighs, because our minds are not deep enough, nor our tongues clever enough, to explain the tragedy of Michael's painful passage.

And so we struggle to reconcile that grief. At least enough to avoid plunging into anger or collapsing in despair.

I don't have to tell you what Michael was like. You know what he was like: charming, bright, talented, loving.

So I thought I might just tell you what he liked during his brief life, some of his "enthusiasms." And so I got up at four o'clock to jot down just a few of the things Michael fancied.

He liked yogurt, with crunchy granola on top.

He liked Starbucks.

He liked electronic devices and gadgets of all kinds.

He liked the latest sneakers and those awful wide-legged pants.

He liked to look "sharp." And he liked the mirror. I wonder where he got that from!

He liked boom boxes with loud speakers, and his cars with hubcaps and wheel rims, and those little jet-propelled scooters that disturbed the tranquility of the neighborhood but got him where he wanted to go.

He liked pepperoni pizzas and takeouts from Deanna's and Italian combo wedges with red hot pepper flakes, onions, the works. And extra oil!

He loved steaks and chicken scarpiello.

He loved Wendy's. And he loved making his mother drive him an extra twenty miles clear across the county to get there!

He loved filet mignons with Béarnaise sauce at "21" and at Mr. Maccioni's. Michael would eat all this, and we would put on the weight!

He was very proud of the new apartment his mother and Emilie O'Sullivan found for him.

He loved sailing his little Optimist sailboat on the Sound with Taylor Boynton on the tiller and Michael at the helm.

And we loved it when he won prizes for sailing—and for swimming—at the American Yacht Club! "Looks like your kid is taking home all the silver!" said one envious Rye WASP parent as Michael gathered up all the trophies one summer evening at an awards banquet.

Mike liked to ride his horses, Bucky and Whitney, up in Waverly in the fall.

And he loved to shoot trap or skeet with his Grandpa on crisp mornings at the Gun Club in Sun Valley.

He loved to ride his lawn tractor and that four-wheeled ATV up at Lordstown, and he loved to go blasting around Lyford Cay in his souped-up golf cart. And that Bahamian woman in the golf shop who was so taken with Mike's smile and manners knew the one he fancied and always saved it for him, the one that went all day without a charge.

He liked piggy-back rides from the top step of that Japanese restaurant in Mamaroneck.

And he liked to pummel Bill during those wrestling matches on the floor of the foyer after dinner at Lord Kitchener.

He loved to sit on Mama's lap—his grandmother's—and pose with Santa during all those Christmas Eves at 50 Inverness.

And he liked to impress Uncle Bernie and Cappy and Mike Miele and Don Foldes and Rob Conte with his knowledge of cars and computers.

He loved to sit in a radio studio as a freshman in high school and read into the mike better than our college interns. He was so good that Don Stevens and Cindy Gallagher put him in charge of all the college guys, while he was still in high school.

He loved dinner alone with his Grandpa at Winged Foot. I wonder what they talked about?

Speaking of which: He liked girls. Did he ever like girls!

He loved playing with babies, infants, and toddlers, his cousins: Andrea and Jack and Bo and Jessie and Ryan and Alex and Katie.

He was a gentle kid. Not mean. Never violent. I never saw him take a swing at anyone.

But make no mistake: He was a guy who could argue and articulate, and advocate and confound, and persuade. Forever!

One of the most famous stories has become legend:

I came home from the station one night to notice three fire trucks in front of the house. Just an ordinary night around our place! Nothing unusual at all.

Apparently, Mike had been sitting in the den watching TV when he noticed smoke billowing up from the basement. So he called 911 to alert the fire department. Shortly after all the fire engines had departed, his mother noticed he was still in a wet bathing suit, sitting in the den.

"Go upstairs and put on some dry underwear, Mike, and start your homework."

"Mom, can't I just watch this show?"

When Nancy had denied his petition and pleading for the third time and told him to "get moving," the ever resourceful Mike—I think he was eight!—uttered this exquisite objection: "Mom, a house! I save! And you won't even go up and get my underwear!"

Maria Cuomo Cole called and said that Nancy was her role model as a mother, as a parent—the other one, of course, being the magnificent Matilda—because as Maria put it, "You are so consistently, insistently, relentlessly loving." Nancy, a great mother. And he knew it. And we all have witnessed her remarkable devotion.

He had so many talents. He was a gifted artist. I'm absolutely persuaded he had the hands and eye of a great architect.

He was a genius at computers though far from a nerd or cybergeek.

He loved to rewire the house in very "creative" ways. He was always fooling with the clickers for the TV.

One day we were dressing for some black-tie occasion. Nancy flipped on the television, and her make-up mirror went on! And it started playing music!

Mike was always somewhat "ahead of the curve." He downloaded music even before it became illegal. And after it became illegal!

The kid loved jokes. Especially if they were at my expense!

It's been recalled what a great athlete he was, on a pair of skis, on a snowboard. And he could throw a baseball. He took the mound for the New Rochelle Youth Baseball League with those awkward Curry hips and stared in at the catcher's mitt with that laser-like focus. He once told his coach he could actually read the writing on the catcher's mitt from ninety feet away! When he got up to bat, he always got on base. And those home runs would sail over the fence into the brook at the Pinebrook Little League field. And we all remember when he was named the Most Valuable Player by the manager, John McDonnell, with Wellington Mara, the owner of the Giants, cheering on the sidelines.

He was a beautiful kid. I remember one rich old dame took a look at him and said, "He looks like a young Tyrone Power in his Speedo bathing suit!"

So we were very proud. He really did have some fun in this life. And he gave us all some wonderful moments. And some great, indelible memories.

Father O'Brien put it all in perspective for us much better than I am able.

But Nancy and I have had two long, sad days and nights to think about all this. And it occurs to me only that Michael is now in a place where no illness or disease can touch him; no clocks can confine him; no doubt or uncertainty can limit or diminish or constrain him.

Michael is, even now, already embraced by all those things we cannot even begin to imagine; the ancient wisdom and teaching of our church, and our preaching, too, assure us they are reserved and waiting, especially for those who have suffered in this life, this "vale of tears," as they call it.

But Mike is not only with God, the Father. He's also with someone else we miss terribly. Say hello to Papa, Mike. He's OK now, Nancy. He's more than OK. Now and forever.

St. Pius X Church
Scarsdale, N.Y.
January 29, 2005

REMARKS OF FATHER JOHN O'BRIEN FOR MICHAEL PASQUALE

This compassionate and uplifting homily was delivered by a great priest on that same sad morning.

Nancy, I can't tell you the depth of feeling I have within myself, and I can only imagine the depth of feeling that's present in *you* and each one of us who has gathered together on this occasion of Michael's entrance into heaven. An occasion you never, ever dreamt you would be present at. You thought, for sure, that perhaps *you* would be on the other side, welcoming *him* to the shores of heaven.

Just a little over two months ago, we gathered together here, in the morning, and we prayed for your *father*, age eighty-four, who had gone to heaven, to his eternal reward. And I remember the first reading was from Ecclesiastes and was a reading that reaches into our hearts, and gives us a sense of comfort and consolation, because we *do* know within our own hearts that there is a cycle of life, and it is that cycle that has to run its course. And when running its course, we can expect death and resurrection into the eternal presence of God, who joined each and every one of us when He gave us the gift of life.

But today things are *out* of the natural order. This *isn't* the way it's supposed to happen; this isn't the way we *see* the gift of life. And so we have to ask ourselves: *What* in God's name is happening? I *can't* say to you this is the will of God, because it *isn't*. It's *out* of the natural order.

Just before Christmas I spoke to the people of the parish. I spoke about a woman who had had a stillbirth, and she shared in *America* magazine, in a very beautiful article, the depth of feelings and pain and anguish she went through at that moment. And with the anger—she was angry at God—there was a sense of loneliness and desertion, and wondering: Has God deserted me altogether? And she said, people meaning well say some of the most unbelievable things at that time, things that didn't *touch* what she was feeling at all.

She said the ones she began to appreciate were the people who approached her and were very honest and straightforward. And *they* said: We don't *understand* this; it's not *fair*; it's not *just*. And she said she began to appreciate *that* sense of expression more than pious platitudes.

One of the very first things, when you study philosophy, you are taught—and it's a very important principle that enters into so much of the way we live out our lives—the recognition that a *thing is received according to the disposition of the receiver*.

And Michael received a gift, a gift of life. And at the very youth and beginning of his life, you could rejoice so fully in that gift of life because you knew as you held that little innocent child in your arms, filled with the love that God filled you with in carrying that child and having that child. You see hope and the *potential*. And then as they begin to grow a little—in little, subtle ways—you begin to see the gift of life given to Michael was not *your* gift; it was *his* gift.

And as he grows in his environment—as he lives, not just within family, which is surrounded with love, but lives in a world that has many temptations—a *thing is received according to the disposition of the receiver*.

And most of us can acknowledge that the gift of life that we received—all of us—we don't have the deep sense of appreciation that we should have for that gift, and there are times when we violate that gift. There are times when that gift seems to be altered and changed because of illness, perhaps, because of an *attitude*, because of a *disposition* that's within us; and I would venture to say that Michael had a *sickness*, and he had a sickness that he was struggling to learn to live with.

There isn't a parent present who can't tell you that their children don't struggle, and they do crazy things at times because they do not know the consequences. And sometimes *we* do things and we wonder how responsible *we* are. But remember: A thing is received according to the *disposition* of the *receiver*, and we're not always in control of our dispositions, are we?

That is, we're growing, and maturing, and developing; and that's what the grace of God is all about. And sometimes we cry out in such anguish that only the power of God can intercede and heal us in mind and in body and in spirit.

We have just completed the celebration of Christmas. And when I was growing up—and I think it's still very much true today—Christmas was *Christmas*, Easter was *Easter*. And the two were *separate*, different feasts altogether. Christmas was a time for—some say presents—but it was a time of *gifts*; it was a time when God, who created each and every one of us, gave us the gift of life, gave His very Self and shared His very Self with each and every one of us. We say: This is wonderful, the love that God has for each and every one of us. And then we put Christmas away, and we come to the celebration of Easter and to the events that precede the celebration of Easter. And we begin to see the suffering and the pain.

The movie *The Passion of the Christ* reminds me of you, Nancy, very much today, as I reflect on the beautiful message it contained of the Blessed Virgin Mary, who held that little child at the manger; and on the road to Calvary, watching her son suffer and in pain, she was powerless, *absolutely* powerless. But she did it with the spirit of faith.

Our lives teach us that *courage* is the opposite of *fear*. But it's not. *Faith* is the opposite of fear, because faith recognizes that no matter *what* happens, everything will be fine. Having that faith is something that doesn't come automatically into our lives. It comes by experience. It comes by the grace of God, and it comes by our own submission to the will of God in our own lives.

When will you get that faith you need, in order to carry you through today and the many, many days of loneliness and pain that you will continue to feel for a long time? Some people say: When you lose your child, you never, *ever* get over it. And in a sense, I understand, that is true.

I remember a few years ago, I had a nephew who was "acting up," and my sister was in a lot of pain and agony trying to decide how she was going to deal with this boy. And I said to her—I never had a family, but I said, "You have to give a little *tough love* here, you have to be *severe*." And she said to me—and I now know how true it is—"Johnny, you *don't* understand." She said she waited eight years in her marriage, wanting every year, every day of her life, to have a child, and she didn't have any. And at the end of eight years, she received a child. And she said, "I carried that child; and on the day that child was born, and the doctors bring that child to you, *something* happens to you—it's a *mystery*—and the power of God's love comes over you." And she said, "I couldn't bring myself to violate that gift, to do anything that could possibly injure the love I have in my heart."

And so, you do what most of us do: You do everything we *know*; we continue to love in a situation like that. We *continue* to love, and love, and to allow the person to *receive the gift according to the disposition that is within them*.

Not true of just a mother either; it's true of a father. I heard Sidney Poitier, one day, mention that he had six girls. One of the interviewers said to him, "Don't you wish you had one *boy*?" He went into a description very much like my sister's and said, "When the doctors hand that little child to you, and you understand what a miracle it is that this gift of life has been given to this child, you know not how, but it is your *gift*, and it is *their* gift, and it is eternal. How could you possibly care about *gender*?"

That gift has been given to you. You nurtured it, and you did your very best with it. You're filled with sorrow now, but faith tells us all is well because His name is Emmanuel: "I am with you always . . . even to the end of the world." It was His name at the beginning, and it is His name at the end. And God is with you today and always, just as He is with that beautiful son of yours, who had fulfilled his life and accomplished what God wanted him to accomplish. He was innocent, trusting, and good. He never hurt a fly, except himself.

So, I come to do the will of my Father. And this is the will of my Father, that I should lose *nothing*, whether it was stillborn, two years of age, twenty-two years of age, or eighty-four years of age.

This is what we celebrate, daringly, in the sacrifice of the Mass. And this is what we pray, and we will persevere in the hope that we will never lose sight of.

God give you all the strength, which I know He will, that you need to receive the loving support of your family and friends, who share the pain today. God bless you, Nancy.

St. Pius X Church
Scarsdale, N.Y.
January 29, 2005

LARGER THAN LIFE: DEPARTED SOULS WHO SPEAK TO US STILL

I escaped from the microphone for a few days last week to stroll along a deserted winter beach with a pretty girl who lost her father last month.

Bernard F. Curry Jr.—Nancy called him "Papa"—was an extraordinary man, personally, professionally, and physically.

At six feet four inches, he was larger than life.

The great Mario Cuomo sized up the man and nicknamed him "Paul Bunyan." Papa, who was always a little more politically "conservative" than his loved ones, returned the favor by calling Mr. Cuomo "Robin Hood"!

As a broadcaster, I encounter many other vivid souls who left us too soon. Some were colleagues at WNEW, WVIP, WVOX, and WRTN. Others I observed from a distance for brief, fleeting moments.

These luminous individuals painted color into our drab existence and belonged to a unique fraternity who fought convention as they pursued their own salvation. Each was *sui generis*, so unique they could be defined only in their own terms. Although they have passed on to a better world, their dazzling turn on this planet lingers in my mind.

Some left us many years ago. My own father passed away in 1974. But they have not irrevocably departed. They instruct and inspire us still from the archives of our minds, often without notoriety or fame.

Although I have listed them below in alphabetical order, this unique roster of disparate, endearing characters is based on my own fading memory without assistance from Lexis-Nexis, Google, or other Internet search engines.

Dying is a solo act. You have to do it all by yourself. But these marvelous characters belong to a rich breed who played and danced to a bold, beguiling music.

And their light still shines:

Val Adams, Spiro Agnew, John Aiello, Ken Ake, Andy Albanese, Ethel Albertson, J. Lester Albertson, Henry Alexander, Mel Allen,

Garner Ted Armstrong, Louis Armstrong, Les Arries, Fred Astaire, Msgr. Terry Attridge, Angelo Badolato, Al Balletto, Edward Larabee Barnes, Andre Baruch, Mort Bassett, William "Count" Basie, Jack Beaton, Frank Becerra, Rocco Bellantoni Jr., Max Berking, Dick Berkoff, Hilda and Bill Berkowitz, Glenn Birnbaum, Sam Bingham, John Bodnar, Gen. Omar Bradley, Paul Braun, Rosemary Breslin, George Burchell, Marty Burke, John Burns, Gordon Burrows, William Butcher, Elizabeth "Miss" Cadoo, Bob Cammann, Jimmy Cannon, Joe Canzeri, Nino Cardinale, John Chafee, John Chancellor, Sir Harold Christie, Stanley W. Church, Rosemary Clooney, Ellen Cody, Roy Cohn, Nat "King" Cole, Cy Coleman, Bill Condon, Frank Connelly Sr., Bob Considine, Terence Cardinal Cooke, Burt Cooper, Howard Cosell, Noel Coward, Pat Cunningham, Immaculata Cuomo, Bernard F. Curry Jr., Shirley Dames, Fred Danzig, Jerry Danzig, Joan Daronco, Judge Richard Daronco, Chuck Davey, Henry de Kwiatkowski, C. Glover Delaney, Matt Dennis, Joseph Paul DiMaggio, Charles F. X. Dolan, S.J., Edwin B. Dooley, John E. Dowling, Hughie Doyle, George Duncan, Perry Duryea, Jean T. Ensign, Mary Ensign, Howard Epstein, Joe Evans, Jinx Falkenberg, Keith Fallon, Bill Fanning, James A. Farley, Jim Farley Jr., Bob Faselt, Mario Faustini, Boris Feinman, Jim Feron, William Fitzgibbon, Bob Fitzsimmons, John "Chippy" Flynn, John Fosina, Mims Fredman, Joe Gagliardi, Lee Gagliardi, James William Gaynor, Arthur Geoghegan, Commodore Bill Gibbons, Anthony B. Gioffre, Charles Goodell, Jack Gould, Milton Gould, Bob Granger, Buddy Hackett, Arthur Hailey, Gabby Hayes, Phil Hollis, John Holmes, Townsend "Tim" Hoopes, Ed Hughes, Jacob K. Javits, Bill Jeffries, Jack Joyce, Helen Kasper, Nancy Q. Keefe, Jane Hoey Kelly, Shipwreck Kelly, Murray Kempton, Bobby Kennedy, Jack Kennedy, Stan Kenton, Katherine Kerrigan, Claude Kirschner, Sam Klein, Fred Klestine, Bill Klinger, Bob Klose, Paul Kovi, Rainer Kraus, Pete Kriendler, Bill Kunstler, Bunny Lasker, William Van Duzer Lawrence, Tom Leahy, Rita LeDuc, Louis Lefkowitz, Fr. Peter LeVierge, Arthur Levitt, John V. Lindsay, Mary Lindsay, Jimmy Lodato, John Loeb, William Luddy, Peter Maas, Gen. Douglas MacArthur, Gavin K. MacBain, John Malone, Squeegie Mangialardo, Ralph Martinelli, Jack Masla, Mary Margaret McBride, Charles F. McCarthy, Bob McCooey, Suzannah

McCorkle, Frank McCullough, Theresa McDermott, Mamie McDonough, J. Raymond McGovern, Br. Joe McKenna, Sandy McKown, Mabel Mercer, Ben Mermelstein, Robert Merrill, Edwin Gilbert Michaelian, Mario Migliucci, Stanley Miller, Alfred Moccia, Archie Moore, Garry Moore, Harry Moore, Walter Moore, Hugh Morrow, Kermit Moss, Arthur H. "Red" Motley, Daniel Patrick Moynihan, William Hughes Mulligan, Jerry Nachman, Eve Nelson, Bud Neuwirth, Richard M. Nixon, Alex Norton, Gus Ober, Jack O'Brian, John Cardinal O'Connor, Harry O'Donnell, Paul O'Dwyer, Paddy O'Neil, Francis X. O'Rourke, Catherine Tucker O'Shaughnessy, Jack O'Shaughnessy, William Mac O'Shaughnessy, Babe Paley, William S. Paley, Gene Paluzzi, Tom Paris, James O. Parsons, Varner Paulsen, Bob Peebles, Augie Petrillo, George Plimpton, Ed Radbill, Tony Randall, John Randazzo, Cary Reich, Carol Fernicola Reilly, Victor Ridder, Volney "Turkey" Righter, Jackie Robinson, Sugar Ray Robinson, Nelson A. Rockefeller, William Pierce Rogers, Kyle Rote, William A. "Billy" Rowe, Br. Darby Ruane, Ken Ryland, Howard Samuels, Lou Sandroni, Ruby Saunders, Irving Schneider, David Schoenbrun, Bill Scott, Paul Screvane, Hugh Shannon, Joe Shannon, Toots Shor, Frank Sinatra, I. Philip Sipser, Walter "Red" Smith, Warren Spahn, Jeff Sprung, Dennis Stein, Gary Stevens, Adlai Stevenson, Martin Stone, Ellen Sulzberger Straus, Al Sulla, Edward O. "Ned" Sullivan, Joan Dillon Sullivan, John Van Buren Sullivan, Sylvia Syms, Sol Taishoff, Larry Taishoff, E. P. Taylor, Harry Thayer, Jack Thayer, Walter Nelson Thayer, Mel Tormé, Neal Travis, Marietta Tree, Dom Unsino, Joe Vacarella, Jerry Valenti, Bill Voute, Bea Wain, Paula Walsh, Will Weaver, Walter Weiss, Ann Whitman, Jock Whitney, Chuck Wielgus, Alec Wilder, George Williams, William B. Williams, Katherine Wilson, Malcolm Wilson, "Admiral" Frank Young.

I will let the priests and rabbis talk about an afterlife. Their sureness eludes a sinner like me. So if you want a little more firepower on the matter, go and bother some guy with a Roman collar for inside information. I celebrate and remember instead the unique sound of these great souls I encountered; some evoked a sweet, mellow spirit, while others were accompanied by loud, raucous night music.

But I liked them all. And loved many of them. Even now.

And I'm absolutely persuaded they're here with us still. The vivid ones last. They go nowhere. It's called "staying power."

December 2004

MR. MARA OF THE NEW YORK GIANTS

Wellington Mara, the patriarch of the New York Giants, was a legend in the sporting world and in the game of Life. Mr. Mara and I maintained a lively correspondence over the years, and he appeared on my cable television and radio shows.

One of my proudest moments occurred when this dear man called me "Coach." It was an appellation I cherish to this day. I've included my own thoughts on his passing, which prompted a lovely note from George Steinbrenner, who wrote, "The world of sport will never see his like again. . . ." Also here preserved is John Mara's beautiful tribute to his father, delivered to a packed St. Patrick's Cathedral.

He went out a winner.

On Sunday, the New York Giants came from behind in the final minutes to beat the Denver Broncos 24–23. And at his home at 67 Park Drive South in Rye, the eighty-nine-year-old Wellington Mara watched the game through a haze of painkillers and medication. The elderly man with the cherubic smile and dancing eyes was in the final hours of an extraordinary life. He was comforted by those who loved him the most, but dying is something you have to do all by yourself.

After he left us early Tuesday morning, October 25, Mr. Mara's passing was covered on the front page of the *New York Times*, whose editors knew the man transcended the raucous, and often brutal, game of football. The life of Wellington Mara was more than just a sports story.

The pages where they celebrated his gentle genius bombard us daily with schedules, scores, and statistics. But the patriarch of the New York Giants was about more than touchdowns, win–loss records, championship rings, or even the Football Hall of Fame in Canton, Ohio, where Mr. Mara is permanently enshrined.

He was the son of a bookmaker when that calling was right, honorable, and legal. And he became an icon of his sport, a pillar of the Roman Church, and a stalwart of the pro-life movement. If Mr. Mara despised anything during his eighty-nine years, it was the taking of vulnerable, innocent, defenseless life, because he believed, with absolute certainty, that it possessed divine potential. And Mr. Mara cared about this cause more than the exploits of his football team.

He was always courteous to doormen, limo drivers and cabbies, waiters, delivery boys, parking-lot attendants, store clerks, and crossing guards, and he always smiled at the caddie at Winged Foot. No one ever had a bad or nasty thing to say about this ontologist, a lover of life.

Possessed of great intelligence, as well as humility and gentleness, he would engage in robust philosophical discussions with Mario Cuomo and other prominent leaders on the great theological and ecclesiastical issues of the day. But he always stayed civil and kept an open mind.

The patriarch of the Giants was the last surviving scion of great football families and legends such as George Halas, Art Rooney, Leon Hess, Sonny Werblin, George Allen, Paul Brown, and Vince Lombardi. Today, few gentlemen remain to preside over this game of choreographed physical battle, with its players operating on the frontier of rage.

Mr. Mara went to all the high school and Catholic Church rubber-chicken dinners, along with the Plunketts, the Smiths, the Gills, the Currans, the Joyces, the Conways, the Egans, the McCooeys, and the Mastronardis. He attended almost every NFL owners' meeting and was generally the last to speak. But Art Modell and Commissioner Paul Tagliabue will tell you his shy, gentle wisdom invariably carried the day.

Mr. Mara hung around Westchester during the football season and visited Winged Foot Saturday nights with his dazzling, luminous wife, Ann. And you would see him at a corner table at Emilio's in Harrison with his daughter, Susan, and her handsome husband, John McDonnell, and, every morning, on his knees at Resurrection Church in Rye.

Mr. Mara made his living in the stadiums and amphitheaters of a ruthless professional sport built on big money. But his neighbors here in Westchester would encounter him on soft, sunlit afternoons in the springtime, as he discreetly perched on one of those tri-corner leather stools at the Pinebrook Little League field, watching his grandson Timmy McDonnell play shortstop. And when north-end parents from New Rochelle would spy the man in an Irish tweed bucket hat, they would inquire, "Aren't you Wellington Mara, the owner of the Giants?!" And the gentle patrician from Rye would tip his hat and say, "Today, I'm only a grandfather!"

The summer was one of his favorite seasons, when he could bunk with his grandson Timmy at the Giants' training camp, near the headwaters of the Hudson.

Mr. Mara wasn't a suave man who moved in a dazzle of haberdashery. But he could make a grand entrance at "21" and at Sirio Maccioni's Le Cirque with the glamorous grandmother of his forty grandkids. And their charisma and presence were very real, drawing from a great reservoir of goodness without haughty glitz, phoniness, or hype.

Edward Cardinal Egan will pray for the soul of Wellington Mara at St. Patrick's Cathedral on Friday morning in a ceremony worthy of the great city. And as he takes the pulpit, the articulate archbishop with the big, booming, resonant voice will proclaim Mr. Mara went out a winner in the game of Life, regardless of the numbers on the scoreboard.

October 26, 2005

"AN IRISHMAN NAMED WELLINGTON WHOSE FATHER WAS A BOOKMAKER": EULOGY TO HIS FATHER BY JOHN MARA AT ST. PATRICK'S CATHEDRAL

On behalf of my mother and our family, I want to thank everyone here to celebrate my father's life. Many of you came from far away, and we are very appreciative. The outpouring of love and affection for my father has been overwhelming.

Also, special thanks to Edward Cardinal Egan for his comforting words; Bishop McCormick, who brought him communion; and Frank Gifford, who has been a true friend to my family for so many years.

Thank you also to those at Sloan-Kettering who took such good care of my father the last six weeks. They treated him as if he were their own father. When he finally decided he wanted to go home and checked out of the hospital, the nurses and staff were all in tears. That is how close a bond they forged.

There is one caregiver who deserves special mention: Ronnie Barnes, whom my mother refers to as her twelfth child. Ronnie spent many days and nights in my father's hospital room. "Is Ronnie coming tonight?" my father would ask. Of course, the answer was almost always, "Yes," and my father's face would light up in response.

We joked with Ronnie about his motivation, accusing him of avoiding the nurses who kept trying to slip him their phone numbers. My father asked him one night, "Ronnie, why are you so good to me?" "Because, Mr. Mara, you've been so good to me," Ronnie replied.

As we made our way over here to St. Patrick's this morning, I thought my father would have been so embarrassed by all this, the police escort, the traffic stopped, the bagpipes; he would have just shaken his head and tried to hide somewhere.

As painful as it is to say goodbye to someone you love so much, to someone who has been such an integral part of your life, I realize my family was fortunate. Wellington Mara was the finest man we ever knew. And he was our Dad.

Many years ago, his good friend Tim Rooney said, "You realize, don't you, that your father is the best example of how we should all live our lives. You will never find anyone better to emulate." Over the years, as I observed my father, I understood what a role model he truly was.

"What can you expect from an Irishman named Wellington, whose father was a bookmaker?" a local sports writer wrote about thirty years ago when we were going through some pretty awful seasons. My father usually ignored criticism from the news media, but those words stung him deeply.

"I'll tell you what you can expect," he said at our kickoff luncheon just a few days later. "You can expect anything he says or writes may be repeated aloud in your own home in front of your own children. You can believe he was taught to love and respect all mankind, but fear no man. And you could believe his abiding ambitions were to pass on to his family the true richness of the inheritance he received from his father, the bookmaker: the knowledge and love and fear of God. And second, to give you, our fans and our coach a Super Bowl winner."

My father's faith was his strength. And it never wavered. He and my mother went to Mass every day and insisted we attend every Sunday and holy day, even long after we were married with children of our own.

When we were young, each year at Christmas, the confession schedule of our parish was posted on the refrigerator door with a little handwritten note: "No confession, no Santa." The past few weeks, as sick as he was, he still received communion every day in the hospital, and his rosary beads were always in his hands.

My Dad's family was his pride and joy. He was married to my mother for more than fifty-one years, and their marriage was wonderful. I can't remember them raising their voices to each other. They met in church when a woman fainted, and they both rushed to assist her. My father later claimed the whole thing was staged by my mother's Aunt Lil. Well, after fifty-one years of marriage, eleven children, forty grandchildren, soon to be forty-two, I would say she got his attention!

Before my parents celebrated their fiftieth wedding anniversary about a year and a half ago here in St. Patrick's, my mother asked him if they could renew their vows. He was very reluctant at first. "The original ones haven't expired yet, have they?" he said. Of course, he eventually agreed, but when Cardinal Egan asked him during the ceremony, "Will you accept children lovingly from God?" the look on his face seemed to say, "Your Eminence, I think that ship sailed a long time ago."

If there was a category in the *Guinness Book of World Records* for most christenings attended, or first communions and graduations, or school plays and Little League games, my father would surely win. He loved watching his grandchildren compete or act on stage. He always stayed in the background without drawing attention to himself, always positive and supportive, setting yet another example.

One of my father's greatest attributes, his loyalty, was freely given to all. He considered Giants players and employees, both past and present, as part of his extended family. If a member of that family was in need, he or she received money, a job, or "just a call from a friendly voice," as he liked to say.

Years ago, he was criticized for that loyalty, and for letting it cloud his judgment. "If that's the worst thing they can say about you," he would comment, "then you must be doing something right." I remember going on countless road trips with him, and he would always make it a habit to call a former player or coach in the town where we were playing. Many of these guys were long forgotten by others, but not by him.

Next to his faith and his family, the thing my father loved most was his team, the team he spent sixty-eight years of his life building. His father suggested going to law school after his graduation from Fordham in 1937. "Just give me one year with the team," he pleaded. My grandfather agreed, and that number turned into sixty-eight. With the exception of four years in the Navy during World War II, he hung around the team and the sport he loved so much. He attended nearly every practice right through the end of the season.

Whether we were 10–2 or 2–10, he was there wearing that old floppy hat, carrying that ridiculous stool, and usually wearing a shirt or jacket almost as old as he was. Each year, our equipment manager would give him new apparel for the season, and it would always wind up in the back of his closet. When we changed our logo several years ago, back to the traditional lowercase "ny," he actually found some of his shirts with that logo from more than twenty-five years ago. "I knew they would come back," he said.

He loved the draft meetings. It was his favorite time. He would sit there as stats were read on every prospect. He wanted to hear everything, and he loved interacting with our scouts, perhaps because he had been one himself for so many years.

I will always remember him sitting alone on the equipment truck prior to Super Bowl XXXV, lost in his thoughts, a scene I witnessed so many times over the years. No pregame parties or festivities for him; he preferred being with his players and coaches, but always in the background to avoid interfering. During our road games, he would sit in the press box instead of a fancy suite, so he could focus on the game.

He always maintained his composure and tried to calm his family down, more often his daughters than his sons! I remember one game, years ago, when a particular player was having a tough day, and some of us became a little exasperated. At one point, I yelled, "What is he doing out there?" My father put his hand on my shoulder rather firmly and said, "What he's doing is the best he can."

My father had a special relationship with Giants fans. It amazed me when he answered nearly every letter a fan wrote to him, no matter how derogatory. "They are our customers," he would say. "They're just demonstrating how much they care about the team, and they deserve a response." For years, the staff joked about fans upgrading their season tickets by writing to my father and claiming to suffer from some physical ailment. The fans knew he was a soft touch.

My father was very proud of his longtime association with the National Football League. He served on nearly every committee and valued all of them, especially the NFL Alumni Dire Need Fund, established to take care of former players who had fallen on hard times.

My father taught us many lessons over the years, maybe none more valuable than in the last few weeks of his life. He fought to live until the end, trying to get out of bed and walk. His faith never waned. On his last day in the hospital, when he realized the doctors could no longer treat him, he summoned me to his bedside. He could barely talk. I held his hand, and he looked at me and smiled and said, "I'll be there when you get there." When he took his last breath, he was surrounded by the family he loved so much and taught so well.

There's a relevant scene from the movie *Saving Private Ryan*. An elderly Private Ryan visits the gravesites of some of the men who died trying to save his life. Overcome with emotion, he turns to his wife and asks her, "Have I been a good husband, a good father, a good person?" Questions I suppose we all must eventually answer. For Wellington Mara, the answers were clear. Yes, you were a wonderful husband; you were the best father and grandfather anyone could ever have; and you were the best example of how we should all live our lives. We came to expect it from the "Irishman named Wellington, whose father was a bookmaker."

He may be gone from this world, and we certainly are grieving over him. But we also rejoice over our good fortune in his long and extraordinary life, and the impact of his spirit as it lives on in his descendants for generations to come. When my father's brother Jack Mara died forty years ago, Arthur Daley of the *New York Times* wrote a column lamenting the loss of his good friend. My father saved that column on his desk. The last line quotes Hamlet: "Now cracks a noble heart. Goodnight, sweet prince, and flights of angels sing thee to thy rest."

October 28, 2005

KIRBY

The cell phone rang as I sat at P. J. Clarke's bar talking to four Catholic priests who work by day as hospital chaplains. They know about death even on this particular Easter Sunday night. Richard Littlejohn, our veteran overnight and weekend manager, only calls with bad news. "I'm sorry to ruin your Easter, Mr. O'."

"Who is it, Rich?"

"Bill Scollon; they found him on the floor in his apartment."

That's how I learned William Kirby Scollon died alone a few days before Easter. He was a slight, elfin little guy with dancing eyes and a stunning intellect who came to our station on Tuesdays to preside over his own radio program.

The New Rochelle Police officers who found him at 6 P.M. on Easter informed us he had been gone "for a few days." According to Frank Ippolito, his radio sidekick, Scollon was preoccupied as recently as Friday afternoon with preparing remarks on immigrants and Iraqi war veterans for this week's show. It was vintage Scollon to the end.

A bit stooped and hunched over from a full life, he spoke in a croak. But Scollon was one of the brightest guys I ever met, an opinion shared by Jack Kennedy, who would call him to discuss the great issues of the day at the Carlyle Hotel—before and after he became president of the United States. Bobby Kennedy also sought Scollon's advice, and Scollon proudly wore the legendary PT-109 tie clip, a staple for Kennedy staffers and admirers.

Scollon became the gray eminence of the Democratic Party in these parts and cranked out thousands of speeches and position papers for local, regional, and national candidates on a wide range of issues. He hung around Miriam Jackson, the Democrats' mother hen who became chair of the Westchester County Democratic Committee, and John DeRario, the Little League czar and a powerful voice on the County Board of Legislators during the seventies.

He was married for a brief time, but for the last several decades reverted to life as a confirmed bachelor. He spent his time over the years at a lonely flat in downtown New Rochelle and would celebrate Easter and Christmas with Bill Mullen, a Verizon executive, and his wife. Thanksgiving was reserved for the elderly councilwoman, Ruth Kitchen; and he regularly shared the Sabbath with our own Larry Goldstein.

In his spare time, William Kirby Scollon *designed* crossword puzzles for the *New York Times* and Gannett. A great wordsmith, he insisted on clarity and precision in both written and spoken English, and would often lecture me on my poor syntax.

A confirmed Democrat, Scollon vigorously objected to WVOX's Republican endorsements and opposed our presence in Vietnam and Iraq.

For many years, Scollon skimmed along the periphery of Democratic politics as chief of staff for Max Berking, the courtly, graceful state senator who later became chair of the Westchester County Democratic Committee. They were a formidable team at the ballot box and in Albany, and they also ran an ad agency on Madison Avenue.

When he wasn't at the Carlyle with the Kennedys, Scollon would hold court at Paddy O'Neil's saloon on Lawton Street. During lunch hour, the bankers and merchant princes of the town would inhabit the place. At night, it became a little less hectic when Hughie Doyle, Tommy O'Toole, and Bill Sullivan came to debate with the little Irishman with the facile mind. And one night, Ken Auletta, the great *New Yorker* writer, came by for advice on Howard Samuels's campaign for governor of New York.

Some people called him "Kirby" because he was related to the Kirbys of Rye, a prominent local family. I just called him Bill. By any name, he emanated a bright aura in every season of his life.

He died alone in an apartment in downtown New Rochelle, and he never made it to Easter dinner at Mullen's house.

WVOX lost a talk show host. But all of Westchester and New York state lost a marvelous, endearing character.

April 17, 2006

DR. STANTON OF CBS

When I read of Frank Stanton's passing, my mind drifted back to a New York afternoon long ago.

The venue was the fabled bar at the "21" Club.

Several network executives were discussing the preeminence of CBS and its lofty reputation as "the Tiffany network." Mind you, this was back a few years.

Wally Schwartz, president of ABC Television; his cohorts George Williams of WABC and Ed McLaughlin, who headed the ABC Radio Network; John Van Buren Sullivan, the classy majordomo of WNEW Radio of sainted memory; Bill Grimes of CBS; plus a few suits from NBC, were all in attendance.

After a few rounds, someone attributed the *real* reason for the supremacy of CBS to the network's CUFFLINKS!

"What the hell do cufflinks have to do with it?" asked one barroom philosopher, stunned by this new-found wisdom.

And then it was recalled that NBC's cufflinks were emblazoned with the peacock; ABC had the alphabet; but CBS had their fabled "eye" in black onyx, mother-of-pearl, and gold. But the CBS cufflinks were "just a little smaller and more discreet" than the other networks', and thus, "just a little classier."

Frank Stanton's doing.

December 27, 2006

NANCY Q. KEEFE: A REMEMBRANCE

Nancy Q. Keefe was the preeminent print journalist of her time in Westchester County, in the Heart of the Eastern Establishment.

She would sit at a Gannett typewriter and fashion words into strong, muscular sentences to make people think and reconcile differences.

She championed many worthy, and often unpopular, causes such as homeless shelters, and supported political candidates who got past her "Bozo" meter. And for about fifty years, she wrote for the *Berkshire Eagle*, in Pittsfield, Massachusetts.

Keefe loved Mario Cuomo and helped persuade him not to run for president, because she believed a good man cannot keep his soul and be president of the United States at the same time.

Nancy Q. Keefe was a brilliant social commentator and had a keen political sense. She stood up for everyday people and would unleash a contagious fury when they were threatened.

I was in Manhattan when our news department called about her passing. I immediately used my cell phone to contact Mario Cuomo, who sat at his desk a block away, looking at a picture of St. Thomas More given to him by Nancy Keefe on Election Day, when he was defeated in his final run for governor.

Cuomo and I make our living with words, he much more artfully than I. But we couldn't think of anything to say about the woman who used words better than both of us.

Except, we will miss her toughness.

And goodness.

March 12, 2004

MAMA ROSE MIGLIUCCI: "THE FIRST LADY OF LITTLE ITALY"

When I gave the eulogy for Mario Migliucci, the graceful patriarch of Mario's, the iconic landmark restaurant on Arthur Avenue in the Little Italy–Belmont section of the Bronx, in 1998, there were more than 1,000 people in the Church of Our Lady of Mount Carmel—fishmongers, bakers, butchers, greengrocers, and the people of the neighborhood in their black. There weren't that many mourners for his dear wife when she passed away last year at ninety-three. But there was just as much love in the Bronx church when "Mama Rose" went off to be reunited with her beloved husband. Nancy Curry O'Shaughnessy once observed, "This was the kind of mother we should all have . . .".

May it please you, Reverend Father Eric Rapaglia . . .

Your posting as pastor here at Our Lady of Mt. Carmel is a great gift from His Eminence, for the parish and for the neighborhood.

And Mama Rose would have been so pleased by the presence on the altar of Monsignor Bill O'Brien, the legendary founder and chairman of Daytop Village, who enjoys a well-deserved international reputation; and also Father Sebastian Bacatan, the parochial vicar of St. Pius X, where he serves the "underprivileged," the "poor" and "distressed" of Scarsdale, N.Y., with another great priest, Father John O'Brien.

Actually, we've been here before in *this* great Bronx church on *another* bittersweet occasion accompanied then as now with a rich admixture of sadness and joy.

It was one month shy of ten years ago that we prayed for and remembered "Pop": *Mario* Migliucci. On that day, January 27, 1998, the people of the neighborhood came together as you have now to bid farewell to another legend of the Bronx. They came out of their shops on that winter day: the greengrocers, the bakers, the bread-makers, the fishmongers, the butchers, and the cheesemongers. That day was for Mario.

And so we are here again to pray for Mario's beloved Rose Bochino Migliucci, to remember our incomparable "Mama Rose."

But it is right, I think, that we also mention Pop as we pray for Mama because you can't really assess the life of one without the other.

They were always, it seems, *together*, ever since that day when a young girl named Rosie Bochino peered out the window of her tenement house—which, incidentally, was directly across the street from Mario's Restaurant. She took one look at Mario, who moved like a graceful ballet dancer, even when waiting on tables or twirling pizzas—sending them airborne with great élan and a certain finesse—at his father's Neapolitan restaurant—his father having come from Cairo to establish a life for himself in these undeveloped, wild, and wooly precincts in the early 1900s. Nineteen-nineteen, in fact.

This was all happening during the days when actual *farms* existed in the Belmont section of what was becoming known as the "Little Italy" we know today.

We all know the story of their courtship, how when Pop started dating Mom—as the popular lore of the neighborhood has it—Mom had *another* suitor who was, in fact, an usher, a very upstanding fellow, who took the collection every Sunday in *this very church*.

And then one day Mario—"Pop"—now greatly taken and deeply in love with Rose Bochino, went to pay this fellow a little "visit" here at the church (I don't think Mario came here to pray that particular day), and legend has it that the man somehow saw fit to transfer his genius at passing the basket to *another* parish! And the rest you know. They lived and loved and flourished for over seventy years together. Rose and Mario. Mario and Rose.

Right here in the Bronx. Right here on these streets, in this fabled neighborhood they call "Little Italy." Or "Arthur Avenue," as some would have it. And, always, on Mondays, by the ocean in Montauk. The two of them.

The papers that wrote stories of her passing last weekend at age ninety-four called Mama Rose a "restaurateur." Well, those of us who knew—and *loved*—her know she was *much* more.

Rose Bochino Migliucci was, essentially, a *teacher*. She taught us all the oldest virtues and verities. She never preached. Rather, she instructed by living, by example, by fortitude, by consistency, by dedication.

She had a quiet charisma, presiding over her domain and her family from that old, wobbly stool near the cappuccino machine from which were drawn the famous "Bochino Cappuccinos" (I could use one tonight, Dominick, and you could spike it too!).

Incidentally, Joseph was *thinking* about closing down in Mom's honor for at least one day. Then he realized that Mama would have been the first to say, "Don't even *think* about it, Joseph!" So he got the message delivered from on high!

To her favorites at the restaurant she would proffer her pickled carrots, her "Mom salad," which she made herself, and her chopped liver (you have to remember: This was an *Italian* restaurant!).

She was always there in every season until late into the night. Feeding people and loving them. And when life turned sad and difficult, when things were spinning out of control, we would repair to her counsel, to her warmth, to her wisdom.

The rich and privileged came from Westchester and Connecticut and even from New Jersey. They came down from their country clubs in Bronxville and their yacht clubs in Rye, because Rose and Mario gave them something they couldn't get in those rarefied precincts.

Mama's goodness and charm brought them to this neighborhood: judges, magistrates, food critics, journalists, merchant princes, civic leaders, the people of the neighborhood who loved her, even a few competitors—other restaurateurs.

One of Mama's admirers—Julian Niccolini, the owner of the fancy, formidable Four Seasons, one of America's most elaborate venues—came every Sunday night to spend his one day off with Mama and Joseph. On other days Julian feeds tycoons and power brokers at his famous landmark Manhattan restaurant. But when *he* wants to dine, he comes straightaway to Mario's because, I think, there's a "realness," an authenticity about the place. He also came for Mama. And I expect he will still come because her spirit is still everywhere apparent.

Mama was so strong, so dignified, so intuitive. Every mother is wonderful and glorious, I know. Yet even after you carve away the excess, you know this one was special. When she walked down Arthur Avenue every afternoon to the bake shop, you knew something very wonderful was coming at you.

She used to regret her lack of education. Maybe it's better she didn't know cybernetics from a salami-slicing machine—or megabytes instead of the struggle for survival. She was better with her intuition than you were with your education and intelligence.

She knew *only* this—that no one could have assembled all this magnificence and all this complication if it weren't going to come out all right in the end. She knew this, and you could not have a mother like this without being awestruck by her strength. She was not of a world where Porsches are parked next to BMWs.

Rose's success as a restaurateur was enough to earn her *respect* but not enough to earn her *love*. She was loved. So today we remember Mario *and* Rose, the charity of their souls and the largeness of their hearts.

I only want to quote from the Book of Proverbs: "Her value is far beyond pearls. Her husband, entrusting his heart to her, has an unfailing prize. She brings him good all the days of her life. She rises while it is still night and distributes food to her household. She has strength and sturdy are her arms. She reaches out her hands to the poor and extends her arms to the needy. She is clothed with strength and dignity, and she laughs at the days to come. She opens her mouth in wisdom and on her tongue is kindly counsel. Her children rise up and praise her. Give her a reward of her labors, and let her works . . . praise her at the city gates."

So it is a remarkable story! A story of generations. A story of a unique Bronx woman as endearing as she was enduring. And, finally, a story of a marriage as strong and remarkable and resilient as any of us has ever seen.

But it was always about family.

And if you didn't have one, or if your own was falling apart, you could come and appropriate her family—and make it your own. You could throw your arms around Rose and have Joseph, who is his father's son, call you "brother" and give you a big, wet kiss on both cheeks. His son, young Mario, has learned that pretty well too!

So she now leaves us Joseph and Barbara. And Diane and Michael. And nine grandchildren and fourteen great-grandchildren. She could not have existed without that family, without all of you to love.

And she leaves us knowing that, essentially, her work was done.

Even to her last day, with everything in her being, Mama loved that family she clung to with a fierceness across ninety-four years.

All of you in that family have your own stories, and you will go off now to share them with one another, and for days and years to come.

Finally, those of you here assembled may not be aware that just before she left, Mama waited up for Joseph to come home at 12:30 from the restaurant last Friday night.

To the very last, she made sure everyone in this amazingly strong family was all right.

And then what happened—my own wife, Nancy Curry, explained, with great sureness, when *she* heard the news that caused us all such exquisite sadness this week: "Mama Rose just wanted to spend *Christmas* with *Mario*."

And that's what really happened, I think, just as Nancy said.

What a remarkable life. What an extraordinary woman.

So, smile for us, Mama. The years are behind you.

And try to make a little room and set a table for us.

Our Lady of Mt. Carmel Church
Bronx, N.Y.
December 17, 2008

ROBERT MERRILL (1917–2004)

The great baritone Robert Merrill, my Westchester neighbor and a beloved member of the Dutch Treat Club since 1946, died at his home while watching the first game of the 2004 World Series. He joined the Dutch Treat (DT) Club soon after his Metropolitan Opera debut, and it remained a constant for the rest of his life. We both lived in New Rochelle and often, around eleven o'clock on a Tuesday morning, he would call me and say, "Let's go into town."

The DT elders would try to seat him at the head table at our prestigious luncheon club. But he preferred to park elsewhere and greet new members. After lunch, we would go around the corner to Pete's Tavern, the oldest saloon in New York. Once in a while, he said, "Let's go and terrorize the '21' Club." We spent many an afternoon there, but, of course, we didn't demolish the place, and he didn't drink all that much. Maestro Emery Davis, the society bandleader, and Bruce Snyder, the Keeper of the Flame of the venerable watering hole, will confirm this account.

Bob loved the showbiz crowd at the Friars Club, but his true loves were the marvelous, eclectic souls who populate the DT. He loved the camaraderie and fellowship, and if we didn't have a performer, he would sing for us. He was always on the bill at our annual dinners and once belted out some ribald lyrics written especially for the occasion by Richard Rodgers.

Merrill grew up in Brooklyn with an undying faith in the Dodgers. He remembered watching them as a boy through a hole in the right-field fence. Bob actually became a fairly good minor league pitcher before singing became his most enduring passion. In addition to performing many baritone roles at the Met, he also starred on the radio, in film, on TV, and, occasionally, in Las Vegas nightclubs.

Because of his love for baseball, he was often asked to sing the national anthem at Yankee Stadium and did so for many years, either in person or through a recording. He prized his Yankees jersey, number 1½, given to him by Billy Martin, and one year, he managed the Yankees in the Old Timers' Day game. In a late inning, with the great DiMaggio at the plate, "Manager Merrill" flashed the bunt sign! The Clipper complied and laid down a perfect sacrifice.

His friendships ranged from the elderly on park benches and at the bagel store in our Westchester neighborhood to celebrities such as Dean Martin and Frank Sinatra. When Sinatra had trouble hitting high notes, he would call Bob and get a "tune-up" over the phone.

When the glory years passed him by, he hung around WVOX, and to this day, we begin every broadcast day with his version of the national anthem. And at the end of the day, we sign off with his rendition of "God Bless America."

How sad the Yanks never made it to the series the year Robert Merrill signed off for good. But his legacy lingers on in the fifty-three albums and CDs he left behind. And in his love for the Dutch Treat.

Robert Merrill was a marvelous man. He was never off-key. On the stage. Or in life. And his wife, Marion, says the sun burst through the clouds at the precise moment he was laid to rest on a Westchester hillside.

With special thanks to Jeremy Main (prepared for the Dutch Treat Club Yearbook).

EMIL PAOLUCCI: "THE MAESTRO"

Professionally, he was known as Emil Powell. Some even called him "Maestro." But we knew him as Emil Paolucci. He was of the neighborhood.

Emil kept the music playing for a long, long time. He was eighty-eight when he died over the weekend in Florida.

As a bandleader and gifted sideman, Emil Paolucci accompanied our seasonal celebrations and courting rites in dance halls and pavilions, at country clubs and cotillions, outdoors at Hudson Park on warm summer nights, in theaters, recording studios, and concerts and church socials in musty school gymnasiums. And always at weddings, bar mitzvahs, and charity dinners.

He played with the big national touring bands and with local music makers like George Hoffman, Ben Cutler, and Hank Carletti. He was there at the Water Wheel and Abe Levine's Larchmont Lodge and for Friday night dances at the Westchester Country Club and the Larchmont Yacht Club.

Emil was always true to the great American classic songwriters. He loved Rodgers and Hart, Cole Porter, the Gershwins, Harold Arlen, Johnny Burke, and Johnny Mercer. The man was a lover and enjoyed playing romantic ballads with the sweet, simple lyrics we could understand and dance to.

He also knew obscure material like "You Are Too Beautiful," an exquisite composition by Rodgers and Hart, known only to musicians, as well as a tender song written by Frank Sinatra and Phil Silvers called "Nancy with the Laughing Face."

Emil played just for you. Some climb up on stage to perform and emote. It's all about basking in the spotlight. But with Paolucci, it was all about the audience having a good time.

He traveled to every state in the Union. But he always came home to Westchester. And he was happiest in that band shell at Hudson Park, with his neighbors listening on blankets or folding camp chairs, as his music drifted out over Long Island Sound on soft, agreeable summer nights.

All of us treasure the music in our lives. We revere and celebrate the musicians who make it, the minstrels of the night. Emil Paolucci,

I believe, provided a perfect example of why we love them so much.

He's gone now after some eighty-eight years out on the road and thousands of songs. He was a music maker. And his music lives on. All the lovely music.

January 7, 2004

A WINTER'S TALE OF FATHERS AND SONS

When Rob Taishoff called to tell me his father, Larry Taishoff, had died, my mind drifted back to a New York afternoon long ago.

I was supposed to be "on assignment"—read: selling radio ads—for John Van Buren Sullivan, the majordomo of the fabled WNEW. Instead, I had somehow found my way to a barstool at the esteemed establishment owned by the late Bernard "Toots" Shor on 52nd Street in Manhattan.

On this particular day, this glorious saloon was also hosting the writers Bob Considine and Jimmy Cannon; Ford Frick, the former commissioner of major league baseball; and General Omar Bradley.

The talk turned to the son of James A. Farley, Franklin Roosevelt's postmaster general, who had somehow failed to appear on time for a dinner date the night before with his legendary father, an icon of the Republic.

Toots, one of the greatest barroom philosophers of his day, opined, "Great men rarely have great sons." We all nodded approvingly at this stunning wisdom. And promptly ordered another round.

It's a nice adage. But Toots Shor never knew Sol Taishoff or his son, Larry. They were both great men, and all of us in broadcasting owe them a tremendous debt.

Larry and his father served as our sentinels on the Potomac, preventing government intrusion into electronic journalism. They kept the drumbeat going for fifty years in *Broadcasting* magazine.

This "Magazine of the Fifth Estate," as they called it, appeared every Monday morning with articles fashioned by Don West, Harry Jessell, and John Eggerton, who shared the Taishoff family's fierce devotion to the First Amendment, which has been described by Jack Valenti as "the most important document ever struck off by the hand of man."

During their stewardship, the words in *Broadcasting* would sing out from the pages and be quoted in the halls of Congress, at the Federal Communications Commission (FCC), and in the White

House itself. They prevented the Honorable Harley O. Staggers from throwing the CBS elders Frank Stanton and Walter Cronkite into a federal jail for contempt of Congress.

For fifty years, Sol and Larry Taishoff published elegant, muscular paragraphs, elevating our profession and transforming us into more than minstrels, performers, or advertising pitchmen.

Their relentless genius was also arrayed against a National Association of Broadcasters deal to accept the dreaded "Fairness" Doctrine in exchange for a reduction in license fees. And their influence put the brakes on a proposal to officially censure Howard Stern.

"We've always had terrible examples to defend," Larry Taishoff told a visitor one day in his ornate office on DeSales Street in downtown Washington, where a giant oil likeness of his late father peers down from the wall.

Many of us were upset when Larry bailed out in the mid-'80s after a $75 million "score" on the *L.A. Times*. And maybe it's a good thing neither Taishoff was in harness when the current FCC threatened us with draconian fines. Even more appalling to them, one is certain, would be our own tribe's awful, deafening silence and abject, obsequious acquiescence in the face of this intimidation.

A generous man by nature, Larry donated a lot of his "score" to Duke University for a new aquatic center, and to combat Down syndrome and diabetes, which killed him. He also created and endowed public parks all over Florida and founded the splendid Library of American Broadcasting at the University of Maryland. Sol was also a patron of the old Broadcast Pioneers, known today as Broadcasters Foundation of America. And Larry was a generous benefactor.

The editors Don West and John Eggerton have described them much more gracefully than I am able. And so has Harry Jessell. But every First Amendment advocate in our tribe mourns the end of this famous father/son duo. The son, Larry, just left us at the age of seventy-four last week, appropriately, in Washington by the Potomac.

They were all business, both of them. But to Larry and his old man, it was always more than an industry. It was a profession.

We won't forget the lessons they taught us.

2006

LAWRENCE BRUCE TAISHOFF (1933–2006)

Eulogy by Don West, president, Library of American Broadcasting.

It is impossible to talk about Larry without speaking in the same breath about his father, Sol, and of *Broadcasting* magazine, inspired by both of them. All three were inseparable. Sol was first generation, an immigrant in swaddling clothes. Larry was second generation and literally lived in the fast lane, a flamboyant Jay Gatsby, tooling around in a British sports car.

I've always been struck by the parallels between the Taishoffs and the Paley family of CBS. Sam Paley, father of the founder, was born in the Ukraine and began a successful cigar company after coming here. Sol had lived nearby in Russia—he would often say he was from Minsk while RCA's David Sarnoff was from Pinsk—and created one of this country's most successful journalistic enterprises. Bill Paley, the son, used his father's fortune to create a communications empire while Larry Taishoff, the son, turned a modest success into a spectacular one.

Larry served as a paratrooper in the Army's 101st Airborne Division, stationed in Germany during the 1950s. He graduated from Duke University, where he was a varsity swimmer, and later endowed a new swimming facility there, the Taishoff Aquatics Pavilion. He served as a director at his first broadcasting-industry job at WTOP-TV in Washington. But soon he was at *Broadcasting* magazine as an apprentice, instructed by his father in every phase of the operation.

Larry flourished on the business side and eventually became president and publisher. He also inherited the family's outside interests, primarily in real estate. DeSales Street, the one-block-long passage alongside the Mayflower Hotel in Washington, became an industry hub after *Broadcasting* moved there in1953. The magazine later built its own seven-story building on the street, widely acclaimed as an architectural gem.

Larry Taishoff spent most of his working life with *Broadcasting* magazine, renamed *Broadcasting & Cable* after his departure. While Larry focused primarily on the business side, he was instrumental in expanding a radio-only magazine to encompass television, cable, and satellite. Larry ensured coverage of the new electronic media, giving status to the wired world, and he sent me to Cannes and Montreux to establish our international coverage.

Larry shared his father's passion for the First Amendment and defended it vehemently in the magazine's editorial policy. To an editor, Larry's policy toward the product was a godsend. "It begins with editorial," Larry would declare time and again, especially when there was a dispute with the advertising side. "Make the editorial as good as you can, and everything else will follow," he would say. We did, and that made all the difference.

After leaving *Broadcasting*, Larry moved to Naples, Florida, where he again became active in real estate. He kept his home on the western shore of Maryland and spent his summers there, near some of his seven grandchildren.

The children, of course, are his proudest legacy. Just as Larry charted an independent course from Sol, his kids did likewise. Rob is a lawyer and a high-ranking captain in the Navy. Randy is a custom jewelry designer in New Mexico. And Brad is a budding music producer.

Both Larry and Sol relied on an unerring intuition. Their inner voices made them decisive and quick to act when they saw the light. They were equally quick to find flaws in a business proposal or a story, making them, respectively, great publishers and editors. Larry's financial acumen was legendary.

Bill O'Shaughnessy, owner of WVOX and WVIP radio up in the New York area, wrote, "Larry Taishoff's passing is an occasion for great sadness for all of us in broadcasting." Erica Farber, publisher of the competing *Radio & Records*, echoed that sentiment. "I am so sad about this," she told me of Larry's death. "He truly made his mark on this business."

Sadness indeed pervades this day, but gratitude moves us, too. Working with Larry wasn't easy, but there was always a love and affection behind his commands. At the end, we can all agree Larry Taishoff achieved the ultimate goal: He left the world better than he found it, and he left us better for knowing him.

November 3, 2006

JEAN ENSIGN

As a young man I was crazy about a woman who was a class act in every season of her life. And even now, as an old man, I'm still crazy about her. And I miss her.

Jean Ensign was a classy woman, a first-rate broadcast executive, and a hell of an actress.

She stood out from the pack in our own profession as a woman of breeding, manners, and erudition.

An inspiration and role model to hundreds of young people, she had her own special vocabulary. If Jean was not enamored of something, she would pronounce it "quite drodsome" (which marvelous word is not to be found in any dictionary, but is absolutely perfect). And she once described a broadcasting station in her care and keeping as "a pristine jewel of a radio station with just a touch of ragtime in its soul."

What a lovely line . . .

She would know.

May 5, 2004

"A DEATH IN THE FAMILY": TIM RUSSERT

This piece drew reaction from all over the country and from many in our profession . . . and a lovely note from Tim's widow—the writer Maureen Orth—and his son, Luke Russert.

His father, immortalized in an endearing and bestselling book, collected garbage and trash from the hard, bleak streets of south Buffalo. And if you came out of that dwindling city in western New York, as I did, you will recognize Tim Russert as a child of the neighborhood.

If you're listening to this in Yonkers (where true love conquers), the Bronx, or even Peekskill or Mamaroneck, you will also feel a kinship with the television journalist who collapsed and died in a studio in Washington Friday afternoon. Timothy John Russert Jr. was the best of what we are as broadcasters. But he did not resemble anyone who ever lived in Scarsdale, Bronxville, Rye, Bedford, or Litchfield.

He was a reassuring, comforting presence you thought would always be there in our lives. And my own tribe, our entire profession, took this hard. Anyone who ever sat in front of a microphone or peered into a television camera feels an awful sadness that is deep and personal. Russert's passing, so unexpected and so sudden, was like a death in the family.

I knew him when he worked for Mario Cuomo. But I am entitled, if not entirely qualified, to get on the radio to tell you about Tim Russert because we also went to the same Canisius High School on Delaware Avenue, the big, broad boulevard that runs through one of the remaining nice sections of Buffalo even to this day.

And although we were in the care and keeping of the German Jesuits some ten years apart, Russert and I both got whacked upside the head by the same worn old leather prayer book belonging to the Reverend John Sturm, S.J., who took most seriously his title and high estate: Prefect of Discipline.

Father John was built like a fireplug. And although an equal-opportunity disciplinarian, he made Timmy Russert his favorite charge almost from the minute he first encountered the personable Irish youngster from south Buffalo with the bright eyes and easy smile. That was back in the sixties, and they have been friends ever since. Canisius has turned out federal judges named Crotty and Arcara, political power brokers like Joe Crangle, big car dealers, stellar athletes including a few Holy Cross and Notre Dame quarterbacks, and doctors and lawyers of great renown. The Jesuits spotted Russert's beguiling potential early on. Even then they knew.

He would go back to Buffalo over the years to see his father and during summers better than this one Tim Russert would sit at Cole's Bar in the Elmwood section to talk sports over a beer and a "beef on 'weck," Buffalo's legendary version of roast beef, a steamship round of which was personally carved by the bartender and then piled on a Kimmelweck roll covered with salt to be dipped in Heinz ketchup. The music in the air on those nights was provided by ancient tapes of Fred Klestine's old radio programs from the fifties and sixties, which survive to this day at Cole's.

They would order another Simon Pure beer or a Carling's ale and talk about the rich girls who went to "The Mount," a boarding school, and about Johnny Barnes, the old Canisius High football coach, and sometimes about Cornelius MacGillicudy, a favorite teacher who owned a bar in the Parkside section over near Delaware Park.

He never lost touch with the Jesuits. And just a few weeks ago, Father Sturm, now in his nineties, sent out invitations to a scholarship luncheon in his own honor with the obligatory picture of his protégé Tim Russert on the cover.

Before his dazzling work on television that made him famous, Tim labored in the service of the two brightest minds in public life during our time: Daniel Patrick Moynihan and the estimable Mario M. Cuomo.

Someone said yesterday on television: "He wasn't exactly a pretty boy." With his cheeks and jowls, Russert was the complete antithesis of all the hyper, vacuous "talking heads" and all the bimbos—male as well as female—who sit each day in those anchor chairs praying the teleprompter doesn't fail lest they be forced to utter something more profound than "absolutely"!

Only Chris Matthews was his equal in terms of depth and intelligence. And maybe Jon Meacham or Lawrence O'Donnell or Peggy Noonan. George Stephanopoulos can hold his own in front of a camera (and in front of George Will). And classy Deborah Norville has a brain. While among the youngsters coming up, William "Billy" Bush and Chris Cuomo are bursting with intelligence and promise. Ditto Bill Geist's kid, Willie. And David Gregory and Tucker Carlson are easy to take. Barbara Walters and Diane Sawyer are class acts in any season. We've always liked Bob Scheiffer and Judy Woodruff. And how can you not like Mike Barnicle and Joe Scarborough (but not the girl with him, the one with the famous father, who talks over everybody)? And I hope Larry King, like Paul Harvey on the radio, goes on forever. Plus I still take pleasure in our infrequent sightings of Dan Rather and Tom Brokaw.

Russert, however, operated on a level far beyond most of them. And he didn't need high-tech production values or fancy overhead lighting in an ultra-modern studio to enhance and amplify his unique genius. He was to network news what Mario Cuomo is to public discourse. And as the great Cuomo himself reminded us, "Tim never forgot where he came from, and he never let us forget it either; and we loved him for it."

He would summer on Nantucket and go to parties at Sally Quinn's in Washington. But Russert never denied his roots in Buffalo. There was a realness about him, a genuineness, on and off the air.

A few summers ago, Russert was the main speaker at an important conference of the New York State Broadcasters Association up at Bolton Landing on Lake George. After his talk he was persuaded by our mutual friend Joe Reilly, the head of the broadcasters in the Empire State, to linger and give out the Association's Awards for Excellence, even as an NBC plane waited on the tarmac at the nearby Glens Falls airport to rush him back to Washington.

There were many awards and citations in every category. But Russert was his usual generous self, and so he stayed late into the night as the awards presentations wore on. And when it was announced that your own WVOX had won the designation for "Best Editorials in New York State" (which we clearly did not deserve), Russert arched his eyebrows and the Irish eyes twinkled as my son David and I advanced to the front of the ballroom to receive our award.

As we posed for the cameras and the flashbulbs popped, Tim asked, *sotto voce*, "How's Mario? How's Nancy? How are the kids? How's the station?" And now as my mind drifts back on this weekend after he died, I wonder if I remembered to inquire about *his* own welfare. I hope so, but I doubt it, given that heady moment in the spotlights. But he remembered.

Russert then thoughtfully pulled away my son David for a shot with just the two of them and said, again on the QT, while still smiling for the cameras, "How the hell did your old man win this damn thing? It must have been by sheer guile! Or did Cuomo write it for him?" As the two of them cracked up with laughter, no one in the audience of more than five hundred had a clue what they were chuckling about.

James O'Shea, who owns The West Street Grill, a high-class saloon (he much prefers the designation "fine dining establishment") in Litchfield, Connecticut, called while I was thinking about all this. According to O'Shea, "Russert possessed the genius of the Irish. Just say he was Irish. People will know what that means. He was *Irish*!" As O'Shea provides libation and sustenance for the likes of Philip Roth, Rex Reed, Jim Hoge, Bill vanden Heuvel, Rose Styron, George Clooney, Peter Duchin, and Brooke Hayward, I will bow to his wisdom. Russert did indeed have the genius of the Irish.

Nancy and I would see him around town of an evening, when he would come up from Washington to do some business at the NBC Universal mother ship at Rockefeller Center or if one of us had to emcee a dinner. And no matter how late the hour or how tired and rumpled he appeared, it was always the same: "How are the kids? How are the stations doing? How's the gov?"

NBC delayed the news of his passing and actually got scooped by the *New York Post* and the *New York Times* until someone from their shop was retrieved to go and inform his wife, Maureen Orth; their son, Luke; and his beloved father, Big Russ. But who, I wonder, had to knock on the door of the old priest in the Jesuit retirement house on Washington Street up in Buffalo to tell Father John Sturm, S.J., that Timmy Russert was gone?

I always thought Russert would have made a wonderful politician himself or a great teacher. Or even a priest. And with his sudden, untimely departure at age fifty-eight, he probably taught us one more lesson learned from the old Jesuits: "You know not the hour or the moment."

The newsman-journalist known as Tim Russert has been mourned by millions and eulogized in all the journals and periodicals in the land. But the most exquisite tribute, and probably the one he would have liked the most, came from Michelle Spuck, a waitress at Bantam Pizza in the Litchfield hills, who told a customer over the weekend, "I'm so sad about this; I never *met* him, but I *knew* him."

He died in front of a microphone.

June 16, 2008

PAUL J. CURRAN

Paul Curran was a famous New York lawyer and a pillar of the Catholic Church in New York. During a long and distinguished career, many tried to make him governor. In fact, Mario Cuomo famously said, "If they put up Paul Curran . . . I won't run." St. Patrick's Cathedral was packed for his sendoff.

The early morning skies over Manhattan were darkening as a west wind came over the Hudson and blew across the concrete and glass canyons on Tuesday, September 9, 2008.

On Fifth Avenue directly opposite Rockefeller Center, the great and the good of New York politics, law, and philanthropy came to St. Patrick's Cathedral to say farewell to Paul Jerome Curran. He was the last Catholic mandarin of the legal profession, and he died last week in a hospital room after the good part of seventy-five years as a prosecutor, corruption fighter, assemblyman, civic leader, U.S. Attorney, and icon of the Republican Party.

With the weather threatening outside, the great cathedral was full up with friends and admirers of this Paul Curran, including many federal judges who had been appointed for life with his imprimatur and blessing. They sat cheek by jowl with the power lawyers, educators, and lay elders of the high church in New York who had come to bury one of their own. There were Plunketts, Donnellys, Gills, and Crottys.

It was a Fordham crowd and Irish that came for what Edward Cardinal Egan called the "celebration" of Paul Curran's life. And it lacked only the presence of Malcolm Wilson, the fiftieth governor of New York, after Nelson Rockefeller. Charles Malcolm Wilson was the greatest orator Fordham ever graduated, better even than William Hughes Mulligan. And Malcolm Wilson must be mentioned here because it was his dream over the years to make Paul Curran a governor of the Empire State too. Back in 1982 it almost came to be.

It is also to be recalled that about that time one Mario M. Cuomo, a Democrat from Queens, a failed baseball player with too many vowels in his name who came out of St. John's, was also being importuned to run for governor.

And in the midst of all this Mr. Cuomo suddenly announced loudly and publicly that if the GOP put up Paul Curran for governor, he would not run. When asked over the weekend why he would say such a thing, the great liberal philosopher-statesman said, "Because he was better than I was."

But Paul Curran never did get the chance to sit where Franklin and Theodore Roosevelt, Charles Evans Hughes, and the magnificent Nelson Rockefeller once presided because the Republican Party chose instead a drugstore magnate named Lewis Lehrman, who merely bought their nomination for $15 million.

As the history books will confirm, Cuomo beat Mr. Lehrman and went on to serve three terms as governor, while Paul Curran settled into what the Jesuit Joseph O'Hare yesterday called "a life of striking public achievements as well as personal fidelity."

"Settled" is probably a bad word I use, because, as Father O'Hare reminded Paul Curran's friends, "he was also no stranger to conflict, trial, or testing."

The graceful former president of Fordham remembered in the huge cathedral that Curran advised the Justice Department and the Defense Department on national security matters and was the first special prosecutor to actually interrogate a sitting president of the United States under oath. It was in 1979 when Paul J. Curran looked right at James Earl Carter and asked him to place his hand on a Bible and swear to tell the whole truth about Bert Lance and the loans to Carter's peanut warehouse.

For over forty years in this town and this state, when the call went out for someone of probity and fairness and good judgment, Paul Curran was summoned. He was a Rockefeller Republican. But such was the respect he enjoyed across a broad political spectrum that even Democrats sang his praises. Mario Cuomo wasn't the only one of that tribe who admired Paul.

He was once Rudy Giuliani's boss when he served as a U.S. Attorney and head of the powerful State Investigations Commission. Father O'Hare said Paul J. Curran "fought for the rights of the poor" and, in a lovely line, even the rights of the "notorious." As a prosecutor he went after Mafia dons, white-collar criminals, nursing-home operators, dirty narcotics detectives, and a few congressmen.

"He was a 'lawyer's lawyer,'" as Robert McFadden wrote in a beautiful *Times* obit over the weekend, "who was most at home in a trial courtroom" where judges and juries knew they were dealing with someone very honest and honorable. The old Jesuits tell you he was *sui generis* in every season of his life and a gifted public man who was dedicated to his faith, his profession, his state, and his country.

He went all the way back in this state to the days of Hugh Carey, John Lindsay, Nelson Rockefeller, Warren Anderson, Roy Goodman, Jack Javits, Charles Brieant, and Daniel Patrick Moynihan. It was a time of civility in politics and public discourse. And only Mr. Robert Morgenthau survives him. And, of course, the estimable Mario Cuomo.

He was absolutely Georgetown and Fordham all the way. There was no mistaking that. They even made him president of the tony University Club. And as a confidential advisor and consultor to archbishops of the Roman hierarchy, Paul Curran helped John Cardinal O'Connor and his successor Edward Cardinal Egan defuse sensitive matters that were of concern to the church of New York during his time.

Thus although it must be acknowledged that Curran was definitely a high-church individual who spent lovely summers along with his handsome family at Spring Lake, a bastion of the Castle Irish down on the Jersey shore, the family, on the occasion of his death, requested that, in lieu of flowers to surround his casket, donations be sent to the Paul J. Curran Fund, which assists schools serving struggling youngsters in minority neighborhoods. Typical for the man. And his family. Beautiful. Just absolutely beautiful.

That's just the way it was. And as the cardinal archbishop prayed in his booming stentorian tone for the soul of Paul Curran, curious tourists and out-of-towners drifted wordlessly along the side aisles of the cathedral, lighting candles and taking pictures of the icons and statues in the alcove altars. (Paul Curran would not have been at all pleased if they had interrupted the flow of visitors by closing the cathedral for his funeral mass.) One of the gawkers whispered, "This must be for someone very special."

It was. And as the incense and hymns filled the great church, a late summer rain began to fall outside on Fifth Avenue as they sent off Paul J. Curran of Spring Lake and Manhattan.

September 10, 2008

EDWARD J. "NED" GERRITY JR. (1924–2009)

Ned Gerrity was a great patron of WVOX and WVIP and many great causes. He was a beloved figure in the corporate world and in Westchester.

May it please you, Reverend Fathers: Monsignor Patrick Boyle, the beloved pastor of this historic church; and an old friend of the Gerrity family, Father Mark Connolly, a great communicator and host of his own coast-to-coast radio program. I will intrude only briefly on this sad morning.

Edward, you are your father's son. I am capable of no higher compliment.

You know, Ned *planned* this whole thing in his final days!

He *knew*—he just *knew*—all of you would be here in this great church. And he is glad you came, as are Nadia and Katharine and Edward III, and all the Bardwils.

I will try to tell you a little bit about this amazing man whom we mourn and whose life we celebrate, if you will allow me.

Gerrity didn't always reside in the rarefied precincts of Rye or among the poor of Palm Beach. (Actually, they *are* poor now!)

He came from the Lackawanna Valley, in the Appalachian mountains of northeastern Pennsylvania: *coal* country. Or, as he liked to say, "*hard* coal" country, as opposed to the much inferior "*soft* coal" country farther west, out around Pittsburgh.

Scranton, Pennsylvania, was his birthplace eighty-five years ago. And it wasn't any kind of hardscrabble beginning. His father was the executive editor of the *Scranton Times* and an elder of the town.

Ned grew up near a bend of the mighty Susquehanna River, which flows hundreds of miles from its headwaters near the Finger Lakes all the way down to the Chesapeake.

This was all before the interstate highways built by Dwight Eisenhower coursed through Scranton and neighboring Wilkes-Barre—routes 84, 81, and 360 all now run to Scranton.

Of course, they had the *railroads* back when Ned was growing up: the Lackawanna, the Erie, and the Lehigh Valley, whose famous "signature" train was the Black Diamond. Young Ned Gerrity's *favorite*, however, was the Lackawanna's Phoebe Snow; "The Route of the Phoebe Snow" they called it.

There were two colleges that still stand today: Marywood and the University of Scranton. Ned went to the university and then came up to New York for his masters at the Columbia Graduate School of Journalism—the fabled Columbia "J" School—where, somehow, the beguiling, brainy Irishman from Pennsylvania with too much charm was elected president of the class of '48. So he became a journalist. A sports writer, in fact.

He also became a *soldier*, during World War II—not a summertime soldier or a behind-the-lines backup soldier or a weekend warrior.

The re-telling of *this* part of Gerrity's amazing life would have embarrassed even shy, modest, retiring Ned himself, but why not come right out and say it? Gerrity was a *hero* on the battlefield against the Germans: an authentic, flat-out *hero* who was decorated three times for gallantry, with a Silver Star and a Bronze Star.

He was there in the cold and snow and mud at Bastogne with George S. Patton's Third Army when it was surrounded. And during much of that mean, desperate winter, Ned would lead patrols out into the night to probe enemy lines and engage the Germans. It's all in the record, the heroism and valor of which I speak. And several books about the siege actually mention Gerrity's own gallantry under fire in the face of great danger.

Tom Brokaw wrote of the Greatest Generation. Ned *lived* it. He was a star of that great generation.

His accomplishments in the *business world* are also the stuff of legend.

He built ITT with Harold Geneen into one of America's first major worldwide conglomerates. Its holdings included telephone, telegraph, and cable companies in South America, Puerto Rico, and Brazil—all over the hemisphere.

Under the ITT banner was Avis Rent-a-Car, the Hartford Insurance companies, Continental Baking, the Canteen Corporation, Sheraton Hotels, and lots more.

The personable Gerrity ran Government Relations, P.R. and Worldwide Advertising out of a spectacular skyscraper at 320 Park Avenue. That magnificent edifice still stands. Only now on the façade are the words "Mutual of America," which means it resides in the care and keeping of Tom Moran and Bill Flynn of the Irish Peace Accords.

And the American flag—"Old Glory"—*still* flies from the halyard of the giant flagpole on the very top of the skyscraper. Gerrity always approved of that.

Ned occupied the entire thirty-third floor, which looked like a war room at the Pentagon or a CNN control room, with row upon row of teletype and tickertape machines bringing in reports around the clock from all over the globe. So advanced was the technology and so extensive were Gerrity's contacts and information-gathering operation that President Lyndon Johnson would often call to check up on the CIA. That really happened. Often.

During those heady years at ITT, Ned battled the Department of Justice and held at bay a series of antitrust lawsuits. Who says *Big* is necessarily *Bad*?

And in one memorable engagement, which is part of the popular lore of the corporate and political worlds, Gerrity took on the Senate Foreign Relations Committee, whose powerful chairman—Senator Frank Church of Idaho—had the crazy idea that Ned had somehow taken an "untoward" interest in the election—or the assassination—of the Chilean dictator Salvador Allende. Can you imagine Ned doing something like *that*?

Needless to say, Gerrity prevailed against the censure. And in later years, he took no small pleasure in telling his pals—and any and all who would listen—that Frank Church *lost* his bid for reelection to the Senate the following year!

To his last breath, Ned swore he had nothing at all to do with *that* election either! He did, however, always hold a kind thought for the good people of *Idaho*, as I recall.

Actually, I kind of wish they'd have *found* him "in contempt of Congress." That would have been beautiful!

He kept his hand in *locally* too. Mr. Justice, now retired, Sam Fredman told me a story when he came in last week to tape his show, "The Rabbi and the Judge." Years ago when Sam was first running for office, Ned volunteered to do press. Judge Fredman said, "They liked the guy so much they almost made *him* the judge! I'm just glad Gerrity didn't have a *law* degree."

He was of a Westchester that's fast disappearing and giving way to so much ordinariness (and many McMansions), and he was around before everyone along Purdy Street was named Buffy, Debby, or Jennifer strolling with their husbands Lance or Chad—where once giants walked the land around here—long before, I guess, we were invaded by those marvelous yuppies.

The names of the vivid souls who shared the stage with Gerrity in our home heath are familiar and known to you, and most of them were most certainly colorful, unforgettable characters like Gerrity.

There was *Vin Draddy*—Vincent DePaul Draddy—the Izod man who founded the Football Hall of Fame; and John McGillicuddy, who left us just last year.

This was the company Gerrity kept: Jim Linen of Time, Inc.; Eddie Egan, a magnificent man who gave us a great congressman and First Amendment champion named Ogden Rogers Reid. And there was another Gerrity pal from New Rochelle: Howard Clark. He ran a little company called American Express. And, through the mist of time: Walter Thayer, Bernard Curry, Frank McCullough, Joe Culligan, Bill Gibbons, Jack Joyce, Bob McCooey. They're all gone now.

Ned spent a lot of time on the fairways with the likes of Freddy Corcoran, who ran the PGA. Gerrity played Winged Foot and Westchester, where he was president of the club.

Mind you, he wasn't exactly the greatest *golfer*. Just last week he admitted that his all-time *lowest* handicap was a 15. "I kinda *talked* my way around the links, if ya know what I mean."

We know what you mean, Ned.

As we've observed, he started as a sports writer. Back in the sixties he ran with Jimmy Breslin (before the great writer stopped drinking) and with Toots Shor and Jimmy Cannon. He also knew the haze of an evening at Mike Manuche's.

Those were the days, Ned told me, when Breslin wasn't drinking any *more*—or any *less*!

Ned influenced the public discourse here at home and across our state with hundreds—nay, thousands—of notes, suggestions, bon mots, and missives to editors, writers, and journalists. Even to governors. And presidents.

I'd often find notes on my desk: "Get this to Sulzberger!" "Here's a good story for Phil Reisman!" "Run this past your friends at the *Post*. Or better yet, let's try to get it to Murdoch!"

Always his intention, his plan (sometimes hatched at Gus's with Charley Steers, Paul Carey, and Del Ladd) was to build someone up, to shine a favorable light on the worthwhile, the meritorious.

No meanness ever accompanied Ned's observations on the great issues of the day.

He was a sucker for the lonely, the forgotten, the hurting. And he was, as he continually reminded us, a *Democrat*.

I spoke earlier about his prowess on the golf course with the big shots, but even to this day the *caddies* at Winged Foot and Westchester will tell you, "Mr. Gerrity always smiled at us; it was always a fun loop." The only one—really, to this day—more popular in the caddy yard was Wellington Mara, also of sainted memory, who addressed his Creator so often in this very church as Ned did and as we now do for him.

Gerrity, Well Mara, Mr. Draddy—we're not going to see their like ever again, I expect.

So as we assess and look back over a marvelous life—Edward Gerrity Jr. was really a *lot* of things; he *did* a lot of things across his eighty-five years. He was a journalist and a military man—a gallant soldier, in fact. He was a stellar Catholic *all* his days: a Knight of Malta and a Knight of the Holy Sepulchre, as Bill Plunkett reminded me. He was a legendary corporate executive, a sportsman, a golfer (all right, a *fair* golfer), a clubman, a commentator, a gentle critic, and a marvelous, witty, colorful character who always, as I've said, smiled at the caddy.

He married two spectacular women, one of whom—Nadia—stayed with him and loved him and sheltered him until the very end of his colorful life. He had a devoted brother, Tom, a college professor, of whom he was so proud; and a beloved daughter, Katharine, and a son, Edward III, in whom he was well pleased. He also took great delight in the accomplishments of the six daughters and son Nadia brought into his life. He was the grandfather of one spectacular ten-year-old named Teddy—Edward Gerrity IV, whom he adored in every season.

I'll mercifully yield and leave you with a story that comes out of a New York afternoon long ago. As the sun set over Manhattan, there were some colorful types assembled at Mr. Bernard "Toots" Shor's emporium on 52nd Street. I'm struggling not to say "saloon."

I think Ford Frick of Bronxville, then the commissioner of major league baseball, was there; Bob Considine, the writer; and, as I remember, I believe *Omar Bradley* was there in his dress blues adorned with the circular cluster of five stars. He had just been named a general of the armies, like MacArthur. Mind you, it was quite late in the afternoon. Considine called it "High Tea." Someone among this august group asked Mr. Shor, the great "philosopher," to identify the "toughest" guy he'd ever met.

After thinking quite profoundly for about a New York minute, Toots Shor replied: "You mean if I were trapped in an alley and wiseguys were coming in after me? Well . . . in *that* case, I'd take Shipwreck Kelly by my side—or maybe Sinatra."

In that exact predicament—and I've been in similar situations, I'm afraid—I'd take Ned Gerrity!

So go off now and tell and savor your own stories of this marvelous man who was such a treasured friend to all of us.

Those are a few of mine.

See you soon, Gerrity.

And do a little "P.R." for us.

Church of the Resurrection
Rye, N.Y.
June 5, 2009

A DAUGHTER'S LAST BREATH
BY JIMMY BRESLIN

Rosemary Breslin, forty-seven, died Monday from a rare blood disease. A writer who crafted scripts for "NYPD Blue" and wrote a 1997 memoir titled *Not Exactly What I Had in Mind: An Incurable Love Story*, Breslin was the third child of columnist Jimmy Breslin and the former Rosemary Dattolico, who died in 1981.

As it was with the mother who went before her, the last breath for the daughter was made before an onlooker with frightened eyes.

First, there were several labored breaths.

And here in the hospital room, in a sight not distorted by passion, was the mother sitting on the end of her bed, as the daughter once had sat on the mother's in Forest Hills for a year unto death. They both were named Rosemary. When the mother's last breath told her to go, the daughter reached in fear, but her hand could not stay the mother's leaving.

By now, Rosemary, the younger, is married to Tony Dunne. He knew she was sick when he married her. He then went through fifteen years of hospital visits, stays, emergencies, and illness at home and all he wanted was for her to be at his side, day and night. His love does not run. And now, in the daughter's hospital room, as it always does, fear and deep love brought forth visions of childhood.

The daughter is maybe four, sitting on the beach. She wants money for ice cream. The mother's purse had money to pay the carpenter at day's end. Earlier, the mother had tried to pay the carpenter by check, and he leaped away, as if the check were flaming. The daughter plunged into the purse and found no change for ice cream. With the determination that was to mark every day of her life, she went through that purse, tossing large bills, the carpenter's money, into the air, digging for ice cream change. She sat there infuriated, throwing money into the sea wind. The mother was flying over the sand trying to retrieve it.

Another labored breath.

Then I could see her later, and with even more determination, typing a script with tubes in her arms. Writing, rewriting, using hours. Clearly, being attacked by her own blood. She said that she felt great. She said that for fifteen years.

I don't know of any power that could match the power of Rosemary Breslin when sick.

Suddenly, the last breath came in quiet.

The young and beautiful face stared into the silence she had created. Gone was the sound of her words.

The mother took her hand, and walked her away, as if to the first day of school.

June 20, 2004

GOVERNOR MARIO M. CUOMO EULOGIZES BILL MODELL

In one of my previous books, I included a lovely eulogy for Michael Modell, scion of one of New York's great merchant families.

In 2008 Governor Cuomo got up once more to remember Bill Modell, the patriarch of the nationally known sporting goods family.

Mr. Modell was a major philanthropist in the New York area. His charitable work continues to this day with the guidance and dynamism of his spectacular wife, Shelby Modell, who is a sheer pure, natural force. Nancy and I adore her.

We all repeat ourselves—but Bill sings a chorus!

It's a cold, clear morning, but one of our brightest lights, who has warmed and enlightened us all, is gone.

Leo Rosten, the famous Jewish writer and philosopher, tells us when death summons a man to appear before his Creator, his greatest advantage will come from his good deeds.

The tsunami of newspaper stories describing Bill's passing call him a "titan of industry" because he transformed Modell's from four stores in New York City to 136 stores in eleven states. He took a modest family retail business and, with the help of Michael and Mitchell, created a national model, envied by all. Even President George H.W. Bush praised him as a brilliant innovator who strengthened our national economy.

For all of his commercial success, for all his iconic stature, those of us who knew him well saw a great deal more. Until now, his virtues and accomplishments have been largely concealed behind a veil of modesty and deference.

He was a distinguished veteran of the Army's Ninth Air Corps in the Second World War; an extraordinary humanitarian and a prodigiously generous philanthropist; a patron of the arts; a civil rights pioneer; a founder and chairman of Gilda's Club; and a co-founder of the tremendously successful Crohn's & Colitis Foundation. Bill was also honored by President Jimmy Carter for his superb skill as a negotiator in drafting the Panama Canal Treaty.

But beyond these specific achievements, Bill was an inspiring, generous, benign, loving person. Our family has known Bill for more than forty years, and we were constantly amazed by his selfless goodness.

Bill was remarkably unflappable. In times of crisis, he remained the same wise, strong, humble, flexible, compassionate man, with a gentle sense of humor.

That endearing sense of humor could occur at any time—to start a conversation, to end one, or to distract you from some unpleasantry. When I was at his bedside, hemming and hawing, he interrupted me and said, "You think I'm sick, what about Goldstein?" And he recounted a marvelous and funny story.

But that was Bill—trying to save you from sharing his pain.

It is, of course, impossible to reminisce about Bill without mentioning Shelby, his soulmate for sixty years, a beautiful, incomparable, effervescent wife, mother, and grandmother, Bill's partner at all times.

They weren't just married; they were indivisible. Poets pray for their kind of love affair, the proverbial match made in heaven. They shared everything: devotion to family, the devastating loss of their son, Michael; and the courage to persevere, founding an organization to help others avoid a similar tragedy.

How special they have been! How very special! Together, they have committed themselves to the two basic principles of Judaism, *Tzedakah* and *Tikkun Olam,* summoning us to love one another and work together to make a better world. And they have done it.

We've all heard great religious leaders motivating their congregations with powerful sermons. But Bill and Shelby chose another path. They lived a meaningful life for all to see. And I'm sure their lovely family—Leslie, Mitchell, Robin, Abbe, Shawnee, and all the other grandchildren—will continue to do so in the years ahead.

Bill retained a deep love and unaffected gentleness to the very end. In those last difficult days, Bill remained unflappable, the strong and loving father, husband, friend, guiding and shielding the flock. With quiet courage, he hid his pain, sparing his loved ones from anguish.

His conduct resembled the way Michael left us seven years ago. They both fought mightily to hold on to life even though they were wracked with pain. In doing so, they stayed alive long enough to spend their last days with their families. The ineffable grace, grandness, and beauty of their lives were gloriously mirrored in the way they left us.

Now Bill is gone from our midst. But no one knows for sure what that means. Thus, we are free to hope for something more. Leo Rosten and others use a ship as a metaphor to describe the meaning of death. This one seems particularly apt:

> I am standing upon the seashore. A ship at my side spreads her white sails to the morning breeze and starts for the blue ocean.
>
> It is an object of beauty and strength, and I stand and watch her until at length, she is only a speck of white where the sea and sky meet. Then, someone at my side exclaims, "The ship's gone!"
>
> Gone where? Gone from my sight, that's all. It is just as large in hull and mast and spar as it was when it left. Its diminished size is in me, not in her.
>
> And just at the moment when someone at my side says, "It's gone," there are other eyes watching for it coming to another shore, and other voices ready to take up the glad shout, "Here it comes!"

And God willing, Bill and Michael will be there on that other shore years from now, waiting for us when the time comes.

Till then, Bill, rest in peace.

We love you.

Temple Emanu-El, New York City
February 17, 2008

JACK NEWFIELD BY JIMMY BRESLIN

It takes one to know one. One great writer eulogizes another.

We bury Newfield today in a meadow on Long Island. It is just as well we do it today. It ends his suffering from a disease that thousands of stories later, still kills as it has for hundreds of years.

And it is just as well he gets peace now because he was being choked by rages at a life around him that he knew deserved only his hatred.

All those years he wrote and talked and demonstrated against a war in Asia that killed 58,000 of our young. Our best hope, his best hope, Robert Kennedy, was assassinated.

Now Newfield finds himself represented by a senator from his own Brooklyn, Charles Schumer, who voted for a war in Iraq.

He is also represented by another senator, Hillary Clinton, who voted in favor of the war in Iraq.

He freed a man from death row and wrote so much about the evil of a government that decides it has the right to execute. It is people's lowest moment.

And he finds himself represented by a United States senator from Brooklyn, Schumer, who favors the death penalty.

He also is represented by a senator, Hillary Clinton, who favors executions.

And the candidate who is supposed to represent him in the state election, Eliot Spitzer, is for execution by state.

So Newfield leaves us the things he hates the most.

But we also inherit something else.

Somewhere a crystal of air snaps, and the tiniest sound causes somebody to wonder where did this come from? What am I supposed to do? Where?

And when the curiosity is raised, it must go naturally to all our Brooklyns. Where the housing for the poor is scarcer than it ever has been in our time. Where the condition of children is worse than at any time since Dickens of London. And hope bursts in the air that the anger and passion of Jack Newfield will prod and push and propel all to take up the great cause of the liberals.

To Assist. Assist. Assist.

December 22, 2004

JACK NEWFIELD EULOGIZED BY MARIO M. CUOMO

I'm one of Jack's older friends who strived to stay on his good side because I expected to receive rather than give his eulogy.

Staying on Jack's good side was prudent for politicians, too; it might not provide immunity, but it might offer a little clemency.

And I'm sorry for all of us because we lost one of our era's most courageous and compelling journalists, a champion of justice when we needed one most.

Since their first tentative steps into politics, the Cuomos have admired and respected the Newfields. After forty years and thousands of conversations about politics, sports, and mutual friends, I came to know Jack about as well as you can know a person.

And in recent years, when he was preparing his memoir, we even talked a little about religion.

Jack was intrigued by C. S. Lewis's famous *Screwtape Letters*, a description of the subtleties of the devil's mind and how evil can overcome you in simple and familiar ways. Lewis writes, "What Hell wants is a man to finish his life having to say, 'I now see that I spent most of my life not doing either what was right or what I enjoyed.'"

Well, Jack has finished his life, and the devil must be terribly disappointed. For the many decades I knew Jack, he did the right thing and enjoyed it immensely.

The Greeks believed the gods' most valuable gift is the gift of passion, and Jack's life bubbled over with it!

Perhaps it was most evident in his profound love for his soulmate, his wife and partner, the beautiful, bright, heroically supportive Janie, and their two jewels, Rebecca and Joey.

His passion infused his life as an investigative reporter, author, commentator, and political analyst. And it forged an enduring bond with his friends and colleagues.

His passion intensified his loves and hates. His love of the city, his country, baseball, music, and his idols, Jacob Riis, Jackie Robinson, and Robert Kennedy.

And his hate of racism, economic injustice, the wars in Vietnam and Iraq, the death penalty, corrupt politicians, and fickle friends.

He probably hated leaving us so abruptly most of all, long before his passion had dissipated. Only weeks ago, Jack appeared stronger than ever, his talents expanding into new media, television, and films, in documentaries and ideas for new books. He was at the top of his game!

And then the game was called on account of darkness.

Jack refused to go gently into that still night. He worked furiously right until the end. Fighting the good fight, and loving it. Just as he always had.

The gods did indeed bless Jack Newfield. And they blessed us, too, by allowing us to share his passion for sixty-six years. For that I think we should all say, "Deo Gratias."

Riverside Memorial Chapel, New York City
December 22, 2004

TRIBUTES TO TONY MALARA

Tony Malara rose from a junior staff position at the most obscure television station in New York state to become president of the CBS Television Network. With his gregarious megawatt personality, Malara charmed CBS affiliate owners all across the country, his bosses at Black Rock, the network headquarters in New York—and all of us.

Mario Cuomo used to kid him about the responsibility he carried as "the highest-ranking Italian in network television"! When Mario ran for governor of New York, Tony returned the favor, albeit quite stealthily, by sending a campaign contribution of a few hundred dollars via a Trailways bus down the Thruway because he didn't trust the clerks in the North Country Post Office not to rat him out.

For, you see, Tony was also an officer of the local Republican Party.

He was also one of the most charismatic and beloved figures in our tribe.

One night when I dropped him off at the Waldorf, three liveried doormen rushed up to our Suburban to escort Malara (they call him "Your Excellency") from the Park Avenue curbside into the famous hostelry. Just before he disappeared through the revolving door, Tony turned, with a big smile: "They think I'm a Saudi Prince." The next morning he called and said: "I don't think we tell Cuomo about that, or Mr. Paley. To them I'm just a guy from Watertown."

Tony emceed every New York State Broadcasters dinner for thirty years—at the Otesaga in Cooperstown, the Gideon Putnam in Saratoga, and the Sagamore in Lake George.

When he died in 2006, the Broadcasters Foundation of America took over the "21" Club for a memorial tribute to this beguiling Italian. It was a fitting venue for a proper farewell to our own born and bred showman.

MARIO CUOMO: I'm batting ninth in this morning's lineup. I hope Tony didn't write out the batting order and put me there. That would make it very difficult for me to be as generous to him as he deserves.

Most Italian young men want to be good-looking, accomplished, smart, and funny. The first eight speakers covered the "funny" part of Tony Malara, but I want to take a more serious tack.

When I was governor, Tony said, "You know, Gov, you always come across as very serious." I was troubled by this observation, and replied, "Do you think it's a problem for me?" He countered, "Well, I've heard you tell jokes at broadcasters' events, and maybe you should stay serious!"

In my own defense, there are many reasons why I seem this way. After all, I spent twenty years in Albany, a place designed to evoke "constant Lent." Still, since it's in my nature, let me add a serious cast to the morning.

Public officials go to a lot of funerals. Often, they involve mass death such as the Lockerbie tragedy, the East Coldenham Elementary School wall collapse, and 9/11. People gather after those events by necessity: The shock and confusion must be shared. Especially when many of the victims were young.

Probably, we should avoid asking why, because it would just increase the torment. The Hebrews reacted with simple resignation, "The Lord giveth, and the Lord taketh away. Blessed be the name of the Lord."

But when it's just one person, like Tony, a different attitude is possible. Without struggling to understand the mystery of life and death, we can magnify the value of a good life by celebrating it!

It reminds me of a simple, lovely poem by a rabbi, recited at many funerals I've attended:

A man stood to speak,
At the funeral of his friend,

And read the dates on his tombstone,
From beginning to end.
He noted first the date of his birth,
And then spoke of the second in tears.
But then, he said, "What mattered most of all,
"Was the dash between those years.
"Because the dash represented,
"All the time he spent alive on Earth,
"And those who knew and loved him,
"Knew how much that little line was worth."

The people here today—Tony's beloved Mary, Toby and Beth, Meg and Scott, Beth and Hammy, his sister Ann, his grandchildren and his close friends—all know just how much that dash was worth.

They've come forward in droves since Tony passed: at the wake, at the funeral, in the press, in letters to one another, and again here today.

We hear their words of respect, admiration, and love, with only the occasional quip about his marvelous gift for dazzling fashion, something I'm sure he picked up from his good friend, the Great O'Shaughnessy, or maybe it was the other way around.

Joe Reilly calls him "Our Big Papi," a leader with charm, a gregarious nature, generosity, piercing intelligence, inherent common sense, courage, and a pleasant wit, in one of the nation's most important and complex industries.

Everyone adds their own affectionate recollections, but they all say virtually the same thing. This consistency is particularly notable because his colleagues, friends, and relatives are known for their candor and forthrightness. Nothing about Tony suggests meanness, selfishness, or vainglorious self-promotion.

I'm speaking from experience. Bill O'Shaughnessy formally introduced me to Tony a quarter of a century ago.

I came to know his many special qualities as I worked with him and many of the other broadcasters here, and saw his intelligence and determination, but his extraordinary sensitivity and affability as well.

And yet . . .

These are things we know and understand. We know how he lived and the way he loved. What he was given, what he gave, and what he has left behind. And we try to satisfy ourselves by sharing our recollections. But some of us yearn for more.

Joe Reilly asked, "What do we do now?" What happens now to all that vivacity, charm, and goodness? Does it die with our memories when we pass away? Does it return to the universe as the Native Americans believe? Is there a heaven?

I don't have any sure answer, but I've lived enough to know that doesn't mean there isn't one. So I'm wise enough not to eliminate any possibilities. But I can choose to believe and call it faith, if I must, if that's what promises meaningfulness.

And I choose to believe what many wise people over all the generations have related: that ultimately the good, the beautiful, and the lovely come together eternally in a better place.

And that means Tony is there, because he earned it in the DASH between 1936 and 2006.

As Dan Rather said so movingly, "He fought the good fight."

Thank you, Mary, for the privilege of being here today with you, your family, and so many of Tony's close friends. And thank you to the Broadcasters Foundation of America.

DAN RATHER: Jim Rosenfield, and Mr. Chairman, Phil Lombardo, Tony's great friend Governor Cuomo, Joe Reilly, and our mutual friend Bill O'Shaughnessy.

You all know about Tony's famous red handkerchief, but let me tell you about the red tie.

When I became the CBS anchor chair in 1981, Tony took me aside and said, "I'm going to give you important advice for your new job."

Tony had researched several focus groups in Australia, of all places, to find out why people watch certain anchor people and not others, and discovered the anchor with a red tie usually gets the "eyeballs."

I contacted Toby Wertheim, the legendary researcher for *CBS News*, to investigate this and found out it was true! So, thanks to

Tony, I have one of the world's largest collections of red ties! (*laughter*)

My wife, Jean, says Tony Malara is the most wonderful man she ever met. You may wonder where that leaves me, and I often have! (*laughter*) But I know why she says that, and so does anyone who ever met the man. Here was this person, always smiling, with an infectious laugh, and a genuine love of people radiating from deep inside. Tony was a nuclear power plant of energy, good humor, good will, and decency.

Just after I became anchor and managing editor of *CBS News*, Tony was chief executive for Affiliate Relations when his alma mater, Syracuse University, invited a competing anchor to give the school's graduation address. Tony swooped in on them like a hawk on a rabbit. (*laughter*) He beseeched; he heckled; he pleaded, "Hey, next year, you gotta invite my guy!" They wouldn't budge. He finally got to them by saying, with a wink and a smile, "Fellows, confidentially, just between you and me, if you don't do it, I will lose my job!"

Many years later, Tony called and said, "Dano, I need a favor." Naturally, I said, "Tony, you got it." Well, he wanted me to emcee the New York State Broadcasters Dinner, far, far upstate. Tony always attended up there in the far-flung reaches of the up country, but this particular meeting was in the dead of winter. "Don't worry, I'll get us a helicopter," he promised. "We'll whirl you up there and back; we'll have a good time, and it will be a breeze."

Well, wouldn't you know, when the scheduled night came, there was a snowstorm of historic proportions! So, no helicopter. We were driven up there and back, and it took hours each way. Well after midnight, we were on frozen roads in driving snow. Tony broke out two cigars; we started puffing on them—nearly asphyxiated the driver. (*laughter*)

Then Tony broke out an "adult beverage," and we sang all the way back. Everything from "Me and Bobby McGee" to "Hello, Dolly." When we dropped him off at his suburban home in Westchester at about 4 A.M., he got out, turned, wobbled ever so slightly, winked, and said, "Debt paid, Dano." (*laughter*)

Then he went into the house, laughing and singing. Now, I don't know what it was like in his house, but mine may best be described as "frosty"! (*laughter*)

This brings us to Tony's unbelievably good wife, Mary, and their exceptional children and grandchildren. How he loved them. A man's family says so much about who he is at his core. So it was with Tony.

Also, every person who knows Tony is amazed by his honesty. I once told him, "Tony you're so honest, I could shoot dice with you over the telephone!" (*laughter*) He just laughed, that deep "within himself" laugh, and said something like, "Alright, Dan, enough of that touchy-feely wisdom."

Then—and folks, sometimes I don't like talking about this—there was Tony's faith. Around and within him. In the words of the old hymn, "The faith of our fathers is with us still. We will be true till the end." And he was, till the end. Tony was never ostentatious about it. Didn't wear it on his sleeve. Didn't have to. Neither did he try to hide it. If you knew him, you knew, just knew, he had it.

He was true to his friends, too. Tony always flew the flag of loyalty. To paraphrase the old saying, "If you had Tony for a friend, you didn't need any others." He wasn't just a sunshine friend. Tony was an "I got your back" friend anytime stormy weather moved in. I witnessed that. This man was oak and iron. When the going got the toughest, Tony was at his finest.

Look how he handled himself in the end. Never explained, never complained, never backed up, and never backed down. He faced a long series of illnesses straight up, head on, eyes and nerves steady, laughing all the way, spreading good cheer and decency. He was, at the finish, as he'd been all his adult life, a man.

The last time I saw him, at the Broadcasters Foundation of America Dinner hosted by Nancy and Bill O'Shaughnessy, not too far from here, it was near the end. He knew it, and he knew I knew it.

In a quiet corner, I said to him, "How you doing, pal, how you really doing?"

"I'm doing great, Dano, just great."

I gave him a long look. Finally, he added, "Let me tell ya something, Dano. Something I once heard an old priest say to an aging lady, 'Don't give up, dear, keep fighting, keep trying, and keep smiling, as long as you have life. After all, you are going to be dead a long time.'" He laughed that huge enveloping laugh and moved back to the center of the party.

You know, I thought about that again last night. I remembered what Saint Paul wrote in a letter, as he lay dying, to his adopted son, Timothy. That saying applies to Tony. "He fought the good fight; he finished the race; and he kept the faith."

If every person helped by Tony brought a flower to this gathering today, he would sleep tonight under a canopy of blossoms.

In his own quiet, good-humored, decent way, there was, there is, no better man.

Come to think of it, the most wonderful man many of us ever met.

Broadcasters Foundation of America Memorial Remembrance
"21" Club, New York City
September 26, 2006

TONY MALARA

Our friend Joe Reilly, president of the New York State Broadcasters Association, gave this lovely eulogy when the colorful Malara was laid to rest in upstate Watertown, whence he came.

Monsignor, Father Robinson, Deacon Mastelon, friends.

We are here to celebrate the life of our remarkable colleague.

Anthony C. Malara was a legend, and it is a daunting task to adequately describe him. He radiated a larger-than-life persona you encounter once in a lifetime if you are lucky. We called him our "BIG PAPI" because he left an indelible imprint on everyone who crossed his path.

Upstate New York is often overshadowed by the bright lights of New York City, but our beloved Tony Malara rocketed himself from Watertown to outshine them all. His gregarious personality put everyone at ease, and he was so talented at making anyone feel his solicitous attention.

No organization, no entity knows that better than the New York State Broadcasters Association (NYSBA), where he served as our president and as emcee of our annual summer conference dinners for over thirty years. His dazzling white smile, his perpetual tan, his folksy charm, and his delightful wit just drew you in to become "one of the gang."

Make no mistake about it, Tony had a wonderful life. He belonged to a relentlessly loving family: Mary; Toby and Beth; Meg and Scott; Beth and Hammy; his sister, Ann; his grandchildren; and innumerable devoted friends.

He was beloved everywhere by everyone, in and out of broadcasting. I know the gang at the NYSBA loved him—Dick, Mary Anne, Sandy, and Barbara—as do the folks at the National Association of Broadcasters (NAB) in Washington. And he reserved a special affection for the humanitarian work of the Broadcasters Foundation of America, represented here today by Phil Lombardo, Gordon

Hastings, Dick Foreman, Nick Verbitsky, Rick Buckley, Ed McLaughlin, and Bill Moll.

But the foundation of Tony's success is sitting in the front row, Mary Frances Theresa Dacey. Mary kept Tony "real," focused, and remarkably humble. She made sure Tony had both feet on the ground. Well, maybe at least one of them. On so many occasions, totaling thousands of nights, Mary escorted Tony into rooms full of broadcasters and celebrities, who all rushed to his side. But you know what? Tony could have entered a room full of strangers, and within minutes he'd have twenty new friends. Mark Russell, the famous political satirist, said he first met Tony at a "home for the chronically adorable"!

Let's reminisce, for a moment, back to the halcyon days of the New York State Broadcasters Association when we gathered at the glorious Otesaga Hotel on Lake Otsego in Cooperstown. Our meetings were populated by the likes of Wally Schwartz, Dick Foreman, George Williams, Bob Mahlman, Phil Beuth, Bob Peebles, R. Peter Straus, Bob King, Bob Klose, Dick Beesmeyer, Les Arries, Phil Spencer, Lev Pope, Marty Beck, Tom Leahy, Walter Maxwell, Bob Williamson, Bob Leader, Perry Bascom, Ed McLaughlin, and so many more.

The regulars included Tony and Mary, the O'Shaughnessy kids, the Champlins, the Noviks, the Reillys, all young, upstart broadcasters in our early thirties. I remember when Tony and Mary invited Carol and me up to Watertown for a weekend. Aside from trying to sleep in a freshly painted guest room—we could hardly breathe!—Carol and I had a ball.

That weekend Tony and I stayed up until dawn talking about our futures. Tony worked for Johnny Johnson, the owner of the newspaper in Watertown and WWNY-TV, but he had a burning desire to be "tested." Well, a few months later, Tony phoned us late on a Sunday night and said CBS offered him a job in Affiliate Relations. I said, "Wow, what's Affiliate Relations?"

Tony accepted that position, and Jim Rosenfield, then president of CBS, invited him to lunch every day for five days so he could get used to the Big Apple. At the end of the week, Tony asked Jim, "How am I doing, boss?"

Jim responded, "Well, how do you think you did?"

"I think pretty well." Then Tony added, "Do you have any comments or suggestions?"

Rosenfield said, "Yeah, do you have any jackets and slacks that match?" (*laughter*)

Jim told us he took a lot of flak when he first hired Tony. Tony would wear blue leisure suits, and he flashed the "Peace" sign to everyone. In fact, he always signed his memos, "Peace, Tony!" When Tony first had business cards printed, they told him not to have his name printed on them so the next guy could use them! (*laughter*)

Tony worked under several chairmen at CBS, including the legendary founder, Bill Paley, John Backe, Arthur Taylor, Tom Wyman, and, of course, Larry Tisch. As one story goes, while Tony was still fairly new at CBS, Mr. Paley called a meeting about adding a newscast at 11:30 P.M., and Tony argued against it.

When Paley asked him why, Tony replied, "Mr. Paley, you don't understand."

The room fell silent, and Paley said, "OK, Mr. Malara, make me understand!"

After the meeting mercifully ended, several attendees informed Tony, "The Boss doesn't like to be questioned." But Tony got a personal note from Paley later on, "It's good to see a young man stand up for what he believes!"

Larry Tisch was quite another story. (*laughter*) Mr. Tisch came from a hugely successful and powerful corporate background. On Tisch's first day, he fired hundreds of senior personnel and was immediately taken to task by Tony. Tisch berated Tony, "CBS does $5 billion a year and employs hundreds of VPs. My company does $12 billion a year with only eighty VPs. Do the math!" (*laughter*)

Tony traveled with kings and was befriended by governors like Mario Cuomo, whom he so admired. But after all of it—the high life, all the glitter, the fancy restaurants, the corporate jets, after exploring the world—he would always return to his beloved Watertown, with its beautiful river and fabled islands here on the Canadian border.

I guess we're all asking ourselves, what do we do now?

How do we fill an unfillable void? Over time, I expect, the memory will dim, but our powerful bond with Tony will remain unbroken.

At the end of the day, broadcasting is about people, not the bottom line. No one understood this better than Tony. In a high-stakes business with fierce competition, scandals, backstabbing, busted marriages, and destroyed friendships, Tony built bridges on the way to the top instead of burning them.

I guess it's not at all surprising that his great heart finally gave out last week up at Wellesley Island, because, you see, that part of Tony got the most use.

His generous, loving heart embraced all of you. And all of us.

"Peace," Tony.

Peace.

St. Anthony's Church
Watertown, N.Y.
August 30, 2006

"TONY"

Here are my own remarks about Tony Malara.

Tony Malara was *sui generis* . . . unique and able to be defined only on his own terms. I never encountered an individual who wasn't crazy about the guy.

Joe Reilly, Dan Rather, Charlie Osgood, and the great Mario Cuomo have spoken of him much more gracefully than I am able. Malara was a pure, natural force. As an emcee, he was one of the two or three best I've observed in front of a crowd. His talent at the podium was informed not alone by the rapier-sharp quickness of his wit but also by the genuine warmth of his marvelous personality.

Governor Cuomo and I used to kid him about the "great responsibility" he carried as the highest-ranking Italian in network TV. But no matter how far up he went, Tony never forgot who he was and where he came from.

As he achieved each high, new estate in a remarkable career, he always went home at night the same guy who came down from Watertown to charm, beguile, dazzle, and love us.

Tony did so much for the Broadcasters Foundation of America.

But his *first* and greatest love—professionally—was always the New York State Broadcasters Association.

December, 2006

GOVERNOR MARIO M. CUOMO ON WILLIAM F. BUCKLEY JR.

I knew William Buckley for more than twenty years and opposed him in his last public debate. I have never encountered his equal as a brilliant, gentle, charming philosopher, seer and advocate. William Buckley died, but his complicated brilliance will live on as long as words are spoken and read.

Governor Mario Cuomo

WILLIAM O'SHAUGHNESSY (W.O.): Governor Cuomo, you and William Buckley are both wordsmiths. Was he a pretty tough guy in a debate?

GOVERNOR MARIO CUOMO (M.C.): Extremely. His was a very subtle and profound intelligence. And he was well read and knowledgeable. Even at a very young age, when he attended Yale and wrote his first well-known book. Buckley was a grandmaster of the English language.

When I debated him in Cincinnati recently, he announced it was the last time he would ever debate publicly. We had a lot of fun, but I was beguiled by his elaborate syntax. I enjoyed his responses so much, my counterpoint was shorter than it should have been.

W.O.: Cuomo and Buckley: opposite ends of the political spectrum. Did you guys get along?

M.C.: Yes, we did. And his magazine, *The National Review*, complimented me on several occasions. We often agreed.

To be candid with you, public officials who diligently study the issues agree on a large part of the dialogue. He was flexible in his beliefs, and our differences were much more subtle. He believed government was a little bit too active, and I felt the opposite. And again, in that last debate, he had me mesmerized.

W.O.: Governor Cuomo, you've told us about your humble beginnings in Queens. Bill Buckley evokes Park Avenue, East Hampton, and Hobe Sound. He acted like a quintessential WASP, but I think he was a practicing Catholic.

M.C.: He was very Catholic and a philosophical Christian. Take the Sermon on the Mount; he probably could have written it better. But he agreed with the substance.

It's a big, big loss. And I have never encountered his equal with the English language. I have every book he's ever written on the subject, and he's written several. They're all on my desk, and if I live to be two hundred, I may begin to understand them.

February 27, 2008

FUNERAL SERVICE FOR OSSIE DAVIS

Mario Cuomo once told me he prays for "sureness." I'm sure of only one thing: Ossie Davis was a saint.

EARL GRAVES: Welcome to our farewell to "Ossie." For that's all you had to say, and people knew you were talking about Ossie Davis.

You could tell from the big smile they gave you, just about anywhere in the nation. There was only one Ossie if you lived in Harlem, where his distinguished stage career began sixty years ago, or at Howard University, or the state of Georgia, or Bedford-Stuyvesant, or St. Louis, or Sag Harbor, or Detroit, or Chicago's South Side, or even Beverly Hills.

And wherever you come from or wherever you've been since his passing, if two or more African Americans were present, you heard the same thing, "Have you heard about Ossie?" Of course, it wasn't just us. The world loved Ossie and Ruby. Again, no last name needed.

I want to say only a few words in Ossie's memory on behalf of his friends. All one billion of us. As Ruby said, "Ossie would be upset if his funeral ran so long that it needed an intermission." (*laughter*)

He achieved many things. A great artist, a fearless activist, a committed educator, a motivator without peer, Ossie considered himself a citizen of the world with an insatiable appetite for knowledge, culture, and ideas. A humanist in the purest sense, he believed our society's commitment to equality and basic justice should be firm and nonnegotiable. Whenever and wherever that social contract was broken or threatened, Ossie stood on the front lines to demand justice. And he was built for the job. Ossie was a formidable man, both physically and intellectually, with a voice God must have patterned after His own.

At the same time, Ossie had a gentle soul and a joyful spirit. Most of all, he was a gentleman, and wherever he walked, he was accompanied by integrity. In this era of caution and compromise,

Ossie's life defied conventional wisdom about the limits on a public persona. He accepted wisdom and avoided contortions and compromise to achieve fame. Ossie served as our moral compass, and if you stood with Ossie, more than likely you were on the right side of the issue.

Unlike other public people, he accepted controversy and unpopular ideas, especially if they meant speaking out in the face of injustice, or standing up for people he admired when things got tough.

He supported Paul Robeson, instead of walking away. He movingly eulogized Malcolm X when other celebrities dissociated themselves from the slain leader's legacy.

But despite his learning and eloquence, he was unable to say no. When you needed Ossie to emcee your event or champion your cause, he was always there. Whether the crowd was five or five thousand, he always made it seem like the most important place in the world. So we are here to celebrate his kindness, loyalty, and generosity. Some of our remembrances and tributes will bring laughter; others will draw tears. Both are appropriate this afternoon.

MUTA ALI: I'm Ossie's oldest grandson. And I figure if all these people are here to say good-bye to him, he's got to be here, right now.

Grandpa, this is my first time talking to you since you passed away. As you probably already know, I was very upset. But that quickly changed, and I felt proud for the rest of the day. I've been avoiding talking to you for two reasons. Number one: I didn't know if you could hear me. And number two: Talking to you without picking up the phone or seeing you with my own two eyes would force me to accept you're gone. I've become detached from the moment, trying to avoid crying; and thinking about the pain others in the family are feeling helps me avoid my own. I remember the last time I saw you. It was Christmas dinner at your house, and before I left, I came to you in the dining room. You were sleeping, and I called your name until you woke up. I said, "I apologize for that." And you laughed and said it was all right. And you hugged me like you always do.

I spoke to you on the phone the night before you left for Miami. You were helping me with something as you always did. Your love is etched on my heart just as your initials are etched on my arm. You've blessed my life for twenty-five years, this earth for eighty-seven. I guess it's the angels' turn now. So, go ahead and bless heaven, Grandpa.

BRIAN DAY: I was his middle grandchild.

He always said if we did his funeral wrong, he was going to get up and do it himself.

I never knew Ossie Davis as the actor or activist, just as my grandfather. And he was the greatest example of a man I have ever known.

For all his greatness, he was so humble. Many people wanted me to tell stories about him, and all I could say was that he liked Fig Newtons and chardonnay.

He would treat presidents and heads-of-state the same way as a beggar or a waiter. Every time we ventured out, he made a new friend. I remember once a lady asked him if he was Ossie Davis. He answered, "I hope so, because I have his wallet."

When I first learned my grandfather died, it was the saddest I've ever been. But now I feel lucky for the twenty years we shared. A lot of people are asking if there is anything our family needs. I usually say nothing. But now, I personally need something. I need everyone here to keep Ossie Davis's legacy alive. I need you to go tell someone about him so he will live far longer than last Friday and far longer than anyone in this room.

MAYA ANGELOU: About ten days ago, Ossie and Ruby asked me to stand in for them at the Kennedy Center in Washington. Ossie said, "It's not much money." And I replied, "That doesn't surprise me."

In the 1960s or 1950s, Ossie and Ruby had a radio show and asked me to write a piece for $50. I still have it, and I said, "I'm going to show it to the world and show how good the writing was, and that you only paid me fifty bucks." Whereupon Ossie said, "Girl, we only had a hundred. We gave you half. We should have given you thirty-three and a third."

And then the heaviest door in the universe slammed shut. And there were no knobs. The season of grief fell around us like the leaves of autumn. When great trees fall, rocks on distant hills shudder. Lions hunker down in tall grasses, and even elephants lumber after safety. When great trees fall in forests, small things recoil into silence; their senses are eroded beyond fear.

When great souls die, the air around us becomes sterile, light rare. We breathe deeply. Our eyes briefly see with a hurtful clarity. Our memory, suddenly sharpened, examines, gnaws on kind words unsaid, on promised walks not taken.

Great souls die, and our reality bound to them takes leave of us. Our souls, dependent upon them, upon their nature, upon their nurture, now shrink wizened. Our minds formed and informed by their radiance seem to fall away. We are not so much maddened as reduced to the unutterable silence of dark, cold caves.

And then our memory comes to us again in the form of a spirit, and it is the spirit of our beloved. It appears draped in the wisdom of Du Bois, furnished in the humor and the grace of Paul Laurence Dunbar. We hear the insight of Frederick Douglass and the boldness of Marcus Garvey.

We see our beloved standing before us as a light, as a beacon, indeed, as a way. We are not so much reduced. Suddenly, the peace blooms around us. It is strange. It blooms slowly, always irregularly. Space is filled with a kind of soothing electric vibration. We see the spirit, and we know our senses. We change, resolved, never to be the same.

They whisper to us from the spirit. Remember, he existed. He existed. He belonged to us. He exists in us. We can be, and be more, every day more. Larger, kinder, truer, more honest, more courageous, and more loving because Ossie Davis existed and belonged to all of us.

HARRY BELAFONTE: Sixty years is a long time to know somebody, a long time to be hugging somebody, and there comes a time when the end draws near, and you realize it's just the blink of an eye.

Tony Bennett is the last great crooner of the American classic songbook and a gifted artist who signs his paintings "Benedetto." At Mario Cuomo's 70th-birthday party, the author looked at Cuomo and said, "I'm just going to sing my greetings . . . because I'd rather *sing* in front of Tony Bennett than try to *talk* in front of you!"

Master of the Flugelhorn: Chuck Mangione has enlivened many a party of an evening.

Nita Lowey has served Westchester, the Bronx, and the entire nation with great distinction in the House of Representatives, where, as a powerful committee chair, she is known as one of the "cardinals." WVOX was a great supporter of hers at the start of her political career. She is seen here with her husband, Steve Lowey.

Below: New York Attorney General Andrew Cuomo, who many hope will become governor of the Empire State, with the author.

Above: A Mother's Love. Nancy Curry O'Shaughnessy and her son, Michael Lawrence Pasquale.

Below: Designer Frédéric Fekkai (right) with the author and Nancy Curry O'Shaughnessy. Fekkai is a generous philanthropist and mentor to many young people in the beauty business.

Maria Cuomo Cole and her husband, designer and philanthropist Kenneth Cole, with the author.

From left: New York power broker Bill Plunkett; Litchfield restaurateur Charles Kafferman; Nancy Curry O'Shaughnessy; Kafferman's partner, the famed chef James O'Shea. Kafferman and O'Shea have operated the estimable West Street Grill on the green in Litchfield for more than twenty years.

Right: "Taken for a Ride!" Mauro Maccioni, the youngest scion of restaurateur Sirio Maccioni, asked the author to hop aboard his Vespa.

Left: the author plants a big one on son David Tucker O'Shaughnessy, president of WVOX and WVIP. He can run them with his eyes closed! Right: the author's oldest son, Matthew Thayer O'Shaughnessy, a young man of many talents. Below: the author and his two sons, Matthew (left) and David, at one of WVOX's legendary St. Patrick's Day community salute broadcasts. Who brought the ketchup bottle?

Above, from left: Jerry Nulty, a videographer, and his wife, Kate O'Shaughnessy Nulty, a licensed clinical social worker; the author; David Tucker O'Shaughnessy, president, WVOX and WVIP; and his wife, Cara Ferrin O'Shaughnessy.

Below: the author receiving an honorary Doctor of Humane Letters degree from Mount St. Mary College in Newburgh.

Above: Atta boy! The author beams approval as his son Matthew Thayer O'Shaughnessy addresses a crowd. Matthew's grandfather the legendary investor and publisher Walter Nelson Thayer ran the *New York Herald Tribune* and was a pillar of the Eastern Republican Establishment.

Below: Extended family. From left: David Kowalski and his wife, the author's niece, Laura O'Shaughnessy; Kelly O'Shaughnessy and the author's nephew and her husband, John O'Shaughnessy.

“G’Pa!” My first grandchild, Tucker Thomas Nulty.

Summer stroll. The author out and about with four of his five grandchildren.

Ossie Davis and I shared a friendship for sixty years and saw many peaks and valleys. And in recent times, when we were on a platform to serve some community or human need, we would notice our lack of energy and exuberance. And when we sat down, we did so a little more slowly to protect our lower backs.

And just a few days ago, Ossie and I reflected on our remaining time. And he said to me, "Harry, if it comes to be that I leave here before you, which is not my intention, nor my expectation, but if that happens, be sure that when you stand before those who are gathered that you don't, for God's sake, put any words in my mouth." I told him it was impossible. In his eighty-seven years, he said just about everything and did so eloquently.

Words cannot express the grief we feel about the loss of our beloved Raiford Chatman Davis. His passing is no simple loss. The vastness of his being, so humbly contained, can only now be revealed. All people embraced him, as he embraced all people. But he was especially loved by black folk and the poor. He was of them, and from birth until death, he was in the midst of their everything.

Among many gifts mastered, he was foremost a master of language. He understood the power of words and used them to articulate our deepest longing to attain oneness with all humanity.

Ossie Davis was born at a time of great promise. With a fervent dedication to justice, he seized every opportunity to uplift the poor, humiliated, and oppressed. He embraced the greatest forces of our time: Paul Robeson, Dr. W. E. B. Du Bois, Eleanor Roosevelt, A. Philip Randolph, Fanny Lou Hamer, Ella Baker, Thurgood Marshall, Dr. Martin Luther King Jr., Nelson Mandela, and many more.

When our America was torn asunder by racial conflict, Ossie stood at the tomb of one of our noblest warriors and delivered a eulogy on Malcolm X and his contribution to the African American struggle for freedom. History has witnessed his uncompromising allegiance to the truth, and Ossie Davis stands validated and revered.

The bond between Ossie and his compassionate and courageous Ruby Dee has been amply blessed. They are inseparable, for their union transcended the physical; their thoughts were one. Their utterances were wrapped in mutual approval, and their love embraced the universe and all its living creatures.

The harmony of their song was filled with trust and respect. Together, their solidarity in the face of bitter struggle was welded to a deep commitment to nonviolence as the most powerful weapon in humankind's arsenal. Their children and grandchildren represent the embodiment of their nurturing love and gift to our world.

In 1917, if a black man could choose, he would avoid being born in Cogdell, Georgia. But this birthplace shaped Ossie Davis's values and courage. He came from a family of achievers, and their dignity and unwillingness to be defined as subhuman enraged the surrounding white community. The Ku Klux Klan's vow to shoot down his father like a dog led Ossie to explore writing as a career.

That quest introduced him to Shakespeare and the theater, and in the thespian world, he found purpose. The performing arts became his rebellion to tyranny. And as an actor, he interpreted our existence in a way rarely afforded to the generations of black artists who preceded him. The few who succeeded, like Paul Robeson, became Ossie Davis's guide to a life of social activism through art.

Black America has survived in a state of siege for four hundred years and has placed its faith in the articles of governance framed by our white Founding Fathers. But exclusion from a zone of special privilege has imprisoned all but a small number of black citizens.

Ossie Davis, though seduced by the privileges of the elite as a movie star and a revered presence in our national culture, refused to distance himself from the vast majority of his people and diligently championed our struggle to sit at the table of America's experiment with democracy.

He despaired at the present state of our nation and detested the lies and deceit in our nation's arrogant and mindless imperial march toward global domination. But he encouraged those who lost heart, saying, "Let us not linger on what is lost, but let us dwell on what we must do. Let us do what we know how to do. Let us forge an unbreakable solidarity and blow the dust off the blueprints of our past victories. Let us reclaim our undistorted moral truth, and turn all of this into a world of peace. Let us reclaim our earth and nurture it with love for all of her offspring. Let us be worthy of our existence and reassert our national humanity. To do anything less would be patriotic treason."

The richness of Ossie Davis's wit and humor complemented his commanding intellect and compelling art. Once in my home, planning for our emerging desegregation battle in Montgomery, Alabama, Dr. King, Stan Levinson, Bernard Lee, Ossie, and a few others were listening to Bayard Rustin, our expert on Ghandian nonviolent methodology. And Bayard showed us what to do if our marches were stopped by state troopers, if we were tear-gassed or beaten, taken in the paddy wagon, booked at the police station, and incarcerated.

We listened carefully and, during the following weeks, organized our demonstrations. In the march for Selma, we planned for tens of thousands of marchers to arrive that night just outside Montgomery at a holding point provided by the Catholic Church, a place called St. Jude. The grounds were quite spacious.

On the morning before the arrivals, to revitalize the marchers, we built a stage using 120 coffins donated by two local funeral parlors. I greeted the chartered flights, crammed with our cultural luminaries from Los Angeles and New York, at Montgomery airport. Stepping off the plane, behind Tony Bennett and Leonard Bernstein and others, was Ossie, and in the near background stood George Wallace's most feared law-enforcement chief, Bull Connor, and his battle-ready Gestapo.

Ossie gazed at the display of force, and at that moment, all of the horrors described by Bayard Rustin danced before our eyes. And just as we were envisioning mad dogs nipping at our genitalia, Ossie, expressing his deepest concern, turned to me and said, "Tell me, Harry, you don't snore, do you?"

I can barely fathom being unable to call upon his wisdom, humor, passion, loyalty, and moral strength in future battles. But just as [with] Paul, and W. E. B. and Malcolm, and Fanny Lou, and Medgar, and Bobby, and Eleanor, his blueprint of courage is now left for us and future generations to absorb and implement by speaking truth to power. Thank you, Ossie. Those whose lives you touched are forever inspired, and we are deeply, deeply grateful.

PRESIDENT BILL CLINTON: Ruby, members of the family, reverend clergy, I want to thank you first, Ruby, for inviting me. Dr. Butts said Ossie could have been a Baptist preacher. He would have also been a very good president of the United States.

I have only this to say. Like most of you here, he gave to me more than I ever gave to him. But whenever I saw Ossie and Ruby, I thought, "They're beautiful, and brilliant, and talented. They're warm and friendly, and they're humble." I always thought, "What is it that they are that makes me feel so good every time I see them?" And finally, I realized that they were free and always have been.

I never was in Ossie Davis's presence, not one time, that I didn't want to stand up a little straighter, speak a little better, be a little more generous. Not very long ago, the great Nina Simone passed on. She sang my favorite song of the civil rights movement: "I wish I knew how it would feel to be free/I wish I could break all the chains holding me/I wish I could rise like a bird in the sky/I would soar like an eagle when I found I could fly/I wish that you knew how it feels to be me/Then you would see and agree, every man should be free."

That lesson is what Ossie Davis taught all of us for eighty-seven years. He labored so other people might enjoy that freedom, but his came from inside, from the greatness of his spirit, from the connection to his maker, from the power of his love with Ruby and their family. And I think I can speak for all of us when I say, thank you, God, for letting us know it.

ATTALLAH SHABAZZ: We live in an America striving for multicultural existence and diversity. But let's hope we maintain the light of Africa, the light of Du Bois, the light of Robeson. And there's Malcolm in that light of Africa. There's Fannie Lou Hamer. And now, there's my Grandpa. There's Ossie Davis who walked among us.

Riverside Church, New York City
February 12, 2005

THE SIMPLE PRIEST

Father John O'Brien was a Westchester priest who presided at the funeral masses for Bernard F. Curry Jr. and Michael Pasquale, my stepson. A tribute to Mr. Curry was published in an earlier book. And my remarks for Michael can be found on page 499.

John O'Brien was a priest of the Roman Church according to the ancient order. He had a marvelous gift, and not since Monsignor Ed Connors have we had someone stand up in front of a Westchester congregation to preach about the carpenter's son with as much grace and eloquence.

O'Brien, a gentle man, spoke with a raspy, gritty croak caused by the thousands of cigarettes that killed him. But he reached into many hearts with that great gift of expression that accompanied him when he went to work in a church.

He was a Christian Brother for many years before entering the priesthood late in life. And so, instead of standing in a classroom before thirty-five rowdy kids, John O'Brien, in recent years, did his teaching and his preaching too in front of many of all ages every Sunday and on the days of obligation.

He didn't speak with the brilliance of a Jesuit orator or the scruffy humanity and relentless compassion of the Franciscans. There was only a stark honesty to O'Brien, who spoke with some intimate knowledge of the long-remembered, timeless wisdom of the church fathers. You could hear the cigarettes, the wheeze, and the rattle in his soft voice as he whispered those ancient truths in stunningly simple homilies.

The old priest was uncomfortable presiding way up in the pulpit lording it over everyone. He always did his best work at eye level on the floor up close to the people huddled in their pews.

I've seen the priest O'Brien in hospital rooms mumbling the rosary for comatose patients who may or may not have been able to hear him. And I observed him consoling a family following the untimely death of a beautiful young man. I also saw the Irishman with the Roman collar go after rich contractors and road builders from Scarsdale, like generous Felix Petrillo, to persuade them to help his parish. He was something to behold when shaking the money tree.

But being Irish, John O'Brien was at his best at funerals, praying and often shedding his own real tears over the deceased and dearly departed ranging in age from eighty-four to twenty-two. But he was gentle and kind and had a great way about him through it all in every season.

I remember one winter day, not unlike this one, when the priest stood in front of grieving relatives at a funeral Mass for that young man:

> Our lives teach us that courage is the opposite of fear. But it's not. *Faith* is the opposite of fear. Having that Faith is something that doesn't come easily or automatically into our lives. It comes by experience and by the awful grace of God.
>
> You're filled with sorrow now. But Faith tells us, assures us, all is well, because His *name* is Emmanuel, and I am with you always. Even to the End of the world. It was *His* name at the Beginning. And it is *His* name at the End.
>
> So, I come to do the Will of my Father. And *this* is the Will of my Father: that I should lose nothing. That you should lose nothing.

He was not a high-church kind of priest. And you could not imagine O'Brien strolling in some Vatican garden taking his constitutional clad in a finely tailored cassock adorned with a purple sash or scarlet trim speaking in hushed diplomatic tones with hands clasped casually behind his back.

And yet, despite his aversion to pomp and pretension, it was announced that several bishops and elders of the church will pray over the Reverend John P. O'Brien at St. Pius X Church in Scarsdale this weekend, including the new Archbishop Timothy Dolan, who, one is sure, is O'Brien's kind of guy. Come to think of it, you couldn't imagine *Dolan* strolling in that Vatican garden with the canon lawyers and diplomats either.

As he lay dying this week at New York University Hospital in the great city, someone sent the priest a note: "You are loved and respected." I hope he got it and understood it through all the tubes and painkillers.

And so Timothy Dolan himself will preside at Mass on Saturday. The archbishop brings a wonderful joy and dynamism to everything he does. But who, I wonder, will reach out and grab people by the throat and tug at their hearts to tell those assembled once more in sadness and mourning just how very special the old priest with the gravelly voice really was?

Before he left us last week, the pastor of St. Pius X Church in Scarsdale sat at his desk in the parish rectory to write a Christmas message. It was to be his last homily. The priest was wracked with pain. But there were many things to do to get the parish ready for the holy season. He knew he was dying, and the very next day John O'Brien would check himself into a New York hospital. So he worked quickly, but carefully. This is what he wrote as he sat in loneliness and silence on that cold day last week in Scarsdale:

> "Silent night, holy night
>
> All is calm, all is bright."
>
> A holy night to be sure, but hardly silent and anything but calm.
>
> The "silence" of that night was shattered by the blood-curdling cries of wild animals roaming the hillsides. In a cold, dark cave a young, frightened woman gave birth to her child while her husband, a carpenter by trade, stood by helplessly.
>
> Finally, amid the bleating of sheep and the braying of animals, the newborn's first cry broke the stillness. This "silent night" was filled with terror, pain, and the bone-numbing exhaustion that sleep alone cannot relieve.
>
> There was no "silence" that night so long ago in crowded, chaotic Bethlehem, bursting with visitors who had come for the great census. In fact, there was no "calm" in all of Israel—only tension and conflict between the Jewish people and their Roman occupiers. Ancient Palestine was hardly a place of "heavenly peace." It was a land torn by oppression, persecution, and terror. Madness reigned.

And yet, on this noisy, chaotic, anxious night, our Savior, the Light of the World, was born. Amid the pain and anguish of a devastated people, new hope was born. The Messiah came at last with transforming joy.

Even though our world today may once more seem far from "silent," our church far from "holy," our personal lives far from "calm," the Prince of Peace has blessed our flawed and fractured world by walking upon it, by loving those in it relentlessly and unconditionally, and by laying down his life for all who pass through it.

For he would rather die than to live in eternity without us.

Emmanuel! God is with us! Let earth receive her King!

He retired with the gift.

December 10, 2009

MARIO CUOMO SPEAKS OF SENATOR TED KENNEDY

WILLIAM O'SHAUGHNESSY (W.O.): Governor, Ted Kennedy—the "Lion of the Senate"—has gone to another and, we're sure, a better world. You've been interviewed by media from all over the world. Your office tells me you've received calls from just about everywhere inquiring about Kennedy. What about his legacy?

MARIO M. CUOMO (M.C.): You said an interesting thing, Bill; you said he's gone to a better world. I suspect he's gone to a world that he's going to *make* better because that's what he did while he was here. He was a true believer in giving service, in the sense of doing for the people around him, for the entire community, everything you can do.

That's the way the Kennedys defined their life, after Joe Kennedy made a "little" money and empowered them with the ability to devote themselves entirely to public life. There was John, Bobby, Ted; and today there's Patrick and Robert Jr., and the younger ones. And they all do it wonderfully well.

He was the last big member of the Kennedy brothers standing. He became the spiritual force and being of the family. And he also became a force in the Congress with both Republicans and Democrats. Of course, whatever people choose to say about him, and especially people who insist on the language of ideology—as in, this guy's a conservative, this guy's a liberal—he was somebody who believes in what Obama believes in. And what I believe in.

And many of us do think there might be a place for ideology, but it's not first place. First place should go to common sense and "benign pragmatism." Benign pragmatism means it works and it works for the good of the people. And that's the way Ted Kennedy defined his own work. In a speech over twenty years ago at Yale, they asked me what *I* was, and I said I strive to be a "progressive pragmatist." That's what Kennedy succeeded in being. That's what Obama is trying to be. And that's what Kennedy *did*—with all sorts of wonderful accomplishments—in the process.

W.O.: Are you saying he wasn't exactly all that "liberal"?

M.C.: I'm saying the word "liberal" doesn't describe him adequately. If you trace the word "liberal" from the very beginning, you'll get very confused because of the people who you now think of with that label. You should ditch most of those labels, but we will continue to use them no matter what I say. What he was is a guy who believed in helping people when people need help.

He was frankly closer to Lincoln than most Republicans are today. Lincoln, of course, ended up calling himself a Republican, but he was at first a Whig. And I say Ted was close to Lincoln because of the way Lincoln described government—as Ted did: government coming together for people to do for one another, collectively, what you could not do as well—or at all—privately.

So if the market won't do it for you, the government *will*. That's what Ted Kennedy believed. That's what he acted on. So things like Medicare, Medicaid, health care, and a new thing called Child Health Plus—which was a New York program, incidentally—which became SCHIP (State Children's Health Insurance Program) because Kennedy liked it. He liked the idea of insuring children that didn't have a family insurance policy. Insuring them at least in terms of primary medicine that is not acute—with regular visitations. And that's what he did. He found that the market system wasn't doing enough, so he worked on getting the government to provide more health care. That's what all the great leaders have done.

Think about it. If the market and philanthropy [had] taken care of all the old people who were sick, you would never have needed Medicare. And if the market took care of poor people who were sick, you would never have needed Medicaid. If the market took care of education, you would never have needed public schools. And if the market took care of outer space or if Boeing would do it for us, you wouldn't need government to spend all that money. And if the market [had] built a highway system that joins the states together for the good of the economy, you wouldn't have needed Eisenhower to do it. And *that's* Ted Kennedy. The things we need and we don't get from the market system. The market comes first. The government system only comes as a last resort. But if you can't get it through philanthropy and the market, then we should do it for you. And that's what Ted Kennedy did. With health care and so many other things.

W.O.: Governor, you've written extensively and beautifully about Mr. Lincoln. You were quoted today on Reuters and the AP that Ted Kennedy was maybe the most influential senator ever in this country. Is that right?

M.C.: Well, it's not such an astounding statement, Bill, when you consider how many years he's been there. He's been there a very long time. Obviously, if you're there a long time you have more opportunity to affect people's judgments.

He made the most of that time—some people have been there for a long time and haven't done a whole lot—by being active for the whole period. He was always one who was involved in the big issues.

Not just health care and other things that were associated with so-called liberal people. Take the creation of a 9/11 Commission. I spoke with Kennedy about that. He was right in the middle of trying to find somebody who would be a good chairman for the Democrats. And he's been in the middle of all these things. Like I said before, he took Child Health Plus and made it a national program by going to another great senator—Orrin Hatch, a Republican.

W.O.: Governor, are you telling me he wanted you to be chairman of the Democrats?

M.C.: No. We were discussing who should be and how it should operate. My point is not whom he wanted to select, but that he was in the middle of every big issue. If he were here now and alive he would be talking about health care, of course. And he would also be talking about Afghanistan. And he would be talking about how long we're going to have to stay there. In all the big issues, Ted Kennedy had a role, and it was a significant one.

W.O.: Ted Kennedy was seventy-seven. You, sir, I think, are seventy-seven. It goes fast, doesn't it? Life, I mean.

M.C.: Well, assuming that I am seventy-seven, O'Shaughnessy, it goes fast. Well, faster than I am comfortable with. And that reminds me of something else—as long as you insist on getting personal—when you talk about Ted Kennedy, it's not unusual for people to end an interview—which I'm sure you won't—with a question: Well, how about *Chappaquiddick*? Or how about this? Or how about things that involve Ted Kennedy's persona as a moral individual?

W.O.: I'll ask the question: How *about* Chappaquiddick?

M.C.: My answer is very simple. If you're asking for judgments on Ted Kennedy and whether or not the things he did—the personal things—were right or wrong, I'm not in that business.

I've been asked that a couple of times earlier today. I try very hard not to judge others. I leave that up to God. I've been in the habit of judging myself for a very long time now, and I'm very uncomfortable with the results.

W.O.: As you pronounce judgment on Mario Cuomo, are you satisfied with *your* seventy-seven years?

M.C.: No, not nearly, Bill. First of all, mentioning my seventy-seven years and Ted Kennedy's seventy-seven years in the same breath is foolish. I'm nowhere near what he ended up being. He was a tremendous force for good at the highest levels of the government of the most powerful nation in world history. That's what he was. He was a powerful force in the most powerful body in the most powerful nation in the world. I was a governor . . .

W.O.: The *Boston Globe* called you "the preeminent philosopher-statesman in our nation," but we'll save that for another day and another discussion.

M.C.: Thanks, Bill.

W.O.: We've lost Ted Kennedy. I'm glad we haven't lost Mario Cuomo's strong, clear, sweet voice.

August 27, 2009

JOHN BRANCA

John Branca, who died this week in Florida at eighty-six, was a beloved Mount Vernon icon. Many knew him as the brother of the legendary Brooklyn Dodger Ralph Branca. But John Branca put up a lot of numbers on the scoreboard of life all on his very own. And for all his laurels and high estate in the world of politics and sports, Johnny Branca was a Westchester townie.

Although he spent his last years in Florida pushing a market basket through Walgreen's and flirting with the silver-haired widows in the Piggly Wiggly supermarket, John Branca will long be remembered around here as a New York state assemblyman and Commissioner of Recreation in Mount Vernon, the land-locked, struggling Westchester city. He was a celebrated high school coach, and Mario Cuomo even made him chairman of the New York State Athletic Commission where he cleaned up the brutal, violent sport called boxing. And, always, he was one damn good friend of this community radio station.

Back in the '60s and into the '70s, "Commissioner" Branca, as everyone called him, would preside and hold daily court on the benches at Hartley Park and listen to the pleadings and importunings of the old men of the neighborhood who would bring him their problems, laden with heavy dialects grown in the hills of Calabria, Guardia Lombardi, and Bari. Branca listened and savored all of it. And tried to assist.

He was a most agreeable figure and a class act in every season. Although he never became mayor of Mount Vernon, John Branca was a powerful political force, and you needed him on your side in every proposition.

Mount Vernon had a lot of vivid and beguiling figures then.

Alan Rosenberg, the legendary Westchester financial guru, played ball at A. B. Davis, which also launched a brilliant guy named Richard Garfunkel. And the great Bob Trupin, who played for Yale, came off those streets. And a brash kid named Jerry Valenti was building up his electrical contracting company even then.

He was of a Mount Vernon when giants walked the land in that city . . . larger-than-life personalities like Joe Vacarella, Augie

Petrillo, the banker Walter Moore, Sal Quaranta, Tommy Sharpe, Judge Irving Kendall, Reggie Lafayette, Tom Delaney, David Ford, Frank Connelly Sr., M. Paul Redd, Frank LaSorsa, and a struggling theater kid named Denzel Washington. Also young rising stars like Gary Pretlow, Jimmy Finch, George Latimer, Roberta Apuzzo, Clinton Young, David Alpert, and Ernie Davis. The great preacher W. Franklyn Richardson, soon to become a revered national figure, would climb up in the pulpit at Grace Baptist Church on Sundays. And Ossie Davis visited his mother every weekend.

For a good, long time, Branca sat before the WVOX microphone, presiding over our Pepsi High School "Game of the Week" as a play-by-play announcer and color commentator. He had a wife named Millie, and she was part of it too, a very big part.

John Branca spent the last two decades in Florida where he never saw his beloved Westchester overrun by insufferable yuppies in their BMWs and Mercedes. These people, who send their kids to Hackley and Rye Country Day School, do not know of Hartley Park where he sat on warm summer nights.

He was a politician the way the people of our parents' time imagined them to be.

This is a Whitney Media Commentary. This is Bill O'Shaughnessy.

July 2010

EPILOGUE: MORE RIFFS, RANTS, AND RAVES (SUMMER EDITION)

My third book, *More Riffs, Rants, and Raves,* like the two before it, was acclaimed far beyond its due. I hated the title, but I'll use it now as a reprise for our annual "End of Summer" column. As the days dwindle down, here then are some meandering thoughts from my notebook:

Just asking: Is it possible **George W. Bush** may have been right all along? I mean, could he actually be a hell of a lot better president than his critics believe?

The rave reviews for **Andrew M. Cuomo** as attorney general surprised everyone. But not his father or mother. Or us.

In the fight between **United Water** and **Louis Cappelli** over paying for the French conglomerate's infrastructure, we're with Cappelli. His generosity and largesse are as apparent as his ubiquitous skyscrapers. The mega-developer has literally saved some of our cities through his care for our neighborhoods. United Water has failed as a corporate citizen ever since it gobbled up the old New Rochelle Water Company forty years ago from its wonderful owner, J. Lester Albertson.

United Water has no community outreach. It eschews conservation, consumer safety, and charity. It's a stealth utility focused primarily on mailing bills, coaxing them slowly upward so the public doesn't notice.

Ernie Davis leads the land-locked, beleaguered city of Mount Vernon with grace and dignity. The multicultural city lacks coastline on the Sound or the Hudson River, but Mayor Davis sings its praises with sincerity and style. *(I like his successor too. Clinton Young is a sheer, pure, natural force.)*

Everybody says **Joe Biden** would make a great secretary of state. What about president? But we're for **Rudy** against all comers.

I loved **Wellington Mara**. And Nancy and I are crazy about his wife, **Ann**, and their daughter, **Susan**. But I hate pre-season football games in August. They remind me of the last gasp of summer. And by the time the season ends for this sport of choreographed violence, it will be a cold, bleak day in January.

We endorsed **George W. Bush** twice. I still admire the guy. But when he declared war on the terrorists, he asked for very little sacrifice from the rich. We're either in a battle for survival, or we're not. Only **Charlie Rangel** dared to mention a draft.

David Patrick Columbia, the magazine editor and social arbiter, and **Robert Zimmerman**, the articulate Democratic National Committee bigwig, are two of the most stylish fellows in New York.

Octogenarian **Bill Mazer**, whom I first heard on the radio when I was in high school in Buffalo fifty years ago, ends every WVOX program with "God Bless America" by **Robert Merrill**. Mazer calls him "the greatest baritone of all time." He was. And they should finally name the **Wykagyl Post Office** in his honor because Merrill had a heart as great as his voice. And we hope **Nita Lowey** convinces the entire New York congressional delegation to petition the **U.S. Postal Service**. As a ranking cardinal of Congress and a powerful committee chair, she's absolutely peerless. (*She did. And the north end of New Rochelle is now served by the Robert Merrill Post Office.)*

I wish I had a dollar for each time **Joe Scarborough** says, "I greatly appreciate" something.

Dick Parsons of Time Warner would make a terrific mayor of New York. So would **Ray Kelly**.

Liz Smith is in the *Post* only three weekdays. I miss her on the other two.

His Honor needs to loosen up a bit. But New Rochelle died and went to heaven when it installed **Noam Bramson** as mayor. Most politicos couldn't make it in the real world, but Bramson's stunning brilliance would shine in any league.

Dr. Tom Fogarty left us last month. The Pelham Manor "family systems counselor" (read: shrink) saved countless Westchester marriages with his goodness and wisdom. His departure didn't make the *Times* or Gannett. But I'll bet he makes it into heaven.

When I was a youngster, **Ángel Cabrera** could have been a jockey or a soccer player. Today, he's a golfer. And a good one.

Political demagogues condemn **Indian Point** but scream and yell when there's a power outage. **Entergy** deserves high marks for its community outreach as statesmen of the nuclear power profession and damn good neighbors.

We lost two magnificent women this summer. **Kitty Carlisle Hart** and **Brooke Astor** could flirt with the best of them but remain ladies. Their contributions to New York state linger still. Meanwhile, we're left with **Lindsay Lohan**, **Paris Hilton**, **Britney Spears**, and **Nicole Richie**.

The two best books of the summer were ***The House That George Built*** by the brilliant **Wilfred Sheed**, who riffed on George Gershwin, Cole Porter, and Johnny Mercer; and ***Imperium*** by **Robert Harris**, a novel about Cicero, Caesar, and ancient Rome. Disparate types, such as **Jonathan Bush** and **Mario Cuomo**, loved it. So did I. *(Harris has a new one out,* Inspirate. *It's the second of a trilogy.)*

Some Democrats are saying New York State Supreme Court Judge **Charles Devlin** is not a "true" Democrat. We believe he's an enlightened and eminently qualified judge, one of the best we've ever had. But don't take our word for it. Listen to the wise counsel of the legendary retired Justice **Samuel George Fredman**, a jurist of towering reputation and former chairman of the Westchester County Democratic Committee. Fredman, now in his eighties, is telling one and all about his enthusiasm and admiration for Judge Devlin's work.

And speaking of politics, **Valerie Moore O'Keefe**, the dynamic Supervisor of Mamaroneck, reminds me of the journalist **Nancy Q. Keefe**, another no-nonsense woman from the same town. Valerie, a phenomenal, local public servant, transcends party labels.

Why can't **"Leshter" Holt**, **John "Robertsch,"** and the young kid out of Salt Lake City for NBC, **Michael Oku**, talk normally instead of sounding like deejays from "Shincinnati"? Or Cleveland?

Speaking of which, **Chris Matthews** is the best on the tube today. But I still miss **Dan Rather**'s passion and gravitas. And **Tom Brokaw**'s quiet strength.

Rick Lazio, with his Hollywood looks, is a big shot with the JP Morgan Chase Bank in the city. But he should be back in public life.

It will soon be autumn in New York, and one good thing about fall is **Daryl Sherman** caressing Cole Porter's piano in the foyer of the Waldorf every evening from Wednesday through Sunday. She's an endearing, enduring songstress.

Don't be put off by the cast of characters on **Maury Povich**'s TV show. He's a lovely guy and the first to write a check to the **Broadcasters Foundation of America**, the national charity headed by **Phil Lombardo** of Bronxville for our down-and-out colleagues.

Sirio Maccioni is seventy-five. But his latest incarnation of **Le Cirque** in the Bloomberg building is again attracting all the beautiful people. I was the oldest guy in the joint, not exactly a great feeling. But at least it's a feeling.

Heard **Mario Cuomo** on **Mark Simone**'s radio show last week. I think he's damn near seventy-five. But his brainpower is unmatched in the republic. Cuomo, a class act in every season of his life, is making some of his best, most profound speeches these days. The *Boston Globe* calls him "the great philosopher-statesman of the American nation." To realize how great the former governor is, just look at the current crop of presidential wannabes.

Our colleagues in the public press had a field day beating up on Lord **Conrad Black**, mostly for his over-the-top lifestyle. But before you condemn the fellow, read the editor-in-chief **Seth Lipsky**'s remarks in the July 17 issue of the *New York Sun*. Lipsky commends Black's journalistic contributions to the security of Israel, Britain, and the United States.

Life is unfair. And there's a whole new variation on that theme from **Martha Coakley**, the attorney general of Massachusetts, who is trying to extort the owners of **Powers Fasteners**, based in New Rochelle and Brewster. It all has to do with a mess up in Beantown called "The Big Dig." The Massachusetts pols are charging the much smaller and long-established New York state company with manslaughter to leverage the Bay State construction giants. We've known three generations of the Powers family, each more ethical and decent than the last. They don't deserve to be in the crosshairs of a ruthless AG or **Paul Ware**, her special prosecutor. **Joe Spinelli** (the former inspector general of New York), a great crimefighter with a sterling national reputation, is defending the Powers family.

Scott Shannon is the best on the radio today. But I still miss **William B. Williams** of the old WNEW, of sainted memory.

Phil Mushnick doesn't hear his melodious music. But **John Sterling** is the best sports announcer since **Mel Allen**.

Abramo Despirito, who runs the little tailor shop on Eastchester Road, says **Mariano Rivera** is one of the nicest people you'll ever meet. And that his wife is even nicer.

And bartenders, captains, and waiters tell me **Johnny Damon** is also a nice man, even when he couldn't buy a hit.

It's time for the ***New York Post*** to dig into its archives again and mine the gold in **Jimmy Cannon**'s columns. He died alone in a room above Times Square. But there would have been no **Breslin** or **Hamill** without Cannon.

I hope Monsignor **Charlie Kavanaugh** can catch a break from his tormentors in the hierarchy of the Roman Church. He's a great priest. And the Church in New York should address the injustice and restore him. Bravo to former Assemblyman **John Dearie** for trying to right a wrong.

David Brooks of the ***Times*** is my favorite columnist these days. Except for **David Hinckley** in the ***News***. But I still read **Cindy Adams** and **Richard Johnson** in the ***Post*** first.

While on the subject of our colleagues in the press, ***The Journal News*** big shots should run **Phil Reisman**'s brilliant columns in the same spot every Tuesday, Thursday, and Sunday, much as the ***Trib*** ran Breslin. It should be "anchored" and "held to the page." They should run it "double column width" on the "left side of the paper." That's newspaper jargon for highlighting a great asset.

My expertise derives from my stint as editor of my army newspaper when I served "overseas" in Staten Island. (I once set a record by running the post commander's picture ninety-three times in one issue!)

Alumni Report: A big Hollywood and New York talent agent tells us **William "Billy" Bush** will be "the next **Johnny Carson**"! The son of **Jonathan Bush**, Billy is a cousin of the prez and a nephew of **President George H.W. Bush**. He started his showbiz career as one of our brightest interns. And even then we knew this talented youngster would go far. Similarly **Rob Speyer**, scion of the **Tishman-Speyer** realty empire (Rockefeller Center, the Chrysler Building, et al.), and his old man, the highly respected New York civic leader **Jerry Speyer**, should be commended. His son and heir, who also sat before the WVOX and WVIP microphones, recently opened the "Top of the Rock" observation deck, offering the best view in Manhattan. I'd like to take 10 percent of their action. But I guess I can only take enormous pride in the accomplishments of these two talented youngsters.

George Pataki's mentor, **Bill Plunkett**, hates it when we call him "the most powerful man in New York state." But we'll be there to cheer when the Rockefellers and landed gentry of Sleepy Hollow honor the Squire of Tarrytown and his spectacular wife, **Caryl**, on Saturday, October 20. **Phelps Memorial Hospital** benefits.

And the week before, on October 12, the **Franciscan Friars of Graymoor** will pay tribute to **Egidiana** and the great **Sirio Maccioni** at the Pierre for a lifetime of generosity to New York.

You still think **George Bush** is a zero? You won't after you read ***Dead Certain*** by **Robert Draper**. That's if you still have an open mind on a guy who's willing to sacrifice his legacy and personal reputation in order to do the right thing.

Marvelous line from the great **Jimmy Breslin**: "This is becoming a 'Between you and I' society."

When a restaurant serves other than **Heinz ketchup** or **Hellmann's mayonnaise**, I wonder where else they're cutting back. Ditto if they don't take **American Express**.

She may be second in line for the presidency, but Madam Speaker **Nancy Pelosi** loses me with that **Paris Hilton–Marcia Cross** hair flip whenever she sees a television camera. **John Edwards** is pretty "flippant" too.

I wish Westchester district attorney **Janet DeFiore** had talked to me before she dumped the GOP and switched to the Dems. But she'll be an ornament of any party.

Nick Sprayregen and **Dan Murphy** have really improved the Martinelli Newspapers. But I still miss fiery, feisty **Ralph Martinelli**, its founder.

All of us in New York radio welcome back **Bob Grant**, the dean of talk show hosts. He's anything but dull, and we're all his students.

I'm glad **Don Imus** took down a score from the timid corporate masters who caved to intimidation and coercion. And I hope he'll be back soon.

Richard Berman of **Manhattanville**, with his shirtsleeves rolled up, is better than any college president in America with all their degrees, academic gowns, tassels, and medals.

How does a staid operation like the Associated Press come up with such graceful CEOs? First **Louis Boccardi**. And now **Tom Curley**. And before them, **Wes Gallagher**.

It's a treat whenever the ***Journal News*** finds some space for **Milton Hoffman**, who brings a keen eye and an invaluable historical perspective every time he sits down at a typewriter.

Flash of déjà vu: When **Eliot Spitzer** sat down for an interview, we gave the then–attorney general several chances to pile on **Jeanine Pirro** during her worst moments. He refused. I hope somebody cuts this well-intentioned (sometimes too dynamic) governor a little slack. And **Darren Dopp**, who served Mario Cuomo with distinction, ain't so bad either. As for Spitzer, anyone who is friends with **William Mulrow** of Bronxville has got to be first class. The Albany establishment threw a shot across his bow. Now, let him get back to governing. He has the potential and heart to be a great one.

Treasures of New York: **Damon Runyon** would have loved Yonkers power broker **"Colonel" Marty Rochelle** and **Murray Richman**, the famed Bronx criminal lawyer.

It is 2007. And **Doug Colety** is now the new chairman of the Republican Party of Westchester, once led by such towering figures as **Frederic Powers Sr.**, **Edwin Gilbert Michaelian**, **Malcolm Wilson**, and **Anthony J. Colavita**. But it's 2007.

I once asked **Nelson Rockefeller**, the Great Squire of Pocantico Hills, "You sustain the Republican Party in this state, don't you?" NAR answered, "No, I contain it."

I'll give you ten other guys to get **Ken Raske** on my side any day. Ditto **Jeffrey Bernbach**, a discrimination lawyer in White Plains. Raske keeps 146 hospitals solvent. And Bernbach, a former Cuomo official, is unsurpassed in the courtroom, especially against the

Establishment. **Henry Berman**, the famed matrimonial lawyer, ain't no slouch either.

Anybody remember the **Ted Heath** Big Band, the swinging English import that blew the roof off Carnegie Hall with several memorable concerts back in the sixties? "You Are Too Beautiful" is an obscure Rodgers and Hart tune known only to musicians. **Johnny Hartman** and **John Coltrane** had the best rendition.

What ever happened to the **Al Belleto** sextet? **Stan Kenton** discovered them in New Orleans. They sang like the **Hi-Los** and played with a Kentonesque dissonance.

Somebody once asked **Louis Armstrong** who was the best female singer of all time. Satchmo replied, "You mean besides **Ella**?" My favorite distaff warblers are **Rosemary Clooney**, **Doris Day**, and **June Christy**. And **Polly Bergen** could belt one out, too. But the greatest of all was **Mabel Mercer**.

The best crooners: **Frank**, of course, **Fred Astaire**, **Nat Cole**, **Matt Dennis**, **Tony Bennett**, and **Louis Armstrong**. **Mel Tormé** belongs on the list too. And you won't believe this, but who the hell knew **Jack Sheldon**, the fun-loving trumpet player, and **Tony Perkins** could sing!

If I could have written just one song, I'd pick "Nancy with the Laughing Face." But **Phil Silvers** and **Sinatra** got there first.

The same people who will tell you **Bill Clinton** is a great speaker also believe **Barbra Streisand** can sing. And they never heard **Mario Cuomo** or **Jack Kennedy** on a flatbed truck screaming into the night in the Garment District while elderly Jewish women hung out of the windows.

I get antsy sitting through most Broadway shows. But I could see ***Jersey Boys*** again. And again.

The beautifully tailored guy smoking a cigar, strolling down Park Avenue with his dog, is **Gay Talese**. Nobody ever wrote better pieces on **Sinatra** or the great **DiMaggio**.

Watch the society dames perk up for the skinny fellow with the camera at 57th and Fifth. He's **Billy Cunningham**, legendary lensman of the *Times* and a living landmark.

Mark for future stardom in Albany: **Jeff Klein** in the Senate, and **George Latimer** in the Assembly. But **Andrew Cuomo** can go as far as he wants in this country. It's in the genes.

This summer we also lost **Murray Grand**, a marvelous songwriter and cabaret performer with a cult-like following. He looked like **Ed Koch** and left us "Guess Who I Saw Today" and "I'm Too Old to Die Young."

Jonathan Schwartz still plays the good ones from the Great American Songbook. He calls it "high standards." By any name, it must be preserved.

One way would be to get **Jim Lowe** back on the radio. He hails from Springfield, Missouri, the "Paris of the Ozarks," and calls his friends, "you old spotted dog." Right now, he's regaling rich old widows in East Hampton. He deserves a slot.

How did I get through this without once mentioning **Hillary Rodham Clinton**?

I once shared an office with **William Kyle Rote** at WNEW. Was there ever a nicer guy in pro football? I last saw him on a hazy afternoon sitting alone at Costello's Bar. And before that, he was walking up First Avenue in a snowstorm, eating a slice of pizza.

Maybe all the local politicians and reporters ought to give the dedicated new CEO of **Westchester Medical Center**, **Michael Israel**, a chance to set things right.

Nick Spano may have lost his Senate seat in a close one. But he remains a politician from a time when the profession was honorable. And I hope he comes back.

Is there a nicer, more generous guy in the fashion world than **Kenneth Cole**? The designer is a star on the runway. And in philanthropy. His dazzling wife, **Maria Cuomo Cole**, is a star, too. Period.

We'd vote for **Robert Morgenthau** even if he were one hundred. The highly effective and nationally recognized Manhattan district attorney is a beloved icon of New York. He's the last lion from the Rockefeller years still in the arena.

Tell Professor **Richard Norton Smith** to hurry up and finish his long-awaited biography of **Nelson Rockefeller**. Smith, who wrote a highly acclaimed biography of Colonel Robert R. McCormick, the

Chicago press baron, has been toiling on the Rocky book for almost ten years. He got sidetracked as the new head of the Abe Lincoln Museum in Springfield, Illinois.

The pope blessed Baltimore when he chose Archbishop **Edwin O'Brien** to replace William Henry Cardinal Keeler in our nation's first archdiocese. O'Brien is beloved in New York, and many Catholics had prayed he would be installed in St. Patrick's.

Did I miss something about **Larry David**, the bald guy with glasses on TV? But then I never got **Jerry Seinfeld** either.

Arrigo Cipriani, patriarch of the **Cipriani** empire, and his courtly, graceful son, **Giuseppe Cipriani**, got a bad break from the taxman. But if the State Liquor Authority moves against the Venetian restaurateurs, at least 1,000 family employees will suffer. We hope the able **Stanley Arkin** cuts a deal so they can keep charging their outrageous prices. The Ciprianis are good people, and they brought a little style and a lot of fun to New York as well as their Bellinis.

Remind **Mario Biaggi**, who served in Congress before he crossed swords with **Rudy Giuliani**, that he was also the most decorated police officer in the history of the NYPD. The Bronx icon will be ninety next month.

Toots Shor would have been damn proud of his granddaughter, **Kristi Jacobson**, who slaved for ten years on the new film named for the famous saloonkeeper. **Tom Brokaw** and **Frank Gifford** subsidized the cinematic love letter, opening in Manhattan this week.

And tell **"Mama Rose" Migliucci**, the First Lady of Arthur Avenue, that she is one of the most beloved women in New York at ninety-three. She's scrambling in Lawrence Hospital in Bronxville.

It's "Autumn in New York." But where is **Bobby Short**?

The great **Jimmy Cannon** started this stream-of-consciousness format with his marvelous piece, "Nobody Asked Me . . . But."

September 14, 2007

IN THE MIDST OF WINTER

> In the midst of winter, I found within myself an invincible summer.
>
> Camus

I've always loved the quote. And in the midst of another drodsome, unforgiving winter, I thought I would try to assemble some of those scattered thoughts I've jotted at all hours in every season on the backs of envelopes and those memo pads jammed in my jacket pockets only to be tossed onto my dresser late at night.

Jimmy Cannon used to call this kind of piece "Nobody Asked Me . . . But." I idolized the legendary sports writer, and although I am not worthy to loosen the strap of his sandal, I thought I might again presume to compile these riffs and notes for you and our other friends who weigh my shortcomings and inadequacies less diligently than you assess any meager virtues I might possess.

Here are my recent jottings.

I wish I had written a song called "I Never Went Away from You." Sir Richard Rodney Bennett did.

Every Little League and Youth Soccer coach prays for just one kid like Derek Jeter.

Whatever happened to Lamar Alexander? And Marc Racicot, who surfaces only during presidential elections?

Keith Olbermann is wound much too tight. But I stay with MSNBC for Chris Matthews.

The grand marnier soufflés at La Grenouille are better than anything in France.

Be kind to any guy whose wife drives a Volvo.

David Hinckley, who writes for the *Daily News*, is the whole franchise. Mort Zuckerman should take out "key-man" insurance on the gifted scribe.

Why does MSNBC's Mika Brzezinski have to "punctuate" (!) every conversation? Is it possible her dad, Zbigniew, never let the kid get a word in edgewise? She's getting even now. *Bimbo Interruptus!* Absolutely!

I've sworn off Dunkin' Donuts. Even the toasted coconut ones the great criminal lawyer Murray Richman brings to the station. But I still fancy peppermint ice cream with Hershey's chocolate sauce.

There is a certain nobility about Mariano Rivera. He is the most graceful ballplayer of our time.

The next guy who tells you he roots for the Mets will have gravy on his shirt and an odd-looking tie.

I miss John Cardinal O'Connor.

Robert Zimmerman should be a matinee idol instead of a would-be politician.

Is there any nicer guy walking around New York than Rick Friedberg?

I can't wait to read *On His Own Terms*, Richard Norton Smith's long-awaited bio of Nelson Rockefeller.

We endorsed Malcolm Wilson for governor over Hugh Carey back in the seventies. But I've been thinking a lot about Carey these days. Peter Goldmark and Jerry Kremer are doing a book on the former gov.

State Senator Jeff Klein is the hardest-working guy in Albany. He's now number two in the state senate.

The pizzas at Mario's on Arthur Avenue in the Bronx are still as good as when Lee Iacocca used to dispatch his jet from Detroit for a stack of them.

The Journals of Arthur Schlesinger is a keeper. Also Jeffrey Toobin's *The Nine*.

There is something very real and very natural about Joba Chamberlain. I hope the money doesn't spoil the kid.

There is something very real and very natural about Sarah Palin. I hope the spotlight doesn't spoil her.

Haters don't poll well in pre-election surveys.

My favorite character in popular fiction is Daniel Silva's Gabriel Allon, the fearless Israeli Secret Service operative, also known as Mario DelVecchio, Venetian art restorer.

If it were my country, I'd hire Joe Biden to run it.

If Cary Grant were around today, his name would be David Patrick Columbia.

Mario Cuomo is making some of the best speeches of his life right now. The *Boston Globe* got it right: The former governor is "the great philosopher-statesman of the American nation."

You can see the wisdom and goodness of David McCullough in his face. And in his books.

Cindy Adams has made a career out of New York "schtick," which obscures the good, thoughtful stuff in the lady.

Radio legend Paul Harvey is ninety. I hope he goes on forever.

Memo to all the pols demagoging on Indian Point: Nuclear energy is the best and cheapest source of power around.

Toots Shor once said if he were trapped in an alley and wiseguys were coming in after him, he'd take "Shipwreck" Kelly (with his fists) or Sinatra (with a broken beer bottle) to help him fight his way out. I'd take the former FBI legend Joe Spinelli. Or maybe Ned Gerrity.

Le Cirque's Sirio Maccioni is a treasure of New York. He just put "roast goose" on the menu "to help the airplanes."

Judge Rory Bellantoni has a lot of guts.

Michael Daly's book about Friar Mychal Judge is a reminder of how much good the Franciscans do.

Nobody walks into a room these days like Nancy Curry. I'm lucky she leaves with me.

Elie Tahari men's jeans are the only ones that fit my expanding waistline.

Edward Cardinal Egan didn't even have to pull out his best stuff to get Paul Curran into heaven at the cathedral last month.

Steve Tenore should be back in politics.

Judge Jeanine Pirro's television shows are better than all the others. Except Judge Judy's. But she's close.

Ralph Martinelli's *Westchester* magazine gets better and better.

The Crabtrees at the Kittle House are the nicest people in the culinary biz in the suburbs. And don't hold that power couple from Chappaqua against them.

The best radio news anchor is Cameron Swayze of WCBS, the classy, articulate son and heir of the legendary John Cameron Swayze. But why do New York stations save their best for the weekends? Mark Simone on WABC is another example.

Manny Ramirez doesn't belong on the Yankees, even if they cut his hair.

We just lost James Brady at eighty. He was writing some of his best stuff for Steve Forbes. He was a great writer. And a marvelous friend. Damn!

The beleaguered Catholic Church is still alive at the Church of Francis of Assisi on 31st Street, where the Franciscan friars forgive you gently and generously. Three Hail Marys for a homicide!

Phil Lombardo of Bronxville is a big television guy with a tough-guy rep and persona. But he reinvigorated the National Association of Broadcasters in Washington. And now he's doing some of the best work of his life raising millions for the Broadcasters Foundation of America.

Leshter Holt of NB-She talksh like a dishk jockey from Cleveland. And he's got kee-yum-pan-ee from John Robertsch of She-NN.

I hope Jack Kemp throws a Hail Mary pass to pick up some yards and a few more years.

Has there ever been a nicer man in public life than George H.W. Bush?

Bruno Dussin, the bantamweight majordomo of Sirio Maccioni's Circo on the West Side, is a heavyweight among maitre d's. His middle name is "Immediately!"

By dumping Nat Hentoff, the *Village Voice* officially ceases to be a newspaper and henceforth shall be known as a bowling alley. The First Amendment has no greater champion than Hentoff, the eighty-three-year-old penman who reminded us that abortion *and* capital punishment demean us as a people. He also writes of jazz masters like Duke Ellington. But his best work celebrates the music of the Founders.

The fast money guys and slicks hate Arthur Sulzberger Jr. But he understands that the *New York Times* is a public trust. He is his father's son.

Speaking of which: Andrew Mark Cuomo grows in wisdom and age with each passing day. I heard a guy call him "maybe the best attorney general we've ever had." He's Mario's son, and he's starting to act like it.

The television genius who put Nancy O'Dell on a red carpet at the Golden Globes without a script and made her ad-lib interviews should change careers.

I never thought I'd live long enough to say something nice about Hillary. But I think she'll make a hell of a secretary of state.

When Rose Bochino Migliucci left at the age of ninety-three, she took the heart out of Little Italy in the Bronx. But her spirit is still at Mario's, her beloved eatery on Arthur Avenue.

Young Rob Speyer, scion of the Tishman-Speyer empire, is a rising star of the real estate world. He's also making his mark as a civic leader like his old man, Jerry Speyer.

Governor George Pataki isn't in the governor's office anymore. But his mentor, Bill Plunkett, is still one of the most powerful guys in New York.

Liz Smith, Bill Mulrow, Col Allan, Tonio Burgos, Jim Cunningham, Howard Stern, Kylie Cappelli, Frederic U. Dicker, Alan Rosenberg, John Spicer, Rich Pisano, Walter Nelson Thayer, Joe Cavoto, Richard Johnson, Phil Reisman, Nancy Palumbo, Kevin Plunkett, Patrick Carroll, Sam Fredman, Al D'Amato, Jeff Klein, Maria Cuomo Cole, Amy Paulin, Louis Cappelli, Arthur Hill Diedrick, Suzi Oppenheimer, Charlie Kafferman, Michele Silva, Steven Butensky, Charles Masson, Bill Kennedy, Billy Jacobs, Ann Dranginis, Brenda Resnik Spano, Andy O'Rourke, Marc Eisenberg, Henry Kissinger, Tom Mullen, Jim Veneroso, Jeff Bernbach, Ken Raske, Jack Rudin, E. Virgil Conway, Wellington Mara, Nat Hentoff, Ned Gerrity, Kevin Falvey, Paul Pellicci, Ogden Reid, Joseph Migliucci, Karen Bernbach, Bill Plunkett, Kathleen O'Connor, Michele Silva, Bernard Curry, Jonathan Bush, and A. J. Parkinson have all done nice things for me and mine. I don't forget.

Former FBI chief Judge Louis B. Freeh is a great American.

At least the Bush people are not stealing the White House furniture or fouling their computers.

Kevin O'Connor, who served as U.S. Attorney for Connecticut and then moved up to number three in the Justice Department, will one day be governor of Connecticut. His spectacular missus, Kathleen Plunkett, would make a good one too.

The Gannett newspaper empire is trimming its sails like everyone else. But they still have Phil Reisman at the *Journal News* in Westchester. He's the best feature columnist in all their two hundred dailies.

The most agreeable bar in New York is Kennedy's on West 57th Street. The loony lefty talk genius Lionel, aka Michael Le Bron, holds court, and the great Breslin himself stops in to grunt and pontificate about the great issues of the day. Langan's, the *Post*-ies' watering hole on West 47th Street, is a pretty good hangout too. And when it comes to saloons, I give the entire East Side to Jimmy Neary, where everyone at the bar looks like Daniel Patrick Moynihan.

It wasn't Sinatra's voice that made him the Chairman of the Board. It was his *phrasing* and the way he landed on a sibilant "s." "Your eye-s-s-s . . ."

I miss Neal Travis. But I'm glad Steve Dunleavy is still around.

Did Fred Astaire ever have an awkward moment?

Was Mabel Mercer ever less than regal?

Jimmy Cannon once described Sugar Ray Robinson getting beat up by a third-rate pug in the twilight of his career: "Nijinsky is dancing in the hallways of Times Square to the sound of a kazoo."

Breslin once called Winston Churchill "a man of beef and brandy and cigars, and the last great statue of the English language."

New York was fun at night when Hugh Shannon sat at a piano in a tuxedo jacket with velvet slippers, crooning, "I'm Too Old to Die Young."

Every time I walk up Madison Avenue, I hear Bobby Short's voice coming out of the Carlyle. "I Can't Get Started with You . . .": "I'm a glum one/unexplainable/I met someone unattainable. . . ." And then I see Kitty Hart coming down the avenue toward me. And it's spring in New York.

When I'm a glum one, I head for the Four Seasons to meet up with Alex Von Bidder and Julian Niccolini. Gerardo Bruno at San Pietro cheers me up too. And so does the great Sirio Maccioni at Le Cirque. And just walking into "21" improves my mood.

I *still* like George W. Bush. Is it possible he was exactly the kind of prez we needed in a tough, dangerous, unforgiving world after 9/11?

The designer Kenneth Cole, a statesman of his profession, is a guy who does well by doing good.

Johnny Mercer was a great songwriter. But he could sing too. With the very best of them.

George, Being George brings back all of George Plimpton's charm and grace.

They tried to put Larchmont mayor Liz Feld in the state senate. But I can't figure her out.

I don't think Assemblyman Richard Brodsky is afraid of anyone. Or anything.

I'd rather give a pint of blood than a college lecture. At Columbia recently a kid with friendly eyes yelled out from the back row during the Q&A: "Who are your *heroes*?" I said, "You mean, besides Mario Cuomo?" Then I mentioned Floyd Abrams, Erwin Krasnow, Nat Hentoff, and a guy from Washington—Patrick Maines—all of them First Amendment champions.

Jamie Dimon of JPMorgan Chase is the smartest banker in the republic today.

The best airline exec is Richard Anderson, CEO of Delta.

I've discovered him late in life, but Franco Lazzari of Vice Versa over on West 51st Street is a darling guy who feeds my body and soul.

M. Paul Redd died last week. He and Napoleon Holmes, Paul Dennis, Ossie Davis, Whitney Moore Young, Joe Jackson, Joe Evans, Pauline Flippen, and Lloyd Jones were lonely voices screaming about "equality" and civil rights when it wasn't fashionable back in the sixties in refined, pristine Westchester. I hope they are all looking down to see Barack Obama sworn as president of the entire country.

Bob Grant should be sitting before a microphone in a radio studio instead of sitting on his ass in front of a television set at his place down in New Jersey.

We'll be hearing soon about the College of Saint Mary up on the Hudson. The new president is Father Kevin Mackin, who moved Siena into the big time.

The best girl singers, besides Ella Fitzgerald and Mabel Mercer, were June Christy, Doris Day, and Rosemary Clooney. Sylvia Syms could sing too.

Richard Gere's new restaurant in Bedford is on the same site where once stood Nino's, the first great suburban eatery, a favorite of Donald Trump; Benny Goodman; Red Smith; Jack Paar; Jerry Vale; Jerry Berns of "21"; Bunny Lasker, the Wall Street lion; and assorted country squires from backcountry Greenwich.

"Art never comes alone," says Egidiana Maccioni. An example is Tony Bennett, the last great crooner, aka the brilliant artist "Benedetto." His stuff is wonderful, on the stage and on canvas.

Another example, I expect, is Charles Masson, the graceful proprietor of La Grenouille, who is also a gifted floral artist and sculptor.

After Sinatra, Dick Haymes has lots of admirers even to this day, and some people still cling fiercely to the belief that Vic Damone had the pipes. But when I call up Central Casting for a crooner, I want them to send Louis Armstrong, Fred Astaire, Nat Cole, or Matt Dennis.

Memo to David Westin and Steve Capus: One of you should grab Geoff Morrell, the brilliant, unflappable, and stunningly articulate "Pentagon spokesman" who does some of his best work on C-SPAN.

Sidney Weinberg, the legendary Wall Street genius who reigned back in the fifties and sixties, was the most sought-after corporate director in America. He served on the boards of some thirty-plus major corporations. When asked what makes for a good director, Mr. Weinberg said, "You sit there and keep your mouth shut for at least two years—they'll think you're a goddamn genius."

The two guys I wanted in the White House never made it. Nelson Rockefeller and Mario Cuomo would have made great presidents. One of them tried too hard. The other didn't try at all.

Being in the care and keeping of James O'Shea and Charlie Kafferman of the West Street Grill up in the Litchfield hills is a lovely way to spend an evening.

Sometimes my mind drifts to Murray Grand sitting in a pencil spotlight over a piano at a smoky cabaret in the Village whispering, "Guess Who I Saw Today?" He looked like Ed Koch.

Marvin Dames, the superintendent of police in the Bahamas, will one day be the prime minister of that island nation. I met him when he was an altar boy. Even then we knew. And so do the Bahamians.

Tell me who is better in front of a crowd at a charity dinner than Liz Smith.

Nancy Pelosi and the Dems should just damn well forget about going after the Bush people. It will ultimately hurt President Obama. And the country.

I'd like to see him back in public service, but Richard Berman, the departing prez of Manhattanville, will be good at whatever he does.

You don't hear much about him, but Assemblyman Gary Pretlow is solid.

This lovely passage, which I've carried in my wallet for years, was from the first inaugural speech by George Walker Bush. Can you get any more eloquent than *this*?

> After the Declaration of Independence was signed, Virginia statesman John Page wrote to Thomas Jefferson: "We know the race is not to the swift nor the battle to the strong. Do you not think an angel rides in the whirlwind and directs this storm?"
>
> Much time has passed since Jefferson arrived for his inauguration. The years and changes accumulate. But the themes of this day he would know: our nation's grand story of courage and its simple dream of dignity.
>
> We are not this story's Author, who fills time and eternity with His purpose. Yet His purpose is achieved in our duty, and our duty is fulfilled in service to one another.
>
> Never tiring, never yielding, never finishing, we renew that purpose today, to make our country more just and generous, to affirm the dignity of our lives and every life.
>
> This world continues. This story goes on. And an angel . . . still rides in the whirlwind and directs this storm.

You heard me right. George W. Bush uttered these lovely words.

I never liked the "Citigroup" moniker. The original name, "First National City Bank," had more heft. But don't bet against them now that Dick Parsons is chairman. The former Time Warner chief and Rockefeller advisor has been a class act in every season.

Nelson Rockefeller would have been 102 this year. So why does it seem like he just left the room?

Edward Noonan Ney, the chairman emeritus of Young & Rubicam, is the Fred Astaire of Madison Avenue. He was also our ambassador to Canada.

Remind Mario Biaggi that he was almost mayor of New York and is still, at ninety-one, one of the best-looking guys in the great city where he is loved.

Did you ever hear Matt Dennis, the West Coast crooner-songwriter, do "Violets for Your Furs"? His best album was *She Dances Overhead* for RCA.

I'm not sure about a lot of things. But I'm certain Ossie Davis was a saint.

Speaking of "sureness," Mario Cuomo once described it: "You're on the road to Damascus and you're struck by lightning; the Lord then appears in all His or Her refinements and says, 'Get back on that horse! Incidentally, your *name* is not Saul anymore. It's now Paul. Oh, and one other thing: you're a *saint*.'" *That's* "sureness," says the gov—a lightning bolt in the tush!

Maybe I'm stuck on 8 10 glossies. But I still hear people talking about John Lindsay, who was a nicer guy after the glory years were behind him. But he was a class act in every season. Even telling stories at the bar of Bobby Van's saloon in Bridgehampton, when he would ride his bike over after telling Mary he was going to the Candy Kitchen.

At the next Super Bowl, and before each and every public sporting event anywhere in the land, they should just put on a record of Robert Merrill singing "God Bless America." Jennifer Hudson was pretty good this year, but I'm sick of the rock star du jour defiling the national anthem, which is difficult enough to sing even if you have a voice.

Even guys who consider themselves fairly literate try to put an "n" in "restaurateur." But the late Jerry Berns of "21" always said, "It don't go there." As the first inductee in the Culinary Institute of America's Hall of Fame, he should know.

Europeans—especially the Brits—love Donna Leon's books about Commissario Guido Brunetti, the appealing and all-too-human Venetian detective. The lady knows how to write.

Why do they have to put raisins in cereal, Mueslix, or trail mix?

General Motors makes damn fine cars and will be around for a good, long time if their new fed "partners" don't ruin things. But I drove a Hyundai on vacation, and it wasn't bad.

William B. Williams was the classiest deejay in the great city for four decades. He called Sinatra the "Chairman of the Board." The music on his WNEW turntables was by the "Duke of Ellington," the "Count of Basie"—and Nat "King" Cole was simply "Nathaniel." William B's theme song was Henri René's "You Are the One," and he opened every "Make Believe Ballroom" show with a gentle "Hello, World!" He walked dusty, dangerous roads in Selma with Dr. King and held high estate at the Friars Club. Sinatra called him "simply the most generous man I know." But he's not in the New York State Broadcasters Hall of Fame. Joe Reilly, David Widmer, Ed Levine, and the elders of our tribe ought to fix that right away.

The fraternity of federal judges misses Charles Brieant, but they have a rising star in Paul Crotty.

A guy I know blames all of today's woes on a former prez named "Jimmy." When Carter made it to the White House, every guy in Yonkers, standing in front of the mirror while shaving in the morning, said, "Hmm, what about *me*?" Forget the helicopters crashing in the desert. I still think it was the name: "Jimmy."

It isn't spring until shad roe appears on Sirio Maccioni's menu. One year he had it in February.

Pitchers and catchers report next week.

February, 2009

HIGHLIGHTS FROM THE HISTORIC WVOX/WORLDWIDE 50TH-ANNIVERSARY BROADCAST

In *The Screwtape Letters,* the great C. S. Lewis wrote that what the devil wants is for a man to finish his life having to say I spent my life not doing either what is *right* or what I *enjoy*. For the many years I've known him, Bill O'Shaughnessy has spent most of his time doing things he ought to have been doing and enjoying them immensely. Blessed with a great, Gaelic gift of words, a sharp mind, deep convictions, a capacity for powerful advocacy, Bill has been able to inspire the faint-hearted, guide the eager, and charm almost everyone he's met. He's a gifted writer of simple truths and powerful political arguments, especially in support of his favorite cause: Free Speech and a Free Press!

He's also an elegant, entertaining, and spellbinding speaker. He might have taken all these gifts and made himself a great political leader or a very rich captain of industry. Instead, fifty years ago he devoted himself to what then was a small and struggling radio station, and ever since then, thanks to his brilliance and dedication, he's created what has become his highly valued and much-praised WVOX/Worldwide and WVIP. He enjoys nothing more than to hear important community leaders describe these stations as perfect examples of concerned corporate citizens, as you will hear on this broadcast. Congratulations WVOX and WVIP. Keep going!

Governor Mario M. Cuomo

I have a great honor to join the many saluting Bill O'Shaughnessy for being an outstanding beacon of light, of sanity, journalistic radio excellence! I remember when I first came to New York, I began on WMCA on the 20th of September in 1970, and it wasn't too long after that I heard about O'Shaughnessy and what he was doing on his stations, WVOX and WVIP. And today Whitney Media is a force to be reckoned with. Bill and I haven't always agreed on everything. But one thing I can tell you: O'Shaughnessy is every inch a gentleman. I join in saluting Bill and his Whitney Media. Straight ahead!

Bob Grant, pioneering talk show host

Very many congratulations on celebrating fifty years on the air! You're the greatest, the absolute best! And we love you.

Novelist Barbara Taylor Bradford and Robert Bradford, movie producer

The broadcasters of New York state—indeed the entire nation—salute you on the fiftieth anniversary of WVOX Radio. You are an inspiration, a beacon in the night for all of us. There has been no more eloquent defender of this country's First Amendment to the Constitution than one William O'Shaughnessy. Here's to the next fifty!

Joseph Reilly, President, New York State Broadcasters Association

The cause of Good Government has no better friend than Bill O'Shaughnessy and WVOX/Worldwide. Congratulations on the fiftieth anniversary of this extraordinary radio station and its gifted proprietor.

Hon. Andrew M. Cuomo, attorney general, State of New York

Bill O'Shaughnessy is one of a kind. He's happiest when he's helping friends. Bill gave my son and heir Billy Bush his start. After one summer with WVOX, Billy knew he had found his calling, thanks to Bill O'Shaughnessy. He's a great guy and a great friend.

Jonathan Bush, brother of President George H.W. Bush, uncle of President George W. Bush, father of TV-radio star William "Billy" Bush

William O'Shaughnessy cherishes language. O'Shaughnessy is a staunch defender of the First Amendment and freedom of speech. He is a protector of broadcasters' rights and has been called "the radio broadcasting profession's conscience." He was among the first inductees into the New York State Broadcasters Hall of Fame in 2005. He is a past president of the New York State Broadcasters Association and served for many years on the board of directors of the National Association of Broadcasters as the point man on free speech matters.

Mount St. Mary College

I think I've known you for maybe thirty of the fifty years. You underscore everything that *we* do: think *global* and also think *local*. WVOX has been very helpful to me when I'm home and continues to be helpful to *me* when I travel around the world. WVOX is a beacon for all of us.

Mario Gabelli, president, GAMCO Investments; Wall Street legend

Happy anniversary to "The Big O." O'Shaughnessy is a New York treasure and a great friend. As Henry David Thoreau once said in defining friends: "They cherish one another's hopes . . . they are kind to one another's dreams!" Bill O'Shaughnessy is a friend of the mighty and of the lowly. He is one of the few media moguls who spend their considerable talents building people up rather than tearing them down. I've always admired his very public and sometimes private embrace of the troubled and less fortunate. If you were down, he'd pick you up. This unique gift is the essence of the man who is better known for his radio shows and his topical and always insightful riffs and for his wonderful books that chronicle the New York scene. To reflect on his brilliant eulogies at the funerals of so many of our mutual friends always gives new meaning to the notion of a life well lived by those who've left us. Bill has been a good friend to Caryl and me for over forty years, and we are better for that friendship.

Bill Plunkett, Plunkett and Jaffe, division of McKenna, Long & Aldridge; New York power broker and George Pataki mentor; advisor to the Archdiocese of New York

Community radio like yours often is underestimated. You have shown how to reclaim the balance of power.

Thomas Curley, president and CEO, Associated Press

I am really delighted to participate in the fiftieth-anniversary celebration of WVOX/Worldwide and pay tribute to Bill O'Shaughnessy. I have known Bill for over fifty years. He is an author, broadcaster, toastmaster. He is absolutely *sui generis*—one of a kind! His radio editorials have inspired us and stirred our emotions. He is the voice of the homeless, the poor, and the forgotten.

His editorials have received national recognition and approval. Most of all, Bill has a good heart that is kind and sympathetic. He is a real champion of all good things, and we love him for it.

Hon. Alvin Richard Ruskin, retired state Supreme Court justice

In my twenty years as CEO of Sound Shore Medical Center, I've grown to have great affection and admiration for Bill O'Shaughnessy. And in large part, it's a result of who he is—in many ways, a "larger than life" character. He is passionate about everything he does. He's passionate about Westchester, about his family, and more than passionate about his wife, Nancy. But the radio station is one of the things that make him who he is. I [was] going through one of Bill's books, and there's a quote in there that does embody what he thinks about his radio station: "Radio is still the medium closest to the people . . . it thus has a very special and intimate relationship with the poor, the hurting, the misunderstood, the disenfranchised in our society. A radio station achieves its highest calling when it resembles a platform, a forum for the expression of many different viewpoints. And when it aspires to be more than a jukebox. . . . Radio can make a community stronger, better—and even sweeter—than it is."

He has made a career out of using that platform to make our community a better place . . . certainly in terms of the hospital and medical center. So many times we had an issue—or crisis—whether it be financial or something dealing with a particular outbreak of a disease, when Bill would call us in and help us get ahead of the issue. He did that because he felt the more the community knew and the more intimate we, the hospital, could get with the community, it would get us all stronger. Bill practices what he preaches. Having him at the helm of that radio station is something Westchester considers a real blessing. It's been fifty years extraordinarily well spent. We all thank him for his passion and his understanding of the dynamics of the Westchester community.

John Spicer, president and CEO, Sound Shore Medical Center Mount Vernon Hospital; director, Westchester Medical Center

W.O. is one of the giants of the industry . . . always standing tall for what really matters: the First Amendment, which makes it possible for all the rest of us to do what we do.

Deborah Norville, "Inside Edition"

There's no mystery about the success of these two stations. They provide a reliable sounding board and an accurate reflection of everyday life in the metro area.

Nelson DeMille, *New York Times* bestselling author

I'll never forget that WVOX was with me at the beginning.

Hon. Nita Lowey, U.S. congresswoman

Happy birthday WVOX and its mastermind, Bill O'Shaughnessy. Bill, you are perhaps the best emcee and interviewer I have ever heard. What a gift you have. You make interesting people more interesting, and human as well. You have one other gift: your beloved Nancy! God bless you both and WVOX.

Judge Charles Gill, Connecticut Superior Court justice

Congratulations to Bill and all the dedicated broadcasters of WVOX—past and present—on their fiftieth anniversary. WVOX has been a staple in Westchester and New York state for ages. I remember selling advertising on the station when it was "Vox Populi" and Bill changed the FM to WRTN, before it became WVIP. This was in the mid-1970s. Bill was a terrific boss and a great public figure in New York. He has done tremendous things for the body politic. The exposure he has given those of good will has been significant. As a fellow New Rochellean, I want to thank Bill for all the efforts he has made on behalf of the public he serves so well.

Bill Cella, president, The Cella Group, Worldwide Television and Media Placement

O'Shaughnessy is a good guy to have on your side—and so are those radio stations—when the chips are down.

Joseph A. Spinelli, president, Daylight Forensic; former Inspector General, state of New York

Congratulations on half a century at WVOX, truly the Voice of the People of Westchester. You made a commitment that your radio station was going to be the people's radio station. It was your insight that radio was local and thus not a jukebox, and you made it work. There can't have been an activist, a clergyman, a politician, a journalist, or an ex-con . . . within a fifty-mile radius who wasn't on your airwaves at one time or another. You wanted every point of view, and for half a century, you made it happen. That's the *public* record.

Some of us had the honor to see how you behaved in *private*. Real stories. A good student underachieved for a few years in high school—you were calling colleges for him. A family that hit hard times—you were chasing job leads for the breadwinner. Someone had a medical issue—you reached out and found the right doctor. So every day the worthy and unworthy were asking your help with this school or that benefit or that cause. The people of Westchester knew you would be on their side. And you never let your staff report these activities. You cherish classiness, those "from the heart" grace notes that make amicable society more amicable. Sometimes at an editorial conference, I would start in on the *policy* of a particular candidate, and you wanted to know about his or her *character* instead.

And, oh those "drodsome" days, as you called them. The sky would be shot with the gunmetal gloaming, the air would be heavier than soft, and you would describe it as "drodsome." The dictionary lists not "drodsome," but it *does* list "drod," a variant of dread. But if you had said of the day as being "dreadful," your listener would have translated "dreadful" to "bad," and the power of the language would be lost. But "drodsome" made this listener look out the window. And yes, Bill, it was a "drodsome" day! And may we have no more of them in the next half-century. Thank you for letting me be part of your life!

Larry Goldstein, legislative spokesman, County of Westchester; former host, "Good Morning, Westchester"

Bill O'Shaughnessy *is* Radio in New York state. He has made community and neighborhood radio relevant in today's world. And he takes a tough stand as their spokesperson for the First Amendment.

Richard Berman, president, Manhattanville College

Let me tell you about O'Shaughnessy: It begins at Fort Wadsworth, Staten Island. Bill and I were stationed there in the late fifties. We edited and published the post newspaper, *The Harbor View*. Although I was "senior" to him, Bill quickly became my mentor. My enlistment was coming to an end, and Bill encouraged me to seek my fame and fortune in radio. He recommended me for a job in Albany. It was the best thing that happened to my family and me. My proudest day in my fifty-year broadcasting career was joining Bill last year as a member of the New York State Broadcasters Hall of Fame. Dr. Bill, here's to fifty more years.

John F. Kelly, former president, Albany Broadcasting; advisor, Siena College

On behalf of our college community, I congratulate WVOX for fifty years of service to the region around us. The College of New Rochelle and WVOX are both dedicated to the education and well-being of Westchester and our region in good times and bad. For fifty years, the people of Westchester have turned confidently to both this college and WVOX for reassurance, for resources, for education and inspiration. We've walked together for a half-century of success, providing wisdom for the life for our extended communities. Congratulations to WVOX, Mr. O'Shaughnessy, and all at WVOX.

Dr. Steven Sweeny, president, College of New Rochelle

I want to congratulate WVOX for fifty years of being the best community station there ever was. As a partner of Clark, Gagliardi and Miller who became president of the Bar Association, I was interviewed often on WVOX. I hope WVOX will be forgiven for interviewing one of their friends! Our firm, two years ago, celebrated our one hundredth anniversary as the oldest personal-injury law firm in Westchester. So to my good friend O'Shaughnessy, I say, Thank you. You are unique and wonderful. I look forward to returning to WVOX in fifty years to celebrate *your* hundredth anniversary!

Henry Miller, Esq., Clark, Gagliardi and Miller; former president, New York State Bar Association

I'm the Voice of the Yankees, but they're clearly the Voice of New York!

John Sterling, New York Yankees play-by-play announcer

The front-running suburban radio station in this whole country!

Larry King

I am grateful for your radio station's friendship of a lifetime. First, for introducing me to the head of the DEA in Washington, and also for using your influence concerning my Yale University Fellowship. I hope to use these experiences to the benefit of the people of my nation.

Superintendent Marvin Dames, Royal Bahamas Police Force

O'Shaughnessy is a patriot who has given so much to our community and to our country.

Dan Rather

WVOX and WVIP are perfect examples of concerned corporate citizens. Each station has the same high level of creativity that appeals to different audiences. The opinions expressed on their "Open Line" talk shows influence the thoughts of local, state, and national officials who have developed a "family affection" for the stations.

Hon. Charles Rangel, chairman, House Appropriations Committee

It seems like yesterday you took a chance on a brash young Irishman. I calculate that was just short of forty-three years ago. I will never forget those wonderful years working at the "Voice of the People." You taught me many things: "Never say no" and "It's not how big you are, but how important they *think* you are." I've found a "little" success in this wonderful business, thanks in large part to the training I received many years ago. We're producing a series of infomercials here today for one of my companies. And if tradition continues, my daughter Molly will be the producer of today's shoot. *Vox Populi!*

Sean Driscoll, former WVOX office assistant; chairman, Madison MediaWorks

Ossie [Davis] and I always felt WVOX's great strength is its relationship with the "townies" of Westchester and the Bronx, those dedicated and concerned citizens with *roots* in the community. He had enormous respect for your principled stands on fundamental things like civil rights.

Ruby Dee

I am so proud to be part of WVOX. Local radio is where it's at! And who is bigger, better, more important, and a greater inspiration to all of us, but Bill O'Shaughnessy! Fifty years of making great radio, producing enlightened entertainment and programming. I salute O'Shaughnessy, and I say fifty more years. Bring it on!

Dick Brennan, "Fox 5 News"

On this tremendous occasion for Bill and his family—what a great opportunity for Louis Cappelli and those who have been a partner with you, to thank you for fifty years of successful broadcasting. What a wonderful way for us to be able to express our gratitude to you and your "family" because you have always run your stations as a family business, and that family has extended well beyond your blood relatives—to include Cappelli Enterprises.

You have been part of our success at New Roc City and in White Plains at City Center and the Ritz-Carlton. And you were the master of ceremonies when we unveiled Trump Plaza. You have played an important role in all our projects. WVOX and its influence have really transcended Westchester, and no matter what your political persuasion or where you came down on the issues, even those you opposed respected you. That's something you can take along with you—a lifetime of memories.

WVOX *is* "Public Radio," a service you provide to everyone. You are one of the most charismatic public speakers and public figures Westchester has ever seen. For those of you twenty, thirty, forty, fifty years from now who are listening to this from the audio archives and who perhaps won't have the opportunity to actually meet Bill O'Shaughnessy in person, let me say he was a one of a kind. His example will continue to inspire. We wish Bill continued success and a wonderful life!

Joe Apicella, Cappelli Enterprises

Bill O'Shaughnessy, the white-haired mogul, has great courage when it comes to free speech. I wish I had worked at WVOX. He's always been there for me.

Howard Stern

In the Westchester market, with all its complexity and diversity, it is virtually impossible to rely on conventional "ratings" to determine the reach, influence, worth, and merit of a radio station like WVOX.

Hon. Edward Noonan Ney, Chairman Emeritus, Young & Rubicam; U.S. ambassador to Canada

I've had the pleasure of knowing Bill O'Shaughnessy for over twenty years. Bill is a very unique and giving individual. I can recall vividly the first time I met him. It was at a grammar-school affair where our kids were going. He was impeccably dressed. Double-breasted suit! And that wavy hair—still to this day—is dashing. But I looked down to Bill's shoes, and they too were unique and somewhat flashy. But I noticed one thing: He wasn't wearing socks! I thought to myself, "There's something wrong with this picture." It wasn't the fact that he couldn't afford them; maybe he couldn't *match* them. My relationship with the O'Shaughnessys has been long, and they are dear friends. Congratulations to Bill and his colleagues for a very happy fiftieth.

Ken Raske, president, Greater New York Hospital Association, a national leader in health care

Congratulations to Westchester's great friend Bill O'Shaughnessy and his WVOX on their fiftieth anniversary. What a fabulous accomplishment! I'm so proud to be the host of a popular and valuable program talking about business development and growth in New York state, all [as a result of] the fact that Bill called us and asked us to be involved. He reached out. We thank you and congratulate you on this momentous and auspicious occasion.

Dr. Marsha Gordon, president, Business Council of Westchester

Bill O'Shaughnessy's unswerving devotion to the First Amendment stands as an inspiration to all who cherish the democratic ideals on which this great nation was founded. His deep belief in freedom of speech, and his personal and professional efforts to strengthen that freedom, are rays of hope to all who view the First Amendment as the cornerstone of our democracy.

Patrick Maines, The Media Institute, Washington, D.C.

Our family has always enjoyed your broadcasts, and our father—Arthur Geoghegan—would be particularly pleased that the faith and confidence he invested in you so many years ago when he was chairman of the old First Westchester National Bank has been well justified by your longevity.

John A. Geoghegan, Esq., Resident Principal, Gellert & Klein

In broadcasting lore about New York state, certain names come up all the time at every media event or conference. And the name and radio stations we always heard about were in Westchester: WVOX and WVIP. Many of us, young in the business, didn't quite understand the importance of what Bill O'Shaughnessy was doing in the media and for the First Amendment. But we do now. And the whole profession is in his debt.

Anthony Rudel, media historian; professor, Manhattanville College

WVOX, WVIP, and O'Shaughnessy continue to provide excellence in the field of broadcast journalism, and they serve as models for the environment we strive to create here at Fordham for our students.

Joseph M. McShane, S.J., president, Fordham University

WVIP, WVOX—and the O'Shaughnessy family—are top-rated with us! Five stars!

Bob Lape, *Crain's New York* and WCBS

I appreciate your station's wit, conviction, taste, and humor.
Michael Feinstein, Feinstein's at the Regency

So few people consistently and fervently support the First Amendment like Bill O'Shaughnessy. It has long been a special treat to hear his editorials and read them again in his books.
Floyd Abrams, America's preeminent First Amendment counsel, Cahill, Gordon and Rindel

The first time I met Bill O'Shaughnessy, I noticed he was larger than life. I knew right away we would be friends for a long time. The second thing I noticed was his Yankee championship ring, and I knew we had a lot in common. After Fordham University Press published his first book in 1999, I always looked forward to his next publications. And now I'm again looking forward to next year because a new book will be published, his fourth from Fordham. Bill is a generous and caring man who loves his family. They are always number one in his life. Congratulations on fifty years, WVOX.
Margaret Noonan, business manager, Fordham University Press

The community is best served when the information given to it is accurate, without drama, histrionics, sensationalism. That's all too common in today's media. But not at WVOX. I want to congratulate Bill O'Shaughnessy and WVOX for fifty years of enlightened service!
Hon. Ernie Davis, former mayor, City of Mount Vernon

I call Bill O'Shaughnessy my "Coach"; we've been friends for a long, long time.
Richard D. Parsons, chairman, Citigroup; former chairman, Time Warner

The king of local talk radio . . . and First Amendment champion!
Westchester Magazine

The stations have a unique style, like their gifted owner.
Sirio Maccioni, proprietor, Le Cirque

Fifty years ago, WVOX was only Bill O'Shaughnessy, broadcasting out of a studio housed in the basement of the Pershing Square Building in downtown New Rochelle. But even then, as now, WVOX was known for its local emphasis and a polished sophistication that I took for granted. Later, when John F. Kennedy was elected president, it seemed as if tall, erudite, charismatic fellows like JFK and O'Shaughnessy had inherited the world we knew—which, at the time, included Schrafft's, Arnold Constable, Scotts, and a Nash Rambler dealer. Now all are gone. Little did we know what the future would turn out to be. But WVOX is still here.

Michael Dandry, philanthropist, civic leader, journalist

Congratulations to WVOX on its fiftieth anniversary! I know a lot of people out there watch me doing the weather on Cablevision, but I don't think too many people are aware that I got my start in broadcasting right here at WVOX! Right out of college back in 1978, I hooked up with a private weather company and one of their clients was WVOX. I had never been on the radio before, never did a single weather forecast, and I must tell you now that in my radio career I was heard in over two hundred radio markets. And before I moved over to television in 1995, I probably did over 200,000 weathercasts for radio stations throughout the United States and Canada. They say when you experience something for the first time, you never forget it. And I'll never forget the time I delivered my first weathercast right here at 1460 AM! And Mr. O'Shaughnessy, about ten years ago we met at a function and you said to me, "Call me Bill." But you know what? I just can't get myself to do that because in my mind you are what Walter Cronkite once said: "The Great O'Shaughnessy is widely heard and heralded in Westchester and beyond." I gotta respect that.

Joe Rao, Cablevision News 12 meteorologist

I've got to be nice to you; my *mother* listens! It's her favorite station!

Ivan Seidenberg, chairman, Verizon

Nelson spoke often of the many kindnesses of WVOX to both of us and the family over the years. He had great affection for you and yours.

Happy (Mrs. Nelson A.) Rockefeller

The gay and lesbian community is grateful to WVOX for so many generous gifts, not the least of which is our unedited weekly forum.

The Loft

DaVinci, Michelangelo, Garibaldi, Verdi, Bernini, Columbo, Caputo, O'Shaughnessy! Bill is appreciated, respected, and loved by the greater Italian American community that listens to all the Italian radio shows on WVOX and WVIP. Thank you on this grand anniversary.

"Uncle Floyd" Vivino, legendary radio–TV host and performer

It is my distinct honor and privilege to be part of the WVOX family. I have known O'Shaughnessy for over thirty years. Who can ever match his effervescent personality and insight! For the past five years, as one of those who have a show on WVOX, he has been the rock we all build upon. Though our views are sometimes diverse, he never censors. While disagreeing, he never overrides. He encourages free thought, with a joy in life that certainly makes him "Mr. First Amendment" in my book.

Murray Richman, famed criminal defense attorney; host of "Don't Worry Murray"

There is only one O'Shaughnessy, and he is the reason we have so much to celebrate with the fiftieth anniversary. There is no imitating Billy O', the one who stood up for so much in our industry, from our First Amendment rights to his stewardship of NAB and its Board. Through his regional support of Westchester and the entire metro area, Bill is everywhere carrying the torch for broadcasting and his fellow broadcasters. One important fact you probably didn't know is that Mr. O'Shaughnessy, for many years, has given of his time, his heart, and his pocketbook to the advancement and development of the Broadcasters Foundation of America. Bill's leadership and example in this vital national charitable organization, which assists broadcasters in dire need, is nothing short of phenomenal. Bill is a leader, a giver, an inspiration.

Richard A. Foreman, president, Richard A. Foreman Associates

Congratulations for fifty years of great radio on WVOX! I've been doing a show on your station since 1991 during my service with Mario Cuomo and Eliot Spitzer, an eighteen-year run. Congratulations for your own fifty years of great radio!

Gary Brown, Westchester Department of Consumer Protection

I'm very proud to be part of WVOX's fiftieth-anniversary celebration. I have known and have the highest respect and regard for Bill O'Shaughnessy for many years. He and I are on the same wavelength when it comes to broadcasting and philanthropy, and how vital it is for this great country. Bill's outstanding presence in our profession has meant so much to so many.

Philip Lombardo, chairman, Broadcasters Foundation of America; chairman, Citadel Television

Bill O'Shaughnessy is my hero. He's always been there for me!

Hon. Rick Lazio, JPMorgan Chase; former member of Congress

Bill and his stations are a tremendous and positive influence on the communications industry. They've been a real leader in trying to help broadcasting confront its equal-opportunity challenges. The stations are led by a man of conscience.

Andrew J. Schwartzman, Media Access Project, Washington, D.C.

Full of the din of the fray, both past and present, the station offers samples from what seems like the forgotten zeitgeist of some distant generation, some strange time when commentators were respectful toward subjects they didn't agree with and criticized ideas, not people.

Asa Fitch, *Litchfield County Times*

Bill O'Shaughnessy's ability to ask the right questions at the right time and get the real answers rank him among the great interviewers like Barbara Walters and Tim Russert.

Louis O. Schwartz, president, American Sportswriters Association

In an increasingly homogenized world encroached [upon] by multimedia corporations, WVOX shines like a beacon over dark waters. A colorful ensemble of characters grace this station, including politicians, other journalists, and celebrities.

Michelle J. Lee, Gannett

I'm so proud of you. You have been a wonderful friend throughout my entire career, first as a councilperson in the 1970s and especially as judge here in New Rochelle. You have been a counselor personally to me, and I send my warmest regards to you and yours. The City of New Rochelle is proud to have you as *its* great friend and champion.

Preston "Sandy" Scher, Chief Judge, City of New Rochelle

I told Charlie Rose he's the Bill O'Shaughnessy of television! That's the least I can do for my hometown stations!

Hugh Price, president, National Urban League

For over five years it has been a pleasure to air my Muslim program on WVOX's airwaves. I have learned so much from so many people on a road filled with trials and tribulations, but with so many good memories for us all. Mr. O'Shaughnessy deserves much recognition and respect for his many years holding true to his vision to provide freedom of speech radio and never forgetting our First Amendment rights. The passionate work of fifty years goes by very fast. May God continue to bless you all for a job well done.

John Nashid, Muslim host, New Mind Muslim Development Project

We're grateful, certainly to Governor Cuomo, but also to your stations for their important role in the naming of the Jacob K. Javits Convention Center for the senator. It was a signal honor for a great man who thought very highly of you and yours.

Marian Javits, Jacob K. Javits Foundation

WVOX and WVIP are two extraordinary radio stations run by a great statesman of our profession.

Erwin Krasnow, Esq., Washington communications lawyer and author

Bill, you have been a wonderful friend. You have this unique quality of being able to relate to anybody. Your insight into various issues has been terrific. You can take the most innocuous topic and make it sound important. There is no question who is on the air when *you* speak on the great issues.

Hon. Andy Spano, former Westchester County Executive, and Brenda Resnick Spano

Congratulations on the golden anniversary of WVOX. This is a true achievement and a great tribute to your lifelong fierce commitment to the First Amendment and the principle of keeping the airwaves free. You are a true Voice of the People!

Phil Reisman, star feature columnist, *The Journal News*

You do so much good for so many.

Andrew O'Rourke, former Westchester County executive, Supreme Court justice, and admiral, U.S. Naval Reserve

Fifty years as the Voice of the People! Any speechwriter would die to have O'Shaughnessy writing their speeches, broadcasting their public service announcements, or introducing the next president of the United States. His circles are amazing: from Le Cirque to the halls of the governor's office. From Cuomo to Clinton, no one knows where they might see Bill O' show up with a microphone or his pen. In the worst of times, he was for the Franciscans at Graymoor and the working poor, with his Irish-Catholic roots celebrating the diversity of Westchester. Jewish, Muslim, Christian—it matters not. Left-headed, right-headed, Republican, Independent—he's there with the people. I'm grateful for who Bill is and for allowing Habitat for Humanity to be heard with so many others on 1460 AM!

Jim Killoran, president, Habitat for Humanity

Re their editorials and pronouncements: I have the utmost respect for Bill O'Shaughnessy's charm and his intellect.

Jerry I. Speyer, Tishman Speyer, Rockefeller Center, Chrysler Building, and Radio City

A radio station is a terrible thing to waste. WVOX was the first station in the entire nation to hold a radiothon for the United Negro College Fund.

United Negro College Fund

We wish we could clone Bill O'Shaughnessy. He's a fighter for the things this magazine holds dear.

Broadcasting & Cable magazine

We're immensely grateful to WVOX and WVIP for using your considerable influence with *both* political parties and for championing our cause with the State Dormitory Authority, which freed up several million dollars that would have been tied up for twenty years. This is no small achievement! Our talented young students owe you a lot.

Walter Luftman, chairman, The Culinary Institute of America–Hyde Park

A strong voice for community service, public affairs, and free speech on the airwaves of New York for some of the country's most influential citizens, politicians, captains of industry, publishers, bankers, businessmen, celebrities, and entertainers. Nationally recognized and acclaimed and the one the broadcasting industry enlists in its recurring fights to stay free of the Fairness Doctrine and other incursions against free speech.

Herbert H. Howard, Ph.D., Professor Emeritus, University of Tennessee

After being a college intern at WVOX in the late 1970s, it is great to be back to tell the stories of the U.S. military and our veterans. From all of us at the American Legion,congratulations on this milestone and for your many years of support for our service and military men and women. I'm pleased to present this special award from the Secretary of the Army.

Ken Kraetzer, commander, American Legion

Freedom to express what's on your mind, knowing no one can silence your point of view! How much is that worth to you? For me, this is the foundation of all the rights we have as Americans. And it's what the rest of the world admires the most about our great country: freedom of speech. For half a century, Bill O'Shaughnessy has been a staunch defender of this bedrock of our Constitution. WVOX is his expression of that freedom, and his eagerness to share it. Thank you for fifty years of guiding "America's Great Community Radio Station" and for a half-century of loyalty and devotion to our country's greatest privilege: that First Amendment right to freedom of speech!

Mike Scully, host, "The Mike Scully Show"

Their parties for charitable causes like the Broadcasters Foundation of America, the Franciscan Friars, and the Police Foundation are among the most sought-after tickets in town.

Joan Jedell, *The Hampton Sheet*

O'Shaughnessy, one of the most sought-after masters of ceremony in Gotham, really knows how to move those tony dinners with style and class, especially when he is presiding in the grand ballroom of the Waldorf-Astoria.

Michael Carney, society orchestra leader

Calling me "my father's son" on your radio stations is high praise indeed.

Arthur O. Sulzberger Jr., chairman and publisher, the *New York Times*

The station's imprimatur is a very signal honor.

Ralph Graves, editorial director, Time/Life

O'Shaughnessy is a throwback to the Golden Age of Radio and a seasoned raconteur. He keeps the banners waving for us with WVOX and WVIP.

David Patrick Columbia, editor-in-chief, *Quest* and *The New York Social Diary*

Bill O'Shaughnessy has been a fixture in Westchester for decades. He has tirelessly championed local, independent radio at a time when more and more stations have been controlled by large broadcasting companies. His commitment to local issues over the past fifty years has been admirable. Thanks to his role in local communications, many voices which may not have been heard otherwise have been given a forum. His dedication to public affairs programming has ensured that listeners have been able to get different viewpoints that relate to national, international, and, most important, local issues. WVOX has taken an active role in the dialogue between public officials and the public they serve.

Joseph Hankin, president, Westchester Community College

I was privileged to hear your commentary about Wellington Mara on WVOX, which so eloquently put into words the heart and soul of a man the world of sport might never see again.

George M. Steinbrenner

Congratulations to all those involved in making WVOX such a successful radio station for so many years. The valuable community information and the opportunity of producing your own radio show along with the professional guidance of "the Ambassador of All Media"—Mr. O'Shaughnessy—have made the station a vital part of Westchester and the Bronx.

Dennis Nardone and Tonny Guido, hosts of "Harrison Live" and "Remember Then"

The most intelligent radio editorials in New York state.

Tim Russert (previously recorded)

Bill O'Shaughnessy's gift for thinking is both broad and deep. So too is his piquant, powerful, and persuasive use of language. He is the scribe of our tribe. As my first mentor in broadcasting, you inspired me with a vision of radio as a Voice of the People, a "Vox Populi." The first "ratings book" I ever saw nearly forty years ago was not a Pulse or Arbitron, but a book of VIP tributes to the open style of local radio created at WVOX. In Greenwich, Windham, New York, and Litchfield County, Connecticut, our own radio endeavors emulating your approach have served our communities well. You are an eloquent thinker, and an elegant writer, and the preeminent conscience and spokesman for our tribe of old-fashioned community service broadcasters. (Our "tribe"—that's *another* notion I've appropriated from Bill's repertoire.) To this day, I'm proud to channel some of what you've taught us about service to the community. You are always so generous in your recognition of others. Now, Bill, it's your turn.

Dennis Jackson, president, New England Media; American community broadcaster

Back in 1959 when Bill O'Shaughnessy started these stations, Dwight Eisenhower was president of the United States, Nelson Rockefeller was governor of New York, and our two senators were Kenneth Keating and Jacob Javits, all Republicans. Today, our president, governor, and senators are all Democrats! Times have changed. In 1959, they were all white males. And today there are two African Americans and two women. Hawaii and Alaska have entered the Union. We were in a Cold War with the Soviets, and Nikita Khrushchev toured the United States. The Russians hit the moon with the Lunar II rocket. Fidel Castro took control of Cuba. The Dalai Lama took control of Tibet. The world's population was almost 3 billion; today it's over 6.5 billion. The United States grew from 173 million to over 300 million. The film *Gigi* beat out *Ben Hur* for the Oscar. The Dodgers whipped the White Sox in the World Series. The Celtics topped the Lakers for the NBA title. And the Colts crushed the Giants for the NFL title. A gallon of gas was 25 cents. The average car price was $2,200.00. A movie was a buck. And a postage stamp was five cents. Buddy Holly and the Big Bopper were killed in a plane crash, and Bill O'Shaughnessy founded WVOX. Since he started this great, unique station, ten presidents have come and gone. But Bill remains.

Richard Garfunkel, journalist, blogger, activist, and host of "The Advocate"

Little did I know, when I left publishing several years ago, that I would end up being a radio talk show host; and it all has to do with Bill O'Shaughnessy, who rescued me from a local station in Connecticut. When I told him what I was doing after my career in publishing, he said, "You have to get on WVOX." He gave me air time to review books and discuss literature. He took a chance on someone who never had done it before, and I made a whole, new career. Bill has been a great mentor. He is a brilliant person with a wicked sense of humor, very caring about what people do and what they think. He has been very supportive and has always been there to answer questions, make suggestions, and tell me if I've got a good idea. There isn't a soul in New York state who doesn't know Bill O'Shaughnessy. Here's to another fifty years.

Joseph Montebello, former editor and creative director, HarperCollins; host of "Between the Covers"

We've spent our entire lives out and about in Westchester. And we can't think of anyone who has had a more consistent and profound effect on public discourse in this area than Mr. O' and his brainchildren WVOX and WVIP. Not the local press, not the institutions of higher learning, and most certainly not the politicians. Mr. O' himself gives you the straight story—no baloney. Just as he sees it. For that reason he never goes unnoticed. And, of course, it doesn't hurt that he has a beautiful shock of white hair, a mellifluous voice, all packaged in perfect sartorial splendor.

What a grand gift he has given all of us: shows hosted by people of every philosophical flavor with a broad range of ethnic, religious, and social backgrounds, every political and cultural stripe. It certainly is a privilege to be part of this family. And a very big family it is. Mr. O' knows everyone, and you can find his fond remembrances of them in his three remarkable books. We can't let pass his enthusiastic support of Westchester's educational institutions, especially those of higher learning. Every college president knows of his devotion to building up our colleges and schools. His support of the mission of our Westchester schools and their graduates is legendary. We are especially reminded of the affection and respect visited on Mr. O' by the late Sr. Dorothy Ann Kelly, president of the College of New Rochelle (CNR), and Nancy Q. Keefe, CNR alumna and editor of the Gannett newspapers.

Valerie Moore O'Keefe, supervisor, Town of Mamaroneck, and Ken Bialo, mayor emeritus, Village of Larchmont

WVOX/Worldwide is like no other station. It reflects the unique spirit and vision of a true community radio entrepreneur. WVOX has long been the place where *all* voices can be heard, not just one point of view. It is the place where the daily dynamics of our local community are highlighted in ways no other station is able to do. It's the place where our area's leaders are featured day in and day out. All this and more is what makes WVOX/Worldwide a special place for those of us who have been lucky enough to be part of the first fifty years, a half-century of extraordinary community radio. Your kind of radio has a future as bright as its past.

Ralph Gregory, president, United Way of Westchester and Putnam

One of the many things I like about WVOX is that I can tune in anytime and hear an interesting person; and I'm impressed by how well, with a couple of questions or well-chosen words, they can sketch the subject's character with amazing accuracy.

Henry A. Kissinger

Throughout his career Bill O'Shaughnessy has been our city's—and to a great degree, our nation's—champion of the First Amendment. Here at WVOX we have a unique and invaluable platform for community dialogue so that more of our residents understand the challenges and opportunities we face as a city. It's very rare to have an individual like Bill who is so eloquent, so articulate, so passionate about what he does and who is willing to pour his heart and soul into a community the way he has here in Westchester for a truly extraordinary fifty years!

Hon. Noam Bramson, mayor, City of New Rochelle; special advisor to Congresswoman Nita Lowey

WVOX is a hell of a lot more than a bloody jukebox, I would say.

Steve Dunleavy, legendary newspaperman and columnist, *New York Post*

Only WVOX has been awarded the Communications Medal by the Archdiocese—*twice*! We consider you a friend. I made my very first speech as archbishop at your behest.

Edward Cardinal Egan, former archbishop of the Archdiocese of New York

WVOX and WVIP—those two splendid call letters—are beacons of enlightenment, especially on free speech and First Amendment matters.

Jack Valenti, president, Motion Picture Association of America (previously recorded)

About fifteen years ago the great Sol Taishoff—editor, founder, and publisher of *Broadcasting* magazine—and I talked about the need for broadcasters to do a better job, because, above all, we're licensed to render a *service* to the public. The legendary Mr. Taishoff opined—rightly so—that the *number one* example in that regard was the estimable Bill O'Shaughnessy for what he had then been doing on the air for years, dedicated to the public's interests. Sol said: "You know, Ward, if O'Shaughnessy's principles of quality service would manifest themselves elsewhere, there wouldn't be all these congressional investigations and Federal Communications Commission [FCC] studies as to what's not being done in public service by radio and television stations." He also said: "Ward, you and I have a great friend in this fellow O'Shaughnessy, a man who believes in the principles on which we should be standing." He also said, "I hope the day will come when people across America, radio and television owners, begin to realize the genius of the work done by this young man and how much can be contributed if we could somehow all do the same thing: serve the public's interests. O'Shaughnessy does it. And he does it with financial success. We can *all* do it and all be equally successful wherever we operate." This broadcaster way out in Chicagoland has the most respect, to this very day, for Bill personally and professionally, and for those radio stations that still reside in his care and keeping.

Ward Quaal, broadcasting's greatest statesman; president, The Ward L. Quaal Company; former president, WGN-Chicago

Congratulations on fifty wonderful, productive, and successful years. You have made Westchester a better place to live and work.

I wish you another twenty-five. We have had a close, special relationship for which I'm very grateful. Bill is a "Triple S" Man—sweet, smart, and special—and loved by all.

Alan Rosenberg, partner, Rosenberg & Chesnov LLP

I'm constantly amazed at the "reach" of WVOX and WVIP and their influence in all the right places.

Kenneth Cole, designer; chairman, Kenneth Cole Productions

As someone who started working out of college at WVOX and got exposed to local government early on, I can't tell you how valuable WVOX has been in my life and in my career. It still serves as a source of information for me and the public.

Charles B. "Chuck" Strome, city manager, City of New Rochelle; former news director and morning show host, WVOX

If it hadn't been for Bill O'Shaughnessy's encouragement, I would have never started my own radio show. "The Health Buzz" allows me to educate the public on the latest natural and conventional medical information. Bill's words of wisdom were: "Alicia, you have the personality to make this work. Don't worry, you're a natural." It's been such an empowering thing. My grandmother, who is over ninety and comes into the studio with me, tells me, "I just love Bill." She talks politics with him; he really makes her day.

Alicia Grande, producer, "The Health Buzz"

I'm a centrist. I believe the United States should lead the world in areas of peace, justice, scientific and social research and advance. There are people of every political stripe on this radio station, and I know of no other station anywhere that has such a range of opinion. Whatever your point of view, you have a voice here at WVOX. Whether you are a host or a caller, your opinion is given equal access to the airwaves, and that is the magic of this station. For fifty years Bill O'Shaughnessy has enforced the essence of the United States Constitution by providing this vehicle for freedom of speech and freedom of the airwaves. I have never heard of anyone being told what to say. And that transcends radio and media and politics. That speaks directly to what it means to be an American.

Bob Lebensold, host, "Environmentally Sound"

I have known and admired Bill O'Shaughnessy for many, many years. He brings back many nostalgic memories. Bill always says it like it is. He has helped Governor Cuomo and the New York state government for many years. And he helped my son become a judge. Congratulations on WVOX's fiftieth year.

Joseph Angiolillo, Esq., father of Appellate Court Judge Daniel Angiolillo

Congratulations, Brother Bill, for being on Whitney Radio for over fifty years. And thank you for doing a great advertising job for us at Mario's Restaurant for over twenty-five years! Mama Rose and Dad loved you. You are part of our family.

Joseph Migliucci, Mario's Restaurant, Arthur Avenue, Little Italy, the Bronx

Congratulations on fifty years, Daddy. I have so many good memories of the radio station, especially when we were little. I remember coming with my best friend, Jennifer Feinberg, and we would record ads for the station. One I remember said, "I like bike riding; I like ice cream; and I like the *new* WVOX!" I also remember coming on school trips, and it was the best field trip of the year because you had the McDonald's truck come and also the Good Humor man. All my friends would be so happy to have Cheeseburger Happy Meals and toasted almond crunch bars at the station. Thank you for all of that and for all you do for the community, for the radio world. And for us. I'm really proud of you, Dad. Big hugs from me and your grandchildren Tucker, Flynn, and Amelia!

Kate O'Shaughnessy Nulty, director, Whitney Media; founder, Mother Nurture Project

WVOX is known nationwide as the epitome of a local station. It is Westchester's own precious gift. Bill O'Shaughnessy remains one of America's greatest champions of free speech and local service.

Westchester EYE

Some years ago, a skinny kid came to New Rochelle to run the radio station. The guy had something very special. He took the little radio station atop the Pershing Square Building—actually, it was in the basement—and almost single-handedly built a giant communications system known throughout the metropolitan area and the world beyond. He helped shape the lives of many, including my own. He truly is "the Voice of the People."

Hon. Leonard Paduano, former mayor, City of New Rochelle

You deserve a lot of credit for keeping those stations going. They are great radio stations.

Rob Astorino, Westchester county executive

I want to congratulate you on a half-century of brilliant broadcasting. It has been an honor and privilege to be associated with you. Jerry and I congratulate you on another fifty years of success!

Lynn Handler, artist and philanthropist

Congratulations on fifty years as a truly local radio outlet. Your legacy of service to New York is damned impressive.

Dennis Wharton, National Association of Broadcasters

Fifty years: WVOX, the Voice of Westchester. We thank you from Zonta Community Radio!

Roxanne Neilson, Zonta International

WVOX has been part of my life, *the* source for local news and announcements. Forty years ago, I was moderator of a team of students from Maria Regina High School in Hartsdale who participated in WVOX's Academic Quiz Show. Today I host "Nora's Neighbors." In between, I've been a guest on other shows and joined in the legendary St. Patrick's Day celebrations. WVOX/Worldwide has been a part of good memories. I've been given the chance to meet interesting people from my neighborhood. Mr. O' has also helped me fulfill a childhood dream. I grew up with Dorothy and Dick, Arthur Godfrey, John A. Gambling, Peter Lind Hayes, and Mary Healy. Growing up, I always wanted a microphone of my own. Thank you, Bill, for inviting me to be a part of

WVOX's family of hosts and for memories and fulfilled dreams and for creating a station that builds up the community and widens horizons.

Nora Murphy, host, "Nora's Neighbors"; former superintendent, Catholic Schools

I *really* enjoy O'Shaughnessy's stations! Richard Johnson and "Page Six" love the guy, and so do I!

Donald Trump

I look forward to reading the history of our times that Bill O'Shaughnessy has captured . . . and lived.

David McCullough, Pulitzer Prize–winning American author and historian

Bill O'Shaughnessy has shown important leadership in the state and nationally in the interest of a free press. His extraordinary radio stations are true forums in the heart of the Eastern Establishment and a cut well above the cacophony.

Ambassador Ogden Rogers Reid, president, Council of American Ambassadors; former U.S. ambassador to Israel

You brought WVOX and WVIP to the forefront of broadcasting, keeping the residents aware and informed in politics, education, city information, fundraising projects, or a needy cause. We welcomed you fifty years ago with our legendary old man, Postmaster John Fosina, and have always considered you a friend.

Mickie and Joe Fosina, partners, Mariano Rivera Steak House

It is my privilege to congratulate Bill on his fifty years of service to Westchester. Sixteen years ago, when I came to New Rochelle, everyone told me, "You must make contact with O'Shaughnessy; he's a key player in this city." And I did. And Bill welcomed me with open arms and a friendship blossomed. Bill was very instrumental in developing our New Rochelle Police Foundation. He was a founding father for the foundation, which has contributed several million dollars to assist and strengthen the New Rochelle Police Department, and that couldn't have happened without Bill

O'Shaughnessy. Bill puts a lot of time and effort into making things right, and the city appreciates it.

Hon. Patrick Carroll, police commissioner, City of New Rochelle; former commander, Critical Incident Unit, NYPD

I have always appreciated WVOX and Bill O'Shaughnessy. I've been a loyal listener of WVOX and O'Shaughnessy for many, many years!

Domenic Procopio, chairman, Municipal Civil Liberties Association; president, Calabria Mutual Aid Society

You are truly the Crown Jewel of the Sound Shore area. Thank you for everything you do for our community.

Frank Micelli, proprietor, Minuteman Press

We came to work with Daddy today to see Grandpa! We want to wish Grandpa a happy fiftieth year in broadcasting. Congratulations, Grandpa, for fifty years!

David and Lily O'Shaughnessy, age four

I would like to wish the "Silver Fox" a very happy fiftieth anniversary for what he has done for the City of New Rochelle and the County of Westchester. I've been there as a legislator, for almost thirty-five years, back when he was getting his start. He had the silver hair then. He still has that great speaking voice. He's just a wonderful person, and totally committed to Westchester and the state of New York.

Hon. Vincent R. Rippa, former mayor, City of New Rochelle; former judge and chairman, Westchester County Board of Legislators

Bill is a true friend of the Italians. For forty years, I've tried to teach Bill how to speak Italian! I'm still trying! I know that his next book is going to include Machiavelli, Marconi, Garibaldi, Columbo, and the great works of Leonardo DaVinci, Michelangelo, Botticelli. I also know that Bill and his lovely Nancy enjoy visiting Italia, and we love you too, Bill, for allowing us to promote our Italian culture and language on WVOX! *Cent Anni!*

Dr. Luigi Miele, host, "Italian Melodies"

You all know me as the owner of Dudley's Parkview on Long Island Sound, which, for the past eleven years, has hosted the popular WVOX St. Patrick's Day celebration. But I've known and loved WVOX/Worldwide for many more years than that, since my high school days, when my children were small and we were involved in politics here in the city. I'd like to congratulate Bill on fifty wonderful years of service to all of us.

Electra Davis, proprietor, Dudley's Parkview Restaurant

WVOX's tent is big. And there is always space reserved for those whose ship came in and drifted back to sea long ago.

Gannett Newspapers

I am so deeply honored to add my gratitude for his service to our city and the County of Westchester to my dear friend of thirty years—the incredibly eloquent, insightful, and always impeccably tasteful Bill O'Shaughnessy. Bill, you've maintained the people's respect, and no one in this community exceeds you in the possession of ability and integrity. You ought to be congratulated for your enterprise, for your unselfishness, and for being an effective force in the growth of this county. You've always had your finger on the pulse of the community and have employed the prestige and strength of WVOX/Worldwide to make this a better place to live. Bill has always believed that participation by the citizens in public affairs is essential. Your awareness of local issues and your powerful advocacy are unparalleled, and you have always been passionate about our people. Seldom do we come across a man more gentlemanly or possessing more charm. On numerous occasions, I have recruited Bill to emcee retirement dinners and charitable functions, and without hesitation, he lent his stature, his wit, and his exquisite use of words to make the evening memorable and never boring. I'd be remiss if I didn't mention his support of our successful Drug Court Program and its graduation ceremonies. We should also never forget that Bill's politics have always been above board. And that his use of the word "townie" has always been with love and affection. Bill, you have been one of the Queen City's biggest supporters. I was privileged to be cited in *It All Comes Back to Me Now,* and I've been privileged to enjoy the pleasurable company of this class act on so many occasions, at Mario's, Le Cirque, Valbella, Edmondo's. You have my boundless admiration and affection. I'll always cherish your friendship and your wise counsel, both politically and personally.

Hon. James Generoso, court clerk, City Court of New Rochelle

Future generations will thank you for your defense of CBS and devotion to the First Amendment.

William S. Paley, founder, CBS (previously recorded)

Bill, nothing can quite equal the buzz you and the gorgeous Nancy O'Shaughnessy create when you enter the room. Any restaurant would be happy to have you, even on a Monday night! Who is that great-looking couple at table 21? And thanks, of course, for all those truly kind and generous things you do for people who needed a helping hand. The world needs a lot more people like you! Continue to keep up your great work.

James O'Shea, proprietor, The West Street Grill

Congratulations on the fiftieth anniversary! You were my mentor. You taught me the importance of city councils, school boards, and going into classes to talk to teachers and kids, and covering all the daily things that had to be reported, from small fires to big fires. I took all that I learned up to Dover-Foxcroft, Maine, to WDME, and we incorporated all that into local talk shows and received the "Broadcaster" and "Station of the Year" awards from the Maine Association of Broadcasters, and we won so many other awards. And I owe lots of that directly to you.

Fred Hirsch, former news director, WVOX; owner, WDME

I'm pleased to be able to do a show on WVOX. The beauty of this show and everything I've done in media, including *The Yonkers Tribune* and the *Westchester Herald*, have been to mimic the efforts of Mr. O'Shaughnessy, because when I looked at the media landscape in Westchester and the Bronx, I realized that Mr. O'Shaughnessy was the only one able to transcend the agendas and the biases that were so evident. He was able to extrapolate on the most basic levels and was able to dissect them and offer different perspectives on the air by allowing people to express their unique points of view. And he did so on a wide range of issues and never pulled away from his responsibility to afford people the ability to hear *all* positions. He did this eloquently, with grace and the thought and need of the public good. I thank him for being my mentor.

Hezi Aris, publisher, the *Yonkers Tribune* and the *Westchester Herald*

The station's interviews, tributes, essays, and thoughts off the top of Bill O'Shaughnessy's handsome head are the stuff of New York history.

Liz Smith, nationally syndicated columnist

BMI is honored to have such a longstanding and beneficial relationship with you and your stations. Please accept this special BMI Golden Record created especially for this occasion as a token of our esteem and to simply say thanks for the support and friendship you have personally extended to our songwriters.

Michael O'Neill, senior vice president, BMI

We gave you a federal judge, and he was a great one. I was pleased to forward your recommendation of Richard Daronco to President Reagan, who obviously agreed with you and appointed him to the federal bench..

Hon. Alfonse D'Amato, former U.S. senator

WVOX and WVIP were on our side from the very beginning, when we wired up Westchester.

Charles Dolan, chairman, Cablevision

Our family and our company have been friends of the O'Shaughnessys and WVOX for more than fifty years. They go all the way back to my grandfather, who was one of their first patrons and supporters, along with the great Nelson Rockefeller, who shared our grandfather's admiration for your radio stations. And for you.

Jeff Powers and the Powers family, Powers Fasteners Worldwide

For fifty years WVOX/Worldwide has set the standard for broadcasters not only in the Westchester area, but all across the tri-state area and New York state. It has also set a national standard for excellence in the broadcasting industry. WVOX has long been a pioneer and leader in the industry. It had its birth here in New York state. For five decades you have informed us, entertained us, enlightened us. But what has really made your mark on broadcasting so truly exceptional has been your strong advocacy for important causes and your special commitment to making the community you've served for over fifty years the very best it can be. It's been a wonderful journey. Half a century!

John Charlson, special assistant to the governor

I always felt WVOX's great strength is its relationship with the "townies" of Westchester and the Bronx, those with *roots* in the community.

Ossie Davis (previously recorded)

I admire your courage. The stations perform to the highest levels of public service.

Walter Anderson, chairman and editor, *Parade*

I am in awe of your ability to be memorable. Your stations are *sui generis*.

Erwin Krasnow, famed Washington communications attorney and counsel

WVOX and WVIP are perfect examples of concerned corporate citizens. They know how to keep their hands on the pulse of the communities they serve. Although the two stations are as different as night and day, each has the same high level of creativity suited to please the different interests of their listeners. The opinions expressed on WVOX's "Open Line" programs are often able to directly influence public officials in the New York area. We salute you for years of uninterrupted community service and an outreach that promotes a free and open dialogue. You exemplify the virtues of a good corporate citizen.

NAACP

When Parliament set about restructuring the whole of broadcasting in Great Britain, we went first to the networks; and then we happened on WVOX, where, incredibly, we learned the most!

Sir Donald Caberry, M.P., and chairman, BBC Task Force, British Parliament

We've been with WVOX for a long, long time. And they have been with us.

Rev. W. Franklyn Richardson, national Baptist leader; pastor, Grace Baptist Church

The great Harold Geneen, who created America's first conglomerate, was also among the first to discover WVOX and WVIP.

Edward "Ned" Gerrity, senior vice president Public Affairs, ITT (previously recorded)

With its strong editorials and High Holy Days broadcasts, WVOX and WVIP have been reliable friends of the Jewish people and the State of Israel.

Rabbi Amiel Wohl, Temple Israel, Westchester

WVOX is like the west wind. It's an elegant radio station with just a touch of ragtime in its soul. Forget their politics. I mean you have to like WVOX, which does so much for Mamaroneck and other swell places.

Jimmy Breslin

The glorious Hudson has a real friend in you and your terrific stations.

Robert F. Kennedy Jr.

For me it's such a blessing to have known you for thirty of those fifty years. You are an amazing man who gives so much of yourself to our world and our community. You've always been a dynamic role model for me. You have given us an opportunity to reach the public regarding a very serious problem—substance abuse—and to allow to us to continue our mission through your airwaves.

Joan Bonsignore, founder, National Council on Alcoholism and Drug Dependence Westchester

All of us in the Fix family congratulate you on this memorable milestone. Fifty successful years in *any* endeavor is an amazing accomplishment and even more so in the world of broadcasting. Providing a true, community-based radio outlet is challenging in the world of mega-corporate media ownership. You should be proud of WVOX/Worldwide and WVIP and how they serve the community. Many years ago, you convinced me to run a few ads for our hardware store on your station. I followed your advice and spoke from the heart about our family business and our connection to the community. That connection is missing in most corporate-owned businesses, whether retail, service, media, or entertainment. Westchester is extremely lucky to still have a large number of strong, locally owned businesses with roots that stretch back fifty years or more. So congratulations, Bill, on your fifty years on the radio! You have truly created a community resource that is sure to endure for many years to come.

John Fix III, third-generation owner, Cornells True Value Hardware

I'll never forget your efforts to have the Wykagyl branch of the New Rochelle Post Office named for Robert Merrill. Mayor Bramson and Nita Lowey were of great help too. But the influence of Bob's favorite hometown radio station was invaluable.

Marion Merrill, widow of Metropolitan Opera star Robert Merrill

I am remembering back thirty years, when I had a fifteen-minute program on WVOX in the old "K-Building"; and at that time I fell in love with WVOX and Bill O'Shaughnessy's charismatic personality—and I've been in love ever since. Congratulations to Bill and his dedicated staff for fifty very superior years on the air!

Hon. Anthony J. Colavita, "Mr. Westchester"—former New York State Republican Chairman

There are, at last count, ninety-three radio stations in this part of the country, and *one* absolutely unique WVOX. And I doubt there's ever been a station conjured up in the mind of man like their WVIP. Both stations feature intelligent discussions about the great issues of the day. I have been "neighborly involved" with Bill O'Shaughnessy for a long time. I never enjoy myself so much than when I turn on his special radio station and he's carrying on about something—it's like coming home.

Ossie Davis (previously recorded)

Nancy and Bill O'Shaughnessy are bright, vivid personalities whose presence often blesses Bermuda. Since my time as Minister of Tourism and Deputy Prime Minister, our country has had no more effective or graceful advocate than Bill O'Shaughnessy and WVOX. I am often called "The Voice of Summer" for my narration of international cricket matches here and abroad. But Mr. O'Shaughnessy is clearly the Voice of New York state, and especially Westchester, which he calls the Golden Apple. By any name, it's the Heart of the Eastern Establishment, and that's a perfect venue for his genius and dedication. He's widely quoted and admired even in my country.

Hon. C. V. "Jim" Woolridge, M.P., commander of the British Empire; Bermuda's "Voice of Summer"

We congratulate Bill O'Shaughnessy on his fifty years of service, and for providing excellent radio to the people of New York state. We hope for fifty more!

Adam Freidlander, president, Insuregy

The New York Giants and the Mara family congratulate Bill O'Shaughnessy and WVOX for fifty years of extraordinary broadcasting. They're truly World Champions! Happy anniversary, Bill, on half a century of really distinctive broadcasting.

John Mara, co-president, N.Y. Giants

The Foresters Club sends anniversary greetings to WVOX with expectations that this great community radio station will be making people happy for at *least* another one hundred and fifty years! For years now, Foresters Club members all over the metropolitan area have been faithful listeners to their favorite radio station: WVOX, "The Voice of the People."

Frankie Lore, The Foresters Club

I fondly recall listening to WVOX with my late husband, William Black, the founder of Chock full o' Nuts. We especially enjoyed Bill O'Shaughnessy's editorials over so many years. I continue to be a fan, and I always have my dial set to 1460 AM out here at my home on Premium Point. Warmest greetings to Bill and WVOX on fifty wonderful years!

Page Morton Black, philanthropist; chairman, Parkinson's Disease Foundation at Columbia-Presbyterian

I'm remembering the times when a white-haired gent came in so many years ago and always got out of his car to come say hello to my father and me. Other customers stayed in the car and just waved! He always came in for a word about the community. I have warm wishes for Bill and his family over those fifty hard-working, productive years!

Ron Harris, Wykagyl Service Station

I've run several businesses in Westchester and was privileged to serve as chairman of the County Board of Legislators—and I even wrote a book (not three like O'Shaughnessy!)—and through it all WVOX has been a constant in my life and in the civic life of the metro area.

Steve Tenore, Lloyd Maxcy & Sons, former Westchester County Board Chairman

September 14, 2009

AFTERWORD BY WILLIAM O'SHAUGHNESSY

All the luminaries and those of high estate, it seems, are here to sing our praises and deliver congratulations, many of them having come a far piece to be with us in person on this historic live broadcast; others by phone or on tape; and even a few were retrieved from our archives. My colleagues here assembled certainly deserve all the plaudits and encomiums. This day is for them and their predecessors, those dedicated community broadcasters whose genius sustained this extraordinary community radio station for five decades.

We've also heard from so many generous and loving friends who have been overly kind to me, people obviously willing to weigh my own many inadequacies less diligently than they assess what they find commendable in my inartful stewardship.

We make our way in broadcasting armed only with words. But I'll never be able to summon up those I need to express my gratitude adequately that we have been privileged to reach this day as a result of the forbearance, love, support, and encouragement of the influential friends who have indulged my enthusiasms for five decades.

So much for the well-founded and those of standing and stature whose blessing and imprimatur have surely helped sustain us as permittees of WVOX and WVIP. We're grateful for all of it. And for them. But it should also be noted that during our remarkable fifty-year run, you, my colleagues, have also won the approval and admiration of those I've always referred to with great affection as the "townies," those who operated out of the spotlight, most of them obscure sidemen in orchestras long dispersed.

On this great occasion I'm thinking of those endearing Runyonesque figures from long ago who painted color and life into our broadcasts. My mind drifts back to Hughie Doyle, Rocco Bellantoni Jr., Teddy Greene, Paddy O'Neil, John Fosina, Bill Scollon, Joe Vaccarella, John Branca, Joe Curtis, Edwin Gilbert Michaelian, Fred Powers Sr., Bill Butcher, Judge Dick Daronco, Napoleon Holmes, Jack Dowling, Hubert Horan, Arthur Geoghegan, Bill Hegarty, Charlie Wendelken, Father Terry Attridge, Charlie Librett, Fred Powers, Burt Cooper, Mike Armiento, Milt Hoffman, Hilda Berkowitz, Dick Ottinger, Brother Jack Driscoll, Jerry Valenti, Governor Malcolm Wilson, "Shipwreck" Kelly, Marvin Goldfluss, Red Motley, Walter Anderson, Milton Gould, Paul Hutton and Winnie Klotz, Jack Kornsweet, Dick Crabtree, Andy O'Rourke, Richie Parisi, Father George Hommel, George Delaney, Jack Gardner, Joe Pisani, Mario Biaggi, Robert Merrill, Ossie Davis, Frank Garito, Stanley W. Church, Elizabeth Rae Lamont, Nick Orzio, Jean T. Ensign, George Vergara, Ned Gerrity, Tom O'Toole, Joe Evans, Nick Donofrio, Ernie Hickman, Murph Streger, Bill Scott, Ad Young, Frank Connelly Sr., J. Ray McGovern, Lynn Ames, Sal Generoso, Walter Moore, Max Berking, Judge Alvin Richard Ruskin, Tony Gioffre, Pat Cunningham, Darby Ruane, Steve Tenore, Herman Geist, Paul Dennis, Mama Rose Migliucci, Mario Migliucci, Paul Lenok, M. Paul Redd, Bill Luddy, Ed

Hughes, I. Philip Sipser, Bob Feinman, Angelo Badaloto, Bob Colwell, Harry Colwell, Owen Mandeville, Vin Draddy, Bob Fanelli, Tom Fanelli, Charlie Seidenstein, Sylvia Ruskin, Ed Carey, Augie Petrillo, George Burchell, Diane and Bill Collins, Joe Gagliardi, Nils Hansen, David Kendig, Paul Hutton, Winnie Hutton, George Salerno, Sid Mudd, James K. Bishop, Alex Norton, Bob McGrath, Joe Anastasi, Al Pirro, William A. "Billy" Rowe, Frank Cartica, Bud Spillane, Rosemary Phillips, Joe Canzeri, Frank McCullough, Bruce Snyder, William Hughes Mulligan, Charlie Brieant, Bill Gibbons, Eddie Egan, Bill Mulrow, Ken Raske, James Mott Clark, Rick Clark, Stew McMillan, John Perone, Burt Campbell, Ken Ake, Nelson Aldrich Rockefeller, Bernard Curry Jr.

In this category could surely go my mother, Catherine Tucker O'Shaughnessy, who was a fierce advocate of this station, and my dear and only brother, John Thomas O'Shaughnessy, who served for many years as a director and wise counselor. As I said, we've been blessed. I've been blessed.

Also missing from today's festivities and remembrances are the thousands of active and concerned citizens among our listeners, and those who came over the years with their petitions and pleadings seeking exposure and assistance from their community radio station. It has been a privilege to provide a forum, a podium for their frustrations, their aspirations, their concerns, and their dreams.

I also want to thank Cindy Hall Gallagher, whose judgment and dedication informs everything I touch. My life doesn't work without this extraordinary woman. I don't thank her enough!

Thanks also to Judy Fremont for producing this glorious day-long broadcast, and also to John Harper and Don Stevens for their technical skill and brilliance and their remarkable dedication to our listeners.

A good chunk of today's day-long celebration will be preserved in *Vox Populi: The O'Shaughnessy Files*, the fourth anthology of my ravings to be published next year by Fordham University Press, the great Jesuit university press in the City of New York. For their blessing and imprimatur, I'm so grateful to Fredric Nachbaur, Margaret Noonan, Loomis Mayer, Eric Newman, Saverio Procario, Rich Hendel, Anthony Chiffolo, the brilliant photographer Courtney Grant

Winston, and the magnificent Jesuit who is president of Fordham, Father Joseph M. McShane, S.J.

Our newest publishing enterprise, incidentally, will again benefit the humanitarian mission of our friends at the Broadcasters Foundation of America. So I hope "Volume IV" will commend itself to your favorable judgment when it comes out next year, even as you've been so generous to the first three collections.

We've sat before these microphones, ladies and gentlemen, dear listeners, in sadness and horror after 9/11 and through blizzards, floods, fires, epidemics, assassinations, days of mourning, and national and local tragedies.

But there were also happy and even thrilling moments of courage, inspiration, generosity, and goodness.

Or as the great Mario Cuomo reminds us, there *was* some *sweetness* that crept out over our airwaves. There was that too. Moments.

Thanks for listening to us—and to me—for fifty years.

I'm afraid I am, after all of it, now really without words.

SUPPORTING CAST

These are some of the great broadcasters and friends—past and present—whose genius, generosity, and sweet voices sustained WVOX/Worldwide and WVIP for so many years and helped amplify the aspirations of our dedicated listeners.

Governor Mario M. Cuomo, Judge Richard Daronco, Nancy Curry O'Shaughnessy, David O'Shaughnessy, Matt O'Shaughnessy, Kate O'Shaughnessy Nulty, Cindy Hall Gallagher, Bep McSweeney, Erwin Krasnow, Frank Connelly Jr., John Harper, Judy Fremont, Luigi Miele, Don Stevens, Bud Williamson, William "Billy" Bush, Jimmy Breslin Jr., Lynn Schlosser, Elsie Maria Troija Walter, Martha Ley, Giorgio Albano, Jim McGinty, Joe Farda, David Grecco, Nat Carbo, Alex Kroll, Paul Lenok, Jeff Bernbach, Stephanie Lombardo, Jean T. Ensign, Cameron Connell, Edwin Gilbert Michaelian, Harry M. Thayer, Walter Nelson Thayer, Ann Wharton Thayer, Monsignor Terry Attridge, Bob Lebensold, Jack Scarangella, Elinor Nardella, Randy Berlage, Fred Hirsch, Col. Marty Rochelle, Judge Andy O'Rourke, Murray Richman, Joe Rao, Nancy Q. Keefe, Phil Reisman, Howard Sturman, Ambassador John Hay "Jock" Whitney, Neal

Travis, Richard Johnson, Jami Sherwood, Chuck Strome, Nancy Amaya, Larry Goldstein, Cindy Adams, Matt Deutsch, Richard Littlejohn, Rudy Ruderman, Mark Mason, Liz Smith, Dr. Kevin Falvey, Dr. Rich Pisano, Col Allan, John Spicer, Louis Cappelli, Tom Luciani, Paul Juergens, Joe Biscoglio, Steven Tito, Ronni Sifer, Jon Lopresti, Ed Dennehy, Ray LeFevre, Geri Latchford, Dominick Gataletto, Lisa Lacerra, Elizabeth Rae Lamont, Davida Rothberg, Lisa Kramer, Michael Dandry, Ed Stelli, John Roma, Jessica O'Connell, Agatha Strome, Amanda Sullivan, Cheryl Dews Brewton, Irene Lemus, Cristine Celenza, Sandy Arnn, Todd Campbell, Ernie Sprance, Kevin VanMeter, Jennifer Irwin, Broaddus "Speed" Johnson, Seymour Sinuk, John Iannuzzi, Roger Cucci, Jeff Crandell, Gregg Pavelle, David Driscoll, Sean Driscoll, Carla Dietz Heller, George Latimer, James Mott Clark Jr., Jesus Valencia, Lynn DiMenna, Richie Hargrave, Bill Shibilski, Joan Cotrone, Jomo Willoughby, Don Sanford, Liddon Griffith, Bob Granger, Matt Murphy, Otto Miller, Courtney Brewton, Mike Scully, Rob Bocellari Jr., Matt Damrow, Inara Bordes, John Boianelli, Albery Bryan, Al Ayers, Robert M. Bennett, Budd Ungar, Matthew Criscuola, Joey Duff, Ray Deenihan, Jim Davis, Lynn DiMenna, Ray Planell, Bill Meth, Tom Mariam, Patrick Maines, Ward Quaal, Rainer Kraus, Dennis Jackson, John Wells King, Floyd Abrams, B. J. Harrington, Nat Hentoff, David Hinckley, Jay Mitchell, John Carideo, Howard Bischoff, Gil Stern, Marjorie Bischoff, John Bojemski, Ermes Bertuzzi, Dean Castellano, Jean Marie Signorelli, Bob Fois, Everard Davis, Judy Sindin, Irma Valencia, Larry Estridge, Bijan Eshangi, Christopher Conway, Lisa Payne, Charles Barton Castleberry, Maria Oliviera, Ken Gaughran, Charles Donegan, Tommy Smyth, Tressa Goodwin, Dennis Nardone, Tony Guido, Burt Korall, Alex Philippidis, Jerry Del Colliano, Tom Taylor, Nick Golden, Russell Mafes, Bernie Dilson, Hank Whittemore, Frank Saxe, Harry Jessell, Chris Sylvester, John Colograndé, Sabrina Castleberry, Jerry Nulty, Cara Ferrin O'Shaughnessy, John Van Buren Sullivan, Phil Lombardo, Frank Boyle, Dick Foreman, Bob Lindner, Don West, Joe Reilly, Ian Berman, Bob Marrone, Nick Sarames, Tom Thayer, Nita Lowey, Jim Cunningham, Irene Masterson, Charlie Massimi, Joe Apicella, Frederic B. Powers Sr., Bill Mulrow, Albert LaFarge, Joseph Montabello, Patrick Carroll, Alvin Richard Ruskin,

Rocco Belantoni Jr., Hugh A. Doyle, Jeff Sprung, Hank Teitel, Bob Hughes, Henry Berman, Sam Fredman, Amiel Wohl, Richard McCarthy, Rosemary McLaughlin, Kevin Elliott, Billy McKenna, John Vasile, Walter Maxwell, Joe Migliucci, Martha Ley, Charlie Kafferman, James O'Shea, Ron Harris, Hon. Ernie Davis, Paul McLane, Bob Doll, Mike Kinosian, John Eggerton, Sol Taishoff, Larry Taishoff, Ebie Wood, Rich Guberti, Scott Fybush, Ralph Martinelli, Louise Montclair, James "D" Tommy Rogers, John Kelly, Debbie Schechter, Sarah Caldwell, Chris Clarke, Heather Dyer, Glenn Francis, Ray Fox, Kathleen Frangeskos, Malissa Martin, Matthew Murphy, Lorraine Werblow, Karl Jantzen, Morgan Kuhl, Kathleen Plunkett O'Connor, Steve Savino, Eric Rhoads, Jim Carnegie, Tracie King, Ira Kleinman, Richard Onayiga, Catherine O'Connor, Eric Miranda, Joseph Lentini, John Lee, Jovan C. Richards, Ronni Sifer, Jon Sher, Eugene Sutorius, Monique Thomas, Keith Vitolo, Sam Wilson, Frank Miceli, Melvin Wilder, Bob Gibson, Carl Marcucci, Stu Olds, Ed Whitman, Patrick Maines, Captain Rob Taishoff, Joe Spinelli, Joe Anastasi, Larry Kaiser, Vincent De Jager, Steven Butensky, Nick Orzio, Richard K. Doan, Mort Dean, Todd Zuzulo, Ed Mancuso, Dr. David Breindel, Arnie Klugman, Denny Haight, Andy O'Rourke Jr., Bob Schaeffer, Joe Candrea, Toots Shor, John Haidar, Colin Burns Sr., Jim Generoso, Jacob K. Javits, William Plunkett, Kevin Plunkett, Vito Verni, John Verni, Bishop James McCarthy, Msgr. Charlie Kavanaugh, Dr. Fritz Ehlert, Dr. Paul Pellicci, Dr. Tom Fogarty, William A. "Billy" Rowe, Alan Chartock, Fred Dicker, Marek Fuchs, Don Pollard, Lisa Foderaro, Ken Auletta, Scott Shannon, John J. O'Connor, and Rocco Bellantoni Jr.

GLARING OMISSIONS

I've tried to say something nice about so many wonderful characters in this book, and it's been a privilege to celebrate their genius. I do, however, acknowledge a few glaring omissions. But I don't take full responsibility for them, and thus I can only hope that someday the following remarkable individuals will somehow surprise me with a splendid gesture that will perhaps convince me I've been wrong about them all along. It won't be the first time I've overlooked real quality.

Tom Connor, Dennis Kucinich, Paul Begala, Lester Holt, John Roberts, James Carville, most of the Roman Curia, Chuck Schumer, Hillary Rodham Clinton, Rosie O'Donnell, Mark Fuhrman, Adam Handler, Ed Schultz, Gordon Medenica, Randy Lex, Larry Schwartz, Amy Garfinkel, Stuart Subotnick, Ernie Sutkowski, Lou Dobbs, Jimmy Haber, Mika Brzezinski, John Zanzarella, John Walsh, Zenia Mucha, Daniel Pelosi, Nancy Pelosi, Raoul Felder, Al Franken, Georgette Mosbacher, Arianna Huffington, Jackie Mason, Susan Estrich, Donna Brazile, Martha Stewart, Eliot Engel, the death penalty, Elie Wiesel, David Ortiz, the New York Mets, Larry Wilson, Adam Lindemann, Zane Tankel, Margaret Sullivan, Gloria Allred, Rod Blagojevich, Dee Dee Myers. And how can I overlook William Jefferson Clinton!

INDEX